ANAND
PANYARACHUN
AND THE MAKING
OF MODERN THAILAND

First published in 2018
by Editions Didier Millet Pte Ltd
78 Jalan Hitam Manis
Singapore 278488
www.edmbooks.com
edm@edmbooks.com.sg

© Editions Didier Millet

Front cover: Photograph courtesy of UNICEF Thailand
Back cover: Photograph by Dominic Faulder

ISBN: 978-981-4385-27-5

For Mia,

ANAND
PANYARACHUN
AND THE MAKING
OF MODERN THAILAND

With much love,

Dominic Faulder

Dominic Faulder

Ponya,

3rd June 2019

edm EDITIONS
DIDIER
MILLET

For my family and friends in the East and the West,
and especially for my sister Clemencia.

CONTENTS

Chapter 5
INDOCHINA FALLS, CHINA BECKONS (1975)

Chapter 6
RETURN TO THAILAND (1975)

Chapter 7
THAMMASAT (1976)

Chapter 8
A NEW CAREER (1977–1991)

AUTHOR'S NOTE

When I met Anand Panyarachun in 2012 for the first of many interviews in his Saha Union office for this book, he asked where we should start. 'The beginning,' I said. We laughed at the time, but neither of us ever imagined that the project – initiated and commissioned by the publisher EDM – would take some six years to complete, and balloon from a projected 80,000 words to close on 220,000. We met over 60 times during the next six years, usually from about 12:30 to 4pm, with sessions often running later. The foundation of this book is therefore well over 200 hours of direct interviews.

I soon realised that Anand's life story could not be told without a quite detailed iteration of Thailand's history during his lifetime. He is deeply woven into the nation's complex fabric, and this is reflected in the book's title: *Anand Panyarachun and the Making of Modern Thailand*. This is not meant to imply that Anand made Thailand, but it should convey the idea that there are very few individuals alive who have interacted so directly with the many influential people who shaped the Thailand that emerged from the 20th century. The project became in some ways a shared journey; I was often perusing periods for the first time, while Anand was revisiting moments and incidents to which he might otherwise never have given another thought. He sometimes went off and checked things again for himself, and would often call me on my way home in the grinding Bangkok traffic with details that had just returned to him.

Of all the people who commented on how long the project was taking (I was also working as an associate editor for the *Nikkei Asian Review* for most of the time), Anand was probably the least critical. He knew that some of the interviews I was chasing would be unlikely to come through, and a few key ones took years to secure, literally. In one way or another, I interviewed over a hundred people, thereby creating for myself the enormous task of weaving so much first-hand material into a coherent narrative.

The benefit of writing a book about Anand is that many people are willing to open their doors to talk about him; this kind of access is rare in Thailand. A major problem, however, was the lack of surviving witnesses to Anand's early career, and often the sparseness of contemporary accounts. Thanat Khoman, his great early mentor as foreign minister, left no autobiography; neither did figures such as *MR* Kukrit Pramoj, Pote Sarasin, and Prince Wan Wathaiyakorn. I am not suggesting that they would have written about Anand particularly, but they could have described so much about the world he travelled through – the world they shared. This is a world most Thais today have not forgotten – it is a world they never knew. Gaps of this kind are not a problem peculiar to Thailand, but the country certainly has plenty of fascinating history that is only slowly emerging. The story of how the Vietnam War ended for Thailand, for example, and the people who worked to put the country on a fresh course is inspiring in many ways. The Ministry of Foreign Affairs took a terrible battering in what was at the time perceived as a battle with existential threats and inner demons – some of which linger to this day.

As you will read, Anand advanced into the top reaches of the Ministry of Foreign Affairs in the late 1950s while still in his 20s. His stellar diplomatic career ended after the terrible circumstances of October 1976, a time when Thailand was riven as seldom before. His relative youth as a diplomat means that many of his contemporaries – for example, ambassadors in Ottawa and Washington, and fellow permanent representatives to the United Nations in New York – were then at the peaks of their careers; they died decades ago. Many people who are still alive, including close relatives and some reluctant members of the military and political establishment, were simply too infirm to meet me. Some I missed very narrowly. For example, Pow Sarasin, one of Anand's close childhood friends, was taken ill the day I was due to see him, and did not recover.

Anand did not embark on this project without some reservations, but always seemed unperturbed by its scope and duration. He was invariably generous with his time and reflections, and for that I am grateful. He also accepted that while the book was principally about him, the authorship belonged to me. This is the nature of an authorised biography, and that understanding was respected. He always made it clear that certain confidences, particularly with regard to private audiences with King Bhumibol Adulyadej, would not be breached. Beyond that, most other matters were placed on the table. He did not ask to sign off on this book, and did not try to censor it, but was kind enough to caution me on areas that might prove treacherous. I have followed my own counsel in that regard. Anand was sometimes squeamish about personal financial details, and I have respected his privacy, even though in my view most of the details in question demonstrated his financial probity. He also requested that I not repeat some of his jokes made at the expense of others, and I have generally followed this advice.

My approach as a journalist has always to been to push for access to key subjects, and to try and let the story then emerge in its own way for the reader to judge. This might sound a bit old school, but in this era of talking heads and glib soundbites I continue to find a detailed storyline more interesting than billowing opinions. Although I am not uncritical, I have not set out to attack anyone; I have never been much enamoured of prescriptive or crusading journalism, particularly in a cross-cultural setting where situations are not always well understood. Perhaps we should all listen harder and pontificate less.

Most of the other interviews were conducted face to face in Thailand, and recorded; these usually lasted at least an hour. Some subjects I visited more than once, and many were helpful with subsequent queries. The interview with the late Suthee Singsaneh was conducted in 1991 when he was finance minister. The rest are all from 2012 onwards. An interview at Saha Union with Damri Darakananda, his wife Jongrak, and other senior company figures was the only one to involve more than one person at the same time. A list of people interviewed is given on p. xvii.

There have been many readers of the text at different stages, all of whom made valuable observations. Ammar Siamwalla, Chaiwat Satha-Anand, and Chris Baker read the entire biography in a very late draft. Others saw various sections of the book at earlier stages. I am particularly grateful to Nicholas Drummond, Paul Wedel, Phongthep Thepkanjana, Tej Bunnag, and David Lyman for reviewing sections that needed clarification.

The Ministry of Foreign Affairs was supportive throughout. The last three director generals of the information department, Thani Thongphakdi, Sek Wannamethee, and Busadee Santipitaks, all helped in whatever way possible. Vijavat Israbhakdi enabled identification of a number of retired diplomats in photographs. There was also assistance at the ministry from Korakot Parachasit, Chulachat Kanjana-oransiri, Nattapong Suwanpakdee, and Panom Thongprayoon; Suwanna Suwannajuta (in the main archive); and Phitchanat Wayakhum, Patcharin Saejiang, and Kanitha Kongdam (in the photo archive).

With the assistance of the late Mike Smith, the former secretary of the Old Alleynians in Bangkok, I was able to visit the Dulwich College archive. Calista Lucy, Soraya Cerio, and Terry Walsh helped with materials at that time, and portraits of Christopher Gilkes, the Master in Anand's day, were provided later. At Trinity College, Cambridge, Jonathan Smith arranged access to the magnificent library, and suggested some useful background materials.

Busarakham Nilavajara, Anand's personal assistant at Saha Union, helped in numerous ways, particularly tracking down names and addresses of interviewees, some of whom were long retired. She was supported in the office and with other tasks by Thanomchit Patrawutsomboon, Kanjana Popak, and Rung Huajiem.

Anand's daughters, Nanda Krairiksh, and Daranee Charoen-Rajapark, also helped in many ways. They ploughed through family albums and archives, providing access to material that would otherwise have remained beyond reach. Daranee's assistant, Ratchada Athakhan, kept track of photographs, many of them irreplaceable, that had to be scanned.

Martin Clutterbuck did some matchless translation work, and unravelled a few particularly complicated sequences. Benjamin Zawacki spent the entire winter of 2014 in Boston reading over 3,000 Wikileaks cables about Thailand for a book of his own, and his detailed pointers were both helpful and collegial. I am grateful to Theerada Suphaphong for assistance in contacting the Kofi Annan Foundation in Geneva, where interaction was handled by Michal Khan. Many other people helped me in small or large ways to fit pieces of a vast biographical jigsaw puzzle together, make introductions, arrange interviews, or to simply check details.

They include: Anthony Davis, Chaiya Richard Holt, Christopher Moore, Chua Siew San, Colin Hastings, Deanna Pajkovski, Desmond Yong, Domenica Piantedosi, George Lerner, Grant Evans, James Osborn, James Pitchon, Jane Kershaw, Jeffrey Race, Joe Horn-Phathonathai, Jonathan Head, Judith Clarke, Judy Benn, Julio Jeldres, Kenneth Barrett, Lachland Thomson, Laurie Rosenthal, Lee Gek Kim, Marina Vaizey, Marko Huhtanen, Matthew Last, Michael Hayes, Michael Vatikiotis, Pana Janviroj, Patchara Benjarattanaporn, Peter Cox, Phil Robertson, Porphant Ouyyanont, Poznan Sorgo, Ray Schonfeld, Richard Graham, Ron Corben, Samson Lim, Scott Bamber, Sheila McNulty, Simon Makinson, Sirin Phathonathai, Steve Heder, Sunai Pasuk, and Tatiana Shoumilina.

Others provided support when it was needed. They include the late Dan White, David Streckfuss, George McLeod, and Nick Nostitz. Greg Lowe gave me invaluable contractual advice. A number of personal friends have also been particularly supportive. They include Tom and Anna Whitcraft, Stephen and Caroline Simmons, Tom Vaizey, and Chris Szpilman. John and Ruth McGee took great interest in the project, but sadly have not lived to see its completion.

My thanks to Sonoko Watanabe, Tetsuya Iguchi, Nobuhisa Iida, Kenji Kawase, Toyoaki Fujiwara, Ken Koyanagi, Gwen Robinson, Satoshi Iwaki, Koji Nozawa, Yasumasa Shimizu, Hiroshi Toyofuku, Hiroshi Koitani, Yukako Ono, Hiroshi Murayama, Marimi Kishimoto, Thanaphorn Daoree, and all my other colleagues at the *Nikkei Asian Review* for their support and goodwill in recent years.

Most especially, I thank my family for their constant love and support: my parents John and Carolyn; my wife Caroline, son Patrick, and daughter Catherine; my older sister Sarah Faulder; and younger sister Clemencia Fergusson, who sadly left us all bereft in 2015; and my in-laws Dr J.P. Dickson and Chalermsri.

Finally, my thanks to the EDM publishing team led in Bangkok by Nicholas Grossman, the person who more than anyone initiated this biography, and juggled numerous other projects as he brought it to fruition. Timothy Auger's careful editing lifted the copy, and highlighted some weaknesses and shortcomings. Nina Wegner sifted the copy meticulously for stylistic issues and inconsistencies. Max Crosbie-Jones was indispensable in putting the book to bed in the final months. Bhimsupa Kulthanan was latterly responsible for research and fact checking; earlier researchers included Grissarin Chungsiriwat, Sutawan Chanprasert, Purnama Pawa, and Ruthai Kritsanapraphan. Annie Teo handled the layout and artwork, and Kay Lyons looked after the indexing and made some fine catches. Charles Orwin and Douglas Amrine contributed in the early days of the project, and Yvan Van Outrive remained a constant supportive presence throughout. Lastly, my thanks to publisher EDM, which had the vision and tenacity to see the project through. For reasons of editorial independence, EDM chose to underwrite the book without seeking sponsors. That kind of commitment is rare in contemporary publishing.

Dominic Faulder
London
27 September 2018

INTERVIEWS

Ammar Siamwalla

Anat Arbhabhirama

Abhisit Vejjajiva

Amnuay Viravan

Arsa Sarasin

Arthit Ourairat

Asda Jayanama

Bhichai Rattakul

Borwornsak Uwanno

Busarakam Nilavajara

Chaiwat Satha-Anand

Chan Bulakul

Charatsri Vajarabhai

Chatrachai Bunya-Ananta

Chavalit Yodmani

Chawan Chawanid

Chirayu Isarangkun Na Ayuthaya

Chutindhon Darakananda

Dalad Sapthavichaikul

Damri Darakananda

Daranee Charoen-Rajapark

David Lyman

Duangtip Surintatip

Ekamol Kiriwat

Gothom Arya

Hasan Basar

James Rooney

Jongrak Darakananda

Kamala Sukosol

Kamol Khoosuwan

Karuna Buakamsri

Kosit Panpiemras

Kraisak Choonhavan

Kullada Ketboonchoo-Mead

Mark Whitcraft

Mechai Viravaidya

Manaspas Xuto

Mike Smith

Narongchai Akrasanee

Nanda Krairiksh

Naowarat Pongpaiboon

Nitya Pibulsonggram

Norbert Eschborn

Nukul Prachuabmoh

Pisit Pakkasem

Phaisith Phipatanakul

Phil Robertson

Phongthep Thepkanjana

Prawase Wasi

Prida Tiasuwan

Pridi Boonyabhas

Pridiyathorn Devakula

Putrie Viravaidya

Saisuree Chutikul

Sarah McLean

Saroj Chavanaviraj

Sean Brady

Simon Hirst

Ralph 'Skip' Boyce

Snoh Unakul

Sompong Sucharitkul

S.R. Nathan

Sriwarin Jirapakkana

Steve Young

Suchit Bunbongkarn
Sulak Sivaraksa
Supakorn Vejjajiva
Supan Jotikabukkana
Supapan Chumpol Na Ayudhaya
Suthee Singsaneh
Suthep Bulakul
Suthichai Yoon
Teddy Spha Palasthira
Tej Bunnag
Thani Thongphakdi

Thant Myint-U
Thepkamol Devakul
Thirayuth Boonmi
Thitinan Pongsudirak
Tommy Koh
Vidhya Rayananonda
Vitthya Vejjajiva
Watana Pechmongkol
William Heinecke
William Warren
Wissanu Krea-ngam

In addition, I communicated with many people at a distance, including:

Bob Nunes
Bruno Huber
David Pratt
Derek Williams
Gareth Evans
James Osborn
Paul Wedel
Peter Cox
Pichai Chuensuksawadi
Piyasvasti Amranand
Steve Kraus
Sompong Charoensak
Uwe Morawetz

A NOTE ON SOURCES AND STYLE

This biography is based on literally hundreds of face-to-face interviews undertaken by the author, and also telephone and email correspondence. To improve the flow of the text, the present tense ("says", "recalls", "remembers", etc.) is used to indicate direct contact with the individual concerned, while the past tense ("said", "recalled", "remembered", "wrote", etc.) indicates material sourced from elsewhere.

Sadly, Chatrachai Bunya-Ananta, James Rooney, Kosit Panpiemras, Mark Whitcraft, Michael Smith, Nitya Pibulsonggram, S.R. Nathan, and William Warren have died since they were interviewed, and therefore their quotes appear in the past tense. The notes and appendices at the back of the book expand on some of these sources, or include additional details that would otherwise clutter up the main narrative.

Thailand has various transliteration systems, and this book intentionally adheres to none of them strictly as they all have their weaknesses and critics. Instead, the author and editors have followed the spellings contained in previous EDM publications on Thailand, which have been vetted already for such style matters.

Thai names in English are often exceptionally long, and their transliteration are a perennial challenge. Even members of the same family sometimes choose to spell their common surname differently. Some Thais also change their names, or the spelling in English, for various reasons.

The correct spelling for King Bhumibol Adulyadej was proclaimed in the Royal Gazette after his accession in 1946, which makes matters unambiguous. Other names are much more problematic. We have used a long version for Field Marshal Plaek Phibunsongkhram, and noted that he is generally referred to simply as Phibun. His son, Nitya Pibulsonggram, used a different spelling. As far as we are aware, we have followed the personal spelling preferences of each individual. We apologise for any errant spellings that might have slipped through.

We use the most common spellings for places like Ayutthaya and Pattaya, but the old spelling of Don Muang International Airport, which was officially changed to Don Mueang early this century. Don Muang was the spelling at the time of the events being described, and is what was used in most contemporary accounts. Similarly, countries are given their name at the time in question; Siam, Ceylon, and Burma became Thailand, Sri Lanka, and Myanmar in 1939, 1972, and 1989 respectively.

We have minimised honorifics and titles as far as possible. The only people identified as doctors have medical degrees. Elaborate and confusing titles and formal courtesies have been avoided, but we do note royal lineage in abbreviated forms. The diminishing royal titles of *Mom Chao*, *Mom Ratchawongse*, *Mom Luang*, are rendered as *MC*, *MR*, and *ML*. The second of these can unfortunately look like a typographical error for Mr, which is not used in the main text. *Khun*, a common honorific used for both men and women, only occasionally appears in quotations. *Khunying* is a conferred lifetime title bestowed on a non-royal woman. *Thanphuying* is the highest lifetime title for a non-royal woman.

CHAPTER I

CHILDHOOD
(1932–1948)

The Panyarachun clan

Anand Panyarachun was born in 1932, a year of revolution and political tumult in Siam, as Thailand was then known. His life spans the development of modern Thailand, an entity he has helped shape in more ways than most. His parents and later a visionary schoolmaster in England were to be the most influential people in his early life.

'We're independent-minded, too proud of ourselves.' Anand vividly remembers the comment, made in idiomatic Thai by his father, Sern. Anand himself puts it this way: 'In my family, we are independent and have our own way of thinking. We don't like to be dictated to or bossed around.'

This family trait no doubt played a role in Sern's decision to quit the civil service midway through his career, in 1933. Anand's four brothers all resigned after relatively short stints as government servants. Sern always contended that the Panyarachuns would never do particularly well in the civil service. He could not have foreseen the future career of his youngest son, Anand.

Anand's parents, Sern and Pruek Panyarachun, were wed in 1913 and shared over 60 years of married life. Anand was the youngest of their 12 children. The oldest child, Rak, 18 years Anand's senior, was studying in France when Anand was born. The Panyarachun family was so large, and so widely spread in age, that there were only three occasions on which all 12 children and their parents were together at one time. The oldest and youngest brothers did not meet until Anand was eight.

Most Thais have a nickname in addition to their given name. Anand is unusual, and has no nickname. Chat, his older brother by four years and the 11th child in the family, was nicknamed Nueng ('One') by his parents. 'They weren't going to call me Song ('Two'),' Anand laughs. The name 'Anand' is Sanskrit in origin and quite short compared to most Siamese or Thai names. It was not chosen by monks, as was the fashion at the time, but by his parents.[1] His parents added an accent later to clip the pronunciation of the name to ensure it did not resemble too closely that of King Ananda Mahidol.

The Panyarachun clan was among titled, non-royal officials collectively known as *khun nang*, although often referred to as *ammart*,[2] which historian Chris Baker regards as a bit misleading. '*Amat(ya)* is an old Pali-Sanskrit term,' he says. 'It is used very loosely in Thai, and very inconsistently over time. It has never been accepted as a word for "class".'

The family was respected and comfortably off, but not especially wealthy. The family name has an interesting history. Its old rendering in English was Panyarjun. It was bestowed on 7 July 1911 by King Vajiravudh (r.1910–1925). *Panya* is a reference to wisdom; Arjun was a heroic king from the *Mahabharata*, a Sanskrit epic that recounts the history of the ancient Bharata dynasty. Running to almost two million words, the *Mahabharata* is much longer than another great Hindu epic, the *Ramayana*, which is known in its Thai version as the *Ramakien*. So the name Panyarjun is arguably better suited than most to a leader, diplomat, or mediator. Arjun's banner depicted a monkey, and he believed fighting among kinsfolk to be morally wrong. The family seal depicts a chariot bearing Arjun and Krishna, an incarnation of Vishnu, the Hindu god. The name 'Panyarjun' was changed to the phonetically more correct Panyarachun by Anand's eldest brother, Rak, in 1956, when he was deputy foreign minister – much to the dismay of Sern.

Large families were commonplace in the early 20th century in Thailand. Although polygamy was not uncommon, in this instance only one wife was involved. Anand's parents both came from smaller families. Born in 1890, Anand's father, Sern, had only one sibling, an older sister; while Anand's mother, Pruek, had two brothers and three sisters.

A father's influence

Nobody was more influential in Anand's early life than Sern, his father. Of Mon ancestry, Sern's family migrated to Siam in 1815 from Mottama, a small town in what is today Mon state in Myanmar.

Sern's own father, Anand's paternal grandfather, Phya Dhepprachun had risen to the position of permanent secretary for defence despite being a civilian. In that capacity, he was also responsible for law and order in Siam's four southernmost states along the Malay Peninsula.[3] At Khao Chong Pran in Ratchaburi province, near a natural lake and massive bat caves, he endowed a temple and a school. The temple in Amphur Potharam was started in 1872 and completed much later by Sern. As a child Anand remembers visiting the temple most years to pay respects to his ancestors.

Phya Dhepprachun, Sern's father, died on 28 October 1894, when Sern was five. His mother, Khunying Chan, the last of Phya Dhepprachun's wives, was quite well off and lived many more years. She had no formal education but kept her accounts using a system of secret codes. Towards the end of her life, she came to live with Sern's family in Sathorn Road in Bangkok, and stored her money in trunks. 'She kept everything to herself,' Anand recalls. After her death, it was found that termites had attacked the banknotes, making many unredeemable. A number of gold items and trinkets were also found to be fake, suggesting she had been duped. Chan lived to an old age, with the consequence that Sern inherited nothing until his late 40s, a good while after Anand's birth.

Sern was a top student at Assumption College and later Suan Kularb School. His Thai education ended at the age of 15, in 1905, when he won a King's Scholarship to Shrewsbury School in the UK. One of Britain's oldest public schools, Shrewsbury was founded by royal charter in 1552. Although scholarships were available, 'public schools' were in fact nothing of the kind, being both private and exclusive. Many of today's public schools were either endowed in the 19th century or evolved from ancient grammar and cathedral schools. Their purpose was in part to educate the functionaries of an empire that once stretched around the world and upon which, literally, the sun never set. Shrewsbury boasts the naturalist Charles Darwin among its many distinguished alumni. Although Sern retained very fond. memories of Shrewsbury, the regime there was Spartan, with a mandatory cold shower each morning. Having started at Shrewsbury some two years later than most of his contemporaries, Sern propelled himself through four normal English school years in just two. During school holidays, he visited Scotland and Wales, studied French in France, and was taught carpentry in Sweden.

Among Thais studying in Britain in Sern's day, only royalty went to Oxford or Cambridge universities. As a commoner, Sern continued instead to the University of Manchester in northwest England to study mathematics from 1908 to 1910. One of the University of Manchester's senior lecturers was Chaim Weizmann, who spent three decades in Britain. Later, in early 1949, Weizmann was elected the first president of the state of Israel. He made a strong impression on the young Sern Panyarachun, whose funeral book includes a photograph of him placing a wreath on Weizmann's grave in the garden of his home at Rehovot, south of Tel Aviv – 'To my old professor from his old Thai student.'

Sern was always grateful for the education in Britain that the royal scholarship had provided. 'He grew up in two cultures, and yet remained 100 per cent Thai,' says Anand.

Sern never completed his bachelor's degree, but he did play football in Belgium for his university team. In 1910, when he was only two years into his course at Manchester, King Vajiravudh recalled him to Siam for service in the Ministry of Education. He started his teaching career at Debsirin and Suan Kularb schools in Bangkok, although his first direct encounter with the king did not come until September the following year.

Even though Sern had no royal blood and was never a member of the inner court circles, he was invited to take roles in plays directed by King Vajiravudh, who himself had spent ten years being educated in Britain and was a keen writer and dramatist. In 1918, the king created a model city, Dusit Thani, at Phayathai Palace where palace officials and civil servants played out democratic roles. These were scripted by the king, who himself played the part of a lawyer.[4] Sern also performed in the occasional *khon* masked dance, and was a noted storyteller. King Vajiravudh once summoned him for an audience at a camp for his *Sua Pa* ('Wild Tiger') Scout Corps, which he had created to train royal bodyguards and feed his own interest in military matters.[5]

In 1916, the king sent Sern to Chiang Mai to establish a Royal Pages School to be run on British lines. There were only mission schools there at the time, and numerous princes from the northern royal family had to be educated.[6] The reason for this posting is not entirely clear. It is thought there may have been some long-forgotten difference of opinion, perhaps over an appointment, and Sern was for a while out of favour with the king. The royal order Sern received said, 'You will do service far away; you must be dedicated to the enterprise I have entrusted to you.' However, the school in Chiang Mai was closed after two years when it was found to be in a malarial zone.

Sern, who had himself contracted malaria, returned to Bangkok and also royal favour, evidently, as he was put in charge of all the royal schools. He was given the title Phya Rajadarunsak in 1918, and in January 1919 was appointed director general of posts and telegraphs, which at that time were administered by a department in the Ministry of Education. A few months later, in July 1919, Sern entered Wat Boworniwet and spent 114 days in the monkhood.

For the next seven years Sern lectured at Chulalongkorn University, then known as the Civil Service College. In the year after King Vajiravudh's premature death aged 44 in 1925, he was appointed headmaster of Vajiravudh College, which was created to honour the late king by his half-brother, King Prajadhipok. The new school was the product of a merger between the earlier King's College (Mahat Lek Luang) and the Royal Pages School, founded in 1910 by King Vajiravudh soon after his accession. Vajiravudh College was a boarding school modelled on the British public school system. The main curriculum was maths, English and Thai; science was not offered.

In 1915 Sern had become the first honorary secretary of the Football Association of Siam, and he dreamed of introducing football clubs to Thailand along the lines of the English league system. He promoted organised sport at Vajiravudh College – an innovation for Siamese schools at the time. Besides games pitches and tennis courts, Vajiravudh College also brought fives and squash courts to the kingdom. Sern was a keen squash player himself. He also introduced carpentry classes – a novelty for a country in which the upper social strata regarded any form of manual work as demeaning.

Sern rose high in the civil service. He eventually became permanent secretary at the Ministry of Education, the top career post. He was granted the title Maha Ammart Tri Phya Prichanusat by King Prajadhipok in 1931 for services to education. However, his tenure as permanent secretary would be brief.[7] On 24 June 1932, six weeks before Anand's birth, a revolutionary coup was staged against King Prajadhipok, ending absolute monarchy in Siam and purportedly launching the kingdom into a democratic era. The princes, educated in Britain at Oxford or

Cambridge, who had served as ministers at the king's pleasure, were swept aside by revolutionaries among the military and civil service who had mostly been educated in France. The usurping commoners called themselves the People's Party and took control of the country's affairs. Four days later, Sern was one of 70 appointed members of Siam's first house of representatives. And so, in the year his 12th child, Anand, was born, everything changed for Sern.

It was a period of political tumult. Six cabinets were appointed in little more than two years. Prince Dhani Nivat, who had been appointed education minister in 1926,[8] was replaced by Chao Phya Thammasak Montri.[9] Thammasak resigned at the end of 1933 to serve as chairman of the house of representatives – only to quit after a few months in a state of disillusionment.

Sern was already gone; he had resigned from the ministry in February, and as headmaster of Vajiravudh College in April.

In 1933, at the age of 43, Sern entered the private sector. With friends, he set up a publishing business called the Siam Commercial Company (Thai Panichakarn). This became a veritable publishing stable, with Thai, Chinese, and English mastheads that included *Satri Sarn*, one of Thailand's earliest publications for women. In his new career, Sern edited the *Siam Chronicle*. It was a precursor to the *Bangkok Post*, of which he was one of seven founding shareholders. Indeed, when the *Bangkok Post* was launched on 1 August 1946, Sern pressed the button on the press that printed the first copy.[10] He was also the founder and first president of the Press Association of Thailand,[11] and the first non-Christian vice president of the Young Men's Christian Association (YMCA), serving on its board from 1948 to 1964. An active Rotarian, Sern also assisted with the setting up of Thailand's first school for the blind in the late 1930s.[12]

Sern was involved in establishing Laemthong Bank, Southeast Insurance, and some other fledgling enterprises. His various business experiences left him with no desire to return to the civil service. He was a royalist, certainly, but essentially uninterested in politics. 'I am sure he had his own political views, but he was not the type to advocate this or that,' Anand recalls. 'Politics was not a subject that was discussed very much.' Anand believes that his father's friendship with Prince Bovoradej, who had been minister of war before 1932 and who led an unsuccessful royalist counter-coup in 1933, may have attracted the interest of the secret police for a while, but this never led to Sern's being harassed. 'My father was devoted to Prince Bovoradej, but it doesn't mean he took sides,' says

Anand. Through his newspaper work, Sern was also close to Kulap Saipradit, a leftist newspaper editor, writer, and activist better known in the literary world as Sriburapha. Kulap would later serve a five-year prison spell for alleged treason before going into exile in China in the late 1950s.

A Bangkok childhood

Anand was born on 9 August 1932, in the Chinese Year of the Monkey. The birth took place at Vajiravudh College in Bangkok, where his father Sern lived with his family in the headmaster's house. After Sern resigned the position of headmaster in April 1933 and left public service, the family moved to a house in Bangrak, towards the western end of Sathorn Road. The compound was not far from the busy Chao Phraya river – at that time the kingdom's most important economic artery. Sathorn Road and its canal had been developed in the 1890s by Luang Sathorn Racha Yuk.[13] The compound faced a bridge crossing the canal from Surasak Road. This was not an ideal situation from a *feng shui* point of view. 'According to Chinese thinking,' says Anand, 'it was inauspicious. So there were two stone lions in front of the house to repel any evil forces.' Today, no trace remains of this compound, obliterated somewhere beneath thunderous traffic at an access point to Bangkok's elevated expressway. Also gone are the spreading rain trees, mud-lined canals, and mansion villas that once made this one of the most desirable residential areas of Bangkok, particularly among European residents and legations.

Anand's memory of his childhood home is of a large, two-storey house, comfortable, albeit of no particular architectural distinction. No photographs of it survive, but Anand remembers walls of concrete reinforced with bamboo rather than steel. The three main rooms on the ground floor were for dining, receiving guests, and family life. The family room contained a billiard table for games on Sundays after large family lunch gatherings. Because of the number of mouths to feed, two sittings were needed for the main evening meal. Apart from the three nannies and their families, the household included a Thai-Chinese cook, two maids, a gardener, and a driver.

The four youngest children in the household were Anand, his brother Chat,[14] his sister Supapan and his niece Charatsri (who was only two years younger than Anand). After they came home from school they would have a short rest and then do their homework together in the family room. The youngest children were sent to bed early, and shared one of four large bedrooms upstairs. The bedding was spread across broad floorboards beneath mosquito nets. Cooling came from electric fans and natural cross-ventilation. Even in the most affluent parts of the city, air-conditioning – or even a steady electricity supply – were still decades away. The children shared nannies and a zinc-floored bathroom. The bathing arrangements were about the only occasional source of friction among them. The nannies were competitive in defence of their charges, and joined in when the children quarrelled. 'All nannies are manipulative,' says Anand. 'They created their own fiefdoms, and always tried to promote their broods – better students, better behaviour. There was an element of jealousy in it but they all meant well.' Some of the nannies had children of their own, who lived alongside the family and were treated very much as their equals. Dee, the daughter of Nom Chuen, one of the many nannies in the household, was sent to the same elementary schools as the Panyarachun girls.[15]

Anand was devoted to his nanny, Ath. She was quick-witted and used to winning in the family rivalries, but died tragically of an incurable brain tumour when Anand was 11. She remained with the family to the end, sleeping in the same room as her charges. Anand recalls Ath's terrible suffering as one of the few traumatic events in his young life.

Sern was a clubbable man and his love of conviviality, good food, and drink would be a big influence on Anand. He enjoyed port and sherry, and making cocktails, a favourite being Tiger's Milk, a concoction of dark rum, brandy, milk, and sugar. He did not smoke. His passions included bridge and Western opera. In the evenings, after cocktails and dinner, he would sit the children down and play records on his gramophone. From time to time, in a schoolmasterly way, he would lift the needle and pause to explain the plots of *Aida*, *Carmen*, *Figaro*, *La Bohème*, *La Traviata*, and other classics unfolding in what must have seemed strangely modulated, utterly alien tongues. Anand also remembers his father cooking Western dishes.

Supapan, Anand's closest sister, remembers her father raising the family like a teacher. Former headmaster that he was, Sern checked on the soap and toothpaste as if he were doing the rounds of a boarding school. She remembers him tutoring her during homework, and the children learning from this example how to help each other. An enemy of rote learning, Sern imbued his children with a spirit of scepticism and inquisitiveness. 'We all spoke our minds and had strong voices,' says Anand. 'When you have three brothers and sisters arguing, outsiders might think it was a quarrel, but it was not. My father taught us to be independent thinkers and honest in every sense of the word.'

The women of the family were equally independent thinkers. Anand's mother, Pruek, was no exception. She was a Jotikasthira, a Hokkien Chinese clan. Her father Phya Dhipakosa, Anand's maternal grandfather, was a businessman and entrepreneur, and a leading figure in the Chinese business community. Their old family home was also on Sathorn Road, on the other side of the canal and not far north of the Panyarachun compound. The mansion survives today as the Burmese embassy. The family was well off. Phya Dhipakosa's enterprises included an early utility company that piped water for washing and laundry to prosperous houses in the Songwat area between Yaowarat Road, in the heart of the Chinese part of the city, and the Chao Phraya river.

Pruek's mother's family name was Lau; her formal title, acquired through her husband, was Khunying Prichanusat. She had limited formal education, but was well read and progressive-minded. She was well travelled by the standards of the day, having visited Rome, Berlin, and other parts of Europe in 1938.

Some people perceived a slightly Eurasian quality in Pruek's face; her strong features with high cheekbones and firm countenance matched her personality. Anand's niece Charatsri recalls that her mother, Pritha, and her young Panyarachun aunts were all good-looking and were courted young. Indeed, Pritha married before receiving her school graduation diploma.

Pruek spoke no Chinese and understood little English but she was always sociable and shared her husband's love for parties. Anand's niece Charatsri[16] remembers her grandparents going to see foreign films even in old age; Sern would lean across to whisper running translations into his wife's ear. 'They were inseparable,' says Anand. 'What strikes me is that my family had real harmony.'

Between Anand's parents there was a clear and even division of duties. As a good Thai wife, Pruek was the disciplined homemaker.[17] 'My mother could not stand lies, but she never spanked us or used force,' says Anand. 'All she had to do was stare in a certain way and we knew where things stood.'

Pruek held the purse strings. She had strong convictions about how the household should be run. When her sons started marrying, Pruek instructed that all their earnings be handed over to their wives. She had a scrupulous sense of order. Books were logically arranged, and suitcases packed meticulously. The children were well scrubbed, properly dressed and nursed at home through chicken pox and other routine childhood ailments. Anand's sister Supapan recalls seven of them coming down with measles all at the same time and her mother taking strict charge of the convalescence. 'My mother was well educated in an informal sense, and cleanliness was her passion,' Anand recalls. To this day, he does not much care for the unhygienic Western practice of shaking hands, and attributes that to his upbringing. With strong genes on both sides, most of the family have always enjoyed robust good health. 'We never went to hospitals or clinics because there were house calls – the doctor would visit us,' says Anand.

Bangkok in the 1930s

The Bangkok of Anand's childhood was almost bucolic. With a population of about 550,000 in 1932, and nearly 200,000 more living in Thonburi on the west bank of the Chao Phraya river, it was Siam's only true city[18] – all the other conurbations, including the northern 'capital' of Chiang Mai, ranked as little more than provincial towns. Siam's main economy was still agrarian, and whatever employment was to be found remained overwhelmingly rural. Few people migrated to Bangkok from the provinces at this time, and the capital was home to only about 5 per cent of the country's overall population.

However, by the 1930s, although it was still not growing particularly fast,[19] Bangkok was starting to become more metropolitan, with an economic life of its own. Siam's hopes for export-led growth were dampened by the Great Depression that afflicted the Western economies: prices of rice, rubber, tin, teak, and other commodities had been driven down. Indeed, Siam's consequent economic woes contributed much to the country's political volatility at this time, and to demands from below for a new, more democratic, businesslike order.

Like most other major cities in Southeast Asia, Bangkok was a port. Although Siam had over 6,000 kilometres of railway lines, most of the rice and teak exported through Bangkok was floated into the port along the Chao Phraya. Unlike many other major cities, Bangkok had no colonial heritage. This meant that roads were not mapped out in the sort of regular grid plan to be found in some other Southeast Asian capitals, such as Phnom Penh or Rangoon. Although the Siamese developed very substantial main thoroughfares and a system of major canals, the lanes and minor waterways in between were much less ordered, giving the city a haphazard, unpredictable quality that has endured to this day.

The city of Anand's childhood featured a network of electric trams dating back to the late 1890s. It ran to over 40 kilometres along seven lines.[20] The trams, with hard teak benches, dinged and rattled up to Banglamphu, along Yaowarat Road, the bustling Chinese mercantile heart of the city, and parallel to the Chao Phraya along Charoen Krung (New Road). Tracks ran above the canal up Silom and along Rama IV roads, connecting back to Hualumphong, the main railway station.

There were some paved roads northwards around Rajaprasong. Fields stretched to the horizon beyond the railway line crossing Ploenchit Road. The surface of Sukhumvit Road was dusty laterite with canals running down each side. The road meandered away to Paknam and ultimately eastwards to Cambodia. Surrounded by nothing more than a hibiscus hedge, the British embassy stood on the very edge of town, and buffaloes roamed nearby. The embassy was opened in 1928 on land next to the compound of Nai Lert, the pioneering founder of the White Bus Company. The mighty flagpole made from a ship's mast ensured the Union Jack was visible in all directions across the virtually pan-flat terrain. Landscaped nearby on crown property was Lumpini Park, one of many grand projects undertaken by King Vajiravudh in the 1920s that indebted the monarchy.[21]

One of Anand's closest friends in later life was Suthep Bulakul, two years his junior, who came from a prominent business family. As a boy, Suthep lived nearby on Sathorn Road and often rode a white horse along the laterite roadway. There were fields and small waterways in the vicinity. Running parallel to Sathorn beneath hardwood trees, Silom Road derived its name from the windmill pumps used to draw water up from the canal.

Almost every year floods afflicted parts of Bangkok. They were particularly severe in 1942, when Anand was ten. For the city's children, the flood was a great recreational opportunity. In those days, boys swam with their friends, ran about in the rain, and got about town on bicycles. The most prized were British Sunbeams and Raleighs, which were washed and serviced at weekends. The canal running along Sathorn Road past the Panyarachun compound was muddy, but relatively clean, unlike its toxic modern counterpart. 'We could still jump down and have a swim,' Suthep recalls.

'Life was very simple in those days,' says Anand. 'There were no real hardships. Chat and I would spend hours reading books my father had collected in his library.' The boys played Thai chess and a lot of table tennis. Sern taught the children bridge, although Anand did not keep it up. Youngsters collected cigarette cards off grown-ups, and played with crickets and fighting fish. Most of their games cost virtually nothing, requiring only marbles, playing cards, or shells. There was no television and very little worth listening to on the radio.

In the Panyarachun household, boxing and cruel pursuits such as hunting birds or squirrels with catapults were not encouraged. 'We were not sissies, but we were to some extent influenced by our older sisters, and my mother would not indulge such sports,' says Anand.

Suthep's mother went even further and banned him from almost all sports. 'In my generation, normally you did not argue with your parents,' he says. 'And in the Eastern world, it is traditionally the mother who looks after the children.' The protectiveness enveloping Suthep was only removed after the end of World War II when he was packed off to school in Hong Kong.

Charatsri remembers mock battles in the garden, with the smaller children riding round on the shoulders of Chat and Anand. Anand knocked some teeth out playing games on a concrete surface. Two or three times a week, when he needed a more rumbustious environment, he would ride his bicycle over to Soi Saladaeng and the household of Pote Sarasin whose wife, Siri, was a niece of Anand's mother and also from the Jotikasthira clan. The Sarasins have long been among Thailand's most prominent bureaucratic families.

Anand addressed Siri respectfully as *pi* because she was his older cousin. Strictly speaking, this made him an uncle to his Sarasin playmates, Pong, Pow, Arsa, Suphat, and their sister, Pimsiri. Arsa Sarasin was four years Anand's junior and Pow three years older. A fifth brother, Bandit Bunyapana, was also part of the Sarasin brood but was adopted and brought up by a childless aunt.

Birthday celebrations and family outings in Bangkok included visits to the cinema and to good restaurants. For upscale Chinese cuisine, there was the Hoi Thien Lao near Yaowarat Road where gilded dragons with red electric eyeballs were painted on the ceilings. Meals often began with melon seeds. For Thai-Chinese food, there was See Fah in Ratchawong Road, which first opened in 1936. On such occasions, a private room with space enough for at least ten was needed for Sern and his family entourage.

Western fare was usually taken at two of the few European hotels of the day, which were among the top places to be seen around town. One was the French-style Trocadero hotel at the bottom of Surawong Road, which was opened in 1927 by Chawee Bunnag, the British-educated daughter of Phya Prapakornwong.[22] With air-conditioning and lifts, and an elegant bar and restaurant, the 45-room property was considered the most luxurious in town. The second was the Hotel Rachathani beside Hualumphong, the main railway station built in the reign of King Chulalongkorn (r.1868–1910). The hotel, opened in 1927 by the Royal State Railways, was renowned for its food and service.[23]

'Anand and I were the youngest and had to sit right at the end of the table,' recalls Charatsri of these special occasions. 'We used to advise each other on which fork to use. I once used one too many, and at the end had to quickly wipe it off with the table cloth and put it back.'

The Panyarachun and Sarasin families spent two months of the year at the beach in Hua Hin, with Anand dividing his time between the two villas.[24] The holiday retreats provided opportunities for fathers normally distracted by their work to reacquaint themselves with their children. Entire households, including kitchen staff, decamped from Bangkok by train bearing all the provisions that might be needed.[25] The boys swam in the sea and rode ponies along the virtually deserted shoreline. Arsa remembers bird hunts with airguns and slingshots, although Anand, mindful of his mother's admonitions, didn't participate.

School days

Anand's earliest formal education was at Surasak School, a five-minute walk from home. He attended the school with his sisters and the children of the nannies and domestic staff. At the age of nine, having finished fourth grade, Anand moved on to Amnuay Silpa School where he spent the three years up to 1941.[26] Because of the distance from home, he was taken to school by trishaw and collected each afternoon by his father in a green Austin car. His most vivid memory from this period is of a teacher named Noon. 'I was a young boy, and attracted to her beauty and mannerisms,' says Anand. 'She was very kind and gentle, and I suppose I had some kind of a crush on her.'

Despite strong family ties, Chat and Anand did not follow their three older brothers to Vajiravudh College and Debsirin School (the latter dated from the 1880s and was closely connected with Wat Thepsirin). 'We often wondered why we were not sent to Vajiravudh,' says Anand. The fact that Sern had not yet received his inheritance may well have been a factor. The family was getting by well enough financially, but there was not a lot of money to spare. Instead, Anand attended Bangkok Christian College, a Presbyterian school. It was located quite close to the old family home of Anand's earliest years, off Sathorn Road, and offered a more modern syllabus.

'I remained a good student,' Anand recalls. 'But the trouble with me was that throughout my entire studies I never enjoyed any particular subject.' He was good at maths but did not like physics or chemistry; and so he opted for the arts curriculum. Then, when he found Pali and Sanskrit not to his taste, he asked to be moved to the science stream.

'He was a regular type, and sociable,' recalls Suthep. 'If he had been a bookworm, you would never have met him.' Anand remained at Bangkok Christian College until *mathayom* seven.[27] Although never the most enthusiastic of students, he always came first or second in class, and experienced no difficulties academically. Among his influences was Ajarn Kamchai, who taught him Thai, and had the rare ability to hold the entire class's attention.[28] There was also a geography master, Ajarn Aree, who enthralled the boys with tales of his travels in the US. Anand encountered other good teachers. However, none had the same impact as his own father, towering above him from the pinnacle of Siam's teaching establishment.

The Japanese occupation

In late 1941, World War II caught up with Thailand. This ruled out any possibility of studying in Britain for over four years. The Japanese occupation began on 8 December at much the same moment as the US naval fleet was, on the other side of the International Date Line, being attacked on 7 December at Pearl Harbor. Under the premiership of Field Marshal Plaek Phibunsongkhram (Phibun), the Thais became nominally allies of the Japanese. Soon after the occupation, Thailand declared war on Britain, although it failed to do so in the case of the US.[29]

Although the Thais faced shortages and rationing, the Japanese presence was initially quite low-key and easy to ignore. A wartime inconvenience for Sern was the scarcity of foreign films and other imported entertainment. Anand remembers being taken off to Yaowarat Road for Chinese opera instead.

'We were not subjected to any violence,' says Anand. 'In general, the Japanese troops were fairly well behaved. They had to observe the fact that Thailand was still a sovereign nation, and they were not running amok as they did in the Philippines, Indonesia, Malaya, or Singapore.' There was little awareness among the general population of the atrocities being carried out in Kanchanaburi province by Japanese military engineers building the infamous Burma Railway, even though labour was recruited locally, much of it Chinese. Occasionally, convoys would enter the Thai capital bearing wounded Japanese troops, evidence of the ferocious war being waged in neighbouring Burma.

Through children's eyes, the occupiers were often objects of amusement. 'The two things we noticed about the Japanese were the way they wore their loin cloths parading around, and their liking for bananas,' says Anand. Even as Japanese official relations with Phibun's government were unravelling, life was peaceful enough until Allied bombing began in earnest in mid-1944. Indeed, the Japanese 18th Area Army, which formed the garrison in wartime Thailand, enjoyed the softest war of any of the theatres in which Japanese imperial forces were present. Its commander, Lieutenant General Aketo Nakamura, had been specially selected for his diplomatic skills and tried to get on well with his Thai hosts.

A few hundred yards from the old Panyarachun family compound on Sathorn Road, the Thai-Chinese Chamber of Commerce was commandeered as the Japanese military headquarters. The British Club on Silom Road was turned into an officers' mess. These were legitimate targets for aerial attacks on Bangkok by Allied bombers flying sorties out of eastern India and Burma. The latter was being retaken steadily by Britain's 14th Army, a multinational force and the largest Allied army assembled in the war. By 1943, Japan was clearly headed for defeat. Other bombing targets included the German embassy on Surasak Road over the bridge from the old Panyarachun compound and, further afield, the power stations at Wat Liab and Samsen. Firebombs fell around the Chinese Association in nearby Yannawa and also along Sri Phraya Road. North of the city, the Don Muang airfield, which was used by the Japanese air force, was bombed and strafed.

Charatsri remembers being caught by surprise the first time an air raid siren went off and everybody dived for cover in the garden. 'It was fun for the children because every house had to have a shelter we could play in,' says Supapan.

By mid-1944, the Allied bombing had become so serious that schools and universities were closed and much of the city evacuated. Suthep and his family ended up in the sleepy seaside town of Siracha, southeast of the capital. The Panyarachuns moved to a big plot of land on Saen Saep canal. This lay northeast of the city near Navathani, on the way to Minburi, and was owned by a Jotikasthira relative. About 20 wooden houses made up the compound. There were several mosques in the vicinity – Bangkok's Muslim communities tended to populate outlying areas. The swimming in the relatively clean canal was good, and tasty noodles were sold from boats paddled by vendors. The journey back into town had to be made by boat.

Anand attended Nantanasuksa School that year, paddling a boat every day for 20 minutes each way. This period was the closest his family ever came to any sort of ordinary village life. Supapan recalls long listless days in the compound with little to do apart from play board games and cards. Though only 12, Anand began to play poker with men many times his age, including Pote Sarasin, taking over their hands when they needed to be excused for a break. According to Anand, his short – but moderately successful – gambling career ended when he was almost 16 and went overseas.

World War II ends

Anand's oldest brother, Rak, had done exceptionally well during his education in France, earning his baccalaureate there followed by a top law degree from the University of Lille in 1940.[31] He returned home and joined the legal department of the Ministry of Defence, attaining the rank of major. Anand's second brother, Kusa, was sent for his education to the more affordable Philippines for 18 months, and moved on to the US, where he attended Williston High School in Maine. The US was drawn into World War II in late 1941. Kusa was unable to join the Free Thai resistance in the US. The movement had been established by MR Seni Pramoj, Thailand's ambassador in Washington, the diplomat who had somehow failed to deliver Thailand's declaration of war to his American hosts.[32] Instead, Kusa was among the very few Thais to enlist in the US army, rising to the rank of sergeant. As the war progressed, the US military developed its contacts with the Free Thai resistance, and with the increasingly influential regent, Pridi Banomyong, whose codename in the underground movement was Ruth. Kusa was soon identified as a potential asset in the Asian theatre, and sent to Ceylon[33] for paratrooper training. He spent eight months there waiting to be dropped into Thailand.

'For some inexplicable reason, he was eventually sent in by submarine,' says Anand, recounting a story that is still a family joke. The US Office of Strategic

Services (OSS), which in late 1945 would become the Central Intelligence Agency (CIA), had found a small island off Thailand's Andaman coast that was habitable but seemingly uninhabited – ideal for establishing a clandestine radio station. Kusa had been assigned the codename King, but was known in Free Thai circles simply as Sarge in deference to his US military rank. After travelling from India in the submarine, Kusa's team paddled ashore under cover of night in a rubber dinghy, arriving exhausted.

The OSS intelligence turned out to be wrong. In fact, the island was inhabited. Kusa and his fellow neophyte spies were found fast asleep by locals who immediately tipped off the Japanese. It could all have turned out very badly. Instead, they were arrested and sent by train to Bangkok, and taken in hand along the way by Thai authorities. Kusa was 'interned' on Phra Arthit Road in the Banglamphu area, but was able to go out at night. Because he was moving about on trust – and because nothing was ever quite as it seemed in the occupied capital – Kusa was not allowed to reveal his presence in the city to his family. Even so, occasionally after dark, he would bicycle down to Sathorn Road and peer over the garden wall into the empty compound, recalling times past. The rest of the Panyarachun family had already moved on.

When the war came to an end in 1945, the Panyarachuns returned to the city and lived in a golden teak house on Chidlom Road that had previously been occupied by a British family. Anand's parents were finally able to sell off the old Jotikasthira property on Sathorn Road to the Burmese government, which would use the large house as an embassy. It had been inherited jointly by Pruek and her three sisters, and the compound could not be subdivided. Anand's aunts had been bought out some years before the sale, which netted about a million baht – a good price for the time. The old Sathorn family compound, Anand's first home, was also sold after the war. Sern went on to buy from Pote Sarasin a plot between Chidlom and Somkid roads that would be divided up equally between the four younger sons.[30]

CHAPTER 2

ENGLAND
(1948–1955)

Beyond Bangkok

On 14 August 1945, Japan surrendered unconditionally. World War II was at an end, and the Thai economy was in shreds. Thailand had been the target of over 4,000 Allied bombing sorties in 1944 and 1945. The power station at Wat Liab was bombed-out, and two Japanese submarines moored in the Chao Phraya were trickle-feeding electricity through it to the grid. Conservative estimates suggest the cost of living had risen by more than six times during the Japanese occupation.

The political situation was fluid. Thailand's last wartime prime minister, Khuang Aphaiwong, had schemed against the Japanese but he soon stood down.[1] The country's diplomatic situation was precarious, and the regent, Pridi Banomyong, moved to shore it up. The country had been caught up with the losing side, and Britain and France now returned as vengeful, potentially resurgent regional colonial powers. The British were bent on exacting reparations from the Thais and prosecuting alleged war criminals among them. To gain US support, Pridi issued a peace proclamation, which asserted that the wartime alliance with Japan forged by Field Marshal Plaek Phibunsongkhram (Phibun) had been unconstitutional, and against the wishes of the Thai people.[2]

Pridi immediately requested that the young King Ananda Mahidol return from Switzerland, where the royal family, including the king's brother Prince Bhumibol Adulyadej, had been waiting out the war. As a conciliatory move towards the victorious Allied forces, it was decided that *MR* Seni Pramoj, Thailand's British-educated wartime ambassador in Washington, who had formed the US branch of the Free Thai resistance movement during World War II, should become prime minister.[3] Seni had returned home in September, and was afforded a hero's welcome in front of the Grand Palace at Sanam Luang, which he circled in a motorcade. Seni remained only four months in his new job before elections were held. Although the US largely thwarted British and French antagonism towards Thailand, Thailand was still required to supply rice to the region and to starving Japan.

In December 1945, Lord Louis Mountbatten, the supreme Allied commander in Southeast Asia, arrived to preside over a parade of Allied forces that had entered Thailand to disarm and intern Japanese remnants. The salute was taken by the young King Ananda, reducing somewhat the sting of national humiliation. His stay in Thailand was subsequently extended for reasons of state, but ended tragically. On the morning of 9 June 1946, King Ananda was found dead in his bed with a bullet through his forehead.[4]

For a few more years, Thailand was officially known again as Siam, but nothing in Thai politics sounded quite so poetic.[5] After King Ananda's violent death, Pridi was forced into exile. After Seni's government, there were two successful coups and four brief premierships before Phibun finally prevailed, fending off resurgent royalists and recovered the power he had yielded in 1944. Phibun's return in April 1948 was the start of almost a decade in power.

Inevitably, during the war, the controversial field marshal was one of the first political leaders to awaken young Anand's political consciousness. However, he never became a role model – for much of Phibun's second stint Anand was studying overseas in an environment much more liberal than Thailand. The post-war prime ministers he would observe more closely were Britain's Clement Attlee and Winston Churchill.

While the war, inconvenience, and expense of foreign education had kept Chat and Anand in Bangkok, the third Panyarachun brother, Prasat, had gone to Tokyo, enrolling in the prestigious Gakushuin (Peers' School) along with the son of Prince Wan Waithayakon, a top diplomat.[6] After two years, Prasat returned to study law at Thammasat University. After the war ended, Prince Wan was appointed ambassador in Washington, and the two young schoolmates went off again together, this time to Georgetown University in the US. Both were planning careers in the foreign service (although, as events turned out, Prasat joined the police).

Chat, Anand's closest brother, planned a career in medicine and enrolled in the science faculty at Chulalongkorn University. He had done well at physics, chemistry, and biology at Amnuay Silpa School. He carried on from Chulalongkorn to do a pre-med at Harvard University, only to discover he could not cope with anatomy lessons in the dissection room. He abandoned the course after a year to study accounting at Boston University. When he returned to Thailand in the mid-1950s, Chat, like his brother Prasat, joined the police, serving for two years as a lieutenant. At the time, serving in the police was a common way for students educated overseas to avoid the army draft.

Dulwich years

Anand's own secondary education, delayed by war and straitened family finances, would be quite unlike anything his brothers experienced. In 1948 he was the only son in the family still of school age. He was almost 16 when, on 30 May, he and five other Thai students took off from Don Muang Airport aboard a KLM Lockheed Super Constellation that had come on the long haul up from Sydney and Batavia.[7]

The youngest member of the group was Chavalit Yodmani.[8] Dressed in shorts, he was four years Anand's junior and in a state of great trepidation. Chavalit's father was a classmate of Rak's and had been taught by Sern. The Yodmani family lived in a compound on Sri Phraya Road that had been firebombed during the war. Although it was not far from Anand's first home, the two boys had not met before, and Chavalit had been given no warning whatsoever of his departure for England. The other four students on the flight were much older men, returning to complete university courses interrupted by war.

In the pre-jet age, the journey from Thailand to the UK by air involved half a dozen stops across Asia, the Middle East, and Europe. The first was Mingaladon Airport, with its noisy steel-plate wartime runway, in the Burmese capital Rangoon. The first night was spent in Karachi, West Pakistan, which had been bloodily partitioned from British India only the year before. The final destination of the KLM flight was Amsterdam. From there, a twin prop took the little party across the English Channel to Croydon Airport, to the south of London. 'It was scary,' recalls Chavalit. His sudden relocation across the world was punctuated by bouts of acute airsickness. Once in London, all the buildings looked the same to him.

He was petrified of losing his travelling companions and hung on to their coat tails, as he put it, 'like a baby elephant'.

Sern had wanted Anand to follow him to his *alma mater*, Shrewsbury, but the school was over 250 kilometres northwest of the Thai embassy in London, and the journey between the two would have involved changing trains. Sern's friend, Phya Sri Visarn Vacha, a foreign minister in the early 1930s, recommended his own old school, Dulwich College, instead. It was located more conveniently in the affluent suburbs of southeast London, a little south of the Thames. Dulwich had Blew House and Ivyholme for senior boarders, and Bell House and Carver House for juniors, but was primarily a day school. Of some 1,100 boys, fewer than 200 boarded. This made the ambience relatively open, less steeped in the traditions of public schools where the boarding culture, which many found challenging, was dominant.

Anand was accepted to start at the age of 16, which was very late. Although 10 per cent of the annual intake was reserved for overseas pupils and sons of Old Alleynians (as former Dulwich College pupils are known),[9] foreigners were still in a tiny minority. The few were a disparate mix from Czechoslovakia, Ghana, India, Iraq, Hong Kong, Nigeria, Turkey, the US, and the Caribbean. 'Dulwich was not stuffy and we were not forced to take cold showers,' says Anand.

Anand had been taught English in Bangkok, but, as he admits, 'I didn't take any entrance exam for Dulwich because my English was virtually non-existent. My English was good for a Thai student, but that doesn't mean anything when you join upper secondary school in England.'[10] His first three months in England were spent acclimatising in the home of a Dulwich schoolmaster, William Darby, his wife Mollie and their children, daughter Frances and son Sheridan. The family lived five minutes from the school.

Darby was himself an Old Alleynian who taught classics and French,[11] and wrote two books about Dulwich. Anand remembers him best as a cricket fanatic, albeit one with limited playing ability. Darby's delight in the game infected his charge. Although Anand never played, he enjoyed the spectacle and cricket's arcane competitive strategies. Anand has retained a lifelong passion for watching team games of all kinds.

In September 1948, at the start of the British school year, Anand entered Blew House as one of 50 boarders under the popular housemaster Eric Parsley and his stout deputy E.C.C. Wynter, who played for Blackheath Rugby Club.

Anand's close West Indian friend at Blew House, Robert (Bob) Nunes, recalls Parsley instilling 'a gentlemanly influence on our upbringing and lives'. Although Parsley's wife, Muriel, appears in house photographs, she played almost no role in Blew's all-male environment.

Anand's house for sports and other activities was Raleigh, one of six athletics houses named after great figures from the reign of Queen Elizabeth I (r.1558–1603).[12]

At Blew boarding house, younger boys slept four to a room while seniors were allotted their own cubicles. The college grounds were covered in soggy leaf mould in autumn, were cold and foggy in winter, and always felt deserted at weekends when the weekly boarders went home. Anand was sometimes invited out by friends. He remembers happy weekends spent at the home of his close friend Hugh Clark, whose parents took the boys off to tennis clubs in Surrey, a county southwest of London.

For someone to whom everything had always come so easily, Anand's first year at Dulwich was one of the most frustrating of his life – a process of unrelenting cultural immersion. 'I would not say it was a trauma, but I was homesick,' he says. 'I was a good student back in Thailand, so when I struggled at Dulwich it was a painful experience. The wretched thing was that it was all because of my lack of English.'

When he joined the upper fifth, Anand had to grapple with the fact that he could often understand no more than a third of anything he read. One reason was that the quality of English teaching in Thailand had declined after the 1932 revolution, especially in the war years. Anand's sisters had been able to read English novels by the time they left St Mary's School, but any such feat was well beyond Chat and Anand, the two youngest boys. 'I was always told that if you have your first dream in English, that is the beginning,' says Anand, recalling his hard grind towards fluency. 'It took me five months.'

Anand was exempted from Latin, history, and French, but did English, biology, chemistry, physics, mathematics, and geography. Science lessons in the laboratories were a novelty. Back in Thailand, everything had been taught from textbooks. In Dulwich's more inquiring environment, teachers and pupils exchanged ideas freely, and there were experiments. For the first time, Anand discovered that lessons could actually be 'fun'. 'It was not a strained atmosphere like in a traditional Thai classroom,' he says. He was particularly struck by the absence of standard texts in history. Boys were given reading lists to choose from, and then debated the various accounts in class. In Thailand, there had been nothing so liberal, and very little attention was ever paid to the impact of historical events. 'History is not just a chronicle of events, but a variety of interpretations,' says Anand. That lesson has stuck with him. He still likes to haul up journalists, and remind them that their work is merely the first rough-cut of history written in the blurred rush of events.

A useful discipline new to Anand was the précis. A good précis reduces multiple pages of text to one page or less without either copying sentences or sacrificing sense. This seemed to him the very essence of comprehension. The process of listening effectively to classes and lectures, he realised, was in many ways a mental précis. Paring down ideas to their core was a novel discipline he still suspects most Thais find tedious. 'That's why we have such a low level of debate in parliament,' he says. 'They don't get the question, so the answers are slightly off the mark.'

Although spared the rigours of Latin, Anand always remained in the room alongside his classmates, often working alone on special remedial English studies. This enabled him to observe history classes without ever actually studying the subject.

The old School Certificate system was replaced in 1950. That year, Anand passed five of the new GCE 'O' (ordinary) levels, which was good enough for him to proceed to 'A' (advanced) level in mathematics. The maths became increasingly demanding, however, pushing him to the edge of his comfort zone.

Although they sometimes appal his family, Anand's recollections of English school life are for the most part extremely positive. He regarded any adversity as simply a part of growing up. Even so, this was austerity-stricken, post-war Britain with unheated houses, rationed clothing, and unspeakable food. 'The British considered rice pudding to be nearly Thai,' recalls Chavalit. 'But rice as a sweet tasted quite strange, and was something we could not get used to.' Apart from dismal, gluey English rice pudding, sugar and meat were in short supply, eggs were restricted to one a week, and confectionery was rationed as well.

Breakfast at Dulwich was grey toast with a sliver of margarine or some kind of dripping and salt. Lunch at noon, the main meal of the day, was called 'dinner'. High tea was at six and featured lots of bread, which had come off ration in 1948.[13] Cocoa and buns were served at bedtime.

Awful food was not the worst of it: the boys shared tepid bath water. 'At first, I was embarrassed about taking my clothes off in front of everyone,' Anand remembers. 'We took a bath in a large tub. Senior boys sat near the hot water tap, and junior boys would have to contend with the lukewarm water and dirt from the older boys. Once a week, we were able to have a private bath.'[14] He shrugs off such 'character-building' experiences: 'That's the way it was.'

As a Buddhist, he was not required to attend morning prayers with the other predominantly Christian boys at assembly in the great hall. Jewish boys had their own private prayer gathering. Anand was also exempted from compulsory chapel on Sunday mornings for boarders and staff. When he became a house prefect, however, he was expected to take his turn in the boarding house reading lessons from the Bible at evening prayers after prep. 'I had to ask a friend to choose a section for me, but I would read it,' says Anand. 'I am not a religious type – not a temple-going Buddhist. I never regard Buddhism as a religion in the normal sense of the word. It is more a philosophy, a way of life. But I believe that I do behave in a Buddhist way.' For some physical reason, he has always found sitting on the floor at a temple in the correct posture most uncomfortable.

Like most of the other boys, Anand had his hair tousled a few times at Dulwich. The Thais have a particular ingrained sensitivity about anything relating to the head, and he did not appreciate this experience. He has, however, no recollection of any bullying or racism. Because of his relative maturity, he arrived at the top end of the fagging system. Fagging was a public-school institution that allowed seniors of 17 and 18 to use younger boys as servants. Juniors ran errands, polished shoes, and made beds and coffee. When seniors clapped their hands, the younger boys dashed up. 'We would shout "junior", and whoever came last got the job,' says Anand. In winter, this included the miserable task of washing muddy rugby kits and cleaning the boots. Many years later, Anand's fag at Dulwich, Roland Dallas,[15] would resurface in New York as a correspondent for Reuters when Anand was a senior diplomat there.

'Some prefects enjoyed spanking the juniors with slippers,' says Anand. 'Canes were only for the masters. Now it is all banned.' He himself was never caned, nor on the receiving end of any corporal punishment, and he never administered it.

Although he missed his family, Anand felt no cultural isolation at Dulwich. He exchanged letters with his family every week, but his Thai spelling began to suffer. Some familiar faces started appearing at Dulwich in 1949, including his nephew Arsa Sarasin – who was four years younger and placed in a different boarding house with some other younger Thais. Arsa always looked up to Anand, and had pleaded to be allowed to attend Dulwich.[16]

Close family members also began to appear in London, including Anand's father. In 1950, Sern became the first Thai to be appointed student superintendent in the UK. With Chat and Prasat studying in the US, Sern could equally have taken the same position in Washington, but opted for the familiarity of Britain where he could be close to his two youngest daughters. He was re-establishing an office that had been closed when Thailand declared war on Britain in 1941. At that time, Thais were designated 'enemy aliens'; Thais stopped studying in the UK for the rest of the war, and the supervision system built up since King Chulalongkorn's reign in the 19th century was suspended. Sern's goal was to become thoroughly acquainted with all the schools attended by Thais.

Sern took an apartment with no central heating on Cromwell Road in south-west London. Later, he moved to nearby Queen's Gate. After ten months, he fell ill. He was ill-suited to the climate and the stress of the job. Among other pressures, there was a scandal involving a teacher and some Thai boys at Romsey College. Unwell, Sern returned home after only a few years.

Anand's sister Supapan, and the nanny's daughter Dee, arrived in London in 1950 along with Pimsiri Sarasin, Arsa's only sister. Five years older than Anand, Supapan moved into the Queen's Gate flat with her parents, which Anand visited on some weekends. She attended a nearby secretarial college, and grew to love London for its broad pavements, parks, Underground, and buses. 'England has a charm that no other country has,' she says, exhibiting a strong Anglophile streak common to many of the Panyarachuns.

Charatsri, Anand's niece and old playmate, also arrived. On her second day, Anand took her to lunch at the Asiatic, a Chinese restaurant near Piccadilly. Of all Sern's children and grandchildren, Charatsri was to be one of the few to follow him into a career in education: she worked at the Ministry of Education and with UNESCO in Bangkok.[17]

Anand enjoyed the bustle and camaraderie of the boarding environment. He made many firm friendships at Blew House, and still talks fondly of Hugh Clark, Taffy Davies, Bob Nunes,[18] John Lowry, and Paul Hitchings, among others. Alan Webb, another close friend, was a dayboy. Although he would lose touch with almost all his contemporaries, Anand has no trouble today picking out their faces in one of the old, framed, black-and-white photographs in his study.

School life outside the classroom was rich and busy. Anand joined the school choir. The head of music was the composer Stanley Wilson, who enjoyed taking on major challenges, such as Benjamin Britten's *Spring Symphony* (1949). Anand took part in a performance in 1952 of Handel's *Messiah* at the Royal Festival Hall, which had opened for the Festival of Britain in the previous summer.

Thirty per cent of pupils at Dulwich opted not to join either the school's scout troop or the Combined Cadet Force, and Anand was among them.[19] Nor did he take up boxing, which was popular at the time. In Thailand, it was rare for boys from such prominent families to enter a boxing ring, particularly for a bout with a stranger.[20] Many led cosseted existences, coddled by mothers, sisters, and nannies. Indeed, when his favourite nanny left after the war to marry, even the fiery Arsa went back to sleeping in his parents' bedroom. Nevertheless, other Thai boys, including Arsa, his brother Bandit Bunyapana, and Pakorn Thavisin, had reputations as formidable boxers. They used natural speed and agility to great advantage in the paperweight and under-seven-stone divisions.

Dulwich joined in quadrangular boxing and fencing fixtures with schools such as Bedford, Christ's Hospital, Eton, Haileybury, Mill Hill, St Paul's, Tonbridge, and Winchester. In a bout in early 1953, Arsa inflicted a memorable defeat on an 'awkward opponent' from Eton, Lord Valentine Charles Thynne:[21] 'Sarasin soon went ahead by superior boxing,' it was reported in *The Alleynian*, the school magazine. 'His fast countering with both hands combined with his quick footwork left Thynne floundering, and a sustained attack in the last round made the decision certain.' Anand vividly remembers the moment when a triumphant Arsa announced that he had decked an English lord.

Arsa's brother Bandit had an unbeaten season in 1952, earning him a glowing profile in *The Alleynian* as a sporting 'character': 'At paperweight, he was far superior to any opponent in boxing ability and fitness. His piston-like lefts and quick rights were lovely to watch but he must sharpen up his infighting and use of the ring.'

Since his earliest days, Anand has often been called Nand or Na Nand ('Uncle Nand') by those closest to him. These include junior cousins, nephews, and nieces close enough in age to be playmates. Arsa recalls Anand taking the role of 'uncle' very seriously, and escorting the younger boys to Chinese restaurants around Piccadilly Circus and Leicester Square in London's West End. Arsa's weekly allowance only bought him four threepenny lemonades, so the outings were major treats.

At school, Wednesday and Saturday afternoons were devoted to games on Dulwich's 18 playing fields. Anand had not himself participated in properly organised team games in Thailand, but he always enjoyed watching soccer. At Dulwich, he was expected to play rugby every Wednesday, usually out on the wing where the chances of out-running trouble were better. The school outing to the Oxford-Cambridge 'varsity' rugby match at Twickenham was an annual highlight.

Far from shunning sports, Anand took pains to identify those in which he might do well, gaining both tennis and squash colours at Dulwich. Other than at Vajiravudh College, Thai schools had not offered these minor sports. Squash – a game his father also played well – was made particularly challenging at Dulwich by the absence of proper courts. The old squash courts had been flattened in 1944 by a German V-2 flying bomb, a liquid-fuelled ballistic missile. Apart from the fives and squash courts, the Nazi blast also destroyed the science block, the rifle range, the armoury, and a new bathhouse. Even by Anand's time, the extensive damage had not yet been rectified and players had to go to nearby Sydenham for games.

Despite such complications, Anand was beaten only once in 1951 in a squash match at Brighton when he developed 'a bad attack of stitch' – a painful cramp of the diaphragm. *The Alleynian* recorded Anand's achievement with a caveat: 'The most successful member of the team, winning his first five matches. Although much improved, he is still rather weak in retrieving the ball from corners, but he has an excellent "kill" shot which won him many points.' Elsewhere *The Alleynian* noted: 'The reasons for his victories lie in his accurate volleying and his very hard and low "kill".'

Anand was captain of tennis, a senior sporting position, for two years. Although there was nominally a master in charge of each sport, it fell to each captain to organise fixtures with other schools and make transportation arrangements. Most importantly, the captain also selected the team. Dulwich was unbeaten at tennis in 1951 in matches against other schools. It also did well in the Glanville and Youll Cups, tournaments in which only King's College School Wimbledon bested Dulwich. In his captain's report, Anand was able to record arguably the most successful summer since tennis had been introduced to the school. J. Aldridge, the master in charge, faulted Anand for a lack of speed and defensive style that was 'a great handicap', but praised his nascent leadership skills: 'As a captain, he has shown himself to be keen, co-operative, capable and most self-sacrificial. His quiet and modest leadership has played its part in the success of both first and second teams.'[22] Anand looks back on his first taste of managerial responsibility with some pride, although he did once have to ask a friend who 'A.N. Other' was on a list of names.

Without stating anything explicitly, Aldridge's very favourable assessment of Anand's early leadership qualities was influenced by Anand's decision to be a non-playing captain in the public schools championship at Wimbledon. Anand assessed another pair as a better playing combination, and left himself on the sidelines, in order to advance the team's overall chances. 'To me it was a matter of fact,' says Anand.

Lifelong friendships were forged among the Thai students in the UK during school holidays, when arrangements were made for get-togethers. Given the expense and distance involved, journeys home to Thailand were generally out of the question. Anand spent seven unbroken years in the UK. Arsa stayed abroad for six years, returned with his mother for a month in 1955, and then went to the US for another four years. Chavalit returned home by sea after four years, but only for long enough to pick up his younger half-brother, Suvit, to escort him back for schooling. After five years spent in Britain before moving to the US, Kamala Sukosol – a society figure later celebrated as much for her musical talents as for her business acumen – ended up marrying an American and did not return to Thailand for another 20 years.

With only a few hundred Thai students in the UK, the youngsters developed a certain pioneer spirit. Some even came to like the food – up to a point. 'No one can beat English toffees, but I have never eaten a Kit Kat since,' says Kamala. She always used to eat her sweet ration – unlike many Thai girls who made themselves popular by giving it to their English friends. Kamala developed a taste for English custard and traditional English puddings with lurid nicknames such as 'dead man's arm', 'matron's leg', and 'spotted dick'. There were also rhubarb pie and trifle on Sundays made from leftover cakes. Kamala lapped up these exotica.

Anand first met Kamala while she was in boarding school at Chislehurst, not far from Dulwich. Following Arsa's example, she began calling him Na Nand. 'I can't recall him saying anything bad about anybody,' she says. 'When we got on the bus, I wanted to find a seat where I could sit next to him, or in his vicinity, because that corner would laugh the most.' Chavalit confirms Anand's popularity among his fellow students. 'Everywhere, he had a nephew or niece, so people called him Na Nand. So did I – although I am not related to him.'

Special holiday arrangements were made by the Thai Student Office at the Royal Thai Embassy in London, then located at 23 Ashburn Place. Thai students from all over the UK were sent off in groups to various out-of-season southerly seaside resorts, mainly in the counties of Hampshire, Sussex, Devon, and Dorset. Miss Harrison, a vivacious spinster known for the noisy bangles on her wrists, supervised the logistics. 'She was a lovely lady, very kind, and loved by all the Thai students,' says Chavalit, whose lifelong attachment to Anand and Arsa, among many others, dates from those holidays. Anand's favourite seaside destination was Eastbourne, on the Sussex coast, where the landlady, Mrs Gurd, had been looking after Thai students for over 30 years. In Bournemouth, on the Dorset coast, there was a couple from the north – the husband had a strong Scottish accent that utterly confounded his Thai guests.

Everybody's favourite landlady was Mrs Bell, in Southampton. The group of young houseguests in her large Victorian mansion included Anand, Arsa, Bandit, Chavalit, Kamala, Tongnoi Tongyai, Thep Chaturachindha, Sombhop Krairiksh, Ungura Puranonda, Supan Jotikabukkana, and Anand's nephew, *ML* Birabhongse Kasemsri – individuals from prominent families who would all one day figure prominently in Thai society. Carefree in the charge of Mrs Bell, they played tennis, went to the cinema, and concocted simple Thai dishes in their rooms.

During the summer holidays, the Thai students in England would meet *en masse* for a ten-day retreat under the auspices of the Thai Students' Association (Samakki Samakhom). Venues included Pinner in Middlesex, Leatherhead in Surrey, Bath in Somerset, and in later years Bryanston School in Dorset.

One of the less enjoyable excursions was to Edinburgh, the Scottish capital, in 1953, the year of Queen Elizabeth II's coronation. Among the new arrivals was Sulak Sivaraksa, who was about to enter the University of Wales, Lampeter. Sulak found the frightful food and bad weather more of a shock to his system than did the others. He was struck by Anand's weak, unpractised Thai more than by his undoubted friendliness.

'I remember it was raining all the time,' says Charatsri. 'We couldn't go sightseeing or anything – it was awful.' She attended three of these get-togethers during her six years in the UK, and remembers that, initially at least, the students tended to stay in their own groups. It was the sportier types such as Anand who mixed the most. There were outings to places of interest, like Stonehenge. The extended house parties included nightly dances, organised debates, games, and plenty of tennis and badminton. Boys outnumbered girls by a factor of three, so the girls were in high demand for dancing. 'The girls were all having a good time,' Suthep recalls. 'There was no time to rest.'

'We were all chasing everybody,' according to Chatrachai Bunya-Ananta, who won the most sports prizes one year to emerge as *victor ludorum*.[23] Sportsmen often went to bed early, and Chatrachai was known to be a particularly heavy sleeper. One morning, he woke up in his own bed – only to find it that had been replanted overnight in the garden. Other pranks included running girls' underwear up flagpoles.

The powerful *esprit de corps* among Thai students abroad was not confined to Britain. After moving to Washington in 1953, Anand's cousins and playmates, Bandit, Suphat and Arsa Sarasin, were core members of the so-called Basement Gang. During their father Pote's posting as ambassador, bunk beds were installed in the bowels of the embassy for Thai students to come and spend the holiday months together. The bonding endured. Kamala Sukosol was the only girl in the Basement Gang's inner circle, and remembers everyone talking to her as if she were a boy. Apart from a month-long visit in 1955, Arsa did not return to Thailand until 1959 and completely lost touch with Anand for six years. Although he was never a part of it, Anand is still regarded as an honorary member of the Basement Gang, and is often invited to its gatherings.

In addition to the service of fags, senior boys at Dulwich had some other privileges. For example, they were allowed to stroll across the school lawns with jackets unbuttoned and hands in pockets. Chavalit Yodmani started his education at Oakwood House and went on to Romsey College. He recalls a much tougher regime there than at Dulwich: 'I remember in my first year I could not put my hands in my pockets. They were sewn up. The prefects had gowns, and in those days they could cane the students. It was brutal and life was tough, but that made the later part of my life very easy. I learned to eat everything and waste nothing – and to think of people who have nothing. It is good discipline for anyone. Children now are spoiled.'

As one of the oldest and most mature boys at Dulwich, Anand was one of some 40 school prefects in his last two years who patrolled the school in search of miscreants in blazers. Anand himself was almost never in trouble at school, but was once called in to see 'the master' – as the headmaster of Dulwich is known – on a disciplinary matter. Anand and another prefect had invited two girls from

James Allen's Girls' School to the annual prefects' dance. After the party, the boys walked their dates home. The rule was to be back at the boarding house by midnight, but they ran a little late. Anand was spotted in an extended farewell kiss by W.C. 'Butcher' Thomas, the unpopular head of junior school and an ardent disciplinarian who that night was lurking in the bushes beside the village pond. 'We were let off with a lecture,' says Anand, admitting that the possibility of being stripped of prefect status did briefly concern the two boys. The master who chose to let the incident pass was Christopher Herman Gilkes,[24] one of the most notable heads of school of his generation.

Without knowing it, Christopher Gilkes was, after Anand's father, perhaps the most important influence in the young man's education. Gilkes became the master at Dulwich in 1941 when his predecessor, Walter Booth, resigned. Booth had been reduced to near-breakdown by the pressures of the war. Among his responsibilities had been some unsatisfactory attempts to evacuate the school from the capital to other schools, including Tonbridge, in 1939.[25] The school lost key staff to the war effort, and the roll dropped from nearly 1,000 boys to about 450 at the worst point in 1940. Bombs were jettisoned in south London suburbs by the German Luftwaffe after failed runs on their intended targets. Among 2,400 houses in the area surrounding Dulwich College, only 400 escaped war damage. Meanwhile, as barrage balloons flew over the cricket pitches, the school was ploughing deeper into debt.

Gilkes restored the school's fortunes, and was the architect of the so-called Dulwich Experiment, which provided full scholarships to boys from south London and the surrounding counties. Gilkes's experiment (dubbed the 'Move Left' by some of his critics) began in late 1947, and bracketed Anand's years there. By the time Anand moved on to Cambridge University in the early 1950s, the London County Council paid for the fees of four-fifths of the pupils without means testing. Headmasters in south London accused Gilkes of creating an 'intellectual aristocracy' by vacuuming up the brightest boys in their catchment areas irrespective of parental status or affluence. Controversially, Gilkes placed great store in intelligence quotient (IQ) tests. He contended that the most intelligent boys – or at least those who scored highest in the tests – would also contribute most in terms of 'citizenship' to other aspects of school life, including sporting and cultural activities.

Gilkes wanted to test two 'half-formed' theories, as he termed them: 'First, that a mixture of social classes in a school is positively valuable provided the boys are all of the same intellectual level; secondly, that a boy of intelligence well below the average of his school gains little from it and gives little in return.'[26]

These ideas were viewed in many quarters as radical, with socialist undertones. There was friction with members of the school's board of governors and staff – including Anand's housemaster, Eric Parsley, whom Bob Nunes recalls as a fierce opponent of the revolutionary scheme. Old Alleynians were also disgruntled, especially after Gilkes was quoted in the press proclaiming that 'the new blood is a great deal better than the old'.[27] The old boys believed, rightly, that a number of Dulwich heroes with indifferent academic abilities would never have gained admission under Gilkes's regime. Scholastic laggards would certainly have included the great Antarctic explorer Sir Ernest Shackleton, who concluded that a year at sea was an education superior to anything offered by Dulwich.[28]

Gilkes found opportunities in all this adversity, but at significant cost to his health. He reversed Dulwich's declining academic and economic fortunes. One enterprising scheme placed 70 boys in scholarships funded by the War Office to learn Oriental languages. As part of their curriculum, these intelligence officers of the future attended the School of Oriental and African Studies (SOAS) for tutoring in Chinese, Japanese, Persian, or Turkish. The rest of their schooling and their board were at Dulwich.

By 1946, Gilkes had eased the overall number of boys back up to 1,000, returning the school to solvency. He decided to repopulate the college with pupils specifically selected for high intelligence – including some 20 boys each year from overseas, such as Anand. Gilkes's meritocratic approach imbued Dulwich with certain qualities associated with the state grammar-school system, which was designed to foster bright but less well-off children.[29]

Under Gilkes's stewardship, Anand's Dulwich years were deeply formative and among the happiest of his life. The move to Britain had opened him up to a much broader and more liberal education than he could have expected in Thailand. Indeed, largely because of Gilkes, education at Dulwich was more enlightened and progressive than at most other British schools of the time.

'It was a learning experience being with UK boys of varied upbringings, religions and backgrounds,' recalls Anand's friend Nunes. 'Most of the "best" public schools comprised mainly aristocratic and upper middle-class lads and few foreigners.' One of the better known beneficiaries of Gilkes's social levelling was the son of a postal clerk, who in the 1990s became governor of the Bank of England and went by the nickname Steady Eddie. 'He was six years younger than me, but I still remember Eddie George as a boy,' says Anand. 'He became a lord.'

As a role model, Gilkes was a formidable combination of administrator, scholar, musician, and sportsman. He particularly loved cricket. An Old Alleynian and former school captain himself, he had also been captain of boxing and a member of the school rugby team. But it was his thinking that left the greatest impression on Anand, who for an unusually long two years was included in the school prefect meetings over which Gilkes presided in the Master's Library. These were a weekly ritual introduced by Gilkes's father a half-century earlier, when he too was the master at Dulwich.[30] The tone was more that of an Oxbridge tutorial. Ideas inspired by the ancient classics would be floated and papers on ethics read. Only towards the end of the meetings were school administrative matters addressed. 'I was very impressed,' says Anand. 'Here was a man of principle and vision. He actually implemented the Dulwich Experiment in spite of any criticism.' Anand particularly admired Gilkes's sharp and assertive style of conversation, and credits him for adding colourful words to his widening vocabulary: 'fiddlesticks', 'humbug', 'nincompoop', 'moron', and 'spineless' among them. Indeed, referring to someone as 'spineless' remains Anand's favourite English term of withering derision. 'Gilkes could be sarcastic, but not in a hostile manner,' he says. 'I don't think we were afraid of him, but he never let you forget that he was in authority – he could put you down.'

Aged only 55, Gilkes died unexpectedly of heart failure in September 1953, the year after Anand left Dulwich. Many believed the strain of the Dulwich Experiment and rebuilding the school through the war years weakened him and contributed to his early death.[31] In an un-networked age when news travelled slowly, Anand heard nothing of his former great mentor's passing until many years later. 'In a way, I had already lost touch with my school,' he says.

Cambridge University

Gilkes had been a classical scholar at Trinity College, Cambridge, where Anand was also bound. Oxford and Cambridge universities are each made up of 'colleges' – 31 in the case of Cambridge at the time of writing. Would-be undergraduates apply for entry to individual colleges. Academic supervision takes place mostly within colleges, although academic faculties and degree examinations operate on a university-wide basis.

Despite his late entry into the British secondary school system and the challenge of mastering English, Anand met the minimum requirement of two 'A' levels. He presumes it was a strong letter of recommendation from Dulwich that compensated for any deficiencies in his interview performance, and helped secure his place in the autumn of 1952, although he cannot be sure that Gilkes was the letter's author. Anand, after all, was but one of many boys in his charge.[32] 'It was, in our day, a little easier to drift into Cambridge,' observed Field Marshal Sir John Chapple, who was a year ahead of Anand at Trinity.[33] 'The housemaster at school, in discussion with parents, played a larger role in making and shaping the application. The process seemed more casual.'

During Anand's remaining years in Britain there would be no guiding force comparable to Gilkes. His time at Trinity was pleasant and enlightening, but Cambridge had a less formative impact on his development than Dulwich. Sern had wished that Anand attend Shrewsbury School and go on to Christ Church, Oxford, King Vajiravudh's college, but Shrewsbury had been ruled out because of its remoteness. Oxford was never an option since Anand had no Latin or Greek, one of which was mandatory for entrance.

Cambridge considered Thai an acceptable alternative as a classical language. However, the required Thai-language exam held an unexpected peril for some. The papers were set by former Western missionaries whose Thai had been learned among northern hill tribes. Most Thai students in Britain spoke the language of the central plains, where Christian missionaries had a dismal record of conversion. 'The rumour was that it was difficult to pass the Thai-language test,' recalls Anand. Indeed, to their utter chagrin, some very well-educated Thais ended up failing a test in their own language set by foreigners in a different dialect. Anand passed.

Cambridge was the furthest north Anand had travelled in Britain at the time. Recalling his first visit, Anand wrote in later years: 'I remember walking through the gate to Trinity's Great Court and being totally captivated by the serenity and tranquillity of the campus environment.'[34] Trinity College's medieval origins make it one of the most ancient seats of learning in the British Isles, an architectural hotchpotch from many centuries. The inner college is a warren of draughty courtyards, passages, and staircases that are damp and cold in winter.[35]

Students could buy their formal attire from Bodger's, advertised as 'the man's shop of Cambridge', and their tobacco in prodigious quantities from Bacon's, which supplied special flat packs of 20 cigarettes bearing the college crest. Anand never smoked cigarettes and hates the smell of them, and only took up cigars and pipes much later. When he drank at this time, it was mostly beer or cider. 'I never touched hard liquor,' he says.

To his dismay, Anand's first year was spent in rooms a ten-minute walk from the college at 28 Park Parade, overlooking Jesus Green beside the sometimes odorous River Cam. A contemporary recalled the riverine aroma 'mixed with the scent of damp leaves and, as often as not, bonfire smoke hanging in the tall bedrooms, windows ritually open'.[36]

When Anand's brother Chat arrived from Boston for a visit, he was shocked to discover Anand in accommodation so basic that bathrooms were shared. There were only jugs of water in the room for washing and shaving. In his second year, Anand moved to 14–17 Green Street, a very short walk from Great Gate, the imposing late-medieval entrance to Trinity. The proximity was a blessing in winter when the East Anglian weather could be freezing.

Like all undergraduates, Anand was required to attend at least four meals in the college hall each week. He often left without dining to seek out more palatable fare at Chinese or Indian restaurants. The Taj Mahal just beside Great Gate was the closest. The refectories at Peterhouse and Magdalene colleges were considered superior to Trinity's, but in general the food in Cambridge was as dire as anywhere else in Britain at that time, as the nation approached the end of a decade of austerity.[37]

One of Anand's good friends from Dulwich, Taffy Davies, studied medicine at Cambridge but they moved in different circles and drifted apart. With some 1,000 undergraduates, Trinity was Cambridge University's largest college and seemed quite impersonal after Dulwich. Anand initially found himself missing the boarding-house life of school – the easy camaraderie that threw people together. On the other hand, his weekly pocket money at Dulwich had been only two shillings and sixpence. With the standard Thai student allowance of £38 a month administered from the embassy by Miss Harrison, rising later to £50, occasional indulgences could be funded: riverbank picnics, punting on the Cam, tea and sherry parties, and the annual May Balls.

There were limits to these extracurricular pursuits. Anand was not attracted to any of the arcane aspects of college life such as the Hare and Hounds Club for horseback hunting or the Magpie and Stump debating society.[38] Nor, despite a facility for public speaking that was already apparent to his Thai friends, did he join the Cambridge Union, or other groups within the broader student body such as the Footlights drama group.[39]

Trinity has a remarkable list of alumni, including the brilliant, the colourful, and the roguish. The great poet Lord Byron attended for seven terms from 1805 to 1807, and as a nobleman was allowed to matriculate with a master's degree the following year without the inconvenience of sitting an exam. The same exemption rule applied at Oxford where there were 'Bloods and Tufts' and 'gold tasselled noblemen who never took a degree'.[40] The notorious British spy H.A.R. (Kim) Philby attended Trinity in the 1930s, forging friendships with four other undergraduates to form the so-called Cambridge Five. Its members had Marxist intellectual inclinations, and later spied for the Soviet Union.[41]

Among Trinity College's many distinguished alumni is Amartya Sen, who would go on to become a Nobel laureate for economic science. He was already a graduate of Calcutta University when, in his late teens, he arrived at Trinity the year after Anand to take a two-year second bachelor's degree in pure economics. 'I admired Anand,' Sen later recalled. 'He was never seen studying but always did well, so obviously he knew something.'[42] Sen viewed Cambridge in the early 1950s as a joyous intellectual battleground.[43] Anand did not, and his problem again was the choice of subjects. Mathematics had been gruelling at Dulwich, so he opted for economics as part one of his Tripos.[44] This proved a major disappointment; he could raise no interest in the tectonic plates of economic theory shifting all around him as the disciples of John Maynard Keynes, Cambridge's most famous economist, squared off against challengers.

Lectures in economics at Cambridge for all undergraduates were very formal and not particularly frequent. The Canadian economist Harry G. Johnson recalled the exceptionally challenging standards: 'They were brilliant lectures, but you had to know at least enough economics for a PhD before you could understand them.'[45]

The economist John Vaizey, who was a don at St Catharine's College in Anand's day, recalled his early encounters with the 'brilliant and ferocious' Keynesian economist Joan Robinson when he was an undergraduate at Queens' College: 'I went to read her my essays, which she dismissed with contempt in supervisions that lasted two hours or more. I walked back through the dark and occasionally cried myself to sleep. I have never thought so hard as in trying to write those essays.'[46]

Like all undergraduates, Anand saw his supervisor each week, and produced essays, but was otherwise expected to find his own way academically. Studying was a tough and lonely enterprise, and he struggled to generate sufficient interest to keep his head above water: 'Economics is a very dry subject, and I found it difficult to understand,' he says.

Anand's salvation was a textbook by an American professor, Paul A. Samuelson of the Massachusetts Institute of Technology. Entitled *Economics: An Introductory Analysis*, it had first appeared in 1948. Although some critiqued the book as leftist, it has run to many editions, made economics more accessible to generations of students, and helped its author become the first Nobel laureate in economic sciences from the US. To Anand's relief, studying economics at Cambridge at the undergraduate level involved very little algebra or econometrics, and he passed part one of his Tripos with a third, the lowest grade.

For part two of the Tripos in his second and third years, he studied law, albeit again somewhat half-heartedly. 'I am a double third and very proud of it,' he says with a laugh. 'When I entered university, my whole interest was just to get a degree – to pass. Whenever results were announced, I would always start looking from the bottom of the list. If I had not seen my name in the third-class division, you can imagine how panicked I would have been.'[47]

'Cambridge was a struggle simply for the reason that I was not interested,' Anand reflects. 'Looking back, I didn't like any subject I studied; but given a chance, I think I would have enjoyed history. In Thai history studies, you talk about what, where, and when, but you hardly ever talk about why or what next – the consequences. Our approach is more like a chronicle.'

Anand did get on well in weekly meetings with his supervisor, Francis Henry ('Harry') Sandbach, whom he recalls as 'a charming and affable gentleman with an impish smile and a dry sense of humour'. Francis Barnes, who was 'witty and illuminating', supervised Anand in his criminal law studies. By contrast, Anand's professor in international law, Sir Hersch Lauterpacht QC, who was born in the Ukrainian town of Zhovkva in 1897, spoke English in immensely long sentences with an impenetrable accent. Lauterpacht has been described as the most influential jurist of the mid-20th century. He sat as a judge at the International Court of Justice, and suggested to the chief prosecutor at Nuremberg that crimes against humanity should be introduced as a new offence into the Nuremberg Statute.[48] Anand found the professor's son, Elihu 'Eli' Lauterpacht, only three years his senior and his supervisor on the same subject, more 'lucid and approachable'.[49]

'I had to study, but I did not study the whole year,' he confesses. 'I would study about five weeks before the exam. I was having a good time. I played tennis and squash, and socialised.' Indeed, Anand played for Trinity in both sports, and the only significant mentions of him in the college journals are for sporting achievements. He was awarded a 'gander' in squash, a minor sport. He found the Cambridge University squash courts an improvement on the Nazi bomb crater at Dulwich, but even so they leaked when it rained.

For his third and final year, Anand was assigned lodgings in the southeast corner of the ancient Great Court. His rooms, I-11, were on a staircase that today leads through to Angel Court: in the 1950s, it was known less attractively as Lecture Theatre Court. Trinity's records of student accommodation only date back to the 1820s, but some historians believe that the route up to the rooms of Lord Byron in the early 19th century is now staircase K, located on the same corner of Great Court as Anand's staircase. According to a 'somewhat unreliable' memoir published in 1827 by J.M.F. Wright, Byron kept a muzzled brown bear called Bruin there as a pet, hoping to secure the creature a college fellowship.[50]

Anand was fortunate to escape the satirical attention of the editors of *The Trinity Magazine*. Its observations on college members were mean-spirited and far removed from the gentlemanly sporting personalities profiled as 'characters' in *The Alleynian*. One fellow was described as 'an unassuming dwarf', and another as 'the undiscovered bore from whom no traveller returns'. Each year, the magazine's creators proffered patently insincere disclaimers: 'The editors apologise considerably more to those who have been mentioned than to those who have been omitted.'

The theme of the annual Trinity College revue in 1953, Anand's first year, was more self-consciously refined: 'Trinity laughing politely at itself.' A rather priggish reviewer observed: 'Its urbane and gentle manner was in marked contrast to the more frenzied entertainment to which we have become accustomed, and it was no less amusing for being civilised.'

Such pretentiousness combined with towering intellects, steamrolling egos, and bruising humour all ensured Anand's Cambridge took some getting used to. But Dulwich had already toughened him up. His experiences in Britain left him with a taste for pointed humour that sometimes catches the uninitiated by surprise. He would later reflect on his time at Trinity rather dryly: 'I acquired a set of values, based on hard work, discipline and diligence which continue to shape and influence my life to this day. For that, I am eternally grateful.'[51]

During his student years, Anand had numerous first encounters with people who would become significant in his career and later life. Nukul Prachuabmoh, a young high flier in Thailand's finance ministry, was one.[52] Anand showed him around London, took him to lunch with friends, and to Hampton Court, a Tudor palace of the 16th century. Nukul, who would later be a key minister in both Anand's governments, was struck by his host's polish and Cambridge accent.

Anand's circle at Cambridge included *MR* Kasemsomosorn Kasemsri, Sakol Vanabriksha, Kosol Sindhvananda, and Sudhee Prasasvinitchai, all of whom became ambassadors. Kasemsomosorn, who was a year ahead of Anand, also became foreign minister. There were also Sombhop Krairiksh, Ungura Puranonda, and Pairat Bencharit. Friends in London included Suthep Bulakul, who was studying at Imperial College, and Supan Jotikabukkana at Regent Street Polytechnic. Anand would find their English-influenced humour a relief once they all got home to Thailand.

There was a small amount of Thai 'society' life in London. Anand was occasionally invited to the Royal Thai Embassy. While at Dulwich in the late 1940s, he had been invited to dinner with the ambassador, *MC* Nakkhatra Mangala Kitiyakara, and met his two daughters, *MR* Sirikit and *MR* Busba, who were being privately tutored. The sisters and their two brothers did not join the other Thai students for the Samakki Samakhom holiday retreats. Anand was at school when King Bhumibol Adulyadej formally announced his engagement to *MR* Sirikit during a party and dinner at the embassy on 12 August 1949, her 17th birthday.

Private life

In Anand's day, colleges at Oxford and Cambridge were still segregated – they were all-male or all-female. Gates were locked at night. 'There were well-charted routes by which one could get into and out of colleges, including the female colleges, after midnight,' recalled Harry Johnson, a distinguished Canadian economist. 'Actually, the rule in the women's colleges was that after 7pm all men are beasts. Up until 7pm, they were all angels, and girls simply had to learn to live with that routine and practise love in the afternoon.'[53]

Anand's girlfriends had all been English except for a Spaniard. During his Cambridge years, he met his future wife, MR Sodsrisuriya Chakrabhandhu, who was attending Queen's College, a girls' independent secondary school in London's Harley Street, where Anand's niece Charatsri also went. She changed the English spelling of the short form of her name from Sodsri to Sodsee for phonetic reasons.

Sodsee's mother, MC Dhityasongklod Rabibadhana, regarded as one of the great beauties of her day, often visited the Princess Mother in Lausanne where King Bhumibol was resident. Sodsee's father, MC Gustavus Chakrabhandhu, was descended from King Mongkut and had attended the Royal Military Academy at Woolwich in England and the Special Military School of Saint-Cyr in France. While her father was military attaché in Paris, Sodsee attended the American Community School. Her friends there included Janet Martin, the daughter of US diplomat Graham Martin, a future ambassador to Thailand and South Vietnam.

In London, Sodsee was staying in the care of the family of Chaloke Kommarakul, the Thai financial attaché. Ungura Puranonda was a close friend from Anand's Bangkok Christian College days when they cycled to school together. The two had lived nearby and had known each from the age of 13. Ungura had come to England six months ahead of Anand in one of the first post-war batches, and attended St Paul's, another academically distinguished London public school. He introduced Anand to the Kommarakul household in Chelsea, and also to Sodsee. During their holiday retreats, Ungura and Anand teamed up for tennis doubles. At the extended Samakki Samakhom Thai student camps each year, the pair's great rivals were Supan Jotikabukkana and Bunying Nandhabhiwat, a Thai junior champion in his day. Supan and Bunying won the prestigious tennis tournament three years running.

'He has always been the closest friend I ever had,' says Anand of Ungura and their teamship. Ungura was seeing Sodsee in a chaperoned, Thai way as part of a group of friends. Anand was smitten without knowing Ungura's intentions. When he revealed his feelings to Sodsee, she responded:

'Your very good friend has been courting me but he never said anything.' Sodsee was puzzled that Ungura – Anand's best friend and tennis partner, no less – had never revealed anything to anyone if his intentions were serious. Nobody knew that Ungura was waiting for his parents to come to London and give their consent before he took matters further and declared his interest.

'I had also fallen for this particular girl, and I won fairly and squarely,' says

Anand. 'I made this intrusion without knowing Ungura's true intention. He was never angry with me.' Anand revealed his feelings to his parents, brother Chat, and Sodsee's guardians in the Kommarakul household, who viewed him as a good match.

In Sodsee's eyes, Anand showed himself to be the more serious of the two. Ungura accepted the situation in a gentlemanly way. Later, he became a senior policeman and married a film star. They remained the best of friends.

'My mother was attracted to my father but she had many, many suitors,' says Daranee, Anand's second daughter. 'She was very beautiful and charming, and he really had to pursue her.' Anand remembers going off to dances with other couples, and visits to the cinema. 'With our limited pocket money we could not afford to go to French restaurants or anywhere,' says Anand. 'We went to Lyons tea houses.' The courtship went on for two years, with Anand visiting from Cambridge, where they attended the annual May Ball.

A second cousin on the Jotikasthira side of the family, Teddy Spha Palasthira, remembers Anand's courtship of the chaste Sodsee as if it were yesterday. Anand was more than five years Teddy's senior. Sodsee was a year ahead of Teddy at school in Paris in the late 1940s, and the object of a major crush on his part. 'I never courted her, I just phoned,' says Teddy, speaking in his crisp English accent. 'I hated Anand for a number of reasons. Firstly, he was brilliant at school and university, which I wasn't. Secondly, he was extremely good-looking. And thirdly, he married the girl that I fancied.'

The pain of Teddy's doomed infatuation with Sodsee was only made worse when his father salted the wound: 'Teddy, I wish you could be like cousin Anand – there's a man you should admire.'[54]

CHAPTER 3

FOREIGN SERVICE, THAILAND (1955–1963)

Homecoming

Sern Panyarachun, Anand's father, regarded the US as the world's dominant power, and would have liked his youngest son to round out his education with postgraduate studies in America. Anand had different ideas, however, having tired of the academic grind. When he graduated from Cambridge in the summer of 1955, he had already spent seven uninterrupted years overseas in England. He wanted to return home and start a career, and to be with Sodsee, his future wife.

Even so, Anand went the long route and took the opportunity to visit the US. He set off in August on a three-month tour with a Cambridge friend, Pairat Bencharit. They were joined by Pairat's two sisters, Sumali and Suchada, who were also students in the UK.

In New York, the group invested in a 1953 Mercury Monterey. They motored to New Jersey and then on to visit the Kessler family in Philadelphia. The Kesslers had hosted Anand's older brother, Kusa, during his undergraduate years after World War II.[1] The four then went on to Washington for the wedding of Anand's closest sister by age, Supapan, whose husband-to-be was studying there. The ceremony was sponsored by the Thai ambassador, Pote Sarasin, a close relative by marriage and someone Anand greatly admired.

'Pote was very popular in America, and he always spoke his mind in a very smooth way,' Anand recalls. 'He was smart, handsome, well dressed, spoke very good English, smoked cigars, and he was one of the few Thai ministers to resign from the cabinet on matter of principle.' When Pote was foreign minister from 1949 to 1951, the Americans somehow convinced Field Marshal Plaek Phibunsongkhram (Phibun) to recognise Bao Dai, Vietnam's former emperor, as head of state. Pote disagreed and resigned. The following year, Phibun posted him as ambassador in Washington for five years.

Continuing south to Florida on their road trip, Anand and his friends passed through St Augustine, Daytona Beach, and Miami, and then drove to Louisiana's New Orleans. The humid climate of the Dixie states was the closest to tropical Thailand Anand had experienced in years, and the young tourists soon realised it was cooler to drive the lumbering Mercury at night. The only bad luck on the entire trip was running over a skunk in the dark – it left a stink nothing could remove.

The informality of the American south as compared to the northeast was appealing despite the obviously racist attitudes to African Americans – which did not seem to extend to Asians. 'Southerners were very warm,' Anand recalls. 'They took a genuine interest in you. I liked the southern drawl.'[2]

On they went through El Paso in Texas and eventually they hit Las Vegas. Eartha Kitt and Frank Sinatra were appearing in concert there, and the great Sands and Flamingo casinos beckoned. Anand did not try his luck, however, having lost his interest in gambling before he went off to England. 'I got turned off then and Dulwich did not convert me,' he says. 'I still never buy lottery tickets.'

The four drove on to Los Angeles and finally wound up in San Francisco where the car was sold for a US$100 profit – despite the lingering aroma of skunk. The flight home to Thailand from San Francisco, on a luxurious PanAm Boeing 377 Stratocruiser, was a series of hops across the Pacific lasting 48 hours. This was a golden age for air travel. The Stratocruiser, developed from the B29 bomber, was powered by four massive radial engines. There were two decks with nearly a hundred passengers seated on top, a bar and lounge below, and a well-equipped galley aft. Smoking was permitted and roast prime rib of beef was served from a trolley. The plane was met in Honolulu by Hawaiian dancers in hula skirts sashaying to the dreamy sound of ukuleles. After Hawaii, they flew to Wake Island, Tokyo, and on to Hong Kong, where the group stopped over for a week. Pairat's father was a prominent rice merchant who spent time at a second home in Kowloon. For Anand, this was a first taste of Asia beyond Thailand.

In late 1955, Anand finally reconnected with his large family in Bangkok. Most of his friends from Bangkok Christian College had gone on to study at Chulalongkorn or Thammasat universities. He slipped back into daily life surprisingly easily, and felt no sense of being an outsider.

The Bangkok to which he returned was actually not much changed from the 1940s. The city was still rather sleepy, the population density low. It was not until the late 1950s that the population would begin to surge beyond about 1.8 million. The roundabout at Victory Monument was still surrounded by open fields. Kao Chan ('Nine Storeys') on New Road near the Chinese business quarter was the tallest building. Concrete shophouses had already begun to proliferate, but residential houses were still typically built of wood. There was barely a handful of small apartment blocks for foreigners, and most of the landlords were minor royalty. Due to the lack of building activity, and limited migration to the city, slums were fewer and much less apparent than in later times. Although the socialites of the day mingled at the Royal Bangkok Sports Club, standards of living were relatively equal across the economic classes, and income disparities far less apparent than they became later.

Some roads had been widened and upgraded. The controversial filling-in of Bangkok's celebrated canal system, created in the 18th and 19th centuries, was starting to gather momentum, but there were still many picturesque waterways beneath broad-canopied trees. Transport options included pedal samlors or Austin A30 vans imported by Diethelm and converted into taxis. Tiny fans over the dashboards struggled vainly to keep the occupants cool, and exhaust fumes and dust poured in through the open windows. Cars were predominantly European with a few American models, mostly Plymouths. A first-class ticket on the tram bought a cushion cover for the teak bench. Arterial roads upcountry were few, unpaved, and generally inferior to those in Cambodia and Vietnam; travellers returned to Bangkok covered in fine red dust. The most comfortable way to travel was by rail. As for air travel, Douglas DC-3s and DC-6s rumbled around the region at speeds not really that much faster than people in the 21st century drive by car. People with money went to Singapore and Hong Kong for shopping, or sometimes Rangoon, Burma's capital from British colonial times.

Bangkok was still treated as a hardship posting for diplomats. The number of foreign residents was so small that they were all pretty much on nodding terms; the Indian doormen at The Oriental hotel knew most of the expatriate community by name. Modern infrastructure was in its infancy, and even the big European trading houses – the East Asiatic Company, the Borneo Company, Anglo-Thai, Diethelm – operated from open-windowed offices without air conditioning. The

Telephone Organization of Thailand served its 28,000 subscribers using five-digit numbers, and overseas calls had to be placed at special booths in places like the General Post Office, or later at the swish new Erawan hotel, which was completed in 1958 and served the best Western food in town. The Chandrphen on Rama IV Road was considered one of the best places for Thai and Chinese seafood.

Although Americans barely numbered in the hundreds, 1956 was the year the American Chamber of Commerce in Thailand was founded. After two years, the entire membership could still meet comfortably around a single large table. The American Women's Group followed a year later. The US dollar bought 20 Thai ticals, as the baht used to be known: 'A tical is a nickel' went the saying. Spacious villas rented for as little as US$100 per month, with bedrooms sometimes air-conditioned. A lot of entertaining was done on screened verandas.[3] After heavy rain, the noise of frogs drowned out conversation.

Saranrom Palace

In the 1950s, the foreign and finance ministries attracted the best-qualified entrants into the Thai civil service. When he was at Cambridge, Anand had tentatively planned to enter the Ministry of Foreign Affairs. It seemed the natural thing to do – almost pre-ordained. He was following his oldest brother, Rak, along this path, and perceived in diplomacy a certain seductive glamour. While economics and law had seriously tested his endurance at Cambridge, Anand was certainly conversant with the subjects. From a late start in his mid-teens, he had acquired an excellent command of English, the *lingua franca* of commerce and law. English had also overtaken French as the language of diplomacy. It was the key to getting ahead in the modern world. 'The first and only conscious decision in my career was to join the foreign ministry, and from then on it was fate,' says Anand. 'It turned out to be the right decision. I had become practically bicultural. I didn't want to live abroad permanently, but to go there every two or three years sounded attractive.'

Saranrom Palace, the stuccoed 19th-century foreign-ministry building in Bangkok, was a former military academy. The white, fortified west wall of the Grand Palace containing the spectacular Temple of the Emerald Buddha, Wat Phra Kaew, stood directly opposite. Because of his foreign degree, Anand was able to enter the ministry at the end of 1955 one grade up from the bottom. Although another Cambridge graduate, MR Kasemsomosorn Kasemsri, was a year ahead of him, Anand was in the vanguard of a train of foreign-educated Thai diplomats who, in the 1960s, would fundamentally change the character of the ministry.[4]

However bright, sophisticated, and outward-looking they might have considered themselves, these aspiring, foreign-educated diplomats were expected to fit right back in and learn the Thai system inside out. Anand was no exception. 'I was an apprentice – some might call it a cadet,' he says. He skipped the paltry first pay grade of 1,200 baht a month, and started on 1,600. The first year was spent in the personnel department working on recruitment and staff development. There were exams to pass and new terms to learn, such as 'territorial integrity' and '*persona non grata*'. Young Thai diplomats were all taught the importance of writing clear, formal Thai.

Anand learned to type and to file papers correctly, and to this day retains a quickness and facility when handling documents. Although the duties were sometimes dull and repetitive, he applied himself with the interest and diligence that had been missing at Cambridge. In doing something with purpose, and upon which others depended, he found focus and an appetite for hard work that would serve him well in the future. When the situation demanded, he would always be prepared to work late into the night to finish a task.

His second year at the ministry was spent in the translation department. This gave him his first exposure to the traffic of diplomacy and the Thai foreign service's growing global network – although at this stage he made no contribution to policy. The translation department was the nerve centre of the ministry's activities. Communications with the embassy network were usually in English, sometimes French. The missives therefore all had to be translated from or into Thai. Clarity was essential, particularly since other ministries lacking language resources were often involved.

Family life

On 4 May 1956, Anand married MR Sodsrisuriya Chakrabhandu. Lively and popular, Sodsee, or Lek as she was nicknamed, was a descendant of the 19th-century monarch, King Mongkut. It was she whom Anand had pursued so intently when he was at university in England. He was only 23 and she 19. Marriage at such a young age was normal for the time.

Monks chose the wedding date, and the marriage was registered in a civil procedure by the *nai amphur*, the head of the local government office. The only Buddhist ceremony held that day was to bless a house in Sodsee's family compound on Sukhumvit Soi 53, where the couple had been given land by Sodsee's parents as a wedding gift. The wooden house built on it was a gift from Anand's parents – in wealthy circles, the tradition is for the parents of the groom to give the first marital home. The wedding party took place in the compound that evening.

A brief honeymoon of sorts came the following year: a visit to Dalat in South Vietnam, the City of Eternal Spring, which French colonials had developed in the 1900s as a hill-station resort. With its temperate microclimate, spruce woods, lakes, and distinctive stepped waterfalls, Dalat left Anand and Sodsee with 'sweet and very personal' memories. Nearly 60 years later in early 2016 when he was 83, and long after the south's capital, Saigon, had become Ho Chi Minh City, Anand gave a very personal speech there as chairman of Siam Commercial Bank at the opening of its first branch in the country. 'I have always had a soft spot for Vietnam,' he said.[5] 'But I had to wait for many more years before I could make a second visit because in the late 1950s and early 1960s Vietnam and Thailand were pitted against each other.'

Sodsee would later tell her daughters that she supported Anand financially in the early years of his career. She worked long hours at the United Nations Economic Commission for Asia and the Far East (ECAFE)[6] beginning work each day at 7am. 'It was a hard life because we had to start very early,' says Anand. After the birth of their first daughter, Nanda, in 1958, the strain only increased. Sodsee used to travel to work with Pruek, her mother in law, while breastfeeding her baby in the back seat of the car. Pruek would then bring Nanda back to the Panyarachun compound in Chidlom and care for her until Sodsee got home in the late afternoon.

Although perfectly happy, and unburdened by rent on their house in the family compound, the couple still had to make ends meet. Sodsee earned a basic salary of 2,500 baht a month; Anand's pay from the ministry brought their income up to 4,100 baht. Since he was allowed to work slightly flexible hours, Anand got permission to give English lessons to architecture and political science students at Chulalongkorn and Kasetsart universities. The various faculties in both universities made individual arrangements for English. Classes were popular and relatively informal, starting at 7am most mornings and lasting two hours, at 30 baht an hour. This way another 900 baht was injected into the family coffers each month. Anand usually reached the ministry for work at about 9:30am.

Foreign graduates returning from abroad were not automatically exempted from military service but given the rank of second lieutenant if drafted. Anand's Cambridge friend Pairat, with whom he had toured the US, joined up and was posted to Chulachomklao Military Academy for two years as an instructor. Alternatives to military service included entering the police force for at least two years, or finding some other public service employment for which the graduate had unusually strong qualifications. One possibility was lecturing at tertiary level, but Anand's elective daily language lessons did not fall into this category.

Instead, he volunteered as a private with the air force at Don Muang for a week's service. After seven days, he was transferred back to the Ministry of Foreign Affairs – which had formally confirmed that as a foreign graduate his services were required there. Anand's very brief, indeed undistinguished, military career left him both poorer and wiser. He had been warned about thefts, and woke one morning to find all his belongings had been stolen by members of his little band of brothers. 'They were all country boys – you had to teach them how to turn right and left,' says Anand without malice.

Anand's first 'real job' in the foreign ministry came in 1957 as third secretary in the division attached to SEATO – the Southeast Asia Treaty Organization.[7] SEATO was an international anti-communist front that had been headquartered in Bangkok since early 1955, and one of the first regional forums in Southeast Asia. It was accorded a visit early on by Anthony Eden, the British foreign secretary at the time who later became prime minister. Among the member states, the British and French tended to take a more moderate view than the US of the People's Republic of China. The old European powers believed that the costly and inconclusive Korean War of 1950–1953 had bled the red-flag Chinese of much of their bellicosity. The national development challenges facing China, a country with over a fifth of the world's population, were monumental enough.

Anand interacted with SEATO, albeit at a low level, from his career's outset. It was there that he met for the first time one of his future great allies and admirers, Snoh Unakul. The young economist, Thailand's future development czar, had recently returned from his studies in Melbourne. 'We were both junior officers and were assigned to help in the secretariat with odd jobs, including arranging documents for the SEATO meetings,' Snoh later recalled. 'Khun Anand had just graduated from Cambridge. My first impression of him was that his complexion was so pink that he could pass for a handsome Eurasian, which would qualify him as a leading actor in a modern-day TV soap opera.'[8] The two ran into each other at parties. Snoh remembers Anand as easy to get along with, even if no deep friendship was struck up. 'He didn't have much time for himself,' Snoh recalls.

SEATO's first secretary general was Pote Sarasin, Thailand's ambassador to the US and the father of Anand's cousins and closest childhood companions. SEATO certainly had its detractors. 'If we had been sufficiently far-sighted in 1954, we would not have joined in founding such an organisation,' Sir Anthony Rumbold, the British ambassador in Bangkok, later concluded. 'The only SEATO commitments we have are those which flow from the Manila Treaty itself and we can interpret those in any way we wish.'[9]

SEATO's presence in Bangkok nevertheless enabled promising young diplomats to cut their teeth in a genuine multilateral diplomatic environment without travelling abroad. 'The threat of communism at that time was real and imminent,' says Anand. Countering it was SEATO's main focus. Laos and North Vietnam were viewed as the frontlines. China and the Soviet Union loomed in the background, competing regionally as ideological sponsors and providers of revolutionary *matériel*. On paper, SEATO was a strategic umbrella organisation concerned with maintaining regional security, providing foreign aid, and improving relations with neighbouring countries. It also had economic and cultural dimensions intended to foster development as a counter-insurgency tool, although it had no real impact on foreign investment or trade.

The SEATO council comprised the foreign ministers of the eight member countries and met annually in Bangkok. There were monthly meetings for SEATO ambassadors stationed in Bangkok who functioned as council representatives. Below that, a permanent working group, mostly first secretaries at the embassies and middle-ranking Thai diplomats, met every week. Anand started at a third level as an alternate to his division chief, who was a member of the working group. Anand also sat on the budgetary working group. He remembers the Philippines always pressing for more funding for SEATO, while France was always pleading to contribute less. Anand soon accumulated far more general exposure to the diplomat's craft than a second secretary in any of the other ministerial divisions could have achieved.

His promotion to third secretary was an important career step into real diplomacy but nevertheless put further strain on his home life. 'We had to socialise more, and that was very tough on my wife,' says Anand. They attended dinner parties and receptions once or twice a week. Sodsee had always enjoyed a lively social life in England, but back in Thailand this proved more strenuous.

Political upheaval

Thailand's foreign minister in 1957 was Prince Wan Waithayakon. He knew Anand's parents and brothers well, and his son was on close terms with Prasat, Anand's third brother. Prince Wan had been educated at Marlborough College in Britain followed by Oxford University, and over a career dating from World War I he had acquired a high international profile. He had become an ambassador at the age of 29, the youngest in Thai history. A formidable diplomat, Prince Wan was sometimes treated warily by his British counterparts, possibly because of Thailand's wartime alliance with Japan.[10]

The Cold War between communist powers in the East and capitalist powers in the West was intensifying, and Thailand entered a critical political watershed that would end Prince Wan's tenure and set the foreign ministry on a new course. It was arguably the most important political upheaval since the overthrow of Siam's absolute monarchy in 1932.

Phibun had dominated the intervening period. As prime minister twice for a total of some 15 years, he had pushed a modernising nationalist agenda that was at times both non-royalist and rightist. Following Japan's invasion of Thailand on 7 December 1941, Thailand was drawn awkwardly into an alliance with Japan, but not as a full Axis member in the Triple Alliance comprising Japan, Germany, and Italy. The relationship enabled Thailand to hang on to the tatters of sovereignty for the rest of the war: there was still a functioning government; the Thai flag flew; the armed forces – such as they were – had an independent chain of command; and the Japanese forces were present as a garrison rather than as an army of occupation.

Pridi Banomyong, another key player in the 1932 revolution, was Phibun's main political rival. Pridi was foreign minister and regent during World War II when young King Ananda Mahidol was resident in Lausanne, and he was prime minister when, on the morning of 9 June 1946, the young monarch died from a single gunshot in the palace. In the muddled fallout from King Ananda's sudden demise, Pridi's political and royalist enemies were able to force him into permanent exile. He eventually passed away in Paris in 1984.

Anand was 14 in 1946, and remembers numerous family dinners at Pote's house when the subject of King Ananda's unexplained death would come up. One uncle was a court doctor, and was of the opinion it was not an accident. 'There were many theories and no agreement,' Anand recalls. 'We lost a king who was very popular, but I was not old enough to think of the political consequences.'

With Pridi gone, Phibun thwarted the royalists and regained the upper hand, but his efforts to introduce an ostensible working democratic system to Thailand were fitful failures that few took seriously. In September 1957, Field Marshal Sarit Thanarat finally toppled him in a coup. Phibun and his key ally, Police General Phao Siyanon, were allowed to go into exile. Like Pridi, both men would die abroad – Phibun in Japan in 1967.

Sarit did not take the direct reins of power until more than a year later. Instead, he appointed Field Marshal Thanom Kittikachorn as prime minister, while he received treatment for a serious liver disease at the Walter Reed General Hospital in Washington, the US military's leading medical facility.[11] During a three-month convalescence after surgery, he was often visited by Thanat Khoman, the Thai ambassador in Washington. Thanat had served in Thailand's wartime embassy in Tokyo under Ambassador Direk Jayanama, and had also been sent to Ceylon in early 1945, as one of Thailand's secret emissaries to negotiate with the Allied powers.[12] Educated in Bordeaux and Paris, Thanat polished up his English while serving as Thailand's ambassador to India. In the US, Thanat translated books and other materials he thought might interest Sarit during his convalescence. The old soldier and young diplomat got along well, and Sarit found the encounters enlightening.

In October 1958, after Sarit had returned to Thailand, he staged a second coup against the government he himself had installed in order to further consolidate his power. Sarit's bold power plays brought change to the foreign ministry. The field marshal wanted to infuse younger, more progressive people into the development of the country. Prince Wan had initially been replaced by Pote Sarasin, who for three months had also served as a proxy prime minister for Sarit. Prince Wan was then reinstated as foreign minister in 1958, although he did not last the year.

'Sarit was one of the worst dictators but he had a lot of good people working under him,' observes Sulak Sivaraksa, one of Thailand's most prominent social critics. For all his flaws, Sarit's sure eye for talent was complemented by his ability to delegate effectively. When he was finally in good enough health to become prime minister in late 1958, Thanat was one of the first people to be promoted. Thanat's statements at that time were strongly anti-communist and consonant with both the US world view and Sarit's. He was made concurrently an honorary army colonel to bolster his status – and also to remind him to follow orders. Or so the field marshal hoped. 'It was not a serious promotion,' says Anand. 'Thanat was made to wear the uniform only once or twice – an honorary colonel has no role or responsibilities.' 'Sarit was a master in selecting young people to work under him. He trusted Thanat's character,' says Vitthya Vejjajiva, a prominent retired diplomat. The consequences of this appointment would soon trickle down the system, and bring a dramatic change to Anand's life.

The most important technocrat at the time was Puey Ungphakorn, a brilliant economist and Free Thai veteran who had completed his education with a first-class degree and PhD from the London School of Economics. Puey later became governor of the Bank of Thailand, dean of economics at Thammasat University, and finally Thammasat's rector. 'Whatever Puey said, Sarit would listen,' says Anand.

In 1960, Sarit took up Amnuay Viravan, a 28-year-old economist with a PhD from the University of Michigan in the US, as a junior member of his advisory team. The field marshal was acting on the advice of Luang Wichit Wathakarn, his effective chief of staff. Wichit, a veteran diplomat, had been Phibun's key wartime propagandist and resurfaced as a special adviser to Sarit. He had been impressed by Amnuay's performance on an advisory body for state enterprises.[13]

Amnuay and Anand would have parallel careers that intersected interestingly at some crucial junctures. After the sudden death of his predecessor, Amnuay became Sarit's key economic advisor. He was given a large office that he later discovered had once been Phibun's. Amnuay's instructions were to generate suggestions for Sarit on macro-economic development. Brimming with ideas, the young economist became a one-man think tank and generated a report each Friday. Not wishing to overburden Sarit, he kept his missives to within two pages. To his dismay, there was no response initially, so he decided to stop writing and see if anybody noticed. The next Monday, Amnuay was visited by a uniformed emissary from Sarit asking after the missing report.

For the next few years, Amnuay's suggestions had to be delivered to Sarit in a sealed envelope each Friday. Only the field marshal could open them. The contents would then be presented to cabinet, often as Sarit's own ideas. Many were aware of Amnuay's role and his 'hot line' to the top man, even though the two virtually never met. Amnuay remembers visiting Sarit's home only once, but he managed to get himself a ring worn only by the field marshal's inner circle of advisers.[14]

Because of Amnuay's weekly direct written contact with Sarit, people often shared ideas with him to get them on the prime minister's agenda. The bones of Thailand's modern economy were being formed.[15] Major institutions launched during this period include the Board of Investment (BOI), the Electricity Generating Authority of Thailand (EGAT), the National Institute of Development Administration (NIDA), and the National Economic and Social Development Board (NESDB) – which initiated long-term national development plans in 1961.[16]

Crucially, the five-year period in which the ailing field marshal served as prime minister cemented an enduring partnership in national development between the military and highly educated technocrats that would last nearly 40 years. The generals wanted a strong say in running the country. They were too powerful to counter, but lacked the expertise needed to fire the economy and stimulate sustainable growth. Rising technocrats and bureaucrats such as Thanat, Puey, and later Snoh were both capable and nationalistic. With no realistic alternative in sight, they were prepared to make tacit accommodations with the military if the country benefited in the bigger picture.

'There were no politicians to worry about,' says Thitinan Pongsudhirak, a political scientist at Chulalongkorn University, of this period.[17] 'Technocrats were able to apply their expertise, and they were a very small number in the finance ministry, Bank of Thailand, NESDB and the Budget Bureau. Puey came from a very modest background and was an iconic personality, the quintessential technocrat. Technocrats were never elected. They were appointed by the military. In the old days, the practice worked well – in fact, it was instrumental in Thailand's development.'

Young technocrats like Anand and Amnuay, who were climbing career ladders from the bottom of the bureaucracy, had to bury their fundamental antipathy to military control and work within a bigger, longer-term framework. Both would eventually run into serious trouble with the military, but their expectation was that economic development and increasingly complex national affairs would in time both constrain the generals and nurture prosperity and greater democracy. In the meantime, from a low base at the end of World War II, Thailand was hitting steady annual growth figures of upwards of 7 per cent.

Sarit's grand plan included facilitating a much greater role in public life for the monarchy, which had been sidelined for over a quarter of a century. Siam's absolute monarchy had been easily pushed aside by the 1932 revolutionary coup that deposed King Prajadhipok, but it was not extinguished. The coup and its fallout led to the king's permanent self-exile in Britain, and eventually his abdication in 1935. King Prajadhipok's successor, King Ananda Mahidol visited his kingdom only twice after his accession, and was not crowned in life.[18]

After King Ananda's death in 1946, his younger brother King Bhumibol Adulyadej acceded and eventually had his coronation in 1950. In the interim, the young king continued his studies in Switzerland at Lausanne University, but these were dramatically curtailed in a car crash in 1948 that nearly killed him and cost him his right eye. In the early years back in Thailand after 1951, Phibun was keen to obviate a royalist resurgence, and kept King Bhumibol's movements and public role strictly in check.

Field Marshal Sarit was from Isan, Thailand's impoverished north-east, and very different from the French-educated Phibun. Indeed, Sarit's view of the monarchy was quite the opposite of Phibun's. Having never studied abroad, he was not influenced by Western notions of egalitarianism, liberalism, and democracy. Sarit viewed the monarchy not as something backward but as a focus for national identity that could be used to bolster defence as well as spur economic and social development.

Many older Thais harbour a certain nostalgia for Sarit's direct and decisive brand of leadership. In fact he was an unabashed military strongman – a dictator who proved himself capable of ordering the summary execution of both criminals and communists. Smiling and charming in private, Sarit always carried a big stick. He could appear in the press talking amicably with a suspected arsonist one day, and the man would be executed the next. With more than a hundred minor wives and his hand deep in the public till, Sarit nevertheless espoused public order. He believed opium consumption was energy-sapping and made Thailand appear backward. He outlawed opium dens in 1958 and staged public burnings of related paraphernalia at Sanam Luang. Even so, opium dens survived along New Road and elsewhere well into the 1960s.

In his five years as premier, the ailing field marshal got on well with young King Bhumibol, and the revitalisation of Thailand's monarchy undoubtedly dates from his pivotal premiership in the late 1950s and early 1960s. Phibun's belated experiments with free speech and pluralism were soon forgotten. Parliament and the constitution were suspended and the press corralled. Puey ruefully remarked once that from the late 1940s to the early 1970s, being a field marshal was the main prerequisite for becoming Thailand's prime minister. If anything, that was an understatement. With only a handful of fleeting exceptions lasting a year at most, every Thai prime minister from 1948 to 1991 was a general.

Thanat Khoman, Sarit's choice for foreign minister, was no booster of military rule – it was simply a fact of Thai life at the time. On account of his education, Thanat was one of the so-called 'French musketeers' in the diplomatic corps, not that their aims and fates were ever much intertwined. Of the three, Thanat's main competitor was Khonthi Suphamongkhon, who became Sarit's personal adviser on foreign affairs and later ambassador to Australia. Bun Charoenchai became Sarit's minister of industry, a position he retained all through the 1960s. When Thanat was abroad, Bun would also stand in as foreign minister.

'Thanat was not anti-military *per se* – they trusted him and listened to him,' Anand recalls. But after hearing Thanat out, Sarit felt no compulsion to follow his young foreign minister's suggestions. Thanat wanted to raise Thailand's diplomatic profile and give it the international voice that had been lacking all through the 20th century. Maintaining a *modus vivendi* with the military was to prove one of the most difficult aspects of his nearly 13-year tenure at the foreign ministry, a period spanning most of the Vietnam War.

Chef de cabinet

The changes Thailand underwent in the early years after Anand's return from overseas were momentous: the military was resurgent, democratising forces were waning, the economy was firing up, and the monarchy was being re-established. These powerful gusts blew very far above Anand's head as a junior diplomat at the bottom of his career ladder, but a dramatic promotion was in store for him.

A few weeks after Thanat returned from the US and was preparing to take up his new appointment,[19] Anand was called in to see the foreign minister designate. As was so often the case in Anand's life, the two had never met but were very distantly connected through marriage – something Anand was unaware of at the time. It was late 1958; Anand was 26 and beginning his fourth year at the ministry. Thanat simply told him that he was looking for someone to work in his office. Initially, Anand failed to grasp what the future minister was talking about. He presumed he was being offered a job as an assistant. 'Thanat said he wanted me to work with him,' Anand recalls. 'I don't think the word secretary was ever mentioned, and that is how I got confused.' Anand asked Thanat who was going to be the secretary. The foreign minister designate looked at him quizzically, and may even have wondered momentarily if he had made such a good choice. 'Well, it's you,' he said quietly.

Taken aback, Anand asked for a few days to think matters over. He went off and consulted an impressive personal network that included, Rak, his oldest brother; Pote Sarasin; and Luang Visutr Arthayukti. Visutr was a former ambassador to France and in charge of SEATO affairs, and his wife was yet another of Anand's relatives. Everyone Anand consulted was positive about the opportunity – and the improved salary would certainly be a boon. Anand always regards himself as a careful person. 'I would not jump into anything without deliberation.' Many times later in his career he would turn offers down, but there was no reason to do so on this occasion, even though he did not know Thanat personally and had absolutely no idea what the position entailed.

Thanat made no mention of anybody having recommended Anand, but the Cambridge qualification was on file. With his experience in the US, Thanat knew he needed someone with an excellent command of English. He was also familiar with Anand's high-flying brother Rak, since both men had top law degrees from France. Rak was married to Chirawat, a daughter of Phibun, and had served as deputy foreign minister to Prince Wan in 1956.

Thanat had long been disenchanted with the chauvinistic aspects of French education, which included different grades of university degrees for French nationals and foreigners. Even so, a French organisational undercurrent would soon come into play with Anand's appointment. His new job title was secretary, but Thanat soon began referring to him as his *chef de cabinet*, a term for somebody of utmost competence and reliability who serves as a right-hand man.

'It was rather a small pool to be selected from,' says Anand with hindsight. 'As secretary to the foreign minister, I was like a gatekeeper. Every paper had to pass through me. My job was to see that those papers were ready to go to my minister's office. It was not merely a transit point, but the first checkpoint. If I found shortcomings, I would make enquiries. That required a high degree of diplomacy because I had to approach the director generals directly.'

Anand's new job catapulted him from third secretary level to a very sensitive and substantive position. In an acutely status-conscious society, it brought him into direct contact with people who were far more senior in years and rank – not just departmental heads but ministers, permanent secretaries, and ambassadors.

Thanat was a sophisticated student of international politics whose perspectives had been broadened by his years in Japan, India, and the US. In his youth, he had overcome a mild stutter. He was a man of great determination, prepared to take initiatives, and he wanted his ministry to be a force to be reckoned with. During the course of his career, he became more driven and forthright in his views. The messages Anand was expected to convey downwards within the ministry were unambiguous – and not always particularly complimentary or welcome. Anand knew he had to be prudent and polite in Thanat's service, but he always engaged squarely and swept nothing under the carpet. 'I would convey the substance without any embellishments,' he says. 'But it would get the message through. It benefited them to know what the minister was thinking. Part of my success in the jobs I was tasked with is that it is a natural habit for me to be truthful.'

Unlike Thanat, who could be blistering in his criticisms, Anand in his early career retained an instinctive tactfulness. He did not gratuitously upset senior colleagues and prided himself on keeping himself in check with everyone, including those under him. 'The moment you lose the respect of your subordinates or juniors, you cease to be effective,' says Anand. 'You lose their trust and confidence. You must speak the truth – but you don't always have to tell the whole truth. Definitely, there are certain truths you have to keep to yourself.' Even as he made such judgments, Anand did not play politics. A benefit of this upfront approach was that it reduced the chances of people trying to circumvent him when they wanted access to his minister.

Anand found his new boss liberal in many ways, and amenable to friendly debate. 'In spite of my age and youthful inexperience, Thanat always treated me with respect.' Thanat would always have Anand sit right beside him when they travelled. The minister was a heavy cigarette smoker, and it was at about this time that Anand took to puffing cigars occasionally. He particularly remembers them being offered round after dinner as part of the full service on KLM flights to Europe.

Another young secretary was assigned to handle Thanat's personal affairs, so there were no distractions from Anand's ministry work.

The relationship between Thanat and Anand would not always follow standard cultural paradigms. For example, Anand never observed the Thai custom of visiting Thanat's house for his birthday or at New Year. This aloofness became apparent early in the relationship. Khunying Molee, Thanat's wife, had stayed on in the US for about three months after his return, looking after their children. When she arrived back in Bangkok, Anand was missing from the airport welcoming party. 'I decided not to go because she did not know me, and I did not know her,' Anand explains. 'That's very un-Thai, but I was quite sincere. Why should I have been there? I was Thanat's secretary, not his wife's.'

On this occasion, when Anand explained himself, Thanat just smiled. While he could be cantankerous and belittle others, the minister was prepared to indulge Anand. If there had been some tension between them, Thanat would simply go quiet for a few days.

Although Thanat had made Anand his 'front door' – thus facilitating an unprecedented career lift in the foreign service – he was by inclination conservative in his other promotions, particularly to higher positions. He was observant, with sharp, discerning ears, a meritocrat operating in a vertical culture strongly influenced by privilege and entitlement. Indeed, Thailand's earliest diplomats and emissaries had been princes and minor royalty. Thanat's assessment of prospective ambassadors could be humiliating for the subjects. He was particularly dismissive of French-educated subordinates if they had poor French or second-tier degrees from France.

When senior foreign-service officials from abroad visited Bangkok and met with Thanat, notes would usually be taken by a second secretary. If the visitors happened to be American, British, or French, the meetings were more likely to include sensitive security issues, and it would be Anand who kept the record. Sometimes, such meetings took place late at night in Thanat's residence.

'I worked closely with him,' says Anand. 'It was often just Thanat and I – there were no department heads. It was a wonderful learning process. I was privy to most of the top-secret conversations. In a way, I was at the pivotal point in terms of the US-Thai relationship on political and security-cum-military issues. I did not take notes. I just listened to the conversation and then afterwards dictated. Sometimes a meeting would last an hour or two.'

Life at the ministry had its lighter moments. It was not all grim, Cold War politics. In the early 1960s, President Charles de Gaulle of France was keen to obstruct Britain's entry into the European Economic Community. A scandal engulfed the government of the UK's Prime Minister Harold Macmillan. John Profumo, the secretary of state for war, had been caught out for having an affair with a 19-year-old, Christine Keeler, who was also sleeping with the Russian naval attaché in London. In 1963, Profumo was compelled to resign after initially denying the liaison. When Achille Clarac, the French ambassador from 1959 to 1968, called on Thanat, he scoffed. The incident illustrated why de Gaulle was right to say the British were not part of Europe, culturally or mentally. They all laughed.

When the British ambassador Sir Dermot MacDermot visited, Thanat relayed Clarac's barbs. 'If a French minister had to resign for sleeping with another woman, the whole cabinet would have to go,' MacDermot fired back. 'My French colleague got it all wrong. British society is supposed to be puritanical, but we have come a long way. That was not the reason. The real cause was that Profumo lied in parliament.'

When the French ambassador returned, Thanat relayed MacDermot's reponse. 'Well, that's even worse,' said Clarac. 'If a politician had to resign for lying in parliament, all the MPs in France would have to go.'

Thai-US relations

Anand particularly remembers a meeting in the early 1960s between Thanat and the US ambassador, Kenneth Young, who had attended Harvard with his future boss, President John F. Kennedy. The talk between Thanat and Young was about US troop deployments in Thailand. When these were to be announced in Bangkok and Washington, Thanat was very clear that the wording should be along these lines: '… at the request of the US government, the Royal Thai government agrees to the stationing of US troops in Thailand.' Anand recalls Young agreeing to this, and there is no reason to believe that the ambassador was responsible for the turnabout that followed. When President John F. Kennedy issued a statement on 15 May 1962, the thrust had been reversed to say US troops were being stationed at the invitation of the Royal Thai Government:

> Following joint consideration by the governments of the United States and Thailand of the situation in Southeast Asia, the Royal Thai Government has invited, and I have today ordered, additional elements

of the United States military forces, both ground and air, to proceed to Thailand and to remain there until further orders. These forces are to help ensure the territorial integrity of this peaceful country.[20]

'These are small things, but the Americans love to do them,' says Anand. For a proud man like Thanat, they were hard to accept and contributed to a considerable souring in his view of the US over the years. He was particularly livid on that occasion, and there was much else to rankle him. As foreign minister, Thanat was never the complete master of Thailand's diplomacy, especially with regard to military relations with the US. Although Sarit relied on Thanat for many international activities, particularly formal diplomacy, he was personally much more vehemently anti-communist. As a result, he preferred to handle regional affairs himself.

'I don't think Thanat was in control of the relationships with the Indochinese states,' says Anand. He believes the US played on Sarit's fear of communism, which could sometimes be extreme. Sometimes it seemed that US ambassadors and other top diplomats, Central Intelligence Agency (CIA) personnel, and senior officers from the Joint United States Military Advisory Group Thailand (JUSMAGTHAI) could show up at Sarit's residence more or less at will and be shown in. Among the key Thai liaison figures used by the Americans was Air Chief Marshal Dawee Chullasapya.

A congenial senior officer at Supreme Command and a military adviser to SEATO, Dawee cut a dashing figure with his film-star looks and a glamorous lifestyle. He had avoided boxing at Chulachomklao Military Academy for fear of the damage it might inflict, and was responsible for installing a full 18-hole golf course beside the main runway at Don Muang Airport. The course was conveniently laid out right in front of the Royal Thai Air Force's main base, where Dawee once commanded a fighter squadron. The kind of access Dawee facilitated for the Americans grated on Thanat. The foreign minister found himself out of the loop on a number of major decisions, such as US troop deployments to Thailand, the dispatch of Thai mercenaries to Indochina, and locating US military bases in Thailand.

'Thanat was a sensitive person,' says Anand. 'If the Americans used the wrong channels, or tried to cut him off, he was much irritated.' How things might have been different had Thanat not been undermined, and had he been allowed a greater role, is a matter of speculation, but Anand retains genuine respect for his mentor, considering all the dilemmas and frustrations Thanat suffered.

'Thanat was not always happy with my father,' concedes Steve Young, son of US Ambassador Kenneth Young. 'Thanat was a patriot – he was determined, he was smart, and he played second fiddle to nobody. I always kind of liked that – and my dad liked it too,' he says. 'Thanat was for a while, and I think rightly so, sceptical of the Americans. Why should the Thais compromise their position and close relationship with the Americans if they were not going to deliver, or work in a crude, ineffective way that had negative aspects?'

Anand attended most of the meetings between Thanat and the older Young. The US ambassador was a counter-insurgency expert who pioneered the concept of 'invasion by seepage'. He believed the front line was in the hills and villages, and that these areas had to be won over by persuasion. 'We would have two or three hundred *kamnan* [village headmen] come to the embassy from time to time,' Steve Young recalls.

The ambassador was on good personal terms with King Bhumibol; they compared notes on many things, from raising young families to strategies for countering communism. Nevertheless, King Bhumibol preferred his own counsel. In Bangkok in 1963, against the wishes of the Americans, he attended the world premiere of *The Ugly American*, a film based on a novel published some five years earlier. Marlon Brando starred as the US ambassador to Sarkhan, a fictional Southeast Asian nation that very strongly resembled Thailand and also benefited from US geopolitical largesse. *MR* Kukrit Pramoj played Sarkhan's wise but usually unheeded prime minister – who happened *not* to be a field marshal. Kukrit would reprise the role of prime minister in real life 12 years later, but even then often introduced himself as a Hollywood star – when he was not describing himself as a 'newspaper man'.[21]

'The film was a critique of stupid blundering people in the 1950s and our inability to relate to village people and nationalism,' says Steve Young. Although the original novel was published before he took office, President Kennedy interpreted the prescient political critique as a personal slight. The president had founded the Peace Corps in 1961, and he felt that the film belittled his commitment to the struggle against communism. Kennedy cabled Ambassador Young requesting that he try to persuade King Bhumibol and Queen Sirikit to skip the opening. Young requested an audience to convey Kennedy's disquiet, and was told: 'I am going to the opening. You, after all, have *The King and I*.'

Not long after, Young and another guest suffered acute seafood poisoning at a private dinner party; the ambassador had to leave his post permanently as a result of severe hepatitis.[22] The US embassy nevertheless continued to promote the monarchy as a bulwark against seeping communism. However irked Thanat was by the easy access to Sarit American officials enjoyed at the time, Young in particular, he stayed with the programme.

'Thanat had spine,' says Anand. 'He should be regarded as a nationalist more than anti-American. He always stood up for Thailand's interests. In our jobs, we deal with governments. We may have been anti-American in some of our government policies, but we were not anti-Americans. I can be critical of my own government, but I can't ever be accused of being anti-Thailand.'

Anand believes the general direction of US foreign policy changed after World War II when the US began to recast itself as guardian of the free world and global policeman. He sees this as very different from the US international agenda in the early 20th century, which was about increasing trade and releasing countries from colonialism, a corollary of the Monroe Doctrine in the 19th century. The US had been more idealistic and altruistic, and Siam had been a particular beneficiary.[23] Siam was also more independent, for example opting not to join the League of Nations in 1919 after World War I. All this changed between 1945 and 1975 when the US became more active in Central and South America, the Middle East, and Southeast Asia, and the CIA came to be viewed by some as a state within a state.

Regional relations

Although there had been serious tensions with Thailand over US support for Phibun before Sarit consolidated his position, anti-Americanism was not on the menu in Thailand, where China was the big issue. On China, Thanat started out much more hawkish than his predecessor, Prince Wan, the consummate diplomat's diplomat and state servant for all seasons who adapted deftly to changing governments and circumstances.

Like the Americans and Sarit, Thanat was staunchly anti-communist in the early 1960s, prior to the Sino-Soviet split. It meant he took a harder line on China than either the French or the British might have done on their own outside SEATO. Although China supported communist parties in countries around the region, its potential belligerence was tempered by the unhappy and costly experience of the Korean War in the early 1950s. The war ended inconclusively in a stalemate, and the peninsula was split along a demilitarised zone that remains in place over 60 years later.

Prince Wan had been cordial in his dealings with China's Premier Zhou Enlai when they met at the Bandung Conference in 1955, and was careful to walk a fine line. He was attentive to Thailand's strengthening Cold War alliance with the US, but also respectful of strong historic Sino-Thai relations. Thailand's concerns about the spread of communism were genuine enough, but in the case of China they needed to be seen in the softer light of cultural and trading relations stretching back centuries.

Thailand's large Chinese population had been through some hard times, but was by far the best assimilated in Southeast Asia. Whatever the concerns about Chinese hegemony, hostility to China could not be considered a healthy or normal state of affairs. To many Thai nationals in the Chinese diaspora, China has always been an ancient motherland. Thanat and Anand themselves both had Chinese forebears of whom they were proud, as did to varying degrees other members of the diplomatic corps, the military, the business and banking communities, most of the other prominent families in the kingdom – and indeed the royal family.

With power plays between Cold War superpowers as a backdrop, Southeast Asia was in the very early stages of evolving any kind of collective geopolitical identity. In 1961, Thanat was the prime mover in the formation of the Association of Southeast Asia (ASA), comprising the Federation of Malaya, the Philippines, and Thailand. Initially, he tried to bring on board all the countries in Southeast Asia other than communist North Vietnam.

As a key member of the working group, Anand was responsible for the early drafts of the agreement. Ostensibly, the aim of ASA was to foster economic co-operation, but little augured well for the association. It encountered strong opposition from President Sukarno's Indonesia, which had hosted the Bandung Conference in 1955 and was a key player in the emerging Non-Aligned Movement. Burma, which strongly supported Bandung and non-alignment, was meanwhile moving towards isolation and xenophobia after the coup by General Ne Win in 1962. For Cambodia, Thailand's prominent position in US-backed SEATO ruled out ASA membership. These were unhappy and divisive times for the region in many other ways. Singapore would experience race riots in 1964, and later find itself pushed out of the Federation of Malaysia, formed in 1963.

Cold War hostilities were meanwhile heating up in Indochina. In early 1962, Thanat included Anand in the Thai delegation he took to Geneva to observe progress on the International Agreement on the Neutrality of Laos,[24] which had got under way the previous May. The talks were co-chaired by Britain and the Soviet Union, and involved 14 nations including China, and three factions from Laos.

Thanat returned to Bangkok after two weeks, leaving the Thai delegation in the hands of Direk Jayanama, Thailand's distinguished wartime ambassador to Tokyo. There were formal plenary sessions once or twice a week, but most of the action took place in private meetings behind the scenes. Anand's job was to monitor the progress of these private sessions through constant contact with different national delegations, all housed in different hotels within easy walking distance. The British were staying at the five-star Hotel Beau-Rivage, and used to disappear in their fine cars for sightseeing at weekends. The Thais were putting up at the modest Hotel Alba, and feeling somewhat put out that the three Laotian factions were all doing much better with generous per diems from their sponsors. 'We led a more humble existence,' Anand recalls. 'I was still a first secretary from a poor, developing country.'

Although Anand only got to see his wife Sodsee when she visited for a fortnight's holiday, Geneva was fruitful in some important ways. 'It was a good experience for me – you learn the intricacies of multilateral diplomacy and the skills. I learned a lot from listening to these people and watching them operate.'

Anand was particularly impressed by Malcolm MacDonald. The veteran British diplomat had been Churchill's young wartime health minister, and then high commissioner to Canada. MacDonald had spent a decade in Southeast Asia in the highest ranks of Britain's colonial administration, and had been instrumental in the formation of SEATO. China's premier, Zhou Enlai, who visited the Geneva conference, once described MacDonald as 'the only capitalist we can trust'.[25]

Adlai Stevenson II, the US ambassador to the UN, made appearances, while W. Averell Harriman, the US assistant secretary of state for Far Eastern affairs, headed the American delegation. Anand remembers hearing Stevenson's frequent quip about the social life of a diplomat being a combination of 'protocol, alcohol, and Geritol'.[26]

In the end, however, sealing off Laos from Cold War hostilities was a hopeless endeavour, and the sparsely populated kingdom's neutrality would soon enough be flouted with recriminations on all sides. In *per capita* terms, Laos went on to become the most heavily bombed country in history.

In March 1962, Anand accompanied Thanat to Washington to meet with Dean Rusk, the US secretary of state. The two foreign ministers issued a communiqué that committed the US to supporting Thailand against communist subversion or direct attack. The communiqué added to the Manila Pact of 1954, which had given rise to SEATO, and other bilateral defence arrangements between the Thai and US militaries. It contained a crucial assurance that in the event of communist aggression, the US would act in Thailand's defence without waiting for the other SEATO member states to react.

'The Secretary of State assured the Foreign Minister that in the event of such aggression, the United States intends to give full effect to its obligations under the Treaty to act to meet the common danger in accordance with its constitutional processes,' the communiqué stated. 'The Secretary of State reaffirmed that this obligation of the United States does not depend upon the prior agreement of all other parties to the Treaty, since the Treaty obligation is individual as well as collective.'

'It was designed to reassure the Thais,' explains Anand, although it was never endorsed by Congress. The communiqué also conveyed the impression that Thanat had some role to play in security relations.[27] It was well received in Thailand, with many regarding it as the equivalent of a bilateral alliance with substantial long-term dividends.

Within just a few days of its signing, it was apparent that the Thai military establishment had misunderstood the purpose of the agreements. US military advisers reported that the Thais were asking for additional funding, believing that the communiqué was in effect a formal treaty.[28]

SEATO was technically the first multilateral grouping based in Southeast Asia, but it could not really be described as regional since Thailand and the Philippines were the only Southeast Asian full members.[29] SEATO was therefore a multilateral defensive grouping, not one based on the other mutual interests of the countries in Southeast Asia. The latter was an area of exploration that interested Thanat much more.

In early 1964, Thanat hosted a landmark, five-day conference in Bangkok attended by the foreign ministers of Indonesia and the Philippines, Subandrio and Salvador Lopez, and the Malaysian deputy prime minister, Tun Abdul Razak. This produced little beyond a communiqué, which was read to the press by Anand as Thanat and the other ministers looked on. The purpose of the conference had been to try and get beyond *Konfrontasi*, the dispute in Sabah and Sarawak (North Borneo) between Indonesia and Malaysia over territories previously controlled by the British. *Konfrontasi* stemmed not from ideological conflict but regional tensions precipitated by the dismantling of colonial legacies in a modernising world. It amounted to an undeclared local war, and ran from 1963 to 1966. The rest of the island, Kalimantan, was under Indonesian rule.

This first dialogue between regional foreign ministers came to be seen as an important precursor in spirit of the Association of Southeast Asian Nations (ASEAN), which Thanat would be instrumental in forming in 1967. It was an example of how Thanat believed smaller countries ought to take initiatives, and chart their own national courses outside constraints dictated by superpower rivalries and the Cold War.

Thwarted diplomacy

Apart from his visits to Geneva and Washington, Anand spent the final three months of 1961, 1962, and 1963 at the United Nations in New York for the General Assembly. Thanat always attended the opening sessions, and was grooming Anand for greater responsibility. 'He wanted to make sure I had good opportunities to work my way up,' Anand says.

Thanat's selection of Anand as his secretary had been based on merit, but it did in some ways reflect his reservations about subordinates educated in France. An exception was Sompong Sucharitkul, ten months older than Anand, and another rising star in the Thai diplomatic corps. Sompong's educational background was untypical by any standards. He attended Oxford University, studied law in Paris, and then went to Harvard Law School. Anand and Sompong had first met in Britain in the early 1950s, on a train heading for a Thai student summer get-together at St John's School in Northwood. Sompong had spent most of the intervening years on his various degrees, and was more qualified academically than Anand. He had put in a stint from 1957 to 1959 working at the International Commission of Jurists in Geneva, giving him experience of international law that was otherwise almost non-existent in Thailand.[30] He lectured in law at Chulalongkorn University, and rounded off his unique *curriculum vitae* with a six-month secondment to Sarit's office. There he undertook special research assignments on international legal issues, but essentially he filled a protocol role. Thanat Khoman always accompanied foreign dignitaries when they met the prime minister, and it was on these occasions that he first noticed Sompong, who, some time after Thanat had appointed Anand as his *chef de cabinet*, arrived at the foreign ministry to work as a legal officer.

Back in Thailand, Anand and Sompong would meet occasionally at the annual Oxford and Cambridge dinners. 'Anand was very articulate,' says Sompong. 'He had a firm grasp and could remember everything that happened in meetings. I was impressed – I could not think of a better person.'

At the foreign ministry there was plenty to occupy Sompong's legal talents. Thailand was embroiled in an international dispute that had dogged relations with Cambodia ever since the 1900s, when Siam signed a number of border treaties with the French. At the heart of the dispute, which continues to this day, was an ancient Khmer temple in the Dangrek mountain range that runs along part of Thailand's eastern border. It is situated on top of a cliff facing into Cambodia. The ruins, on a patch of otherwise barren high ground covering some 4.5 square kilometres, were known to the Thais as Khao Phra Viharn (or Wihan) and to the Cambodians as Preah Vihear. Thailand argued that the watercourse at the cliff's base provided a natural and logical border between the two kingdoms. The Buddhist temple astride the watershed on top of the cliff was indeed Hindu-Khmer in origin – as are a number of other sites much further inside modern Thailand. The Thais considered Phra Viharn to be on Thai soil. Indeed, its cliff-top setting meant it could only really be accessed from Thailand.

Unfortunately, a French colonial map from the early 1900s placed the temple inside Cambodian territory. From this fact, an increasingly bitter international legal dispute arose within a larger mix of contested lands. Siam had ceded to Cambodia the provinces of Battambang, Siem Reap, and Banteay Meanchay in 1907, but was allowed to repossess them in World War II during the Japanese occupation. The three provinces were restored to Cambodia after the war. Following Cambodian independence from France, Phibun's irredentist ambitions revived and Thailand took control of the temple area in 1954. The Cambodians disputed the Thai move and in 1959 took their case to the UN's International Court of Justice (ICJ) at The Hague in Holland. In June 1962, the judges ruled 9:3 in favour of Cambodia's claim to the ruins.

Although the dispute has gone through long dormant phases, Thailand's overall handling of the Phra Viharn issue had been marred by poor judgment. Siam had failed to dispute French maps in the first place, and during the reign of King Vajiravudh even officially reproduced a French map of its own borders that showed Khao Phra Viharn inside Cambodia. This occurred partly because Siam did not have a map-making department of its own until the late 1920s. In 1928, Prince Damrong Rajanupab was sent by King Prajadhipok to clarify the situation along the border, and was received officially at the temple by the French commissioner in Preah Vihear province beneath a fluttering French tricolour. 'Prince Damrong accepted that Preah Vihear belonged to French Indochina,' observed Charnvit Kasetsiri, a distinguished Thai historian.[31]

Anand believes Damrong, confronted by the overbearing French, had little choice at the time. 'It was under threat that he had to accept this,' he says. 'It was a trap.'

Siam had never been colonised – unlike every other country in Southeast Asia. This was always a source of national pride; but it brought vulnerabilities and deficits in experience when it came to dealing with the outside world. At this juncture, Thailand had no Western power to turn to quietly for coaching on helpful precedents in law and international relations. 'My personal view is that having not been colonised, we have often been left roaming around in the wilderness,' says Anand. Siam, he notes, had appointed foreign advisers on agriculture, finance, transport, irrigation, security, but 'international relations was a different terrain'. He believes this has also had a detrimental impact on relations with neighbouring countries. 'We have been estranged not by geography but by history,' he argues, noting that even in the 1980s Thais rarely visited Burma.

Sarit inherited the revived dispute over the temple from Phibun, but his government's response was muddled. The Thais had on their team Sir Frank Hoskice, a former British attorney general, and other distinguished legal counsel; but there was still infighting. The Cambodians meanwhile fielded Dean Acheson, President Harry S. Truman's formidable secretary of state a decade earlier, to argue their case in court. 'That was a shock,' Anand recalls of Acheson's appointment. 'I personally thought the Cambodians made a very clever move.'

At the Ministry of Foreign Affairs, Sompong was the key man reporting to Thanat Khoman. He was even taken up to the border by Colonel Kriangsak Chomanand for a site inspection. With his own perspective on international law, Sompong could see the Thai position was precarious. His preference was for a protracted legal war of attrition. He firmly believed Thailand's first shot should have been to challenge outright the jurisdiction of the ICJ. Thailand did make a preliminary objection, but lost.

Unfortunately for Thanat and Sompong, the case was not being handled by the foreign ministry but by a national group formed by the justice ministry. The minister of justice, Phya Arthakarinibhonda,[32] had appointed *MR* Seni Pramoj – somewhat remarkably, his partner in a private law practice – to head the group. Without doubt, Seni had a good legal mind. Indeed, he had won a 300-guinea prize when he qualified as a barrister at Gray's Inn in London at the top of his year, 'first of firsts' in the British bar examinations.[33] However, he had no experience in international law. Seni was very confident Thailand would win the case at the ICJ, which raised Sarit's expectations. Indeed, Sompong was horrified to learn through the grapevine that Seni had said – he hoped in jest – that the young lawyer should be shot for suggesting otherwise, particularly as his father was a close friend of Seni.

Sompong considers the Sarit government's handling of the case to have been a blunder. 'We should have fought every step of the way.' As Anand recalled, 'Thanat and Seni never saw eye to eye. There was an element of unfriendliness.'

Anand meanwhile lacked Sompong's legal credentials, and was spared detailed involvement in the Phra Viharn case. As Thanat's gatekeeper, he nevertheless had a privileged view of the fallout from the slow implosion of Thailand's legal case at The Hague. 'Sarit blew his top – he wanted to invade and alerted the troops,' Anand recalls of the verdict that was so disastrous for Thailand. 'Pote Sarasin and Thanat rushed to Sarit urging caution and saying it would be unwise to take that course.' Sarit was advised that the best diplomatic approach was to respect the court's decision but reserve the right to differ in the future. The prime minister cooled down and announced on television that the ruling had to be respected, at least for the time being. 'With blood and years, we shall recover Phra Viharn one day,' he promised.[34]

From Anand's relatively lay perspective, it seemed 'normal and irrefutable' that the watercourse at the foot of the cliff should have played a decisive part in delineating the border near Khao Phra Viharn. But it was not the merits of the case that struck him so much as the weaknesses that Thailand's conduct of it exposed. It now seemed isolated in the international arena. Siam had long suffered from predatory French colonialism along its borders. Having played an indispensable role in causing the problem in the first place, the French remained supportive of Cambodia. Their interest in winning was not simply on account of Cambodia's great ancient culture, but a vested stake from colonial times. The French inevitably saw the dispute as partly their fight.

Even though Thailand lost at The Hague, Sompong had made his mark with Thanat, impressing him with, among other things, polished draft submissions in English and French. 'Civil servants who were competent enjoyed working for him – he instilled pride,' says Anand.

Because of his own constant presence within Thanat's orbit, Anand's experience with top-level diplomacy had bounded ahead, both at home and abroad. His professional development had run well beyond his years. Thanat had mentored him and also been generous with the opportunities he opened up.

The time had come to push Anand to another level. When Thanat arrived in New York in October 1963 as usual for the annual General Assembly, he had two men at his side. The secretary from Cambridge was his outgoing *chef de cabinet*, Anand. The secretary from Oxford, Sompong, was to be Anand's replacement, the second of three *chefs de cabinet* during Thanat's 13-year tenure as foreign minister.

Anand would soon be back in New York, working in Thailand's permanent mission to the United Nations. After almost nine years at the foreign ministry, Anand's first foreign posting, a career milestone, might have been slow in coming, but New York was a pinnacle most diplomats would not attain in a full career.

CHAPTER 4

FOREIGN SERVICE, NORTH AMERICA (1964–1975)

North American postings

When Anand entered the foreign service at the end of 1955, one of its attractions was the 'glamour' of diplomacy, as well as the promise of a cosmopolitan life with regular postings abroad. He would spend almost 12 years in North America, occupying a succession of different and increasingly important positions in both the US and Canada. Such an extended absence from home on a single continent was unprecedented in the Thai diplomatic corps, and has never been repeated.

In posting Anand to the US in 1964, Thanat was pushing his top protégé and most trusted subordinate into the furnace where a key part of Thailand's relations with the outside world was being forged. Thanat was convinced that the US, and particularly New York, which was the global hub of multilateral diplomacy, was the best testing ground for young diplomats. The fact that Anand had been constantly at his side meant that he could place in North America arguably the person most familiar with his worldview. For nearly five years he had mentored Anand in a particularly close and mutually respectful relationship.

The Thai foreign ministry in the 1960s had fewer than 500 people in total; most knew each other both professionally and socially. Though it raised a few eyebrows initially, Anand's stellar rise was inspirational for some, particularly those arriving home from study overseas. He was only 32 when he was posted in 1964 as a first secretary to the Permanent Mission of Thailand to the United Nations in New York. A year later, he was promoted to counsellor, the deputy head of mission. In 1967, he was promoted as Thailand's acting permanent representative to the

UN with the personal rank of ambassador. Concurrently, he became Thailand's ambassador to Canada, although he did not take up residence in Ottawa until 1969. In 1972, he would become the Thai ambassador in Washington.

Thailand and Canada had established diplomatic relations in late 1961, but initially with the Thai permanent representative to the UN in New York serving concurrently in the two posts. Prior to Anand's move to Ottawa, his close friend MR Kasemsomosorn Kasemsri served there as *chargé d'affaires* in the absence of an ambassador. Given their friendship, Anand was loath to outrank Kasem, but Thanat would have none of it. 'It doesn't matter,' he told Anand. 'Friends are friends but you are going to be the ambassador.'

Although the Canadian International Development Agency (CIDA) had several projects in Thailand, including faculty exchanges between the University of Manitoba and Khon Kaen University in the Northeast, bilateral trade was small and included such items as newsprint, which greatly favoured Canada. In 1967, when Anand became non-resident ambassador to Canada, there were other reasons to warm the relationship. King Bhumibol and Queen Sirikit were to pay a three-day state visit in June. This included viewing two magnificent Thai pavilions erected in Montreal for Expo '67, which ran from April to October and attracted over 50 million visitors from 62 countries. The Thai structures had originally been erected at the New York World's Fair, which ran for 18 months from April 1964. One was described as a reproduction of an 18th-century Buddhist shrine, and the other was an elongated pavilion with gabled roofs designed to showcase fine arts and crafts. For the royal visit, Apasra Hongsakula, who in 1965 was Thailand's first Miss Universe, modelled the silks.

All through his five years as ambassador to Canada (1967–1972), Anand remained Thailand's acting permanent representative at the UN in New York, and he was often teased about the title. 'I was acting permanent representative for so long that many of my Asian colleagues started calling me "permanent acting permanent representative",' he says.

He had replaced Upadit Pachariyangkun, a future foreign minister, who was then appointed as ambassador in Lagos. It was a malaria-ridden posting in those days, where roaming animals howled through the night. Thanat sent Upadit there after he received complaints directly from a permanent representative of a neighbouring Southeast Asian country that Upadit was being insufficiently pro-active at the UN on the Tibet question. Though whispers dogged Anand down the years, there was no truth in the gossip that he was in some way involved in Upadit's temporary career reversal. Instead, it showed what a taskmaster Thanat could be – he was tough with everybody.

In July 1972, when he became ambassador to Washington at the age of only 39, Anand was also finally confirmed as permanent representative at the UN, a position he technically retained for four more years. He likes to point out that his final promotions in the US were made under a new foreign minister, not under Thanat, his main mentor – 'a great honour that the National Executive Council has placed trust and confidence in me', he told a reporter.[1] His career achievements, he has always maintained, were his own and not steered by patronage.

Family life

For Anand, the move to the US in 1964 was an immense wrench from his close family life in Bangkok. Nanda, Anand and Sodsee's first daughter, was six and attending kindergarten. Daranee, their second child, was only two, and thereafter would spend her entire childhood in North America. Both daughters had to work hard to develop their Thai-language skills with tutors and annual summer visits to Thailand, and today retain noticeable American accents.

Nanda remembers the move to New York in 1964 vividly, because she was so seriously ill at the time. Probably as a complication from measles, she was afflicted by *thrombocytopenic purpura*, an illness causing a perilous drop in blood platelets and susceptibility to bruising and bleeding. It is potentially more serious than the mosquito-borne dengue fever, a common disease in Southeast Asia. Nanda's illness required risky transfusions and blood supplements from the US. She doubts she would have survived without therapies that were generally unavailable in Thailand at the time. Anand also got help from a friend in the US Central Intelligence Agency procuring a machine that stimulated platelet generation.

Because of Nanda's illness, Anand travelled ahead on his own. Sodsee followed with the girls, stopping in Tel Aviv en route to Copenhagen to see her parents. Nanda developed a serious rash in Israel, and, fearful that the illness was recurring, Sodsee decided to press on directly to New York. Anand was waiting for them at the airport with an ambulance, but Nanda's condition had calmed. Instead, they went to a hotel on 86th Street. A stranger, Edna Hirst, had helped Sodsee during the flight from Tel Aviv. She astonished everybody by appearing for breakfast at the very same hotel next morning. The family kept contact with the warm-hearted New Yorker during their time in the city. Nanda meanwhile needed two more years of regular check-ups, and remains vigilant to this day.

The family would live for five years in New York until Anand finally became Thailand's resident ambassador to Canada in 1969. With the girls by then moving towards adolescence, Ottawa offered a more wholesome environment than the Big Apple. The residence at 489 Acacia Avenue was a large mock-Tudor house in Rockcliffe Park, a quiet, well-to-do part of the Canadian capital with several diplomatic residences. The large garden iced over in the deeply cold winters, morphing into a private skating rink. The schools were close enough to reach on foot. 'It was good for the kids,' Anand recalls.

With Sodsee and the girls in Ottawa, Anand maintained an apartment on 82nd Street for his working periods in New York. His life was split between the two North American cities. He flew from Ottawa to New York via Montreal. The journey usually took about four hours, but on a few occasions in deep winter he got snowed in at the airport. 'Anand has infinite energy – he did the commuting with his laundry,' observes Tej Bunnag, a future foreign minister.

During the General Assembly months from September to December each year, Anand would only return to Ottawa for three or four weekends. The New York apartment had a small room where he watched National Football League games. Anand's lifelong passion for all kinds of team sports made him an avid spectator of American football in the US, and ice hockey in Canada – neither of which he played. As time went by, he found himself less drawn to watching tennis, which had been his sporting passion at Dulwich and Cambridge. He never found an interest in golf because of the amount of time it consumed. Squash was ideal for quick, efficient exercise.

When the UN was not in session, Anand tried to spend as much time as possible in Ottawa. Daranee remembers the long evening dinners when he was home, and this was probably the most treasured family time. The girls followed a ritual of visiting their parents' room for a bedtime chat before going off to sleep. It was a warm family environment, and they never felt neglected, but both girls had to learn how to always make the most of the limited time available with their father. 'It's how I learned to speak clearly and concisely,' says Nanda. 'He was strict in some ways, and not others. What was very important was that he inculcated independent thinking in us.' Daranee remembers her father personally organising annual family holidays, sometimes to remoter parts of Canada, with 'quiet meticulousness'. Anand always took great interest in the girls' education, and at one point considered sending Nanda for schooling in Britain.

'There were no secrets between us,' says Anand. 'We were concerned about the drugs and sex questions later on, but they had a healthy school life throughout.' Sodsee nevertheless sometimes worried that her daughters would become completely westernised and end up marrying foreigners. She need not have worried. 'Somehow our fate was to find Thai men,' says Nanda. Daranee says she never considered staying abroad. 'Thailand was always home, although when I came back, everybody thought I was *dek farang* [a foreign kid]. I always had French fries and spoke a lot of English.'

For Sodsee, the three years in Ottawa were the toughest, and the furthest from home, during the almost 12 years the young family spent in North America. Although there was the *chargé d'affaires*, Kamthorn Udomritthiruj, his wife Samphan, and two other junior diplomatic staff for company during Anand's frequent absences, as well as social activities with other diplomatic wives, Sodsee was on her own for significant periods. Far removed from Thailand's bottomless pools of domestic staff, she did most things for herself, including driving her car into town for shopping.

Daranee remembers her mother then as stylish with beehive hairdos. She also recalls having more contact with her father's side of the family than with her maternal grandparents, both of whom were of royal lineage. Her grandfather, *MC* Gustavus Chakrabhandhu, a great grandson of King Mongkut, was a military officer and diplomat who had served in France and Denmark. Although Sodsee always applied herself, there was a greater sense of entitlement on her side of the family. Indeed, Sodsee's father had been given a house with land by King Prajadhipok when he married. Her parents were close with Queen Rambhai Barni, King Prajadhipok's dowager queen (who was widowed in 1941 and lived until 1984). 'They spent their lives in a more leisurely manner,' says Daranee of her maternal grandparents, who always doted on their energetic son-in-law.

Even overseas, the girls saw more of Anand's parents. In their later years, Sern and Pruek travelled abroad every year, and often came to the US. The governor of the 'Commonwealth of Kentucky', Louie Nunn, even commissioned Sern as a Kentucky Colonel. 'I hope your appreciation of Kentucky and its many fine attributes will continue to grow,' he wrote. The elderly couple visited Europe frequently, particularly Rome, Vienna, and Paris, where Sern could immerse himself in opera and classical music. There were lighter excursions for burlesque at the Lido and Crazy Horse revues in Paris, and visits to other curiosities, such as a restaurant situated at the border of three countries.

Their second son, Kusa, who operated World Travel Service (WTS), handled the elderly couple's itineraries. The company was blazing Thailand's inbound tourism trail, but also handled much smaller numbers of Thai outbound travellers. One of the more exotic WTS trips made by Sern and Pruek was to Treetops in Kenya. The elderly couple were among the first Thais to visit the remote African resort where Princess Elizabeth had learned of her accession to the British throne in early 1952 after the early death of her father, King George VI.

Nanda and Daranee spent their summers back in Thailand, staying in the large Panyarachun family compound on Chidlom Road. Nanda remembers the often-remarked noisiness of the Panyarachuns *en masse*, and her father's siblings hotly debating anything and everything, often regrouped in the alliances formed decades earlier in the time of shared nannies.

Nanda recalls Pruek's devotion to all her grandchildren, and how she indulged them. 'She was even more doting later to my own daughter, Tippanan.' Sometimes, Pruek would arrive with special treats of shark's fin soup or Peking duck.

During their visits from the US, Nanda and Daranee spent hours both morning and afternoon listening to the recollections of Sern, a man who had lived long and fully. 'We just enjoyed being with our grandparents,' says Daranee. 'We weren't told that we had to go into my grandfather's room twice a day. It was all very natural. We have a very open kind of family, and that comes from enjoying people.'

Sern's fondness for travel and international goodwill earned him the Skål Club of Bangkok's Skålman of the Year award in 1970. In his declining years at Chidlom, where Anand's brothers Prasat and Chat also kept their homes, he continued to welcome guests. On one occasion, 200 members and friends of the Gourmet Club gathered in the garden for one of their periodic dinners. Sern barely had time to eat himself, and passed among his guests with a large box of cigars extolling the digestive merits of smoking Havana leaf.

'His knowledge of food and wine was extensive and expert,' Robert Caro recalled in Sern's funeral book. 'His tastes embraced the good things in Asia as well as Europe, and he was equally at ease hosting one of his Italian luncheons at the top of the World Travel Service building as he was in his own home enjoying a Thai meal. His personal favourites were the great white wines of France, and his son Rak tells me that, even in the last months of his life when he was under intensive medical care, he unfailingly drank a glass of one of them with each meal.'

In 1974, at the age of almost 84, Sern died, and Queen Rambhai Barni presided at the cremation. Pruek went to live with Rak, her eldest son. Daranee was then 16, and spent a lot of time at her grandfather's bedside. To this day, Sern remains for the two sisters a model for lifelong learning. Nanda believes the family's strong work ethic and discipline were instilled by her grandfather. 'My father absorbed all that,' she says. Anand remembers finding all his father's pocket diaries intact after his death, and believes he has inherited the same habit of storing things.

'I had been in Canada two years earlier when there was a widespread rumour in Bangkok that I was to be appointed ambassador in Washington, and my father was ill,' Anand recalls. 'It was time for me to come back for a visit, and he was looking forward to that, but I delayed my return in case it looked like a move to accelerate the appointment process. That was a great regret in my life – that I did not return in time. I was devoted to him, and he played a major role in developing my character. His death was not unexpected because he had been ill for quite a while, but for most of that I was not with him. I was very much bereaved, and that sense of loss persists up to this day.'

Sern had 'a long, full, and extraordinarily happy life and I suppose he was ready to go,' Rak wrote to family friends. 'But he was the head of our family for 61 years and we miss him badly. Even though confined to his bed for over a year, he was astonishingly vital right to the end, and his interest in his projects and the affairs of his family never flagged … I don't think anyone else in the world could have been the father that he was.'[2]

Diplomatic life

Anand's replacement at the foreign ministry in Bangkok, Sompong Sucharitkul, had an outstanding legal mind and was a brilliant linguist. When Sompong was posted as ambassador to Tokyo in 1968, he was replaced in turn by ML Birabhongse Kasemsri, Anand's nephew and childhood playmate. Birabhongse, the son of Anand's oldest sister Suthira, was only three years younger than Anand himself. His family had lived in the lower Silom Road area near the old Panyarachun compound on Sathorn Road.

Under his grandfather Sern's guiding hand, Birabhongse attended Shrewsbury, Sern's old school in England, on a foreign ministry scholarship and went on to Christ Church, Oxford, the college attended by King Vajiravudh. Unlike Anand, and much to his grandfather's further delight, Birabhongse also opted to pursue postgraduate studies in the US, attending the Fletcher School of Law and Diplomacy at Tufts University. As secretary to Thanat, and later in Washington and New York, Birabhongse was a benign, familiar shadow through much of Anand's diplomatic career.[3]

Many viewed Sompong as a genius, but he had a knack for alienating colleagues and stepping on toes. 'Academically, Sompong and Birabhongse were miles better than I am,' says Anand. 'Birabhongse was always a scholarly type.'

In 1965, Thanat visited the US on a speaking tour supporting the increasingly embattled administration of President Lyndon Johnson. He was stewarded for much of the trip not by Anand but by his friend James Linen, the former publisher of *Time* magazine who throughout the 1960s was president of Time Inc., the magazine's parent company. Linen was well connected politically. He had an astute wife, Sara 'Sally' Scranton Linen, with strong links to Pennsylvania's political establishment and a brother in the senate. Linen took a keen interest in Thailand and the region, and once visited with a large fact-finding mission in tow.

Thanat made a presentation that greatly impressed them. In the US, Thanat was an articulate, assertive outside voice supportive of the Vietnam War, and Linen ensured that doors everywhere were opened to him. He organised an appearance for Thanat on *Face the Nation*, the current affairs flagship of CBS News. After his forthright performance, Thanat got a personal call from President Johnson in the White House thanking him profusely; Anand was sitting beside Thanat when it came through. Linen laid on an executive jet and arranged a speaking tour for Thanat that ran from Arizona to California. There were introductions to people such as Clare Boothe Luce, the influential journalist, diplomat, and wife of Henry Luce, the publisher of *Fortune*, *Life*, *Time*, and *Sports Illustrated*. Anand accompanied Thanat throughout the tour, and remembers the despairing pair being served chicken at every meal.

Thanat's speaking tour culminated in San Francisco where Bernie Yudain, a member of Linen's staff, was assigned to draft 'without haste and occasional decorum' a mock treaty of amity between the kingdom of Thailand and Time Inc. The so-called 'Declaration of the Pacific' spoofed the Rusk-Thanat Communiqué of March 1962, and talked a lot about golf. The declaration identified among many common enemies Prince Sihanouk of Cambodia, the rice weevil, and the editors of *Newsweek*. The signatories promised not to poach staff or serve each other chicken, with penalties ranging from a 'diplomatic protest to a measured nuclear response', and to restrict responses to requests for information to 'ten words in English or 15 words in Thai'. 'It was all in jest,' Anand recalls.

Linen was nevertheless serious enough about Thailand to later invest personally in the *Bangkok World*, which had been founded by Darrel Berrigan, an American correspondent and former US intelligence operative. The new paper was conceived as a serious rival to the *Bangkok Post*.[4] Despite his friendship with Thanat, Linen once lightheartedly attempted to recruit Anand to Time Inc., a move that was explicitly banned under the second article of the mock Declaration of the Pacific. 'Thanat would not let him do that, and I was not interested,' says Anand. Indeed, over the years his career both at home and abroad has been filled with corporate and political offers that, if accepted, would have taken Anand in radically different directions.

Thanat's staunch anti-communism raised his international profile – and Thailand's – in sometimes unexpected ways. The Hungarian Freedom Fighters Association of the United States recognised him for his services to world freedom. More than 200,000 Hungarian political refugees had fled abroad after the brutal Soviet suppression of the Hungarian Uprising in late 1956, and many had found their way to the US. Unable to attend the awards ceremony, Thanat sent Anand on his behalf. It was a fine summer evening, and Anand arrived from New York at a Sheraton hotel in Washington with two journalist friends, Inge Galtung, a Norwegian correspondent at the UN and good friend of Thanat, and an American radio correspondent. The trio found everything utterly disorganised, and the shambolic proceedings meandered along until well past midnight. 'If there was any doubt that the Hungarian uprising was spontaneous, tonight proved it,' a Hungarian journalist working at the UN commented ruefully as they set off home exhausted.

Working at the UN

Anand found the North American working environment generally enjoyable and challenging. He had no difficulty making friends among delegates from all manner of political orientations and religions. Many were from non-aligned nations and were considerably older. 'When I was at the UN, I was in my late 30s and early 40s, and all my close friends were already 50 or 60,' says Anand. 'Many have passed away.'

Life at the UN involved three months of intensive work for the General Assembly in the final quarter of each year. Anand continued to have personal access to Thanat, who was usually in New York at least twice a year and always attended the beginning of the General Assembly. Anand's position also gave him contact with all the other high-ranking Thai officials visiting North America. Having attained the rank of a departmental director general, Arsa Sarasin remembers attending the General Assembly eight or nine times. Most other Thai diplomats travelled far less, however. Given the expense and distance, there was no official paid home leave in the system. At that time, postings seldom exceeded three years. Indeed, Anand was only occasionally recalled to Bangkok for official consultations during his first six years abroad.

During Anand's first year at the UN, Thailand's permanent representative, Upadit Pachariyangkun, often received speaking invitations that did not interest him; he was happy to pass these along to Anand. Such approaches came from many directions, including the World Affairs Council, the Brookings Institution, television and radio stations, high schools and colleges.

'Most prominent missions would view speaking as part of their normal duties,' says Anand. Thanat wanted his assignment in New York to make Thailand more visible and proactive. 'It was a golden opportunity. We needed to do a lot of public relations work in terms of promoting Thailand's position in world affairs,' Anand recalls. New York always attracted good public speakers; he sought them out and observed closely, hoping to rekindle the oratorical promise that Thai friends had first noticed during his years in England. Acting very much on his own brief, Anand started taking up the speaking invitations, initially from borough high schools in places like Brooklyn and the Bronx, where he drove himself.

'My English was adequate, not perfect, and I learned on the job,' he says. 'I didn't have to do much homework and started speaking extemporaneously. I am sure I made a lot of mistakes, but it was good training.' He was quite surprised by how readily he could speak impromptu in both English and Thai. After about a year, he 'graduated' himself from schools and began talking at colleges. He started coaching Thai students participating in the mock UN. This was also the time he began to get more involved with the Western press. He made himself available to wire services and major newspapers, and engaged with journalists. 'I was very much involved with the institutional image of Thailand. It opened up a new chapter in my life. That's why I find it very easy to get on with the press. I can be very candid with them. It was good fun.'

At that time, Thailand was little known in the West. To help rectify this, Anand organised the kingdom's first special supplement in *The New York Times*. This included an unattributed contribution from William Warren, a young American lecturer at Chulalongkorn University in Bangkok who was only too happy to supplement his modest income with some editorial moonlighting. Warren wrote colourfully about how the sudden vast inflow of US dollars as a result of the growing American presence in Thailand was transforming the city and upcountry areas near military bases. Warren received a stiff written rebuke from Anand stating that Thailand had not benefited by 'so much as a dollar' from the American military's arrival. Warren was chastened – and not just because his authorship had been so casually revealed. However, when they next met, Anand told a somewhat wary Warren that he had been instructed to write the letter and he was not to give the matter another thought.

War in Indochina

In retrospect, Anand believes diplomats had a narrower brief in the 1960s and 1970s than their modern counterparts, who need to be much better versed in economic affairs. In the 1960s, Anand's diplomatic activities were inevitably bound up with the Cold War, a polarised ideological conflict. The positions adopted by small powers such as Thailand tended to be responsive to the superpowers – the United States, the Union of Soviet Socialist Republics and the rising People's Republic of China. Through SEATO, Thailand was already well established as one of the foremost US allies in Asia; Thai boots were on the ground in both Vietnam and Laos. The creeping war in Indochina was never popular in the US, and became less so as the free-spirited 1960s progressed, and anything that smacked of the *status quo* was ripe for challenge. Viewed from the UN, Indochina was the hottest place in the Cold War world. U Thant, a former headmaster and diplomat from Burma, was UN secretary general from 1961 to 1971. He knew Southeast Asia exceptionally well and was openly critical of US activities in Vietnam.[5] This brought him up against the hawkish Thanat who railed against advocates of appeasement in Southeast Asia as 'instigators of doubt, of confusion and defeatism … masquerading as princes of peace'.[6]

One observer at the UN noted: 'Mr Thanat Khoman of Thailand, like Mr Thant of Burma, is one of those outspoken and blunt Asians who disprove the still persisting occidental misconceptions of Asian subtlety, double-talk and inscrutability. The difference between Thanat Khoman and U Thant is, of course, that they collide head-on in their respective approaches to the Vietnam War.'[7]

'Being in the UN, you got to know different points of view,' says Anand. 'I had to immerse myself in matters relating to the Vietnam War. I didn't have much trouble propagating our particular official line, but my feelings about the war began to change when I saw the protest movement in the US. Then we began to see the atrocities and the "body count" strategy.'

'It made life a little uncomfortable,' Anand continues. 'In the UN context, we were castigated as "running dogs of US imperialism" by the Chinese propaganda machine. Of course nobody was so directly critical of Thailand with me, but I knew that some of our non-aligned friends were looking at the Thais in a different light. Gradually, I started to ask questions. I began to worry about the strength of the American resolve to see the war through. That affected my thinking. If Thailand were to hitch along all the way without asking any questions, we would end up in hot soup. It was a turning point for me.'

Anand's concern about the American resolve to stay the course was shared by Thanat whose hawkishness was becoming increasingly reinforced by his irascibility. Sir Anthony Rumbold, the British ambassador at this time, described Thanat as 'vain, touchy and disputatious' on many fronts. ' Any allusion to peace talks in Vietnam makes him shiver. He is a strong adherent of the American alliance and supporter of American policies, though his attitude towards the United States is qualified by xenophobia and the Americans find him difficult to handle. He is a vigorous promoter of all forms of regional co-operation.'[8]

Thanat was well aware that the US could lose heart in the war on communism in Asia and return home. The Thais, on the other, had nowhere to go and would eventually have to find accommodations with their neighbours – whatever their political hue and whatever the outcome of the conflict.

There was considerable concern about competing Soviet/Vietnamese-backed and parallel Chinese-backed communist insurgencies on Thai soil. These had started to rumble in about 1964, but few Thais subscribed to the so-called Domino

Theory being peddled by the US, even when a more sustained, armed domestic insurgency flared in 1966.[9] This was partly a matter of mindset. Through astute diplomacy, the Siamese had seen off predatory British and French colonial powers in the 19th century. They had later witnessed at first hand the failure of Japanese expansionism based on supposed cultural supremacy during World War II, and the collapse of Western colonialism. Throughout, Siam and later Thailand had always struggled through to a better day.

'As time went by, as I saw more brutality, more atrocities, and the insanity of war, I began to feel there was no military solution,' Anand later recalled. 'And then I saw more and more Americans were turning against their government. To me, that spelled disaster for Thailand – to be overcommitted to something which was being eroded every day by internal forces, particularly by the US congress.'[10]

'You began to see that the American government and the administration were playing a dangerous game,' says Anand today. 'In the UN context, the Americans were not really interested in small powers. They were playing a game of *realpolitik*.' This meant showing respect for an economically ascendant Japan, and for India and Indonesia with their enormous populations. Less powerful, Thailand was vulnerable to US fickleness. Anand realised that Thailand could all too suddenly become 'baggage'.

Southeast Asia coalesces: from ASA to ASEAN

Thailand was not the only country that needed to bulk up its profile in the region and further afield. Thanat went a step beyond the failed Association of Southeast Asia (ASA). This comprised Thailand, the Philippines, and the Federation of Malaya, but not Singapore (which became part of the Federation of Malaysia in 1963). In 1967, the five charter members of the next regional grouping, the Association of Southeast Asian Nations (ASEAN) were Malaysia, the Philippines, Singapore (which had been pushed out of the Federation of Malaysia in 1965), Thailand and, crucially, Indonesia. Indonesia's new post-*Konfrontasi* leader, General Suharto, and his more outward-looking foreign minister, Adam Malik, were happy to see Thanat's lame-duck ASA superseded by a more inclusive, mutually beneficial, new regional grouping that they hoped might one day provide a foundation for Southeast Asia's collective dealings with the world. After the failure of ASA, Thanat's orchestration of ASEAN was an attempt to create an effective regional grouping. 'At that time we were not fully open with the world,' Anand notes. 'ASEAN came as an economic and cultural association, but the motive behind it was political, and the objective was political.' The grouping's political objectives included pushing the quagmire of *Konfrontasi* into the background.

'Indonesia had to be involved – it was a very calculated move,' says Anand, who knew Thanat had been close to Tunku Abdul Rahman, the Malaysian prime minister, certainly more so than to Sukarno, the former president of Indonesia. 'I knew that whatever Thanat did, he always had regional interests in mind. He did what he could one step at a time.'

Thanat assigned Sompong, Anand's replacement as his secretary, to chair the Thai working group and drafting committee. Sompong's team produced the original draft joint communiqué for circulation among the prospective partners. The Thais agonised over a name for the organisation that would produce an acronym sufficiently dissimilar to ASA or SEATO. They came up with SEA-ARC for the work in progress: Southeast Asia Association for Regional Co-operation. Sompong remembers the Thais successfully doing the rounds of Kuala Lumpur, Singapore, and Manila. In Jakarta, however, Foreign Minister Adam Malik said Indonesia – by far the largest and most populous country in the region – would only sign on with an additional clause stipulating that all foreign military bases in Southeast Asia should be impermanent.

Thailand and the Philippines both had bases used by the US military. In the case of the Philippines, the immense naval facility at Subic Bay and the Clark Air Base were leased under a 1947 treaty. In Thailand, listening stations were a grey area but the air bases used by the US air force were all technically under Thai command. Indeed, Graham Martin, Kenneth Young's successor as US ambassador from 1963 to 1967, was summoned in person to confirm this arrangement to the Thai cabinet. The British had naval facilities at Sembawang in Singapore, and the Australians had an airbase at Butterworth in Penang, Malaysia.

Even so, it could be argued that there were no *permanent* foreign military bases hosted by the five original member countries, and this opened the way to Indonesia joining. Indeed, the Indonesians did not just come on board but turned out to be the most active in cobbling together support and smoothing out obstacles within the group. Malik's assistant, Anwar Sani, virtually pioneered shuttle diplomacy in the region in the run-up to the Bangkok Declaration that established ASEAN.

The new regional grouping's final communiqué was hammered out at a government resort in Thailand near the sleepy seaside village of Bang Saen, half-way along the eastern seaboard between Bangkok and the Royal Thai Navy's immense US-built air base at U-Tapao. Thanat included plenty of games of golf between negotiating sessions, setting a more collegial, friendly tone for such gatherings that has endured.

Away from the resort, a young Singaporean diplomat, S.R. Nathan, immediately picked up on the corrosive effect of the US military presence. 'It was so unlike Thailand,' he recalled some months before his death in 2016. 'The people wanted the US dollar rather than the baht.'

Singaporeans were particularly sensitive to any untoward US influence. Their founding prime minister, Lee Kuan Yew, believed that the US was keeping bad company in South Vietnam and waging a hopeless campaign. 'He was clear-eyed in knowing it was an unwinnable war, and had no fear of being contrarian,' recalls Professor Tommy Koh, one of Singapore's most distinguished former diplomats. As a 'pragmatic socialist', Lee did see in the US presence some benefit, in that it bought other countries in Southeast Asia time for economic development and institution building.

'We were trying to detach ourselves from any affiliation with the Americans,' said Nathan, whose long, multifaceted career in public service was to culminate in the presidency of Singapore. 'The whole purpose of the exercise was to develop a relationship with Vietnam as a collective body – it was all about what to do with Vietnam after the war,' he recalled.

Singapore's foreign minister at the time, S. Rajaratnam, openly described any perceived US involvement in the new grouping as the 'kiss of death'.[11] 'The basis of ASEAN was political but it had to be given an economic face,' recalled Nathan. The Singaporeans pressed for more than just a declaration. They wanted clauses on joint tourism and other forms of economic co-operation. The Thais were less keen on such specific inclusions at that time, and pushed back most of these proposals. 'After that, we learned that we should keep a low profile,' said Nathan.

'It was in a way collective defence, but we didn't want to use those words,' says Sompong. 'It was about peaceful co-existence.' The Bangkok Declaration was signed at the Thai foreign ministry on 8 August 1967. It was Thanat who announced the new regional grouping's name – the Association of Southeast Asian Nations (ASEAN) – but he credited it to Malik. Nathan recalled the name coming as a revelation to most of the people assembled, and this played into speculation about who was influencing the course of events most. Apart from Thanat and Malik, their fellow foreign ministers Narciso R. Ramos of the Philippines, Tun Abdul Razak of Malaysia, and S. Rajaratnam of Singapore were all formidable individuals.[12] 'My sense was that it was really Thanat Khoman who felt that ASA did not work – it had to be expanded,' said Nathan with hindsight. 'To what extent the Tunku was involved, I do not know. The one who ran it was Malik.'

Some have dismissed ASEAN's formation as a US plot to encumber and distract Thanat – a strand of thought to which some Thai academics still subscribe. Nathan remembered being buttonholed at the time by a Russian diplomat who observed that the name ASEAN had appeared in a US academic tome in the early 1960s. He was correct.[13]

'Success has many fathers, but from Singapore's perspective we were not inspired by the Americans,' observes Tommy Koh. 'Lee Kuan Yew and S. Rajaratnam thought this was the right thing to do – we should get the non-communist countries together. It all started from a fear of communism. We also needed peace among ourselves.'

Sompong was in his element drafting communiqués and travelling the region. When he met Lee, the Singapore prime minister admitted openly to a recurring nightmare that Thailand might one day get around to actually building a canal across the Isthmus of Kra in the South. A kind of Suez or Panama canal for Southeast Asia, it would have dealt a severe economic blow to Singapore.[14] 'It wasn't funny – he was serious,' recalls Sompong.

Lee and Thanat had some rough moments in Singapore's early days, but patched up a working relationship after meeting face to face. 'Perhaps they didn't like each other,' speculates Koh, who regarded the Thai foreign minister as a Cold War warrior. Lee by contrast started his political career championing workers' rights as an anti-colonialist, ostensibly on the left. 'He was a pragmatic socialist, and bound to clash with Thanat,' says Koh. 'Thanat had to do what he had to do in the kingdom's interests. He made an impressive person and was very intelligent. He had a certain sense of his persona and status, but he was very ideological and very right wing. He would later change.'

Lee once complained to Koh about Thailand's shifting loyalties of convenience. 'The Thais are always on the side of the angels,' he said. Koh remembers chiding him for insensitivity, and for not phrasing it better. 'They are actually admirable,' he told Lee. 'With skilful statecraft and diplomacy, they have escaped being colonised. We should compliment them.' In fact, Lee had been even less diplomatic, referring to Thailand publicly as the 'organ grinder's monkey' – the US being the organ grinder. Nathan remembered arranging a meeting for Lee and Thanat, who was passing through on a trip to Australia. 'We hoped the matter could be closed,' he recalled of the organ grinder slight. 'It was not even brought up: the meeting turned out to be very positive, with an emphasis on working together in the future.'[15]

In New York, Anand played a key role in expanding the reach of ASEAN. 'I was active in forming the ASEAN working group,' he recalls. The early ASEAN missions were pretty threadbare affairs. Nathan remembered other delegates dropping the Singaporeans off at the Waldorf Astoria where they would 'sweep grandly in through the front door and a few minutes later creep surreptitiously out again'. There was a blossoming of regional awareness at the UN, and a new camaraderie developed among the ASEAN representatives. Nathan recalled arriving as a 'practically raw' delegate to the UN in 1967, and being very impressed with the Malaysian and Thai teams. Enduring friendships were forged. Anand and his colleagues were nicknamed the Thanat Khoman Boys. 'As far as I was concerned, I was learning from them,' said Nathan. 'Although Anand was a bureaucrat, he had very statesmanlike qualities.'

Nathan remembered Anand, who was dividing his time between New York and Ottawa, turning up only for important sessions. 'He was very seasoned and prepared to share his views, but he was also a bit aloof. He used to make sarcastic remarks and laugh them off. He once commented, "You Singaporeans talk a lot."' The Singaporean diplomats found him inclined to attribute every idea emanating from the island republic to Lee Kuan Yew.

The UN was particularly important to countries with a limited network of legations around the world. Singapore at that time had nothing in Africa, the Middle East, or South America. Six years younger than Anand, Tommy Koh arrived at the UN for the first time in 1968, and soon came to regard Anand as 'my older brother'.[16] 'He was brilliant, still relatively young, good-looking,' says Koh. 'To be a successful diplomat, your EQ[17] needs to match your IQ. He was proud of himself obviously, but he controlled his ego very well. I would say Thailand had more influence there because of Anand.'

The ASEAN *esprit de corps* at the UN predated Koh's arrival. He remembers being struck by how 'very close' the five Southeast Asian missions had already become, operating as a small club within the much larger UN club. 'It was a surprise that there was already quite a sense of community among us. We got on well as individuals and friends,' he says, recalling teas in the delegates' lounge and dinner parties at each other's homes.

Koh remembers feeling closest to Anand among all his ASEAN colleagues, but it was sometimes tough keeping up. When Koh's second posting to the UN came up in 1974, Lee Kuan Yew was greatly impressed by Anand's combining his position as permanent representative to the UN in New York with the ambassadorship in Washington. 'Why can't you do that?' he demanded of Koh. In Singapore's case there was a greater chance of conflict of interest, Koh responded defensively. The Thais after all were supposed to be good US allies and thus more compliant, providing less chance of friction. 'What you do at the UN might not please Washington,' he advised Lee.

Anand in fact found running the two posts extremely taxing, and at one point the plan was to have Sompong Sucharitkul replace him in New York. The two even exchanged correspondence on the matter. Sompong, who was more prone to tangles with senior people, however, ended up being posted to The Hague for reasons that were never explained to Anand.

The Vietnam War's spilling over into Cambodia presented ASEAN with several problems. Tommy Koh vividly recalls a moral dilemma after General Lon Nol's US-backed removal of Prince Sihanouk in 1970. Although Lon Nol clearly had more control of the territory than Sihanouk, the question of recognition, including at the UN, was particularly sensitive for Singapore. When Singapore was pushed out of the Federation of Malaysia in 1965, Sihanouk had great empathy for the fledgling republic and its People's Action Party (PAP). The bond was strong enough for Sihanouk to promise Cambodia as a refuge for a government in exile should Kuala Lumpur ever attempt somehow to force federal rule on Singapore. 'Sihanouk and Lee Kuan Yew were bosom buddies,' Koh recalls of Singapore's dilemma after Lon Nol's putsch. 'Sihanouk felt betrayed, but he was also a supreme realist.'

'In certain situations, I prefer a direct approach to get things done,' Anand recalls. In his view, Lon Nol had clearly taken over and there was little choice but to recognise him and move on. 'There was no real argument within the group – they knew my line was the only way. Neither Indonesia nor Singapore was in a position to say anything against it. Thailand was the only country that could talk sense to Lon Nol.'

As his Singaporean colleague vacillated, Anand dismissed Koh's moral reservations over recognising the Lon Nol government. 'For my country's interests, I am willing to sell my own grandmother,' he said, using a very English – and intentionally humorous – turn of phrase. Koh reproved him with mock sternness. 'Anand, I am shocked by you – I would never sell my grandmother for anything.' 'That remark has stuck in my mind all these decades,' he says. 'Anand was a realist.'

Royal visits

King Bhumibol Adulyadej and Queen Sirikit visited North America together twice. On the first occasion, in 1960, Anand was only peripherally involved. He remained in Bangkok while Thanat went to Europe during the five-month extended tour that followed the US leg. On the second royal visit, in June 1967, the Thai ambassador in Washington, Sukich Nimmanheminda, was responsible for the Washington arrangements, which included a dinner at the White House hosted by President Johnson. Anand handled everything else, which included the stays in Canada, New York, and Los Angeles.

The visit began the day after the outbreak of the Six-Day War[18] between Israel and three of its immediate Arab neighbours. The crisis in the Middle East compelled Anand to head hurriedly from Canada to New York where the UN Security Council had gone into session. Anand particularly recalls the inspirational oratory there of Abba Eban, who had become Israeli foreign minister the previous year, and played a key role in formulating UN Security Council Resolution 242, adopted that November, 'emphasising the inadmissibility of the acquisition of territory by war and the need to work for a just and lasting peace in which every state in the area can live in security' – a state of affairs yet to be realised.[19]

There were other unexpected complications. When Anand arrived ahead of time to inspect arrangements for a benefit in Los Angeles for the World Adoption International Fund (WAIF),[20] he was dismayed to find two large Buddha images installed as decorative Oriental items. He lost no time getting them removed. 'I had to be quite blunt,' he recalls. 'Just imagine if you came to a grand ballroom in Thailand decorated with Jesus on a crucifix. Then they got the message.'

The second part of the trip included four days in Canada and five along the US east coast. As guests in Canada of the governor general, Roland Michener, the royal party travelled to Ottawa and Quebec. Relations between Quebec's dominant

French-speaking and minority English-speaking populations were tense at the time. There were also tensions between the regional and central governments, and a trade minister had recently been assassinated.

With sensitivities raised, the protocol in the bilingual nation was for the first paragraph in a speech to be given in French or English, and the rest in whichever language was most dominant in that particular area. This put Anand at a disadvantage because, to his lasting regret, he had never learned French. Having been brought up in Switzerland, however, King Bhumibol spoke both languages fluently – and always preferred French. The king made light work of the official functions. 'That was the first time I met with the king,' Anand recalls of the North American visit. 'I found working for him was very smooth and pleasant. It was a good starting point to get to know him. It was also daunting – things could have gone wrong easily.' Sodsee felt the pressure just as keenly.

Anand knew many of the people in the entourage. The former permanent secretary at the foreign ministry had become the king's principal private secretary. Princess Vibhavadi Rangsit was a cousin of Anand's father-in-law, and Poonperm Krairiksh[21] was lord chamberlain. Thanat was also on hand as minister in attendance.

Initially, Anand would join the royal entourage at the rear, letting older and senior people go first. One evening the king wanted to know something, and called him to the front. He then told Anand to walk right behind him. Everyone then knew Anand was there by instruction and not because he was pushing himself to the fore. Anand spoke to the king in Thai and remembers often having to stretch himself to find the right words. He had never been schooled in *rajasap*, the court language derived from ancient Khmer. Anand helped draft some of the official speeches, and in the process found the king to be open-minded and a good listener. One night, well past midnight, King Bhumibol came across Anand working on a speech and was concerned by the lateness of the hour. 'It showed he cared,' says Anand.

After Canada, King Bhumibol and Queen Sirikit went for a few days' holiday in Maine, staying at the beachside home of John Watson, the former chairman of IBM and a friend of James Linen, the influential president of Time Inc. Linen, an alumnus of Williams College in Williamstown, Massachusetts, was the mover behind an honorary degree awarded there to the king.[22] He was also instrumental in laying on a high society reception in New York for 700 at the Metropolitan

Museum of Modern Art, hosted officially by the museum's trustees and Time Inc.

Though an ambassador, Anand was still only 34 at this time, and Sodsee around 30. Both were grateful to Thanat's wife, Khunying Molee, who arrived in New York to help out in the background of what had changed from a state to a working visit.

The visit went off smoothly. King Bhumibol was evidently satisfied with the arrangements. Royal decorations were routinely conferred on ambassadors on such occasions, and Anand received a Royal Cypher Medal, third class. Three months later, however, he learned that he had been made a knight commander, second class, of the Most Illustrious Order of Chula Chom Klao, and Sodsee fourth class. This royal decoration is not routine – unlike the various grades of the Most Exalted Order of the White Elephant, for example – but is the personal gift of the king. It is therefore rarer and much more highly coveted.

Anand visited the palace for a reception later in 1968, and spoke with the king informally for about ten minutes. He did not see the king again for nearly five years. The next opportunity came in 1973 when, as Thailand's permanent representative to the UN, he attended a formal luncheon in Bangkok hosted by King Bhumibol for Kurt Waldheim, U Thant's successor as UN secretary general.

Changing geopolitics

At the end of 1972, Anand was sent to Paris as an observer at the Paris Peace Talks for Indochina, in which Thailand was not included but Indonesia was. The negotiations resulted in the signing of a peace agreement in late January 1973 by representatives of the US, and of North and South Vietnam. The agreement was never ratified by the US senate, but facilitated the withdrawal of US forces and 'peace with honour', in the words of President Richard Nixon. Henry Kissinger, the US national security advisor and future secretary of state, was very controversially awarded the Nobel peace prize that year for his efforts in Paris. His counterpart, North Vietnam's Le Duc Tho, was also awarded the prize, but declined it on the grounds that peace had yet to be achieved. The subsequent departure of US forces from the Indochina theatre brought no peace, however, and US bases in Thailand were maintained on a reduced footing. Indeed, the fighting in Cambodia, Vietnam, and Laos did not end until mid-1975 with the final communist takeovers. Phnom Penh and Saigon fell within a fortnight of each other in late April.

Even as the wheels came off the US military adventure in mainland Southeast Asia, key elements in the Thai military were quite happy to continue as beneficiaries of the vast amount of military aid involved. Thanat and his brain trust in the foreign ministry, including Anand, had been deeply sceptical for a long time. Anand was also viewing events from the US where strong anti-war sentiment had dogged the Johnson and Nixon administrations. The war in Indochina was viewed with unparalleled immediacy on television and in the rest of the media, and by the late 1960s US public opinion had turned strongly against it. Some dodged the draft by going to Canada; returning veterans found themselves being vilified as murderers and baby killers.

The background to the peace talks dated to early 1969 when Richard Nixon took office with the promise to end the unpopular war – which in fact would outlast his political career. The new president visited Thailand in July, commenting: 'Asia can, and must, increasingly shoulder the responsibility for achieving peace.' Under this so-called Nixon Doctrine, the US would honour its treaties and provide *matériel* support to its allies, but primary fighting forces had to be raised locally. Nixon's shift would lead to Vietnamese forces taking over the fighting in South Vietnam. With Thailand facing armed insurgencies on three fronts, and China promising to step up wars of 'national liberation', Thanat was concerned that domestic security problems should not be muddled with the Vietnam War being waged from US military bases in Thailand.[23] There were some 48,000 US troops still in Thailand, three-quarters of them air force.

Even as Nixon broached troop reductions, Thanat was clear that there remained a role for the US military in the region. 'It would hardly be conceivable that a nation which has succeeded in sending men to the moon should withdraw from [this] corner of the globe,' he said on US television. 'I do not think it would be in the interest of the American nation to leave Vietnam or Southeast Asia entirely, and leave the whole scene free for others to take over.'[24] But the tide was running out on the US war effort – raising the long-feared possibility of Thailand being left beached. The reports reaching Thanat from Anand in the US were therefore often dismaying.

'Thanat knew the Americans well, but they were using each other in a way,' says Anand. 'When we saw the winds of change, we had to adapt ourselves to the new geopolitical landscape. Towards the end of his ministerial career, it was Thanat who initiated secret talks with the Chinese through me in New York.

That took place long before the government adopted a formal position. I was instructed secretly by him to start making contact with the Chinese after their entry into the UN in October 1971.'[25]

As instructed, Anand held three or four secret meetings lasting up to 45 minutes each with Huang Hua, China's first permanent representative,[26] in the underground meeting rooms at the UN headquarters in New York. With Chinese interpreters present, Anand's brief was to open back channels without discussing matters of substance – which would inevitably have included the Chinese-backed communist insurgency in Thailand. Each day, a radio station in Kunming blasted vituperative propaganda supporting the guerrillas of the Communist Party of Thailand (CPT). From his meetings with Huang, Anand tried to glean impressions of how China viewed Southeast Asia and its vision for future engagement.

'It was sizing up – getting to know each other,' says Anand. 'It was definitely not peace talks. The euphemism is "confidence building" – it's about understanding respective viewpoints. The Chinese would never admit they were supporting the communist movement in Thailand, so we refrained from arguments about the past and started afresh. We said what our concerns were.'

Anand's reports were carried back to Bangkok in the diplomatic pouch. The brief, low-key meetings with China at the UN attracted little attention. It gave Anand the chance to rekindle his acquaintance with Huang, whom he had met before in Canada. In February 1971, during the run-up to China's readmission to the UN, Huang was posted as ambassador in Ottawa. He was re-emerging after being purged in the Cultural Revolution and spending time in internal exile.

Although Thailand–Canada relations were fairly minimal at the time, the Canadians were pleased to have Anand physically present for at least part of the time from 1969 onwards. He had been non-resident ambassador since 1967, popping up from New York as needed. 'That was the kind of thing that was never appreciated by Canada,' recalls Sean Brady, a young Cornell graduate who embarked on his diplomatic career at 27 in mid-1970. 'We would almost have preferred to have people not there than do this kind of shuttling.'

'The very first cocktail party I went to was at Anand's place, and he was the only one who was pleasant to me because I was so junior,' recalls Brady. 'He was highly respected as a diplomat but not a player on the China scene as far as we were concerned.' Normalisation talks were at that time under way between Canada and China in a neutral third country, Sweden, and these produced a very short formula for establishing relations. Canada's communiqué with China was signed on 13 October 1970, and within six weeks 26 other countries had followed its lead by using the same formula.

Brady remembers Huang, China's top diplomat, as urbane and sophisticated, and not given to making jokes. His subordinates were equally disciplined: 'There were no personal relationships with those guys – they were very strictly controlled.' The Chinese arrived in Ottawa with US$50,000 in cash in a bag, and are still remembered for sending out meals to the Royal Canadian Mounted Police assigned to trail them incognito.

Saroj Chavanviraj ranked third in the Thai mission to the UN. He and his colleagues played no role in Anand's quiet warming of relations between China and Thailand during three or four secret encounters. Saroj remembers sensing 'the drift of history' in all the excitement that year surrounding the China vote in the assembly, but he also noticed how little debate it stimulated in Bangkok.

'Nobody was interested,' says Saroj, who eventually served as foreign minister for just two days in 2008.[27] 'There was very little political involvement. If it was today, there would be a lot of arguments.' He believes the foreign ministry at that time could often direct official policies without the kind of political oversight that would now be imposed. But while Anand was running his own day-to-day show in most ways, he was also always following broad, overarching directives from Thanat in Bangkok.

'We are not looked at in the same way as we used to be,' says Saroj mournfully. 'We have lost some of the glitter we used to have – we used to be one of the ministries people thought highly of.' Saroj believes Thailand's stature in the region has also diminished since the 1970s, and that it is still often seen as America's poodle. 'The US always takes us for granted,' he says. 'It is so many things put together – we can always be persuaded.'

Asda Jayanama[28] is also wistful for the kind of diplomacy Anand exemplified in his UN days. Asda became Thailand's permanent representative at the UN in the 1990s and found himself dealing with rather more specialised matters than Anand had in the same position, such as development financing, Security Council reform, and nuclear non-proliferation, of which the first two Asda had played important executive roles. Trained in the US as an economist on a foreign ministry scholarship, Asda first met Anand at the UN in the early 1970s when Anand arranged internships for his young colleague at the International Monetary Fund and the UN. The encounter left a strong impression. Anand, he remembers, firmly believed diplomats on the ground should make clear recommendations home that could be placed on the record. 'When you come to multilateral diplomacy, people in Bangkok don't know enough,' says Asda. 'In the UN, things move very quickly and you can't just abstain all the time.'

Anand was good at thinking proactively and making suggestions, an exemplar for those who dared to follow. In the case of the UN, the representative in New York is more senior than the director general of international organisations at the foreign ministry in Bangkok.

'You have to have your own mind and make inputs,' Anand counselled Asda before he left for New York. Anand believed his role was to generate properly grounded policy inputs that would help thinkers at higher levels. Asda believes this approach is past; today's politicians are much more likely to be presented with options – a sort of multiple choice – than any clearly argued recommendations.

'You should have it on paper forever that you had already presented an idea,' says Asda. 'An ambassador should use his judgement. If Bangkok doesn't think you are good enough to make a decision, better not send you. Unfortunately, they also sent a lot of incompetent people.'

In his early work with SEATO, which was created to contain the perceived China threat, Anand's diplomatic schooling had been hard-line anti-communist. But nearly two decades on, the mood was changing, rusting the ironclad thinking of the early post-war years. Thailand had already begun opening embassies and normalising relations with Eastern European countries, and Anand played an important part in facilitating this at the UN. It was meanwhile dawning on him that much of the tension between China and the US was based on positions adopted uncritically during the Cold War amid shrill propaganda exchanges.

'One began to see the shallowness of this accusation that China was the yellow evil or wanted to dominate all of Asia,' says Anand. 'The Chinese knew the Americans wanted to contain them – they knew the Americans had put up a line of defence – so it is debatable whether it was they who took the initiative or were merely being reactive to the situation. At that time, they kept on saying they had no designs on Asia or any part of the world. They adhered to the ten principles of the Bandung declaration.[29] So you don't know which came first – it was a chicken-and-egg situation. If you look at history, the Chinese were never really aggressors.'

Thailand had another good reason for re-evaluating relations with China in the early 1970s. The US was already shifting towards a rapprochement with China without even a passing reference to Thailand, its ally in mainland Southeast Asia.

'If anyone knows about changing winds, we Thais have never failed to perceive them all the way back in history,' says Vitthya Vejjajiva, who was then a rising figure in the foreign ministry. Vitthya sees some parallels in the shifting allegiances of the early 1970s with the end of World War II, when Thailand was technically allied to Japan, an Axis power by then clearly on the losing side of history. 'Things went on while the Japanese were here, and they had some inkling,' says Vitthya, referring to the way Thailand courted the Western allies in the mid-1940s as World War II approached its conclusion.

In July and October 1971, Henry Kissinger, the US national security adviser, paid visits to China for talks with Premier Zhou Enlai. These were aimed at restoring diplomatic relations between the two countries after a freeze of over 20 years. The first trip was made secretly from Pakistan. Kissinger went out of his way to make his trip through Asia 'excruciatingly boring' for his press entourage, keeping them in the dark. 'We were down to one Associated Press reporter by the time we left India,' he recalled.[30] Kissinger feigned illness after a dinner in Islamabad. This enabled him to drop out of sight and make a secret 4,000-kilometre flight at 4am to Beijing for a 48-hour visit. Pakistan was the perfect co-conspirator. It was active at the UN and a key facilitator in the warming of relations between the US, the world's largest democracy, and communist China, the world's most populous nation. Meanwhile India, Pakistan's main regional rival, was constantly at odds with China and pro-Soviet.

A Kissinger aide, Winston Lord, was sitting at the front of the aircraft. 'As the plane went over the border, I was the first American official in China for 22 years,' he later recalled. 'Henry never forgave me.'[31]

Anand recalls the UN General Assembly at the time. 'Kissinger's first visit was kept so secret that even George H.W. Bush Senior, their permanent representative at the UN in New York, was not aware of the meeting,' he says. 'We were all still working on the Chinese representation question, advocating continued recognition of Taiwan.'

In February 1972, President Nixon made his historic visit to Beijing and met with Chairman Mao. His arrival broke the ice dramatically, but the follow-up was dissipated by his re-election campaign and the Watergate scandal it precipitated. Watergate ultimately led to Nixon's downfall in 1974, marking him down in history as the only US president to resign from office. Indeed, it was not until early 1979 in the early post-Mao years that Deng Xiaoping and President Jimmy Carter finally exchanged embassies in Beijing and Washington. In the meantime, the Thais had pushed ahead, charting an independent course.

'I was committed to the normalisation of relations with China,' recalls Tej Bunnag, who was then a young officer working on the East Asia desk in Bangkok. His task was to try and track China's moves during this unusually turbulent period. 'You had to do a lot of work to see where the problems were,' he says. One of his more onerous duties was lecturing sceptical audiences in the military, at defence colleges, and in the Ministry of Interior on how China might be repositioning itself. Despite enormous historic links with Thailand, China was unpopular with the country's entire security establishment, and indeed with swathes of the general public.

'There was always a lot of anti-communist feeling,' says Tej. This was hardly surprising. A domestic communist insurgency ran hot in Thailand from 1966 to 1975, and did not finally fizzle out until the 1980s. The general public's suspicion of leftists and liberals was often underpinned by anti-Chinese sentiments, and this could extend to Thai-Chinese families who had lived in Siam/Thailand for generations.

Tej always regarded the General Assembly vote on China as essentially a piece of theatre intended to make the process appear more democratic.[32] China had always been represented, after all, and the question now at hand was by whom – the nationalists or the communists? Four of the five permanent members of the UN Security Council had already lifted their block, imposed on the mainland after 1949, when Mao took power.[33]

For Thailand, the most particular problem in normalising relations with China was the kingdom's good relations with Taiwan, the resourceful, capitalist Republic of China, which was about to lose its UN seat to China, the communist People's Republic. After the 1949 revolution, nationalist, or Kuomintang (KMT), forces belonging to the 93rd division had refused to surrender and headed south from Yunnan province. They eventually took refuge in northern Thailand around Mae Salong on the border with Burma,[34] establishing the hilltop town of Santikhiri. Subsequent Taiwanese largesse included donations to royal charities.

Thai-Chinese themselves were split over whether to support the mainland or Taiwan – or neither. Those with connections to Hong Kong were important pivots. They included Lenglert Baiyoke, and people working for Bangkok Bank, including Prasit Kanchanawat.

Another key early supporter of mending Thai relations with China was Field Marshal Praphas Charusathien, Field Marshal Thanom Kittikachorn's deputy prime minister. Praphas served as interior minister and army commander in chief, and few doubted that it was he who was really running the country. Although things would later go terribly wrong, many at the time regarded his nominal boss, Thanom, as a pliable, rather pleasant old fellow. Even Thanom, a loyal royalist, had spoken of starting a dialogue with China. But when Thanat once remarked that it was about time Thailand sat down and talked with the Chinese, it triggered a hostile reaction in the Thai press. The journalists were quite unaware that this was exactly what Thanat had already instructed Anand to do in New York.

When the time finally came in late 1971 to vote in the UN General Assembly on China's admission, Thanat abstained. He was caught between a rock and hard place. Outwardly, he wished to be seen walking a middle line between an old friend, Taiwan, and an important potential new one, China. In an interview with *The New York Times*, Chinese premier Zhou Enlai gave special recognition to the Thai abstention, casting it in a constructive light. But Thanat's diplomacy backfired on him at home, and set off another storm of criticism in the Thai media.

'By 1971, Thanat was already very unpopular and always shouting at the Thai press,' recalls Tej Bunnag. This growing mutual hostility had erupted in public on a few occasions, with Thanat berating reporters for being sub-standard and not reading press releases properly. When they responded by asking if he had ever considered resigning, Thanat was dismissive, demanding to know who they imagined would ever be able to replace him.

'Thanat was very much for opening up with China, even before the government,' says Kullada Ketboonchu-Mead, a political scientist at Chulalongkorn University, noting Thanat's mauling in the press and parliament when he floated the idea of establishing relations. 'I still cannot make up my mind whether they attacked him because they hated him or because they thought it was a bad policy. He had so many enemies.'

Not everybody felt that way. Thanat was sometimes seen joking with Anand about getting into 'hot water' with on-the-record comments to the US media. 'He has very good relations with the press, which quite clearly likes him for his abiding courtesy, good humour, perfect manners and willingness to answer questions, however delicate they may be,' noted one observer at the UN, clearly unaware of Thanat's difficult relations with the Thai press.[35]

However brilliant, Thanat was increasingly embattled and isolated at home. It was not only the press he riled. Even some within the ministry felt he had a tendency to look down on Thais in general, and was careless about offending cultural sensibilities. He never liked people coming to his home with food and flowers, a common show of deference to seniors. Candidate ambassadors for postings overseas were terrified of the questions Thanat might hurl at them during vetting, and he could be reluctant to confirm senior promotions. There was a lingering sense that he lacked faith in his compatriots.

'In terms of human relations, Thanat was not so good – he could be very sarcastic and cruel,' says Asda Jayanama, now a retired diplomat. On the other hand, Asda notes that Thanat always defended people he respected, Anand included. 'It was an easy relationship in that sense,' he says.

A change of minister

Although Thanat was ahead of the curve by recognising the importance of normalising relations with China – and may have been one of the first to guess this was already in the US State Department's pipeline – he would not remain foreign minister to see the process bear fruit. Within a month of China's re-entry into the UN in October 1971, Field Marshal Thanom staged a coup against his own government. Among those who did not figure in the new revolutionary council was Thanat. Technically, Thanom himself replaced him as foreign minister.

Some believe US President Nixon was pleased to see the back of Thanat, noting his ouster in the margin of a briefing paper on the coup: 'This is what really matters.' This may simply have been an acknowledgement that Thanat's departure would have important consequences, but Kullada believes the US had by then come to view Thanat as 'impossible' to deal with. Anand views this as too speculative, and doubts such mutual antagonism existed. Both sides, after all, were still involved in prosecuting the Vietnam War. There is also speculation that Thanat's downfall was related to US military aid being fed through the Thai military for operations in Cambodia and Laos. Anand never found out why Thanat was removed. 'It came to me as a surprise,' he says.

Thanat's dismissal left him bitter and sometimes openly critical of those who followed him as foreign minister. But in the immediate aftermath, it was all hands to the pumps on a sinking ship. Pote Sarasin, as a former prime minister and veteran diplomat, was put in to run the ministry with his son Arsa serving as his secretary. Even Prince Wan resurfaced to offer counsel.

At the time of Thanom's coup, Manaspas Xuto was on one of his frequent visits to New York. An alumnus of the Fletcher School of Law and Diplomacy at Tufts University – and one of the few Thai diplomats to receive training in intelligence from the US – Manaspas had been an early contemporary of Anand at the foreign ministry. Anand always held Manaspas in high regard. Although he never worked in Thanat's office, Manaspas used to be assigned specific projects, and was instrumental in the development of the Voice of Free Asia (now Saranrom Radio), using a 1,000-megawatt transmitter donated as aid by the US.[36] The radio station broadcast news and information in Cambodian, English, Lao, and Thai. As young officers, Manaspas and Anand often lunched together, and were clearly among Thanat's high flyers. Suddenly their bold mentor, the man who had shaped their careers, and focused their minds for more than a dozen years, was gone, a victim of opaque Thai feuds and shifting geopolitics. They were now on their own.

In New York, Anand was asked to talk about Thanom's coup on NBC's morning television programme, and he invited Manaspas to accompany him. Driving his own Chevrolet, Anand collected his colleague on the west side of Central Park. As they drove to the studio, Anand outlined his talking strategy. They both knew that as a civil servant he could not criticise whatever had just transpired in Thailand, however baffling a self-coup might seem to the outside world. Anand planned to be direct and reasonably abrasive. He was clear in his own mind about what needed to be said, irrespective of the actual questions. 'He put most of the questions back to them,' Manaspas recalls of the interview. 'They were all courteous, but the transcript showed a lot of cross-talk.'

Manaspas remembers being impressed not so much by Anand's fluency but the sharpness of his political instincts, and his ability to fend off criticisms that might invite ridicule of Thailand. Whatever his personal reservations might have been, Anand remained the loyal diplomat, parrying the talk show hosts with allusions to English constitutional history and other distractions. He argued that it was unrealistic to expect perfection of a country at Thailand's state of political development. The situation was nevertheless far from clear, even to Anand years later: 'I don't know what prompted Thanom to leave Thanat out,' he says.

Thanat was ejected to an advisory position as a special envoy on Pacific affairs. Despite his closeness to his old boss and mentor, Anand had no reason to fear for his own position, particularly with Pote effectively in charge.

The situation back at the ministry was borderline chaos. 'Over the years, power was concentrated in the secretariat,' observes Tej. 'It grew and grew until it was bigger than any department in the Ministry of Foreign Affairs. It was Thanat Khoman and the secretary who ran the ministry in every way. By the time of the coup, there was no one else working at our level.'

'Thanat did not trust some senior members of his political department,' says Manaspas. 'He did not think they were always up to par.'

Tej and Nitya Pibulsonggram, both future foreign ministers, had been expecting their first foreign postings. Instead, they were held back to help sort out the paperwork. Tej remembers Birabhongse clearing his office and nobody then knowing where anything was, including many of the China files. 'People like Nitya and me were having to go into the secretary's office to rummage around and find out what Thanat and Birabhongse had been doing,' says Tej.

The Washington years

If Anand's meteoric rise in the foreign ministry occasionally ruffled feathers, he never stumbled, and kept rising. The only Thai diplomat to have become an ambassador at a younger age than Anand was Prince Wan at 29. 'I think it was recognised that I delivered,' Anand reflects. In 1972, at only 40, he was promoted to Thailand's top diplomatic posting of the time, the ambassadorship in Washington. Concurrently, he was finally confirmed as Thailand's permanent representative to the UN, a job he had already been doing since 1967.

'Because of my youth and inexperience, Thanat kept me as acting representative for six years,' says Anand. He recalls there were two older diplomats in the running for the Washington post. The decision to promote Anand over their heads was made by Thanom himself, further proof, Anand asserts, that his rise had not simply been by dint of Thanat's patronage.

Anand had never had much contact with Thanom. When the prime minister came to New York in April 1968 on his way back from a visit to Brazil, Anand arranged a meeting with UN Secretary General U Thant. '[Thanom] did not speak English too well,' Anand recollects. Deputy Prime Minister Pote Sarasin and Thanat were both concerned that a speech Thanom was to deliver at a dinner sponsored by the Asia Society might not be understood. The solution was for him to make the opening and closing remarks, and for Anand to read the rest. Bunchana Attakor, the ambassador in Washington at the time, was none too pleased with Anand's involvement, and felt the speech arrangement demeaned Thanom. The field marshal, however, was much relieved, and spent a few days in New York. Anand remembers him as a man of little military bearing who was civil, simple, and polite. He recalls Thanom's deputy, Praphas, as a rather 'jolly character' who liked parties.

By the early 1970s, the young Anand who had been so diplomatic and deferential as secretary to Thanat had developed into somebody far more confident and assertive. He was always loyal to Bangkok, but he had also long been compelled to think on his feet and act independently. The no-nonsense working style that so many came to associate with him in later years was already well developed.

'He is a Leo – always a leader,' says Saroj, who got to know Anand well in New York. 'Once he takes something up, you feel confident he will see it through. He is very tense at work and very direct. He says what he wants to say, and never holds back. He can't stand people who just talk and talk or don't answer him directly – particularly when they are at fault or haven't accomplished something. He would shout at them: "Stop, answer me! I asked you this!"'

'He can criticise you but he is a very straight person, very decisive,' says Pridi Boonyobhas, who first worked under Anand in Washington in 1972 as a third secretary. One of Pridi's talents was being able to read Anand's tight handwriting and type up his speeches.

At the embassy in Washington, Anand always made a point of not disturbing his staff if at all possible after work or at weekends. Given his own workload and travel commitments, weekends were precious family time with Sodsee and the two girls. Anand had a staff of seven or eight; his policy was to rotate all the junior officers in the embassy so that everyone was familiar with all the tasks. Although he wanted to trust people to get on with their work, he tested them first. Never the aloof bureaucrat, he took possession of everything he worked on.

'If he instructed me to do something, I had to do it right away,' says Pridi. If a message needed to be sent, it had to go immediately and its arrival needed to be confirmed. Anand delegated efficiently, and still retains a knack that many remark upon of putting the right person in the right job. He values competence and loyalty above everything, and in that order.

Saroj has no recollection of Anand spending hours at his desk. 'I didn't see him reading too much but he was always ready and well informed,' he says. Like many others, he attributes this partly to Anand's adeptness at quizzing people – and perhaps more importantly at identifying the right people to quiz. There were regular staff meetings at the UN, with 'morning prayers' each day when the General Assembly was in session.

The only people at the embassy in Washington with whom Anand did not have much to do, in management terms, were the military attachés. These included an army lieutenant colonel, Suchinda Kraprayoon, a mid-career officer who had been the brightest and most influential figure to emerge in 1952/3 from Class Five of Chulachomklao Royal Military Academy. This is Thailand's equivalent to West Point in the US, or the Royal Military Academy Sandhurst in the UK. The attachés moved in different circles from the other diplomats in Washington, spending much of their time at the Pentagon. People at the embassy recall Suchinda as being civil but also somewhat distant. Nobody could possibly have guessed the role he would play in Anand's life two decades later.

'He was a clever person, but we were not in the same society,' says Pridi. 'He had his group of military and business people around him.' Vidhya Rayananonda, a close aide to Anand, remembers Suchinda attending receptions or dinners at the embassy most weeks, and getting along with Anand without being too close. 'Suchinda is a good man and very sharp compared with other people in the armed forces,' he says. 'He was never too serious.'

Anand remembers some personal social interaction with Suchinda at the time, and no antipathy between the two. Most importantly, the overlapping postings gave Suchinda direct insights into Anand's character and calibre. These would have significant – but wholly unforeseeable – consequences for both men two decades later.

When Anand looks back, there are few regrets he will admit to, but one thing that clearly bothers him is that he could sometimes be too brutal a taskmaster.

'I could be hard on my personal staff,' he says. 'In New York, you had to work against time and stay up late to get things done. I had an Australian secretary and I made her cry two or three times. I was very quick-tempered. She was a very nice person but not that resourceful.' At the time when Taiwan and mainland

China were vying over the UN seat, he remembers writing a letter to one of the ambassadors concerned and his secretary mishandling it. 'I forget which, but she sent it to the wrong ambassador,' he says. There are stories of junior Thai diplomats appearing for work at the UN improperly attired. On a short fuse, Anand blasted them publicly. They were sent home to change, and such basic mistakes were never repeated. 'He liked his officials to be like ping pong balls in water,' says Manaspas. 'When the hand was moved, they sprang back up. For him, substance was very important. He was very direct and not afraid.'

However, Anand's direct style and outspokenness could catch people unawares and was not always appreciated by older diplomats and military figures. 'It's not a Thai way of doing things,' says Saroj. 'He didn't care about upsetting people. He was abrasive – but mostly to people who deserved it.' Saroj remembers being snapped at once himself by Anand for shuffling papers loudly while he was chairing a meeting in New York. 'Stop that noise – I can't concentrate,' Anand suddenly thundered in a room full of strangers.

'He is not always careful with his choice of words,' says Saroj. In English, Anand's most withering criticism of anybody, he recalls, is to call them 'spineless', the derisive term Anand first heard in the Master's Library at Dulwich tripping off the lips of Christopher Gilkes, his headmaster. Although Saroj only remembers Anand calling him this once, and being mortified, he readily took sheets out of Anand's management manual. 'I liked it, and I took it as my own practice when I became more senior,' says Saroj.

'I think it comes out spontaneously without any ill meaning,' says Pridi. 'It's not personal. Afterwards, he completely forgets everything.' Saroj still marvels at Anand's ability to separate work and play, and set disagreements aside. In the office, Anand might be tense, absorbed, wary, and combative, but after office hours he would be friendly and straightforward – 'a great guy'. 'On the same day, he could be very explosive in the morning but very relaxed after five with a drink,' says Saroj. 'When he laughs, he laughs his heart out.' 'He is a very sincere man,' says Vidhya. 'After work, we are all friends.' Vidhya arrived at the Washington embassy in 1970, and was taken up by Anand as a close aide when he became ambassador. To this day, he has no idea why he was chosen or if anyone recommended him to Anand, a boss quite different from any other.

Anand could also be remarkably tolerant and soft. William, his driver in New York, was a looming African-American with failing eyesight. 'William was very old and well past retirement,' says Saroj. 'Anand was always complaining about William's driving but didn't do anything. It proves his mouth might be fast, but his heart is always good.'

Old William meanwhile put up with Anand's penchant for smoking cigars in the back of the car as they negotiated New York's terrible traffic. Saroj remembers William driving them to a party one winter's evening with Anand puffing away happily. 'It was very cold and the windows were up,' he says. 'I almost died that night.'

In New York and Washington, Anand always much preferred to unwind after work with junior colleagues than attend diplomatic functions. He retains a lifelong dislike for cocktail parties and diplomatic small talk, but enjoys a lunch or dinner with an ambassador and small group of interesting guests. Naturally gregarious, he has always loved real parties and meeting new people, especially younger ones. 'He says it sharpens his mind,' says Pridi.

Anand therefore made it a point to meet Thai students arriving in the US, particularly those with scholarships. One was Wissanu Krea-ngam, who in 1973 found himself arraigned before the ambassador among a jet-lagged group freshly arrived from Thailand. Missing from the gathering was a young police officer, Thaksin Shinawatra, who was about to start work on a doctorate in criminology at Sam Houston University, Texas, that was sponsored by the Royal Thai Police. On such occasions, Anand's predecessors usually gave pep talks lasting a few minutes before dismissing the disorientated and jet-lagged students. Anand was remorseless, and kept them on their feet for an hour.

'I have intentionally spent 60 minutes because I want to test your tolerance,' he lectured. 'That is why I have not asked you to sit. Good students, like good diplomats, have to be tolerant and not complain. This is your first lesson, now go back to sleep.'

Wissanu recalls: 'Anand impressed me and my friends a lot. He did not act like an ambassador but an older brother or parent.' Many years later, after Wissanu had served as a secretary to his cabinets, Anand recollected perfectly their first encounter in Washington.

Anand has an endless repertoire of jokes, many of which are delivered at the listener's expense, an immediate test of their ability to laugh at themselves. 'I like to pull their legs,' says Anand. He always checks the professions and nationalities of unfamiliar faces when he sits down to dinner with a new group. Someone from Malaysia or Britain might hear the tale of an old colonialist negotiating with a

Malay-Chinese. 'You have to remember, the sun never sets on the British Empire,' says the old British imperialist. 'Of course not, because God does not trust the Brits in the dark,' the Malay retorts.

Sometimes Anand's teasing gets him in deeper than expected. At a White House reception, he was in conversation with Senators Mike Mansfield and William Fulbright, both powerful critics of the war in Vietnam. During the Kennedy administration in the early 1960s, Mansfield had been one of the first to question the expenditure of US treasure on a war in Southeast Asia. The Thai stance officially was supportive of the US in Vietnam, but Anand and the two senators were discussing the notorious body counts the US had adopted as a gauge of the war's progress.

'At the back of my mind, I was quietly critical of the US policy then and making fun of the US intelligence system,' Anand says. He told Mansfield that he doubted the value of body counts because US intelligence was usually unreliable. In fact, he speculated mischievously, if the corpses were all added up they would probably exceed the actual population of Vietnam. To drive home his provocation on flawed US intel, Anand related the old Panyarachun family joke: the story of his brother, Kusa, being captured as an enemy combatant during the war by the Japanese on a Thai island the OSS had wrongly identified as uninhabited. Kusa had been trained as a paratrooper, but the Americans decided instead to deliver him to occupied Thailand in a submarine.

'We all laughed,' Anand recalls. 'One guy happened to overhear what I said and turned round and introduced himself as someone high up in US intelligence. He asked if my brother's codename was by any chance King. I said yes, and he said it was he who changed the plan. I was so taken aback that I did not ask why.'

Anand liked to tell an old East European joke about the Polish nationalist who dies and goes to heaven. At the Pearly Gates, St Peter grants him three wishes. The Pole's greatest wish is that China should invade Poland and then go home. When he repeats exactly the same wish two times, St Peter is bemused and wants to know the reason. The dead Pole explains that for China to invade Poland it will have to arrive and depart through Soviet territory each time. When Anand got to the punch line, everybody chuckled except for a senior diplomat from China. The diplomat reproved his smiling young Thai counterpart dryly: 'But Mr Ambassador, China would never invade any country.'

Political unrest at home

'Anand enjoyed Washington, no doubt about it,' says Saroj. Thailand, meanwhile, was becoming increasingly restive. After Thanom's coup against his own government in 1971, students and workers were agitating, stymied by political inertia and the absence of a long-promised constitution. Heightened xenophobia led to protests against one of Thailand's biggest foreign investors during Anti-Japanese Week. There was also hostility to China and mounting resentment towards the apparently semi-permanent neo-colonial US military presence.

Student-led demands for constitutional reform mounted. In mid-October 1973, Bangkok was witness to the biggest demonstrations in its history. Violent attempts to suppress the political unrest forced thousands of students to seek refuge in the grounds of the Chitralada Villa of Dusit Palace, the main residence of King Bhumibol. At one point, crowds were machine-gunned from a helicopter that was believed to be carrying Colonel Narong Kittikachorn, Thanom's son.

King Bhumibol could see the hostility to the military government and the mounting violence; he appeared sympathetic to many of the demonstrators' demands. Indeed, the ousting of the military regime in 1973 was one of only two popular political triumphs seen in Thailand in the 20th century.[37] In the Thai tradition of political losers, Thanom, Praphas and Narong, the so-called Three Tyrants, were allowed to go into exile overseas. King Bhumibol appointed Sanya Dhammasakdi, the respected former rector of Thammasat University (and president of his Privy Council) as prime minister to replace Thanom. Later that month, he granted an audience to student leader Seksan Prasertkun, and reportedly commented: 'It is really strange that in Thailand [really] good people do not seek power while on the contrary there are a lot of corrupt people who try every way possible to get power.'[38]

The Communist Party of Thailand was critical of the new government. In a clandestine broadcast on the Voice of the People of Thailand, it declared that more radical change was needed, but it was careful not to attack the monarchy. 'Our country did not have independence and democracy,' the CPT said. 'Our society was rotten while the working people were poor and troubled. This was due to the reactionary administration that contained elements of imperialism, feudalism, and bureaucratic capitalism. The problems of the country will never be solved if the root causes are not entirely dug up and destroyed. A partial change will lead to nothing.'[39]

As foreign minister, Thanom was replaced by Charunphan Israngkun na Ayudhya, a gentle and conciliatory individual. One of Charunphan's first instructions was for Anand to meet Thanom in Boston when he arrived there to begin his exile. It would be unseemly for even a disgraced former military strongman to be ignored by his own people and left on the street. Anand carried out the instructions sent by Saranrom Palace and met Thanom, only then to find himself being attacked as an alleged Thanom sympathiser by radical students studying in the US.

'You have to understand the storm was too strong at the time,' explains Anand. 'They all knew me in person, but still they accused me of being one of a Gang of Four Tyrants.' Anand received death threats, and somebody even fired a shot in the direction of his residence. The Federal Bureau of Investigation was called in. Although Anand did not feel particularly threatened physically, he did feel badly let down by the new government, which failed to confirm that he had been officially assigned to meet Thanom at the airport. Back in New York, he was steaming over the 'spineless' treatment afforded him, and drafted a letter of resignation. Saroj talked him out of submitting it.

Despite the tensions, Anand tried to maintain good relations with elements of the Thai student body in the US. When members of the Thai Students Association in California invited Sulak Sivaraksa on a tour of the US, Anand attended for a panel discussion. 'He was kind but I was a little naughty,' Sulak recalls. 'I said he spoke wonderful Siamese with a Cambridge accent.' Sulak felt that Anand was at that time somewhat out of touch with political developments in Thailand – but the criticism has to be placed in the context of Sulak being one of the best informed observers of the day. In 1963, he had started editing the influential, CIA-funded *Social Science Review*,[40] which had been officially tolerated despite on occasions being 'severely critical of military rule'.[41]

For Anand, the most important personal consequence of Thanom's departure as nominal foreign minister was not Charunphan's appointment but that of his deputy, the newly promoted Major General Chatichai Choonhavan, who became *de facto* foreign minister. Chatichai had become a diplomat in the late 1950s by force of circumstance rather than any intent. When General Sarit staged his coup against Field Marshal Plaek Phibunsongkhram (Phibun) in 1957, Chatichai was a cavalry commander who remained loyal to the government. He was also the brother in law of the police chief, General Phao Siyanon, who was arguably Sarit's main target. Chatichai soon discovered he was in the wrong coterie; when he ordered his tanks to move against the rebels, nothing happened. Both Phibun and Phao were forced into exile and would die abroad. As the son of Field Marshal Phin Choonhavan (who led a successful coup in 1947), Chatichai the loyal, battle-hardened officer was a potential threat to the new government. He was therefore reassigned to the foreign ministry and dispatched as ambassador to Buenos Aires, a form of gilded exile. 'I was told that he was mad,' recalls Manaspas.

'Isn't there anywhere further away?' Chatichai growled angrily as he left. His continuous postings abroad lasted 16 years. In Argentina, he tangoed, rode horses, and attended great parties. In Vienna, he acquired a Lamborghini. He was also later Thailand's ambassador to Turkey, the Vatican, Switzerland, and Yugoslavia, and permanent representative at the UN in Geneva. All the while, he was waiting to come home from a stint abroad that exceeded even Anand's North American marathon – but one spent on more continents.

'Actually his mind worked better than we thought,' says Manaspas of this supposed *bon viveur*. People underestimated this playboy at their peril. Chatichai had an excellent intuitive understanding of people. In the case of Anand, this was a particularly good thing because their first professional meeting in New York was more of a collision than an encounter. Chatichai's son Kraisak, a student at George Washington University, witnessed it. Kraisak and his future wife already both knew Anand quite well socially. 'Anand was very opinionated,' says Kraisak of the young ambassador. 'He abhorred military-type thinking. Everybody knew he was a progressive nationalist – very pro-democracy.'

At his first meeting with Chatichai, Anand was still smarting from the foreign ministry's inept handling of the exiled Thanom's arrival in the US, and the unjustified attack upon his integrity and the physical threats. 'I only listen to my old boss, Thanat Khoman,' Kraisak remembers Anand telling Chatichai bluntly when they met. 'I don't listen to anyone else appointed by the military or whoever.' Kraisak recalls that he was strangely impressed: 'I thought, wow, this guy has guts. I was taken aback, but my father took it in his stride. He was quite a character – not one of those people who takes offence.'

In return, and with no hint of anger or irony, Chatichai calmly complimented Anand on his skills as a diplomat and spoke of the great esteem in which he was held in the foreign ministry.

And it was Chatichai who would steward Anand to his next career peak.

CHAPTER 5

INDOCHINA FALLS, CHINA BECKONS (1975)

Regional pivot

Early 1975 was a time of great flux in Southeast Asia with the Vietnam War drawing to its shambolic, but decisive, conclusion. Anand was drawn inexorably into a series of events that by year's end would see him return to Thailand after more than a decade in North America.

Thai politics had been seething since the ouster of Field Marshal Thanom Kittikachorn's government in October 1973, when King Bhumibol Adulyadej stepped in to appoint Sanya Dhammasakdi, the president of his Privy Council, as prime minister. Amid considerable difficulties, Sanya succeeded in putting in place a long-delayed constitution, resolving one of the issues causing political unrest. Sanya's efforts opened the way to elections, and an analyst at the US embassy later credited him with presiding 'over the transition from authoritarian to democratic government'.[1]

After Sanya stepped down in February 1975, there were two general elections and three elected governments in a 14-month period, with the Pramoj brothers[2] playing musical chairs as prime minister. In March, MR Seni Pramoj, who had also been prime minister for a four-month period in 1945, replaced Sanya but was unable to form a stable coalition. After only three weeks, his younger brother, MR Kukrit Pramoj, replaced him, presiding over a fragile goverment. Although his Social Action Party had only 18 of 269 seats, Kukrit, despite his impeccable establishment credentials, in fact pushed some radical and progressive policies.

An echo of 1932, this was to be another false democratic dawn for Thailand. In eight centuries of Siamese and Thai kingdoms, the Pramojs were the first properly elected heads of government – but they were deeply competitive. In the early 1980s, Australian journalist Robert Woodrow met both men on successive days without revealing his arrangements to either, and profiled them:

> In temperament and political outlook, no two men could be less alike. Kukrit is flamboyant – extravagantly, sometimes outrageously so. Seni is cautious, self-deprecating, seemingly almost timid. Seni is a true democrat, an old-style liberal. Kukrit is an arch-monarchist and conservative, not at all averse in his old age to authoritarianism. They have been bitter political foes, and only see each other now on official occasions or at family weddings and funerals. Each has led political parties that detest each other. Seni headed the Democrats, political heirs to the liberal wing of the revolutionaries who toppled Siam's absolute monarchy in 1932. His brother led the Social Action Party, which he founded himself.[3]

While the beacon of constitutional democracy was flickering in Thailand for the first time in a generation, it was further than ever from being ignited in Indochina. Seen from the free world's perspective, the Vietnam War was ending catastrophically, as Cambodia, Vietnam, and Laos fell in quick succession to communist rule.

Meanwhile, Anand was still in post as Thailand's ambassador in Washington and permanent representative to the United Nations in New York. For him, one of the most important personal developments at this time was Kukrit's appointment of Chatichai Choonhavan as foreign minister. Foreign Minister Charunphan Israngkun na Ayudhya had been close to Sanya, and Chatichai had earlier succeeded him as ambassador to Vienna. Chatichai had been respectful of his senior, but he was always the driving force at the ministry during Sanya's premiership. Kukrit now formally elevated Chatichai to foreign minister as Thailand's foreign policy took a more independent turn. In his opening policy statement to parliament, Kukrit announced his government's intention to close the remaining US military bases in Thailand within a year – a shorter time frame for the process than his brother Seni had envisaged – and of normalising relations with all neighbouring countries. Kukrit also stated explicitly that diplomatic relations would be established with the People's Republic of China.

Anand had already played a crucial role in the warming of relations with China from his perch at the UN. Initially, Anand's contact was secret, but it became public knowledge after the Chinese invited him to a reception in New York in November 1971. Anand had attended with the open approval of the National Executive Council, Field Marshal Thanom Kittikachorn's junta.

Important political figures who were elected after Thanom's ouster in 1973, including prime ministers Seni and Kukrit, and the foreign ministers Chatichai and Bhichai Rattakul, were all of a mind on foreign policy. They could see that the American war in Indochina was lost, and that rehabilitating relations with neighbours of whatever political hue was essential. By mid-1975, the Indochinese outer dominoes had fallen but not the rest of mainland Southeast Asia; the consequences for Thailand were uncertain.

Events moved faster than anyone expected. Barely a month after Kukrit took office in March 1975, the Cambodian capital Phnom Penh fell to the Khmer Rouge and the Democratic Kampuchea regime of Pol Pot installed itself. The nominal president was Khieu Samphan. Prince Norodom Sihanouk, the communist front's former figurehead, was locked up in his palace along with his wife, Princess Monineath and one of their two sons, Prince Norodom Sihamoni.[4] Less than two weeks after the fall of Cambodia, victorious North Vietnamese tanks crashed through the gates of Independence Palace in Saigon, with its basement bomb shelter and rooftop nightclub, gambling dens, and cinema.[5] In May, the Pathet Lao overran Vientiane and abolished the Laotian monarchy, confining members of the royal family to gulags where they would die from medical neglect and starvation.

All of Indochina was now indisputably communist, Burma was lost to a dark and baffling 'socialist' odyssey and at war with virtually all its minorities, and the Communist Party of Malaya was still active along Thailand's southern border. Unlike, say, the Philippines, Thailand was not sitting somewhere out in an ocean. Ultimately, it would have to co-exist with Indochina whatever the region's political complexion. This would mean coming to terms with an ancient rival: Vietnam.

'The domino theory scared the hell out of us,' recalls Asda Jayanama, a young foreign-service officer at the time. 'A lot of rich people took their money abroad.'

Indeed, some wealthy Thais took the unpatriotic step of making provisions for themselves overseas. Hitherto, even corruptly gained wealth had usually been stored at home, not in Swiss, Hong Kong, or Singapore bank accounts. Among Thais, being a crook was no bar to patriotism. There was also a flight of foreign capital and stock values slumped. Rice prices were down and energy costs up.

'I never believed in the domino theory for Thailand, but you have to look after your own interests,' says Bhichai Rattakul, who succeeded Chatichai as foreign minister in 1976. The mood at the time was gloomy. Everybody was hunkering down.

The permanent secretary at the foreign ministry in 1975 was Phan Wannamethee, a highly respected individual who had joined the service in 1943. He was a skilled diplomat who, as head of the political department, had accompanied the Thai badminton team to Beijing in 1973. Phan was in no way blocking moves to normalise relations with communist neighbours and the mainland Chinese. However, Chatichai had numerous ambitious plans, particularly on the China front. He wanted someone more vigorous and assertive in the position, not a classic old-school diplomat.

Energetic and much more feisty, Anand was Chatichai's obvious choice but he was very resistant to returning home. Anand had been ambassador in Washington for three years, and was Thailand's top diplomat overseas, enjoying freedoms that were normally unthinkable in the Thai system – particularly at the age of just 43. His daughters were in American schools and doing well. Life in Washington and New York was stimulating and enjoyable. He was widely respected and very much the captain of his own ship. He had no desire to return to suffocating Thai bureaucracy. 'Being in Bangkok is a hardship posting – too many bosses,' Anand once told his key aide in Washington, Vidhya Rayananonda. He admits that he was never a great admirer of the Thai civil service system. 'Had I not been kept abroad for 12 years, I could not have risen so high.'

Tipping point

Preoccupied as he was with the fall of Indochina, Chatichai's plan to promote Anand to permanent secretary was suddenly overtaken by events: the Vietnam War turned out to be not quite over, and the 'last battle' had still to be fought.[6] On 12 May 1975, the SS *Mayaguez*, a US-flag freighter, was en route from Hong Kong to Sattahip, the main Thai naval base located on the Gulf of Thailand's eastern seaboard. It was intercepted just inside Cambodian waters seven miles off the island of Poulo Wai,[7] some 270 miles southwest of the Cambodian port of Kompong Som (Sihanoukville). The Khmer Rouge made the intercept in old US gunboats that were among some 900 naval vessels left behind in the aftermath of the Indochina conflict.

The unarmed American freighter was piled high with containers of general cargo, including PX supplies for a US military department store in Bangkok. Distress signals were transmitted by the crew before it was boarded and seized. The Khmer Rouge directed Captain Charles Miller to moor off Poulo Wai, and the next day to move to Ko Tang, a larger island halfway to the mainland.

The seizure of the ship and its crew was a major international incident, offering considerable potential for further humiliation of the US in general, and of President Gerald Ford and his secretary of state Henry Kissinger personally. An earlier incident had set a bad precedent – in January 1968, a navy vessel, USS *Pueblo*, was seized by North Korea, and its crew held hostage for months.

The Ford administration was determined to recover the ship and crew, and teach the victorious Khmer Rouge a lesson. Like everybody else, the Americans knew very little of recent developments inside the revolutionary new Democratic Kampuchea. A Panamanian freighter had also been intercepted a week before, and was initially referred to as the Unid – until somebody realised this was actually an abbreviation for 'unidentified'.[8]

Following Operation Eagle Pull in April, in which US Ambassador John Gunther Dean and his staff were extracted by helicopter from Phnom Penh, the US no longer had any direct diplomatic contact with Cambodia. After the seizure of the *Mayaguez*, diplomatic notes were instead delivered via the US liaison office in Beijing headed by a friend and former colleague of Anand at the United Nations, George H. W. Bush, a future US president. Bush passed messages to the Chinese foreign ministry and the Cambodian legation, but to no effect.

The little former kingdom was already being taken back to 'Year Zero' in one of the most ambitious and ill-conceived political experiments in history. In their unbridled arrogance, the Khmer Rouge leadership believed themselves to be model revolutionaries who could revisit China's disastrous Great Leap Forward and Cultural Revolution – and succeed. Ostensibly to pre-empt vengeful US carpet-bombing, the populations of the capital Phnom Penh and larger provincial centres had already been hurriedly evacuated into the countryside by Cambodia's new Maoist government. Many of the weak and old died in the mass forced exodus. The rest went hungry and sickened fast.

Ford, the only unelected president in American history,[9] was under tremendous pressure. He had controversially pardoned Nixon for Watergate, and was overseeing a humiliating withdrawal from the failed war in Indochina that had pushed Kissinger into a deep gloom. Ford was also dealing with a ravaged domestic economy, an uncooperative Congress, and immense public disillusionment with government in general. Bolstered by the War Powers Act (which defined his authority to act in times of national emergency without congressional approval), and determined to demonstrate leadership, Ford convened four National Security Council meetings during the course of the three-day *Mayaguez* crisis, which included a 14-hour battle on Ko Tang as fierce as any seen in the entire Indochina conflict.

The Americans were determined to recover the ship and crew, and teach the Khmers a lesson. Their presumption was that the Thais would be compliant in allowing military assets in Thailand to be used in the rescue operation. However, such an action ran entirely counter to the policies and goals of the new Kukrit government. The last thing this ambitious, elected – but very thinly stretched – government wanted was any hint of aggression towards neighbours with whom it hoped to patch up relations. Permission to use the American-built air bases at Nakhon Phanom and U-Tapao was immediately refused. Nonplussed, the Americans appealed to the Thai military and National Security Council, where green lights flashed on immediately. This issue of whether the military (a state within the state) or the elected civilian government administered Thailand would become a major preoccupation for Anand when he returned home as permanent secretary.

US marines and special forces were brought to U-Tapao from Okinawa and the Philippines for the rescue mission. Marines aboard the USS *Holt* were dispatched to recover the *Mayaguez* off Ko Tang, which was unpopulated but turned out to have robust defensive emplacements along its beaches. The *Mayaguez* crew had been run ashore on the second day in a gunboat similar to the ones being strafed by US aircraft. Rescue forces were flown to Ko Tang from U-Tapao in transport helicopters brought down from Nakhon Phanom. One crashed into the sea, killing 23 on board. The island was also far better garrisoned than expected, and two more helicopters were lost to hostile fire while landing forces.

US aircraft meanwhile sank four Khmer Rouge gunboats, two in the approach to Kompong Som harbour. Over 30 Khmer fighters were killed or wounded in the hostilities. American casualties were significantly higher, however, with another 18 killed on the island and over 40 wounded. The dead included three marines who were left behind and subsequently executed by the Khmer Rouge, two by bludgeoning.

In the general confusion that followed the loss of their gunboats, the Khmer Rouge authorities had decided to cut their losses and release the 40-man *Mayaguez* crew. Aboard an impounded Thai fishing boat, they were returned under a white flag to another warship, the USS *Henry B. Wilson*.

With men still unaccounted for and troops on the ground, the Americans dropped the last and largest bomb of the Vietnam War, a 15,000-pound BLU-82 that caused a massive detonation in the middle of Ko Tang – to no military advantage.[10] It could almost have been a metaphor for the entire Vietnam War.

On the mainland, the port of Kompong Som and Ream Naval Base were also bombed, even after news of the crew's release. It later emerged that clearance for a B-52 bombing on the Cambodian mainland, of the type the Khmer Rouge had spuriously used to justify the evacuation of Phnom Penh and other populated areas, had been authorised by Ford and Kissinger. It did not happen – Secretary of State James Schlesinger and an air force general were probably responsible for suppressing the order. Ford fired Schlesinger six months later, and his opposition to the B-52 bombing order is thought to have been among the reasons.

Even though so much went wrong, Ford and Kissinger did well in terms of public approval. Kissinger regarded the Khmers as 'thugs', and a second *Pueblo* incident had been averted. In some respects, the aggressive action to recover the crew even looked better with time – a subsequent US hostage crisis, in Iran, blighted the presidency of Ford's successor, Jimmy Carter. The Khmer Rouge meanwhile went on to slaughter anyone crossing into their territory, including several unsuspecting foreign yachtsmen. One was burned alive with car tyres outside the infamous Tuol Sleng interrogation centre in Phnom Penh.

Apart from the loss of life and limb on all sides, the other significant casualty of the three-day *Mayaguez* crisis was Thai-US relations. These had been declining for years but now they finally hit rock-bottom. The Thai press was vitriolic about the intrusion of US forces, and anti-American protests kicked off in Bangkok. Outside the US embassy, student leader Thirayuth Boonmi was immediately at the fore of some 10,000 protesters, a third of whom lingered for two days, but the embassy's back entrance was left open as a courtesy. Kraisak Choonhavan, the son of Foreign Minister Chatichai, believes the protests were important not simply for bringing people out on to the streets overtly against the US, but because the students involved had tacit government support – quite the opposite of what would transpire in October the following year at Thammasat University. 'It was quite historic in a way,' he says.

On the afternoon of 13 May, the second day of the crisis, the Kukrit government had unequivocally informed the US that bases in Thailand were not to be used in any actions against Cambodia, and that the newly arrived US troops were to be removed. When Edward Masters, the deputy head of mission and *chargé d'affaires*, met Kukrit, he was warned: 'I know how you Americans feel about freedom of the seas. And we respect all that. But whatever you do to get this ship released, leave us out of it. We've got our own problems. And I ask you to not involve Thailand in this process.'[11]

Masters was never entirely in the picture during the *Mayaguez* crisis. He was personally unclear if this was an oversight or deliberate. 'Did somebody say, "Let's not tell Masters. What he doesn't know, he can honestly say he didn't know"?' he later ruminated.[12] After giving Kukrit reassurances that day, Masters got back to the embassy to find a press report that some 1,200 marines had already been dispatched from Okinawa to U-Tapao. 'I don't want this kind of problem,' Kukrit told him on the phone. 'All hell's going to break loose if you stage a military action out of Thailand.'[13]

Kissinger was certainly aware of Thai sensitivities, but they were the least of Ford's concerns, and he chose to ignore them. Brushed aside, the Kukrit government was outraged by what it viewed as a cynical and deliberate violation of Thai sovereignty at an unusually sensitive time. It felt snubbed by the continuing dual-track US relations with Thailand. A tight bilateral military pact had been used to ride roughshod over a democratically constituted government.

'You will recall that about 48 hours before the act of retrieving the *Mayaguez* and its crew, Prime Minister Kukrit Pramoj called in Edward Masters, the *chargé d'affaires* of the United States embassy, and told him in plain language that the Thai government would view with serious concern if there should be an attempt by force to retrieve the ship and if the operation was launched from our territory,' Anand told a correspondent. 'One has to realise that there has been a fundamental change in the decision-making process in Thailand. Here we have a fully elected government and the government has to keep its commitment to the parliament and its people. This is a democratic Thailand.'[14]

'We were very angry with the US for coming in out of the blue and taking over U-Tapao without asking permission from Kukrit Pramoj,' says Tej Bunnag, who was running the East Asia desk at the foreign ministry. 'They asked Kriangsak and the military agreed of course.'

From Washington to Beijing

In the wake of the *Mayaguez* incident, Anand's life immediately moved in a new direction. By way of formal protest, a diplomatic note was handed to Edward Masters, the US *chargé d'affaires*, on 17 May.[15] More importantly, Kukrit recalled Anand in protest from Washington for consultation. Before leaving, Thailand's young ambassador appeared twice on *Agronsky & Company*, one of the most influential political TV talk shows in America at the time. He defended Kukrit, who had bluntly stated that Thailand could not be friendly with the US when it sent in marines uninvited.

'I think one can understand the extent of his disappointment – and perhaps even anger – at an action of a friendly country and a friendly government against the expressed wish of his own government,' Anand told Agronsky. But he was also conciliatory, saying 'friendly relations' between the two countries would be salvaged: 'I think that all countries in the area still very much welcome [the] US diplomatic, economic, and financial presence.'

It was an important point. Remarkably, Thailand's various military and diplomatic frictions with the US in the latter part of the Vietnam War seldom had any tangible impact on business relations between the two countries. 'It was like the military was here but not really here,' recalled James Rooney, an American Chamber of Commerce president in the early 1970s. 'Having the military didn't make an awful lot of difference – I think most of us were generally so busy it wasn't the foremost thing on our mind.' Although there might have been an element of false bravado in all this, Rooney recalled few foreign businessmen giving much credence to the Domino Theory. Most of his peers viewed the Thais as poor planners but always adept at weathering crises. Thailand might have setbacks but it would never be defeated.

At this rather unlikely moment, Anand also predicted on the record with Agronsky that Cambodia, Laos, and newly reunified Vietnam would one day join ASEAN, whatever the obstacles: 'Of course, all of these countries, both the

ASEAN group and Laos, Cambodia, and Vietnam, also have to readjust their policy in order to accommodate [each other's] interests.'

Anand's recall from Washington brought Thai-US relations to a dramatic low, but fell well short of cutting them altogether. But at this important tipping point, Anand unexpectedly found himself briefly back in Thailand with the home team.

'For the first two weeks, there was nothing for me to do,' Anand says. Then Chatichai summoned him to his office, and said normalisation of relations with the People's Republic of China was to be pursued. He wanted Anand to go to Beijing without delay. Kukrit's policy statement about China at the opening of parliament had been clear enough, but Anand wanted to know if there had been a cabinet decision to take it forward. Chatichai did not answer the question, but observed that if they were to go through normal processes, the National Security Council would have to be involved. 'He implied that it was the decision of a smaller group of cabinet members,' Anand recalls.

The China play

Chatichai viewed Anand as the obvious negotiator for establishing diplomatic relations with China. Such a rapprochement would happen sooner or later anyway, but after the *Mayaguez* fiasco it was the perfect grand gesture to demonstrate that Thailand was henceforth charting its own independent course in foreign relations. A better relationship with China could also provide useful levers in repairing regional relationships, and undermine domestic insurgencies.

Politicians had for some time agreed that normalisation with China was desirable, and other ASEAN countries were pursuing the same policy. At the time of Anand's recall, the policy was a given – certainly in the view of Bhichai Rattakul, a senior Democrat Party member. 'I think the Thais took that decision immediately after we knew Kissinger had been to China through Pakistan,' he says.

The Thai military and security apparatus naturally harboured reservations. They were dealing with two communist insurgencies backed separately by China and North Vietnam, the latter with Soviet support. These remained clear and present threats. Even so, Kukrit and Chatichai wanted no more equivocating on China, which quietly continued to woo Thailand.

After Kukrit replaced Seni as prime minister in early 1975, Bhichai was one of five Democrat Party MPs invited to Beijing on a familiarisation trip. Even though Seni's Democrats were by this time in opposition, the broad parliamentary alignment on foreign policy meant that Kukrit himself not only knew about the trip but also endorsed it. In informal talks with senior Chinese officials in Beijing, the main sticking point turned out to be their desire to normalise government-to-government relations while maintaining separate party-to-party ideological and revolutionary relations. On the basis of recent experience, continued fraternal party-to-party relations of this kind with the Communist Party of Thailand could only be construed as fundamentally hostile to the Thai state.

Since Bhichai was in Beijing as a guest politician, not a negotiator, he could easily adopt a hard stance. 'I cannot accept that,' he told his Chinese interlocutors. 'You are putting on two hats. How can I go home and explain this to my people?' Bhichai got no answer on that occasion, but as a sitting MP he was happy to place his obvious dilemma on the record.

The only question really remaining was how long normalisation would take. At the UN in New York, Anand had for four years been ploughing a complementary furrow, progressively warming relations with China's top diplomat. By early 1974, his dealings with Ambassador Huang Hua in New York were being openly reported in the Bangkok press, but it took the political drive of Kukrit and Chatichai, and the outrage generated by the *Mayaguez* incident after the fall of Indochina, to prod matters to a conclusion.

For Thailand, the visible thaw had begun three years earlier in September 1972 with so-called 'ping-pong diplomacy'. Thailand was among a few dozen national teams from Asia and the Middle East invited to participate in the Asian Table Tennis Championships in Beijing. Thai businessmen also attended the Canton Trade Fair that year.

Prasit Kanchanawat accompanied the table tennis team in 1972. He was *de facto* commerce minister to the National Executive Council, Thanom's junta, and was described by Pote Sarasin, the assistant chairman, as 'my deputy'. Prasit was a veteran politician who would later become house speaker and then vice chairman of Bangkok Bank. He was one of the junta's most senior advisers, and close to Thanom's deputy, Praphas Charusathien, who personally announced the visit. 'We have to be friends with the Chinese people,' said Praphas, affirming that Bangkok would be receptive to trade initiatives and support sporting and cultural exchanges.[16]

The Chinese took special care of Prasit and gave him separate accommodation.

'His midnight meeting with [Zhou Enlai] was without any forewarning as to the personage involved,' the US Statement Department later recorded in a conversation between Secretary of State Kissinger and Pote Sarasin. 'It was a correct and formal meeting. [Zhou] sent best regards to His Majesty the King and Field Marshal Thanom. Pote noted as interesting one item that Zhou mentioned, that the Thai must be very careful about Russian interest in the Kra Canal. The Chinese, Pote said, evidently tried to be very nice to the Thai visitors.'[17]

Prasit's meeting with China's premier was an ice-breaking event that constituted the highest-level official encounter between Thailand and China since Anand's well-publicised attendance at the Chinese reception in New York two years earlier. Prasit's interpreter was Sirin Phathanothai, the daughter of Sang Phathanothai, a close aide to Field Marshal Plaek Phibunsongkhram (Phibun). Sirin and her brother Warnwai had been sent to live in Mao Zedong's China in the 1950s, and were placed in the care of Zhou Enlai. They witnessed the tumultuous Great Leap Forward and Cultural Revolution from the late 1950s through the 1960s.[18]

More tangible negotiations got under way in August 1973 when Phan Wannamethee was director general of the political department and Tej Bunnag had been promoted to head the East Asia division. A young career officer still only in his late 20s, Tej had made his early mark as a historian. He was saved from an academic career because his scholarships at Malvern College and King's College, Cambridge, had been provided by the foreign ministry, which then required his services. He had been working on China relations since 1972 as a second secretary in the East Asia division. The pair accompanied the national badminton team to China amid a large entourage that included Police General Chumphol Lohachala, who had led the table tennis team the year before. 'It wasn't secret,' says Tej. 'Everybody saw us leaving and coming back. It was a huge group.' Even so, it would still be another two years before this warming led to formal diplomatic relations when the geopolitical landscape had been transformed by the end of the Vietnam War and the *Mayaguez* incident occurred.

Amnuay Viravan, an adviser to the finance ministry at the time, accompanied the badminton group in 1973,[19] and some trade discussions were conducted alongside. Initial enquiries were made about procuring light-grade crude oil from China. Thailand's need for energy would soon become more urgent. The global energy crisis deepened in October after the Organization of Arab Petroleum Exporting Countries introduced sanctions because of US support for Israel in the

Yom Kippur War. Anand was instructed by Chatichai to talk directly with Huang Hua in New York to request 1.2 million barrels immediately, and 27 million for 1974. The upshot was that Deputy Prime Minister Dawee Chullyasapya and Foreign Minister Chatichai were invited in mid-December to Beijing at the head of a fuel procurement delegation by the China Council for the Promotion of International Trade. Parliament was by then being readied to dump Revolutionary Party Announcement No. 53 (1959) which prohibited Thailand trading with communist countries.[20]

In the wake of the fall of Indochina and the *Mayaguez* incident in 1975, Chatichai was keen for Anand to go to Beijing as chief negotiator directly, but Anand informed him that preparations for such a visit needed to be made through Huang Hua, China's permanent representative at the UN in New York. Anand set up a committee to draft a working paper for cabinet approval. This was sent to Huang Hua with a request that it be passed to Beijing. Because they had got to know each other over the years, Anand recalls this all happening very quickly. 'By that time, we were all on very friendly terms in New York, and Beijing knew that,' he says. 'We did not have to meet secretly any more.'

China was the main backer of the Khmer Rouge, supplying them not only with revolutionary templates but military *matériel* and advisers. The *Mayaguez* incident temporarily muddied the slow-moving but warming waters with the US, but it had no effect on China's improving relations with Thailand. The response from Beijing was that Anand's negotiating team would be received.

Anand received cabinet approval to proceed to Beijing on 16 June 1975, a Monday, with the four other members of his working group: Chawan Chawanid, the newly appointed deputy director general of the political department; Suchinda Yongsunthorn from the treaties department; and Tej Bunnag and Thanit Akrasut, both from the East Asia division.

There were no direct flights to Beijing, of course, so the group travelled from Bangkok to Hong Kong. An old friend and colleague of Anand, Manaspas Xuto, was doing a two-year stint there as consul general. His unusual talents included never forgetting telephone numbers. Sitting on mainland China's doorstep as Thailand's eyes and ears, Manaspas missed nothing. He handled the normal traffic of consular affairs, and took good care of visiting VIPs and parliamentary delegations. Among others, he saw Bhichai and Anand pass through – but he never entered the People's Republic himself. Any messages that needed to be channelled to Beijing were sent through Xinhua, the official Chinese news agency. Manaspas's contact in the Xinhua 'bureau', the mainland's *de facto* embassy in the British colony, was a man who had been second secretary in the Chinese embassy in Indonesia during the late Sukarno years. 'He was known to carry a gun in Jakarta,' says Manaspas, recalling a much more shadowy world of diplomacy, a time when anti-communist and anti-Chinese sentiments in Indonesia were about to explode.

Manaspas confirmed that Anand, Chawan, Tej, Suchinda, and Thanit were expected in Beijing. They spent the first night in Hong Kong and next morning took a train up to Luohu on the border with mainland China. The team crossed the bridge on foot to Shenzhen, which at that time, as Tej recalls, had only three brick buildings. The diplomats were then picked up by police cars and taken across the mouth of the Pearl River by ferry. Another train took them to Guangzhou where they spent the second night before boarding a domestic flight to the capital.

Tej put on record the two-day journey.[21] 'It was like going to the moon – a different world,' he says. Negotiations finally got under way in Beijing on 18 June, the expedition's third day out from Bangkok. 'It was a tough week,' says Chawan, recalling the tight schedules.

This was Anand's second visit to Beijing. He had passed through briefly in 1974 as deputy head of a Thai trade delegation to North Korea led by his friend Prasong Sukhum, the minister of commerce. On that occasion, the Thais went on to spend three days in Pyongyang on a 'warming up' mission approved by Prime Minister Sanya Dhammasakdi. Anand was struck by the total regimentation, and the rigid way in which children were educated and trained. The central heating in the airless VIP accommodation in the North Korean capital had been so excessive that they had to throw open their windows. Anand recalls that nothing of substance came from the North Korea visit.

The much more fruitful talks in Beijing on Wednesday and Thursday, 18–19 June, were held in a beautiful 19th-century building on Rue Hart that had once been the Austro-Hungarian legation. The Maoists had allocated the building to their foreign policy think tank. There was a courtesy call and some preliminary discussions with the man responsible for China's affairs in Asia, Deputy Foreign Minister Han Nianlong.

Han had received Bhichai and the other four Democrat MPs on their familiarisation trip a few weeks earlier. A legendary figure in both the Communist Party of China and at the Ministry of Foreign Affairs, he was a veteran of the Long

March in the mid-1930s and one of several generals turned diplomat. One of his claims to fame from his early revolutionary days was introducing Mao Zedong to *maotai*, the fearsome white liquor made from sorghum used for interminable toasts at official functions.

Anand negotiated with Ambassador Ker Hua, head of the Asian Department: 'a very nice, soft-spoken man,' he recalls. There was no shortage of thorny issues on the table. They included ongoing Communist Party of China support for the Communist Party of Thailand; the kingdom's long-standing good relations with the Republic of China (Taiwan); and the status of Sino-Thais, particularly the Nationalist Chinese Kuomintang remnants of the 93rd regiment in northern Thailand. (Chatichai, as a young officer in the Phayap [Northwest] Army in the Shan States during World War II, had himself fought alongside the Nationalist Chinese forces of Generalissimo Chiang Kai-shek that were defeated by Mao's communist mainland Chinese in the late 1940s.) By 1975, there were 316,235 Chinese nationals living in Thailand with alien permits.[22]

The main objective was to draft the final communiqué in Chinese, English, and Thai to reflect the steady improvement in Sino-Thai relations, and to lay the foundations for future formal diplomacy. Malaysia had signed its joint communiqué with China in May 1974, and kept its ASEAN partners informed of developments. The Philippines followed suit in June 1975, a few weeks ahead of Thailand. All three communiqués had six main components: the basic premise of the agreement; the basic principles of détente; peaceful settlement of disputes; the one-China principle and principles of nationality; trade and economic relations. The Sino-Thai Joint communiqué differed from the other two in that it acknowledged 'the amity that characterised the relations of local Chinese with the Thais, somewhat atypical of Southeast Asia'.[23] Indeed, the document states: 'The Government of the People's Republic of China takes note of the fact that for centuries Chinese residents in Thailand have lived in harmony and amity with the Thai people in conformity with the law of the land and with the customs and habits of the Thai people.'[24] For that reason, the Thai communiqué substituted the word 'resume' for 'commence' when describing diplomatic relations between the two countries.[25]

As Anand chipped away at the negotiations with his Chinese hosts, Tej fretted over the nuances of translation, searching for elusive Thai terms to reflect accurately the English working text. 'We were still finalising the Thai text and couldn't agree on certain words,' says Tej. 'Anand was in another room. We took such a long time that at one stage he came in to find out what was holding things up.' Tej vividly recalls Anand's exasperation. 'You are a real *agent provocateur*,' Anand hissed in his ear. 'Use any word. Get it done.' As it turned out, Anand later spotted one word poorly translated into Thai. 'I gave them hell,' he recalls.

The negotiations in Beijing were finished by Thursday, and the long journey back to Bangkok beckoned. Before Anand's departure, the Chinese made it clear that a delegation led by Kukrit himself would be welcome. China's door was finally open for Thailand's prime minister.

The journey home on Friday 20 June took just one day, with no overnight stops in China. Anand's group flew to Guangzhou and were then driven hard for five hours to the border with Hong Kong. From there, British authorities arranged a transfer that would not have gone amiss in a James Bond film. The Thai diplomats were collected in two ultra-light military helicopters with Plexiglas bubble canopies and flown over the British colony to Kai Tak Airport. There, an Air Siam flight bound for Bangkok had been held by Manaspas. An irritable supreme-court judge was among the passengers kept waiting. 'Anand was in the lead helicopter and I was in the other,' says Tej. 'We were dropped literally at the stairs of the aircraft. That was a truly memorable trip but very rough.'

By Friday night the successful emissaries were back in Bangkok, and Anand was able to brief Chatichai. 'We had to finalise everything domestically before Kukrit was to go,' says Tej. 'I have never worked so long and so hard in my life. We had meetings morning, afternoon, and night.'

The National Security Council met on Monday, and Tej remembers liaising there with Group Captain Prasong Soonsiri, its hawkish number two. There were no immoveable obstructions to normalisation, but a significant amount of detail – including disestablishing diplomatic relations with Taiwan, the Republic of China. These dated from the years after the war when Thailand negotiated its entry into the UN and also established relations with the Soviet Union. In a compromise in 1975, the Taiwanese would retain a *de facto* embassy in Bangkok in the form of a trade office. Thailand, while signing up to the one-China policy, retained a similar office in Taipei.[26] Kanit Sricharoen, Thailand's *charge d'affaires* there, was recalled late that month.[27] Taiwanese citizens were issued certificates of identity, and mainland Chinese citizens were later told they could continue living in Thailand or apply to become naturalised Thai citizens, but they could not have dual nationality.

Meeting Mao

Kukrit's cabinet met on 24 June 1975, a Tuesday as usual. Chatichai was anxious to move ahead as quickly as possible with Kukrit's historic visit, and brought the departure date up by two days to 28 June, a Saturday, and just eight days after Anand had left Beijing with the agreed communiqué in hand.

It was still not quite two months since the fall of Saigon, which had been renamed Ho Chi Minh City. Soviet naval vessels were already moored in the Vietnamese port of Danang near China Beach (My Khe), where US forces had once surfed and partied during breaks from the fighting. It was one of a number of potential naval bases for the Soviets in the relatively warm waters of the South China Sea. During the war, Soviet ships had used the great northern port of Haiphong to supply North Vietnam, and that made it a constant target for US bombers.

Kukrit did not want to glorify China, or admit that Thailand had to kowtow in any way after the communist victory in Indochina. In typical style, he later told the press that the Peking duck served at the Scala, a restaurant in Siam Square, was still better than anything to be found in China's capital. Nevertheless, this momentous diplomatic initiative was to prove the most historic event of his premiership.

He insisted that all 15 permanent secretaries accompany him, including Amnuay Viravan, who had just been promoted to the position at the Ministry of Finance in April. Apart from top civil servants, over 100 people boarded the special Boeing 707 flight to Beijing, including businessmen, celebrities, diplomats, and journalists. It is doubtful that so many key figures would be allowed to board a single aircraft in modern times. 'We were all replaceable,' jokes Anand.

'It was a comprehensive social and political drive into China,' says Vitthya Vejjajiva. 'For Kukrit, it was a young person paying respects to an elder, just like we Thais do.' However, the two most important elders in this instance, Chairman Mao Zedong and Premier Zhou Enlai, were ailing. And, as Kissinger had discovered on his ground-breaking secret visit in 1971, there was no precise schedule for anything.

The Chinese were also receiving others at this time. On June 21, Mao had met with Cambodia's new revolutionary leadership – Pol Pot, Ieng Sary, Ney Sarann, and Siet Chhê – beside the private swimming pool at his home in the Forbidden City. Mao quoted Kumārajīva, the fourth-century Buddhist missionary from India, to Pol Pot: 'If you copy everything I do, it will be a fatal mistake.' It is not clear what Pol Pot said or took on board from the encounter, but according to Philip Short, a biographer of both Mao and Pol Pot, 'Mao sought to convey the idea that the Cambodian leaders should open their minds and place their revolution in the context of the wider world.'[28]

'You have scored a splendid victory,' Mao told Pol Pot. 'Just a single blow and no more classes.'[29] Whatever misgivings they may have harboured, the Chinese had decided to give the Khmer Rouge their support, bolstering them against their shared historic enemy Vietnam, which was now providing the Soviet Union with a solid toehold in mainland Southeast Asia. If Thailand was seeking amicable relations with both China and Cambodia, that was all to the good in Beijing's eyes.

For Kukrit and the Thai delegation, the two main events were a hoped-for meeting with Chairman Mao at some stage, and the signing of the communiqué by the two premiers, Kukrit and Zhou. As they waited, the Thais were treated as honoured guests and shown the sights. On the third day, during a visit to the Institute of Minorities, security personnel arrived unheralded and escorted Kukrit, Chatichai, Anand, and Prakaipet Indhusophon (secretary general to the prime minister) away. 'Chairman Mao is now ready to meet with you,' they were told.

It was a hot day, and many in the Thai group had thrown their jackets over their arms. The four smartened themselves up and were taken off to meet a very elderly Chairman Mao, who by that time was afflicted with Parkinson's disease, among other ailments. Veteran correspondent Clare Hollingworth, who had been posted by London's *Daily Telegraph* to Beijing in 1972, reported that Mao suffered a stroke in 1974, but did not reveal her sources for the story. 'Her prediction that the coming leader was Deng Xiaoping was also greeted with some scepticism,' the paper later conceded.[30]

Anand recalls Mao standing 'quite erect' but there was no meaningful exchange as they shook hands. 'Mao mumbled a few words nobody could understand,' he says. The encounter was over in 30 seconds. After being introduced, Anand and Prakaipet withdrew, leaving only Kukrit and Chatichai with Mao, his long-serving translator Nancy Tang, and some other Chinese interpreters.

'At that age and in that condition, you don't expect Mao to discuss substantive matters,' says Anand. 'It was a courtesy call.' By one account,[31] Mao began by asking Kukrit, 'Aren't you afraid of meeting a communist like me?' Kukrit replied, 'No, I have always admired you. I am not a communist, but I am meeting a friend.'

According to Kukrit, Mao had a speech impediment, and the extra Chinese interpreters were needed to catch his utterances. He was able to rise unassisted, however, and walk alone. Kukrit formed the impression of a very elderly man who could switch in and out of the moment. 'We got on very well because I used the Thai manner of approaching, the idea that "you are older and you are better",' Kukrit recalled later. 'I didn't sit full in the chair, just on the edge ... I had my hands in my lap and I did not cross my legs. I think he took a liking to me for that reason. After that, he talked and joked with me as though I was a very minor relative.'[32]

Kukrit said Mao asked him if he was not concerned to visit after what had befallen Nixon, who left office in disgrace but for unrelated reasons. Given the ongoing Chinese-backed revolutionary activities in Thailand, Mao somewhat contrarily then counselled Kukrit on ways to defeat communism. He said the best defence was to ensure people are happy.

'See that they are well fed, that they have work to do, that they are satisfied with their work and their station,' advised Mao. 'Then the communists cannot do anything.' He then ruminated on the characteristics of insurgents. 'They won't listen to you – they are thick-skinned, these people,' Mao said. 'Killing them off would be equal to calling more people to be killed. They'll come to get killed – they like to be killed.' According to Kukrit, Mao also advised against sending troops into the jungles. Eventually they would have to return to their barracks, and the communists would creep back.

'Nobody knew what was actually said and what the responses were,' says Anand, pointing to the absence of a transcript from this historic meeting. It is unfortunate that he was ushered from Mao's library ahead of the 58-minute encounter. With his years of recording sensitive conversations for Thanat Khoman, and experience of conducting and reporting high-level exchanges, Anand would have been the ideal recording secretary. Although they did speak of the meeting, Kukrit and Chatichai were not the sort of people to take notes, so exactly what transpired has never been known on the Thai side. There remains, however, a lingering suspicion that the US-born Nancy Tang, after so many years at the Great Helmsman's side, could easily have reeled off stock lines on behalf of a by then virtually incoherent Mao. There were, after all, few subjects she had not heard him discuss, and she went on to become a senior figure in the foreign service and party hierarchy.[33]

Towards the end of their encounter, Mao told Kukrit: 'I am not strong. Sitting and standing is painful – I will die soon.' 'Don't say that,' said Kukrit. 'The world cannot do without its number one villain.' Mao laughed, but his attention soon wandered.[34] 'When I shook hands he didn't even look at my face,' Kukrit admitted. Their hour was up and it was time to leave. '[Mao] looked at the ceiling and was obviously gaga. He went back to his old age quite suddenly.'[35]

Among the invited journalists in Beijing was Suthichai Yoon. 'Nancy Tang, the interpreter, was probably running the whole country,' he jokes. Suthichai remembers Kukrit's extraordinary press conference after the encounter. 'Mao told me the Thais are hopeless communists,' Kukrit declared. 'Kukrit said he told the chairman that Thai people are lazy and not committed to anything. It was all half-joking,' Suthichai recalls.

Later that year, Kissinger was keen to know about Kukrit and Chatichai's encounter with Mao. 'Did he form words when you met with him in Peking?' the US secretary of state quizzed Chatichai during a lunchtime meeting.[36] 'They used interpreters,' Chatichai explained. 'There was a very nice-looking girl, Nancy Tang. When we came into the room, we did not see Mao at first. He was sitting in a chair. Then he stood up and greeted Prime Minister Kukrit. During the conversation, there was interpretation for Chinese to Chinese to English. Sometimes he would write things.'

'It was the same way when I saw him,' said Kissinger.

While some dismiss Kukrit as an opportunist showboat, Suthichai believes his humorous, cajoling, very human approach was essential to pulling off the normalisation of Thailand's relations with China. Ultimately, that drove a deeper wedge into the Communist Party of Thailand, already split between its Soviet/Vietnamese and Chinese patrons. 'I think if it was not for Kukrit, that policy would not have worked,' says Suthichai. 'It was not easy. He had to convince the military, the palace, and he had to deal with China. There was no way the Thai military could change.'

According to Suthichai, 'Kukrit was a good performer, but he would not go into details.' Nor would Chatichai. 'Chatichai was a clever guy but I don't think he was very deep in all this analysis,' he says. Suthichai regarded Anand as the indispensible, steady technician in the background keeping everything on track. 'Anand did all the work for Kukrit – Anand was controlling the mechanism from behind. Anand could have blocked it. He went all out with his team and plunged deep.'

Thailand's prime minister was on triumphant form that night, and regaled his compatriots with a colourful account of what Mao had said to him, describing the tremendous personality he had encountered – a true force of history. The following day, 1 July, he led the Thai delegation to the Forbidden City and a villa that served as a hospital. It was home to China's declining premier, who had less than six months left to live. Tej recalls that the atmosphere in the room was exceptionally sombre. He acted as Kukrit's aide, laying before him the historic documents for signing in three languages. Anand stood directly behind Kukrit, beside Chatichai and Zhou's deputy, Deng Xiaoping.

'Zhou Enlai took ages to sign the three copies because his hands were so shaky, whereas Kukrit took no time at all,' says Tej. After his years manning the East Asia desk at the foreign ministry, he recalls the day as a personal peak: 'It made my career. I did many other things but this was my greatest achievement and contribution.'

That night, it was Deng Xiaoping who hosted a banquet in the Great Hall of the People for the Thai delegation. To the relief of his Thai guests, who were fearful of Chinese hegemony in Asia, Deng's lengthy speech focussed on Asia as a zone of peace and neutrality free from foreign interference. Speaking to Kukrit, Chatichai, Siddhi, and Anand, the chain-smoking Deng punctuated his assurances against hegemony[37] with hearty contributions to the nearest spittoon.[38]

Kukrit in his speech played up the historically close Sino-Thai relations: 'At the risk of being unduly boastful, I feel in all sincerity that the success with which Chinese and Thai have lived together is something we should take pride in, because it is unique and this should be generally known.'[39]

'It was a huge table with about 20 people,' says Anand. 'After 16 maotai, you couldn't remember anything.' 'It went on and on,' Suthichai recalls. 'It must have been 12 or 14 courses with wine, beer, and everything – the Chinese wanted to show the whole world.'[40]

After Beijing, the Thais flew south to Shanghai. Large crowds had been rallied to cheer as the foreign visitors were transported through the great port city in a 96-car motorcade. Their host was Hua Guofeng, the minister of internal security, who the following year would succeed both Zhou and Mao in their respective positions.[41] Next stop was Guangzhou for a tour of the lychee orchards, followed by an excursion to Kunming in Yunnan province, close to the borders with Vietnam, Laos, and Burma. The region had strong ethnic and cultural links to

Thailand, which Chatichai later made light of in Washington.

'When I asked to go to Kunming, they asked why I wanted to go there,' Chatichai told Kissinger. 'I said that it was the former Thai capital and I wanted to liberate it. It was very poor; the food there was the same as in Chiang Mai in northern Thailand. The people speak a Thai dialect. When I got there and they raised a Thai flag over the place where we were staying, our escort said, "See, you have already liberated Kunming."'

Kunming held another particular fascination for the Thais: it was home to the propaganda radio transmitter for the Thai Liberation Front. With their flag flying, the Thais were put up in a guesthouse about a kilometre from the radio station. A broadcaster in the group, Arkom Makkarondh of TV Channel 4, tuned in during the day for an unusually clear reception of the vitriol being broadcast against his homeland. The poison-tongued, Thai-speaking broadcaster then spent the evening translating the sweet language of diplomacy to many of the same people she had just been vilifying. One of the requests Kukrit made, now that China and Thailand had formal relations, was that these propaganda transmissions should cease. Soon they did become less virulent, and they tapered off after about a year.

The Thais themselves were not complete neophytes in radio propaganda warfare. In an earlier job, Anand's old colleague Manaspas had set up Voice of Free Asia (now Saranrom Radio) at the foreign ministry. A transmitter donated by the US was used to broadcast in different directions according to the time of day. Manaspas was delighted that the breakthrough normalisation of Sino-Thai relations was 'blasted to the mountains, the caves, and the forests' from his former station.[42] 'I think Kukrit was a genius in approaching Zhou Enlai and Mao Zedong,' he says.

Later, when thought was being given to posting an ambassador to Beijing and there was speculation in the Thai press as to who it might be, Anand got a distraught call from his mother, Pruek. She was a victim of the anti-China propaganda that had been splashing around – about old people being killed and turned into manure, and the like. Many Thais of Chinese origin had been bombarded with such fake news and fallen for it. 'I forbid you to go to China,' Pruek told her youngest son, offering to take care of the family if this forced his resignation. Anand reassured her, and said he would not be going himself – but he would certainly have a say in who got the posting.

CHAPTER 6

RETURN TO THAILAND
(1975)

Final months in the US

After a frenetic spell of bilateral diplomacy on the hoof in June 1975, Anand was able to return to Washington and resume more normal duties at his official posts. That included explaining recent developments in Thai foreign policy to a wider world. In August, the Thai embassy in Washington put out a press release. It was a transcript of an interview Anand had given to an unnamed correspondent of the *Bangkok Bank Monthly Review*, a less-than-mainstream publication even in Thailand. Anand's interviewer was Paul Sithi-Amnuai, Bangkok Bank's representative in New York. Paul was a graduate of the London School of Economics, and a protégé of Boonchu Rojanastien, Kukrit Pramoj's finance minister.

The 12-page document set out Thailand's position on a number of key issues, including increasingly multipolar diplomacy, normalisation of relations between China and Thailand, détente (the negotiated reduction in Cold War tensions), the withdrawal of US forces from Thailand, and the importance of ASEAN and regional unity in Southeast Asia. It also included some frank personal observations by Anand on a number of topics, including political development, corruption, and the importance of democracy.

'There was a story to tell,' Anand says. 'I knew Paul well, so who else would I talk to?' The interview served a clear purpose. Quotable observations in such depth would not easily have found their way into, say, *The New York Times* or *The Atlantic Monthly*. This press release is one of the best early examples of a favoured Anand tactic: always get important matters on the record – particularly when most people are not paying attention and are unlikely to read them properly. Ideas can always be referenced later and cited.

Anand harboured no illusions about Thailand's very limited influence in world affairs. As an ally of the US, it had played a major facilitating role in the Indochina conflict but ended up being taken for granted and essentially ignored. The *Mayaguez* incident, and the insouciant disregard Ford and Kissinger had displayed for Thai sensibilities in general and the express wishes of the elected Kukrit government in particular, amply demonstrated this.

'If we have learned at all from our history, then all of us, especially in Indochina and Southeast Asia, must realise that we have no real alternative but to learn to live with and to adjust to one another in the spirit of tolerance, mutual confidence and trust,' said Kukrit in a speech the month before Anand's interview.[1]

Kukrit explicitly laid out his policy to make peace with old adversaries and promote relations with socialist and communist nations in the region, the Soviet Union, and China. Anand himself had been involved in low-key contact with North Korea in 1974. In an oblique swipe at the US, Kukrit referred to the 'warm and hospitable' reception he had recently been afforded in Beijing.

'We share the same goals: to develop peaceful and friendly relations between us, based on the principles of mutual respect and non-interference in each other's domestic affairs,' Kukrit said of China. 'Furthermore, we are both of the same mind that no country, large or small in any part of the world, should attempt to impose its will and domination over any other country; that, in fact, it is an inalienable right of the people of each nation to live in accordance with their own dictates and values.'

'The present government, elected by the people's representatives, no longer wants "stability at all cost" but, rather, orderly and wilful changes which are long overdue,' Kukrit declared. 'The recent trend of Thailand's policy has uncharitably been referred to by some as "bending with the wind". It is in fact a culmination of the process of orderly and rational development that, we hope, will be judged by posterity as a real contribution to the peace and wellbeing of the region as a whole.'

Anand had been a key instrument for advancing these new policies. In his main job as ambassador in Washington, he maintained good relations with Philip Habib, a US State Department assistant secretary responsible for Asia-Pacific, although he rarely interacted with Habib's boss, Kissinger. The secretary of state was more preoccupied with *realpolitik* – the interaction between great powers and their interests – or fire-fighting various crises around the world in hot spots such as Bangladesh (formerly East Pakistan), Chile, East Timor, and parts of the Middle East. The US was a world power with 170 countries represented by diplomats in Washington. The secretary of state rarely had time for ambassadors from minor countries.

'I never expected to be received by Kissinger,' Anand recalls. 'I was not an ambassador of Britain, West Germany, or Japan. Most other ambassadors never saw Kissinger – it didn't cause me any concern. Kissinger viewed Thailand as an appendage, not as an ally in the normal sense of the word. I don't think he paid it much attention. You cannot judge him just by one period of history, but by his overall performance. When he was very much involved in the US government, in his overview of the geopolitics of the world, there were five main centres of power: the US, Europe, the Soviet Union, the Middle East, and China. Elsewhere in Asia, there were Japan, India, and Indonesia. Kissinger belongs to this group of people who advocate the balance of the great powers, the balance of interests. Small countries rarely figured in his mind – they were just pawns in a way.'

This view crystallised in Anand's mind during his later Washington years. Thailand was just 'a tiny spot on Kissinger's radar, a useful ally'. Anand recalls: 'I was critical of American policy, and I think personally Kissinger was quite angry – this young man from a small country, this upstart talking back to the US.'

Anand did, of course, get to meet Kissinger when his minister was in town. There was talk at the US embassy in Bangkok that Anand felt personally slighted by Kissinger's aloofness towards peripheral players. One of the people who later picked up on the rumours was US Air Force Brigadier General Harry C. 'Heinie' Aderholt, who took command of the Joint US Military Advisory Group in Thailand (JUSMAGTHAI) in May 1975, and oversaw the final US drawdown in Thailand. 'Anand is very anti-American,' Aderholt later told a Thai reporter. 'It goes back to the way he was treated in the States when he was ambassador.'[2] Even in Bangkok, a city that has always gorged on toxic and false gossip, this was overkill.

Anand was with Chatichai for a lunch meeting in Kissinger's personal dining room at the State Department on 26 November 1975.[3] The lunch occurred three weeks after Kissinger had been relieved by President Ford of his concurrent position as national security adviser,[4] so it would be fair to say the German-born secretary of state had a little more time at his disposal. The encounter is notable in many ways, particularly for the fact that the *Mayaguez* incident gets no mention – except very obliquely when Kissinger talks about the US desire to push Laos and Cambodia into China's camp rather than Vietnam's. 'Yes, we would like you to do that,' Chatichai said. 'And then after we do it you can kick us around,' retorted Kissinger sourly. 'You can call Ambassador Anand home and thereby keep the students happy.'

Chatichai ducked the barb adroitly, and made an almost prophetic observation: 'The right wing is what we really have to worry about, not the left.' He also corrected Kissinger, pointing out that Laos and Cambodia were already two quite different propositions: 'The Chinese are 100 per cent in support of Cambodia's being friends with Thailand,' he said.

During his time as ambassador, Anand recalls many of his compatriots arriving in Washington smiling with their hands out.[5] This may well have explained Chatichai's reticence about mentioning the *Mayaguez* incident. He was there, essentially cap in hand, with an agenda: securing US *matériel* and support after the military drawdown in Thailand was completed.

The conversation started off with quite frivolous references to Vietnamese haircuts and the quality of the ambassador's residence in Bangkok. Kissinger complained that while Ambassador Charles Whitehouse was a very nice man, 'he is giving things away so fast we'll soon have nothing left in Thailand'. He went on, 'I say we should keep enough there so that you will have something to yell about to us.'

'We have guns and aircraft but no bombs or bullets,' Chatichai complained, pulling up a mental shopping list before his somewhat exasperated host. Kissinger then reminded everyone that it was an 'informal lunch', and suddenly proposed a toast: 'We feel that Thailand is an old friend and we appreciate your support during a difficult conflict,' he declared. 'We will not forget what you did, and we will not forget Thailand.'

After the toast, with everybody sitting down again, Chatichai came back strong with his charm offensive on Kissinger. Thailand felt 'alone', he said. Its armed forces needed re-equipping and re-organising; the economy was down in the dumps and desperate for foreign investment. The US should help. Chatichai also wanted US assistance to turn U-Tapao into an international airport for civil use, and to build an ammunition plant that could serve all ASEAN's needs. Chatichai registered his dismay that President Ford would not entertain even a refuelling stopover in Bangkok on his forthcoming visit to Asia. Was Bangkok suddenly too far off the beaten track? Hovering in the background during the meeting were Kissinger's deputy Philip Habib and Brent Scowcroft of the National Security Council, wringing their hands over the expense of it all and the fiscal tightness of Congress. Kissinger reminded everybody how much he hated losing wars and pleaded poverty.

'This Congress is impossible,' Scowcroft growled. Everybody in the room hoped an election would bring change and, searching around for a common enemy, they agreed that the liberal media were an even bigger nuisance. 'The press is impossible,' complained Kissinger. 'Ours is also troublesome,' Chatichai sympathised. 'The problem is now that we have too much democracy.'

Anand was listed second in seniority on the Thai side. 'I was embarrassed at that meeting,' Anand recalls. He uttered barely a word, but as usual took everything in. Although it does not appear in the transcript, he vividly recalls Kissinger listening to Chatichai run through his shopping list, and then leaning over to one of his aides and saying under his breath: 'Give them toys.' 'Kissinger was quite correct, too,' says Anand.

In his interview with Paul Sithi-Amnuai, Anand presents an outline of ASEAN and regional cohesion that would not really begin to manifest itself until the late 1990s. His vision was not for a Southeast Asian replica of the European Economic Community:[6]

> I think ASEAN leaders are realistic enough to believe that each state in
> the region does not count very much in regional and world affairs, but
> that together and collectively, in spite of the differences that we may
> have on this or that issue, ASEAN would be a force to be reckoned
> with. If we don't stick together to exchange views, to co-ordinate or
> synchronise our policies, we will be the losers in the future structure
> of peace and stability of the region.

Although his language was considered and diplomatic, Anand was firm on the sovereign right of all nations to adjust policies to new circumstances, and bold on two issues: the wrongness of viewing Thailand as a flighty fair-weather ally, and the absolute need for US forces to withdraw from Thailand by a fixed date.

'For a long time now, some people have been making complimentary, or perhaps sarcastic, remarks about Thailand's traditional policy of "bending with the wind",' he said. He argued that Thailand's normalising of relations with China was far from a sign of fickleness, but followed on from the initiatives of Kissinger and Nixon: 'That was when this wind of change started,' he said. 'When great nations like the United States and China cause a gale to start blowing, we small states have no alternative but to adapt ourselves to the changes that originated, not from our doing, but from the actions of major powers.'

After digressing about Thailand's ability to defend itself and manage its own affairs, Anand reached the key message on the drawdown of US forces:

> With regard to my government's request that the US withdraw its forces from Thailand by March 1976, some may feel that the US is complying with this request rather reluctantly.

Diplomatically, Anand described the end of the war in Indochina not as a military defeat but as a political one:

> The withdrawal was therefore a political decision based on the lack of political will to back up the military will.

Anand's parting shot was delivered with a quick history lesson that would certainly have met with the approval of Thanat Khoman, his mentor in diplomacy, followed by some incontrovertible logic:

> We must not forget that in 1961 it was President Kennedy who asked the Thai government to accept 10,000 US marines in the northeast of Thailand, and that in the middle 60s it was President Johnson who asked that we accept the expanded American military presence here in connection with the war in Vietnam. Before that, there was no question of a foreign military presence in Thailand. So, when we ask the Americans to withdraw, for the very obvious reason that the Vietnam War has come to an end, there is no question of Thailand

being anti-American. There were no US troops here before, and no one suggested that Thailand was anti-American then.

This argument had been deployed consistently over the years. As far back as 1972, when Anand was still Thailand's acting permanent representative to the United Nations, *Newsweek* had carried a letter from him on the topic. Taking issue with an article from 3 July, 'The War In Indochina', by Maynard Parker, Anand wrote: 'US military personnel and planes are in Thailand only for the duration of the Vietnam War. Unless circumstances drastically change, there is no reason to expect US military personnel and Air Force units to remain in Thailand after the Vietnam War.' *Newsweek*'s editors responded that within Thailand there appeared to be differing views on the matter than those held by Anand. 'Senior officials of the Thai government, both military and civilian, told Mr Parker that they wanted US forces to remain in their country after the end of the Vietnam fighting in order to insure the security of Thailand.' The editors went on: 'As for *Newsweek*'s statement that a number of Thai officials have benefited financially from the US presence in their country, Ambassador Panyarachun can find no documentation for that in several reports of the Foreign Relations Committee of the US Senate and the General Accounting office of the US Government.'

Sweetening the bitter pill, Anand had written in his letter, 'The other US presences, economic, diplomatic and cultural, are still as warmly welcomed in Thailand as they were in the past. I do not think that the occasional displays of anti-American feeling by certain groups is a reflection of the true feelings of the majority of the Thai people.' Although he was unquestionably the messenger carrying Thailand's official national policy at the time, Anand's high profile and unusually confident presentations gave some people the impression that he was not just a deliverer of policy but an important initiator. Right or wrong, this notion was to have serious consequences for Anand when he returned to Thailand.

Homeward-bound

In September 1975, Chatichai came to New York for the UN General Assembly as usual, and pressed Anand to return to Bangkok as permanent secretary at the foreign ministry. Anand declined for all the same reasons. He also felt it would be unfair on Phan Wannamethee, the incumbent, whom he respected.

By November, as the General Assembly was drawing to a close, Chatichai had had enough of Anand's evasiveness, threw persuasion to the winds and simply ordered him home. Phan would be reassigned to Bonn – West Germany was already Thailand's largest trading partner in Europe. For Anand, it was part of an emerging lifetime pattern: another job had been given to him without being sought. 'It was all preordained in a sense – fate,' he says. Anand was not particularly keen to come home. 'I had plenty of freedom to operate in the US, and my kids were still in school,' he recalls. However, there was no room for debate.

On one of his last nights in the US before a farewell dinner with colleagues, Anand was having drinks in the Oak Room bar at the Plaza hotel in New York. He was with his colleague and friend Saroj Chavanviraj, Thailand's number three diplomat at the UN. Saroj was concerned about what awaited Anand in Bangkok.

'Mr Ambassador, when you return to Bangkok please be careful,' Saroj cautioned. 'Don't be too *farang* in your approach and your thinking.' Saroj remembers getting Anand's attention and, looking back, is still impressed by his chutzpah that evening. Anand never forgot his young colleague's prescience. 'Saroj was the one who warned me in New York,' Anand told people at a party in 2011. 'It was out of real concern.'

Saroj and his colleagues were largely inured to Anand's management style. Although it could be brutal at times, at least it toughened them up in the bruising, treacherous world of multilateral diplomacy. They also knew from Anand's gregariousness outside working hours that his treatment of them was not personal: it was all about developing competence, testing mettle, and getting the best from people. They knew that Anand was also always loyal to people who had proved themselves capable and trustworthy. Indeed, he brought Pridi Boonyobhas, his dependable assistant, back with him from Washington.

Although Anand had been happy in Washington, there were some personal compensations in his return. 'My father had already passed away, and my mother was getting old,' he recalls. 'It was good to be back with the large family – the clan. My concern was whether we could afford to keep the girls in school, but my mother always chipped in.'

Anand moved back into the Panyarachun family compound created on Soi Chidlom by his father, Sern, after World War II, renting out the larger house he and Sodsee had built further out along Sukhumvit Road. The move back was disruptive, with Sodsee remaining on her own in an apartment in the US for three months looking after their daughters.

Anand was looking forward to the challenge of running the foreign ministry, and working at the head of a particularly talented team. 'I was quite excited,' he recalls. 'I had no hesitation in assuming the role. Kukrit had already made a statement in parliament about new policies and initiatives. I happened to agree basically with him, and was looking forward to being part of a new foreign policy. I knew Kukrit a little, and admired and respected him. There was an agenda. It was a new ball game – a period of adjustment with our neighbours.'

'I had become a little more forthright in my critiques of American policies, be it the *Mayaguez* incident or the Vietnam War,' Anand recalls. Indeed, a number of influential people had already privately concluded that Anand had become fundamentally anti-American. They included Air Chief Marshal Siddhi Savetsila, who had been a member of the Free Thai movement in the US during World War II, and was a friend of Anand's brother Kusa.

As head of the National Security Council (NSC), Siddhi was heavily reliant on intelligence provided by the CIA, and was indisputably one of the best friends the US had in Thailand. But Siddhi was also on close terms with Chatichai and his Rajakhru Clan.[7] Kukrit, a natural debunker and tease, was much less impressed with American intelligence. When Siddhi presented the prime minister one day with a CIA file concerning the latest happenings in Phnom Penh, he claimed the intel was so good that a pin could not drop unheard in the Cambodian capital. Unimpressed, Kukrit snorted back that the system obviously hadn't been good enough for the Americans to hear the Vietcong clumping around the Cu Chi tunnels in Saigon.

Soon enough after his return, Anand detected coldness creeping into his contacts with both the US and Thai militaries and the NSC. '[The Americans] became very rigid,' says Anand. 'They never recognised that there had been a sea change in Thailand in terms of the decision-making process.' All of them were carrying on almost as if the war, which had ended six months earlier, was still going on. The fall of South Vietnam was meanwhile proof enough that US support was never the defence Thai hawks claimed.

On the Thai government's side, there was a feeling that its legitimate concerns and stated positions were not being taken into account. The US dawdled over loose ends as the deadline for the complete US departure approached. Kukrit had originally given the Americans a year, but after the *Mayaguez* incident he threatened irritably to close everything down in 30 days.

Ruffling feathers

Anand's predecessor at the foreign ministry, Phan Wannamethee, got on well with most people, including the military. So did Arsa Sarasin, one of Anand's relatives and oldest personal friends, who was by then head of the ministry's Southeast Asia division. Like Saroj, Arsa was concerned that after his return Anand would be too 'Western' and insensitive in his dealings with other Thai institutions. Their fears were fully justified. If Anand had his way, the usual Thai sensitivities, vagaries, and ambiguities would be swept aside, and business would no longer be 'as usual'. He was determined to shake things up and make his mark.

'I would not allow the foreign ministry to take a secondary role to the military and intelligence community,' says Anand. 'My idea was that we should play the role that we were entitled to.' He was well aware of the implications of his actions at this time. He knew what he was doing, and was a stark contrast to his predecessor, the conciliatory Phan. As a result, he soon came to be viewed as outspoken, cynical, brash, and sometimes plain rude – and not only by the Americans.

Tej Bunnag recalls attending a meeting with the NSC when the issue of disarming the Kuomintang's 93rd regiment came up for discussion as part of normalising relations with China. Anand wanted to know why these foreign soldiers were still armed on Thai soil. A full general close to General Kriangsak Chomanand, the army chief, was present; he responded that he was still 'awaiting orders from those above me'. As Tej observes, 'In Thailand, there is always somebody above.' Siddhi was chairing the meeting; Anand was blunt and antagonistic, and persisted, even raising his voice as he queried who could possibly be above the NSC in this instance. The incident got back to Kriangsak, and Anand's relations with the general dropped another notch.

This relationship was further damaged by an incident in which Anand forwarded to cabinet for approval the name of a general to take the place of Kriangsak on the Thai-Malaysian Joint Border Committee. Anand was technically correct to do this. Kriangsak had been promoted out of the *ex officio* post in question when he ceased to be army chief of staff. However, Kriangsak detected no deference or tact in the way Anand handled the matter. 'I think he was hurt by that in a Thai way,' says Anand. On the surface Anand was playing the good bureaucrat, but his approach was underpinned by a deeply ingrained personal scepticism towards the military. He was also riding roughshod over many Thai norms.

Tej is among those who dispute the notion that Anand is somehow 'un-Thai'. 'Anand is very Thai but of a certain kind,' he says. 'He is the youngest son of a very distinguished family and full of self-confidence. You can even use the word "cocksure". He is a Thai aristocrat – a leading member of the Thai establishment. To understand why he is that self-confident, that cocksure, you would have to do some analysis of the way he was brought up.' Anand disputes the notion of Thailand having an 'aristocracy' in the European sense. He points out that royal ranks diminish to insignificance as generations pass, and that most honours cannot be handed down.

A new broom

When Anand took over at the foreign ministry, his subordinates were immediately reminded of his appetite for hard work. By the time most arrived for work at 9am, Anand had already been through all the overnight cables from the embassies, marking them up with orange ink in his neat, tight script. Thus his mark was already on the incoming flow of information for all to see. Sometimes, just a solitary word or phrase that conveyed some important drift would be underlined.

Anand's relations with the military continued to worsen. When he was six months into his new position, after Kukrit had failed to gain re-election, a number of generals took their grievances directly to Seni, the new prime minister. Bhichai Rattakul, Chatichai's replacement as foreign minister, conveyed Seni's concerns to Anand, whose response was blunt. 'Tell the prime minister to either trust me or back off.' Anand describes himself as an 'angry young man' at that time.

Within the defence establishment, one of the few supporters of the official government position on regional relations and the US military drawdown was the new army chief of staff, General Charoen Pongpanich. 'He was a very logical man who knew exactly what we were trying to do,' recalls Bhichai. But if Charoen could make sense of a foreign policy formulated by civilians for national survival, he was in a very small minority in the military. Anand made no effort to court Charoen's fellow generals. He considered self-evident the rightness of the strategy he had been charged with executing by the elected government of the day.

Anand was not a member of the NSC, and only attended if his minister wanted him there for some reason. Every time he was present, he would later recount to Arsa some further frustration with the military. 'I advised [Anand] to be very cautious, and not to go too far,' says Arsa. 'I was very much aware that Kriangsak did not like Anand.'

Arsa himself had come to know Kriangsak quite well when he headed the foreign ministry's Southeast Asia department. The pair collaborated on a number of regional issues, which, since the premiership of Field Marshal Sarit Thanarat, had been kept increasingly under military control. On one occasion, Arsa and Kriangsak were due to visit a Kuomintang village in the north. As the helicopter came in to land, they both noticed a portrait of General Chiang Kai-shek on prominent display. To register their displeasure with such a tactless show on sovereign Thai soil, the pilot was instructed to fly on without landing.

After crossing swords with Kriangsak over his position on the Thai-Malaysian border committee, Anand faced more problems associated with the southern region. Chin Peng, who led the Malayan Communist Party, financed his movement partly by extorting Thai-Chinese businessmen. The area could be lawless, and there was a six-kilometre corridor along the border in which hot pursuit of insurgents was permitted under a bilateral agreement. This enabled Malaysian security forces to chase Chin Peng's cadres into Thailand. These chases upset Thais along the border. Surin Masdit,[8] a Democrat minister attached to the prime minister's office with special responsibility for the South, was sent down to placate protesting locals. Without reference to anyone else, Surin promised that Malaysian troops would no longer be allowed to pursue suspects across the border.

Anand immediately raised concerns about Surin's undertaking with Bhichai and Seni. He was then dispatched in person to assuage the Malaysians, who rightly felt that a bilateral agreement had been very publicly broken. Anand had to put matters right but without embarrassing the government in Bangkok. 'I had to be defensive,' recalls Anand. 'We looked at Malaysia with suspicion and Malaysia likewise us. Perhaps they thought I had a hand in it. That was another incident that did not endear me to the Thai military or the Seni government.' Anand was on a dangerous course. He was far more in the Thai public eye than he ever had been as ambassador in Washington or as permanent representative to the UN in New York.

In Anand's early days back in Bangkok, Chatichai was mainly responsible for his heightened profile. The relationship between the two men strengthened, although they could hardly have been more different in temperament. Chatichai was an instinctive personality with a keen understanding of what makes people tick, particularly Thais. Anand has a talent for penetrating inquisition, but always found it hard to keep Chatichai on any subject.

'Chatichai could never take part in any serious conversation, and he was not interested in what you were talking about,' says Anand. 'He was totally unfocussed but he had good horse sense and made good decisions. Never ask him what motivated him or why he made a decision because you would be totally confused. Chatichai was a prime example of a pragmatist who might not have his own ideas but who knew how to put ideas into action.' Wissanu Krea-ngam, who later served Anand's two cabinets, was often struck later by Anand's fondness for Chatichai and admiration for his intuitive powers.

Chatichai often signed papers vetted by Anand after reading them cursorily. He had complete faith in Anand's capabilities and powers of communication. He always liked to be surrounded by people and ideas, and would often summon Anand to his home at weekends to brief journalists who enjoyed gathering at his spacious compound on Soi Rajakhru. Chatichai would quickly sketch out the big picture with the media and then hand over to Anand for more detailed explanations. The upshot was that Anand was constantly being quoted in the press and began attracting considerable attention, not all of it favourable. He found himself being attacked by some rightist columnists, and was once burnt in effigy. 'In a way, they were all ganging up against me,' he says. 'Chatichai was a good foreign minister in terms of making decisions, but not a technical person. That's why people thought he was under my influence.' However, Anand was at all times working at the behest of Kukrit and Chatichai, and subsequently Seni and Bhichai. Like Chatichai, Kukrit did not have the time or inclination to explain technical details to the electorate.

'The job of explaining often fell on me as the permanent secretary, the front man,' says Anand. 'So the military viewed me as the one who really pulled the strings. I knew that I was gradually getting into a very, very untenable position because of my high profile, either in promoting or explaining the decisions or policies of Kukrit's government, or Chatichai's foreign policy.'

Another person receiving unfavourable attention from similar quarters at this time was Puey Ungphakorn, the former governor of the Bank of Thailand and by then rector of Thammasat University. Even though the two were never close, Puey was concerned by the enemies Anand seemed to be making. 'Khun Anand, you had better watch out,' Puey warned one day. 'In our society when a lie is repeated often enough, people believe it.'

Puey's warning was prescient. However correct Anand might have felt his own approach to be, he was sailing into a perfect political storm, one more severe than anybody could have envisaged.[9]

Grating the Americans

The US military presence in Thailand had mainly been air force. During the 1960s and early 1970s, the US Air Force upgraded six Royal Thai Air Force (RTAF) bases and one Royal Thai Navy (RTN) base located in central and northeastern Thailand. The bases remained under Thai command with gentlemanly protocols in place, but operations were under US control. The two oldest bases, at Don Muang and Takhli, had been in use from 1961. Don Muang, the RTAF headquarters just north of Bangkok, was phased out by the US in 1970. Among other things, its location directly opposite Bangkok's international and domestic civil aviation terminals made Thailand's involvement in the raging Indochina conflicts obvious to all. It disquieted the Thais, and did not sit well with an expanding tourism industry.

The USAF pulled out of Takhli and Ubon in 1974, and Korat in 1975. Only three bases had a continued US presence until 1976. Two of these were in the Northeast close to communist Laos: at Udon Thani and Nakhon Phanom. Udon Thani was mainly used by reconnaissance aircraft in its later years.

Nakhon Phanom, on the west bank of the Mekong River, which forms much of the Thai border with Laos, was home to large helicopters that used to be dispatched for covert missions and to pick up downed pilots in Laos and Vietnam during the war. US pilots visiting from bases in Vietnam, such as Phu Cat on the coast 230 kilometres north of Saigon, found a 'wonderland'. Whereas Phu Cat offered red dust and occasional incoming shells, Nakhon Phanom had sturdy buildings apparently made of mountain redwood with white picket fences, grassy playing fields for softball, gyms as good as any in the US, and a huge officers' club.[10]

By far the largest base was U-Tapao, which belongs to the Royal Thai Navy (RTN). The vast airfield was located not far inland from the RTN's home port and headquarters at Sattahip, some 30 kilometres southeast of the once sleepy fishing village of Pattaya. During the war in Indochina, massive quantities of American aerial ordnance were offloaded at Sattahip and hauled up a specially built road to the B-52s parked on U-Tapao's extra-thick concrete aprons. The runway was designed for B-52s taking off fully bomb-laden, and it remains to this day one of the world's largest.[11] The massive bombers needed half the runway to gain sufficient speed just to level the droop in their wings. They were usually dispatched in threes, and required refuelling immediately after take-off and also for the homeward leg. The Boeing KC-135 Stratotankers used for the aerial fuelling operations also operated out of U-Tapao. By 1976, these mammoth aircraft had already been deployed to Guam or back to the US, and only reconnaissance aircraft remained. Overall in 1975, there were an estimated 27,000 US military personnel (down from some 34,000 in March 1974) and 300 US aircraft still in Thailand.

In August 1975, Anand had delivered a reminder in Washington about the closure of all US bases in Thailand by March the following year. By May 1976, Prime Minister Seni Pramoj was able to assure a Japanese correspondent that the question of the US troop withdrawal from Thailand was at an end. 'Since January 1976, the were no US combat troops or aircraft [left] in Thailand,' Seni stated. He did, however, concede that the US government negotiated with the Kukrit government to keep some 3,000 technicians in place at various communications installations.[12]

Indeed, on this final issue of withdrawing technicians, the US had shown little inclination to follow the previous government's schedule. In early February, Foreign Minister Chatichai therefore presented Ambassador Whitehouse with a seven-point document relating to the command of military remnants. The 'unprecedented proposal', which threatened to trample over existing military agreements, sought to place all US military personnel and facilities under Thai jurisdiction and command, 'including the highly secretive intelligence monitoring apparatus'.

Grumpy and bemused, the US embassy responded point by point. The Thai bluff was unworkable for many reasons, including the lack of time available for approvals from Washington. It nevertheless put the embassy back on notice that the Thais were very serious about a full US departure. Events had also taken a spectacular, unexpected turn early in the year when it emerged that there was one base hardly anybody knew about: Ramasun. 'It was so secret that the foreign ministry was not aware of it,' says Anand. 'In fact, few Thais were.'

Ramasun was a listening station built on 1,200 rai (192 hectares) of Thai real estate about 20 kilometres south of Udon Thani in northeast Thailand, and nearly 480 kilometres from Bangkok. Equipped with some of the most advanced surveillance equipment of its time, the base was staffed exclusively by US technicians, who enjoyed all kinds of immunities and privileges, and was meant to be entirely off-limits to Thais. For the elected government the shock of Ramasun's existence was all the greater because its establishment had apparently never been approved at cabinet level. Instead, a secret agreement had been signed 'for the government of Thailand' by the deputy defence minister, Air Chief Marshal Dawee Chullasapya, and by the US ambassador, Graham Martin. It was presented as being pursuant to Thai-US military assistance agreements signed in 1950 and 1964. The principal clause stated:

> The Government of Thailand undertakes to authorize the conduct by the Government of the United States of America of a Radio Communications Research and Development effort in Thailand with a personnel ceiling not to exceed one thousand except as may be specifically authorized by the Government of Thailand. In addition the Government of Thailand agrees to make available for unrestricted use by the Government of the United States land near Udorn, not to exceed five hundred acres, as may be required for this purpose. It is understood that title of this land will remain with the Thai Government and that it will remain available to unrestricted United States Government use as long the United States requires it. The Government of United States shall provide funds for the acquisition of privately owned land by the Thai Government as required by the United States.[13]

Ramasun began operations in 1966, manned by 50 men from the US Army's Fifth Radio Research Unit. Although the US paid for the land without laying any claim to owning it, the agreement's lack of an expiry or renewal date was remarkable. 'It was given to the Americans in perpetuity,' says Anand. 'We were not allowed to go in – we did not know what they were doing. The agreement had to be revised. At least we should not be treated as foreigners in our own land, and we could no longer allow a surveillance station to spy on our neighbours. It had to go, and the Americans did not like that.'

Having secured a copy of the controversial agreement, Anand feared that if he asked Siddhi and the NSC for an opinion they would most likely sandbag the issue and set up some kind of committee. Instead, he went straight to Kukrit and Chatichai, forcing the matter directly into the cabinet's view. 'Obviously Siddhi was not happy at being bypassed,' says Anand.

The secret base rubbed up against all sorts of national sensitivities. The Thai security establishment was heavily dependent on the US for its regional intelligence, and the Ministry of Foreign Affairs had long been unhappy with the close relationship between the NSC and the CIA. There was a lot of mutual suspicion. Anand was also doubtful about the value of the information provided to the NSC by the US, such as photographs of Russian naval vessels at sea that could have been taken anywhere in the world.

On one occasion, when Anand and Siddhi were both on an overseas trip, Anand talked about all the intelligence documents the NSC received, and said that he had heard that the CIA briefed Siddhi every day. It was a fact, but an inconvenient truth for Siddhi. 'There were four or five people sitting there, and I think he felt rightly that I was being impudent, and had exposed him. Being forthright or candid is one thing, but being too aggressive is something that is not acceptable in our society. Having lived in England for seven years as a student, and the US for 12 years as a diplomat, I had gotten used to pulling people's legs. I did not know Siddhi too well and it was not appropriate humour on my part. Siddhi was very angry that night and would not talk to me for the rest of the trip.'

After a copy of the controversial Ramasun agreement and a working paper had been sent to all cabinet members, copies of the documents exposing the listening station quickly found their way to the *Far Eastern Economic Review*, a Hong Kong weekly magazine covering regional politics and economics. Although the leak could have come from any member of the cabinet or its secretariat, the finger of blame was predictably pointed at Anand. He was far from surprised but professes innocence to this day. He points out that with so many copies of the document flying around, he didn't actually need to leak anything. Twenty-five copies had been sent to the NSC and another 20 to the cabinet. 'I would not be surprised if Siddhi thought I leaked it,' says Anand. 'Kriangsak was under the impression that I leaked it, which was not true. He never forgave me for that.'

There is some reason to believe Kriangsak's suspicions were misplaced. Suthichai Yoon, the young editor of *The Nation*, recalls that Anand was always meticulous in his dealings with the press, and that nothing ever showed up with his fingerprints on it: 'Anand was always very correct and very careful,' he says. 'He would never give you any secret documents – he would never be caught in that way. He would never whisper something in your ear.' There was anyway no need for Anand ever to leak anything himself. 'Mid-level diplomats were quite co-operative,' recalls Suthichai of press relations then. 'Foreign ministry officials at that time were afraid that this kind of information would be kept secret forever.'

According to Suthichai, sensitive intelligence matters were also frequently divulged unintentionally. 'The best sources were sometimes not connected to the stories,' he says. The cabinet leaked everywhere. Reporters cultivated ministers who each week received stacks of photocopied briefing documents ahead of the Tuesday cabinet meetings. Much of the material was irrelevant to most of the ministers, who had little grasp of its wider significance. Tame news-hounds sniffing through the materials related to the cabinet agenda could find much of interest. Leaks therefore occurred easily through unrelated ministries such as commerce, health, or education, and were impossible to trace.

One of the very few Thais to gain access to Ramasun was Foreign Minister Bhichai Rattakul, who was taken personally for a visit by Ambassador Whitehouse. 'I was shocked,' says Bhichai. A forest of aerials and surveillance equipment confronted him; the largest formation was called the Elephant Cage – by coincidence it vaguely resembled an ancient Siamese elephant corral.[14] News of his trip got out, and Bhichai found himself under attack in the local press and from leftist students for travelling in the ambassador's limousine.

Despite such tensions, both Bhichai and Anand got on well on a personal level with Whitehouse, a much decorated US Marine Corps pilot in World War II and veteran CIA operative who had been transferred to the State Department. Whitehouse had been ambassador in Laos previously. Anand's frequent written communications with the ambassador were always businesslike, and betray no signs of any underlying personal tension. His relationship with Whitehouse's effective predecessor, Ed Masters, had been more abrasive.

'The guy who made lots of trouble for me was Ed Masters,' Anand recalls. 'I think he genuinely believed I was anti-American.' Masters, as *chargé d'affaires* during the *Mayaguez* crisis, had been *de facto* US ambassador for some time, and was reassigned to Bangladesh after Whitehouse's arrival in Bangkok. 'Frankly, I was not filled with great joy,' Masters later recalled. 'I had been operating, in effect, as an ambassador to a much bigger country, and a much more important country than Bangladesh.'[15]

Some believe Kukrit was slightly dismissive of Whitehouse, and viewed him as an Anglophile who was more British than the British. Bhichai, however, warmed to him: 'Damn good man. I liked him so much – we were able to talk to him closely. I think that inside he felt uncomfortable about the whole thing. He knew that the steps taken by the Thai government were correct. It was very obvious that we had to re-establish relations with our former enemies.' This, however, would be compromised by Ramasun continuing to function, and by a significant US military presence within Thailand.

Prime Minister Seni met Whitehouse for two hours in early June to discuss Ramasun and other bilateral issues. He was conciliatory, and stated in a brief televised address afterwards that there appeared to have been a misunderstanding over Ramasun being used in an offensive role when in fact it was for signals monitoring. Seni said that century-old Thai-US relations remained 'cordial as before'.[16] The government nevertheless stuck to the 20 July deadline set previously by his brother Kukrit's government for the final US withdrawal. The original date had been 20 March, but by June there remained some 4,590 technicians at Ramasun and other bases – a somewhat higher figure than he had offered the Japanese correspondent a few weeks earlier.[17]

Non-US-Thai relations

After the normalisation of relations with China, the Thai plan was for similar initiatives vis-à-vis neighbouring countries. In May, soon after the fall of Saigon, the Vietnamese sent over a delegation led by Phan Hien, the vice foreign minister who had attended the Paris Peace Talks in 1973. They were seeking war reparations, but got nowhere. In October, Chatichai received Ieng Sary, the Cambodian foreign minister and Pol Pot's brother in law, in Bangkok, where he arrived in a new Chinese jet. The foreign ministers signed a joint communiqué to re-establish diplomatic relations and border liaison offices, but impediments to following through included border disputes and the continuing US military presence.[18] They met again subsequently just over the border in Poipet, but made little further headway on bilateral normalisation.

It would fall to Chatichai's successor, Bhichai Rattakul, to renew conciliatory overtures to Cambodia, Laos, and Vietnam. As a district governor of Rotary, a philanthropic club for businessmen, Bhichai had a long-established network that stretched through seven countries in the region.[19] Among prominent Thais, Rotary was at the time regarded as a significant vehicle for promoting international understanding.[20]

Indochina was Bhichai's immediate priority (he never visited Burma). His efforts at regional rapprochement began with a secret trip across the border into Cambodia at the Aranyaprathet-Poipet crossing. It had been delayed by fighting between Cambodian and Vietnamese forces in the northeastern Cambodian province of Ratanakiri, near Laos and Vietnam. Bhichai, Anand, and Chawan Chawanid travelled from Poipet to Sisophon to meet Ieng Sary. Bhichai found the Khmer Rouge foreign minister to be 'a very straightforward man', but obsessed that Thailand might be involved in a plot to cause crop damage using 'Yellow Rain'[21] or Agent Orange, the highly toxic chemical defoliant developed by the US during the Vietnam War.

Paranoia of this kind was to be a hallmark of the Democratic Kampuchea regime, which ended up purging thousands of its cadres, particularly in the country's eastern zone bordering Vietnam. Bhichai tried to assure Ieng Sary that there were no grounds to fear a chemical strike from Thailand – and that he was much more interested in bringing order to their long and lawless shared border, and in preventing landmine proliferation. 'Believe me, Ieng Sary, we are not your enemy,' Bhichai remembers telling his Cambodian counterpart. 'Your enemy is Vietnam.'

Bhichai's trip into Cambodia with Anand produced an agreement in principle for the two countries to open embassies, but it would take time. Ieng Sary eventually opened the Cambodian embassy in Bangkok in 1978, not long before Pol Pot was overthrown by the invading Vietnamese.

The brief access granted to Bhichai and Anand was very unusual. The Khmer Rouge allowed the Swedish ambassador to tour some of the provinces, and there were often technical advisers from China in the background, but foreigners were generally unwelcome, and regarded with deep suspicion. Bhichai, who was better travelled in the region than Anand, was disturbed by the ominous atmosphere in Kampuchea, as Cambodia had been renamed, and the sullen distance of ordinary people. 'You could see at once it was not normal,' says Bhichai. 'Everything was so quiet. The people were scared. I knew they were not happy at all. You did not see anybody in the villages. Something was bad.'

Anand's recollections of the visit are much the same as Bhichai's, but he has no sense of how far inside Cambodia they actually were. 'In a remote village in Thailand, the atmosphere would be much more lively – laughing, arguing, fighting,' he says. There was no evidence of atrocities, however, and he did not form a negative impression of Ieng Sary at that time.

As part of his efforts to normalise regional relations, in August Bhichai took Anand with him to Vientiane, the Laotian capital. 'We already had diplomatic relations – it was a change of regime,' Anand recalls. 'The visit was to reset the relationship.' Tension had arisen late the previous year when Laotian forces fired on a Thai patrol boat, killing its captain. Fighting lasted a day, and the Thai ambassador had been recalled to Bangkok.

A document to address some cross-border trade problems was signed, but it was obvious to both men that Laos was completely in the thrall of Vietnam. During their meetings, the Vietnamese ambassador was downstairs at all times, functioning as a virtual proconsul. Dismayed by the lack of progress, Bhichai pondered the extent to which Thailand might have pushed land-locked Laos into Vietnam's arms by exploiting its single-market control over the sparsely populated former kingdom's meagre exports, and by charging usurious overland freight charges. 'We must abolish all this nonsense,' Bhichai remembers telling Anand as they left, irritated by the avaricious, short-sighted habits of so many Thai businessmen.

From Vientiane, the Thai delegation went to Hanoi for the largest and most public of the regional diplomatic initiatives. There was much more to discuss, even though the two countries shared no borders. Personally, Anand saw the trip as an opportunity to prepare a platform for better regional understanding. 'What was important was peace and stability in the region, and this could only be achieved with Vietnam and Thailand co-operating,' he says. Before the visit to Vietnam, Anand, Arsa, and Chawan all warned Bhichai that the military would be on the foreign ministry's back if they went ahead. 'Bhichai thought about it, but said, "No, I must go,"' Anand recalls.

Bhichai included Siddhi's deputy, Group Captain Prasong Soonsiri, in the delegation. There was some concern in the security establishment that Anand might make concessions to the communists.

The joint communiqué Bhichai took with him had originally been drafted under his predecessor, Chatichai. It included a clause on the repatriation of Vietnamese from Thailand, which Bhichai considered vague and problematic. The military was concerned about support for the Communist Party of Thailand (CPT) from Vietnam, which made ethnic Vietnamese settled in Thailand subject to suspicion.

'The CPT was still very active, and I agreed with the military that we had to get rid of them,' says Bhichai. But beyond that, as he admits, he sometimes found the Thai military harder to deal with than the regional communists.

Candidates for repatriation under the proposed clause included, at the military's request, some 40,000 Vietnamese who had been assimilated into Thailand long before. Anand and the foreign ministry took the lead in the plenary sessions in Hanoi with everyone present. These started slowly, and appeared to be going nowhere. The pilots were therefore told by Bhichai to prepare the aircraft to fly the delegation home next day. Word of this instruction got back to the Vietnamese negotiators, who had Thai speakers posted to listen. The Vietnamese then requested more informal talks with a smaller group.

At the request of the Vietnamese, the final talks, led by Anand, were confined on the Thai side to foreign ministry officials, and lasted until 2am. To Anand's satisfaction, a protective clause governing the modalities of any Vietnamese repatriation from Thailand was included.

To Prasong's annoyance, he was left out of the final interaction, and might have been concerned about what Anand would offer. 'I suspect that Prasong felt that I upstaged him,' says Anand. He concedes that the Vietnamese regarded Prasong as belligerent, but maintains it was appropriate for the foreign ministry to lead the talks for Thailand. Anand remembers telling the Vietnamese frankly that he had come with 'empty pockets', and had nothing to give them. His goal was only to normalise relations. Thereafter, issues between the two countries could be handled through proper diplomatic channels.

Anand rejects any notion that he was a soft touch. 'We did not agree on any solutions,' he admits. 'But without that communiqué we would not have been able to proceed on all the problems that existed. We never believed we could resolve all those issues at one meeting. It was at least a start.'

The communiqué agreed in Hanoi as a foundation for future relations resembled the one signed the previous year in Beijing. It was all approved over a radio link with Seni's cabinet sitting in Bangkok. Practical dealings and interaction could proceed thereafter.

The agreement was something of real significance, but the message the Thais wanted to convey – 'forgive the past, move on' – did not resonate in a battered land that had just lost three million people to war. The Vietnamese were greatly interested in the return of aircraft flown out of the former South Vietnam by fleeing airmen, and in discussing possible compensation for war damage.

For their trouble, Bhichai and Anand were both attacked in the press as well as by politicians, including by a Democrat Party firebrand, Samak Sundaravej. They were rebuked on their return for appearing too positive and conciliatory towards Vietnam, a historic foe unlike China. Indeed, Bhichai was given a Vietnamese nickname. Some of his colleagues believe it was the Vietnam visit that really marked Anand out for reprisal in the months that followed. 'Anand was supposed to be the brain behind Bhichai,' says Vitthya Vejjajiva. 'That is when he began to get himself into trouble with these right-wing radicals and got labelled a leftist – that's when it all started.'

The US military send-off

A major point of friction with the US was the Joint US Military Advisory Group in Thailand (JUSMAGTHAI), located near a major intersection at the top of Sathorn Road in central Bangkok. Nearby was a Hungarian restaurant, Nick's No. 1. The restaurant served as an unofficial canteen for US Air Force officers and spooks, and the countless name cards pinned up in the entrance area proved that plenty of military business got done there. It was at JUSMAGTHAI that a large part of the bombing of Indochina was planned. Unlike Ramasun, the squat, windowless building running alongside the road was obvious to all and no secret.

With the Vietnam War over, a forward-looking, new bilateral status-of-forces agreement between the US and the Royal Thai Government was needed. The main issue was appropriate residual staffing and concomitant diplomatic privileges.

'We didn't have any figure in mind, but it would be in accordance with the size of the military assistance programme,' Anand explains. A number that floated up from the Thai side was a maximum of 270, which harked back to the original US-Thai Military Assistance Agreement of 1950. The US had in mind a figure of around 3,000 overall, most of whom it wanted to station at U-Tapao. Apart from Ramasun, the Americans also wanted to maintain a seismic sensing station near Chiang Mai to monitor for underground nuclear tests in China.[22]

The US Air Force general commanding JUSMAGTHAI was Heinie Aderholt. 'A crimson curtain had come down on the Vietnam War, but there was work yet to be done,' wrote Aderholt's biographer. 'General Aderholt's primary mission now was to tie up all loose ends in Thailand and see that the remaining US forces there were withdrawn in an orderly fashion and without incident.'[23]

Aderholt was a charismatic Cold War warrior, a courageous, barnstorming veteran of the 1961 Bay of Pigs fiasco in Cuba who went on to command the First Air Commando Wing and make his name bombing the Ho Chi Minh Trail through North Vietnam and Laos in 1966 and 1967. One of the more remarkable aspects of his dislike for Anand was that the pair barely knew each other. By Aderholt's account, Anand once came up to him at a cocktail and delivered a quick dressing down: 'You're Aderholt,' he recalled Anand saying. 'Well, you guys stop conniving with the Thai military; you should be dealing with the foreign ministry.'

This could have been a verse from Thanat Khoman's songbook in the early 1960s. Ironically, Thanat and Aderholt were getting along fine at the time. 'I treasure [Thanat's] friendship very highly,' said Aderholt. 'I've known him for many years. He spoke out against the American presence at one time, and you know I never condemned him for that, and yet now he speaks very strongly that we should remain ... We were never less friends when [Thanat] had some critical things to say ... We talk long and hard privately about what we want for Thailand ... and we are not far apart, never have been.'[24]

Aderholt had identified a so-called Gang of Four in the foreign ministry, with Anand as the ringmaster, whom he believed – quite correctly – to be fundamentally opposed to the continued US military presence in Thailand. Anand's fellow 'gang members' were Kosol Sindhvananda, the director general of the political department; Kosol's deputy, Chawan Chawanid; and Woraputh Jayanama, who ran the American desk. Despite his closeness to Anand, Arsa was overlooked by the Americans because his responsibility lay with economic affairs, not politics.

With a ringside seat and friends in the foreign ministry, Sulak Sivaraksa admired the Gang of Four for their sheer pluck and lauds it as Anand's 'masterpiece'. Recollecting the feisty foursome, Kraisak Choonhavan says, 'They were sometimes labelled the "untouchable angels" of the foreign ministry, because they always gave interviews against government policy and the US presence. They were not expelled but Thai history overwhelmed them in the end.'

'We had the same approach,' Anand recalls. 'We were all excited to be a part of the new foreign policies. They argued, yes, but once I made a decision they all followed.'

'I always felt we were the cutting edge of the foreign ministry at that time,' says Chawan. He was firmly of the view that junior diplomats who returned from foreign scholarships should not be perpetuating pre-1955 practices. The ministry was professionalising, and no longer a club for the children of nobility. 'We were the same age group and worked very well together. We could communicate with each other and had a lot of mutual respect. We did not hesitate to take action. We were from the free world – it was quite natural that the military did not trust us.'

Indeed, Chawan remembers being summoned once along with other young firebrands from the ministry for lunch at Supreme Command so that the military could get a better handle on what it might be up against. Like many of his colleagues, Chawan believed the military had its own agenda that did not always serve the national interest.

Chawan argued strongly that the foreign ministry and parliament, and not the military, should be the entities responsible for negotiating and approving national borders. The job of the military, he believed, was to defend national integrity. Local commanders should therefore not be fraternising with their foreign counterparts, or be involved in cross-border business. Fourth Army Region officers in the south sometimes crossed into Malaysia for games of golf in Ipoh.

The Gang of Four wanted to stamp the foreign ministry's authority and independence. When Anand became permanent secretary, there were a half-dozen ambassadors in posts overseas who were from the military. Although some were capable individuals, they were viewed as a burden to the foreign ministry with its crop of ambitious professional diplomats.

Chawan recalls that the military ambassadors were a particular 'point of friction'. The process of rotating them out of their postings after Bhichai replaced Chatichai as foreign minister was quite involved. Anand did not regard it as so contentious. 'It sounds worse than it actually was,' he says. 'It was a matter of principle.' After all, his own father-in-law was a military diplomat, and Chatichai had been a major general at 31 before being sent to Argentina as ambassador in the late 1950s. Most of the generals concerned had been found diplomatic postings because they did not belong to any particular clique; they were not fighting generals. Some were minor royalty who had peaked at the rank of lieutenant general, and would never be given command positions. 'Bhichai was a good Rotarian, and earnest in his job,' says Chawan. 'I think he wanted to prove he was equally as good as Thanat. He had courage – a bureaucrat would not have dared remove a militarily appointed ambassador.'

To this day, the feisty, principled Chawan still chides the military for inflexibility. 'These people didn't have a sporting spirit,' he says. 'We didn't think much of our comments – it was done for the good of the country. We didn't want to be dictated to.' He still believes the US military and CIA were improvising in late 1975 after the end of the Vietnam War, and lacked a clear policy in Thailand.

Aderholt firmly believed that Ramasun – the no-longer-secret listening station planted by the US and Thai militaries in the Northeast with nobody else's knowledge – should remain. He considered the facility essential to regional security. 'He's really sabotaged us,' Aderholt complained of Anand. Referring to the US's other perceived antagonists at the foreign ministry, he went on, 'They're bright young men, alright, but they're moving in the wrong direction.'

Aderholt also accused Anand of being in cahoots with the outspoken editor of *The Nation*,[25] Suthichai Yoon. '*The Nation* is a very anti-American paper,' he said. 'You know who writes the editorials? No, not Suthichai Yoon – Anand. Or else Anand directs him every day. But I am sure Anand writes them.'

'This is a joke,' says Suthichai, nearly 40 years later. 'I believe there was this document – a CIA briefing. According to this allegation, Anand was writing editorials in *The Nation* to close down the bases. I never actually saw it. When I met Anand, he told me about it. We were laughing. Anand never had any role in our editorial policy. He gives interviews but doesn't like writing – every time we ask him for an article or an opinion piece he says, "No, I don't write."'

While Aderholt blasted away at diplomatic barn doors, at least he never stooped to smearing Anand as a leftist. 'Let me just say from the American side that no one has ever, ever, ever said [or] indicated that he's communist. We think he is a nationalist and we think he is a very brilliant individual. He just, we think, has different ideas than ours, but he's Thai and we're American. That's understandable.'

The scuttlebutt spread by Aderholt and others was that Anand wanted to give American diplomats their comeuppance, and have the last word. Under Anand's new rules of engagement, administered by Woraputh, US diplomats and officials would henceforth have to go through the foreign ministry in all official dealings.

There was no question that Anand wanted these rules applied, particularly with regard to the military, but interpreting the new protocols as personal and petty was very questionable. Anand could see that the US embassy in Bangkok had become used to functioning more in the manner of a country than a legation, with diplomats behaving as if Thai ministers and senior officials were their direct counterparts. Although his enemies painted him as overbearing, egotistical, and vengeful, Anand was trying to bring some order to a chaotic relationship at a problematic time.

There were also those in the foreign community who viewed Anand's approach as principled and quite reasonable. James Gormley, the US embassy's financial reporting officer in Bangkok, had a rare perspective. Through his close dealings with Thai bureaucrats, particularly in the finance ministry, Gormley had formed a high opinion of their capabilities. He dealt with graduates of Oxford, Cambridge, MIT, and Harvard. When he conferred with these individuals to report back to Washington, 'nine out of ten times the person I was dealing with would know more about the issue than I did, which was not true in any other country I served in'.

Gormley, who was a source for the *Far Eastern Economic Review*, regarded his ambassador, Charles Whitehouse, as 'a very bright man' but also as a Newport playboy and dilettante who never took Asians seriously. The urbane Kukrit, with his impeccable English manner and wit, ran circles around the ambassador. Whitehouse did not grasp that Anand's doggedness over closing the US-built bases and the troop drawdown was entirely consonant with Kukrit's personal views and his government's policies. Gormley heard the embassy gossip that Anand felt he had not been taken seriously as ambassador in Washington. Anand was basically 'a dog in the manger about the United States, so this list of conditions was just a reflection of Anand's pique and not of Thai policy'. Although this was nonsense, Gormley recalls Whitehouse going to see Kukrit to 'straighten out Anand'.

'Kukrit, like a good Thai, says, "Don't worry, there's no problem." What Kukrit is telling him is, I don't have a problem – you may have a problem,' Gormley recalled. 'It was a number of weeks later that it finally dawned on him that this was the Thai position, it was not Anand.'[26]

As permanent secretary, and with Kukrit's support, Anand implemented a 'hard access regime' to stop the US ambassador bypassing both the permanent secretary and foreign minister. 'It was not a question of preventing access,' he explains. 'It was the level that was the issue – the proper channels. What it meant was that requests for access should go through the foreign ministry.'

The appropriate levels of access remain fresh in Anand's mind to this day. The ambassador should have access to the prime minister and his ministers; deputy chiefs of mission, political and economic counsellors to the permanent secretaries; cultural and other attachés to director generals; and first secretaries to division chiefs.

'I wanted to make sure the embassy interacted properly with the foreign ministry, and that the ambassador also sometimes saw the permanent secretary,' Anand says. 'I suppose they were not too happy.' Anand certainly had Kukrit's support in blocking direct access to him and his ministers, but he knew he could never prevent the militaries intermingling – keeping the government permanently in the dark about what was going on between them.

The foreign ministry administered diplomatic privileges, even in theory down to vetting maids and drivers, and this became an increasingly thorny and impractical interaction when hundreds or more 'diplomats' were involved. 'We cannot allow 4,000 US diplomats in Thailand,' Kukrit once remarked testily. His government was faced with hundreds of US technicians and operatives asking to be afforded diplomatic privileges. At one point in early 1976, there were some 600 applicants to the foreign ministry's relatively junior protocol department for privileges and immunities, of whom only about 100 received them.

As permanent secretary, Anand was right at the heart of this tension, increasing his unpopularity with many Americans in Thailand. 'Instead of having an adequate American embassy of the size of, I don't know, 150 or 200, it turns out there is an American embassy which has about 4,000 people,' Anand told a group of reporters. 'This situation is not conducive to the promotion of more honest and, shall we say, mutually beneficial co-operation between our two countries.'[27]

The last straw

Apart from overseeing the closure of the US bases, Anand also became embroiled in a much less obvious problem with the Americans: ammunition in Thailand (AIT). All the major ammunition dumps were under US control, including the main one in Korat that was believed to contain a nuclear-proof command bunker. Without access to the ammunition dumps, the Thai military could only expect to fight for two days, three at most, if there was a full-on invasion. Under an article in the US constitution, ammunition could only be stockpiled overseas under direct US supervision. In the most unlikely event of a communist invasion, without access to ammunition the army would have had insufficient firepower to mount any kind of defence. Whether or not the Thai military would succeed in a battle was thus a moot point. This was a disquieting realisation for the Thais, and the impasse required time-consuming negotiations.

Anand viewed the AIT problem as in some ways the 'last straw', and was annoyed that it came up so late in the day. 'It was one thing after another just to make the negotiations more difficult,' he recalls. 'All these things were brought up by the Americans.' Both militaries must have known about the AIT issue all along, yet it only surfaced when the US was looking for another lever to gain flexibility in the final withdrawal. 'This was a dirty game,' says Anand. 'The military should have warned us that the US presence was related to AIT.' He ended up negotiating directly with Ambassador Whitehouse on ammunition already stockpiled inside Thailand worth around US$67 million.

In March, he wrote to the ambassador: 'What is posing a problem for the Thai military authorities is not only what quantity is available, but also how readily available [it is] for actual use. The crux of the matter is that the Thai military authorities do not have possession of nor control over the use of AIT.' Like Bhichai, Anand got along well enough with Whitehouse. He addressed him, 'My dear Ambassador,' in his first note, and 'Dear Charlie' as matters relating to AIT drew to a mutually acceptable conclusion in April.

Although he did not work with him, Whitehouse's deputy chief of mission, Daniel O'Donohue, later described Aderholt, Anand's nemesis, as an almost 'impossible' chief of JUSMAGTHAI. He recalled the US military withdrawal from Thailand as 'one of the two worst negotiations I had ever seen conducted by the [State] Department and the rest of the US government'. (The other was the later 'fiasco' of the US military bases in the Philippines.) His verdict was highly critical of both sides:

> There was a combination of arrogance in Washington and utterly confusing signals coming from the various agencies in the US Government, as well as ineptitude in the Thai civilian government which engaged in the negotiations. Both sides, in effect, wanted to keep a residual American military presence. However, by the time that we were through with the negotiations, we had no alternative but to leave entirely as a result of [a] foolish ultimatum by the Thai government.
>
> From our point of view, this failed negotiation turned out to be strategically a benefit because it gave us great freedom of action from that point on. We could determine the extent of our involvement in Thailand. From the Thai point of view the failed negotiation was

viewed, particularly by the Thai military, as a disaster. The US had been already forced to leave Vietnam, the South Vietnamese Government had collapsed, and a resurgent and united Vietnam had come into being under communist control with the US withdrawal. Thailand had thus lost the anchor for what had determined and dominated its foreign and security policy since 1945.[28]

While the Thai military certainly shared this view of the US departure, the elected civilian government, the foreign ministry, and Anand did not. Anand was on the leading edge of a policy decision relating to national sovereignty. 'Perhaps I was too effective,' he says in hindsight. 'At certain times, you could say that I was against certain US policies, but not anti-American. You have to know your own position.'

As it turned out – and not for the last time in Thai history – the Thai military would not be fighting foreign forces with live ammunition, but alleged enemies within the state. Anand and his so-called Gang of Four would be high on the military's hit list.

CHAPTER 7

THAMMASAT
(1976)

Student massacre

Prime Minister Kukrit Pramoj, the head of the Social Action Party, had constantly found himself undermined by coalition members on his right, and by repeated coup threats from the military. He finally dissolved parliament, lost a general election, and in April 1976 was replaced by his elder brother, Seni. With all the stress, Kukrit became seriously ill and was hospitalised.[1] Anand spent only four months as permanent secretary under Kukrit's foreign minister, Chatichai Choonhavan. He then worked for Bhichai Rattakul, who was foreign minister for six months until 6 October 1976, when Bangkok was witness to terrible violence.

Having gone one way in late 1973, when a military government was toppled in a popular uprising, by 1976 the pendulum of public opinion had swung markedly. There was widespread public opposition to assertive students, farmers, and workers. Rightist and ultra-monarchist groups were now in the ascendant, espousing simplistic, short-term world views and endowed with very thuggish appetites. They included Village Scouts, Red Gaurs, and Nawaphon – all well organised with links to the military's Internal Security Operations Command (ISOC) and the paramilitary Border Patrol Police. Complementing these groups, vocational students formed a rightist rabble; they had a predilection for street fighting and mindless violence. Many of them resented their more academic peers, particularly those from Thammasat University, who formed the bedrock of the Student Federation of Thailand and were openly leftist.

August 1976 saw the return from exile in Taiwan of Field Marshal Praphas

Charusathien, the former deputy prime minister and most powerful member of Prime Minister Field Marshal Thanom Kittikachorn's successive cabinets in the 1960s and early 1970s. His return prompted violence at Sanam Luang near Thammasat University, leaving two dead and scores more injured. Following an audience with King Bhumibol, Praphas reluctantly went back into exile.

The following month, Thanom himself arrived from Singapore. After his exile in Boston in late 1973, Thanom had returned briefly to Thailand a year later. He was again told to leave, and moved to Singapore. The late S.R. Nathan, who in 1999 was to become Singapore's president, was at the time director of the security and intelligence department at Singapore's Ministry of Defence. By chance, he once met the fallen dictator carrying a shopping bag around the supermarket at Plaza Singapura, a popular mall, accompanied only by his son in law, Suwit Yodmani.

The two met on later occasions. Nathan was well aware that most important Thai visitors to Singapore at the time paid a visit to Thanom, and they included the army chief, General Kriangsak Chomanand. One day, Thanom informed Nathan that he would be entering the monkhood as a novice at the Thai temple at Bukit Merah in Singapore. He then requested help – he wanted to go back to Thailand where his elderly father was ailing. From Singapore's perspective, the former strongman's presence in Thailand was a matter for the Thais themselves. However, according to Nathan, there was concern that Thanom's return might cause a diplomatic incident and another embarrassing deportation. The Singaporeans wanted assurances that if he went home, Thanom would not be told to leave Thailand for a third time.

The key go-between between the governments at this time was Samak Sundaravej, the right-wing deputy interior minister from the Democrat Party. He assured the Singaporeans that the disgraced field marshal would be welcome. Samak also told an emergency cabinet meeting convened by Seni that 'Their Majesties had personally approved Thanom's return'.[2]

'We made all the arrangements, had the passport chopped and put him on the plane,' Nathan said. He personally saw the former military strongman off from Paya Lebar Air Base. After arrival in Bangkok, dressed in the saffron robes of a novice monk, Thanom was taken straight from the airport for ordination at Wat Boworniwet, the temple with some of the strongest historical links to the royal family. King Bhumibol regularly met for dhamma studies with the abbot, Phra Yanasangvara,[3] a future supreme patriarch who had been the king's spiritual guide when he was ordained for two weeks as Bhumibalo Bhikku in October 1956.[4] On 23 September 1976, King Bhumibol and Queen Sirikit, soon after returning to Bangkok from the South, visited the temple. Thanom's presence there ratcheted up tensions dramatically, and caused increasingly large demonstrations at Sanam Luang, which the Grand Palace overlooks.

Despairing of the situation, Seni tendered his government's resignation. This was not accepted by the king. Meanwhile Thanom remained ensconced in the temple under the protection of Red Gaurs. After two activists were found hanged in Nakhon Pathom (with the police apparently involved), their hangings were re-enacted by demonstrators at Sanam Luang. Photographs of the staged event were printed in a rightist newspaper. One of the students in the picture resembled Crown Prince Maha Vajiralongkorn. This further inflamed public opinion, even though witnesses to the mock hanging noticed no resemblance.[5]

Dr Prawase Wasi was a progressive figure in the medical establishment, an activist who had become interested in issues he considered directly related to public health: economics, politics, and education. A specialist in haematology, he worked at Siriraj Hospital, which was across the river from Thammasat University. Prawase sensed from the anti-leftist hysteria and inflammatory broadcasts on the military's Armoured Brigade Radio Station – which attacked Anand by name on occasions – that something terrible was about to happen to the students. 'Actually, I warned them the night before to get out because things were looking bad,' he says. 'When Thanom came as a monk, I realised something fishy was going to happen. Fear leads people to do terrible things.'

According to Prawase, both students and teachers at Siriraj, Thailand's oldest and pre-eminent teaching hospital, were very divided politically, and they were not alone. In the great confusion of the period, students at Ramathibhodi Hospital had a reputation for leftism while many of their teachers were inclined to the right.

As a personal precaution, Prawase called at the local police station to warn its commander, a relative, that he himself expected at any time to be denounced as a communist by people at Siriraj. This duly occurred – despite his lack of interest in communist ideology: 'I had read one page of *Das Kapital*, and could not understand it,' he says.

Chaiwat Satha-Anand, a Bangkok-born Muslim of Indian extraction, had been a part of the broader student movement at Thammasat University since 1972 when he embarked on a political science degree. In September 1976 he became a junior lecturer there. Despite his background, he says, he was not really a radical in any sense. He vividly recalls his last visit to the campus on 5 October: 'I had a feeling that something terrible was going to happen.' His intuition was correct.

Matters came to a head early on the morning of 6 October, a Wednesday, when security forces and rightist groups laid siege to Thammasat University after failing to persuade student protesters to disperse. *The Washington Post* carried a detailed report of what followed:

> At 6 am, when the negotiations failed, the police entered the campus and, according to Thai journalists and photographers who had spent the night with them, they were fired upon by students from the roof of the four-story faculty of accounting building. The police reportedly pulled out without returning the fire.[6]

An hour later, having regrouped and presumably been given authorisation, a 'massive armed attack' was mounted. Border Patrol Police fired a recoilless rocket launcher through the university's front gates, while ordinary police took pot shots through the campus railings. They then set about shooting, beating, and lynching students. The bodies of two students taken from the university were hung from trees on Sanam Luang and mutilated by the mob, which some accounts put as high as 15,000. Bodies were piled on top of each other and immolated in public. On campus, students were rounded up, stripped to the waist, bound, and made to lie face down. Those with spectacles had them smashed.

Although some shots were certainly fired early on from inside Thammasat, the political violence that day soon became one-sided and ranks as some of the very worst ever seen in Bangkok. By official count, 46 people died, but many have speculated the figure was at least double that. Apart from the dead and injured, some 3,000 students were arrested. Reuters reported that at least 4,800 people had been arrested nationwide by 19 October. Up to 3,000 students fled to the forests to hide out, and of these over 1,000 joined the Communist Party of Thailand. Puey later noted that while the figures were woolly, some 6,000 people went missing from regular education at this time:

> The number does not matter as much as the quality. The communists have never been blessed with so many qualified people: medical

students, engineering students, educators, communications students and so on. In other words, the *coup d'état* that was launched in the name of anti-communism, helped the communists in the jungles of Thailand to become stronger.[7]

The final toll on the day will never be certain, but Chaiwat believes the actual number of dead is less significant than the manner of their killing. Officially, more people may have died in political violence on the streets of Bangkok in 1973 (70), 1992 (52), and 2010 (91), but they were killed in clashes: casualties in a violent narrative. The killings at Thammasat in 1976 were simply a massacre. 'It was not the number but the barbarity and the way Thai society seemed to tolerate it,' argues Chaiwat. 'It was done in broad daylight. It was not the killing – it was the glee.' There was bloodlust in the air. 'It exploded the myth of Thai society as peaceful – it is not angelic. What we are very good at is self-deception.'

Some onlookers shown in film footage appear happy and to be applauding the mayhem. Cameraman Derek Williams was on assignment for CBS News. 'I had never seen uniformed men and militia run amok like that before in such a frenzy of fury and hatred,' he says. 'It was the day the "Land of Smiles" myth was shattered for me.'[8]

From Siriraj, across the Chao Phraya, Prawase could see desperate students jumping into the water. Thousands were trapped on the campus; some managed to escape the deadly Sanam Luang area. 'It may be Thai culture, but many conservative teachers helped the students when the police and military came after them,' he recalls.

Government House was besieged by 6,000 rightist demonstrators. Seni was inside, a vacillating force now spent.[9] That evening, his government was toppled in a coup with Admiral Sangad Chaloryu as head of the new junta, the National Administrative Reform Council (NARC). 'The government cannot govern,' Sangad announced over the radio. 'To keep Thailand from falling prey to the communists, and to uphold the monarchy, this council has seized power. The country is under martial law.'[10] Heavy censorship was imposed, and newspapers did not reappear until Sunday.

Despite the gruesome scenes, not all foreign coverage was critical. 'The violence of yesterday's clashes may have shocked the inhabitants of Bangkok, but the "silent majority" one can approach – neighbours, drivers, market sellers, small shopkeepers and businessmen – welcomed the return of law and order,' reported Joel Henri, a correspondent known for his anti-leftist views.[11]

'For Thais, the most attractive part of the military administration will be its avowed "law and order" platform,' predicted Alan Dawson, a United Press International correspondent who had reported the fall of Saigon the previous year. 'A large majority of the nation, and particularly residents of Bangkok, is clearly tired of the constant student demonstrations and labour unrest which democracy brought in the past three years.'[12]

The rightists strike back

The most powerful military figure in play was not Sangad but the army chief, General Kriangsak Chomanand, whose strong dislike for Anand was common knowledge. Initially, however, Anand was ignored, even as people and institutions deemed remotely leftist were purged. Unions and political parties were disbanded. On five occasions between 6 and 26 October, special branch police seized and burned in all more than 45,000 books from the Suksit Siam shops and warehouses in Bangkok of Sulak Sivaraksa, a leading intellectual and social critic. These included six copies of Thomas More's *Utopia*: it was written in 1516, centuries before the advent of communism. In an outraged letter from London to UNESCO in Paris, Sulak listed every last volume, protesting the flagrant flouting of Article 19 of the Universal Declaration of Human Rights.[13]

On the morning of 6 October, Anand was at Saranrom Palace, the old foreign ministry, on the other side of Sanam Luang, but arrived for work after the shooting earlier in the morning had subsided. 'I knew it was serious, but I did not have the whole picture,' he recalls. 'What I heard was horrifying. We had been living under the illusion that we were a Buddhist country and that there should be more compassion, kindness, and humane treatment of people. At that time, you could not talk sense to either the student leaders or to the military – it was out of control. It was one of the saddest days of my life. Suddenly, I felt ashamed of the Thais.'

During the period after a coup when military juntas deliberated on the reassignment of seized ministerial portfolios, the usual practice was to make the permanent secretary in each ministry acting minister. This meant that by default Anand replaced Bhichai, and for the next fortnight served as Thailand's foreign minister.

During Anand's tenure as acting minister, the ministry monitored international reaction to the coup, with detailed analysis of reports appearing in the foreign media. Thailand was as sensitive as ever about its image, which had been severely battered by the barbaric scenes at Thammasat. *The Washington Post* spared nothing when it related how 'police and rightist mobs crushed a leftist student protest in an orgy of shooting, lynching, beatings and immolation'.[14]

The Vietnam News Agency strongly rebutted allegations being put about of a communist plot. Police General Chumphol Lohachala was quoted in a Thai TV report alleging that Vietnamese identification cards had been found on the bodies of protestors killed at Thammasat. Hanoi's state media expressed concern for the safety of Vietnamese living in Thailand. 'Vietnam's policy vis-à-vis Thailand and the other Southeast Asian countries is quite clear,' the agency said. 'Since the new rulers in Thailand have made brazen ludicrous charges against the Vietnamese people, we must warn them against inciting anti-Vietnamese feelings. We warn them against taking advantage of the coup to suppress Vietnamese nationals, who are living honestly and scrupulously respecting Thai law.'[15]

The following day, Thursday, it fell to Anand to provide ambassadors with the names of 18 officers in the original NARC, but the list had to be revisited on Friday when six more generals were added. There were evidently competing factions in the upper reaches of the military, and disagreements about how soon there should be a return to civilian government – if at all. Just the Sunday before the coup, General Chalard Hiranyasiri was dismissed from active duty by the defence ministry and placed in the military reserves. Only 53, he had been promoted to deputy army chief six months earlier, and then demoted. Chalard was reported to be at odds with Sangad, and part of a group loyal to Thanom.[16]

NARC belonged to the military faction that was evidently not bent on entrenching a ruling junta and proceeded quickly to a civilian solution. Within two days of the Thammasat bloodbath, Tanin Kraivixien, a right-wing judge in the Supreme Court, was named prime minister designate. Tanin was well regarded in palace and military circles for his no-nonsense approach and staunch anti-leftism. He was best known publicly for his weekly TV programme, *Democracy Talks*.

Anand had first met Tanin in England where the latter studied law at London University and Gray's Inn.[17] He was president of the Samakki Samakhom, and Anand was in charge of the debating section at one stage, but the two had lost touch back in Thailand. 'He is a good man, honest, forthright – a man of integrity and strong convictions,' Anand wrote to his daughters soon after Tanin's appointment. 'Let's wish him [the] best of luck. He will need it in his new job.'[18]

Although, surprisingly, only three portfolios in the new line-up would go to the military, Anand rightly predicted that Tanin's cabinet would have ministers selected for their strong anti-communist credentials. The authoritarian cabinet was exceptionally small with only 17 members, most of whom were 'politically inexperienced, unknown figures'.[19] Tanin ignored suggestions for the cabinet made by the military; and the only politician to be included was the rightist former Democrat, Samak Sundaravej, whom Seni, in a last gasp on the way down, had managed to expel from his cabinet. Superficially, the most innovative aspect of the new cabinet was the inclusion of Khunying Lursakdi Sampatisiri as minister of transport, the first woman to hold a Thai cabinet portfolio.

Tanin's cabinet was initially expected to last four years: 'a long period of quiet stability', Anand wrote. Tanin later said it would take 12 years for him to put the country on the correct path to democracy.

Like many others at the time, Anand was putting a bright face on a very disturbing situation. In letters to his daughters, he expressed relief that calm had returned after the violent collapse of the Seni government: 'There was a total breakdown in the previous government,' he wrote. 'Its indecisive prime minister, lack of political leadership, petty disputes among politicians, the return of [the] former premier, students' unpopular actions, and many other factors all combined to bring about the inevitable.' The 'inevitable' was arguably the most gruesome military takeover Thailand has ever seen. The US embassy took a similar but more hawkish view:

> The takeover of the [Royal Thai Government] by the NARC was not really a coup: the political situation had deteriorated to the point where the Seni Government was no longer capable of governing and a complete breakdown of public order seemed imminent. Members of Parliament and other politicians within the former government had actually created new corruption instead of instituting reforms to prevent corruption. The squabbling and bickering that had gone on under the Seni Government had led to indecisiveness, discontent, civil disorder, and actually threatened the nation's integrity and its ability to withstand insurgent threats and pressures from abroad.[20]

Many had been accepting of the coup, including to a degree even Anand in his letters. Thailand's first real attempt at parliamentary democracy since the immediate post-World War II period had, after all, been chaotic. Three weak governments had been elected in less than two years. Widespread public support for the students and reformists gained in 1973 had been eroded. There was fatigue with leftist dogma and constant agitation, and fear of the communism manifestly spreading through the region.

'Getting rid of Praphas [Charusathien], Thanom and Narong [Kittikachorn] had been a positive act in nearly everyone's view, but the social disorder that followed their departure was viewed as negative,' argued the political scientists David Morell and Chai-Anan Samudavanija. 'The rightist leaders and their new organisations were committed to destroying the students and their leftist allies, and by October 1976 most Thais were ready to tolerate such a move.'[21]

Even Puey, who had commended the students for their idealism, could see where they had erred. 'The accusation that the students are destroying the nation is a slanderous accusation in order to destroy their important force,' he wrote in a letter in late October 1976. But Puey was also critical of their doctrinaire tactics and arrogance. 'They took up every single issue and made a big thing of it. Their overdoing made the people tired. For example, whenever and wherever there was a rally, there must be a scolding of the government in power. In the US military withdrawal issue, there were ceaseless rallies, even though the government had promised the dateline of withdrawal ... Instead of seeking popularity among the people, the students thought that the people would side with them forever. Instead of strengthening their own force, they became weaker.'[22]

'In the initial stage, there were some ugly scenes which should best be forgotten,' Anand confided in a letter to his daughters. He moved on immediately to his instinctive response at such times: 'The main question now is where do we go from here?'[23]

Anand was asking this question as acting foreign minister during the week before Tanin, the prime minister designate, actually announced his new cabinet. He was completely unaware of what would soon befall him personally.

The axe finally fell on the foreign ministry on 21 October. The blow came in one of the final directives issued by the junta before it transformed itself into a 24-member advisory body to the incoming appointed cabinet. Without much evidence, the foreign ministry was viewed by the resurgent rightists as a hotbed of leftist sympathisers, which had courted communist powers and leaked state secrets. Anand – the diplomat who had negotiated with China and shown the American military to the door – was at the top of the list of alleged leftist malefactors. He was suspended for vaguely described leftist sympathies pending a formal investigation.

A 'high-ranking source' told the *Bangkok Post*: 'If Anand is cleared of these charges, he will be reinstated, but not as [permanent secretary].'[24] Nobody actually knew what the 'charges' were. Anand's fall made international headlines. *The New York Times* reported: 'It was clearly a political move against Mr Anand, who in fewer than two years in office, is understood to have alienated virtually every major faction in the military that seized power in the October 6 coup here.'[25]

Anand's numerous adversaries closed in on the foreign ministry. Kosol Sindhvananda was also relieved of his position as political director general, as was his former deputy Chawan Chawanid, who had recently become head of the ASEAN section.[26] No diplomats were actually fired. Anand's Gang of Four were all put in limbo while a high-level, three-man civil service panel[27] was convened to look into the charges that might be brought. Anand was undoubtedly the main target, but nobody doubted the whole foreign ministry was under attack. There was also little doubt as to who was behind the purge.

'Kriangsak never took a liking to me,' says Anand. 'It followed that after 6 October he was partly, if not directly, responsible for my removal. I have nothing against Kriangsak.'

The allegations that would lead to Anand's suspension were not revealed to him until December. Speculation at the time included his alleged communist tendencies; establishing relations with East European countries such as Bulgaria, Romania, and Yugoslavia; allowing more Soviet diplomats into the kingdom; permitting *Pravda*, the Soviet newspaper and communist party official organ, to establish a bureau; and leaking national secrets to the press. Anand still mulls over 'the irony of the whole sordid period', with its echoes of McCarthyism and the anti-communist witch-hunts in the US in the 1950s. He finds it particularly absurd that he was allowed to serve as *de facto* foreign minister for a fortnight when charges of leftist subversion were about to be laid against him.

'If they thought I was a communist, they would have known two weeks before when they made me foreign minister,' he points out. 'A "communist" suspect could have done a lot more damage during his 15-day tenure!'[28]

Few experience the trauma of an official purge – discovering very publicly who is for you and who is not. Up to October 1976, Anand had enjoyed a stellar career with no reversals. Promotions had seemed to come naturally. He had risen on merit and through hard work, with no obvious sign of personal ambition. He had even attempted to decline the job of permanent secretary, the role that had got him into so much trouble.

Anand had suddenly been felled, and his future was in the hands of others, some of them extremely hostile. It was a stunning blow that would temporarily rob him of any initiative with regard to his own life – although he had already concluded that his career would have to change course. 'I knew I could not work with the military,' he says, reflecting on the fortnight he had spent as acting foreign minister. 'I was looking forward to the day the government was formed, then I could resign or asked to be reassigned.'

Perhaps to keep the more acerbic tendencies of Thanat Khoman in check, Anand's mentor was invited back inside the tent as an adviser on foreign affairs to Tanin's new government, a role he accepted. Thanat had been permanently embittered after being sidelined in Thanom's 1971 self-coup. The former foreign minister vacillated over Thailand's relationship with the US, and sniped from the sidelines; he rarely had anything good to say about his successors. Although he had supported normalising relations with China from the earliest stage, he came to believe that Chatichai and Bhichai had gone too far in alienating the US while ingratiating Thailand with Beijing. He was deeply critical of both men in private. Not that it had much effect: it was water off a duck's back for the ebullient Chatichai. Bhichai, for his part, never cared for what he considered Thanat's tendency to 'zig zag'. Anand himself felt that Thanat's constant carping sometimes went a little too far. He remembers once getting an earful about the shortcomings of Thanat's successors and protesting, 'Minister, I am a career man – I cannot choose my master.'

Thanat for his part spoke of undoing the damage of the previous three years, and obliquely chided Anand for being high-handed with the US. 'When you're dealing with the great powers, you don't go around giving ultimatums,' he remarked.[29] 'I was disappointed,' says Anand of the implicit criticism. 'Thanat was kind to me and supportive, but he did not fault the military at all. In a way he showed sympathy for the events which led up to the October backlash.'

When the US embassy spoke with Thanat on 14 October, he gave the impression of being mostly concerned about Thailand improving the investment climate. 'It was obvious, in his opinion, that foreign capital would flow to a well-run nation which provided such an environment, just as it had in the case of Singapore,' the cable noted.[30]

The list of people who were prepared to come out in public and support Anand was extremely short. 'Nobody in the civil service would help him,' recalls Asda Jayanama, a young diplomat at the time. 'They were all survivalists.' Arsa Sarasin, however, did try and rally support at the foreign ministry for Anand and the Gang of Four. 'I don't know what they had in mind,' says Anand, who was never consulted.

Anand suspected that Group Captain Prasong Soonsiri, the new head of the National Security Council (NSC), who had been so unhappy with the way Anand handled the official visit to Vietnam in August, had been involved in his removal. On his own initiative, Arsa approached Siddhi Savetsila, Prasong's predecessor at the NSC. But Anand had also upset Siddhi with some brusque official encounters and ill-advised jibes about Siddhi's close relations with the CIA. Siddhi was not vengeful, but certainly believed Anand had a case to answer.

Some believe that Kukrit had run into trouble pursuing overdue political reforms and mooting abolition of the Anti-Communist Act. Matters had only worsened when Kukrit made an ill-judged remark that seemed to make light of Thai security personnel falling victim to landmines along the Cambodian border. Kukrit quipped that the army might have done better to send in real 'buffaloes' for mine-clearing operations. In Thai culture, it is more than usually offensive to compare people to animals, particularly buffaloes and monitor lizards. The official narrative at the time was that of a nation threatened by the crimson tide of communism, with frontline areas bravely and selflessly protected by the armed forces. The armed forces were also key supporters of the monarchy.

Anand was one of many officials who attended occasional lunches at the palace, particularly when foreign guests were being received and a related topic might arise. King Bhumibol and Queen Sirikit could be briefed about developments on these occasions. Anand recalls being asked for additional information by Kukrit a few times – and providing some blunt insights into inconvenient truths. 'I had to present certain facts,' Anand recalls. Looking back, he believes his observations were honest but were not always well received.

Anand's leading role in the US military withdrawal had certainly made him grave enemies in the security establishments of both countries, and these people were happy to observe from the shadows his very public downfall. He was one among many casualties of one of the darkest phases in modern Thai history.

'I was a victim,' says Anand. '[The whole episode] left a very unfortunate scar on the political process in Thailand.' He still mulls over the possibility that there was a conspiracy among his foes to foist blame on others to conceal their own involvement, and he traces the root of much anti-monarchist sentiment to this period.

Many murky scenarios have been put forward. A member of the so-called Gang of Four at the Foreign Ministry at that time, Chawan Chawanid, believes that the CIA might indeed have played a role in Anand's removal, and he dismisses suggestions that the palace was anti-foreign ministry in 1976. He believes spurious allusions are often made to the royal family and other senior people to conceal or justify wrongdoing by others. However, the foreign ministry's evident eagerness to normalise relations with previously hostile powers had certainly been noticed. Normalisation was the policy of both the elected Kukrit and Seni governments. Subsequently, regional normalisation was also endorsed by the unelected government of Kriangsak.

Some of those who publicly suggested that the CIA was involved in the bloodshed of 1976 were predictable but not credible. For example, *The Moscow News* claimed: 'This is the 14th military *coup d'état* in Thailand since the Second World War; the US CIA was directly involved in all of them.' In fact there had only been ten coups attempted in that period, seven of which succeeded.[31]

Unlike Anand, Arsa was not the target of any direct attack, but he was viewed as tainted simply by virtue of their personal closeness. He was transferred to Brussels as ambassador to Belgium and the European Economic Community for two years. He remembers being advised to enjoy the fine chocolate and keep his head down. 'Arsa gets along with everybody,' says Anand. 'He always maintains very good relations with the military – that is his virtue.'

Arsa had been concerned that Anand's enemies would press for his dismissal, replicating the fate of Amnuay Viravan, the permanent secretary for finance, who infringed on vested military business interests and ended up being fired. If Anand was to be disciplined, Arsa argued, it should be done with a transfer of some kind. Inevitably, however, this would be to a lesser post.

'It was quite clear they were going to get us,' recalls the pugnacious Chawan, the son of a provincial official who had risen entirely on merit and hard-won scholarships. He was – for quite the briefest of moments – appointed to head the SEATO department. At almost the very moment the appointment was signed, he received a punishment posting abroad – as ambassador to Addis Ababa, Ethiopia. 'It was the highest possible posting in our ministry at the time because it was 8,000 feet above sea level,' he says.[32]

Chawan's former boss in the political department, Kosol Sindhvananda, was initially posted to Ankara, Turkey. After complaining, Kosol ended up cooling his heels in a Hanoi hotel room that passed for an embassy. Even so, they all considered themselves lucky to survive as ambassadors, and not end up shuffling papers in some diplomatic backwater as counsellors or ministers.

The day after the junta ordered Anand's suspension, Prime Minister Tanin Kraivixien appointed Upadit Pachariyangkun as foreign minister. Upadit, 55, had recovered from his exile by Thanat to Lagos in the 1960s, and was back on track as a senior career diplomat. After he had completed his studies in Switzerland, his early postings had included a wartime spell in Berlin, from 1942 to 1945, and two years in the early 1970s as permanent representative to the United Nations in Geneva. More recently, Upadit had replaced Anand as ambassador in Washington in 1975.

Chawan recalls Upadit being 'happy to be appointed' as minister. With the experience of a transfer from New York to Lagos behind him, Upadit knew all about demotions. He actually brought his unfortunate personal experience up during a dinner before Chawan's Ethiopia posting, and consoled him that Addis Ababa was a better fate than Lagos.

Upadit and his wife, Apira, had known Anand's daughters during the family's early years in New York, and were fond of them. Anand told his daughters that Upadit had been shocked when he heard the news about his (Anand's) suspension from the foreign ministry: 'He was not consulted, nor informed in advance. He was totally uninvolved in this matter. He is a good and decent man.'[33]

Anand believes that Kukrit discreetly lobbied on his behalf, but it was an indignant Bhichai Rattakul who was his most voluble defender. The former foreign minister was outraged that Anand was being hounded for his efficiency in implementing government policies sanctioned by parliament. 'I am quite willing to take all responsibilities for Anand,' Bhichai told reporters three weeks after the junta's purge at the foreign ministry. 'He was just carrying out my orders.'[34]

Bhichai remains emphatic. 'We can't blame Anand. Blame the government, blame Seni, blame me as foreign minister,' he roars nearly four decades later. In his late 80s, Bhichai's still-powerful voice cracks with emotion. 'Anand was doing his job as a government servant. I was the only one who stood up very strongly defending him. I thought he did the right thing, and he did what I told him to do. Anand was the key player in implementing the policy of the two governments. I was so proud of this young man. He did it with distinction. The whole ministry of foreign affairs was accused of being communist.' Despite his combative stance, Bhichai took some time out travelling overseas while things cooled off.

In his letters to his daughters, there is always a sense of Anand searching for the decency in others, but there was very little to be found. Anand had brought his trusted aide Pridi Boonyobhas back from Washington when he became permanent secretary. Pridi never doubted that the situation would somehow right itself, or that his boss would rebound. Pridi continued to work for Anand in the small office that had been assigned to him at Saranrom Palace. Anand and the others accused were left on 'fly-swatting duty' with nothing to do as the investigation dragged on. Anand took the opportunity to undergo a thorough dental overhaul.

When Tej Bunnag returned to Bangkok from his posting in Jakarta for a visit, he found the mood in the ministry broken and demoralised. He knew only too well that, had he remained in Bangkok, he would also have been a prime target for purging because of his key role in establishing diplomatic relations with China. 'I was on the list, but I wasn't around for them to sack,' he says.

Family hurt

It was a dark time. Anand recalls working off some of his tension through explosive games of squash at the Royal Bangkok Sports Club with Thai friends, the Pakistani military attaché, and Douglas Latchford, a long-term British expatriate who played for Brighton College when Anand was at school at Dulwich. For some years previously, he had had little time for the game. The string of letters to his daughters began to take on an uncharacteristic, slightly distracted air at times. The handwriting was larger and more rushed, but it told only part of the story. Anand had new concerns. His attention was turning from his sudden career reversal to the failing health of his wife.

The political violence at Thammasat and the subsequent political witch-hunt against her husband took a severe emotional toll on Sodsee. She had dedicated two decades to Anand's career, including three quite isolated years in Ottawa. She was devastated that, after all the sacrifice and commitment, her husband's integrity should be called into question. For Sodsee, the attack on Anand could not have been more personal. It was a violation of everything they had worked for together, and their place in public life.

'When I was accused of being a communist, it was the greatest shock of her life,' says Anand. 'For anybody who knew me, it was obviously a trumped-up charge, but my wife was afraid that there was a conspiracy by certain individuals in the military to stitch me up. It was a period of persecution. Up to this day, if I were to accept anything political, this sense of persecution would come back. It was very traumatic for her.'

Sodsee suffered a breakdown and was hospitalised for three months. Anand's focus shifted from the dark shenanigans engulfing the foreign ministry to his wife's hospital bedside. He had to decide how much to tell his daughters, who were both still in the US. Nanda was in her first year at Tufts University, near Boston, Massachusetts; and Daranee was at Madeira, a boarding school for girls in Virginia, near Washington.

Daranee had returned to Thailand when Anand became permanent secretary, but she disliked her new school environment so intensely she would wait up late for her father and implore him to send her back to the US. Anand relented, and ways were found to fund Daranee's return to the US. After Madeira, Daranee attended Pine Manor College.

Far from Bangkok, the two girls had first learned of their father's sudden fall separately from the front pages of *The Washington Post* and *The New York Times*. 'We tried to call and couldn't get through,' says Daranee. 'He finally called us and one of the embassy officials also got in touch.' The girls found their father cagey and tight lipped – he was concerned the telephone lines might be tapped. However, 'one thing that had been instilled in us was never to lose hope in times of adversity,' says Nanda. The girls gradually pieced things together, and Nanda was able one day to get a call through to her father from Boston.

'Everything was bugged,' she remembers, wiping away a tear. 'I still remember that afternoon.' It so happened that she had been studying the McCarthy political witch-hunts of alleged communists in the US. 'That helped me a lot, because I think at that time Thailand was going through the same phase. In that way, I could rationalise the situation, but I still felt he was being persecuted and wrongly accused with bogus charges. It was right after the *coup d'état*, and he was going to be investigated by a totalitarian regime. I was concerned about him because I knew he had dedicated his life to his country.'

Anand could not reveal to Nanda and Daranee how badly their mother had been affected. He was going through a private hell worse than most could see, and had no inkling of how lasting the effects on Sodsee would be. 'It was devastating for her,' says Nanda. 'She cares very much about what others think and say.'

'Mum has been very upset but she is bearing up,' Anand wrote to his daughters, giving the first hint that something beyond politics was amiss. 'All our relatives and friends have rallied to our side.'[35]

Vidhya Rayananonda, another of Anand's trusted aides from Washington, who looked after the family whenever Anand went to New York, visited Sodsee often at this time. 'I was very close to this family,' he recalls. The strong professional and personal bonds he formed with Anand in the 1970s would again come into play when Anand became prime minister – and have lasted to the present day.

Amid the uncertainty, Anand told his daughters not to worry about their finances, reassuring them that their grandmother, Pruek, would help out if necessary. He commiserated with Daranee over the misery of studying economics. 'The same thing happened to me many years ago,' he consoled her.

Well before any conclusion to the inquisition had been reached, Anand finally opened up in a letter on one personal matter: 'My foreign service career probably has come to an end,' he wrote. 'I have no regrets. Perhaps the decision is forced upon me sooner than I would have wished. You know that I have been thinking of retiring from the service for quite some time. After 21 [years of] devoted service to the government, the reward is not commensurate with the dedication that I gave. Nonetheless, I still have self-respect, satisfaction that I made a contribution to the nation and that I have been honest with myself and with others throughout my career.'

Anand was 44 when he wrote this. He had served as an ambassador for 11 years before he returned to Bangkok, and from time to time had vaguely considered early retirement from the foreign service – perhaps at the age of 54 or 55 when all his family commitments were met. By then, his daughters would have long since completed their university education, embarked on careers, and in all likelihood be married. So long abroad, Sodsee also always yearned for a more settled family life in Bangkok. Before he became permanent secretary at the end of 1975, Anand had viewed the possibility of being an ambassador for over 26 years until retirement with little relish. If he retired in his mid-50s, he had a good chance of finding his way on to some large corporate boards as a non-executive director, and putting funds aside for his retirement. He recognised that he would be unsuitable for any direct management role in the private sector.

'Ambassadorial duties are quite fun, and I had the benefit of being stationed in interesting places, but I was being worn down by all the social functions and protocols,' he recalls. 'I was working very hard. There was very little home life for a period of ten years. I needed more private time – it was time to see the other side of the world.'

But now, it appeared the career-changing decision had been made for him by the new government. In a letter written while he was acting foreign minister, Anand alluded to the possibility of a demotion somewhere small and quiet overseas. Denmark was the sort of place he had in mind. Perhaps for the first time in his life, he was grasping at straws. 'At the moment, nothing is definite, but let's hope things work out the way we all want (the four of us),' he wrote.[36]

Official investigation

The accusations against Anand were finally sent to the investigating committee on 10 November. There was no specific mention of relations with China, Eastern Europe, or the USSR, just an observation that 'the accused had shown a tendency of wanting to establish relations with communist countries'. There were also allegations that he did not like the US because Kissinger did not invite him to meetings, that he had mishandled the ammunition issue, and that he thought the Thai armed forces wanted the US military presence to continue for their own personal benefit.

The main issues, however, were two specific leaks of secret information. The first pertained to the agreements between Thailand and the US concerning Ramasun, the no-longer-secret listening station in the Northeast. The second related to a National Security Council meeting Anand attended in May when permission for US aircraft to refuel at Takhli had been discussed. Anand was blamed for a report appearing in the *Bangkok Post* about the NSC meeting. He was also held responsible for sending 50 sets of documents about Ramasun to the cabinet secretariat. The latter were duly reproduced in the *Far Eastern Economic Review*, *The Nation*, *Bangkok Post*, *Prachachat*, and beyond. The Ramasun documents, it emerged, had originally been sent to the foreign ministry by Supreme Command in 1970, and were not intended for wider circulation. It was all confirmation of how badly Anand had riled the Thai and US intelligence communities.

The inquisition against him got off to a wobbly start when the secretary general of the Civil Service Commission, Colonel Chinda na Songkhla, asked to be excused because his wife, Pimsiri Sarasin, was a relative of Anand. He was replaced by Captain Charoen Charoen-Rajapark, permanent secretary at the Ministry of Communications.[37] Nobody guessed at the time that 15 years later Charoen's son Chatchawin would marry Daranee. The committee was headed by permanent secretary to the Office of the Prime Minister, Lieutenant General Boonruan Buacharoon, and also included Siri Atibodhi, permanent secretary of the Ministry of Justice.

Anand was confident of being exonerated once given the opportunity to present 'full and factual information'. In the meantime, he talked of taking Sodsee on a short holiday to Singapore or Kuala Lumpur, places she had never visited. The trips did not happen (and with hindsight Anand believes the superior shopping in Hong Kong would probably have appealed to her more).

'I'll be thinking about our future when the whole mess is cleared,' he confided to his daughters. 'I take a dispassionate view of the whole matter. Just a nightmare that everybody has to go through in his or her lifetime. I hope that the experience will enable me to be a wiser and better man. I hold no personal grudges or feel bitter against anybody. I hope and pray that Mom and both of you feel the same.'[38]

With plenty of spare time, Anand read *The China Hands* by E.J. Kahn, a book about the terrible treatment afforded some American experts on China in the 1940s. These Asia veterans simply reported what they saw, which included unflattering commentaries on the Nationalist leader, General Chiang Kai-shek. For all their professionalism, these dedicated US foreign service officers ended up being hounded and vilified in their home corridors of power. It was an episode that hinted at the McCarthy era that was to follow, and their tribulations resonated. 'It is very similar to what is happening to me now,' Anand confided to his daughters. 'I find the book very enlightening and consoling.'[39]

Whatever his own problems, Anand's fortnightly letters to Nanda and Daranee were warm, sometimes cajoling, reminding them to eat properly, take care of their health, and write home more often, particularly to Pruek, their ever-indulgent grandmother. Money was tight, he admitted, but ways would always be found. Indeed in November, their grandmother, or *khun ya*,[40] contributed much-needed funds. Anand warned that there might not be enough money for airfares home in the summer. Amid references to blouses from Mexico sent as gifts and gentle admonitions for occasional disappointing grades, there was more talk of holidays abroad for Sodsee that never happened.

By late November, there had still been no progress in resolving his case, and to make ends meet Anand was contemplating selling the wooden house given by his parents as a wedding gift, 'if the price is right'.[41] It was eventually sold for 750,000 baht. There were also – for him uncharacteristic – visits to monks with Sodsee to see what the portents held. There was only a passing reference to the effect the inquisition was having on his wife and mother: '*Khun Ya* and Mom are very much affected by the whole incident (and all our relatives have been most helpful), so your letters have cheered them up.'[42]

December arrived and Anand had still not been called to give an account of himself. 'I suppose they have not been able to make a case against me,' he speculated. 'The longer the matter drags on, the more ridiculous it has become. Anyway, do not discuss the matter with anybody. Just pretend that I have not told you very much about it.'[43]

Not that Nanda and Daranee had to pretend: their father had told them only so much. Anand ends one letter triumphantly with mention of a job offer with a decent salary and 'profit sharing opportunity', but admits that he had still not made up his mind about what to do next.

Finally, in the second week of December, Anand was called to give testimony. He could see that the accusations against him were going nowhere. 'When I saw the charges, I was quite relieved,' Anand recalls. They were manifestly false. Had they been more cleverly fabricated, however, he could easily have found himself in a much more dangerous situation, with people trying to frame him as a communist.

'Thank God my father had died, otherwise he would have been broken-hearted,' says Anand. Sodsee was still in hospital, and this continued to be his main personal distraction. It had left him uncharacteristically passive – he let the attack roll over him. Under more normal circumstances his response might have been more spirited. 'The charges are absurd and hardly substantiated,' he wrote to his daughters, without going into any detail. 'The committee was very understanding and knew in their hearts that I had got a raw deal. Be that as it may, my case should never be discussed with anybody. You should continue to say that I have not explained very much to you.'[44]

To his relief, Thanat, Chatichai, and Bhichai all testified. Anand hoped everything would be cleared up by New Year, but Sodsee was still 'anxious'. The couple had been taking trips to the seaside at Pattaya and Hua Hin, but Anand still did not reveal to his daughters how serious their mother's condition had become. 'I don't think she will be coming to the States as she planned,' he wrote, adding vaguely: 'In her present mood, it is better that she stays with me.'[45]

Anand did mention that Crown Prince Maha Vajiralongkorn was getting engaged and would marry in early January, and that they might join the 72nd birthday party the following week for Queen Rambhai Barni, the dowager queen of King Prajadhipok – hardly items suited to the diary of a crypto-communist.

There were still numerous loyal supporters in the background, including in the US. In early January, Professor Frank Darling wrote to lend moral support: 'I was especially troubled when I heard about your removal from the Ministry of Foreign Affairs. Like many Americans, including those working in official missions in Thailand, I agreed with many things you were doing in reorienting Thai foreign policy in the new international environment in Southeast Asia.'[46]

Anand's network from his UN days also rallied. UN Secretary General Kurt Waldheim even telephoned to see if he was interested in a senior position as chief of protocol, or in the United Nations Development Programme, but Anand politely declined both. The Swedish ambassador, Jean Christof, called upon Prime Minister Tanin at the urging of his permanent secretary in Stockholm, a former colleague of Anand's in New York.

A much closer old friend at the UN, Singapore's permanent representative Tommy Koh, tried to buck him up in a letter: 'Please let me know if there is anything at all we can do for you from here.'[47] In the background, Lee Kuan Yew had personally gone to Anand's defence. The Singapore prime minister made a point of asking after Anand every time he met a senior Thai official. He also instructed Koh to see if any position might be available for Anand at the UN, but he too did not consider the chief of protocol position good enough.

'This was a rare case,' Tommy Koh recalls. 'I have never seen Lee Kuan Yew take an interest in someone – show concern and be willing to go out of his way to help a person.' Anand was unaware at the time of Lee's efforts on his behalf. He attributes Lee's awareness of him to his time as Thanat Khoman's secretary, a period when it was almost impossible to see one without the other. 'Everybody knew I was very close to Thanat. I was treated as if I was the number two man in the foreign ministry.'

'For the New Year, it is my sincere hope … that we shall soon see you again either on the circuit of the "ASEAN Mafia" or in some other capacity,' wrote Tan Boon Seng, the deputy secretary for political affairs at Singapore's foreign ministry. 'It is difficult to keep a good man down.'[48]

Nightmare's end

Tan's letter was prescient. By the second week of January, the public ordeal was finally over. None of the allegations against Anand had been substantiated. 'Under regulations of the Civil Service Commission, Mr Anand will be back in active service soon,' reported the *Bangkok Post*.[49] The newspaper also referred to 'an informed source' saying that the foreign ministry was considering posting Anand as ambassador to the UK.

Many breathed sighs of relief. 'I never had the slightest doubt that you will emerge with flying colours convinced as I am of your integrity and patriotism,' wrote General Carlos P. Romulo, foreign minister of the Philippines.[50]

The Israeli ambassador, Reuven Dafni, interpreted Anand's exoneration as a victory for Thailand as much as for Anand: 'There are not many countries in the world, especially not in Thailand's vicinity or for that matter in most countries of the so-called "Third World", in which this could have been possible.'[51]

A particularly warm handwritten note was signed 'Charlie'. Charles Whitehouse, the US ambassador, and his wife Molly expressed their delight at the outcome. 'I can only guess at what a discouraging and dispiriting time this has been for you, but I can assure you that your friends have all been impressed with the patience and fortitude you have displayed.'[52]

Anand immediately wrote to his daughters with the good news, which he had known was coming a little ahead of time: 'It is a great relief that this long and trying ordeal has come to an end. All those who know us appear to be happy and joyful about the news. They all seem to expect us to leave for London soon. I do not make any comment about the paper reports concerning London. All we say is that it is up to the foreign ministry.'[53]

Foreign Minister Upadit would not confirm the London rumour, saying only: 'Mr Anand will have to come back to the ministry before any decision is made on his future postings.'[54] He was clear on one point, however: it would be technically a full re-instatement: 'He will return to the foreign ministry to take up a post equivalent to that of undersecretary of state.'[55]

Since there was already a new permanent secretary in place, the Civil Service Commission allowed Anand to become a special ambassador with C11 rank and salary (ambassadors normally hold C10 rank).[56] The condition for this special position was that it be abolished when Anand vacated the post. Anand took up his new post in early February 1977, becoming the most senior 'ambassador at large' or 'special envoy' in the ministry, pending a posting overseas. He had been reinstated at the ministry with full seniority and salary – although not in his old job.

The new duties were not all onerous. Anand participated in the second US–Thai Bilateral Forum at Berkeley California in early June (the first had been held in Bangkok). Although relatively informal, papers were presented at these precursors of modern-day workshops. They provided an opportunity for interested players from different sectors to get to know each other. Among the small number of foreigners attending as part of 'Team Thailand' was James Rooney, the former AmCham president who had first arrived in Bangkok in 1968 with First National City Bank, which later became Citibank. The group bonded over rather poor meals at one of the few Thai restaurants in California at the time. Like many members of the diplomatic and foreign business community, Rooney admired Anand's principled conduct as permanent secretary and had been appalled by the attack on him. Some of the group ribbed Anand that they might not be allowed back into Thailand if they were seen with him, and took to referring to him by an alias, John. Anand took the teasing in good heart.

Another member of the Thai group arrived in less good humour. At the first session, Thanat Khoman blasted the Americans. 'There was no humour behind it,' Anand recalls. 'Many of my American friends came to me and said, "What happened to Thanat? Why did he become so anti-American?"' That evening, Thanat invited Anand for drinks and dinner, and Anand broached the subject.

'I started speaking softly to him, and referred to the incident. He was not arguing but just listened. I said something to him about how much I respected and admired him.' Anand remembers warning Thanat of the danger of being taken for an 'angry old man', and how the words left a sour taste in his mouth as he spoke them. Thanat took the advice to heart, and next morning was friendly to all.

Anand felt that he needed to get away from Thailand for a period of recuperation. 'I would have loved to go to London. It's one regret in my life that I never served in the UK. That would have been a very happy ending to my diplomatic career.' But it was not to be. When his next posting was finally made public in early June,[57] it was to Bonn, the capital of the Federal Republic of Germany, which ranked as high as Paris or London. Phan Wannamethee, Anand's predecessor as permanent secretary, had been posted there when Chatichai brought Anand back from Washington. History was repeating itself: another demotion without disgrace for a Thai permanent secretary, both posted to the same place.

By tradition, Thai ambassadors who are about to be posted overseas are granted a royal audience. For Anand, there had been no direct personal encounters with King Bhumibol since the visit to North America in 1967. He was present at the luncheon honouring UN Secretary General Kurt Waldheim in 1973, and for several other palace functions after he became permanent secretary, but the encounters were formal and distant – not private audiences. Most of the people close to the king at that time were members of the Royal Chitralada Yacht Squadron, and sailed with him from the beach at Klai Kangwon ('Far from Worries'), the seaside palace at Hua Hin.

The coup leader in October 1976 was Admiral Sangad Chaloryu. A year later, he visited Bonn with a number of naval officers and arms dealers. Anand invited them all to dinner at his residence. The arms dealers did not attend, but Anand found the admiral friendly and talkative. He could not resist asking about the suspension order signed against him when he had been acting foreign minister.

'Khun Anand, there were so many papers passed to me to sign at that time,' the admiral protested. In a play on Thai words, the foreign ministry had indeed nicknamed the junta's chairman Sun Yat Sen, because of his willingness to sign anything, irrespective of consequences. Even so, Anand believes the admiral must have been well aware of what he was signing in the junta's last hours – even if the order did not originate from him. That night in Germany, Sangad did allow that he had been told Anand was 'anti-military', but Anand responded that this was only if they were corrupt. Sangad proceeded to London, and a vice admiral in his group was said to have been most displeased by Anand's forthrightness.

Before the Bonn announcement, Foreign Minister Upadit had told Anand that he was planning to send him to London, but that Tanin Kraivixien had vetoed the idea. Years later, Anand asked Tanin directly if he had vetoed the London posting. The former prime minister was vague, and like Sangad claimed to have no recollection of the matter. Apparently, there was some concern that Puey and Anand might join forces, and even rally students exiled in the UK.

Puey had resigned as rector of Thammasat on the morning of the bloodbath, and went into what would turn out to be permanent exile in the UK.[58] He gave his own account of his narrow escape later that month.[59] Anand had once spent three agreeable days together with Puey when the great technocrat passed through Ottawa in the late 1960s, but they never had the occasion to develop a deeper relationship. 'The government viewed him as being anti-government and anti-military,' says Anand. There were some very ugly, disrespectful scenes at the airport before Puey was allowed to leave for Europe. 'I learned about it the next morning,' Anand recalls. He was well aware of the justifiable alarm with which embassies viewed the whole situation.

Even after Anand was exonerated, in the paranoid climate of the time there were some in power who felt it better to keep these sharp and critical personalities apart. Puey suffered a stroke soon after going into exile[60] that left him with a withered arm, but had borne stoic witness in his speeches and writings in the US and UK against the violent political unravelling in Thailand.

In hindsight, had things been different, and had he been sent as ambassador to London, Anand doubts that he would have forged a close personal relationship with Puey. He would have been in London as a career diplomat. Despite everything he had been through, Anand had less reason to feel embittered than Puey. He was not as well known as Puey, and had simply not been treated as badly.

CHAPTER 8

A NEW CAREER
(1977–1991)

European interlude

In late 1977, Anand arrived in Bonn, the 'provisional capital' of West Germany while the city of Berlin remained divided up between the capitalist West and communist East Germany. Although he would have preferred to be in London, Bonn was substantively Thailand's most important embassy in all Europe. His loyal assistant Pridi Boonyobhas, who had stood firmly alongside him during the 1976 inquisition, remained in Bangkok. Pridi was absorbed into the personal staff of Foreign Minister Upadit Pachariyangkun for 18 months, and then posted to Vientiane, capital of the newly minted People's Democratic Republic of Laos. During the intervening time, he quietly handled Anand's personal affairs in Bangkok.

Anand arrived in Germany firmly set on leaving the foreign service. His plan was to resign after nine months, and then work out the mandatory three-month notice period. In the Thai civil service protocol, the absence of any response to a letter of resignation means it has been accepted. Arsa Sarasin was there to meet him – he had recently been appointed ambassador to Brussels, just a couple of hours' drive along some fine autobahns, and he would still be there after Anand left his post in Bonn and quit diplomacy. As he was not expecting to be there for more than a year, Anand made no effort to learn German – a slight handicap in day-to-day matters, but not professionally. 'I had no difficulty – they all spoke English,' he recalls.

Prior to its reunification with communist East Germany in 1990, the Federal Republic of Germany was already Thailand's largest trading partner in Europe.

Anand was assigned as chief negotiator on behalf of the Association of Southeast Asian Nations (ASEAN) in their emerging relations with the European Economic Community (EEC). He handled mostly political relations between the two groupings, and Arsa dealt with economic interactions. The first of 11 annual meetings of West European and ASEAN foreign ministers was held in 1978. In the second half of that year, Chancellor Helmut Schmidt of West Germany assumed the EEC presidency, which rotated among member countries every six months. As ASEAN's chief negotiator, Anand drafted the political section of the working document. His experience, particularly in endless committee work at the United Nations in New York, made him well suited to the task.

Nevertheless, personal matters weighed heavily on Anand's mind. Close friends in Thailand were aware that he planned to resign when the right opportunity presented itself, and feelers were being extended discreetly on his behalf in the business world. An oil company in the US approached him. Given his lack of business experience, it was Anand's international credentials that were in demand. The drawback from Anand's point of view was that the companies that would make offers with that experience in mind would inevitably be those that had to deal with the government.

An early offer came when Bancha Lamsam, chairman of Thai Farmers Bank (now renamed Kasikornbank), was on a visit to Germany to open a new branch in Hamburg. He personally offered Anand the position of vice chairman of Loxley, one of Thailand's foremost trading conglomerates, where Chatchanee Chatikavanij (*née* Lamsam) was president and chief executive. Anand was already close to the Lamsam family, and the prospects would be good at Loxley. The bank opening in Hamburg provided Anand with his first encounter with Ekamol Kiriwat, a deputy governor of the Bank of Thailand whom he would come to know much better. Ekamol was impressed, and remembers Anand engaging openly with Bancha. 'The main reason for my leaving was to get as far away from the government as possible,' Anand says.

Then, in late 1978, Anand received a visit from Amnuay Viravan, who had come to Bonn with Damri Darakananda, the founder of Saha Union, already a major conglomerate primarily focused on textiles. Anand invited them to stay at the residence. Although they had not been close colleagues, Anand knew Amnuay – they had been permanent secretaries of their respective ministries (the finance ministry, in Amnuay's case), and their terms had overlapped. 'You might say we were technocrats in different fields,' says Amnuay.

Only a few months older than Anand, and also born in the Year of the Monkey, Amnuay was one of the 14 permanent secretaries Prime Minister Kukrit Pramoj had taken with him to China in 1975. He is pictured standing directly behind Anand when Kukrit and Premier Zhou Enlai signed the historic communiqué establishing formal relations between the two countries on 1 July 1975. Amnuay actually entered mainland China earlier than Anand, having been in the entourage of the large badminton tour in 1973. In 1976, he returned again at the head of a delegation to conclude a Sino-Thai trade agreement.

At an early juncture in his storied career in public finance, Amnuay had served a stint as secretary general of the Board of Investment. In that capacity, he pioneered road shows overseas for Thai companies scouting for business. Damri often joined Amnuay on those trips, and the two struck up a firm relationship. The two men were in Germany on this occasion to secure a licensing agreement from the German sportswear manufacturer Adidas for the Saha Union conglomerate to produce athletic footwear in Thailand. Adidas was family-owned, and always deliberated long and hard on decisions.

Like Anand, Amnuay had had a bad run-in with the military. Prior to being permanent secretary at the finance ministry, he had been director general of the customs department. In that capacity, he came down hard on a company owned by military top brass that was cheating on its declarations. He fined the company heavily and bankrupted it. The generals came after him. 'They tried to destroy me,' says Amnuay. 'They charged me with all sorts of things. If they had only come to me and said, "We want you out," I would gladly have resigned. I didn't want the job – I didn't want to be in government in the first place.'[1]

Like Anand, Amnuay was exonerated, but he was quicker to exit government service. Unlike most other civil servants of their generation, Amnuay and Anand would emerge from these setbacks dealt by the military with a rare qualification: after ending top-flight careers as civil servants unhappily, they both rebounded with successful second lives in the private sector.

By Amnuay's account, the very evening he stepped aside after falling foul of the military, Damri arrived at his home to offer him the executive chairmanship at Saha Union. Amnuay accepted. Soon after, Damri's brother-in-law stood aside to allow Amnuay the full chairmanship. 'I knew that Saha Union was one of the few companies with an impeccable reputation,' says Amnuay. 'They would never cheat the government on taxation. They had honesty and integrity. That's what I liked about Damri.'

Now, in Bonn, Anand had a surprise for Amnuay. '[He] said he wanted to leave the government and find a job in the private sector,' Amnuay recalls. 'He asked if I could help him.' It so happened that at the time, Amnuay was setting up an international trading company as a wholly owned subsidiary of Saha Union. 'I thought he had potential, so I told him, "Yes, certainly."'

Amnuay viewed Anand as an ideal prospective chairman for the new trading company and also as a vice chairman for Saha Union, despite his lack of prior commercial experience. He and Damri offered Anand the job on the spot. 'Khun Anand was a bit upset with the civil service at that time,' Damri recalls of the encounter with Anand through Amnuay. 'Both men are good people and intelligent. When Amnuay first resigned, his friends all disappeared knowing he had been forced out. When friends are in trouble, I always want to help. I didn't really care what people thought of me.'

'It was the first time I got to meet Damri,' says Anand, 'and I think we liked each other.' The Saha Union conglomerate was in many ways exactly what Anand had been seeking. It had started out manufacturing buttons and zippers and then branched off into textiles with integrated spinning and dyeing. The textile business involved some operational contact with the commerce ministry, but little beyond that. There were no government procurement elements in Saha Union's business that required 'tea money' or payoffs. The business hinged on foreign export quotas that could be accumulated on competitive merit, capacity and reliability rather than by corrupt means. The company stood independently on its own merits. It only had to worry about doing business, paying taxes in full and on time, meeting its obligations to its employees, and then hopefully turning a profit.

'Our guiding principle as a company is to do business morally, focussing on quality and on creating benefits,' says Damri. 'There are many businesses we cannot participate in exactly because of this. If I didn't care, I would be far richer by now.' Similar sentiments are expressed by Jongrak, Damri's wife. 'We only have one set of books,' she says. 'We don't do anything that is not straightforward. We have nothing to hide – many business people do.'

Having spent slightly longer in Bonn than the year he had originally planned, Anand quietly wrapped up his diplomatic career at the end of 1978. Anand had been happy with his work in Bonn, but was looking forward to his new career.

'I left with no regrets, no resentment,' he recalls. 'What is past is past. It was a blessing in disguise.' No discreet attempt was made to dissuade him from leaving the institution he had joined in 1956, devoted half his life to, and at one point ran.

Anand's new life at Saha Union began early in 1979. He often refers to this pivotal moment as his 'second birth'. And not for the last time in his career, he started at the top in a position for which he had no previous experience.

Second birth

Anand was bridging two worlds that seldom understood each other. He was making a transition from a world in which advancement usually came through regulated promotions and appointments into a more meritocratic environment, where talent needed to be identified and nurtured for efficiency and economic gain; a world that did not disburse budgets but generated wealth.

In personal terms, Anand was suddenly much more comfortably off than he had ever been as an ambassador, with his basic income almost tripling. He and Sodsee were now settled in the new family home – like the first, on Sukhumvit Soi 53 – which had been built during his final years in Washington on land given by Sodsee's parents. Initially, it had been rented out to a Japanese family by one of his sisters who helped with his financial affairs. Back home, Anand found himself free to socialise with old friends he had lacked the time and money to go out with in the past. He enjoyed the clean break he had made with government, and generally took no interest in politics.

Although these years were dryer professionally, and much less dramatic than Anand's career peaks in international diplomacy, they were key to his future understanding of the way Thailand works as a society, particularly in terms of business and politics. The next 12 years would provide first-hand insights into Thailand's enormous economic potential – and also its aching shortcomings.

Like many countries, Thailand has a long history of civil servants taking up lucrative private directorships when they reach retirement. Directorships in the same sector as former ministries carry a strong whiff of payoff, but the practice is so common globally as to be unremarkable. Although civil servants retiring early, with transfers to the private sector, became more frequent in Thailand in the booming late 1980s and the 1990s, when foreign capital flooded into the country and sent corporate salaries through the roof, it was most unusual for such a senior public servant to enter the corporate world at such a young age. Thai civil servants normally retire at 60; Anand was only 47.

Amnuay's shift to Saha Union was perhaps the only comparable example, although Amnuay arrived much better versed in private-sector principles, numbers, and finance. Anand could not have hoped for a better mentor – and Amnuay has never been shy of taking credit for tutoring the future prime minister. 'Anand is very knowledgeable about European history and cricket,' he says. 'He was not trained as a businessman. When he joined me at Saha Union, I had to teach him how to read balance sheets.'

Anand willingly concedes the point. 'All through his career, Amnuay had always been in touch with the commercial world,' he says. 'I was totally clueless. I did not have a financial background. I had to learn new words and simple things. It took me about two years to learn the ropes and how to read balance sheets.' Anand recalls their relationship as always more mutually respectful than intimate. 'Amnuay was not arrogant, but not always a good listener,' he says.

Soon after joining Saha Union, Anand visited Jakarta on a textile industry mission. He was staying at the Mandarin Oriental next to the Thai embassy, and looked up Tej Bunnag, the China expert he had worked with in 1975 and subsequently posted to Indonesia when he was permanent secretary. The posting had spared Tej the post-Thammasat purge of the foreign ministry.

'I remember Anand saying that he was very grateful to Amnuay Viravan for bringing him in,' Tej recalls. 'He intended to work for Saha Union full time and not be just a decorative item. He was determined to really master the private sector.' Tej also recalls a former Indonesian diplomat at the United Nations asking after Anand.

'He is a captain of industry now, sir,' said Tej.

'He is a captain of everything,' laughed the Indonesian.

Saha Union is very much a Chinese conglomerate, but its logo features the Venus de Milo, the famous classical Greek statue of the Aphrodite of Milos with both arms now missing. The semi-nude of the Greek goddess of love is on show at the Musée du Louvre in Paris. By Damri's account, an image of the sculpture caught his eye on a trip to Europe. 'When I began the business, I started with zippers,' says Damri. 'Zippers are largely used by women, so we chose Venus. When we went into garments, I kept Venus because she is a symbol of beauty and brought us a lot of business success and prosperity.' A small reproduction of the

Sern and Pruek Panyarachun, formally titled Phya and Khunying Prichanusat, with nine of their 12 children in about 1930, before the birth of Anand in 1932. Three of Anand's brothers are present: Rak at the back, Kusa in the middle, and Prasat on the left. Six of his seven sisters are present: from left, Suthira, Koonti, Karnthana, Chitra, Pritha, and Dusadee.

TOP LEFT: *Anand (front left) with his parents. Sitting on Sern's lap is Anand's eldest niece,* ML *Suratee.*

TOP RIGHT: *Anand (standing left) with his sister Supapan and brother Chat. Sitting in front are Anand's nieces (from left) Nantha, Charatsri,* ML *Suratee, and Aporn, and his nephew* ML *Birabhongse (second from right).*

ABOVE: *Anand (left) and Chat (right) with nieces* ML *Suratee and Charatsri and nephew* ML *Birabhongse in between.*

(ALL PHOTOS FROM THE PANYARACHUN FAMILY COLLECTION)

TOP: *Sern Panyarachun presenting a book to King Ananda Mahidol in Lausanne, Switzerland, during Sern's visit to Europe in 1938. Prince Bhumibol Adulyadej is looking on.*

ABOVE: *A postcard sent from Europe to Thailand showing Sern and Pruek Panyarachun with their two oldest sons, Rak (left) and Kusa.*

(BOTH PHOTOS FROM THE PANYARACHUN FAMILY COLLECTION)

TOP: *Anand (centre background) with other Thai students on a Samakki Samakhom students' retreat in the UK in 1949. From second left, Arsa Sarasin, Thep Chaturachinda, Chavalit Yodmani, ML Birabhongse, with MR Tongnoi Tongyai in front.*

ABOVE: *Blew House, 1951, Anand's boarding house at Dulwich College in London. Housemaster Eric Parsley is seated in the front row with his deputy E.C.C. Wynter standing behind him. Anand is seated second from left with other prefects.*

(BOTH PHOTOS FROM THE PANYARACHUN FAMILY COLLECTION)

ABOVE: *Portraits of Christopher Herman Gilkes, the Master at Dulwich College, showing how dramatically he aged during the time he ran the school from 1941 to his early death in 1953.*

(BOTH PHOTOS WITH THE KIND PERMISSION OF THE GOVERNORS OF DULWICH COLLEGE ©)

BELOW: *Anand (front row right) was captain of tennis at Dulwich College in 1951 and 1952.*

(PANYARACHUN FAMILY COLLECTION)

Anand graduating from Trinity College, University of Cambridge, in 1955.
(PANYARACHUN FAMILY COLLECTION)

TOP: MR *Sodsee and Anand on their engagement day in early 1956.*
ABOVE: MR *Sodsee and Anand on their wedding day, 4 May 1956.*
(*BOTH PHOTOS FROM THE PANYARACHUN FAMILY COLLECTION*)

LEFT: *Thanat Khoman, Thailand's foreign minister from 1959 to 1971.*

BELOW: *Thanat Khoman hosting President Lyndon Johnson during a visit to Thailand in October 1966.*

(BOTH PHOTOS FROM THE MINISTRY OF FOREIGN AFFAIRS ARCHIVE)

TOP: *UN Secretary General U Thant received King Bhumibol and Queen Sirikit during their visit to New York in June 1967. Foreign Minister Thanat Khoman is standing left. Anand (right) was at this time the newly appointed ambassador to Canada and concurrently Thailand's acting permanent representative to the United Nations in New York.* (MINISTRY OF FOREIGN AFFAIRS ARCHIVE)

ABOVE: *UN General Assembly 1967. Front row from left, Sompong Sucharitkul, Anand, Thanat Khoman; back row from left, MR Kasemsomosorn Kasemsri, Nissai Vejjajiva, and Klos Visesurakarn.* (PANYARACHUN FAMILY COLLECTION)

TOP: *Anand, during his tenure as Thailand's ambassador to the US, presents his credentials to President Richard Nixon, 1972.*

ABOVE: *Anand presents his credentials as Thailand's first ambassador to Canada to Governor General Roland Michener, 1967.*

TOP: *Anand and* MR *Sodsee with UN Secretary General Kurt Waldheim in December 1972.*
(MINISTRY OF FOREIGN AFFAIRS ARCHIVE)

ABOVE: *UN General Assembly, 1973. Middle row from left, Permanent Secretary Phan Wannamethee, Anand, Foreign Minister Chatichai Choonhavan; behind from left, ACM Siddhi Savetsila, and Sukho Suwansiri.*

(PANYARACHUN FAMILY COLLECTION)

TOP: *Anand's seven sisters (from left in ascending age) Supapan, Karnthana, Dusadee, Chitra, Koonti, Pritha, and Suthira in the 1960s.*

ABOVE: *Anand's entire immediate family with their spouses and parents (seated centre). The brothers in the front row are (from left) Rak, Kusa, Prasat, Chat, and Anand.*

(BOTH PHOTOS FROM THE PANYARACHUN FAMILY COLLECTION)

TOP: *Anand and MR Sodsee with their daughters, Daranee and Nanda, at an embassy fair in Ottawa. In the background is Samphan Udomritthiruj, the wife of Kamthorn, the* chargé d'affaires.

ABOVE: *Sern and Pruek with all 12 of their children in 1972, on one of only three or four occasions the entire family was together.*

TOP: *Anand welcoming Huang Hua, China's first permanent representative to the United Nations, to a reception marking King Bhumibol Adulyadej's birthday in December 1972. The two diplomats had initially met secretly in New York.* (MINISTRY OF FOREIGN AFFAIRS ARCHIVE)

ABOVE: *Anand (second from right) aboard a train in 1974 during a visit to Pyongyang, North Korea, with Prasong Sukhum (front left) the deputy commerce minister.* (PANYARACHUN FAMILY COLLECTION)

TOP: *Anand briefly met with Chairman Mao ahead of an hour-long meeting Mao had with Prime Minister MR Kukrit Pramoj, standing in the centre.* (MINISTRY OF FOREIGN AFFAIRS ARCHIVE)

ABOVE: *Anand and MR Sodsee with the assistant military* attachés *at the Thai embassy in Washington. On the left is Commander Paisarn Punyasanti of the Royal Thai Navy with his wife Chomsri; on the right, Colonel Suchinda Kraprayoon with his wife, Wannee.*

(PANYARACHUN FAMILY COLLECTION)

Prime Minister MR Kukrit Pramoj (front right) waves as the official Thai delegation is given a major reception led by Deputy Prime Minister Deng Xiaoping (front left) at Beijing airport when it arrived on 30 June 1975 to establish diplomatic relations with China. Behind Kukrit in dark suits are (from right) Chawan Chawanid (partially obscured); Foreign Minister Chatichai Choonhavan; Prakaipet Indhusophon (partially obscured), secretary general to the prime minister; Anand; and Sathit Sathirathai, the chief of protocol. The Thai army officer behind Kukrit is General Fuangchaloei Aniruth-Deva (partially obscured). (MINISTRY OF FOREIGN AFFAIRS ARCHIVE)

In a speech later in the Great Hall of the People responding to Deng, Kukrit said: 'The government of the Kingdom of Thailand is convinced that even though the Kingdom of Thailand and the People's Republic of China have differing political, economic, and social systems, that should not constitute an obstacle to the development of peaceful and amicable relations between our two countries and peoples on the basis of the principles of pancha sila.'* [Peking Review, No. 27. 4 July 1975]

* The five principles of pancha sila in international relations are: mutual respect for each other's territorial integrity and sovereignty; mutual non-aggression; mutual non-interference in each other's internal affairs; equality and cooperation for mutual benefit; and peaceful co-existence.

Venus de Milo still peeps out on top of a cupboard in the hallway of Amnuay's large home in central Bangkok.

When Anand entered beneath the Venus de Milo at the old Saha Union head office in Lart Phrao, northern Bangkok, he was immediately assigned a personal secretary, Busarakham Nilavajara, 26, who had studied geography and education at Chulalongkorn University. At Saha Union, she was involved in programmes to teach the Thai language and some non-curriculum subjects to employees, and she also tutored a Singaporean executive in Thai. Busarakham did not answer to any particular boss before Anand's arrival. 'I was assigned to him maybe because I was the only person who spoke English,' she says. 'He had been a permanent secretary, and that scared me. I was very worried about how I could do the job. I remember making lots of mistakes and thought of quitting many times in the first year.'

'I work very fast, and sometimes private staff cannot catch up,' says Anand. 'I used to be very hot-tempered with my office people. Sometimes I was too harsh on them. I had become a slave master. They understand me, my subordinates. They know my temperament, which is at fault, but basically I am a decent guy. If I blow up, that's it – it's past. As time went by, I instilled more self-discipline in myself otherwise I would burst out. If I made a slip – perhaps chose a wrong word – if I felt I made people uneasy, I would apologise. Never be afraid to apologise, never be afraid to admit mistakes – and never be afraid to make mistakes either.'

Anand had reduced secretaries to tears in the past, but not Busarakham. Now he was on a fresh path, acquiring new skills himself; perhaps he was finding it easier to empathise with others who were also finding their way. Busarakham went forward step-by-step, gaining confidence, and after the traumas of the first year found that things improved. 'He was very patient and gave me encouragement,' she says. 'When he sees you are efficient, he gives you freedom to get on with the work. That gave me confidence.' She has remained with him ever since, even in retirement.

Anand seldom arrived early at the office but always stayed late until his work was done. Busarakham observed a quick learner who listened attentively at meetings and contributed ideas. 'He enjoys everything that he does,' she says. 'He is something of a workaholic who works fast and thinks fast.'

Damri continued to serve as Saha Union's president and it was he who ran the company. Despite all the directorships of subsidiaries he took on, particularly in the late 1980s, at no time in his 24-year career with Saha Union would Anand ever be involved in operations. His contribution was more strategic; his value lay in his ever-expanding contacts at home and expertise in international relations. He was well known in China for his diplomacy in the 1970s, and in the late 1980s and 1990s Saha Union went on to increase its presence there significantly. 'I have a special place in China,' says Anand. 'They knew who I was and that was very useful.'

At home, Saha Union assigned him to liaise with the Thai Chamber of Commerce and the Board of Trade. In 1980, he was appointed vice chairman of Union Textile Industries, the Saha Union subsidiary Amnuay and Damri had originally earmarked for him at the meeting in Bonn. In 1981, he became chairman of the Association of Thai International Trading Companies (ATITC), a position he occupied for the next 10 years.

At the same time, he was invited to become one of two vice presidents of the Association of Thai Industries (ATI). The other was Pong Sarasin. ATI belonged to the ASEAN Chambers of Commerce and Industry (ACCI), which had four other members from counterpart organisations in Indonesia, Malaysia, the Philippines, and Singapore. Brunei contributed a fifth when it joined ASEAN in 1984.

In 1982, Thailand's turn to chair the ACCI was 18 months away, and a problem loomed. The ATI president, Thavorn Pornpraphas of Siam Motors, lacked the English-language skills for the job. Deputy Prime Minister Boonchu Rojanastien, a former president of Bangkok Bank, approached Anand and asked him to get involved. In 1982, he became the ACCI president for a two-year term. He continued as vice president there until 1989.

From 1982 to 1983, Anand chaired the Task Force on ASEAN Co-operation. This was charged with charting a course for greater economic integration within the group, and was an early stirring of what would develop into the ASEAN Free Trade Area (AFTA) in the 1990s. This initiative always had strong intellectual backing from Singapore, but as a geographically minor member of ASEAN the island republic lacked the clout to take the lead in such matters. Indeed, economic harmonisation was always treated with the greatest indifference by Indonesia, the most populous and powerful member of the six-member regional grouping, and the member with the largest economy.

From 1986, Anand chaired the ASEAN section of the US-ASEAN Center for Technology Exchange, which he had joined in 1985 at the time of its establishment. President Ronald Reagan was in office, and the centre enjoyed strong US corporate support. Its purpose was to foster technological transfers and direct investment from the US into ASEAN.[2]

As with many similar accommodations that were to follow, Saha Union was happy to go along with its vice chairman's numerous external endeavours. Anand's networking activities at home and abroad over the next 12 years were prodigious – and remained so over the following three decades. He joined the international council of the Asia Society in 1980 and served on it for six years, and later served for four years as a director of the John E. Peurifoy Foundation, which funds Fulbright scholars from Thailand. In the year he joined Saha Union, Anand also became a council member of the influential National Institute of Development Administration (NIDA), serving until 1991.

Anand's foreign networking contributed to Saha Union's expansion as an increasingly diversified conglomerate. He had good relations with IBM, which brought in computer hard-disk manufacturing, a very profitable line of business. There was also the Nippon Industrial Fastener Company (NIFCO), which established Union Nifco, a subsidiary owned jointly with Saha Union, in Thailand in 1988. NIFCO's president from 1967, Toshiaki Ogasawara, had taken his masters at Princeton University's Woodrow Wilson School of Public and International Affairs in the 1960s.[3] Anand also got to know Phil Knight of Nike, whom he visited in Portland, after Saha Union took on contract manufacturing for the US sportswear company. Nike was another of Amnuay's initiatives.

Outside Saha Union, Anand was spreading his wings. In 1982, he became chairman of Star Block, a property development company founded by Suthep Bulakul. He was also appointed a director of Sime Darby, a Malaysian conglomerate founded in the 19th century by British planters. Two years later, he joined the board of Siam Commercial Bank.

In 1990, Anand became a trustee of the Asian Institute of Technology. He remained involved until 2006, and served as chairman for the last six years. He was also appointed a member of the World Management Council at this time, and in January 1991 became a member of the Business Council for Sustainable Development.

At various times in the mid-to-late 1980s, Anand served with the University Bureau Committee, the Science and Technology Development Council, the advisory council of the Sasin Graduate Business Administration Institute at Chulalongkorn University (a position he holds to this day), the Export Development Committee, and in the early 1990s the Chulalongkorn University Council. He also sat on various parliamentary standing committees for foreign affairs and trade. At the request of Arsa Sarasin, he joined a high-powered selection committee vetting applicants to the Ministry of Foreign Affairs.

The wide-ranging networks Anand built up at this time among technocrats, business people and academics, and with institutions dealing broadly with national development, would be key to structuring his unusually effective cabinets when he later became prime minister.

Thailand's transition

One of the most influential people with whom Anand came into contact in the 1980s was Dr Snoh Unakul. In 1984, Anand became a trustee of the new Thailand Development Research Institute (TDRI), a development think tank created by Snoh, the head of the National Economic and Social Development Board (NESDB). NESDB had generated Thailand's five-year development plans ever since their launch in the early 1960s under Field Marshal Sarit Thanarat.

After the Thammasat massacre in 1976, Puey Ungphakorn, the great economist and long-time governor of the Bank of Thailand, returned from self-exile in Britain just once, in 1997. In his absence, Snoh became Thailand's most prominent technocrat. He served as the national development czar during the governments of Prem Tinsulanond, the retired general who had served as Thailand's unelected prime minister from March 1980 to August 1988.

After the tumultuous, divisive, and violent politics of the 1970s, Prem's eight-year stewardship was a crucial period of national economic repositioning against a background of relative political calm and moderated democratic development. Prem had five cabinets, each with progressively more elected politicians as ministers and fewer appointments from outside. He survived a number of assassination attempts. There were also failed coups – in 1981 and 1985 – staged by the Young Turks of Class 7, junior officers who had backed his predecessor, General Kriangsak Chomanand, at crucial junctures. Guided by Snoh, Prem's governments tackled an economic slowdown in the mid-1980s, strove to build up manufacturing, and fostered export-led growth.

'By keeping macroeconomic fundamentals strong, with low inflation, a sound fiscal policy, manageable external debts and a low current-account deficit, the soldiers and technocrats managed to make Thailand part of East Asia's economic development miracle,' explains Pavida Pananond, a professor of business.[4] 'The foreign investment-led transformation of the predominantly rural economy into a production and export base for heavy industries was the formula that led Thailand to double-digit annual economic growth in the late 1980s.'[5]

With its contiguous landmass, Thailand had an immense inbuilt advantage over countries such as the Philippines and Indonesia when it came to developing infrastructure, particularly highways, water supply, and power. But even with the vision of men like Snoh, who got things done no matter which government came or went, Thailand's development was often chaotic and crisis-driven: airports were only upgraded when they were handling double their capacity, and expressways arrived only after Bangkok had experienced countless hours of pure gridlock.

'The problem in Thailand is there is no incentive for taking action,' says Bill Heinecke, a billionaire American businessman and long-term resident who took Thai nationality. He believes people in Thailand are quick to point fingers and more than usually suspicious of self-serving motives in others. 'What you really want is a benign despot,' he argues.

But if they are to succeed, Thailand's benign despots must be able to ride a number of dragons; they must contend with self-seeking politicians, a voracious and often unprincipled business class, fiercely competitive factions within the military, idealistic students, and politicised labour movements.

'Thailand has given a gift to the world by showing how little governance is sometimes necessary to run a country,' counters Jim Rooney, a businessman and former AmCham president. 'One of the things that amazes me is that Thailand can tick along irrespective of what the government does. This may be because, unlike other countries of Southeast Asia, Thailand has assimilated the Chinese quite well into the fabric of the country – and the Chinese will always find a way to do business.'

Jim Rooney maintained a warm friendship with Anand throughout Anand's early Saha Union years. He found the new vice chairman increasingly visible at business functions and always refreshingly open. Their interests also overlapped beyond Thailand. In the 1980s, Rooney chaired the Asia-Pacific Council for American Chambers of Commerce, and often visited Washington for networking. 'You got a feeling of a lot of energy,' he recalls of Anand. 'You always took something away from a meeting with him.'

Bill Heinecke, one of Rooney's successors as AmCham president, was keen to tap that energy for the chamber. 'Anand was quite a dashing man,' says Heinecke, who had first met Anand in the early 1970s when he was ambassador in Washington. 'He was always the elder statesman – the guy you admired for what he did and how he balanced things, and for the sacrifices he had made for the country. He was always very keen on foreign investment in Thailand and the positive influences of foreign involvement.'

Heinecke had started his business in the late 1960s when he was still a minor, and the multi-billion-dollar corporation he built up is still known as the Minor Group. An irrepressible entrepreneur with passions for fast cars and planes, Heinecke was initially refused entry into AmCham because of his youth. Having once been rebuffed, he was determined to leave his mark. In 1981, at 32, he became the youngest president in the chamber's history. He regarded the chamber as a rather insular gentlemen's club.

For all its shortcomings, AmCham was influential in the Thai business world, and aspired to being more so, although it would soon be eclipsed by its Japanese counterpart. In the 1980s, the chamber was much more involved in lobbying and producing position papers on customs, taxation, and business processes, and less with the charity and social diversions it undertakes today.

'I tried to get incredible speakers,' Heinecke recalls of his presidency. 'I said, "Let's have some Thais here who actually know what's happening in the country instead of a bunch of *farangs* [Westerners]."'

Heinecke wanted to break the AmCham mould and induct influential, highly informed Thais on to the board of governors itself. The tough part was convincing his conservative expatriate board that top-drawer locals should be *invited* to join and not be expected to run for office. Heinecke's thinking was that they were doing AmCham a favour, not vice versa. 'They don't want to join your private club,' Heinecke told his board. He regarded it as a great coup when Anand agreed to come aboard as a governor in 1981 for three years along with Amaret Sila-on, an executive with Siam Cement, and Tarrin Nimmanahaeminda, the president and chief executive officer of Siam Commercial Bank.

The timing was good. Among other things, the US was pushing anti-corruption legislation that threatened to cramp American corporations operating overseas. It was a very tricky issue, particularly in the Thai context.

'How could you be against the Foreign Corrupt Practices Act?' asks Heinecke rhetorically, raising his eyes and hands comically to the ceiling with a helpless shrug. Everybody knew competitors such as France and Japan would not play by the same rules. Heinecke believed it would be better if Thais themselves explained the law's shortcomings and pitfalls to US legislators. In particular, he remembers Amaret meeting with Senator Edward Kennedy and explaining the cultural significance of gifts in Thailand, and how Thais would never take kindly to foreigners telling them who could give what to whom and when – particularly when donations to royal charities or projects were involved. Facilitation charges, for example, might not have been legal in the US but they were normal in Thailand. Reasonable account had to be taken of such local business conditions or US businesses would simply be unable to function.

Even as Congress threatened to tie US multinationals up in knots, plenty of companies remained bullish on Thailand. Unocal[6] was opening up vast natural gas fields in the Gulf of Thailand and Northrop Grumman was offering to build a new airport for Bangkok at Nong Ngu Hao – at no cost.[7]

Nobody doubted that AmCham benefited considerably from the involvement of Anand, Amaret, and Tarrin, with their deep understandings of commerce and finance – but the three-year experiment was never repeated. Comparable personalities on both sides were never in the mix again.

The benefits of this cross-pollination were by no means one-sided. Even after stepping down as a governor, Anand maintained a connection. In 1985, he led an AmCham team that briefed eight visiting US congressmen and an aide to President Reagan on the unsoundness of a protectionist bill, the Textile and Apparel Trade Enforcement Act, being tabled by Congressman Ed Jenkins. It seriously threatened the Thai textile and clothing industry, including Anand's own industry-leading company, Saha Union. The Jenkins Bill, as it was dubbed, was defeated the following year.[8] In 1988, Anand joined an *ad hoc* committee for a year advising the US congress on the Omnibus Trade and Competitiveness Act.

'Those are the sort of people I grew up admiring, my heroes so to speak,' says Heinecke of Anand and his generation. 'The nice thing is the Thais accept you. They were never colonised and therefore don't have a chip on their shoulders. If you are smart enough to make some money, good for you. They don't mind.'[9]

Thailand during the 1980s was seeing rapid economic growth. It was a time of incremental democratisation stewarded by Prime Minister Prem Tinsulanond, a former army chief famous for a smile that disguised a steely inner resolve and great tactical shrewdness. Grappling constantly with difficult party politics, Prem oversaw a crucial transformational period in Thailand's post-war history, shifting it forever beyond being a simple commodity exporter.

Prem had surfaced as a pragmatic force after playing an important part in the late 1970s, cajoling leftist students from the forests back into the fold. He brought political stability after a rollercoaster decade that produced eight governments, three coups and considerable bloodshed. It was his predecessor as army chief, General Kriangsak Chomanand, who had engineered Anand's removal as permanent secretary at the foreign ministry in 1976, but Kriangsak steadily lost support, particularly in the military, after taking power himself in 1977. Prem's consolidation of power at that time forced Kriangsak's departure, and has been described as an 'invisible coup'.

'Above all the new premier is a staunch monarchist, serving as royal *aide de camp* in both 1969 and 1975,' a foreign correspondent wrote of Prem's ascent. 'His appointment as premier is said to have delighted the king.'[10]

Heinecke was optimistic about Thailand's prospects under Prem's leadership, but his enthusiasm was sometimes doused. In 1981, he accompanied Prem to the US and drafted one of the speeches he was to give during stops in New York and Dallas. One day, Snoh brought Heinecke to Prem's suite at the Waldorf Astoria hotel in New York, only to be refused entry by Chamlong Srimuang, the prime minister's secretary. 'He didn't like foreigners and was very protective of Prem,' Heinecke recalls of Chamlong's blockade.[11]

Prem, for his part, was always circumspect and retiring, and not just with foreigners. 'General Prem was very reluctant to have any session for the press to ask questions,' recalls Mechai Viravaidya, who served in Prem's final cabinets and was one of Thailand's most media-savvy operators. When Mechai once organised a get-together with reporters, Prem, who always looked so benign in public, reproved him sternly afterwards: 'Never again.' When Chatichai was about to replace 'Pa Prem' as prime minister in 1988, Prem told the press, 'Go back home, children.'

'Prem was much admired not because he talked but because he did not talk,' reflects Manaspas Xuto. He remembers him listening to Chancellor Bruno Kreisky of Austria talk for 45 minutes about world affairs, including the Cambodian situation. Prem did not say a word.

'Prem was very easily piqued,' according to Manaspas. When he, Manaspas, was ambassador to Austria, he was exceedingly careful with preparations when Prem visited. 'He loved anyone who called him "Pa",' Manaspas recalls, so when the band happened to strike up "Oh! My Papa" one night, it went down very well.[12]

One of Anand's most high-profile positions was as vice president of the Association of Thai Industries (ATI) from 1980 to 1987, when it became the Federation of Thai Industries (FTI). He served as vice chairman of the FTI until 1990, when he became chairman, replacing Paron Israsena Na Ayudhaya. In the late 1980s, Anand played a key role in recasting the ATI as a federation. This required an act of parliament, and the young Chulalongkorn law professor drafted in to advise on technicalities was Wissanu Krea-ngam, one of the jet-lagged students Anand had lectured mercilessly for an hour in 1973 when he was ambassador in Washington. It was the first of many dealings between the two men in the years to come, many of which would be much more serious in substance.

In meetings, Wissanu noticed that Anand assumed a natural leadership position, and was the only member of the ATI board to really probe him. 'I asked somebody if he was a lawyer,' Wissanu recalls of one meeting. 'Anand asked deep and practical questions, and spotted loopholes. I was very surprised because I had just shown him the draft without preparation.'

Wissanu was also struck by Anand's constant concern about creating a level playing field. 'You should start with fairness from the outset, otherwise people will abuse it,' Anand lectured him. He always wanted ambiguous wording removed: 'may' became 'shall' or 'must'.

The bill to upgrade the ATI to federation status had to be submitted by the industry minister, Ob Vasuratr, who was initially sceptical. He had himself been the ATI president, and could see no problem with the old status. Wissanu knew that if Ob could not be convinced, the bill would not reach parliament. Anand was the ATI board's choice for talking the minister round, but Wissanu feared he might be too abrasive: 'That is his character.' He thought Paron might be more persuasive, and even at one stage volunteered for the job himself; but Paron stuck with Anand. When Anand met Ob, he was humble and polite and used lots of analogies and lucid explanations. He reminded Ob that the association had far fewer members in his days as president, when it could fall back on his personal *baramee*.[13] Times had changed and the new law was essential, Anand contended.

'We need more *baramee*,' Anand told Ob. 'Okay, I shall give you more *baramee*,' the minister promised. Persuaded by Anand, Ob supported the bill vigorously in parliament and helped see it through. 'That was a lesson for me about convincing older people,' says Wissanu.

Saha Union hit its peak in Thailand in the 1980s and 1990s, but has since shrunk as the business sectors in which it could compete have diminished. In the late 1980s, the company's focus began shifting to China with its vast market and low costs. Saha Union still manufactures hard disks, and is an independent power producer, but it no longer has a relationship with Nike, and textiles are a sunset industry facing fierce price competition. Indeed, Saha Union has made no serious investment in Thailand in the 21st century. Anand's relationship with Damri Darakananda has weathered the years well, however.

Damri enjoyed a close relationship with Chin Sophonpanich, the founder and chairman of Bangkok Bank. However, he always refused to join the bank as a director, saying that his assured goodwill was enough. Chin once asked Damri personally to take over a troubled business. This became Union Textile Mill, with Damri as president; it complemented Saha Union's plans for integrated textile production with spinning, dyeing, and weaving.

Amnuay too was close to Bangkok Bank, and accepted an invitation to become a full-time board director. After Amnuay moved over, Anand continued as vice chairman of Saha Union, although he did not become chairman until January 1991. Some tension had developed between the two men over how to address various business problems. Saha Union became over-extended at one point, and Amnuay was determined to cut marginal companies. 'Anand and the others did not understand the intricacies of finance,' he says.

Anand's main recollection of Amnuay's departure was wishing that he would stay. 'Amnuay made a much larger contribution to Saha Union's business success than I ever did,' he says. 'I never played that central role in the Saha Union hierarchy. I was a good addition – I filled up some weak areas in terms of connections and liaisons with foreign companies.' This was particularly true in China, where there was recognition of the role Anand had played in normalising relations in the earlier part of the 1970s. 'In China, they say people always remember the man who dug the village well,' says Anand.

'Frankly, Saha Union is not a product of any particular president or chairman,' says Damri. 'Every manager and every employee at all levels contributed to its creation. Khun Anand contributed to this particularly by focusing on good governance – he worked a lot on that. At Saha Union, ideas tend to be initiated from the bottom, and trickle up rather than down. It was not Anand giving them ideas – employees gave him ideas.'

'Damri recognised Amnuay's contribution,' says Anand. 'In my case, I did not contribute so much but he knew that I was genuine. In a way, his character and mine are compatible. I always told him the truth.'

Damri was well aware that Anand had declined ministerial appointments on several occasions. He always gave Anand a remarkably free hand to pursue other activities, both domestic and regional, which were unrelated to Saha Union's core business. 'We at Saha Union did not take any leadership role but gave him freedom to engage in these national issues,' says Damri. 'Damri let Anand do whatever he wanted,' says Suthichai Yoon. 'He never publicly claimed any authority over Anand although technically he was the boss. Anand was lucky that he had all these good people who let him do the things he wanted.'

Saha Union's approach to industrial relations, outwardly congenial, has always been essentially paternalistic and distrustful of unionised labour. 'We can help [the workforce] solve problems, making it unnecessary for them to join unions,' says Damri. 'I have grown up with the workers from all levels, so I understand their needs. I tried to set up a proper welfare system so each factory could take care of its own workers, which might be better than joining a union. An employee committee looks after benefits and management is highly involved. When employees have problems, they can always be heard.'

During the 1980s, Saha Union's desire to keep outside organised labour movements at bay earned it a reputation for being anti-union, and this led to protests. Staff who wanted to quit with compensation – an entitlement that only came with dismissal – had long known that the best way of securing an exit handshake was to air the topic of unionisation on a Saha Union factory floor. A full departure package would materialise soon enough, and the factory door was courteously opened.

However, Kamol Khoosuwan, Saha Union's former head of personnel, disputes the notion of an actual union ban. 'If employees wanted to form unions, they could,' he says, noting that some of the many companies in the Saha Union conglomerate are in fact unionised. But it is clearly on sufferance.

'We believe if we take good care of employees, be fair, sincere, and open, allow employees to have opportunities to express their views, then management at higher levels can recognise them,' says Kamol. 'At Saha Union, this plays a vital role promoting a working relationship between management and employees. They don't need to go to an outside body to get access to top management.'

Kraisak Choonhavan sees a harder side to Anand when it comes to trade unions. 'I don't think this will even figure in history,' he says. 'Most Thai people will see Anand as a man of good judgment, intelligence, wit – somebody who was able to make sense out of very difficult situations in Thailand.' Kraisak was sympathetic to the attacks on Saha Union over its labour policies in the 1980s, although he never condoned or participated in personal attacks on Anand at that time. 'The protesters did that for themselves,' he says. 'I will always consider [Anand] very close and dear to me.'

Some commentators are more critical. 'Anand Panyarachun is known to be extremely anti-trade union and his Saha Union factories banned all unions,' charged Giles Ji Ungpakorn, a Chulalongkorn University academic and the youngest of Puey's three sons.[14] Giles sees a broader problem. 'Trade union and labour rights are limited, both by repressive laws and actions of the state, but also by the political weakness of the labour movement itself.'

Anand also views Thailand's labour movement as weak and fundamentally flawed. The issue for him is structural, and he traces the issue back to the movement's roots in the 1950s and 1960s, when state enterprise unions were established by Phibun and Sarit – neither of whom brandished progressive credentials.

'[The problem] originates from Phibun's idea of building up a democratic experience, but he was not sincere,' says Anand. 'As a result, all the state enterprise unions were not unions in the right sense of the word. They were tools of politicians. They were not representing workers. The heads of the unions in state enterprises had very friendly and profitable relations with state enterprises, and the army as well. That left a bad taste.'

Anand believes the distorted union experience in the public sector affected perceptions, and stunted the movement's development in the private sector. Thai labour unions did not develop from grassroots, and so they have always been treated with suspicion and hostility by managerial, technocratic, and government elites. Over the years, there have even been attempts to promote industrial estates as union-free zones.

'If they were real unions, I don't think the Thais would object too much,' says

Anand, with more scepticism than hostility. 'We've been accustomed to unions being politicised by the government, the politicians and the military. The other factor is outside interference.'

Above the fray

Unlike Anand, Amnuay had political as well as business ambitions. In 1980 he became finance minister in the first Prem government, serving for three years. Along with Amnuay, Prem appointed another powerful figure with a background at Bangkok Bank: Boonchu Rojanastien of the Social Action Party, who became deputy prime minister. Boonchu at one point approached Anand to test his interest in becoming foreign minister, but Anand declined. Indeed, the position was held all through the Prem governments until mid-1988 by Air Chief Marshal Siddhi Savetsila, the head of the National Security Council in the 1970s whom Anand had antagonised with jokes about his intimate links to the CIA during the Vietnam War years. Siddhi went on to learn the job of diplomacy well, and was held in high regard, particularly by the US. Vietnam, however, would never trust Siddhi because of his hawkish history, and little progress on reconciliation with Indochina was made on Prem's watch.

A more serious attempt to co-opt Anand into the cabinet was made in late 1986, when the prominent businessman and founder of Bangkok University, Surat Osathanugrah, was forced to step down as commerce minister. Kukrit Pramoj, still the most senior figure in the Social Action Party, personally offered Anand the portfolio, but again it was declined.

Anand had strongly held reasons for not accepting. He had no party loyalties, and no desire to enter politics, particularly as an unelected minister in a fractious coalition cabinet. But the reason he gave Kukrit for declining was his wife Sodsee's continuing ill health.

Refusing to accept the unencumbered offer of a ministerial portfolio was fairly remarkable. 'In Thai culture, anybody offered the job would take it without hesitation,' says Anand. Indeed, the assumption was so commonplace that Anand's name was already on the list of the reshuffled cabinet submitted to the palace for King Bhumibol's signature. The document had to be hastily called back for adjustment. Nevertheless, Kukrit immediately accepted Anand's reason.

Amnuay charted a very different course from Anand, who had an almost visceral loathing of party politics. His political career was already well under way and lasted into the mid-1990s. He would come to look back on it with very mixed feelings.

'For me, politics requires sacrifice – of family life, of financial assets for the good of the nation – and you really have nothing to gain,' Amnuay says. 'I say sacrifice because I never made any money from politics. I never accepted any bribes, and I always tried to fight against corruption. That is why I am not well liked, and have a lot of enemies, but I am glad I did what I did.'

CHAPTER 9

A TALE OF TWO COUPS
(1991)

Land of coups

Coups have a special place in Thai political history. King Taksin, Siam's ruler in Thonburi after the fall of Ayutthaya, lost his throne, and ultimately his life, to a coup in 1782. On 24 June 1932, General Phraya Phahol Pholphayusena, leader of the People's Party, staged a revolutionary coup that ended Siam's variant of absolute monarchy. It was the start of a very rocky road to constitutional democracy that has yet to reach its destination. A year later, the same general staged a second coup to quell restive elements in the party. Over the next five years, there were three royalist counter-coup attempts, all of which failed. Since 1932 overall, 22 coups have been attempted, of which 13 have succeeded and nine have failed.[1]

Coups are remarkably easy to stage in a country with an unarmed population, provided there is unity in the military. When they later step aside, the generals concerned have also invariably awarded themselves full pardons, which so far have never been challenged. The leaders of failed coups, or those on the losing side, have been penalised with exile abroad, sometimes permanent but usually relatively brief. Only one officer has ever been executed for attempting a coup, General Chalard Hiranyasiri in 1977; and his crime was murdering a brother officer during its commission – thereby violating an unpublished code respected by the military's senior ranks.

A major problem for Thailand is the abrogation of constitutions each time a coup is successfully staged. Since 1932, Thailand has had 20 constitutions, four of which were interim and 16 purportedly 'permanent'.[2] The lengthiest also lasted the longest: the so-called People's Constitution drawn up in 1997 with Anand serving as chairman of the drafting committee, but it was abrogated with the coup of 2006. None of these charters has so far provided a defence against a military that intermittently casts itself as the final arbiter of the national interest. Some coups, as in 2014, can be justified for averting probable bloodshed, but the military's part in precipitating violent political crises must also then be examined.

It must be said, the generals do not always get everything their own way. The popular ouster of the government of Field Marshals Thanom Kittikachorn and Praphas Charusathien in October 1973 – as close to a coup by the people as Thailand has ever seen – was related to the junta's failure to produce a new constitution after a decade in power.

In October 1977, Admiral Sangad Chaloryu headed his second coup in little over a year to oust the unpopular government of Tanin Kraivixien, which his first coup had installed. There were two failed coups in 1981 and 1985 against governments headed by Prime Minister Prem Tinsulanond, himself a retired general. As the 1980s went by, some political pundits predicted there would be no more. Thailand had outgrown them, they asserted. How wrong they were.

Coup on a plane

Anand's great career setback in October 1976 followed Sangad's first coup, which was underwritten by General Kriangsak Chomanand, the army chief. By 1991, Anand was leading an entirely different life as one of Thailand's most prominent businessmen and industrialists. He had devoted a good part of the previous decade to nurturing Thailand's international business prospects and credibility. All through that time, he had had no dealings with the military. Tin hats, tanks, uniformed businessmen, and coups did not figure in the image that Thailand's economic liberals wished to project. Meanwhile the military had grown rich, and they were far from done with political interference. 'General Suchinda's Class 5 group, in particular, had its own investment managers, and the military used intelligence sources for market research,' wrote a leading foreign correspondent from the time.[3]

In 1988, after the general election in July, Prem Tinsulanond declined a sixth term as prime minister. He was replaced in August by another retired general, Chatichai Choonhavan, the former foreign minister. Unlike Prem, Chatichai had been elected to parliament; he led the right-of-centre Chart Thai Party. As prime minister, Chatichai performed a remarkable balancing act, perched precariously atop a political coalition brimming with venal competing interests.

Outwardly congenial and easy-going, Chatichai had personal unfinished business with the military. This dated back to September 1957, when he had been on the wrong side of the coup staged by Field Marshal Sarit Thanarat against Field Marshal Plaek Phibunsongkhram. Chatichai was himself the son of a field marshal, Phin Choonhavan, who had staged a successful coup in 1947; his opposition to the coup in 1957 could not be overlooked by Sarit and his new order. Chatichai was packed off into exile as ambassador to Argentina, and spent the next 16 years recovering his position in a series of increasingly important diplomatic postings.

As prime minister, Chatichai could be charming but elusive, disarming sceptics with a signature 'no problem' riposte to awkward questions. His key policies included normalising relations with Indochina, which he and his successor as foreign minister, Bhichai Rattakul, had first attempted to do in 1975 and 1976 when Anand was permanent secretary at the ministry.

As prime minister, Chatichai wanted to curb the power of the military and technocrats, allowing the free-wheeling private sector to play a greater role in economic development. He was helped by exceptionally favourable tailwinds: economic growth was in double digits; the property and stock markets were booming as never before; and as a competitive manufacturing hub Thailand was benefiting from overvalued currencies such as the Japanese yen and New Taiwan dollar. Booms in Japan and other parts of East Asia made these countries desperate to move some manufacturing offshore. Thailand offered cheap labour and reasonable infrastructure. Since 1987, foreign investment had dwarfed previous inflows.

It seemed that Thailand only had to leave its doors ajar, and foreign money would come flooding in. There was palpable overconfidence. Dubious fortunes were amassed on the stock market and openly flaunted. Parts of state enterprises were being earmarked for privatisation and modernisation. Civil servants were being seduced into the private sector with massive salaries and perks.

Moves by Snoh Unakul, Prem's economic development czar, to privatise state enterprises were causing serious friction with the military, given its myriad vested interests. He was sidelined soon enough in 1989, after one of the wives in his technocrat group coined the term 'buffet cabinet' to describe the more corrupt elements in Chatichai's government. When the snipe appeared in a newspaper column, Snoh was dismissed by a furious Chatichai.

Snoh's stature was enormous. Technocrats from the Thailand Development Research Institute (TDRI) had been immensely influential since Snoh founded it as chairman in the mid-1980s. Ammar Siamwalla, one of Thailand's most distinguished economists, recalls that during Prem's time, TDRI was very much a part of the government. 'We were almost a ministry. At every cabinet meeting, we had an inner group of technocrats sitting around.'

Snoh was replaced by his reluctant deputy, Pisit Pakkasem, who was touring US nuclear power plants when he received the news. Pisit wanted Snoh to be left to retire quietly at the end of the year, but Chatichai was adamant. It was a lesson in the perils that stalk public figures. 'When you are walking uphill, say hello to everyone because you will meet them again coming down,' says Pisit, sharing the widespread Thai technocrat disdain for politicians.

In one of many departures from Prem's governments, which had placed great store in old-school technocrats, Chatichai took his cues from an unelected group of young advisers, some of whom were appointed senators. His admiration for them was not unqualified. They included his own son Kraisak, who was regarded as left of centre and more socially conscious. Chatichai once described Kraisak to Anand as an 'air-conditioned socialist', after waking up one Sunday to an empty house. Kraisak, he complained, had given all the servants a day off.

Among the other advisers were Pansak Vinyaratn (a future key adviser also to Prime Minister Thaksin Shinawatra and subsequently to Thaksin's youngest sister, Yingluck); Borwornsak Uwanno, a law academic; and MR Sukhumbhand Paribatra, a great-grandson of King Chulalongkorn, a future deputy foreign minister and two-term governor of Bangkok.

Chatichai's youthful think tank was named after its operating base at Baan Phitsanulok, an Italianate building near Government House. Both buildings date from the reign of King Vajiravudh in the early 20th century. Baan Phitsanulok is technically the official residence of the prime minister but, apart from a few uncomfortable nights spent there by Prem, is not used as such. US diplomats at the time referred to it as the Tree House, in view of the young age of its technocrat occupants. The irreverent Americans also assigned them punk musician nicknames. Kraisak was known to some as Johnny Rotten and Pansak as Sid Vicious.

Despite his rank and ancestry, Chatichai's relations with the business-savvy military were uneasy. There was tension with a former army chief, General Chavalit Yongchaiyudh, who harboured such enormous political ambitions that he eventually broke with military tradition and established a political vehicle, the New Aspiration Party, to carry him forward. Chavalit curried public favour by publicly renouncing coups as a means to achieving power, but Chatichai was not about to stand aside and let the retired general have the premiership.

In 1990, Chavalit joined Chatichai's cabinet as minister of defence, a position previously held by the prime minister himself, but soon resigned as his efforts to play civilian politics failed. Chavalit was unpopular with Class 5. The Thai military had always divided into factions competing for promotion. These divisions had become fiercer and more ideological in the difficult period of transition from American tutelage, and had been bottled up during Prem's long period of domination. In the late 1980s, the tensions erupted in contests between members of different classes from the military academy.

Chatichai wanted to promote Chavalit's predecessor as army chief, General Arthit Kamlang-ek, in the hope that he would be more malleable. Arthit had become prominent after shielding the royal family in Korat during the 1981 'April Fool's Day' coup attempt. Subsequently he had been promoted to army chief and supreme commander. His star eventually faded and Prem replaced him with Chavalit.

Arthit was unpopular with both Classes 1 and 5 in the military, which were competing for power. Both these classes hated Class 7, which failed in coup attempts in 1981 and 1985 to unseat Prem. The key figures in Class 7 were Prajak Sawngjit, Manoonkrit Roopkachorn, Chamlong Srimuang, and Pallop Pinmanee. Unwisely, as it turned out, Chatichai gave Manoonkrit a senior advisory position in the Ministry of Defence.[4]

Another problem had been created for Chatichai by his deputy education minister, Chalerm Yubamrung, a former police colonel. Chalerm served Chatichai well as a flak to critics, particularly during no-confidence motions, an almost annual performance in the Thai parliamentary theatre. Chalerm would appear in parliament with piles of police files in front of him covering the various transgressions, actual and alleged, of the hectoring members of parliament before him. Sifting through the dossiers in public was a remarkably effective technique for quelling dissidence. Chalerm's sheer pugnacity sent a chill through the chamber.

Mobile phones were still in their infancy at that time, but Chalerm's diligent monitoring of the rich, powerful, and disruptive extended to a mysterious Mass Communications Organization of Thailand (MCOT) van that could supposedly intercept telephone calls. Class 5 began to suspect that Chalerm and Manoonkrit were listening in on their conversations. There was further outrage over an allegation that the van had been in operation in a car park near the Chitralada Villa of Dusit Palace, the royal family's main residence in Bangkok.

A deadly brew of military self-interest, government corruption, and rumoured threats to the royal family was bubbling away. Suddenly, after over 13 years without a successful putsch, talk of an impending coup did not seem quite so far-fetched. In fact, many people expected one, particularly when the army chief, General Suchinda Kraprayoon, publicly berated the government for its policies concerning the stock market and state enterprises.

Although Chatichai's 'buffet cabinet' was widely derided as corrupt, he himself was bluff and popular with much of the public. When necessary, he would shuffle ministers to stave off public opprobrium towards graft and put his coalition partners off balance. Chatichai had seemed to lead a charmed existence, outwitting his enemies, but he was was always stalked by serious problems.

A rumour was being spread that suggested his son, Kraisak, had been involved in a plot nearly ten years earlier to assassinate Queen Sirikit and Prem. An 80-page Special Branch report had been compiled which included the comings and goings at Kraisak's home on Soi Rajakhru, right beside Chatichai's residence. The visitors included leftist figures from the 1970s, who from time to time did indeed impose themselves on Kraisak's hospitality, often overstaying their welcome.

A 30-minute video recording was brought by police Special Branch officers to Borwornsak Uwanno. Borwornsak was a young law lecturer at Chulalongkorn University, a senator, and a member of the Baan Phitsanulok group. He also served as Chatichai's deputy secretary general. Although Borwornsak had his own excellent police connections, he felt that bringing supposed confessions to him personally was inappropriate. Any evidence of a plot should go straight to Government House. He therefore took the tape to Chatichai.

The prime minister and some of his other young advisers, including Kraisak and Surakiart Sathirathai, gathered round and watched the video. With photographs of the king and queen displayed in the background, flanked by the national flag and that of the Royal Thai Police Force, an alleged breakaway officer from the Class 7 group described the rumoured plot to kill the queen and the premier a decade earlier. He tried to implicate Kraisak as a co-conspirator.

Two things were immediately apparent to all. However implausible, such a serious attack on Kraisak was in reality an attack on Chatichai – and defending his son could be construed as treason. More immediately, the filmed confession, however oddly staged, was exactly the kind of evidence to present as justification for a coup.

Late that night, a senior policeman visited Borwornsak. As a friend, he suggested that the young senator take a holiday overseas until matters blew over. 'I am not going to flee because I have done nothing wrong,' Borwornsak responded.

Earlier that week, Anand had lunched with Chatichai at the Princess hotel in Larn Luang, a favourite haunt of politicians due to its proximity to the government quarter. Anand recalls Chatichai being in a good mood. Outwardly, he was his usual dismissive, avuncular self, unfazed by his problems with the military and the coup rumours rumbling around town.

At the time, Anand was deeply preoccupied with personal commitments of no global significance whatsoever. In 1989, he had taken on the presidency of the Old England Students Association (OESA) and inherited its various financial headaches. To replenish the coffers, months of planning had gone into a fund-raising gala dinner at the five-star Shangri-La, a riverside hotel.

OESA functions are generally rather Thai affairs and rarely involve many old students who are actually British. Apart from the banquet, the format for the evening would be a standard array of door prizes, and celebrities and well-known public figures singing, as well as lots of dancing. Anand had high hopes that the event would put the OESA finances firmly back in the black, and he had every reason to believe that Saturday 23 February would be a night to remember for all the right reasons. He was looking forward to a good party among old friends.

But Saturday 23 February 1991 was not normal by any stretch, and would not soon be forgotten. The world's attention had been far from Thailand in the preceding months. After a massive build-up of allied land forces in the Middle East, and weeks of aerial bombardments of Iraq from mid-January, softening up President Saddam Hussein's defences, US General Norman Schwarzkopf was on the verge of launching a land offensive that would retake Kuwait and oust Iraqi occupying forces.

Operation Desert Storm was launched on Sunday 24 February. A massive invasion force poured across the desert out of Saudi Arabia. It was so overwhelming that a ceasefire was declared within 100 hours. On the Friday before the invasion, US President George H.W. Bush, Anand's colleague from their days as permanent representatives at the United Nations in New York, issued a final ultimatum to Saddam: he should withdraw his forces from Kuwait or be removed. A complete global news blackout was in force until midnight the next day in the Middle East, Saturday 23 February, which was early morning Sunday Bangkok time. At this momentous juncture, journalists in Thailand and almost everywhere else were looking for stories to fill up pages rendered blank by developments in the Middle East. One of the largest military movements since World War II was going unmentioned because of the embargo.

That Saturday morning, Chatichai set off from his Rajakhru residence, just north of Victory Monument. It was early, and the prime minister was bound for the VIP wing of the Royal Thai Air Force Base, which faced the civil aviation terminals of Don Muang International Airport across twin runways and a Vietnam War-era golf course. The prime minister's party included General Arthit Kamlang-ek, his newly nominated deputy defence minister. The party was bound for Chiang Mai for an audience with King Bhumibol. The king was residing upcountry at Bhuping Palace, one of five provincial palaces used at different times of the year by the royal family.

The night before, while a senior policeman who suspected an impending coup visited Borwornsak, Arthit had called separately on Chatichai at his home. Arthit's confirmation was the reason for their journey to Chiang Mai, and he suggested requesting a postponement of the royal audience. Chatichai rejected the idea. 'What would we tell the king if there is no coup?' he reasoned. Chatichai had also rejected the idea of flying north on a commercial Thai domestic flight. He did not want to risk dragging innocent bystanders into a political brawl.

The party was accompanied by lightly armed police bodyguards from Special Branch, and was due to fly in a modified C-130 transport plane. A curtain divided the aircraft's cargo bay, and the smarter section in front contained a horseshoe-shaped bench. Chatichai settled into the forward area with Arthit, Anan Anantakul, and Yongyuth Sarasombath. As they boarded, Borwornsak recalls very lax security. Apart from the police bodyguards, there were at least ten air force security personnel at the back of the plane. In total 40–50 people were on board.

As everybody strapped themselves in on the C-130, and the hold was sealed, nothing seemed amiss. Borwornsak was sitting behind the curtain, reflecting on how he actually had no reason to be in Chiang Mai. 'I did not want to go but Surakiart called me every hour,' he recalls.

The prime minister's aircraft was cleared to move from the apron on to the taxiway leading to the older, short runway. Suddenly, the plane came to a ferocious halt. Everybody was pitched forward against the restraints. At that moment, Borwornsak remembers, air force commandos burst from the back of the aircraft and a machine gun was put to his head. He thinks it was an Uzi. In the commotion, Chatichai drew back the curtain. 'What's going on, Borwornsak?' he growled.

The answer was immediately obvious. A coup was under way. The man in charge on the ground outside was the air force chief himself, Air Chief Marshal Kaset Rojananil. Another 20 air force commandos jumped off trucks and offloaded the passengers from the grounded transport plane, escorting them back into the air force terminal – there was no question of any resistance.

Chatichai, Arthit and a few others were taken into the reception area on the ground floor. The rest were taken upstairs; Borwornsak was called out by name and told to open his bag. Some mid-level officers rummaged through his papers. Apparently they could not find whatever it was they were looking for. They started muttering about missing documents. Borwornsak asked what they were after. They would not be drawn, but he knew well enough. 'There was a rumour that the visit to Chiang Mai was to transfer Class 5,' recalls Borwornsak. 'That was completely false.'

For those behind the coup, this was a bad start. The absence of any transfer papers prepared for King Bhumibol's signature immediately discredited one of their justifications. Chatichai later told Borwornsak that when Kaset was informed downstairs that nothing had been found, he was almost contrite. For a moment, it seemed he might let them all go as if nothing had happened. Chatichai was enraged, however, and Kaset realised it would be impossible to pretend, somehow, that the hijacking of an aircraft with 50 people aboard had never happened.

At about 9am, as the drama at the airport was unfolding, General Sunthorn Kongsompong, the supreme commander of the Royal Thai Armed Forces, was making offerings to the spirit house in his garden in a military district in Bangkok's northern suburbs before heading north to the airport. He was accompanied by his personal head of security, Colonel Watana Pechmongkol, who often doubled as his driver. Sunthorn had graduated in Class 1 from the Chulachomklao Military

Academy, and was a contemporary of General Chavalit Yongchaiyudh – not that the two were close.

As a former commander of special forces, Sunthorn wore a prestigious maroon beret. He was very much a soldier's soldier and popular with his subordinates. This placed him apart from the more business-minded younger officers of Class 5, who were led by army chief General Suchinda and his brother-in-law, the army chief of staff General Issarapong Noonpakdee. Air Chief Marshal Kaset, the air force head, was also a Class 5 alumnus in the air force academy. He had been suddenly recalled the previous day by Suchinda from a trip to South Korea.

When General Sunthorn's car was a few kilometres short of the airport, it ran into road works and a typical Bangkok traffic snarl-up. As the car crept forward, it dawned on Sunthorn that he was running late for his own coup. He remained calm in his immaculately pressed uniform, which a tailor had modified with zips to replace buttons for a perfect body-hugging fit. Sunthorn often carried his cigarettes in his sock to avoid unsightly bulging pockets (a ferocious smoker, in 1999 he would succumb to lung cancer). An aide followed him everywhere with a special case from which were dispensed at regular intervals exact measures of Scotch whisky and ice.

When Sunthorn finally arrived at the air force terminal, he found Chatichai sitting in a chair, far from pleased with the end of his 'no problem' premiership. The supreme commander dropped to his knees and gave the former prime minister the deepest possible *wai*, apologising for the inconvenience of it all. Chatichai, momentarily mollified, said that if Sunthorn really felt that way, he should immediately reverse the coup. Arthit, well aware that he was a significant part of the problem, belatedly offered to stand down from his new post as defence minister – if it would help.

Sunthorn was friendly but resolute. He said the pair would remain guests of the military for a little while, and that everything would be done for their comfort. As everybody in the room knew full well, particularly Kaset despite his momentary vacillation, there can never be any question of putting a successful coup into reverse.

Arthit asked for the bathroom. Inside, he noticed a door exiting the building directly, but it was locked. The old general threw his full weight against it, banging the side of his head in the process, but it did not budge. He emerged with a bruised face, and a story soon got out that he had been beaten. Sunthorn's security aide, Colonel Watana, was blamed and received death threats before the misunderstanding was cleared up.

News of the coup, one of the most surreptitious in Thai history, filtered out as the morning went by. Six old tanks were briefly put on the streets in the Dusit government quarter of Bangkok, and then returned to their bays in the cavalry barracks. Lightly armed infantry and some anti-aircraft units were deployed around Government House. The soldiers shooed away photographers who arrived belatedly to try and capture images of a coup that had actually taken place hours before and had been consolidated behind closed doors.

A foreign correspondent in Bangkok was dozing after eating a fine Malaysian curry when a call came through from a Scottish expatriate in Cyprus. The BBC was reporting a coup that morning in Bangkok. Was it true?

'Never on a Saturday,' the correspondent retorted instinctively, switching on the television. He was wrong. Martial music was already playing. Senior officers were reciting announcements from an old military playlist most imagined had been torn up years before. The process was pretty standard: application of martial law, dissolution of parliament, disbanding of the cabinet, abrogation of the constitution. So too was the coup-plotters' reasoning: the government was corrupt and the monarchy was in danger.

Thailand's newest junta identified itself as the National Peacekeeping Council (NPKC). Observers commented on the name's disconcerting resonance with the State Law and Order Restoration Council (SLORC), the junta in neighbouring Myanmar that had come to power so bloodily in September 1988. The announcements were being made by Sunthorn, the junta's chairman and Thailand's *de facto* new head of government, but there was no question that the most powerful general in play was, as always, the army chief, Suchinda – who had not been present that morning at the airport.

The coup had all sorts of long-term implications for Thailand, and the damage that would be done to the nation's image. It was attracting disproportionate global interest because of the news blackout in Kuwait, and its relatively early timing in the global news cycle. Attracting more attention than would otherwise have been the case, it was easily the biggest foreign news story playing in the Sunday papers next morning all over the world. If the Thai generals had for a moment hoped to topple the country's elected government while all attention was focused on a massive news event in the Middle East, they failed spectacularly. In practice, the timing was entirely determined by Thailand's goldfish-bowl politics.

For Anand, the timing was a disaster. His problem that Saturday was not the derailing, again, of Thailand's slow train to democracy, but the OESA party scheduled to take place at the Shangri-La in the evening. The expectation was that, following a coup, the capital would be under martial law with a curfew in place. Anand enlisted those with the military contacts he had so deliberately shunned over the previous decade to place some calls. Reassurances were made by the NPKC that the OESA party could go ahead as planned. In its haste to prevent Chatichai and Arthit reaching King Bhumibol in Chiang Mai, the new junta, which already had enough problems on its hands, had probably not anticipated upsetting the social arrangements of so many influential people.

Despite that morning's coup, the OESA party was well attended. Among the guests was a young lecturer from Thammasat University, Abhisit Vejjajiva, who was contemplating a career in politics with Thailand's oldest party, the Democrats. At the dinner, Anand said little from the rostrum about the events earlier in the day. It was after all a social gathering. As the host, he moved around the tables and shared his dismay more privately with the guests, who included some family members there to support him.

'We were all so excited and upset,' recalls Charatsri Vajrabhaya, the niece and childhood playmate Anand had looked after in London. 'I remember that Anand looked depressed because he thought the entire political situation had gone backwards. Probably he thought there were better ways of handling things, but he couldn't leave the party because he was the president.' Abhisit had a similar sense: 'I can't remember the words but certainly the impression was that he was not pleased with what had happened, and obviously very concerned.'

Next morning, Anand woke quite late. Sunday is always a family day in the Panyarachun household, and outside invitations are usually not accepted. Anand nevertheless took an urgent call from a friend. The press was reporting that the NPKC planned to establish an advisory committee, and that Anand's name had been included on the long list of technocrats. The names of Snoh Unakul, Amnuay Viravan, Anat Arbhabhirama, Kasem Chatikavanij, and Suthee Singsaneh were also there. According to the papers and radio broadcasts, the committee's first meeting was scheduled for later in the week.

Anand felt somewhat irritable when he arrived a few days later at the large hall in Sanam Suapha. This is the First Army area, near Royal Plaza, where the colourful Trooping of the Colour ceremony was performed early each December for King Bhumibol's birthday. The military had summoned some 80 technocrats for lunch. Anat, an engineer and former governor of PTT and TDRI president, had been travelling upcountry when he heard his name on the radio. He recalls a room full of military officers and civilians networking in numbers too large to take fully on board. The gathering was like a fish tank: a large pool of experts from which the military planned to reel in a cabinet.

Anand knew that the junta had said it would instal a civilian-dominated cabinet. On that basis, he told anyone who would listen, as he circulated among the junta's prospective ministers and advisers, that the group's first move should be to disband itself. A decent civilian cabinet, he reasoned, would not need any outside coaching. Others less voluble than Anand suggested waiting to see what actually transpired. After all, they cautioned, nobody yet knew whom the NPKC had in mind for prime minister, let alone the cabinet rundown.

The unexpected prime minister

In the days immediately following the coup, things did not go well for General Suchinda. He had immediately ordered a senior and impartial police officer to look into the alleged assassination plot supposedly involving Kraisak against Queen Sirikit and Prem. Within a matter of days, the policeman returned to report that the plot was a smear and completely without substance.

Kraisak had nevertheless taken no chances; he had good reason to believe his life was at risk and fled Bangkok within hours of the coup. With just 15,000 baht in a plastic bag and four changes of underwear, he headed for the Thai-Malaysian border. Later, with the heat still on, he was taken across the border for his own safety. Chalerm also fled the country and spent some time in exile in Denmark as a political refugee.

Suchinda was deeply irritated when he received the police report scotching the plot rumour. After the missing transfer papers for Class 5, this was another embarrassing blank. Although there could be no question of putting the coup into reverse, the powerful general was facing a simple reality: that the coup had no demonstrable justification.

To make matters worse, Suchinda's two leading prospects for nomination as a civilian prime minister to replace the elected Chatichai were not panning out.

Influential people who had had business dealings with Ukrit Mongkolnavin, a former senator and dean of law at Chulalongkorn University, conveyed to the junta strong opposition to his possible nomination. An alternative, Arsa Sarasin, was already being embarrassed by congratulatory phone calls, even though no formal approach was ever made to him by the NPKC. Arsa's leadership qualities and his record as a top diplomat were never in question, but he lacked private-sector business experience – and this was arguably one of the most business-interested juntas in Thai history.[5] 'I was not convinced,' Arsa recalls. 'I had nothing to do with the coup and did not know Suchinda that well.'

Suchinda began casting around among his wide network of friends for more candidates. Unlike the many generals who had attended the Armed Forces Preparatory School before entering Chulachomklao Military Academy, Suchinda had been educated in ordinary schools, such as Tri Udom. He was bright and had completed the first year of a medical degree before joining the military. As a result, one of his closest friends was Dr Phrao Nivatvongs, who along with Dr Attasit Vejjajiva, the father of Abhisit, had set up the Prommitr Hospital in an affluent residential part of Sukhumvit.

One evening in the middle of the week after the coup, Suchinda invited Dr Phrao and some other friends to dinner at one of his favourite European restaurants, the Fireplace Grill, in the basement of what was then the President hotel. Dr Phrao had a good idea of what Suchinda wanted to discuss that evening. Trawling for names to put forward to Suchinda for prime minister, Dr Phrao had consulted an old friend, Chan Bulakul, a businessman and cousin of Suthep Bulakul. Chan's recommendation was Anand. Chan himself had only really got to know Anand after his move into the business world at Saha Union.

In the restaurant, when Dr Phrao mentioned Anand's name, it was a 'light bulb' moment for Suchinda. Although they had never been close, Suchinda had served as deputy military attaché at the embassy in Washington when Anand was ambassador. They had seen each other perhaps four or five times in the intervening years, including when Suchinda attended the funeral rites for Pruek, Anand's mother. Whatever had transpired in 1976, with the Thammasat bloodbath and Anand's being hounded out of the foreign ministry, Suchinda personally had no doubts about the former diplomat's capabilities. But he had no idea how Anand might react to being asked to take on the premiership – or whether he might have residual feelings of antipathy towards the military. It was not in his nature, but Anand had every reason to hate the generals.

On the Thursday evening, a nephew of Anand's, MR Charnvudhi Varavarn, telephoned him at home. What he had to say was completely unexpected. He had been told that Anand's name had been put forward, and he was testing the water. How would Anand feel about being asked to be prime minister? Taken aback by such an astonishing question, Anand said he had never given the matter any thought; and he would not answer a hypothetical question – one of his trademark responses. Anand said he would need to hear the proposition directly to make any comment.

'I treated it as nonsense,' Anand recalls. 'On a matter of such importance, you can't have somebody just ring you up. I did not give it another thought.'

On Friday, day six of the NPKC's rule, the technocrat advisory group assembled once again at Sanam Suapha. Despite the phone call from Charnvudhi the night before, Anand had no reason to change the view he had expressed so firmly at the previous meeting – that a competent civilian cabinet did not need advisers constantly chipping in. As the discussion among the technocrats continued, a colonel in full dress uniform approached Anand and asked him politely to step away with him for a moment.

In some neighbouring countries, this could have foreshadowed a bad ending behind a bougainvillea bush. Instead, Anand stepped out to find Suchinda waiting for him in person. They adjourned to a more private area where Suchinda cut straight to the main item of business: would Anand be willing to serve as prime minister?

The meeting lasted about an hour, and ended with no more than an agreement from Anand that he would consult with his family over the weekend. After that he would provide a definite answer.

This was a pivotal moment in Thailand's modern history. In inviting Anand to become prime minister, Suchinda was asking him to overlook a grievous old wound that had caused pain to Sodsee, Anand's wife, every day. Meanwhile, Anand, the man who had never sought political office, was on the verge of taking the biggest risk of his life. Snoh remembers Anand returning to the group in a very pensive mood. He seemed distant, and his hand was cold to the touch. 'He wouldn't talk,' Snoh recalls. 'He was in deep thought.'

Anand invariably consults his two daughters when major decisions have to be made. He knew better than to worry Sodsee at this juncture. Having confided in no one, he left the gathering of technocrats and went immediately to see his first daughter, Nanda, who lived nearby. She was at home having been unwell in the previous months. They spent the next hour discussing with her how the country might be rehabilitated after the coup, which both agreed had been 'a step backwards'.

'We talk on the phone all the time, visit regularly over the weekends, go out to dinners together – we consult on everything,' says Nanda. She remembers the meeting vividly: 'He was actually torn apart. Obviously, he did not believe in the military takeover, and by accepting he would be associated with it, but at the same time he saw it as an opportunity for political reform. My advice was, "Go for it."'

Anand then placed a call to Singapore where Daranee, his younger daughter, was on holiday with her husband, their two children, and three other couples. 'He would not have accepted without discussing this with the family,' says Daranee. 'It is part of the way the family deals with things – talking about everything. My main concern was Mom, and the effect this would have on her health.'

Daranee immediately confided in her husband but they revealed nothing to their travelling companions. 'I remember walking up Orchard Road after I had gotten the phone call from my dad,' she says. 'My friends were speculating as to whether it would be Arsa or Ukrit, but nobody mentioned Anand's name. It was really too strange.'

Anand had twice before been asked to join the cabinet, and had twice refused. Those offers could never have been accepted for personal reasons. He had always known how distressing accepting any political position would have been to Sodsee, and to a lesser degree to his daughters, given the political savaging he had endured after Thammasat. Sodsee remained deeply mistrustful of the society that had betrayed her husband.

Anand viewed the coup as a national catastrophe that had precipitated an acute political crisis. He still vividly recalls the many questions in his own mind. Apart from a fortnight as acting foreign minister in October 1976, he had no cabinet experience. Could he handle the steep learning curve as prime minister? What would be the limits of his authority? Would he be able to restore any balance to the situation? What would be the price of failure? He remembers pondering his dilemma, and wondering whether he should just walk away. After all, at this stage nobody but his daughters knew what was on the table.

As he mulled things over, Anand realised that this time the situation was very different. If he was not going to accept, he had to come up with a good reason for declining – and there were certainly some to consider. Critics would rightly say that his appointment occurred outside any legitimate political process, even though he had not been involved personally in any way with the chain of events leading up to the coup. Critics would also say that this was another instance of technocrats colluding with self-serving military interests, baling them out after yet another half-baked military intervention in politics. Was there not now an opportunity to leave the military high and dry, and expose their fundamental ineptitude in political and economic affairs? The easy personal option would have been to adopt the high-minded position that coups are invariably bad and the military should stay out of politics: beach the generals and teach them a good lesson.

But how would that help Thailand out of the mess it now found itself in? 'I had to think of a reason for saying no, and I couldn't,' says Anand.

Matters started moving quickly. On the same Friday evening, Anand went to a business reception where he met up again with Staporn Kavitanon, the secretary general of the Board of Investment who had also attended the afternoon meeting at Sanam Suapha First Army headquarters. The two adjourned to the Imperial hotel on Wireless Road, which was owned by Akorn Hoontrakul, a *bon viveur* fond of his wine but also a politically wired personality. The old hotel lobby had good food with a band in the evenings, and was a popular meeting place. Anand told Staporn about Suchinda's request, and the two discussed the situation.

Anand remembers getting home late that night. To his great dismay next morning, however, he discovered that Suchinda had not told him everything. The NPKC's appointed assembly had already been chosen, and the names were being floated in the press. The assembly would be charged with the task of drafting a new constitution. This was unnerving. It robbed Anand of any say in the composition of the unelected legislature – and of direct influence in drafting a new constitution.

With this major new concern playing on his mind, Anand received a call at about 10am from General Issarapong Noonpakdee, whom he had never met. Issarapong asked if he was available to speak with Suchinda. Anand said he was, and Suchinda called five minutes later. Time was not on the army chief's side. He had an audience scheduled with King Bhumibol in Chiang Mai at 5pm, and it would look bad for him if a week passed without the nomination of a viable premier.

'You never mentioned this,' Anand said to Suchinda when he came on the line, pressing him to explain how such an enormous omission from the discussion the previous afternoon could have occurred. 'Brother, I don't know,' Suchinda responded, trying to play down the significance of the appointed assembly and reassuring Anand that it would not affect his role.

'Suchinda pleaded with me and tried to ease my concerns,' says Anand. He remembers being shocked by the vagueness of it all – the fact that something so major could somehow not have been mentioned in their face-to-face discussion. Suchinda must have known about plans for the assembly when he met Anand. Maybe he did not consider it much of an issue – it was easy enough to be cynical about legislative assemblies and drafting constitutions in Thailand, after all.

At this point, with Suchinda waiting on the other end of the line, Anand could easily have said that he had been misinformed and turned the general down. At the same time, the belated revelation had a powerful counter-intuitive effect: it reinforced Anand's view that the situation was 'chaotic' and would get even further out of hand if somebody did not take charge.

The legislative assembly was important in another respect. Although it had never succeeded once in Thailand's history, an elected parliament would normally start out with the intention of completing a four-year term before the next election came due. An appointed assembly charged mainly with redrafting the constitution, on the other hand, would have trouble justifying its continued existence after all the amendments and changes had been completed and the revised constitution had been drafted.

The fact that Anand's government would have no direct say in this process meant that it would not be able to set the direction for the new constitution. It also meant the NPKC retained a crucial element of control over timing. Anand's personal instincts were always for a relatively quick exit, but the pace of the constitutional revisions would ultimately circumscribe his government's term. An Anand government would come with the NPKC's assembly and leave with it – unless Anand was dismissed by the junta first.

The phone conversation was tense. However, to Suchinda's great relief, Anand set aside his serious misgivings over the assembly and said he would accept the general's nomination. 'My greatest concern was that the country was drifting,' he explains. 'Suchinda was the brain of the class, and it is my assessment that my appointment was his sole decision.'

'They chose him because of his reputation for being independently minded, and for his international experience,' says Nanda. 'I think they were very concerned about the international reaction. Suchinda was probably being very practical.'

Sunthorn and Suchinda flew to Chiang Mai for their audience with King Bhumibol late the same afternoon, and returned with the king's signature on the proclamation naming Anand as prime minister. In Thailand, the prime minister designate does not attend such audiences, but receives the proclamation at a solemn ceremony elsewhere and presents himself subsequently.

The normal dress code on such occasions is a white high-collared tunic, the formal style of senior public servants. This presented a problem: Anand did not have the right attire. When he left the foreign ministry in 1978, he had disposed of all his white civil service uniforms. 'I had totally done away with my official career.' Sunthorn and Suchinda returned to Bangkok the same evening for the ceremony at which Anand was to receive the royal proclamation. It was followed by a dinner in Suan Ruen Rue Dee, the junta's base of operations. Anand arrived in a western-style business suit. He was unfamiliar with the buildings in the military part of town. All six members of the junta were waiting, accompanied by some top military aides.

Anand entered the room. 'The members of the military council had all lined up,' he recalls. Then a thought struck him. 'As I walked through, I realised I did not know any of them except Suchinda.'

Indeed, Anand was an anomaly to the military. He had not attended the National Defence College when he returned to Thailand as permanent secretary at the foreign ministry in 1975. That was a normal rite of passage for civil servants of his rank – who were usually considerably older. Courses run by the college are designed to create familiarity between key military figures and senior technocrats, civil servants, and key executives in state enterprises. Exceptionally busy in 1976, the youthful Anand had missed out on the networking.

That night, Anand had in mind some initial requirements for taking on the job. These included the lifting of martial law, the unconditional release of Chatichai and others, and a free hand to select his own cabinet. Suchinda had raised no objections earlier to the latter demand, but made it clear that ministerial portfolios relating to national security would have to be filled by the military.

'I could take that,' says Anand. 'It was to be expected with defence and interior, but with the others it had to be a free hand.'

After they had dined, General Sunthorn as the host, junta chairman, and *de facto* head of government, courteously invited Anand to say a few words.

Anand began by asking if anybody had informed Ukrit, the former senator and dean of law the military had first considered for the job. He was told that this had not yet been done. Anand then said he would keep his comments short because he wanted there to be no misunderstandings.

'Many of you do not know me personally,' he said. He briefly explained how he knew Suchinda from their Washington days, and offered a thumbnail sketch of himself as a person of great candour who was 'neither poor nor wealthy'.

'I am a very independent man,' he went on, warming to his main theme. 'My being prime minister will be viewed by many people in Thailand as not being legitimate.' In view of that, Anand said he would have to be judged by what he did: any legitimacy he gained would derive from the trust he earned. He would therefore try his best to explain his actions to everyone – including the military.

Anand then set out the three key rules of engagement with the military that would apply for the duration of his government: 'Firstly, whatever I do as prime minister, I will try to explain it to you. Secondly, I will never stab you in the back – and I expect you not to stab me in the back. And thirdly, I am the prime minister.'

'I don't think they had met a man like me before,' Anand reflects on this odd encounter. Here was a lone technocrat-cum-businessman in a city suit squaring up to the generals in their crisp uniforms, earnestly informing them that he had every intention of doing the right thing and being the best prime minister possible. In essentially his first directives since being named prime minister, Anand then asked for emergency rule to be lifted and for Chatichai to be released immediately.

After the week of uncertainty and confusion following the coup, the generals must have derived assurance from Anand's confidence and poise. Whether any of them at this stage realised that a second, invisible coup had just taken place right under their noses is a matter for conjecture.

'I am not a product of the coup,' Anand told his uniformed audience, wrapping up his off-the-cuff address. 'I am the outcome of the coup.'

CHAPTER 10

FORMING THE FIRST ANAND GOVERNMENT (1991)

A new dawn

The day after King Bhumibol signed the proclamation confirming him as prime minister, Anand assembled a small working group at his home that over the next three days would help him draw together the most technically qualified cabinet in Thailand's history.

The date was Sunday 3 March 1991, the eighth of the 409 days during which the National Peacekeeping Council (NPKC) officially governed Thailand. Anand's younger daughter, Daranee, was photographed that morning on a flight home from Singapore holding a newspaper. The front-page news was her father, the new prime minister. She had learned of his nomination by phone the day before, but had not told the couples travelling with her. Nobody could doubt Daranee's ability to keep a secret. When they reached Bangkok, she sensed a certain excitement in the air, but also a palpable sense of relief. The confusion surrounding the coup was beginning to clear.

General Suchinda Kraprayoon's decision to nominate Anand as prime minister had caught everyone by surprise, but it drew immediate praise from prominent members of the foreign business community. Over the years, many of them had interacted personally with Anand. Australian businessman Raymond Eaton, an incorrigible Thailand booster and chairman of the Export Development Trading Corporation (a regional agency for Walmart, the giant US retail chain), immediately lauded the appointment. 'Why is everybody so surprised?' he chided a group of foreign correspondents.

Just days after the coup, the lawyer David Lyman, a former AmCham president, had said to Anand in a characteristic throwaway remark, 'You know, they should make you prime minister.' He would have won a tidy sum on Anand's nomination if he had thought to place a bet. The two men had been fellow members of the original board of governors of the Heritage Club.[1] Soon after Anand was appointed prime minister, their paths crossed there again. 'David, it's all your fault,' Anand ribbed Lyman. 'Anand may have been a compromise but in my view he was the only candidate,' says Lyman.

Such reactions suited the NPKC. Many people could accept that Thailand's political system needed cleaning up and a new approach, but few advocated coups as a route to reform. Given Anand's credibility, the possibility of a competent civilian administration immediately damped down widespread criticism of the military. Anand had the right bureaucratic pedigree. In times of crisis, the foreign affairs and finance ministries, along with the judiciary, had always provided pools of competence.

'Anand has a good grounding in terms of principles,' says fellow diplomat Manaspas Xuto. 'He is very scrupulous, which is rare in Thailand. There may be more people like him, but they have never shown up.' Indeed, nobody had once questioned Anand's probity; no hint of financial scandal had ever attached itself to his name.

While the diplomatic and foreign business community respected Anand for his broad experience, approachability, candour, and integrity, they also realised he was taking an immense personal risk. Nobody felt this more keenly than Anand himself. 'Don't forget that I could have been removed at any time by the military council,' he reflects. 'I always had a shadow opposition, and that was the NPKC.'

Although the two sets of circumstances could not be more different, a prime minister appointed in the wake of a coup has much the same job as one appointed after a general election: to form a durable government in as short a time as possible. In most countries, an elected prime minister selects ministers from among newly elected members of parliament. On this occasion, the NPKC had already appointed its 292-member assembly without any reference to Anand. Of these, 51 per cent were active or retired military officers.

While the appointment of the assembly bothered Anand, it did not impinge on the composition of his cabinet. At their initial meeting, Anand had extracted an undertaking from Suchinda that he would have a generally free hand in the cabinet selection; exceptions, for national security reasons, were the interior and defence portfolios.

There was an upside. As an appointed prime minister of an unelected government, Anand did not have to concern himself with party politics in the selection process for the other portfolios. Unlike his predecessors over the previous two decades, he could bypass what he calls the 'shareholdings and percentages' involved in cobbling together a Thai-style cabinet coalition – carving up the cake of ministries in terms of their value, both political and economic, among the competing parties. Comparisons with other prime ministers are not entirely fair. Anand himself readily admits that not having to negotiate with party leaders speeded up the selection process – but this was a pre-condition he had shrewdly extracted from Suchinda. He was free to make selections on the basis of competence and integrity.

Like Anand, General Prem Tinsulanond, in office from 1980 to 1988, was never an elected prime minister; but Prem had always been legally endorsed by parliament in accordance with the constitution of the day. Even he had to worry constantly about balancing parties in his cabinets and their competing, often venal, interests. This problem followed him through three elections and five cabinets. However, as his cabinets rolled by, the number of unelected ministers steadily diminished – a manifestation of the incremental democratisation that Thailand underwent in the 1980s. As it became tougher to hand out cabinet positions to outsiders, Prem urged people he wanted in the government to run for political office. He told his dependable foreign minister and old schoolmate, Air Chief Marshal Siddhi Savetsila, to join a political party if he wanted to stay in the cabinet. Siddhi went off and got himself elected under the Social Action Party banner.

The brothers Kukrit and Seni Pramoj in the 1970s, and Chatichai Choonhavan in the 1980s, were elected prime ministers ground through the coalition mill. Kukrit's tenuous premiership in 1975, a watershed for elected government in Thailand, was founded on the Social Action Party's 18 elected members of parliament. Chatichai as head of the Chart Thai (Thai Nation Party), the most successful in the 1988 election, headed a five-party coalition. Managing coalitions was a full-time job for Kukrit, Seni, Prem, and Chatichai, and had eventually defeated them all.

Even so, the task of assembling a cabinet was not without problems. In the past, while formulating cabinet mixes had always been testing, there was never much difficulty finding prospective ministers. Securing a lucrative portfolio was the goal of most Thai politicians. Anand faced the possibility of the opposite problem – not finding prospective ministers.

By 1991, coups were considered *passé* by the intelligentsia. They were meant to be out of date. There was definitely an antipathy to governments that emerged from coups among technically well qualified people – civil servants, technocrats, lawyers, businessmen, bankers. Like Anand himself, they had wanted to believe that Thailand had progressed beyond such things. Clearly it had not. 'He had to convince them, and ask them to please come and help,' says Chan Bulakul. 'People did not know if he could do it. He had no track record – it was not as simple as some imagine for him to form his cabinet.'

While Anand could approach those he considered to be the best people, there was no guarantee they would accept. In the final reckoning, however, he was turned down by only one person, and that was for a perfectly legitimate personal reason.

The cabinet Anand formed in the first week of March 1991 had 34 members,[2] some of whom were previously known to him only by repute. This cabinet included no professional politicians. Anand's concerns about who should and should not be included in his cabinet went beyond money politics and vote farming. There were also no trade unionists, labourers, factory workers, or farmers. His selection was patrician: an elite, educated, hopefully incorruptible, top-down cabinet that could make no claim to being representative of the general population it set out to serve. It had not emerged from any sort of representative process, and there was not enough time for the luxury of tokenism. Anand surrounded himself with people he knew personally or by reputation, people he felt he could work with. Any legitimacy the new cabinet acquired would not be derived from the ballot box; it would have to be earned on merit and performance. It could only come from positive results as perceived by the general population.

Unlike politicians, technocrats such as Anand and Snoh tried to follow the uncompromising principle of 'MBO' – management by objective. They believed that the right objectives should be achieved through correct processes without compromises, deviation, or corruption. This is a tough course to chart not only in Thailand, but anywhere. One of the biggest challenges is to determine who decides what is 'right'.

In Thailand's case, in the rush towards modernisation and development, technocrats had helped build vast dams upcountry, plant industrial estates in flood plains, fill waterways with toxins, and pave over the old canals of Bangkok. As roads penetrated the hinterlands, forests that had covered more than 70 per cent of Thailand's land area at the end of World War II were now decimated. Even Anand's own birthplace had vanished beneath a sea of tarmac.

With hindsight, had enough thought been given to this process and its consequences? Were the wise, beneficent technocrats not also fallible? In his twilight years, Snoh, Thailand's great development czar, admits to being haunted by the environmental damage done by the accelerated economic development he himself did so much to engineer.

It can always be argued that while a fragile democracy such as Thailand's does not always produce optimal development, the country did not suffer the worst effects of rapid change. A relatively safe, bumbling mediocrity had emerged instead. The cityscapes of modern Thailand are ravaged by unsightly power poles and phone lines; water pipes pop from the ground at all angles; dual carriageways scar the landscape. However, nobody can say the daily needs of most people are not, for the most part, adequately met. Nothing is perfect or efficient, but the legacy of the technocrats is a robust, nationwide infrastructure. Everything works well enough, the aesthetics aside.

Anand wanted ministers who could convince him of their honesty and competence. They also needed practical experience in dealing with the civil service to avoid being obstructed by bureaucrats. Instinctively, he sought liberal-minded personalities who understood how business could promote the national interest. He wanted ministers with public service achievements already under their belt – evidence of their effectiveness as operators. 'They had to think in the same language as me – we had to be on the same wavelength,' says Anand. 'I am not saying they had to agree with me on everything, but I needed doers who would not procrastinate. I could not afford to spend time managing people, so I called on people I knew could deliver. It was not a crony thing.'

The technocrats return

Anand's first call was on Snoh Unakul, the former head of the National Economic and Social Development Board (NESDB), which had been formulating Thailand's five-year development plans since the premiership of Field Marshal Sarit Thanarat in the early 1960s. Snoh was chairman of the Thailand Development Research Institute (TDRI), which Anand had joined as a founding member of the council of trustees in 1984. TDRI had always been Snoh's baby; he knew better than anyone the strengths and professional qualifications of its senior members. As it turned out, almost a third of Anand's cabinet was drawn from the higher reaches of the TDRI.

After Snoh, his next key call was to Staporn Kavitanon, secretary general of the Board of Investment (BOI). Anand had a good, work-related relationship with Staporn that dated back five years. In his capacity as vice chairman of the Federation of Thai Industries, Anand sat on a BOI subcommittee. Staporn had been present when Anand was called out to meet Suchinda and was offered the premiership: the pair had spent the evening together at the Imperial hotel weighing the situation, before Anand gave his final agreement to the NPKC the next morning.

Staporn was regarded as a sharp, pragmatic operator with particularly good connections to the military. He had an excellent understanding of the real workings of the Thai economy, including aspects of the polity that Anand had often consciously avoided. For Anand, the military was always going to be the elephant in the room that somehow had to be handled. Staporn had the connections, diplomatic skills, and knowledge to deal with much of that for Anand, and this made him the obvious choice for the job of secretary general to the prime minister.

Anand also called in two trusted aides dating back to his time in Washington. The first was Vidhya Rayananonda, who had already been first secretary in Washington for 18 months when Anand became ambassador in 1973. Vidhya was only too glad when Anand recalled him to duty. After two years as consul general in Los Angeles, he had been Thailand's ambassador designate to Kuwait when Saddam Hussein invaded in early August 1990. He had never been able to take up the posting. Instead, he found himself wandering around the ministry in Bangkok as an 'ambassador at large'. Vidhya was to become deputy secretary general to the prime minister, and would function as Anand's special assistant and confidant, attending virtually all meetings, and liaising particularly closely with the foreign ministry.

The second loyal aide to be drafted was the self-effacing Pridi Boonyobhas, whom Anand had brought back with him from the US when Chatichai recalled him in late 1975 to become permanent secretary at the foreign affairs ministry. Pridi was now working at the ministry as an assistant permanent secretary. Pridi was well tested and completely dependable.

Government House was not yet ready for a new administration, so most of the cabinet selection over the next few days was done from Anand's home at the top of Sukhumvit Soi 53, and also at Saha Union. He worked through the cabinet formation in his study and office, running an informed eye down lists of familiar names. He contacted most by telephone, followed if possible by a brief personal meeting. Pridi remembers spending virtually the whole week at Anand's house, with Sodsee supervising meals and looking after him.

Anand was being assisted primarily by Snoh and Staporn, but others were consulted. The recommendation for Saisuree Chutikul, the only female member of the cabinet, came from Anand's daughter, Nanda, who held a senior position at the United Nations Economic and Social Commission for Asia and the Pacific (ESCAP). Saisuree was a special inspector general for women's and children's affairs in the Office of the Prime Minister. She was attending a conference in Vienna when she took a personal call from Anand at 6am, telling her to contact the ambassador immediately and arrange tickets for the first flight home. Before this bewildering wake-up call, Saisuree had not even been aware that Anand had been appointed prime minister.

The call to Nukul Prachuabmoh, Anand's choice for the communications portfolio, interrupted a late steak and wine dinner Nukul was enjoying at a club in Hong Kong. Nukul's wife sent a message from the Mandarin Oriental hotel, where the couple were staying, telling him to call Anand immediately. Nukul was utterly mystified, but, expressing his regrets, excused himself from the table. 'I did not have the slightest idea that he would ask me to join his cabinet,' he recalls.

That night Nukul quizzed Anand over the phone about who else would be drafted in, and asked with characteristic forthrightness whether Anand forming a government would actually be a good thing for the country. In the event, Nukul was never seen to smile in public once for as long as he was minister. A finance technocrat and former governor of the Bank of Thailand, he had an exceptional reputation for probity and toughness. He had retired early, at 55, following a dispute with Prem's second finance minister, Sommai Hoontrakul, over what Nukul deemed to be inadequate regulation of a troubled bank, Asia Credit Trust. People joked that Nukul was so straight he would walk up one side of a palm tree and down the other rather than step around it. His was to be one of the two most embattled portfolios of the Anand governments. Indeed, Nukul was one of the most frequent visitors to Anand's office.

Nukul gave Anand a warning: 'It is not easy to get good people nowadays who can also work.'

This remark was particularly apposite. The only way the new cabinet could be effective was by delegating everything possible to competent people and letting them get on with their jobs. This had always been Anand's style, however, and he enjoyed a reputation for spotting good people. Effective delegation would also free him up to devote attention to problem areas where he could make the most useful personal contribution. This meant appointing deputy prime ministers with responsibilities for particular areas. Snoh was the obvious choice for all the economic portfolios – including finance, commerce, industry, agriculture, and science, technology, and energy. Anand selected General Pow Sarasin – 'Pi Pow'[3] as he always called him – to oversee the security portfolios. These included interior, defence, and transport and communications. Pow was a former director general of the police department who was widely respected for his competence and integrity.

Meechai Ruchupan was enlisted as the third deputy prime minister for the remaining portfolios and for his legal mind. 'He was always the legal brain after every coup,' says Anand. Indeed, Meechai Ruchupan had an almost embarrassing wealth of experience redrafting constitutions, but this also made him a good link to the legislative assembly.

There were no ministries of labour or 'social development and human security' (welfare) at the time. To cover these areas, Saisuree was made one of four ministers attached to the prime minister's office. The other three were MR Kasemsomosorn Kasemsri, like Anand a Cambridge-educated diplomat; Phaichit Uathavikul, an academic specialising in environmental affairs; and Mechai Viravaidya, an expert on population and development. Mechai believes one of the reasons for his inclusion was his earlier success in turning around the Provincial Water Authority. He was well recognised for family planning initiatives – these were so successful, in fact, that the common Thai word for a condom is mechai.

Instead of a 'kitchen cabinet' so beloved in British political memoirs, Anand ended up with a 'noodle cabinet', which lunched together at Government House, usually three times a week. Mechai and Saisuree were its most constant members, but the other two ministers attached to Anand's office and his three deputies also attended. The meals seldom lasted even half an hour, but ideas were tossed around to provide Anand with context and lively sounding boards.

Anand selected Arsa Sarasin for foreign minister. With Anand at the helm and taking a particular interest, Thai diplomacy was now firmly in the hands of the so-called 'Dulwich mafia'. As Arsa's older brother, General Pow, was to be deputy prime minister, Arsa playfully quizzed Anand on the wisdom of having two Sarasins in the cabinet. Anand reassured him the next day: 'Well, I talked to Suchinda and he doesn't mind.'

Anand did not invite Amnuay Viravan to join his cabinet, despite their friendship and recently intertwined careers. Amnuay says he never asked Anand why he, with all his experience as a deputy prime minister and finance minister in the Prem governments, was not approached. After all, other key figures from the Prem era were there, most notably Snoh. 'He proved to be a very good political leader, and I admired him for that,' says Amnuay. Ekamol Kiriwat was a deputy governor of the Bank of Thailand at the time, and saw Amnuay as his mentor. 'Khun Amnuay loves Khun Anand,' he says, 'but I don't think he believes Khun Anand is better than him.'

Anand did in fact consider Amnuay for the finance portfolio, and discussed it with Suchinda, who had nothing against him personally. Amnuay's technical brilliance was widely recognised, but he had been associated with General Chavalit Yongchaiyudh's New Aspiration Party – a very heavy black mark against him from the NPKC's perspective. 'It was well known that Suchinda and Chavalit did not get along,' says Anand.

Anand's pick for finance minister, Suthee Singsaneh, was suggested to him by Suchinda, and played well in many quarters. Suthee had been Prem's third finance minister, and was noted not just for his experience but also for his charm, and his talent for chivvying complex matters along. He was willing to humour people, including the press and the military.

The man chosen as deputy finance minister, Virabongsa Ramangkura, was also well regarded and progressive. Media-savvy and gregarious, Virabongsa liked nothing more than rehearsing his ideas in front of public audiences, preferably large ones.

Suchinda, with his old connections to the medical community, made another cabinet recommendation: Dr Pairoj Ningsanonda for health minister. Anand was acquainted with Pairoj as a classmate of his brother Chat, and went along with the suggestion.

The toughest portfolio allocation was the transport and communications ministry, which was coveted by Air Chief Marshal Kaset Rojananil. Kaset had executed the coup against Chatichai at the airport, and was considered the second most powerful figure in the junta after Suchinda; he was its key political strategist. Although there was arguably a security dimension to the communications portfolio, Anand felt that allowing a member of the junta to fill the position would seriously undermine his cabinet's credibility. It would be clear proof that the military's vested interests were in play.

Anand broached the problem with Suchinda, who was reticent, saying that the position had already been promised to Kaset. Although Suchinda was not prepared to tell Kaset to stand down, he had no objection to Anand dealing directly with the air force chief. When the two met, Kaset proved unexpectedly accommodating, and agreed to withdraw – a sign, perhaps, that the junta knew it had to be flexible enough to keep Anand on board. Anand did compromise, in allowing two of the three deputy ministers to be NPKC nominees: General Viroj Sangsanit and Air Chief Marshal Suthep Teparak.

With Kaset out of the line-up, Anand ended up with eight members of the military in his cabinet. Suchinda's brother in law, General Issarapong Noonpakdee, was interior minister with Air Chief Marshal Anan Kalinta and Admiral Vichet Karunyavanij as his deputies. Admiral Prapat Krisnachan was made defence minister, and General Wimol Wongwanich and Air Chief Marshal Pisit Saligupta were his deputies. The appointments had all been agreed with Suchinda. During his own tenure as prime minister, Chatichai had done his best to keep the military at bay, but the generals eventually struck back. In the Anand cabinet, in a Thai, post-coup context, the military appointments were not particularly controversial.

Anand was able to secure all the other ministries for high-flying civilians drawn from academia, the civil service, and the other upper reaches of the technocracy. Sipphanondha Ketudat was given industry, much to his own surprise. He had been expecting education, which went to Kaw Swasdi Panich. Amaret Sila-on was given commerce, and Dr Attasit Vejjajiva became deputy health minister under Dr Pairoj.

In the final tally, technocrats and high-powered civilians outnumbered the military by nearly four to one. 'It may be a gross exaggeration to label the first Anand cabinet as the TDRI cabinet, but it certainly contains some truth,' Snoh later recalled – without any reference to the key role he himself played at the time.[4]

'I think Suchinda was sincere,' says Arsa. 'Anand was picked as a very able person, and was able to appoint his own cabinet. They happened to be honest people, and they worked for him, not the military.'

Accommodating the military

The NPKC promulgated its interim constitution on 1 March 1991, the day before Anand received the royal decree from King Bhumibol appointing him prime minister. Anand's cabinet was ready for its appointment with the king on Wednesday 6 March. By the time of the royal audience, a tailor had made Anand the white tunic suit of a government servant to replace the ones he had discarded in 1978. Fast off the blocks and unfettered by parties or coalitions, Anand had rolled out a government in just five days from the time Suchinda first asked him to be prime minister. It was a remarkable feat, and a taste of the pace and businesslike approach that would characterise the next year and 16 days. The first Anand cabinet was to be in office from 6 March 1991 to 22 March the following year, serving in a caretaker capacity until 7 April 1992.

On its first day, it convened for a face-to-face meeting with the NPKC at its Suan Ruen Rue Dee headquarters. Anand made some brief general statements about what he hoped could be achieved. Suchinda responded but took an unexpected line: he asked Anand about Thailand signing up to the United Nations' Convention on the Rights of the Child, which had been adopted by the General Assembly in 1989 and came into effect in 1990. The army chief wanted to know the implications. Could Thailand meet its obligations if it signed?

Anand made some comments off the cuff, but knew he was not well versed on the topic. He deferred to Saisuree, who was unfazed. Saisuree happened to know one member of the NPKC quite well: Kaset, her former classmate. She quickly ran through the ins and outs of signing up to conventions, and the need for exempting clauses if the supporting domestic legislation is missing or inadequate. As a principle, she advocated signing conventions quickly and then catching up, but noted disapprovingly that conservative elements within the foreign ministry generally liked to take things much more slowly. According to Saisuree, the problem areas for Thailand included its laws on nationality and compulsory education. In her view, about five exemptions would be needed for signing up – and the sooner the better.

Suchinda was satisfied, both with Saisuree's response and the proof sitting before him that Anand had filled his cabinet with competent people.

The NPKC and the Anand cabinet never met again. Many of them did, however, gather more informally soon after at Don Muang International Airport to send Chatichai into soft exile overseas. 'The amazing thing is that when Chatichai left Thailand, nearly everyone was at the airport, including Prime Minister Anand,' US Ambassador Daniel O'Donohue recalled. 'So the new cabinet, put in office by the Thai military, all turned out at the airport to say goodbye to Chatichai. The old cabinet, which had been deposed, was also at the airport, and the military leaders were there. This was truly a Thai-style coup.'[5]

In his first administration, Anand ran the executive branch as an appointed prime minister. He was not, strictly speaking, the head of government. As supreme commander and chairman of the National Peacekeeping Council (NPKC), it was General Sunthorn Kongsompong who technically filled this role. However, in practical terms, Sunthorn's was a nominal role, much to his frustration at times. Anand's relations with Sunthorn were courteous and proper on the surface, but there was no real empathy beneath. Although Anand says he sensed no animosity, the two men were products of different, alien worlds.

At private social functions with King Bhumibol presiding, protocol dictated that Sunthorn be placed beside the king, the head of state, with Anand sitting one place removed. This was indeed the arrangement on one or two occasions. However, Sunthorn found King Bhumibol and Anand talking across him, leaving him extraneous to the conversation. One day, Anand arrived to find the name tags reversed. He was now sitting between the king (head of state) and Sunthorn (head of government). Anand pointed this out to the chamberlain. The response was, 'Well, you had better talk to the king.' In fact, Sunthorn was not in the least bit bothered by the rearrangement. 'I think in his mind he was happier,' says Anand.

Interior Minister Issarapong was also cut from an entirely different cloth to Anand. At a dinner with Anand, Staporn, and Suchinda, the general once brought up the issue of Article 27 in the interim constitution. This gave special, extrajudicial executive powers to the head of government during unusual political times. Field Marshal Sarit Thanarat had used a similar, more lethal, clause (Article 17) to personally authorise executions nearly a dozen times in the 1960s. Anand was adamant that the NPKC should not be allowed such power, and that the phrase 'with the approval of the prime minister', which had been included in the NPKC's interim constitution before it could receive King Bhumibol's signature, had to remain – not as a softener but as an effective veto.

Issarapong believed the article should be invoked to allow for executions for the most heinous crimes committed by both military and civilians, but Anand refused to go along with it. 'I am the prime minister, and I will not give approval,' he told them at the table.[6] 'I put my foot down.'

Rather than debate the matter, Issarapong stood up abruptly, saluted, and marched off. 'Next day,' Anand recalls, 'Issarapong came and apologised for leaving dinner early – he was always courteous to me.' The incident was never raised again. As a cabinet minister, Issarapong was the only member of the junta who watched Anand operating at first hand. No matter how much he might have disagreed with Anand on particular matters, his inclination was to avoid public divisions and maintain civil working relations. Sunthorn, Issarapong, and Air Chief Marshal Kaset Rojananil respected their chosen prime minister. That did not mean that they liked him, and the relationships became publicly testy at times. Without Suchinda's steadying, pragmatic influence, many believe Anand might have been removed before the year was out. 'I think I created a constituency of my own, but with Suchinda alongside it would have been difficult for the military to remove me,' says Anand. The importance of Suchinda's role is confirmed by Arsa Sarasin. 'Suchinda was respected by his colleagues very much,' he recalls. 'He was the stabilising factor as far as Anand was concerned, and helped a lot.'

In the NKPC, 'Sunthorn was the figurehead and Suchinda was running the show,' Anand recalls. 'My determination was to strike up a workable, co-operative relationship with the military. It was important to set the tone from the beginning. Suchinda was helpful in smoothing out some of the viewpoints or feelings of hard-core military members of the council.'

When problems arose, the intermediary with Suchinda and the military was usually Staporn; if they involved foreign affairs, it was Arsa. It was not always necessary. Anand remembers Suchinda feeding him useful information on occasions to circumvent problems. 'We had very good personal relations,' he says. 'Even Staporn did not know everything.'

Anand was aware of one particular trait in Suchinda: 'He takes care of his friends.' Loyalty to friends, classes, and clans are powerful Thai traits. The military's network of friends extended deep into the state enterprises and business world. Anand realised that it was essential that sensitive bills should be fully discussed with the generals ahead of time. Consequently they never felt that they had not been properly informed. He cannot recall them being deliberately excluded from any issue. 'I never wanted to put them on the spot. I dealt with sensitive issues quietly, sensitively, and confidentially. They were interested in results. So long as I delivered, they respected me.'

Anand blocked the junta's attempts to increase the national defence budget, and to develop land owned by the military in Bangkok for commercial purposes. This caused friction with Sunthorn and Kaset, which received publicity, but it passed. Anand always downplayed the issue, noting his regular interactions with Suchinda and Sunthorn. In September, he told *Siam Rath*'s magazine that he was working comfortably with the junta, and being given 'the territory that a prime minister should have'.

Team coach

Saisuree Chutikul recalls Anand prepping his cabinet like a team manager before a big match. 'I hand-picked you all; therefore I trust you will do your work well,' he said to them. 'You are not going to tell me you don't know about something. There is no time for learning – this is the time for action.'

'Khun Anand told us that we were not under anyone's orders,' says Saisuree. 'We were going to do what we thought should be done for our country.' Although she had never been a minister before, Saisuree in fact had far more cabinet experience than most of the people in the room on that first day, particularly Anand. She had served as a deputy government spokesperson under Prem. In that role, she attended cabinet meetings, sitting in the centre of the horseshoe formed by the ministers, preparing papers and summarising meetings.

'I was angry about the way they sometimes spoke about women,' she says of the all-male Prem cabinets. Its members, like the cabinet of Chatichai Choonhavan that followed, saw no great role for government in women's affairs. 'These are your mothers and sisters,' she used to protest to anyone who would listen. Nevertheless, she had got on well with Prem, the retired general, whom she found to be direct, if somewhat abrupt and military in manner. She would put cut flowers in his home after being shocked to find no living things there. During her time working with him, she made it her business to read every folder that went through the cabinet office.

With the appointment of Anand as prime minister, she now had the chance to help set the national agenda herself. The irony for Saisuree and her colleagues in the first Anand cabinet was that a great deal of overdue, progressive legislation was passed through the compliant, military-dominated National Legislative Assembly. 'The military are not used to long debates,' says Anand. 'They just wait for decisions and orders to follow.'

When he moved into Government House in the first week of March, Anand inherited a permanent staff of civil servants left by Chatichai. The cabinet secretary general, Yongyuth Sarasombath, who had been on the hijacked C-130 with Chatichai, had been replaced by Group Captain Sopon Suwannuruji, a slightly older schoolmate of Anand, albeit one whom he barely recalled. They got along well enough, but Anand was reluctant to trouble him with anything minor or errand-like.[7] Daily run-of-the-mill work was instead assigned to the deputy cabinet secretary general, Wissanu Krea-ngam, who had been appointed only a month before the coup.

Wissanu was a lecturer in law at Chulalongkorn University. He had been delighted at the opportunity to serve in Chatichai's elected government, hoping to research the workings of democracy first-hand. When, almost immediately, this possibility was snuffed out by the coup, Wissanu was disappointed. He was inclined to return to Chulalongkorn, where his old position remained open. Hearing of Wissanu's dilemma through Sopon, Anand asked him to shelve his reservations. He remembered Wissanu's quality legal counsel to the Federation of Thai Industries, and respected the young man's intellect. 'We will leave together,' Anand told Wissanu.

Anand did advise Wissanu to carry on lecturing to keep himself sharp intellectually. Over the next 18 months, he sometimes used Wissanu as an intellectual stalking horse. When all sides of an argument needed to be explored, Wissanu would often be appointed to the role of 'presumed enemy' to argue the other side. 'Anand is a strange person,' Wissanu recalls, thinking of their intellectual jousts. 'But I am too. I asked many questions and he answered them all. He once said, "Keep asking."'

Anand brought Busarakham, his personal assistant, together with another secretary from Saha Union to handle his personal affairs, but they did not become involved in any government business. Four secretaries occupied the area outside Anand's office. Although there was much protocol and bureaucracy in the daily traffic, Busarakham did not find her work arduous, and there were always plenty of competent people available to help. However, she did find the hours extremely long. Anand would normally leave home at 8:30am, peruse papers in his car and arrive at about 9am. He came in earlier than at Saha Union, and generally stayed much later, sometimes until midnight. He also came at weekends, something he had not done since his UN days. 'Even if I was not in the office, I would be working at home,' he says. 'I am lucky that I always enjoy whatever I do.' When Anand worked late, he would emerge for an informal dinner with his staff and put out of his mind whatever issue was engrossing him. While everyone was eating, the conversation was usually frivolous, with plenty of laughter and jokes. Then Anand would draw the social curtain and return to his desk, with his cigar smouldering. 'The work had to be done, no matter what,' says Busarakham.

Being prime minister

On his appointment, Anand had had to step aside as chairman of Saha Union. The company worked on Saturdays, and Anand went to the office in the afternoon to tell Damri Darakananda that he had become prime minister. It was an unusual situation, and Anand apologised for the lack of warning. ' All of a sudden, Khun Anand came to see me and told me the country needed him as prime minister,' Damri recalls. 'I thought if anyone is fit for the job, it's him. I was very supportive of him. He left. We were happy for him, and that was that. Saha Union never asked for any favours from the government.'

Anand's new salary as prime minister was, however, significantly less than Damri had been paying in the private sector. He had to step down from other remunerated positions, too, including the directorship of Siam Commercial Bank. 'My monthly income went down drastically,' he says. He had been appointed prime minister out of the blue, and had made no financial provision. Although his daughters were both career women, married, and taking care of themselves, he nevertheless found his personal finances squeezed.

His friend Chan Bulakul stepped in with a personal loan of a million baht to tide Anand over, on the understanding that it could be repaid whenever convenient. Chan viewed this very much as a personal matter between friends, something to be handled, at least initially, with discretion, and he told nobody. Anand, on the other hand, found his predicament quite amusing, and was soon dining out on the story that he had had to borrow a million baht from a friend to be able to afford the privilege of being prime minister. 'He told so many people,' says Chan, 'that I thought I might as well do so myself.'

Anand was quite unusual among Thai prime ministers in that he emerged from his term of office poorer than when he went in. The loan from Chan had to be repaid. Fortunately, Anand and Damri had earlier bought two plots of land in a housing estate, alongside one another, with a view to their eventual retirement. Later, he made good on his debt to Chan by selling his plot to Damri.

Although Anand had had no previous cabinet experience, he had little difficulty in handling the weekly meetings on Tuesdays. He had sat in on countless committees at the United Nations in the 1970s, and had even chaired a few as a member of the Law of the Sea working group. Over the years, and in many settings, he had had the chance to observe some very skilled practitioners at work, and had tried to absorb some of their good practices. There were also many tedious experiences with self-important windbags who went off-topic. 'People say Anand is arrogant,' says Ekamol Kiriwat. 'I don't think he is, but he won't suffer fools.'

At the first cabinet meeting, Anand laid out his rules of engagement, much as he had done with the NPKC a few days earlier. Everybody, he promised, would have the chance to make their case on the issues that arose, but the final decision would always be his. Cabinet members who found themselves on the losing side were to accept Anand's decisions in good grace. There was to be no talking outside cabinet, politicking, or backbiting. Anybody uncomfortable with these conditions could resign. There was also to be no corruption – full stop. 'They kept their promise,' says Anand.

A joke got around soon enough that Anand's idea of democracy was to listen to everybody's point of view and then for him to make the decision on their behalf. In fact, that was exactly how the cabinets functioned. Arguably Anand took the prime minister's prerogative to make the final decisions in cabinet more seriously than other prime ministers. The three deputy prime ministers and other senior ministers were expected to have smoothed out possible divisions ahead of the Tuesday cabinet meetings, and a clear consensus usually existed on most issues.

'They knew the etiquette and rules,' says Snoh of Anand's cabinet protocols. 'They would fight, but once things were settled it was over.'

There was already a well-established tradition in Thai cabinets of not taking votes. There had been an exception to this protocol only once. During Chatichai's government, Samak Sundaravej was in a minority opinion on a matter relating to the State Railway of Thailand, which fell within his remit as minister of transport and communications. He wanted the issue put to a vote. 'Historically, we never vote in cabinet,' Chatichai countered. 'Why don't we start?' argued Samak. 'I disagree with the summary of the meeting.' 'Okay,' agreed Chatichai, warily. 'But let's vote first on whether we should vote.' The cabinet then proceeded to vote overwhelmingly against voting. Thus, the only vote ever taken by a Thai cabinet was not to vote.

Wissanu, who would be cabinet secretary to six more prime ministers after Anand, believes this consensual, rather gentlemanly practice may owe a little to the wartime cabinet of Field Marshal Plaek Phibunsongkhram, which never formally voted to join the Axis alliance after Japan invaded in 1941. Nor did it subsequently vote to declare war on the US and Great Britain.

As to the dress code to be adopted by ministers, Anand did not go as far as Singapore's premier Lee Kuan Yew, who had favoured semi-casual attire, including open-necked white shirts. However, he did encourage them to make themselves comfortable. 'I am going to take my jacket off, and you are at liberty to do so too,' he told them.

Mechai Viravaidya had been a deputy industry minister under General Prem. He recalls that Anand was more assertive in the decision-making process outside cabinet than Prem, whose inclination was always to listen quietly at meetings and let trusted ministers take the lead in reaching decisions. 'The telephone was always there to be used,' says Mechai of Anand. Like others, he found that Anand did not mind being bothered at all hours. 'He has the skill to get 120 per cent out of you.' Mechai remembers Anand calling him once to tell him that he would be siding with an argument counter to the position that Mechai was advocating. 'I was totally behind whatever decision he made,' says Mechai. 'He wasn't a dictator – it was all explained.'

'The opportunity to speak out was always there, and Anand encouraged people to do it,' said Kosit Panpiemras, the deputy minister of agriculture and co-operatives. As Kosit recalls, Anand rarely had any need to be tough on his ministers as by the time a matter reached cabinet their positions were seldom too far apart. 'He talks people around,' says Nukul.

'You have to earn the respect of your colleagues in cabinet,' says Anand. 'They must have faith in you – trust you.' Although he consciously structured the cabinet to keep disputatious parties apart, the cabinet room was filled with discussion –

even when conclusions had been reached earlier. Anand cannot remember any cabinet exchanges that led him to change his mind on an earlier decision.

'Although certain decisions had already been made, my approach was that I wanted people to hear all sides in the cabinet meeting,' says Anand. 'I wanted to maintain the debate but in a reduced form. They had to be prepared to live with a decision – to tolerate it. If I did not feel consensus, I would let the debate go on. I am not the dictatorial type – there had to be "collective ownership".'

But there were limits. 'I never allowed them to repeat arguments – I was very strict on that,' says Anand. 'It was important not to waste time. They could let off steam in smaller groups outside the cabinet, but once they were inside they had to raise matters in a less incendiary way. When I noticed the temperature rising, I would tell a joke to distract them. A chairman has to be in control without stifling debate – it has to be stage-managed. I like to listen to arguments, but there is a thin dividing line between arguments and quarrels.'

Anand was very careful not to play favourites, particularly in the context of close friendships with people such as Nukul and Snoh. 'I separate personal relationships from working relationships.' He believes people noticed his impartiality.

Sopon Suwannuruji, the secretary general of the cabinet, scheduled the cabinet agendas, assisted by Wissanu. The Tuesday cabinets were sometimes relatively brief, but they could run through lunch, and ministers would be served where they sat. Anand would occasionally call breaks when he felt there was a need for private talks or bathroom visits. 'I did not allow smoking during cabinet meetings. Nor was there any smoking break. If anybody wished to smoke, he had to go outside.' Some meetings ran from 9am right through to the evening, usually due to a long order of business rather than lengthy debates on individual issues. Kosit recalls agendas being got through briskly. 'Anand was very good at details. He has the capacity to explain why, and that's a quality that is difficult to find. I felt comfortable under him, and I liked the challenge. If he could prove me wrong, I accepted it.'

'There were a lot of subjects to discuss,' says Pridi Boonyobhas, Anand's close aide, who was always stationed outside the cabinet room. As secretary general to the prime minister, Staporn was always in attendance, constantly moving back and forth between the cabinet room and the prime minister's offices with papers, ensuring that precious time was not wasted. Pridi viewed Staporn as a 'very capable man'.[8] The son of rice merchants from Nakhon Sawan, Staporn shared Anand's unusual disdain for golf – 'a waste of time', preferring badminton and basketball. He was a gourmet and appreciated fine wine. Like Anand, Staporn was a voracious reader.[9] Anand admired his sharp mind, quick grasp, and ability to get things done. There had sometimes been quite strong disagreements during their Board of Investment encounters, but this was not a lingering issue on either side.

Looking back on one of the most interesting years in his career, the relatively junior Kosit was struck by Anand's unabashed bluntness: 'If I said things like he did, it would get me into a lot of trouble. I don't know if it's charisma or what his secret is.'

The communicator

For Prime Minister Prem Tinsulanond, silence was always golden. He believed that the less was said, the less chance there was of a mistake. Chatichai was more outgoing and avuncular but he also never exposed himself by speaking publicly in any detail. 'No problem', his constant retort to reporters, became his nickname. His policy on Indochina was real and significant, but articulated as a single, concise sound bite: 'From battlefield to marketplace.' Anand's approach was different.

For Anand, communication was everything. 'In the first six months, I devoted a lot of effort to building bridges to the public,' he says. 'I was speaking publicly once or twice a week. I gave interviews every day. I put my agenda across, explained, and tried to get people to understand issues and policies. I never criticised the military deliberately. I said it was my duty to raise issues and explain. That was a psychological move on my part. Thais don't like people talking about themselves.'

He certainly had sceptics to win over.

'When Anand was first in office, we felt very far away from him,' recalls Karuna Buakamsri, a second-year student at Chulalongkorn University at that time and a rising official in the Student Federation of Thailand. After the NKPC coup, the Chulalongkorn Student Union had immediately called a press conference to denounce it, but reporters who turned up found themselves vastly outnumbered by plainclothes policemen. 'Anand was from a noble family and a diplomat,' Karuna says. 'He had a reputation for arrogance, and of not really knowing the man on the street. He was a *phudee Ratannakosin* – upper class. He was serving the military so I was against him. So he was not a good person – my attitude was not very positive.'

The foreign media were also initially sceptical, certainly much more so than the foreign business community. Soon after Anand's appointment, the Ministry of Foreign Affairs sent its head of information, Sakthip Krairiksh, with a team to the Foreign Correspondents' Club of Thailand (FCCT)[10] to give a briefing. The relationship between Thailand and the foreign press was generally frigid and mistrustful. Although both Prem and Chatichai had followed a tradition of making occasional formal keynote addresses to the FCCT, contact with the government for most correspondents was confined to renewing their annual accreditation and applying for one-year visas. Prickly areas in the relationship included coverage of the royal family and access to the Thai-Cambodian border, where a tripartite guerrilla force was based, waging a civil war against the communist government in Phnom Penh headed by Prime Minister Hun Sen.

The foreign affairs ministry wanted – or more accurately had been told by Anand's office – to turn over a new leaf. Sakthip was solicitous towards the foreign press corps: the new government wanted to establish a more cordial working relationship. Correspondents were duly invited for drinks on a spectacular balcony at Saranrom Palace, the foreign ministry, overlooking the Grand Palace. Across the way, the twinkling stupas of Wat Phra Kaew and its main structure, the Temple of the Emerald Buddha, were fully illuminated, sparkling in the clear dark sky.

That evening, Mechai, who had always been accessible to foreign journalists, acted as an informal master of ceremonies. Thus, the first steps were taken towards improving Thailand's relations with the foreign press. Meeting many of the correspondents for the first time, Anand made it clear that he would be giving interviews, and that he also intended to address the FCCT as soon as possible.

He made good on the promise on 25 April with a keynote address to a packed ballroom at the Dusit Thani. The event was beamed out live on Channel 9, with production standards unusually high for the time. *The Nation's* Suthichai Yoon provided live commentary, as Anand spoke without interpreters and answered unvetted questions from the floor. He described his premiership as 'one of the greatest accidents in history'.

Afterwards, he adjourned to Library 1918 beside the hotel's main lobby to relax with a brandy and a cigar. He engaged informally for well over an hour with about 20 senior correspondents. Although *MR* Kukrit Pramoj had always been a witty and polished speaker when it came to the foreign press, Anand's directness, tone and informality were unprecedented – and indeed have not been replicated by any Thai premier subsequently. Meanwhile the foreign journalists quickly realised that there was the junta and there was the premier – and that they did not seem to be playing from quite the same score.

Soon after his evening with the FCCT, Anand made a similar address to the Joint Foreign Chambers of Commerce of Thailand (JFCCT). A highlight was his open invitation for recommendations on legal and procedural improvements. This resonated with a jaded community used to fruitless lobbying, arcane bureaucracy, and demands for tea money. Anand suddenly seemed to be talking the language of free markets, liberalism, and level playing fields. But was this a tropical mirage? Coups were usually associated with conservative backlashes.

Anand would return to both the FCCT and the JFCCT before the year was out. He also took any opportunity he could to talk directly to Thai audiences. Ever since his early years in the US, he had always enjoyed speaking in public – but ironically he had accumulated almost no experience doing so in Thai. Speaking publicly in Thai was a source of particular personal satisfaction. 'That was an asset I never thought I had,' he says.

'Winston Churchill once said that to be a good speaker you need a vocabulary of only 5,000 words,' says Anand. 'When you speak, you make use of the available material in your head, jokes, and punch lines. I read about international affairs, biographies, and history. I remember bits and pieces and it is all stored in my head. Of course, my weakness is that I only read what interests me. I never read scientific books.'

Looking back, Anand estimates that only 30 per cent of his speeches were formally drafted. The rest were delivered extemporaneously and with growing facility, often based on talking points prepared by Staporn. He would often speak off the cuff, and confesses that he does not read speeches very well. He also sensed that people listened more closely when he spoke his mind and engaged visually with his listeners. Thai public speakers he admired were Prince Wiwat Jayant, MR Kukrit Pramoj, and Seksan Prasertkun – the latter two both writers as well as political figures. Seksan rose to prominence in 1973 as a student leader. 'His statements always make sense,' says Anand. Prince Wiwat was the first governor of the Bank of Thailand, and Anand recalls his eloquence addressing annual Oxford and Cambridge dinners in Bangkok.

The foreign media were surprised by Anand's accessibility, and his unusual sharpness and frankness. It was timely because a prestigious international event had been thrown into question by the coup. Thailand had committed itself to hosting the World Bank/International Monetary Fund (IMF) annual meetings in October. These autumn meetings are held two out of every three years in Washington, and the third is staged somewhere overseas. The project was being shepherded through by the finance ministry's Nibhat Bukkanasutr.

Nibhat had played an important role in the devaluation of the baht in 1986 under Prem. That did much for the national economy, but nearly triggered a coup by the then army chief, General Arthit Kamlang-ek, who had not been forewarned. The general felt national prestige had been damaged. As Arthit fumed on television, Nibhat booked into a suite at The Oriental, and vanished from sight.

In 1991, Nibhat was devoting strenuous effort to completing the Queen Sirikit National Convention Centre (QSNCC), the venue for the IMF and World Bank meetings. In its day, the QSNCC would be rated one of the top ten conference centres in the world. Fortunately for the NPKC and the Anand government, these gatherings of global finance officials and bankers were not yet the target of the anti-globalisation protests that have routinely afflicted them since the late 1990s. There was, however, a problem nobody could miss. Directly opposite the QSNCC stood the ramshackle remnants of Pai Singto, a slum in the heart of the city that had resisted various clearance efforts – including arson – over the years. The mostly wooden buildings were typical of slums all over Bangkok, including Klong Toey, the largest, close by in the port area. Pai Singto's tumbledown structures had their own story to tell about Thailand's development.

Mechai Viravaidya was soon up and running with a campaign about Bangkok having some of the nicest slums in the world. Paint was judiciously applied to spruce up the urban eyesore, which survived into the 21st century. The official response was nimble and humorous, and sidestepped a potential public relations disaster. After the coup, there had been serious talk of taking the annual meetings elsewhere.

'That would have been a lot of added negative publicity for Thailand,' Anand recalls. Failure to complete the QSNCC on time was not an option; this was to be the first internationally visible meeting in Thailand after the coup and everybody was keen to play down the negative signals that had gone out. 'It was well attended – all the big shots were here,' says Anand.

CHAPTER 11

ANAND'S FIRST TERM: FOREIGN RELATIONS (1991–2)

On familiar ground

As Thailand's prime minister during a critical period in Cambodian history, Anand was able to witness and participate in the final throes of the Cold War that had so shaped his career as a young diplomat. He was well versed in Cambodia's tragic experience since the late 1960s, when it became caught up in the Vietnam War. He also had personal diplomatic experience from the 1970s of working to normalise relations with China, Laos, and Vietnam. He was therefore in a position to keep his own counsel, and also to play a low-key role as events unfolded in the region. Cambodia was Thailand's greatest regional concern, as it had been in the time of Chatichai and his young Baan Phitsanulok advisers.

'I was engaging in adhocracy,' he says. 'I assigned myself a role of being not so much a facilitator as a moderator. I was involved behind the scenes, and worked with the Cambodian parties individually and collectively.'

Anand picked up the threads of Thailand's overall foreign policy with relative ease. His foreign affairs team was unusually robust and seasoned, despite having been delivered into office by a coup. One of four ministers in the prime minister's office, *MR* Kasemsomosorn Kasemsri was a former permanent secretary at the foreign ministry with a similar Cambridge background.

Anand had also had a close relationship since childhood with Foreign Minister Arsa Sarasin. Arsa had survived the 1976 purge of the foreign ministry, and had remained a constant presence there; he was a solid anchor after the rapid succession of foreign ministers since August 1990, when Prime Minister

Chatichai Choonhavan offloaded Air Chief Marshal Siddhi Savetsila in a cabinet reshuffle. The departure of Siddhi, the old national security chief and CIA ally turned diplomat, caused some dismay to the US State Department and its embassy in Bangkok.

Anand's deputy secretary general, Vidhya Raiyananonda, was also a senior diplomat, and devoted much of his time to liaising between Government House and the foreign ministry. Arsa recalls that Anand knew on a daily basis about whatever had been discussed at the foreign ministry.

As army chief, General Suchinda Kraprayoon also played a part in regional foreign policy. He continued the military tradition of close involvement in relations with neighbouring countries that had been fostered by Field Marshal Sarit Thanarat and General Kriangsak Chomanand, among others. Military involvement in foreign affairs was one of the issues that had so rankled peppery diplomats such as Chawan Chawanid at the foreign ministry in 1976.

Recalling the first Anand government, Arsa says: 'I had a really close relationship with Suchinda because I recognised that you could not work without the military.' Suchinda was particularly important in relation to Cambodia where the Thai military controlled the flow of foreign military assistance from China, the US, and others, to the tripartite guerrilla coalition fighting the Phnom Penh government of Prime Minister Hun Sen. Indeed, the Cambodians fighting along the border trusted Suchinda more than some of his predecessors to actually deliver their weapons and other *matériel*.

Suchinda would call at the foreign ministry to see Arsa at least once a month at around 6:30 or 7am. The visits preceded 'morning prayers' – a routine 8:30am meeting at the ministry that set the agenda for the day. During their early-morning conversations, Arsa says, Suchinda 'would listen very hard and make suggestions sometimes'. Because Suchinda came calling, Arsa remembers, other members of the junta did the same thing, including General Issarapong Noonpakdee, the army chief of staff and minister of the interior.

Cambodia

The smallest country by landmass in mainland Southeast Asia, Cambodia was occupied by Vietnam at the end of 1978. The Vietnamese invasion was the issue that gave ASEAN unprecedented cohesion throughout the 1980s, even though the regional grouping had not been formed to deal with security issues. The common regional focus on ending Cambodia's occupation was the key topic at numerous ASEAN meetings, and paved the way to the establishment of the ASEAN Regional Forum for 'security issues of common interest and concern' in 1994.

One of the key Cambodian figures was its former king, Prince Norodom Sihanouk, who had abdicated in favour of his father in 1955 to become prime minister and later head of state. General Lon Nol pushed Sihanouk into exile in a US-backed move in 1970. Following a historic broadcast from Beijing, Sihanouk then became the nominal head of the Khmer Rouge front that took control of the country so disastrously in 1975. The Khmer Rouge regime, Democratic Kampuchea, was responsible for the deaths of an estimated 1.8 million people – more than a fifth of the population – during its rule from April 1975 to Christmas Day 1978, when Vietnam invaded. Sihanouk's personal reward was to be imprisoned in the palace in Phnom Penh for more than three years. Subsequently, he discovered that the Khmer Rouge had murdered 14 members of his family.

Sihanouk cultivated many international leaders in the years that followed, and was eventually given residences in two communist capitals, Beijing and Pyongyang – his royal pedigree was evidently not an issue. After periods of peripatetic exile in France, North Korea, and China, in 1984 Sihanouk became president of the Coalition Government of Democratic Kampuchea (CGDK) ranged along the Thai-Cambodian border. This government in exile and tripartite guerrilla coalition comprised the communist Khmer Rouge (Democratic Kampuchea) backed by China; and Sihanouk's royalist FUNCINPEC party[1] with its Armée Nationale Sihanoukiste (ANS); and the Khmer People's National Liberation Front (KPLNF). The latter was led by Son Sann, who had been a prime minister in the late 1960s. The KPLNF was non-communist and backed principally by the US.

For Thailand, the most enduring legacy of the Vietnam War was refugees. After the fall of Indochina in 1975, some 150,000 people fled communist rule in Laos and Cambodia by seeking refuge in Thailand. Some Thai entrepreneurs, both civilian and military, eventually profited from the refugee business, supplying vast amounts of food and materials, and trucking water. The camps were rooted in misery with the lives of their occupants left on hold. Successive Thai governments were reluctant hosts; they always grasped for ways to shut down the camps through repatriation.

When the situation deteriorated further in Cambodia in 1979, a time when large numbers of refugees fleeing Vietnam by boat were also a mounting concern, there had been strong official resistance to allowing ever more refugees safe haven. Some 40,000 were forcibly repatriated by the Thai military in June that year. The month before, UN Secretary General Kurt Waldheim had visited the border to confirm personally that the refugees were genuine, and vouched for them to Prime Minister Kriangsak. 'Kriangsak told diplomats that the policy of repatriation would be stopped only if the world paid attention to Thailand's predicament at the forthcoming Geneva Conference on Indochinese refugees in July,' William Shawcross later reported in *The Washington Post*. 'In the event, Thailand's problems were practically ignored, as was Cambodia itself, at Geneva.'

> By mid-October there were at least 100,000 starving Cambodians on or along the Thai-Cambodian border. On Oct. 18 Kriangsak visited the area and, obviously moved by the misery he saw, expanded the government's new policy. Thailand would now have an "open door" and would allow entry to all Cambodians who wished to come. They could either stay along the border, where they would be fed or be moved into "holding centers".[2]

Thereafter, Thai governments continued to view the refugee problem as a serious national burden. At their height, the border camps contained some of the largest Cambodian population concentrations outside Phnom Penh. The dusty Thai border town of Aranyaprathet, opposite Cambodia's Poipet, had become capital to an entrenched refugee industry supported by the United Nations High Commissioner for Refugees (UNHCR), the United Nations Border Relief Operation (UNBRO), and numerous non-governmental organisations, mostly Western.

The disconnected, abandoned railway line at the Aranyaprathet-Poipet crossing symbolised in many ways what the Chatichai government – and then Anand's – wanted to reverse. They wanted the refugees to be able to return home safely, and normal cross-border relations to be re-established in a climate of peace and mutual prosperity. As the civil war continued, conditions safe enough for even partial repatriation remained elusive throughout the 1980s. There was always a debate going on in the background over whether the camps provided relief from or abetted the fighting over the border – or both.[3]

During Chatichai's premiership, efforts were made to break the deadlock, improve relations with Hun Sen, and to make Sihanouk a less overbearing presence. Hun Sen visited Bangkok for the first time in 1989, was shown the Grand Palace and other sites, and was treated as an honoured guest.

The ice had been broken at the Jakarta Informal Meetings in July 1988 and February 1989, and the Paris Conference on Cambodia in July and August 1989. The Paris talks were co-chaired by Foreign Minister Ali Alatas of Indonesia, and were intended to set the stage in Cambodia for the period after Vietnam's impending withdrawal in December that year.[4] Although 19 international players attended the talks – a major step forward – this was not enough to break the deadlock. As to the warring Cambodians, each group was 'immensely distrustful of all the others', Australia's then Foreign Minister Gareth Evans later observed.[5] US Secretary of State James Baker, who attended only the opening ceremony in Paris, was deeply and openly ambivalent about any future role for the Khmer Rouge in the country.[6] The Thais were more inclined to give them the benefit of the doubt to move the process along. Foreign journalists who brought up the Cambodian genocide would sometimes be lectured privately by Thai officials on the need to move on and bury the past.

One of the largest remaining camps was Site B in the Northeast's Buriram, which is among Thailand's most impoverished provinces. The camp was controlled by Sihanouk's ANS. Not long before Vietnam pulled out, US Congressman Stephen Solarz, the energetic chairman of the Asian and Pacific Affairs Subcommittee of the House Foreign Affairs Committee, visited and floated the idea of a transitional government for Cambodia run by the UN. His thinking had failed to gain traction in Washington, but UN involvement could circumvent the problem of power-sharing, which had been an insurmountable obstacle in Paris.

As always, the elephant in the room was the Khmer Rouge. Using the good offices of the UN would give China a diplomatic means to distance itself from its internationally reviled client. Solarz discussed the idea with Australian Foreign Minister Gareth Evans, who immediately wanted to run with it, and in November 1989 Evans presented an outline plan to the Australian senate.[7] Prince Sihanouk's son, Prince Norodom Ranariddh (who in 1983 had made the unlikely transition from being an associate professor of law at the University of Provence in France to ANS military commander)[8] presented the peace plan to his father. Sihanouk was favourable. In January 1990, the five permanent members of the Security Council accepted the proposal.

After the Jakarta and Paris talks, a meeting had been set up in Tokyo in 1990 by Chatichai's Baan Phitsanulok advisers, but these lacked a coherent script. The thinking had essentially been to bring the Cambodians all together in a room in the hope that everything would flow from there – the fact that the parties were still literally at war with each other notwithstanding. As Western diplomats watched a non-event unfolding in Japan with little sign of the parties engaging, General Chavalit Yongchaiyudh was flown in. Chavalit was Suchinda's predecessor as army chief, and one of the very few people familiar with the Cambodian factions and the other parties involved. On his way to the top, he had been involved in the formation of the CGDK, which had been formally established in Kuala Lumpur in June 1982, and lasted until 1993.

It was during Chavalit's thankless mediating efforts in Tokyo at the behest of Chatichai in 1990 that Chalerm Yubamrung, the firebrand communications minister, publicly disparaged Chavalit's wife, Khunying Pankrua, insinuating corruption. 'Although avoiding the use of names, Chalerm called Mrs Chavalit a "walking jewellery box",' Reuters reported. 'She responded by calling him a moron.'[9] An outraged Chavalit demanded a public apology and resigned from the cabinet. When King Bhumibol granted Chatichai an audience, and the opportunity to give his account of the fiasco, Suchinda accompanied the prime minister. Thailand's tense political situation again turned volatile; the military locked in behind the maligned Chavalit, rattling sabres, and threatening a coup. When the coup finally came early the following year, resulting in Anand's appointment in March 1991, Chalerm fled into ignominious exile in Sweden and Denmark. Chalerm's contribution to setting the scene for the first Anand government can never be underestimated.

UN peace plan

During Anand's watch in early 1991, international efforts to bring peace to Cambodia acquired new momentum. The financial collapse of the Soviet Union in the late 1980s had ended its military adventure in Afghanistan and proxy war in Cambodia. Vietnam had withdrawn its forces from Cambodia over a year earlier, but the low-intensity civil war ground on between Hun Sen's forces and the three guerrilla forces operating from the Thai border backed by China, the US, ASEAN, and some European powers. Despite Vietnam's withdrawal, refugees and displaced persons allied to different CGDK factions lingered on in the Thai border camps. These families had always provided the Thai military and other powers with the headcount for the guerrilla forces used as proxies against the occupying Russian-backed Vietnamese, and later Hun Sen's forces.

While the Cambodian peace process was under way after decades of war and devastation, it had snagged on some thorny issues. The Khmer Rouge, for example, did not want to acknowledge their involvement in a genocide. Even so, complex international diplomacy was finally bearing fruit and productive outside intervention on the ground looked possible. Arsa firmly believed that Thailand's most useful role was as a facilitator. 'I told my ASEAN friends, leave them alone to discuss their own country,' he recalls.

China-Thailand relations were on the up at this pivotal time. In June 1991, the elderly President Yang Shangkun arrived for a six-day state visit, with 40 officials and 20 journalists in train. Threatened protests by Chinese dissidents over the suppression of China's pro-democracy movement in Tiananmen Square two years earlier failed to materialise. When Foreign Minister Qian Qichen met with Foreign Minister Arsa, the situation in Cambodia was at the top of their discussion agenda. Bilateral relations were improving across the board. Qian's deputy Xu Dun Xin, and the vice minister of trade Wang Wen Dong, met Commerce Minister Amaret Sila-on. Bilateral trade was already worth US$1.2 billion annually, and Thailand was China's eighth-largest trade partner – with a deficit in China's favour for a fourth year running. It had reached US$452 million the previous year.[10]

With his villa in Beijing, Sihanouk was on good terms with the Chinese, who tacitly approved his steadily improving relationship with Hun Sen. This understanding was marginalising the Khmer Rouge. In June 1991, Sihanouk finally convened in Thailand the 12-member Supreme National Council for the first time since its formulation the previous September in Jakarta. With Sihanouk as president, it comprised six members from Hun Sen's side in Phnom Penh, two from the KPLNF, one from FUNCINPEC, and two Khmer Rouge. As hosts of the meeting, the Thai government chose the luxurious Royal Cliff hotel in Pattaya, a raucous seaside resort better known for its nightlife than as a setting for international diplomacy.

'My government's interest was to see peace and order restored in a neighbouring country,' says Anand. Suchinda, he recalls, was happy to leave arrangements to Anand and his team. 'Suchinda was acting as a facilitator to ensure all factions in the Cambodian dispute were involved directly or indirectly.'

'In a way, I drew a lesson from the Chatichai government's Baan Phitsanulok experience,' Anand recalls of his approach to Cambodia. 'They were always trying to publicise whatever they wanted to do. I didn't need the limelight. It was not my way of dealing with a very sensitive issue. I preferred quieter diplomacy.'

According to Gareth Evans, Sihanouk used Pattaya to broker a series of agreements between the four Cambodian parties, confirming their support for the Permanent Five framework and a central role for the UN in achieving a comprehensive settlement.[11]

But Sihanouk, Hun Sen, Ranariddh, and Son Sann were not the only members of the Cambodian factions making decisions in Pattaya. The Khmer Rouge delegation's nominal head, Khieu Samphan, the former president of Democratic Kampuchea, was the group's 'presentable face' for the purposes of international relations. In reality, it was Pol Pot who was making key decisions on behalf of the most powerful CGDK faction nearby – but from outside the Royal Cliff. Pol Pot's physical proximity to the process would have been impossible in Jakarta, Paris, or Tokyo – or indeed anywhere outside Thailand.

Pol Pot, whose real name was Saloth Sar, was a French-educated electrical engineer in his pre-revolutionary days. After Vietnam displaced his regime in 1979, he had operated along the Thai border, received medical treatment in Thai hospitals, and occasionally holidayed at Bang Saen, the Thai seaside resort where ASEAN was put together in 1967. The only access to Pol Pot – and conceivably to a settlement of some kind in Cambodia – was therefore through the Thai military. Sihanouk might have been president and titular head of the CGDK, but the Khmer Rouge, whose diplomats continued to occupy Cambodia's seat in the UN General Assembly on behalf of the CGDK, remained the fighting core of the guerrilla coalition. Even by the undiscriminating standards of Cold War alliances, the Khmer Rouge presence at the UN was deeply unpalatable to most governments.

Of the negotiations, *The Asian Wall Street Journal* reported that Pol Pot himself was inside the hotel. The management strongly refuted this. 'Pol Pot did not come,' a hotel spokesperson told *The Washington Post*. 'Everyone would have recognised him. There was only Khieu Samphan and about seven others in the delegation. No one stayed and hid out in their room.'[12]

'There was no reason for Pol Pot to be there,' says Anand, pointing out the solid Khmer Rouge presence. Nearby was good enough. Anand himself was at the hotel for the full duration of the talks and never went offsite. 'The suspicion was that he was in Bang Saen, but I intentionally did not want to know where he was because people kept asking me, particularly the press,' says Anand. 'I knew he was somewhere nearby.'

There were many secure places Pol Pot could have been. On the evening of 25 June, Khieu Samphan left the hotel, and it was presumed he was on his way to a meeting with the Khmer Rouge leader. Within a 30-minute drive of Pattaya, there was reputed to be a Khmer Rouge safe house, as well as two secure military facilities: the Royal Thai Navy's headquarters at Sattahip, and its massive, underused airbase at U-Tapao, from which US B-52 bombers had flown sorties over Cambodia and Vietnam during the war. The Thai navy connection extended to the guards outside Khmer Rouge-run refugee camps and military bases along the border; these were often marines and widely regarded as some of the best-trained Thai military units.

Saroj Chavanviraj, formerly Anand's younger colleague at the UN in New York, and now a member of the Thai contingent, remembers getting acquainted with Hun Sen during smoking breaks. 'The army people told me Pol Pot was there, but they didn't say where,' he recalls. A Khmer Rouge diplomat, In Sopheap, and others in the Cambodian delegations, later confirmed independently that the fanatically secretive Pol Pot was holed up somewhere nearby. [13]

With the UN, China, Japan, the US, Australia, Hun Sen, Sihanouk, Thailand and the rest of ASEAN all finally pushing in the same direction, Pol Pot was by this time left with little choice but to go along – although some argue the UN-backed peace juggernaut would have gone forward with or without his approval. He had certainly outstayed his welcome in Thailand, which wanted finally to normalise relations with Cambodia. That was the policy first unsuccessfully attempted by Chatichai as foreign minister in 1975 and 1976, when he brought Anand on board as permanent secretary.

As backers of the two non-communist factions in the CGDK, US officials were especially keen to keep their distance from the Khmer Rouge. Indeed, Ralph 'Skip' Boyce, the political counsellor at the embassy in Bangkok, spent much of his time ensuring that Assistant Secretary of State Richard Solomon was not photographed with any member of the Khmer Rouge delegation.

While everyone got to know each better in Pattaya, the summit was not without its trials. At the end of dinner on the last night, Sihanouk was invited to sing even though it was well past 10:30pm. To everyone's discomfort, the past and future king proceeded to croon for over an hour. 'He had the time of his life,' one attendee recalled. As Sihanouk warbled into the historic night, Charles Twining, the Khmer-speaking future US ambassador to Cambodia, was contemplating his impending posting to Phnom Penh. Twining's colleague Kenneth Quinn, another Cambodia veteran and future ambassador, leaned across and whispered in his ear, 'Every night, Charlie, every night.'

'[Pattaya was] was very important in getting things moving again in June 1991 – but the crucial player here was Sihanouk,' says Gareth Evans. He viewed Thailand as helpful but not a key driver of the process. 'Indonesia and Vietnam were the regional players who mattered most,' he says.

'Evans is correct, but he did not understand the role we decided to play,' says Anand of Thailand's place in the proceedings. 'We had a discreet role acting as a go-between. In UN parlance, we were providing "good offices". The key word is "discreet". We never intended to be a key driver of the process. That is a Western mentality.'

Evans later concluded:

> At the heart of the idea of giving an unprecedentedly central role to the United Nations in the actual governance of the country during the transitional period, was that this would give China a face-saving way of withdrawing its support from the Khmer Rouge, which would then wither on the vine. And it was essentially this solution – although there was a long diplomatic road ahead with many twists and turns – which unlocked the conflict and brought long-awaited and desperately needed peace to the country.[14]

Cambodia had experienced US carpet-bombing, the Khmer Rouge holocaust, and more than a decade locked in civil war. In late October 1991, the Paris Peace Accords – agreements on ending the war and a comprehensive political settlement – were signed, paving the way for a ceasefire, a peace process, a start on national rehabilitation, a new constitution, and ultimately a general election. This was all to be the responsibility of the United Nations Transitional Authority in Cambodia (UNTAC), which cost the international community almost US$2 billion, much of it paid for by Japan.

The UNTAC operation was finally approved by the UN Security Council in February 1992, more than two years after the Solarz-Evans plan first arrived in its in-tray. It was put into effect the following month, in March. A veteran Japanese diplomat, Yasushi Akashi, began serving as the UN secretary general's special representative and *de facto* proconsul. He arrived to oversee an interim bureaucracy numbering over 1,000. Australia's General John Sanderson commanded a huge multinational peacekeeping operation from 45 countries with 16,000 troops and nearly 4,000 police.

UNTAC was the biggest UN operation in history, and the only occasion the international body technically administered an entire country. Cambodia's sovereign interests were represented to the UN by a transitional body, the Supreme National Council of Cambodia presided over by Sihanouk and located in Phnom Penh. But all the while, Hun Sen, Cambodia's wily, chess-playing prime minister, maintained his hold on the levers of power: the military, police, judiciary, civil service, and the communist Cambodian People's Party, which had ruled under a Vietnamese umbrella since 1979.

In early 1992, with an international stamp of approval, Thailand was finally able to empty all the camps and repatriate its Cambodian refugees safely by bus. The Khmer Rouge later refused to disarm, and opted out of UN-supervised elections. To the outrage of Hun Sen, the general election was won by Ranariddh's royalist FUNCINPEC. To avoid a conflagration, Sihanouk brokered a compromise government with two prime ministers, Ranariddh as first prime minister and Hun Sen as second prime minister. For a while, the two got along unexpectedly well. The UNTAC interregnum was crucial to turning Cambodia around and putting it on a rocky path to peace after more than two decades of devastation.

Sihanouk was later asked if Gareth Evans and his dynamic diplomatic team should get the Nobel Peace Prize for their unstinting efforts on Cambodia. Sihanouk praised the Australians to the sky, and then impishly added a long list of other people who also deserved credit, including the Thais. Looking back, Arsa notes with satisfaction that the Thai foreign minister and other officials were among the first to be invited into Cambodia by Sihanouk after his return. It was left to Solarz to make good on a promise that he would nominate Evans for the Nobel if he succeeded in bringing peace to Cambodia. 'Which, I should gracefully acknowledge, he duly did in 1992, albeit not to any discernible effect in persuading the judges,' Evans later recorded in his memoirs.[15] Solarz himself never took any public credit for his initiative.

Soon afterwards, Sakthip Krairiksh, a senior diplomat who had once worked under Siddhi Savetsila at the National Security Council, was made ambassador in Phnom Penh to foster bilateral relations between two countries that had been at odds for centuries despite their closely shared cultural roots. Sakthip's Cambodian counterpart in Bangkok, Ambassador Roland Eng, was a former aide to Sihanouk and Ranariddh's brother in law, and would regularly call on Prem Tinsulanond, president of the Privy Council. Sihanouk ascended the throne again in 1993, and diplomatic relations between the two kingdoms in the mid 1990s were probably better than they have ever been.

Many years later, Anand was the keynote speaker for UNICEF at a conference in Siem Reap that was opened by Cambodia's indefatigable prime minister. During his address, Hun Sen noted Anand's presence and made a point of mentioning the vital role the talks in Pattaya in 1991 had played in setting Cambodia on a new course. In Hun Sen's estimation, Anand had done 'many good things for Cambodia'.

Anand remembered feeling relief at the successful conclusion of the Pattaya meeting, and some quiet satisfaction. 'I was relieved, but I never knew my role was appreciated until I went to Siem Reap and Hun Sen recognised me publicly. It was after so many years.'

Beyond Cambodia

In December 1991, Anand made his first formal visit to China since 1975; he had visited frequently on Saha Union business. That month he also led a 40-member business delegation to Japan. He continued from there, with a much smaller entourage, to Washington for a working visit.

The US had changed since the Cold War, and by this time took a jaundiced view of military takeovers and unelected governments. Promoting cordial relations was nevertheless a plank of Anand's foreign policy. Having served a stint as ambassador in Washington in the 1970s, Anand felt that his visit was a fleeting homecoming of sorts. He was on first-name terms with President George H.W. Bush as a result of their years together as permanent representatives to the UN in New York during the Vietnam War. They had always been friendly and sometimes socialised away from work. Anand remembers being invited on one occasion to

Bush's private box at the Metropolitan Opera, along with France's permanent representative, Louis de Guiringaud.[16]

Anand's connection to Suchinda's coup ruled out his visit being termed official, and therefore proscribed a night in the Lincoln Bedroom at Blair House. 'I was invited as head of government on a working visit, and that automatically disqualified me from staying at Blair House,' Anand recalls. 'It was just a matter of protocol.' There were no other protocol issues during the visit, however, and Bush received him in the Oval Office ahead of their lunch. It was a reunion of old friends in unexpected circumstances, and for Anand a moment of personal satisfaction. Afterwards, Bush gave Anand a tour of his private quarters at the White House.

Anand was well aware of the festering wounds in Vietnam's relations with both the US and Thailand. In January, a few weeks after his visit to Washington, he visited Hanoi and was received by Vietnamese Prime Minister Vo Vian Kiet. With the US trade embargo still in place – it would not be lifted until February 1994 – Anand called for better relations between Vietnam and its old enemy, the US. 'As long as one remains obsessed with the past and mistrusts, there can be no progress,' Anand told reporters.[17] Arsa hewed to the same line, and remembers making jaws drop at a meeting with his Vietnamese counterparts. He told them it was time to get over the war and 'let bygones be bygones'. A break was called while his interlocutors withdrew to recover their composure.

With time so short for the Anand administration, Thailand's diplomatic agenda was dominated by its immediate neighbours. Impoverished Laos had to be content with receiving half of Thailand's modest US$8-million foreign aid budget, but official relations improved when President Kaysone Phomvihane, the ethnic Vietnamese strongman and Pathet Lao leader during the Vietnam War, visited Bangkok in January 1992 for a ten-day state visit. This warming of relations was remarkable in light of a three-month border war around the start of 1988 over a disputed village, Baan Romklao. The fighting took place when Chavalit was still army chief, and is believed to have claimed 1,000 lives on both sides, the majority Thai. 'Kaysone got on very well with our king,' Anand recalls. Indeed, the Hanoi-educated Lao president was honoured with a state banquet, and awarded the Most Auspicious Order of the Rajamitrabhorn. He died in December the same year.

The Order of the Rajamitrabhorn was created in 1962 by King Bhumibol to be bestowed exclusively on heads of state. Its previous recipient was Emperor

Akihito, who paid a five-day state visit with Empress Michiko in September 1991. Akihito had visited Thailand before as crown prince, but this was the first time a Japanese emperor had set foot on Thai soil.[18] Although born of a coup, the Anand government carried off a large amount of such formal diplomacy, consolidating established relationships and expanding newer ones.

In common with the rest of ASEAN at this time, the Anand administration was viewed internationally as soft on the widely vilified junta, the State Law and Order Restoration Council (SLORC), in Myanmar (as neighbouring Burma had been renamed in 1989). After five weeks of massive pro-democracy demonstrations there, the military had struck back on 18 September 1988, establishing SLORC under the chairmanship of Senior General Saw Maung, and leaving over 500 civilian alleged looters dead, many of them youngsters. At least 3,000 people perished that year in nationwide political upheavals.

ASEAN's official policy towards Myanmar was one of 'constructive engagement'; this avoided direct criticism of the regime, ostensibly because a more confrontational line was seen as potentially counterproductive and culturally inappropriate. The stance was widely condemned in the West, particularly by the US and UK, and predated Anand's government. The term 'constructive engagement' had been coined in the 1980s, in the early years of the first administration of Ronald Reagan, for an alternative to sanctions in dealing with South Africa. Condemned widely by the vocal anti-apartheid global lobby, the expression was also adopted by the government of Prime Minister Margaret Thatcher in the UK. The US reversed its policy in the latter part of the decade; constructive engagement, which had been favourable to foreign business interests in South Africa, was abandoned.

Constructive engagement was a collective approach by ASEAN, Anand points out, noting the deliberate irony in ASEAN's use of the term given its origins among Western democracies. 'They reproached us when it didn't suit them – condemned us,' he says. 'These people are hypocrites.' ASEAN's engagement with Myanmar permitted, or at least did not prevent, commercial engagement, and some in Thailand continued to exploit the pariah nation's isolation. After Chavalit visited Saw Maung in Rangoon in December 1988, numerous logging and fishing concessions were signed by suitably connected Thai businesses. 'That did not play too well with our neighbouring brothers and sisters [in ASEAN],' Anand recalls. These questionable Thai-Burmese business arrangements remained in place, however.

Anand and Arsa both knew that Myanmar, which had been subject to stultifying, economically inept military misrule since a coup in 1962, was unlikely to take any leaps forward during their brief window in government. A general election in May 1990 had been unfavourable to the generals, producing a landslide victory for opposition leader Aung San Suu Kyi's National League for Democracy (NLD). The military's proxy National Unity Party was utterly trounced. However, the military simply ignored the result.

In October 1991, Suu Kyi was awarded the Nobel Peace Prize. As secretary general of the NLD, she had already spent over two years under house arrest. At a dinner in Bangkok with foreign correspondents, Anand did not disparage Suu Kyi but openly expressed puzzlement at the award being given with no peace or political settlement in Myanmar to show for it.[19] 'You had to recognise her courage and determination in confronting the military, and give her credit for that, but not the Nobel Peace Prize,' Anand says. 'Perhaps some other prize would have been more in order.'

During his time in office, Anand made no attempt to visit Myanmar, and offered no public comments on the country's internal situation. 'I said to my Western friends, "We cannot move away from Myanmar",' Anand recalls. 'We wanted to have peaceful engagement with Myanmar, but I didn't get involved myself. My policy was that I would have no direct relations with their leaders, but I would have no hesitation in sending my foreign minister – I delegated to Arsa.' He remembers being disappointed to learn from President Suharto that the Indonesian military did not have particularly close relations with its Burmese counterparts. Privately, he hoped that Japan would have more success persuading the country to open up.

ASEAN free trade

In late May 1991, Anand paid a two-day visit to Singapore. He was received at the Istana, built in the 19th century as a residence for the British governor. After independence, it became the Republic of Singapore's presidential palace and also housed the office of the prime minister. The president at the time was Wee Kim Wee, whose republican credentials did not diminish his personal view of King Bhumibol as a great man of his time.

Anand's counterpart and host was Prime Minister Goh Chok Tong, who had only come into office the previous November. Goh had replaced the Republic of

Singapore's founding prime minister, Lee Kuan Yew, who now occupied the newly created post of senior minister. With characteristically meticulous foresight, Lee had in set place a smooth succession plan almost a quarter of a century ahead of his death, which eventually came in early 2015. He remained in this consultative capacity until 2004, when Goh replaced him as senior minister, and Lee Kuan Yew's son, Lee Hsien Loong, in turn replaced Goh as prime minister. Lee senior remained as minister mentor until 2011 when, after the death of his wife Kwa Geok Choo, he finally lowered his public profile and retreated into old age. All the while, however, Lee retained an office close to the prime minister's, and remained a figure of towering influence.

Lee Kuan Yew and Thailand's former foreign minister, Thanat Khoman, had had a thorny relationship. Anand had always been at his mentor's side during Thanat's encounters with Lee in the early 1960s and later in New York at the UN. 'Lee Kuan Yew knew me when I was just a junior officer,' Anand recalls. Unusually, Lee had lobbied quietly on Anand's behalf in late 1976 when the Thai foreign ministry had fallen victim to the military's bogus anti-communist witch-hunt, with Anand as the main target.

Lee, the newly minted senior minister, was on the list of people to see Anand during his visit. 'You are now prime minister,' Lee told Anand. 'I am just a senior minister – it is I who has to come and call on you.' The situation was not without irony: here was Anand visiting as a prime minister installed by the military that had once effectively evicted him from government service – to Lee's great dismay at the time.

As always, there was purpose in Lee's meticulousness. He certainly wanted to give Anand a fitting welcome, but he also wanted to remind Singaporean officials that things had really changed, and that he himself had moved on. Lee's visit to the hotel that day was no mere courtesy call. As one of the world's most astute geopolitical observers, he was there to discuss matters of mutual significance, including Cambodia. There had been a special relationship between Sihanouk's Cambodia and the newly sovereign Singapore in the 1960s. As a small, vulnerable country, Singapore was particularly appalled by Vietnam's invasion of Cambodia. After all, such military adventures might give others ideas.

Another, broader, topic was regional trade. Singapore's march up the world's economic ranks was (and is) based on its astute development as a trading entrepôt, a transport and shipping hub, and as an increasingly high-tech manufacturing centre and regional financial capital, as well as its attractiveness to highly qualified expatriates. Promoting trade and economic relations was therefore core to Singapore's vision for ASEAN.

Lee was well aware that among many quasi-public roles in the 1980s, Anand had chaired the Task Force on ASEAN Co-operation in 1984–5 with a view to charting the future course of ASEAN economic relations. Its recommendations had been presented at the ASEAN Summit in Manila in 1987. It was a chaotic period in the Philippines; President Corazon Aquino had been swept into office with the 1986 People Power Revolution and her predecessor, Ferdinand Marcos, had been forced to flee abroad.

The new ideas had been met with caution by Indonesia. Brunei, Malaysia, Singapore, and Thailand were receptive enough, but less ready to deal with the challenges these posed, particularly in terms of the inter-ministry frictions that would inevitably be triggered. 'They accepted the recommendations with a pinch of salt, but nothing was done subsequently,' Anand comments. He felt not enough people in Manila were paying much attention to ASEAN at that time.[20] 'I knew the timing was not right.'

Even so, Lee had liked Anand's report and proposal, and now saw an opportunity to revive the ASEAN Free Trade Area (AFTA) agenda. 'For the first time in the history of ASEAN, we have a prime minister who has had a career in the bureaucracy and spent some time in the private sector,' Lee said to Anand during their *tête-à-tête*. 'In my view, you have another chance.'

'I had never thought of that before,' Anand said, reflecting back at the time of Lee's death. 'That was not Lee's only purpose in coming to see me, but it got me thinking. He planted the seed and I did act on it – it was a difficult task.'[21] Because of Lee's encouragement, Anand moved forward on AFTA immediately.

Lee spent 90 minutes in the hotel suite before Anand escorted him to his car to see him off personally. They never met formally again. Always conscious that he was not a professional politician, Anand did not call on heads of government and statesmen during his future travels. 'It would have been presumptuous,' he says. After all, he had no political ambitions, and no expectation of being prime minister again.[22] However, if senior ASEAN figures visited Bangkok and asked to see him, they would meet.

Strategically, Lee and Anand both knew AFTA could not be promoted as any sort of Singaporean initiative. 'It never was,' says Anand. 'If Indonesia and Malaysia had known the idea was discussed at my meeting with Lee Kuan Yew, it would have been a problem and treated with a degree of scepticism.' Indonesia felt it should always take a leading role in ASEAN affairs, which is one of the reasons the grouping's secretariat had been established in Jakarta in 1975. Meanwhile Malaysia has always been suspicious of anything with Singaporean fingerprints on it.

Lee was circumspect about his meeting with Anand. 'He understood the economics of trade and investment in an interdependent world,' Lee later wrote. 'To avoid lingering suspicions about Singapore's motives, I advised Prime Minister Goh to get Anand to take the lead to push for an ASEAN Free Trade Area.'[23]

Lee had actually been quite dubious about ASEAN initially. In the title of a chapter on ASEAN in the second volume of his memoirs, *From Third World to First*, he used the words 'unpromising start, promising future'. Singapore's relationship with Malaysia has always been prickly, but it was usually businesslike. Other factors had gone Lee's way to brighten the regional picture. Most importantly, under President Suharto, who had come into office in 1968, Indonesia had become an increasingly benign and stable neighbour that was growing economically, and benefited from Singapore's developing commercial and financial sophistication.

As to Thailand, Lee had got on well with Field Marshal Thanom Kittikachorn and General Kriangsak Chomanand, the soldiers who dominated Thailand in the 1960s and 1970s. He also admired the steady statesmanship of Prem Tinsulanond, Thailand's unelected prime minister for most of the 1980s.

Geographically, Thailand was not one of Singapore's immediate neighbours, and posed no geopolitical or significant economic threat. Indeed, it competed weakly in areas where, arguably, it should have had natural advantages. Japanese and Western multinationals found Singapore a far more efficient environment in which to headquarter regional activities, and Bangkok always came an expensive second to Singapore as an aviation hub for Southeast Asia.

Before ASEAN's formation in 1967, Lee once admitted to Sompong Sucharitkul, Anand's successor as *chef de cabinet* to Thanat, that the prospect of a canal across Thailand's Kra Isthmus, in the mould of Suez or Panama, actually woke him up at night. It would have diverted shipping from the congested Strait of Malacca, and enormously undermined Singapore's principal natural advantage – its location at a maritime crossroads. Thailand never built the Kra Canal, although the possibility is revisited from time to time.

The rate of development in regional trade was always dictated by Indonesia

– the world's fourth most populous nation, which to this day accounts for 40 per cent of the combined ASEAN economy. Indonesia during the early 1990s was still a very closed economy and protective of its industries; but without its involvement there was no point talking about ASEAN free trade.

The imperatives in 1991 were stronger than in 1987 when AFTA failed to gain traction in Manila. The Uruguay Round of the General Agreement on Tariffs and Trade (GATT) was taking multilateral trade negotiations into new areas, including agriculture, services, textiles, and intellectual property; a final draft text was delivered in December 1991. Canada, Mexico, and the US were pushing ahead with the North America Free Trade Area (NAFTA). New markets were emerging in Eastern Europe, and the Single European Market was consolidating itself, bolstered by the reunification of Germany in 1990. Closer to home, ASEAN was directly involved with emerging multilateral economic structures, including Asia-Pacific Economic Cooperation (APEC) and the East Asia Economic Caucus (EAEC).[24]

Because of its multicultural identity and lack of natural resources, Singapore is arguably more affected by such adjustments to the global economy than any other country in ASEAN. 'We are a creation,' said S.R. Nathan, Singapore's former president. 'We are the only people who have to tell others what we are not. It will take one or two centuries before that will strike root. It is very important that our economy must never go down because when that happens the divisions will come. Every time the world market is in crisis, it is a crisis for us.'

'I always told the Singaporeans that Singapore needs ASEAN more than ASEAN needs Singapore,' says Anand. 'They just laughed, but it's true.' Despite its strong economy and no-nonsense administration, Singapore has always kept a wary eye on its neighbours. As it relentlessly raised education standards, the little island republic became in some ways a think tank for ASEAN. For all the intellectual brilliance Lee and his cabinets brought to the table, Singapore lacked the geopolitical clout to set regional agendas. With its free economy and liberal tax system, it was also often regarded by other ASEAN members as suspiciously 'Western'.

In terms of political protection and economic survival, Singapore probably had the most to gain from AFTA, but it could not afford to be seen as AFTA's leading advocate. That is where Thailand came in. Dispassionate and removed, the second largest economy in ASEAN, Thailand often proved Singapore's vital, quiet ally. In many ways, the encounter between Lee and Anand in the hotel suite was a crystallisation of this relationship.

Once Lee reseeded the AFTA initiative in his mind, Anand formed a working group to move it along. Within the Thai cabinet, the three most relevant ministries were finance, commerce, and foreign affairs, and there were turf complications to be considered. For example, tariff reductions were a matter for the finance ministry, not commerce; while anything to do with foreign relations was in the remit of the foreign ministry.

Finance Minister Suthee Singsaneh, Commerce Minister Amaret Sila-on, and Foreign Minister Arsa Sarasin were all driving, effective personalities, and not mutually antagonistic. They all had effective people skills, and did the rounds of ASEAN for AFTA. However, they inevitably had different priorities, and also numerous other commitments. Anand's most important selection, his point man for the working group, was Narongchai Akrasanee, a Thammasat University economist.

Narongchai had been working in the background for Prime Minister Kukrit Pramoj in 1975 when he first encountered Anand, someone he regards as coming from the older generation of 'super technocrats', the era that preceded that of professional politicians. These older technocrats included Puey Ungphakorn, Snoh Unakul, Amnuay Viravan, and Suthee Singsaneh.

He had been a student of Professor Béla Balassa, an influential economics professor at Johns Hopkins University who advised the World Bank on trade and development. Another influence was Professor Seiji Naya, the Japanese-American chief economist at the Asian Development Bank (ADB) in the early 1980s who had taught at Thammasat University in Bangkok in the 1970s. Naya was a powerful proponent of economic cooperation in Asia, including ASEAN, and chaired a pioneering joint study on ASEAN free trade that Narongchai helped write up in Manila. The Philippine capital was the location of the headquarters of the ADB, backed principally by Japan and the US.

Narongchai's relationship with Anand developed with the ASEAN Task Force in 1984-5, for which, in his own estimation, he had been 'a natural choice', and through which he had built up a vast network of contacts in the region. Narongchai travelled widely, meeting with the representatives of both the public and private sectors. 'Nobody objected to any study – they co-operated,' he recalls. Narongchai believed that trade should be 'not completely free but liberal', that bigger economies tended to be more competitive, and smaller ones were either completely open or completely closed. He also believed that people tend to be nationalistic about professions and services, and that it is easier to start breaking down barriers with merchandise. He considered Thailand as already more open to imports than most other countries in the region were to Thai exports.

'In my game plan, things don't happen by themselves,' says Narongchai. 'You have to force them.' The biggest block to AFTA was Indonesia. 'They still did not think free trade was good.' In a conversation that took place during a three-day mission to Jakarta, one minister's declaration was short and to the point: 'Indonesia no free trade, Indonesia no free trade.' 'In the old days, whatever Indonesia said we all went along with,' comments Anand. 'It carried so much weight.'

Despite Indonesia's underlying scepticism, Anand's AFTA initiative soon gathered momentum. At the 24th ASEAN ministerial meeting in Kuala Lumpur in July 1991, the final joint communiqué noted: 'The foreign ministers welcome as a matter for serious consideration the initiative of His Excellency the Prime Minister of Thailand, which was supported by the Honourable Prime Minister of Malaysia [Dr Mahathir Mohamad], that ASEAN moves towards a Free Trade Area by the turn of the century and agreed that the senior officials of ASEAN undertake further study and discussion for submission to the forthcoming ASEAN Summit.'

With hindsight, Anand finds the communiqué's wording slightly odd, since all the ASEAN countries had to be supportive. This was not a bilateral meeting. Encouraging as it sounded, not all the members of Suharto's cabinet were as outward looking as Indonesia's foreign minister, Ali Alatas. 'Anand had to get involved in Indonesia,' Narongchai recalls of September 1991. 'He did not have to intervene in other countries.' Anand visited Indonesia twice to broach the subject of AFTA with a dubious President Suharto, with whom he had had little previous contact.

'Suharto was not like Sukarno – he was a different generation,' Anand recalls. 'At whatever cost, we had to get the Indonesians on board. In practical terms, if the Indonesians did not play ball we could not get going.' Suharto was accessible and friendly enough, but his reaction on Anand's first visit was not that positive. 'He did not say yes or no, but definitely he was not too happy,' Anand recalls.

Soon after, Amaret was dispatched to Jakarta to lobby ahead of the next ASEAN ministerial meeting, due to be held in Kuala Lumpur in October. 'Most people believed Indonesia would say no,' Narongchai recalls. The pressure was building, and everybody would lose face if Indonesia, with its heavily protected markets, stymied the proposal. Some believe that Indonesia increasingly viewed China's economic rise as a threat to its foreign investment prospects, and felt it had no choice but to open up.

'I just flew in, flew out twice,' Anand recalls. 'The actual agreement to the proposal by Suharto was given to me on my second visit. I did not ask him what changed his mind but just accepted his words. He always had his suspicions about Singapore, and knew that Indonesia was not at the same level of development with it, or with Thailand and Malaysia, and possibly even the Philippines. I think he was worried that these countries would push for progress faster than he was willing to accept. I made it clear that we would take that concern into account, and that we would not run as fast as the most developed country – Singapore – might want. I also impressed on him that this project could not fly if Indonesia did not come on board.'

According to Anand, it was agreed by all the parties that ASEAN should not be changed into a supra-national body, and that it would not be another European Union. 'Eventually, we offered the 20-year transition period in order to get the Indonesians to go along. I did not have an actual time frame in mind – just as soon as practicable.'

At a later meeting in Chiang Mai, it was the Indonesians who could see more clearly the practical benefits of AFTA, and they pressed to actually speed up the process. Anand always believed that the problems of unequal development within ASEAN impose an absolute requirement for flexibility. 'The answer is to do things gradually,' he says. 'We should not be tempted into radical propositions.' Big steps can lead to bigger mistakes, he reasons, whereas smaller ones inhibit damage and are more easily corrected. For that reason, he argues against making time frames sacrosanct. 'You put up a date that everyone can aim at. If it works, fine. You don't have to be right all the time.'

AFTA was formally endorsed on 28 January 1992, at the fourth ASEAN summit held, appropriately enough, in Singapore. The host, Prime Minister Goh Chok Tong, was of course strongly supportive, his views being consonant with those of Senior Minister Lee. ASEAN declared it was moving towards 'a higher plane of political and economic cooperation', and a framework was adopted for a free trade area by 2008: it involved a common effective preferential tariff (CEPT) scheme with intra-ASEAN tariffs ranging from nothing up to 5 per cent.[25] A ministerial-level council was created to oversee implementation of the CEPT agreement.

'The ASEAN summit in Singapore elevated Thailand's status in the family of nations at that time,' Anand says. The summit was historic in other ways. It endorsed October's Paris Peace Agreements for Cambodia, and got firmly behind the UNTAC plan for Cambodia with its Supreme National Council. Unusually progressive noises were made about education, women and children's affairs, sustainable development, the environment, 'transboundary' pollution, narcotics, non-government organisations, aid, and HIV-AIDS. The ASEAN secretariat was upgraded and the ASEAN secretary general promoted to ministerial level. Overall, there were some clear echoes of the reforms Anand was pushing in Thailand. Indeed, Anand recalls Mahathir once teasing him at a meeting in Hong Kong: 'I had retired, but he said, "You have given us elected politicians a bad name."'

To this day, Thai schoolchildren learning by rote the main achievements of Thai prime ministers are taught that Anand was responsible for AFTA. What this might mean to them is unclear, but its ramifications are certainly still being felt. In late 2015, ASEAN took another step towards regional economic integration with the ASEAN Economic Community (AEC) to promote global competitiveness, free movement of labour and capital, and a unified market and production base. The AEC will take a long time to bed in; it falls well short of the European Union model, which it has never aspired to emulate, and there is no prospect of political or monetary union. Nevertheless, the AEC is grounded in AFTA and the work of Anand and other pragmatic economic liberals in the 1980s and 1990s.

Anand's AFTA journey produced the brief, decisive encounter with Senior Minister Lee with whom comparisons are sometimes drawn, possibly because both men were so technically adept. S.R. Nathan, Singapore's former president, saw no similarity between Anand and Lee, however. From the 1950s, starting with a blank sheet of paper, the latter worked on the complete transformation of Singapore. While Anand has been a vital and influential part of the Thai establishment, he never courted power or attempted to position himself as an indispensable nation builder. Indeed, uniquely in Thai history, Anand would twice relinquish power when many would have been quite happy to see him retain it.

Like Nathan, Anand sees Lee in an entirely different light. 'I was fond of him and have high respect for what he did for Singapore, and his achievements, but he was an autocrat – and a very good one. It was the right time to be an autocrat in Singapore in the 1950s and 1960s.'

While some countries – notably China – look to Lee's Singapore for inspiration, Anand doubts that the Singaporean model for economic development is anything intrinsically remarkable. He believes it was Lee's application that was so crucial, citing 'his vision, his foresight, his leadership, his decisiveness, his integrity, his honesty'. He continues: 'One has to understand that Lee Kuan Yew was no democrat, but having said that doesn't mean you have to be negative about his credentials or aspirations. Having paid proper compliments, there is no way anyone can tell whether if Lee had become prime minister of a larger country he would have been equally successful.'

CHAPTER 12

ANAND'S FIRST TERM:
TELEPHONES, UNIONS,
& HIV/AIDS
(1991–2)

Telecoms tangle

According to ancient Greek mythology, a fearsomely complex knot tied by Midas, the son of King Gordias, was released only when Alexander the Great sliced through it with a single stroke of his sword. In 1991, Thailand was facing numerous 'Gordian Knots', one of which was made of telephone lines. Outside Anand's office at Government House, four secretaries sat at desks arranged in an L-shape, and the visitor they saw pass by most frequently was Nukul Prachuabmoh, Anand's assiduous minister of transport and communications.

Nukul's predecessor during Chatichai Choonhavan's premiership, Montri Pongpanich, had been deeply involved in a controversial project to bring a million telephone landlines to Bangkok, and two million more to the provinces. In September 1990, the state-owned Telephone Organization of Thailand (TOT) passed over two foreign bids from France's Alcatel and Sweden's Ericsson, and awarded the contract to Telecom Asia. Today known as True Corporation, the company was a subsidiary of Charoen Pokphand (CP), the multi-billion dollar agro-industry conglomerate of Dhanin Cheeravanont, one of the richest men in Thailand.[1] There had been 22 telephone concessions to the private sector during the Chatichai administration; the one for Bangkok awarded to Telecom Asia was worth an estimated 9.78 billion baht, the most valuable ever in Thailand for the sector.[2] Telecom Asia was to be one of the most nettlesome issues of Anand's first premiership, and one of the handful of problems he felt compelled to deal with directly.

Nukul's intention was not to stop the project – which was badly needed – but to ensure that it worked to the public's benefit. The unsigned contract had too many loopholes and invited graft. Thailand's dysfunctional telecommunications industry had always been a web of corruption. In 1991, the mobile revolution was still in its infancy. Normal applications for private and commercial telephone landlines took years to go through the system and often produced nothing. Desperate would-be subscribers were forced to buy on a black market with quasi-official connivance. Ordinary lines in Bangkok's business district went for US$500 while those with international subscriber dialling cost more than US$1,000. Although they stayed in the background, the military was deeply involved: the chairmanship and other board positions at the Telephone Organization of Thailand (TOT), were effectively 'owned' by its top brass, with national security being one justification.

The original contract signing had been scheduled for late January or February 1991, but a fortune-teller advised Dhanin that a date in the period March to May would be more propitious. Because of the delay, the deal, which had already attracted considerable controversy, became entangled with the coup. The project would have placed CP at the centre of Thailand's telecommunications boom, and also of speculation about corruption. The whole imbroglio had forced Chatichai to reshuffle his cabinet, and was one factor leading to the coup itself.[3] When he came on the scene as prime minister, Anand was not happy with the opaque bidding process, nor with the concession terms. These were unclear, and he wanted the unsigned contract sent back for fresh tendering.

As prime minister, Anand considered himself neutral. As is typical in Thailand, there were rumours and insinuations that he had ulterior motives for re-opening the bidding. For that very reason, he made sure that the Telecom Asia negotiations were kept very public. 'To get things done in Thailand, you have to do that,' says Ekamol Kiriwat, who at the time was deputy governor of the Bank of Thailand. The renegotiations spanned half of Anand's first premiership, and in the government's closing months featured frequently in the press.

Dhanin, the head of CP, visited Government House personally for discussions with Anand. Others present included Nukul and Wissanu Krea-ngam, the deputy cabinet secretary general.

Initially, Wissanu was mystified by the need for his presence. He was unaware that Anand had consulted Deputy Prime Minister Meechai Ruchupan about how to handle the issue prudently. 'I need a lawyer who is very neutral to sit beside me whom I can consult,' Anand told Meechai, who had been advising prime ministers on legal matters for two decades, including as secretary general of the Judicial Council. Anand had some names in mind, but immediately accepted Meechai's suggestion: Wissanu. Anand called Wissanu in and told him there would be meetings once or twice a week – and told him not to say anything to anyone.

'What is my duty here?' Wissanu asked. 'To keep you company or something?' Anand replied: 'No, I want a witness for when I leave.' Among his concerns was the possibility of being sued when he left office. 'I want you to be the witness that there is no ambiguity here or under-the-table talk.'

If Anand had simply wanted technical advice, Nukul would have been the obvious choice. Wissanu was a permanent official with a fine legal mind. Anand knew that he could not be expected to know about everything that happened in cabinet, but that he had a 'very good memory' for the things he did know about. Anand would sometimes test him with questions about discussions at previous meetings.

At the meetings with Dhanin, Wissanu observed Anand's negotiating tactics for the first time. The talking was done for the most part sitting at a table, but Anand sometimes suggested moving to more comfortable armchairs. He would then digress and ask Dhanin about his children, talk about hobbies, music, painting. Initially Dhanin seemed bemused, interested in getting back to negotiations. But Anand just talked about his own family life, or something else off-topic. Wissanu recalls that when Dhanin began to relax, Anand would say, 'Okay, let's go back to work.'

As things turned out, a new round of bidding left Telecom Asia with only a million lines in Bangkok, with the rest redistributed among other bidders. Many believe Dhanin's fortune-teller served him exceptionally well. Because of the delay, Telecom Asia jettisoned the financially marginal upcountry component, and got the benefit of some technological advances for the lines it retained in Bangkok. 'If Dhanin had signed the original contract, he would have lost a lot,' says Nukul. 'Outside Bangkok, there was no way he could have made money.'

In this treacherous environment, Anand had firmly blocked the military's moves to make Air Chief Marshal Kaset Rojananil minister of communications. 'Keeping Kaset out of the cabinet was very remarkable,' says Mechai Viravaidya – who later observed General Issarapong Noonpakdee, the chairman of TOT, interior minister and the only senior junta member in the cabinet, also being kept in check. 'Khun Anand held him down very well.'

Military oversight of telephones was never really a security issue, according to Nukul. He nevertheless believes his portfolio was the most sensitive in Anand's cabinet. 'It affected the economy. I created many enemies during my term – Anand knew that I was not afraid of anyone.'

Indeed, Nukul had an exceptional reputation for probity. He had first met Anand passing through London as a mature student in the early 1950s on his way to the US. Back in Thailand, their paths crossed socially from time to time in the early 1960s, and during the 1980s a good friendship developed between them. Pote Sarasin made Nukul deputy director of the highways department in the early 1960s, and he remained there for a decade. As an economist, not an engineer, Nukul could never rise to head the department. Instead, imbued with a powerful sense of public service, he managed funds from the World Bank and Budget Bureau building Thailand's first arterial highways.[4] Prior to these, the biggest road in Thailand was the US$140-million Friendship Highway up to Isaan, in the Northeast, built in 1958 for strategic reasons by the US.

Nukul returned to the Ministry of Finance in 1974, and became director general of the revenue department. He eventually succeeded Snoh Unakul as governor of the Bank of Thailand (BOT) in late 1979. Nukul remained governor until 1984. After falling out with Prem Tinsulanond's second finance minister, Sommai Hoontrakul, over the handling of a distressed bank, he took early retirement.

Nukul's five-year tenure as governor had been longer than average, but fell well short of that of his former boss, Puey Ungphakorn, who held the post for 12 years (1959–1971). Nukul considered himself lucky to have been mentored by Puey in his early career, communicating with him frequently and learning how to seize opportunities 'to do something useful for the country'. Puey himself never showed any interest in becoming a minister, prizing more highly his positions as dean of the faculty of economics, and ultimately rector, of Thammasat University. Nukul also never aspired to being a minister, until Anand asked him to become one.

After resigning from the BOT, Nukul moved into the private sector, and spent two years as executive chairman of Siam Motors, turning around its debts. He helped generate 200 million baht in profits in his second year, but he was always an outsider and the relationship was not comfortable. 'I thought it was better to resign before they asked me to leave,' he says. He took on the chairmanship of a small brokerage, First Asia, and resigned from that in 1991.

Throughout his career, Nukul had displayed a dispassionate and principled doggedness. This meshed well with Anand's requirements. Like Mechai, Nukul did not get on particularly well with Staporn Kavitanon, the former head of the Board of Investment whom Anand had made his secretary general. They both viewed Staporn's relations with Dhanin's CP and with the military as too cosy. But with Staporn and Nukul both reporting to him, Anand felt he had two streams of information relating to telecoms, and would be in a position to assess developments from both sides. Just to be sure, he also set up a working group outside the prime minister's office. 'I got the benefit of three corridors of information,' says Anand. 'In a way, Nukul was the first line of defence. It was a war of attrition.' The game plan was to have Nukul wear down Dhanin and the military, and raise the prospect of no contract at all. Shifting final negotiations to Anand then seemed to increase the chances of a successful outcome.

Although Anand successfully renegotiated the Bangkok lines with Telecom Asia, he still ran into problems with the redistributed provincial lines and the military-dominated board of TOT after some initial progress had been made. 'All of a sudden it stalled,' Anand recalls. 'I suspected the military wanted to wait for a more compliant government. Eventually they would win out – that's when the real deadlock came.'

Nukul clashed with the military in other areas too. One was the taxi business, a vast, dark industry of vested interests controlling vulnerable drivers – men often with very few choices for livelihoods. The so-called 'black plate' unlicensed taxis that operated for years from Don Muang Airport had always been linked to the air force. Ordinary taxi drivers in the capital generally rented their vehicles by the day from the owners, paid their own fuel costs, and took home whatever was left from their takings. It was a miserable, insecure life, stuck in traffic interminably with little certain income at the end of it. A key issue was the liberalising of the licensing system. The military wanted to ice their cake and expand the taxi fleet within reason. The matter came to Nukul, who simply chose to liberalise the system in a controlled way and remove the cap entirely. 'I did not limit the number of licenses so they could not make money with it,' Nukul recalls. He remembers one of his deputy ministers, General Viroj Saengsanit, a Class 5 member and future supreme commander, being very angry and attacking him in the press.

Anand was away in Singapore at the time. He called Nukul and told him not to resign. 'He should have known me better,' Nukul says. 'Nothing would frighten me. I had so many enemies afterwards!' However, despite his outwardly unflappable demeanour, this was a challenging time for Nukul. When his daughter married at the Dusit Thani, there were bomb threats and all the wedding gifts had to be screened.

'The job had to be done. I did it. I have no regrets,' reflects Nukul.

'Anand would think of VAT and so on, but to me liberalising the taxis was the most radical thing that he did,' says Ammar Siamwalla, Thailand's most prominent economist at the time. 'In one day, about six billion baht of wealth was destroyed – the wealth that had gone into the yellow taxi number plates. It becomes an oxymoron, but Anand is also the most political among the technocrats. He knows what will fly and what won't. Within that context, he is very radical.'

The taxi liberalisation also brought better regulation, which benefited passengers. Meters were introduced for the first time, to great public approval. It was a system nobody thought could ever work in Thailand, but it became embedded. Other reforms enjoyed less success. 'The one I thought wouldn't work was the motorcycle helmet law,' says Abhisit Vejjajiva, a Democrat member of parliament and political neophyte at the time. 'It still doesn't.' Anand disagrees. He contends that his government's making helmet use compulsory has worked to a significant degree. Motorcycle taxi drivers in Bangkok all now wear helmets, though their passengers usually do not. The level of compliance varies greatly elsewhere. Anand remembers a group of surgeons he once encountered joking that he had ruined their businesses. The doctors complained that the helmet law had cut off their supply of young, healthy organs for transplant operations. 'It was all in jest,' he says.

Anand believes he dealt fairly with the military. 'Theoretically, I was beholden to them because they could have removed me at any time without reference to any other authority,' he explains. 'I planned from the very beginning to have a sincere and honest relationship with them, and throughout the entire administration I never criticised them publicly. I would hold private talks with them on a one-on-one basis, or with a group of council members. That kind of relationship helped convince them of my sincerity. I gained their trust.'

The military expressed misgivings from time to time, but they came to nothing. 'Sunthorn admitted a few times he wanted to get rid of me, but he had no power, and Issarapong was very loyal to Suchinda,' Anand recalls. 'Even Kaset never said bad things about me. Suchinda would occasionally joke about the mistake he made making me prime minister.'

Whatever its reservations, the NPKC came gradually to appreciate that any legitimacy the government had came from Anand. The junta's primary motivation had been to get rid of Chatichai and his cronies, and that had been achieved immediately. 'After about seven months, I was never at any time concerned that I might be removed,' says Anand. 'I never threatened them with quitting – I stayed cool. I had the backing of the people who, I think, believed I was not doing anything for my personal benefit. I won their hearts in a way.'

Procurements were always sent to Deputy Prime Minister Pow Sarasin for deliberation, a process that took a few weeks, particularly if there were whiffs of corruption. The paperwork was then forwarded to the economic ministers. 'Military procurement was the most bothersome question,' Anand recalls. 'All we could do was stall the process.' The cabinet managed, however, to prevent commercial development by the military around the Sanam Pao area of Bangkok. 'That would have been a precedent for them to commercialise military-held land all over the country,' says Anand.

To this day, the military controls substantial amounts of land. It has large tracts in Bangkok's northern suburbs, around the Viphavadi-Rangsit Highway and Paholyothin Road; and significant swathes upcountry. They also control entire islands in the Gulf of Thailand, many of which remain pristine. The justification is national security. The title deeds are often held through the Treasury Department, which is part of the finance ministry. According to research in late 2015, the amount of land controlled by the Ministry of Defence totalled 2.66 million rai (4,230 square kilometres).[5] The Treasury Department at that time owned another 9.85 million rai, for a total of 12.5 million rai of state-held land.

The military land greatly exceeds the holdings of the Crown Property Bureau, which controls many of the assets of the monarchy. These holdings tend to attract far more scrutiny. Of the 41,000 rai owned by the Crown Property Bureau, 8,300 rai are in Bangkok. Many of the plots in the capital are in prime locations, including the central business district, and therefore comprise much of the most valuable real estate in the kingdom.[6] In terms of bald overall acreage, however, the military holds 0.824 per cent of Thailand's total land mass, some 65 times more than that owned by the Crown Property Bureau.

Unions and state enterprises

With its appointed parliament, the junta wasted no time cracking down on perceived threats. 'Getting rid of the state enterprise unions was the first thing that came out of the NPKC gate,' says Phil Robertson, a Thai-speaking US labour relations expert.[7] Almost immediately, the junta's legislative assembly enacted the State Enterprise Labour Relations Act (SELRA) to dissolve state enterprise unions, replacing them with associations that were not allowed to engage in collective bargaining or industrial action. State unions, with a membership of 186,000, had previously been covered by the 1975 Labour Relations Act, which had provided the first legal basis for organised labour under *MR* Kukrit Pramoj's government. Prior to SELRA, state enterprise and private unions were unified in one congress. The state unions were more secure and their members better paid, and they were trying to give succour to their private sector peers. All the unions had done relatively well during the Chatichai years, when social security legislation was enacted for the first time. Announcement 54 in the NPKC's interim constitution amended parts of the 1975 act that affected private unions, which only had 152,000 members.[8]

Robertson describes SELRA as 'perhaps the most crushing blow ever for the Thai labour movement'. It was part of 'a military process,' he says. The army and the labour movement were old foes, and any time the labour movement got strong, the military viewed it as a threat through an anti-communist lens. 'You didn't hear a peep from Anand about that,' says Robertson. He notes that subsequent elected governments did not repeal SELRA. The relatively brief, unelected Anand governments were meanwhile geared to the thinking of technocrats, not unionists.

Anat Arbhabhirama, Anand's minister of agriculture, is also clear that while it was the junta that was most fixated on steam-rolling the unions, there was very little sympathy for the unions in the cabinet either. 'I think everybody agreed,' he says. 'They were sick and tired of the unions. The problem is still around now, but a lot less than when Anand took over.'

Anat had experience of working with four unions when he ran PTT, the state energy conglomerate. 'They gave me a lot of headaches,' he recalls, casting his mind back to the difficulty of formulating business strategies with constant interference from bureaucrats, politicians, the military, and unionists. 'If the chief of an organisation cannot control the human resources, he is dead,' he says.

Chatrachai Bunya-Ananta, the executive vice president of Thai Airways

International, the national flag-carrier at the time, took a more pragmatic view. He was dealing with highly qualified technicians who had to be of international calibre and rewarded adequately. Chatrachai recognised that the airline's technicians needed effective collective bargaining to satisfy their needs. 'There is nothing wrong with that if they are confined. We talked – negotiated salaries and benefits even though technically they were extra-legal,' he recalled. 'Maybe they retarded our progress in some areas.' For Chatrachai, a bigger concern was political influence and the involvement of strong personalities.

There was another agenda that state unions did not play into particularly well: privatisation. In June 1991, Thai Airways International was partially privatised amid doubts that it had actually been profitable in 1990. Other candidates for partial, or what Anand called at the time 'backdoor', privatisation included the Electricity Generating Authority of Thailand (EGAT) and the Telephone Organization of Thailand. 'We can sell down to 51 per cent and it still remains a state enterprise,' said Finance Minister Suthee.

Thailand at the time of writing has 58 state enterprises with 300 subsidiaries. Many remain a drain on state resources – they cannot be allowed to fail. Among state enterprises that run perennial losses that the state is legally required to cover, the State Railway of Thailand (SRT) is the most notable. Others have ditched their social mandates and gone after profits.[9]

In 1991, Suthee was concerned about their rigid, unimaginative managements, and access to the substantial capital needed for their development. 'We think we should allow the private sector to handle this,' he said. 'They know when to borrow, and they know how to repay debt.'

Suthee recognised that some state enterprises might always have to remain public, including the sports and tourism authorities, and the public always expected access to water to be cheap. But laws and ideas would need to change. 'Thinking is one thing,' said Suthee. 'Putting your thinking into action calls for changes which may not be achievable in a few years.'

Apart from a privatisation plan for EGAT, independent power producers (IPPs) that could sell power to the national grid were launched at this time. Saha Union was one of the bidders for a coal-fired power station, which later led to some predictable personal snipes at Anand. 'People used to believe that electricity generating could not be privatised, but lately they have changed their minds,' said Suthee. He was a firm IPP advocate who believed that privatisation would lead to greater efficiency, reduce the cost of doing business, and give producers better access to finance.

The most serious individual casualty of the NPKC's antagonism towards unions was Tanong Po-arn, the outspoken president of the Labour Congress of Thailand, and a vice president of the International Confederation of Free Trade Unions Asia-Pacific. In June 1991, Tanong was due to address the annual meeting of the International Labour Organization in Geneva, Switzerland. He made it clear that he intended to blow the whistle on the NPKC's measures to suppress organised labour. 'He was basically left with just a shell and quite angry about that,' says Robertson. 'At a time when nobody was saying anything against Suchinda and the NPKC, he was standing up there and blasting them.'

One night, Tanong did not come home from work. His car was found outside his office with the door open. There were signs of a struggle. There was speculation that the 55-year-old labour leader had been taken to a military area of Don Muang for some 'attitude adjustment', collapsed and died through a medical misadventure – he suffered from diabetes that required regular medication with insulin. Nothing was ever proved, including whether he was assaulted after his abduction. Tanong was never seen again. The disappearance provoked international outrage, and has permanently tarnished Thailand's image.

Military elements were also suspected in the ambush and murder of Klaew Thanikul and his bodyguard upcountry in early April. As president of the Amateur Boxing Association of Thailand, Klaew was among the most flamboyant but least influential of some 20 known 'godfathers' in the Thai underworld. That was enough, however, to win him a place on the military's list of conspicuously wealthy individuals in the darker reaches of Thai society. His car was fired upon by heavily armed men in a pick-up truck, and dozens of people in a nearby restaurant were wounded. 'Klaew Thanikul died as any self-respecting gangster should – in a hail of bullets,' *The Economist* reported. 'The intriguing question is, did the army order the hit?'

Perhaps a more pertinent question was the level from which the order came. The army had been plagued by hot-headed colonels all through the Prem years. Both Tanong's disappearance and Klaew's murder occurred very early in the first Anand government, and the tensions that arose between Anand and General Issarapong Noonpakdee, the interior minister and army chief of staff, concerned the best way of dealing with gangster elements in the military.

Issarapong was all for a show of military justice. He thought military wrongdoers should be tried and executed, and an example made of them. Anand considered all executions inappropriate. The NPKC did not have the authority to execute criminals, as Field Marshal Sarit Thanarat had done summarily 40 years previously using Article 17 of the then constitution. Under the interim constitution signed by King Bhumibol, executions would require the approval of the prime minister. Anand made his views clear at dinner with senior members of the junta, and also at a later meeting with the entire NPKC.

At the dinner, when he realised this prime minister would not be persuaded, Issarapong stood up, bowed, saluted Anand, and marched off. 'Don't worry; he's always like that,' said Suchinda still sitting at the table. Issarapong later apologised profusely to Anand, explaining that he believed there should be no distinction between a civilian and a soldier guilty of a serious crime. The issue would later preoccupy the second Anand government in the aftermath of serious bloodshed by the military in May 1992. Throughout, Anand always felt the prime minister should veto any kind of summary justice on principle. 'You are dealing with the life of a person,' he says.

Critics of Anand say he should have done more to curb the military's more brutal tendencies; his supporters say his restraining hand prevented more such incidents. Whatever the truth might be, these issues were all indications of the chaos Thailand risked, and that Anand feared, had he not accepted Suchinda's offer of the premiership.

Social reforms

In striking contrast to the military's tougher manoeuvres, Anand's government made significant headway on social issues not previously addressed. Saisuree Chutikul was crucial to pushing this agenda. She was only the third woman ever included in a Thai cabinet, and was fully a match for any of her male colleagues. 'I felt lonely in a way,' she says. 'I don't dislike anybody but, if you are against my position, let's fight.' One of her causes was to have Thailand a party to the UN Convention on the Rights of the Child. Anand fully supported this, and signed up.

Saisuree pushed Deputy Prime Minister Pow Sarasin to get civil service regulations amended so that women ceased to be explicitly barred from many official positions. 'Ajarn [respected teacher], don't you have anything else to do?'

Pow once chided her wearily.

Saisuree refused to be bowed by smug male chauvinism among her colleagues. On one occasion, the importance of breastfeeding was debated, and the affable Suthee found himself for once out-manoeuvred on technical details. He suggested nursing mothers could express their milk and leave it in the fridge when they went to work. 'You say that without being a mother,' Saisuree admonished him.

Saisuree succeeded in getting maternity leave introduced for the civil service, after struggling with Suthee and his deputy, Virabongsa, over whether it should be for 90 days. She wanted more, while they were concerned about the economic impact. Former Prime Minister Kukrit Pramoj supported her in his *Siam Rath* newspaper column, pointing out that men could take three months off to go into the monkhood.

Anand was initially non-committal on the issue of maternity leave. 'It was his corporate background – it was a money issue,' says Saisuree. Could Thailand afford it? Is it a luxury or an investment in healthier, happier children? Saisuree was very upset when the proposal was voted down in her absence. Anand reprimanded those responsible for bringing it up without her, and it was reinstated at a subsequent meeting when she could argue her corner. On a better day, Saisuree pushed through Thailand's first legislation against sexual harassment, although 25 years on there remains much to be done in the area of gender-equality legislation.

Some of the issues Saisuree addressed were rooted in outdated norms. At Anand's suggestion she met, privately, with a prominent law professor who was considering a campaign to reduce the legal age of marriage from 15 to 13. Saisuree remembers an extraordinary lunch at a Chinese restaurant. The professor arrived with a female friend, with whom he conversed exclusively as they ate, and said not a word to Saisuree. Because she also said nothing, she presumed her powerful counter-argument communicated itself telepathically, because the professor went no further with his campaign.

Saisuree also took on entrenched problems of nationality and discrimination, some of which were not particular to Thailand. For example, when 150 women and girls from Myanmar were rescued from a brothel, only 95 were accepted for repatriation after vetting by Burmese officials. Those denied were all from Shan state in the eastern part of the country. Anand suggested that Saisuree take the matter up directly with the Burmese ambassador in Bangkok. Some of the girls were eventually taken safely across the border. Others went to a halfway house in Yangon. Saisuree helped when money was sent to benefit other distressed Burmese in Ranong. It came via the Swedish ambassador from Michael Aris, the British husband of Aung San Suu Kyi, Myanmar's Nobel peace laureate who was under house arrest in Yangon.

The Pearl S. Buck Foundation in Thailand existed primarily to help Amerasian children fathered by American servicemen during the Vietnam War. Saisuree found teenagers there with Thai mothers but no citizenship. 'It just broke my heart,' she says. 'If you are a non-person, what does it mean?' Many of these children were treated much better than others in a similar situation in Vietnam and elsewhere in the region, but they were often denied their basic right to education. Saisuree pressed for the rules to be relaxed. She took on school principals, arguing that they often did not understand their own admission criteria. She found such prejudice particularly ironic in Thailand, a country of migrants clearly ignorant of their own histories. The present-day population includes many ethnic Chinese whose own antecedents may well have arrived 'illegally'.

Gender also played a part in the discrimination against children of mixed race. Under the nationality laws, children of Thai mothers by foreign fathers did not enjoy the automatic entitlement to citizenship given to children with Thai fathers and foreign mothers. 'What is the difference?' Saisuree demanded. 'Do you want to analyse their blood?'

Thailand had actually been quite liberal until the 1960s, giving citizenship to anyone born legally in the kingdom. However, as refugees started arriving in ever-increasing waves from Indochina during the Vietnam War, the pre-1973 regime of Thanom Kittikachorn reacted with the restrictive Decree 337, withdrawing automatic rights to citizenship.

After the fall of Indochina in 1975, the refugee problem worsened; hundreds of thousands of refugees were pouring in from Cambodia, along with boat people from Vietnam, and Hmong from Laos, many of whom had worked and fought for the US Central Intelligence Agency. There were growing numbers of Karen, Karenni, Mon, and Shan refugees along the Burmese border, fleeing the brutal suppression of ethnic insurgencies there. During the 1970s, the multiple flows of refugees from all round had become a serious national security issue.

Saisuree held round-table meetings at Government House with the National Security Council and the ministries of education, foreign affairs, defence, and the interior. The most entrenched party was always the defence ministry, and she recalls employing suitably bruising tactics at times, once accusing a general of not loving children. There were also procedural issues on nationality. The interior ministry had discretionary power when it came to awarding citizenship, but always insisted on the children having a Thai name. Saisuree succeeded in getting this requirement eased.

The HIV/AIDS epidemic

In 1991, Thailand faced a health crisis. Although it was not officially acknowledged, there was a galloping epidemic: acquired immunodeficiency syndrome (AIDS). The disease had first been described in the US in 1981; the first properly documented case of infection with the human immunodeficiency virus (HIV) in Thailand had arisen with a diplomat at the US embassy in 1984.

As in every other country, the evidence of an HIV/AIDS threat in Thailand was deceptive because infection could be asymptomatic for many years. Indeed, official statistics revealed only 433 full-blown AIDS cases in 1991 and 1,349 in 1992 – with less than 6,000 cumulatively by 1994. While deaths due to AIDS were still in the low thousands, new infections were soaring. Indeed, these actually peaked in 1991, at 143,000. By the end of 1990, infections were already believed to number cumulatively at least 400,000 overall. A study published by the Thai Red Cross estimated between 660,000 and 825,000 by mid-1993.[10]

The Prem and Chatichai governments had both failed to really engage with this great issue. The disease gathered momentum initially in the male gay community and among people injecting drugs; but it spread later into the heterosexual population through commercial sex. Vested business interests, particularly in the tourism industry, initially pressured for it to be treated as an illness that only affected foreigners. When this proved false, one health minister suggested turning a leper colony into a half-way house for people affected with HIV. The Chatichai government did, however, establish the National Advisory Committee on AIDS, in 1989.

In 1990, elements in the Ministry of Public Health favoured draconian legislation, which led some international experts to boycott a conference hosted by Thailand and opened by Princess Chulabhorn, the youngest daughter in the royal family. In his address to that congress, Tanin Kraivixien, a former prime minister and privy councillor, called for strict control of 'irresponsible' people, such as prostitutes, homosexuals, drug addicts, and prison inmates.[11] A draft anti-AIDS bill had to be aborted.

Vested tourism industry interests were keen to suppress the issue, and the Tourism Authority of Thailand (TAT) essentially buried its head in the sand. TAT's job was to market Thailand as a safe and appealing destination, and HIV/AIDS had come along at a particularly awkward time. Visit Thailand Year in 1987 concluded in December with King Bhumibol's 60th birthday, which many Thais consider the most important in a lifetime. Within the global travel industry, Visit Thailand Year came to be regarded as one of the most successful tourism promotions in history. Other celebrations followed. In 1988, King Bhumibol became the longest-reigning monarch in Thai history; the following year, when Prince Franz Joseph II of Liechtenstein died, the king became the longest-reigning living monarch in the world. By 1990, these historic national milestones were in the past; yet the official silence on HIV/AIDS persisted.

The disease touched deep sensitivities, and was linked to taboo topics such as drug abuse and the ubiquitous commercial sex industry, both of which were illegal. 'I think many Thais were a bit in denial about the sexual diversity of their own culture, and also about the sexual networks in Thailand,' says Steve Kraus, the head of UNAIDS based in Bangkok.[12] 'We were all very well aware that the epidemic was a wildfire in 1989, 1990, and 1991.'

Fortunately, Thailand had monitoring mechanisms in place, and some excellent doctors and epidemiologists. A robust Sentinel Surveillance programme was mapping the spread of the disease, extracting reliable data from a network of clinics dating back to the 1960s and 1970s that had been set up to deal with venereal diseases. 'It was a huge asset,' says Kraus. 'It was a product of the sexually transmitted disease work done during the Vietnam War era.'

By 1991, seven years since HIV/AIDS had first been detected in Thailand, something radical had changed in its pathology. 'We knew that the vast majority of the infections – more than 95 per cent – were taking pace in the context of commercial sex: unprotected vaginal intercourse,' says Kraus. It was being transmitted primarily through the sex industry, with the epicentre of the crisis in northern Thailand. A survey in June 1989 had revealed that 43 per cent of sex workers in northern brothels were infected. By June 1991, the median figure for brothels in all provinces was 15 per cent. Among military conscripts nationally, 3 per cent were infected. In the North, the figure was double that.

This was social and political dynamite, particularly in a country where commercial sex was illegal. Infected brothel patrons were a threat to their wives, their partners, and their unborn children. Epidemiologists were taking note. This was the first time in Asia that HIV transmission on such a scale threatened the mainstream heterosexual population. Previously, vaginally transmitted HIV had been seen on a large scale only in Sub-Saharan Africa.

Recognising a problem is one thing, finding a solution quite another. Nobody in Thailand's political establishment wanted to go anywhere near the crisis. Mechai remembers lobbying Chatichai on a golf course. 'I'll let you brief the cabinet,' Chatichai said. And so he did. Mechai recalls: 'They listened – I don't know whether they believed me or not.'

Meanwhile, the disease was seeping indiscriminately through Thai society. One very prominent Chatichai-era minister subsequently died from the disease. A C10-level civil servant – the most senior rank – was admitted to the first AIDS hospice discreetly set up by the health ministry in Thonburi. The facility had a crematorium attached, where corpses wrapped only in white sheets were cremated while they were still warm. The ashes were placed in cotton sacks, and stacked in a mournful wall of white sandbags built from forgotten lives.

Thailand's unacknowledged AIDS epidemic was Mechai Viravaidya's main preoccupation. With no vaccine or cure in sight, contracting HIV at that time was a certain death sentence. The only weapon was education, but Mechai had failed to get Chalerm Yubamrung, among many, to take the problem seriously during Chatichai's premiership. Chalerm was minister of the Office of the Prime Minister, and responsible for the Mass Communications Organization of Thailand – a state-owned broadcasting enterprise run by the Office of the Prime Minister that regulated mass media. Mechai did better with General Chavalit Yongchaiyudh, who until 1990 was chief of the army, which controlled a significant part of the nation's broadcasting capacity.

In the early days of the epidemic, there was a ban on information about HIV/AIDS on radio, television, or any government-owned media network. The six free-to-air television channels and some 488 radio stations at that time were not only controlled by the NPKC, but in many instances actually owned by the military. Proprietorship benefited the military commercially, and could be conveniently justified on national security grounds. Controlling the airwaves was particularly important during coups.[13] Mass-media organisations were therefore generally self-censoring, and did not require much prodding from above.[14]

'I tried to overcome this objection, but those were difficult days,' recalls Mechai.

As always, any critical coverage of the government and the junta was to be found in the much more independent and feisty print media. Even so, the mass media blockages were cramping chances of an effective AIDS alert. 'We faced a very serious future,' Mechai recalls. He feared that between two and four million Thais would become infected.[15] 'Very small amounts of money were provided. At that time there was very little financial and no political commitment from the government. Some of us recognised that this failure to commit resources would destroy all the advances in public health that had been made over the past few decades.'[16]

While Chavalit had been receptive to using military-controlled radio and TV stations to broadcast some public information spots, it was far from enough. Others pushing to get the issue addressed included Jon Ungpakorn, the World Health Organization, foreign governments and charities, and various emerging civil society groups. The Thai Red Cross Society has also always played a vital role, including programmes with sex workers and gay men and transgender people, voluntary counselling and testing.

Surveys meanwhile showed that AIDS-awareness activities, far from driving tourists away, had exactly the opposite effect and provided reassurance. 'Mechai took the tourism people's figures to prove that countries which tackled the AIDS question seriously found themselves to be more attractive destinations,' Anand explains. 'There were a lot of heated arguments with the ministry of public health,' he recalls.

The medical profession was searching for treatment regimes that at the time did not exist. Anand remembers letting all parties vent steam in discussions, but always coming down in favour of education and prevention for all. People simply needed to be properly informed. 'There was nothing started before my time,' he recalls.

Mechai knew he lacked the personal clout and resources to drive a really effective public-information campaign. It would take strong leadership and political will – there had to be central ownership of the problem. Fighting AIDS needed to be treated as nothing less than a national security issue. He wanted Anand as prime minister to be head of the national AIDS-response community. And so the National AIDS Prevention and Control Committee was established to better coordinate the national response. It operated within the Office of the

Prime Minister with Anand as chairman. The minister of health, Mechai, other ministers, and various experts attended the committee's quarterly meetings. 'I was the architect, Anand was the final decision maker,' Mechai recalls.

Funding followed. By 1991, the government was already financing 72 per cent of its anti-AIDS programme, and the proportion continued to rise. Effective steps were being taken to protect the blood supply, and the following year a five-year national AIDS plan was put in place.

'If you had not had an arbiter, a real leader up there, then some of this wrangling would not have been resolved,' Anand later recalled. 'Political leadership, the willingness to view the problem in a holistic manner and the understanding that AIDS has far-reaching social and economic implications were all key. At the working level, you needed people with passion, people who really cared, who knew their business. You had to provide sufficient funds, make sure you could rely on accurate statistics, and ensure the health infrastructure was adequate. In these respects we were quite fortunate.'[17]

The success of the Anand government on the HIV/AIDS front was huge, according to Kraus and many other experts. Complacency and denial were thrown out the window, and proper budgets were assigned for the HIV/AIDS national response. Thailand's national HIV/AIDS budget went from US$2.7 million in 1990 to US$25.5 million in 1992.[18] 'It was like a breath of fresh air,' Kraus says. The essence of the new policy was: 'Let's not say this is too sensitive to address – let's get the best information to the entire population.'

Its war on AIDS transformed Thailand from a state in denial to arguably the world's most honest and transparent country on the topic. Where politicians had failed, others had already been trying to make a practical difference. Dr Wiwat Rojanapithayakorn was a health official responsible for seven provinces, and the chief architect of Thailand's 100 per cent condom programme in the context of commercial sex. In the province of Ratchaburi, west of Bangkok, Wiwat's campaign dropped sexually transmitted infections from 13 per cent to 1 per cent in a two-month period. The challenge Wiwat had to overcome was taking this up to a nationwide campaign.

Mechai meanwhile became the lead advocate, engineered the national education campaign, and read a simple bottom line to the recalcitrant business community: 'Dead customers don't buy much.'

'We did a study to determine probable scenarios from 1990 to 2000 if nothing was done about HIV in Thailand,' Mechai recalled. 'The projections indicated that we would have almost four million HIV-infected people by the year 2000. We would lose about 25 years of productive work from each person, and 20 per cent of our gross domestic product annually. That would be far greater than any economic downturn that Thailand has ever experienced or anticipated.'[19]

The media were enlisted. Every editor and reporter was educated about HIV and its pathology, and every hour of broadcasting on every channel included 30 seconds of HIV/AIDS information. Condoms were thrown around like confetti. By Mechai's account, police were put through a special 'cops and rubbers' programme to make sure condoms were used in brothels and massage parlours. The penalty for non-compliance was closure. Even soap opera scripts were vetted to ensure only correct AIDS-related information went to air. All branches of government cottoned on, got with the programme, and saw positive results.

'It worked well because of the collaboration between government departments at national and provincial level,' says Sompong Charoensak, a leading Thai epidemiologist. 'At the provincial level, the governor, the public health officer, the Ministry of Labour, Ministry of Social Development, were all involved. The police, who had to deal with brothels and prostitution, worked hand in hand.' In 1992, 60 million properly stored condoms were given out for free.

'Anand was the first Asian leader to recognise HIV/AIDS as a major development challenge and to mount a nationwide programme in 1991 to combat the epidemic in Thailand,' according to the UN. 'As a result, Thailand was able to significantly reduce the number of HIV infections.'[20] The World Health Organization (WHO) estimates that by 1993, Thailand had seen over a million people infected with HIV/AIDS, many of whom were already dead.

The nation's AIDS crisis was not solved, but it was dramatically mitigated. '[The people in government] who talked openly and honestly and put their money where their mouths were, invested heavily in the national response, and in the end saved millions of lives – no doubt about it,' says Kraus.

Nobody can be entirely sure how massive the decline in HIV infections was. Afterwards, Thailand reverted to more lackadaisical ways, and cut funding for some of its anti-HIV campaigns, including free condom distribution costing just US$1.5 million per annum following the 1997 Asian financial crisis. One model for averted HIV infections suggested that by 2004 there would have been over eight million people affected 'if behaviours had not changed' – an extreme assumption. The study, which tracked HIV infections as they climbed from 1985 and peaked around the turn of the century, suggested a differential of over seven million – which, as Mechai points out, is considerably bigger than the population of Singapore. To this day, he is in no doubt that Anand's decisiveness was core to averting such a dramatic scenario.

What happened on Anand's watch was 'a global best practice example about leadership, investment, and national ownership', says Kraus. 'Thirty years ago, Thailand served as a model to the world about what happens when a government and its communities take ownership of the response, move quickly beyond denial, and move programming to where the virus is.'

Anand took possession of the issue rather than simply leaving it to the ministry and medical profession and hoping for the best. 'If something makes sense and you can demonstrate its worth, Anand will back it,' says Mechai. 'You need that political commitment, then financial commitment.'

There would be ample payback, not just in terms of the countless lives saved, and incalculable grief avoided, but economic benefits as well: fewer breadwinners were lost, more families remained intact, and there were long-term healthcare savings. These were all wins for Thailand – and some would argue for the world.

CHAPTER 13

ANAND'S FIRST TERM: ECONOMIC & LEGISLATIVE REFORMS (1991–2)

Economic agendas

'For me and for many others, the economic and associated legislative reforms were the most dramatic achievements and most lasting legacy of the Anand governments,' says historian Chris Baker. He points to the liberalising of trade, energy, and finance; the first legislation on the environment; the easing of the business environment for foreigners and educators; and the sheer volume of legislation. Considerable thought and hard work went into these advances, and they did not always come easy.

Anand made Snoh Unakul his deputy prime minister responsible for all economic portfolios, and there was much to preoccupy him. Snoh worked late into each night, driving himself relentlessly. His wife Nongnuj (Nui), a dentist whose patients included Anand, often had to ask people to fetch her husband home from the office. She was only too well aware of Snoh's history of overworking.

While governor of the Bank of Thailand under Prime Minister Kriangsak Chomanand in the late 1970s, Snoh had faced an oil crisis, interest rates spiking to over 20 per cent, and foreign reserves down to only US$350 million.[1] The Bank of Thailand turned to the World Bank and International Monetary Fund for the first time, and syndicated loans were brought in from the commercial market.

At that stressful time, Nukul Prachuabmoh hoped Snoh would steel himself to stay on as governor. He clearly recalls their last meeting at the Bank of Thailand in late 1979: 'Snoh looked healthy and promised he would not resign.' However, after a sleepless night and a meeting with his family, Snoh stepped down the very next day. 'They all agreed it was not fair on Thailand to have a governor of the Bank of Thailand who had not slept all night,' recalls Snoh.

'I knew so much had to be done,' says Snoh. During the year of the first Anand government, some moments felt like the happiest of his life; others were among the most sorrowful. Working with Anand was a contrast to the wilderness Chatichai years, when the young Baan Phitsanulok advisers usurped the old technocrats. 'This group did not listen,' he says. 'They did not even let me speak any more. Chatichai was a nice man, but his ministers were doing whatever they wanted.' Snoh reckons he was the first one they wanted to get rid of after the eight years of Prem – a golden time for him as head of the National Economic and Social Development Board (NESDB).

Snoh's world was shattered again soon enough. After only a few months in office, he suffered a serious stroke that required a convalescence of three months and left him without the use of his right arm.[2] Even when his condition improved, Snoh did not relish public appearances. 'I was so ashamed,' he says. 'I didn't want to face the press with this kind of thing.'

Initially, Snoh could not walk from his car. Anand ordered that ramps be installed at Government House for the first time. But at the first cabinet meeting he attended after his stroke, Snoh had to lie down and rest after just ten minutes. 'I need to be here,' he told everyone.

From the outset, all economic issues were reviewed by Anand's economic ministers before being sent to cabinet. This process was part of Snoh's remit. After partially recovering from his stroke, he took to convening sub-cabinet meetings at his Sukhumvit home. The exceptionally long table that once seated 16 ministers and their staff remains in place to this day, running down one side of his sitting room. It overlooks a neatly tended garden and a shaded fish pond.

Later, as Snoh's recovery continued, an even worse disaster befell the family. His youngest son, Abhinand ('Pok Pak'), home for the New Year from studies in the US, was killed in a car accident on 5 January. 'It was terrible,' says Snoh. 'They come together, disasters and opportunities.'[3]

As Prem's most influential economic adviser, Snoh had always considered the fifth plan in the early 1980s to be transformative. In its later stages, it brought extra dividends following the appreciation of the Japanese yen in 1985. To remain competitive, many Japanese factories moved abroad, opening a window for Thailand to develop its industrial sector and build supply chains.[4] Although inbound investment in the 1980s favoured industry over agriculture and the service sector, the tourism industry boomed mightily with the Visit Thailand Year promotion in 1987, bumping foreign arrivals up 24 per cent, to 3.4 million.[5]

The physical core of Snoh's plans was the Eastern Seaboard, stretching eastwards from Bangkok down the Gulf of Thailand to Sattahip. To liberalise the economy and energise the industrial estates and factories that were springing up, the whole regulatory structure needed change. The Anand government, with Sipphanondha Ketudat as minister of industry, streamlined procedures for setting up factories. This was crucial to positioning Thailand as a manufacturing hub, particularly for automotives and electronics, in the decades to follow.

'We consider Thailand to be one of the least protectionist markets in the world,' said finance minister Suthee Singsaneh at the time.[6] He wanted it to be even more open, in order to press domestic industry to be more competitive. The tariff on automobiles, for example, was 600 per cent on imported cars powered by engines over 2,300cc. He described the barrier as 'quite normal in this part of the world'. Protectionist tariffs had been in place for decades, to help build the local assembly industry. But car prices were also high partly due to the domestic inefficiencies. Suthee dropped the tariff to 200 per cent, ramping up foreign competition, forcing in new technology, and ultimately bringing car prices down.

Thailand emerged from the Anand years as an increasingly important global automotive manufacturing hub, and is today one of the world's top producers of one-ton pickup trucks. It made the crucial crossover from assembly to manufacturing, with thousands of supply companies coming into operation. 'That's how the automotive industry of Thailand was founded,' says Anand unabashedly.

The country's entire administrative structure needed overhauling. Snoh viewed bureaucrats as far too powerful and business-unfriendly. 'An economy cannot function at the discretion of bureaucrats,' he says. Archaic laws were a breeding ground for corruption. Meechai Ruchupan, secretary general of the Judicial Council, was one of the reliable, 'very good' legal minds Snoh had often turned to in the Prem years, and he was at hand once again as a fellow deputy prime minister.

There was further housekeeping to be done. Price-control barriers for commodities were removed, and quota procedures made more transparent. The Bank of Thailand relaxed regulations on the international movement of funds, and made it easier for foreign banks to establish branches.

Foreigners working legally with work permits were no longer required to produce a tax clearance certificate every time they wanted to leave the country. Suthee saw high personal tax, 50 per cent on income over two million baht, as a deterrent to foreign business. 'That level of income is easily exceeded,' he said. 'That does not encourage people working here at all. I would say that quite a number do not declare their full income – they have ways of being paid elsewhere. Something needs to be done here so that income tax stimulates doing business and working hard – we don't want to allow the income tax system to be the thing that sends them away.'

Corporate and income tax were reduced, but the most important step forward was the introduction of value-added tax (VAT) to replace an obsolete system of business taxes. 'The old system was impractical and people could cheat,' says Snoh. 'We had to come up with something else.' The advantages of a VAT system, which passes the burden on to the end user, had been clearly identified in the mid-1980s, but governments were not strong enough to overcome vested interests and implement it.

A flat VAT rate replaced a mixed bag of business taxes. Previously, contractors paid only 3.3 per cent while manufacturers paid 9.9 per cent. Adding to the administrative complexity, hotels paid 11 per cent on rooms and restaurants, but 16.5 per cent on restaurants with music. Snoh wanted a flat 10 per cent VAT rate, but 7 per cent was the level finally approved in cabinet – and it has not been adjusted in over a quarter of a century.

'We expect to lose revenue in the first two years, and we can afford that because of our present treasury surplus,' Suthee predicted as he tailored Snoh's high hopes to reality. As Mechai Viravaidya recalls: 'Suthee had great skill in saying no to you – and you thanked him.' But Suthee also had a reputation for being more willing to compromise than Anand, and sometimes Mechai won. He wanted tax exemptions for charitable donations increased, and got Suthee to lift the figure from 1 per cent to 2.

Farmers and small shopkeepers were exempted from the VAT system for practical reasons. 'A lot of people did not know how to keep accounts anyway, and Anand knew time was short,' says Snoh. 'With value added tax, if we hadn't allowed these exemptions, it might have taken a few more decades.' Indeed, Malaysia was unable to implement a more modest 6 per cent goods and services tax until 2015; and in India the economically progressive government of Prime Minister Rajendra

Modi struggled to get state government approvals for a much more complicated goods and services tax regime that finally came into effect on 1 July 2017.

In the bigger picture, Suthee streamlined customs tariffs to 5 per cent for raw materials, 10 per cent for semi-finished products and 20 per cent for finished products. He later waived VAT on books, and pressed for zero tax on computer equipment compared to 40 per cent previously. 'I personally intend to make this country more computer-literate. With a reduction in tax, everyone can own a computer,' he said.

With a background in the civil service and business, Anand could claim no real insight into the lives of farming families. Anat Arbhabhirama, the minister of agriculture, felt new agrarian policies needed at least five years if they were to stand a chance. 'You can only lay foundations in a year,' he says. Kosit Panpiemras, Anat's young deputy minister of agriculture, was therefore quite surprised to be given significant time with Anand. 'If you can convince him, it is very quick,' he recalls. 'He had strong interest in the welfare of rural people. He was also interested in following up. I found out later that he did that to many people.'

Kosit found Suthee supportive enough in terms of budget, but with strong views on fiscal discipline. 'A finance minister can never please everybody, but he was hugely respected,' says Kosit. 'Suthee could reach difficult solutions without creating enemies. Part of it was his great sense of humour. His idea was that dialogue and transparency were much better than fighting and having decisions made behind closed doors.'

At the outset, Anand had reminded his ministers that their term was short, and they should focus on attainable goals. Kosit wanted to make the agriculture ministry more effective in planning and production. He felt it should help farmers mitigate risk by advising them to select only the most suitable crops for their farms and to avoid monocropping, a process known as integrated farming. Farmers were perennially burdened with debt, had problems with land rights, and suffered as younger family members migrated to the cities. One possibility Kosit floated was creating a land bank that could be used for rentals to needy farmers, but this was a huge undertaking well beyond the reach of a short-stay government. Indeed, it was not taken up by any of the elected governments that followed.

There was more success with rubber in the South where a central market was set up in Had Yai. This placed justifiably sceptical farmers alongside buyers and exporters, all together under one roof. 'The idea was to cut through several layers of middlemen,' says Kosit.

Such liberal initiatives recognised that a strong economy required fairer income distribution to stimulate aggregate demand, and fairer deals all round in a country notorious for some of the world's highest income disparities. Grassroots stimulus efforts included increasing the minimum wage by 15 per cent, and lifting public sector remuneration, including at state enterprises, by 20 per cent. Six billion baht was also allocated for discretionary spending at village level, a direct stimulus approach that would be used again a decade later under the Thaksin Shinawatra governments. At the time, Anand said he hoped a system for local tax levies could be devised so that provincial administrations could get a better handle on their own budgets [7] – a theme to which he would return in the following century with his national reform proposals.

There was also a need to try and remedy the damage often done by accelerated economic development. Thailand was choking on the damaging byproducts of prosperity, with pollution and deforestation among the main problems. As deputy prime minister with responsibility for all the economic portfolios, Snoh was personally haunted by the environmental degradation associated with careless economic development and industrialisation on his earlier watches. 'That was my bad mark,' he says. 'It was a mess and we had to accept that. I felt I owed the environment – but we had to run to make it happen.'

The cavalier official attitude towards the environment had been dramatically illustrated in early March 1991 within a week of the coup. An extremely noxious warehouse blaze erupted inside Klong Toey Port in the heart of Bangkok, close to one of the city's largest slums. Improperly stored chemicals, including methyl bromide (an insecticide), and trichloroisocyanuric acid (an industrial disinfectant), ignited in a toxic cocktail and spewed a plume of choking white smoke and ash over the capital. At least three people died and many suffered long-term health damage; nearly 650 slum dwellings were destroyed. Suchinda visited the disaster scene in person, but there was outrage when the military subsequently ferried the remaining chemicals for burial near the Thai-Burmese border. 'We're a fast-developing country,' said one official dismissively. 'This is one of the prices we pay.' [8]

Phaichitr Uathavikul, the minister of science, technology, and energy (later environment) battled such irresponsible attitudes. Aided by industry minister Sipphanondha Ketudat, Phaichitr was instrumental in overhauling the energy sector's muddled management. Despite its title, the National Energy Administration

(NEA) within his ministry was only actually responsible for small hydropower projects and pumping water. The ministry also oversaw the National Environment Board, which played no role in controlling air pollution. The Electricity Generating Authority of Thailand (EGAT) came under the Office of the Prime Minister. The provincial and metropolitan electricity distribution authorities answered to the Ministry of Interior, as did PTT, the state-owned energy conglomerate, and the Public Works Department, which regulated petrol stations and oil storage. The Ministry of Commerce set retail energy prices and product standards.

There had long been considerable disagreement on how to streamline this dysfunctional structure. One option was to create a dedicated energy ministry. Instead, Prime Minister Prem Tinsulanond had issued an order in 1986 to establish the National Energy Policy Committee (NEPC) under his chairmanship, with the National Energy Policy Office (NEPO) as its secretariat. These fell under the Office of the Prime Minister, but being temporary they were at political risk. The Anand government quickly set about drafting the National Energy Policy Act to make the NEPC and NEPO permanent. 'Resistance was strong among permanent officials of the various energy-related ministries, but the prime minister and his cabinet were determined,' recalls Piyasvasti Amranand, a former secretary general of the Thai National Energy Policy Office who later became energy minister.

The National Energy Policy Act and related amendments finally went through the National Legislative Assembly in February 1992, recasting the NEA as the Department of Energy Development and Promotion, and the old Ministry of Science, Technology and Energy as science, technology and environment. As a permanent fixture, the NEPC could now continue providing strong leadership. 'A truly unified decision-making progress on energy was created for the first time,' says Piyasvasti.

Deregulation of oil prices, a radical reform in the energy sector, was implemented much earlier in the first Anand government. Thailand depended on imports to meet 90 per cent of its needs, and suffered severely in the 1973 and 1979–80 oil crises. While petrol costs were kept high for motorists, a costly oil fund was in place to subsidise diesel, kerosene, and liquefied petroleum gas for the benefit of poorer consumers. This led to severe price distortions and misuse of fuels. It also left successive governments politically vulnerable. Indeed, the energy crisis played a significant part in bringing down Kriangsak Chomanand's government in March 1980.

'The only permanent solution was to cut the link between oil prices and politics – allowing domestic oil prices to move in line with world prices,' says Piyasvasti. The government moved very quickly in May 1991 to deregulate retail prices with NEPO continuing to control ex-refinery prices until August. Once market mechanisms came fully into play, the oil fund had no role to play. As a result, 1.5 billion baht was released in 1992 to fund the Energy Conservation Fund, and 4.5 billion baht was given to the new Environment Fund. The first Anand government pushed through Thailand's first environmental protection legislation with the comprehensive National Environmental Promotion and Conservation Act in March 1992, drafted principally by Phaichitr. Although it would be widely flouted, this was a very important start. Among other things, it established a National Environment Board chaired by the prime minister, and created space for non-governmental organisations to play a role.

The Anand governments did not have the time to deregulate the liquefied petroleum gas market, and this was not completed until 2017 – evidence of the radical nature of the 1991 reforms for other fuels. Anand's government also made the energy sector more competitive. Caltex, ESSO, PTT, and Shell dominated fuel distribution, so barriers to entry were lowered. For example, a regulation that no petrol station could be within a kilometre of a PTT station was dropped. Caltex and Shell were both allowed to build new refineries and ESSO to expand its existing plant. This increased competition and promoted national security – at that time Thailand was importing 40 per cent of petroleum products from Singaporean refineries.

A related success was the introduction of lead-free petrol over a three-year period starting from 1 May 1991. Unleaded petrol was more costly to refine, and older vehicles could not use it. Anand recalls the struggle to find a way to make it less expensive, thereby giving drivers of new vehicles an incentive to switch. The solution was to follow Singapore's example and use excise tax to ensure the price of leaded fuel was higher than unleaded. While the move to cleaner fuel got under way, the government required that from the start of 1992 the lead component should be reduced by almost two-thirds to 0.15 gram per litre, and that from September 1993 all new cars should be fitted with catalytic converters. These measures had an enormous impact on air quality, particularly in severely polluted Bangkok. By the end of 1991, 21 per cent of premium gasoline sold was unleaded, rising to 37 per cent by the end of 1993. 'The policy was highly successful as oil companies competed to import unleaded gasoline,' says Piyasvasti. The sale of leaded petrol was finally banned in 1996.

There was also some success in bringing better oversight to infrastructure development, and improving transparency. One particularly problematic project, the Bangkok Elevated Road and Train System (BERTS), was an integrated elevated highway and rail link from the capital to Bangkok International Airport at Don Muang. It was the brainchild of Gordon Wu, an engineer and international infrastructure entrepreneur who operated through Hopewell Holdings in Hong Kong. The project was to be built mostly on land owned by the State Railway of Thailand. An agreement had been signed in November 1990 by Montri Pongpanich, the minister of transport and communications, but there was much that needed to be clarified.

Under the Chatichai government, Wu had extracted a private understanding that the land could be developed with Board of Investment (BOI) privileges. Anand took the view that this was a matter for the BOI to decide, not the cabinet. The BOI duly turned down Hopewell. Anand happened to be chairman of the BOI as well – it was one of the hats he wore as prime minister. The hopelessness of the Hopewell project remained evident after the Anand government finally suspended it in early 1992, but it was not permanently cancelled until 1998. Periodic attempts were made to revive it, or incorporate the hundreds of pillars left behind into other mass transit systems. Some of the concrete relics were demolished, others collapsed of their own accord in 2012.

Legal reform

A month after Anand formed his cabinet, Snoh Unakul was invited to lunch by the presidents of the foreign chambers of commerce. Snoh, his technocrats, and the foreign business community had been frozen out during the bullish, self-confident, go-it-alone Chatichai years, when policies were driven by the group of young Baan Phitsanulok advisers, and Thai businessmen imagined the world should take lessons from them on how to grow economies.

During the lunch, the affable, always modest Snoh tried to make amends. He said that one of the most important contributions foreign chambers could make was providing lawyers from the private sector to advise on draft legislation to remove business and development bottlenecks. It was a gracious gesture, a dim echo of the foreign advisers drafted in during the fifth and sixth reigns in 19th-century and early 20th-century Siam.

A few days later, senior members of the American, British, and Japanese chambers called on Anand at Government House. 'He asked that we be as specific as possible, give him the text of the changes, being realistic and reasonable,' recalled lawyer David Lyman. The former AmCham president was soon to become coordinator of what was dubbed the Law Changes Project. 'In essence, the prime minister asked the foreign chambers of commerce to give him our "wish list",' Lyman recorded at the time.

There was enormous enthusiasm for the project initially. Here was an opportunity to cut through the complex web of legislation and bureaucracy – an incubator for corruption – that many foreign businessmen believed stymied not only their personal commercial opportunities but also the Thai economy in general. Suddenly, foreigners had a chance to contribute to the development of Thailand in a manner that was not too overtly self-serving. There was an unexpected sense of shared adventure.

The foreign chambers conferred and set about the project with gusto. Reports were promised in English, with Thai translations to follow: on areas of high priority by the end of May, medium priority by June, and less pressing agendas for the end of July. A daunting 39 areas of interest were initially identified; these ranged from criminal liability facing company directors to ship mortgages. A Foreign Chambers of Commerce Working Group (FCCWG) was set up. Five international law firms with a steering committee headed by Lyman were involved,[9] as well as nine chambers of commerce.[10]

While Anand unequivocally endorsed the Law Changes Project at the outset, he was more aware of its constraints than most, particularly the limited life span of his government, and the full legislative calendar waiting at its end. The pace of legislation being undertaken by his government was unprecedented. With new laws and reforms relating to bankruptcy, the environment, industry, land reform, the stock market, trade, trademarks, taxation, and more, Anand's cabinet was barrelling forward faster than any hastily assembled coalition of commerce chambers and law firms could match. In the period 1 March to 6 December 1991, 127 laws were enacted compared to 105 over 30 months in the Chatichai government.

Lyman was never naïve; his gut feeling was that such an opportunity would never come again. 'I still retain a nagging thought that all our work may be for nought,' he ruminated. 'We will probably not have a better opportunity in the near future to effect the changes to legislation that we deem needed. In this context, the current cabinet is the best government we can expect.'

The project proved very heavy going. The May deadline for the high-priority topics was missed. Actual recommendations to the government only started flowing in August and September, but by then the realisation had dawned that the project was chewing up enormous resources and had become unsustainable. The areas-of-interest list had already been cut back to 37, and the FCC presidents decided in August to suspend work on anything beyond 16.

The government was meanwhile making good progress. In early June, it submitted a new draft trademark bill to parliament, which passed on its first reading. In early July, a condominium act also sailed through. There were some significant developments outside parliament. In reviewing the foreign business law, the Judicial Council adjusted the definition of an 'alien' juristic person. The Ministry of Commerce then faced the task of tracing the beneficial ownership of all Thai-owned shares. This was a significant issue given that foreign ownership was generally restricted to 49 per cent, apart from under the 1966 treaty of amity for US citizens. The cap was routinely circumvented using Thai proxy shareholders. Indeed, Japanese investors had built up the economy on the understanding that proxy ownership would always be quietly ignored. 'For existing companies the nightmares could only be just beginning,' Lyman reported ominously. 'I am told this ruling has not yet been made public.'

By September, Lyman and his team were preparing to sign off and walk away. In the final reckoning, only eight of the remaining 15 reports were sent out. These went directly to Anand's office and were courteously acknowledged by Vidhya, his deputy secretary general. On September 16, Lyman issued one of his final directives: 'With the completion and submission of these works, the Law Change Project is now shut down, except for the preparation of legal fees and expenses bills … '

Payment was a moot point. There had never been any question of the government paying. Snoh had asked for suggestions; the project was never a paid consultancy. The bill was supposed to be footed by the chambers, and AmCham had said it would pay 'its share'. In the end, however, the law firms acted *pro bono*. 'It was approved by the foreign chambers of commerce who said they would pay us,' says Lyman. 'We did not see one baht.'

In the end, the task of remedying Thailand's legislative shortcomings far outstripped the resources Lyman and his foreign legal and business cohorts were able to marshal, and also the life expectancy of Anand's government. 'There just wasn't enough time to enact all the laws we recommended here,' says Lyman.

One of David Lyman's personal lifetime missions has been reducing the excess of criminal liability facing company directors in Thailand in areas he believed should carry civil penalties, a situation of 'vicarious criminal liability'. He lectured on the topic frequently, headlining it: 'Who wants to be a Thai director?' Lyman counted about 100 laws that imposed criminal penalties on directors if something went wrong.

Lyman's project was a torturous exercise. In a letter to Anand, he wrote: 'We have to find a way to create something new to Thai jurisprudence – the civil offence and its corresponding civil penalty – and make them acceptable. This idea had to be moulded in such a way as to use the existing principles of Thai law, satisfy the needs of the regulator (i.e. the bureaucrats) as well as the regulated (i.e. the businessmen), be perceived as retaining all the trappings of control to placate the government's legal scrutinisers, and be of a form and substance acceptable to members of the National Legislative Assembly. Ours was an exasperating effort in the practice of the art of the possible.'

After so much proved to be impossible, perhaps one of the lessons of the Law Changes Project was that foreigners offered the chance to effect change in Thailand would inevitably be overwhelmed and doomed to failure.

CHAPTER 14

BLACK MAY
(1992)

Royal audiences

By 1991, Anand had not been granted a private audience with King Bhumibol since he left for his final diplomatic posting as ambassador to Bonn 15 years earlier. His first audience as prime minister was at Bhuping Palace in Chiang Mai, when he was accompanied by the entire cabinet for the formal swearing-in. At tea afterwards, the king's chief *aide de camp* came up and inquired if Anand had anything else to say to the king. Anand was not expecting a further meeting, but the officer just stood, waiting for him to follow. 'I stayed another hour and a half,' Anand recalls. 'It was a private audience.'

Anand had spent a third of his life abroad, and was not always comfortable with the more arcane aspects of Thai protocol. He therefore consulted *MR* Kukrit Pramoj about further audiences. 'Don't bother him,' the former prime minister advised. Kukrit himself greatly missed the audiences of his premiership.

Anand let matters rest for three weeks. 'And then there was a signal,' he recalls.

The normal protocol was to request an audience through the Office of the King's Principal Private Secretary, *ML* Thawisan Ladawan, which would then be granted – or not. In Anand's case, there would sometimes be oblique invitations. For example, Foreign Minister Arsa Sarasin might be presenting a new ambassador and the king would ask him specific questions about the government's policy. 'I think he wants to see you,' Arsa would tell Anand later.

'I never told the public I was going to see the king to discuss this or that,' Anand says. He also never gave press interviews when he emerged from the palace. The audiences took place on average once a week, with Anand always dressed in a business suit – he had had seven made by a local tailor after he first became prime minister.

In an interview with *Matichon* newspaper in June 2017, a year before his death, Police General Vasit Dejkunjorn, the former chief of court police, was interviewed about the tradition among British prime ministers of visiting the monarch once a week. According to Vasit, Anand was the only prime minister to come close to this in Thailand. 'Apart from [Anand], I do not know of anyone else who had regular meetings with the king,' he said.

People close to Anand say he sometimes alludes to the audiences in general terms, but he never recounts conversations in any detail; there are no breaches of confidentiality.

Normally, it was Anand who would raise points, and the king would respond. Topics were always from the present day, and never about historical events. 'If the king ever initiated a discussion about something from the past, it would always be to do with the constitution,' explains Anand. 'He knew I had some very serious questions in my mind.'

Anand found King Bhumibol to be scrupulous in remaining apolitical, and not passing judgements on others. He offered advice on broad principles only. 'He set aside personalities, and just addressed the issues raised. He never showed favouritism.' The king, of course, had enormous experience in the affairs of state. 'He educated me on many matters,' admits Anand. 'He was the foremost constitutional authority in the country. I learned a lot from him: tolerance, fair-mindedness – learning to let go.'

Unlike his predecessors, Anand brought to the encounters a well-informed world view, a unique personal experience of the military, and familiarity with the world of business. In a later speech, Anand described part of the context of such audiences in more formal terms: 'As a constitutional monarch ... the king possesses three discretionary powers: the right to be consulted, the right to encourage, and the right to warn. Under normal circumstances, he exercises these prerogatives through private audiences he grants to the prime minister of the day. What transpires during these meetings remains private and confidential – and even after the statutory silent period, part of the consultations may never be known.'[1]

For Anand personally, these very private audiences were clearly among the most treasured aspects of his two premierships. He had never worked in the palace, and only been close to the king on occasion, such as during the king's visits to Canada and the US in 1967. 'What I remember most was that I got to know my own king. I am glad I had that opportunity from my heart. It was a rare and precious opportunity.'

Although Anand quite intentionally moved into the public eye during the premiership, many remark on how little his personality changed then and when he left Government House. He still found time to carry on some of his social life, dining sometimes with friends. Manaspas Xuto remembers a relaxed dinner one night at the Imperial hotel, with the prime minister requesting songs. There was no sign of stress. 'Khun Anand just exports it,' says Kosit Panpiemras.

Soon after his appointment, he arrived at a regular dinner for old boys of Dulwich College as normal. This particular Old Alleynian get-together was held at the Fireplace Grill, the restaurant where it had so recently been suggested to Suchinda that Anand might be just the person he needed as prime minister. 'Anand just breezed into the room,' recalls Simon Hirst, the club secretary at the time. 'There was no big police escort or security outfit. He is a very direct guy, a straight-shooter, and he expects other people to be the same.' One Thai Old Alleynian with military connections, Major General *MR* Mahisorn Kasemsant, complimented Anand on his appointment, referring fulsomely to the honour it had brought to Thailand and to Dulwich College. 'That's not what you were saying when they were accusing me of being a communist,' Anand responded sharply, alluding to his miserable experience with the military in 1976. Then he laughed, and moved on quickly with an old joke about military intelligence. 'We all thought it was incredibly funny,' says Hirst. But he did wonder about the advisability of making such jokes.

Democratic manoeuvres

The president of the constitution drafting committee, Deputy Prime Minister Meechai Ruchupan, was close to Ukrit Mongkolnavin, the president of the senate. However, Anand and the rest of his cabinet were not involved in the process of drafting the new constitution. 'It was a contentious issue when I decided to accept the premiership, and always a disappointment to me,' says Anand. Ministers would, however, sometimes attend the National Legislative Assembly appointed by the junta to explain bills and answer questions. There was also a separate constitution-scrutinising committee reporting directly to the junta that had nothing to do with the cabinet.

'I think Anand kept quite a distance from the political side of the coup makers – the constitution and so on,' says Abhisit Vejjajiva. Although the issues arising from the drafting process were hotly debated in the press and academia, they were fairly unremarkable in the Thai context: the size of the senate, how it should be created, what powers it should have, and how the president of parliament should be selected. Two other issues raised concerns: whether serving military officers and senior public officials should be allowed to hold political office, and whether the prime minister needed to be elected. These constitutional matters – particularly the large senate and its powers relative to a fully elected lower house – did cause Anand disquiet. When the doubts he aired surfaced in the press in November, they were simply ignored by the junta.

Meanwhile the prime minister's office was receiving faxes related to the most contentious aspects of the draft constitution. They appeared to originate from the palace. Anand decided the situation could easily be misconstrued, and needed to be raised at an audience. He wanted to find out whether the faxes had been sent on the king's instructions. When he asked, the king passed no comment on the faxes or their substance, and replied: 'Khun Anand, do you know how many fax machines we have in the palace?' 'By not responding to my question directly, the answer covered all my concerns,' says Anand.

As the year went by, Anand had from time to time given public assurances that elections would be held, and that there would be an orderly return to democracy. With no sense of irony, the interior ministry controlled by General Issarapong Noonpakdee – the army chief of staff, interior minister, leading member of the NPKC, and brother in law of Suchinda – was promoting efforts to educate the grassroots in democracy. The programme was cobbled together hastily and predictably ineffective. *The Nation* reported: 'Surveys of villages where the project had been implemented show no sign that villagers are more politically informed than they were before.' It quoted Squadron Leader Prasong Soonsiri, the hawkish former secretary general of the National Security Council: 'It was definitely the wrong way to educate people about democracy.'[2]

For once, Anand and Prasong were on common ground. Historically, votes were delivered to parties by arrangement with the *kamnan*, the village headman. The cabinet had the power to change ministerial regulations affecting the way laws were applied, even when laws themselves could only be adjusted or changed by the legislative assembly. To counter the power of the village headmen, the Anand government pushed through rules requiring they be re-elected at regular intervals, and not allowed lifetime tenure.

As 1991 passed, there was speculation that Suchinda might return to power as prime minister – even, some feared, while remaining army chief. Anand linked up with Gothom Arya, an electrical engineer whom he had met as a member of the Chulalongkorn University Council. Gothom was an early civil society activist who strongly opposed the constitution being drafted by the military. 'We were very apprehensive that some of it would not be democratic,' he says. Gothom collected signatures against the draft, and organised a demonstration at Sanam Luang in November 1991. The interior ministry responded with its own signature campaign, and managed to collect even more names supporting the draft.

Anand always remained apart from the constitution-drafting process.He did, however, attend a dinner with Suchinda that had been initiated by Gothom. 'We somehow reached an agreement that our main objections would be heard and corrections made in the draft,' recalls Gothom. 'Khun Anand said he would support the change in the draft and General Suchinda would exert his influence so the changes would be made – and he kept his word. A better draft was promulgated.'

Overall, Anand viewed the emerging constitution as 'not perfect but workable'. King Bhumibol also took this view, observing that it could be amended in the course of time. 'Any rule can be changed,' he said in his birthday speech in early December, shortly before the constitution was passed without referendum.[3] This proved to be essentially true: the constitution of 1992, albeit with some amendments, remained in place while five governments were elected. The biggest elephant in the room initially, however, was the possibility of an unelected prime minister taking power. Suchinda promised he would not take the premiership. His subsequent breaking of that vow haunts him to this day – a step much too far for the usually forgiving Thai public, certainly in Bangkok.

The military always argued that the general election which produced the Chatichai government had involved vote-buying – a view almost nobody disputed. Once the new constitution was in place, the generals were proposing to deploy village headmen to curb money politics. It was akin to turning poachers into gamekeepers and hoping they would suddenly turn honest. 'You need other kinds of volunteers,' says Gothom.

Anand wanted somebody such as Gothom to create independent machinery that would disrupt the various influential groups who controlled the election process; monitor canvassing and voting; and expose malfeasance through the media. Thus, PollWatch was created with Gothom as its first secretary. 'It was a special arrangement,' Gothom explains. 'Its implementation was more like a civil society project.'

PollWatch was initially funded from the Office of the Prime Minister with a special budget allocated as a lump sum. The International Foundation of Electoral Systems (IFES) later assumed PollWatch had started out as a non-governmental organisation. After the 1996 election that produced the government of General Chavalit Yongchaiyudh, IFES reported: 'PollWatch grew to become a government-funded entity which utilised tens of thousands of volunteers in each election to help draw attention to election irregularities, particularly the practice of exchanging money for votes.'[4] This misconception, after the event, was understandable. PollWatch's creation during a military-installed government was certainly counter-intuitive. As Gothom puts it, 'Very paradoxically, this unelected prime minister was supportive of popular movements.'

Democratic process

The general election that took place on 22 March 1992 produced nearly 2,700 complaints to PollWatch over the whole election period from January. Although the voting went off uneventfully, it generated a slightly skewed result. Chavalit's New Aspiration Party won the popular vote with almost ten million ballots, but garnered only 72 seats. Samakkitham, the military's proxy party, emerged with 79 seats, but with over 1.4 million fewer votes.

The electorate had nevertheless had some say, and Anand had fulfilled his promise to the people. His departure from office was unusual in one respect. In the last days, King Bhumibol sat for a picture with the entire cabinet – something he had not done before, and never repeated.

'Those were exceptional days, in fact an exceptional era, and, as you know, all eras come to an end,' says Nanda Krairiksh, Anand's older daughter. 'It was a difficult period for our family, particularly for my mother who likes to lead a quiet life. While we were proud he had fulfilled his mandate for the public good, we were certainly happy that his term as prime minister had come to an end. We felt there had been enough sacrifices in the family.'

At the end, Anand and Sodsee were invited for an audience and afternoon tea with the Princess Mother. She had known Sodsee's parents in the 1930s and 1940s in Lausanne, where she raised Thailand's two future kings and their older sister, Princess Galyani.

For Anand, it was the conclusion of an unexpected, but eventful, 14 months. All he really wanted by then was to relax and take his wife on holiday to Italy. He would be able to puff cigars at a favourite café at the foot of the Spanish Steps in Rome while Sodsee went off to shop, indulging in some overdue retail therapy. As an anonymous Asian gentleman at leisure, Anand could then recover some of the anonymity torn from his life in Thailand. After the break in Italy, he would return to his old life, reassuming his chairmanship of Saha Union. He had certainly enjoyed the public service stint, but there were no regrets, no hankering for power – it was time to move on.

'He is basically a very democratic person – very straightforward,' says Ekamol wistfully. 'I wish Anand had been there [as prime minister] for five years.' Many shared this view, but not Anand. He knew perfectly well that many – including the politicians who often approached him – would have supported him stretching his stay at Government House to a four-year term, but that it would have set a terrible precedent. 'I did not have that mandate,' he says. 'I was sure I would not be doing the right thing by prolonging my term. My assumption of the position of prime minister arose from a *coup d'état*, with which I basically disagreed.'

Anand has never regretted stepping aside, and never wonders about what might have been. 'I don't believe in hypothetical questions,' he says. 'The past is the past. Once I leave a job, it is *finito*.'

Political revolts

Military coups have punctuated Thai politics since 1932. However, on three occasions governments have been brought down following rebellions on the streets, in what one might term 'civilian coups'. All three were quite different in character.

The first, in October 1973, was a student-led uprising that toppled the government of Field Marshals Thanom Kittikachorn and Praphas Charusathien, and forced them into exile.

The most recent, in early 2014, saw anti-government demonstrations in Bangkok undermine the caretaker administration of Prime Minister Yingluck Shinawatra, sister of ousted prime minister Thaksin Shinawatra. Led by a former Democrat Party deputy prime minister, Suthep Thaugsuban, the unelected People's Democratic Reform Committee prevented a general election that would almost certainly have returned Yingluck to office. Instead, she was removed by a court ruling,[5] and her government was subsequently ousted by the military in a coup.

But perhaps the 'civilian coup' that made the greatest impression upon the global consciousness was the second, which took place in May 1992. Mass demonstrations in Bangkok forced the resignation of the prime minister, Suchinda Kraprayoon, the unelected former army chief, and his permanent retreat from public life. If it was Suchinda's good judgment in 1991 that brought Anand unexpectedly to the premiership, it was ironically his very poor judgment the following year, in 1992, that was to bring about an unpredicted, brief second term for Anand as prime minister.

A pivotal figure in the events of May 1992 was Arthit Ourairat, a somewhat unconventional personality in Thai politics who harked back to the heady idealism of the mid-1970s. Arthit quit the civil service commission in 1975 brimming with optimism, took a failed run at the Bangkok governorship, and acquired his first experience of party politics during Kukrit's tumultuous time as prime minister (1975–6). 'The politics of that period was very noble,' he recalls. 'I thought it was for the service of the country. I was very naïve.'

Arthit was elected to parliament in 1988 when Chatichai Choonhavan became prime minister. In late 1990, after one of Chatichai's regular reshuffles, Arthit became foreign minister for about three months. Although he oversaw some routine diplomacy with Malaysia, his feet barely touched the ground at Saranrom Palace. He was not long enough at the post to achieve anything of substance. The foreign ministry was a much-changed place compared to the decade Siddhi Savetsila had spent there as foreign minister to Prem and Chatichai. 'Siddhi had been the rock who we always went to, and then suddenly we started having "foreign minister of the month",' laments a retired US diplomat.

With little inside knowledge of the military's role in politics, and no background with the intelligence community, the neophyte Arthit was caught off-guard by the coup that unseated Chatichai. He never saw it coming.

After losing his ministerial post, Arthit spent the next year setting up a hospital with his father. He returned to politics in the Ekkaphap (Solidarity) Party led by Narong Wongwan, a wealthy businessman from the North with interests in tobacco and hotels. Narong, who had held cabinet positions in the 1980s under Prem and Chatichai, had been tainted by a logging scandal, and had few supporters in the press or the central business community. Ekkaphap was an amalgam of four small parties that merged into the larger Samakkitham (Justice Unity) Party during the course of 1991 with Narong emerging as its leader. A key political broker in this process was a former air-force officer and businessman, Thiti Nakorntab. He had strong links to Suchinda and the National Peacekeeping Council (NPKC) but did not run for election.

Arthit never doubted that Samakkitham was essentially a vehicle for advancing the military's political ambitions, but such connections between political parties and other interest groups were not unusual. He was not himself part of the party's inner core. After the March election, he found himself placed further from the centre as speaker of the lower house and president of parliament. This was because another member of parliament from his province, Chachoengsao, east of Bangkok, wanted to be in the cabinet, and prime ministers generally found it politically prudent to ensure that all regions were represented among the ministerial portfolios. As a former minister, Arthit remained senior in party terms but somewhat detached due to the broader responsibilities he had assumed as parliament's leader. Initially, it seemed that he had little more power than to bring down the gavel when members of parliament got too rowdy.

After the election in March 1992, the natural choice for prime minister was Narong, who was the leader of Samakkitham, the largest party in terms of seats. However, his nomination derailed spectacularly. At his first press conference, Narong was challenged with an allegation that he had been blacklisted by the US in connection with a visa application. The US Drug Enforcement Agency (DEA) evidently had reason to believe his businesses in the North had links to narcotics. 'I was shocked,' Arthit recalls as Narong floundered in front of the reporters. 'Narong did not understand the meaning of the question. After that, he was desperate.'

Narong's questioner was Tan Lian Choo, a correspondent with *The Straits Times* of Singapore, who had recently been elected president of the Foreign Correspondents' Club of Thailand (FCCT). Her tip-off had come from the US embassy. 'It wasn't much of a leak – it was pretty much an open secret,' says a retired US diplomat from the period. Indeed, the rumours of connections to the drug trade dated from the Prem years, and it soon emerged that the Australians would also have rejected any visa application by Narong.

The press conference collapsed in uproar. Tan was denounced by Samak Sundaravej, who had been looking forward to a cabinet position in a Samakkitham-led government. There was an appeal to the US embassy for clarification, but the new ambassador, David Lamberston, said he was powerless to assist. Demonstrations were staged outside the embassy's gates in central Bangkok. 'For visa applications, you are guilty until proven innocent,' explains the former diplomat. 'It's pretty much the opposite of everything else in American society. We don't need proof. All we have is intelligence, and we're not going to put that out there.'

Thanat Khoman, Anand's great mentor in foreign relations, emerged from the wings to denounce the US for meddling once more in Thai affairs, as he saw it.

'Nobody seriously thought Narong Wongwan could ever become prime minister,' says Abhisit Vejjajiva, a newly elected Democrat member of parliament at the time. 'It was made to look like an accident. The party was put together to support not Narong but Suchinda.' There was speculation that Narong had been deliberately set up to get him out of the way, but the conspiracy theorists came up with no evidence. Indeed, the discrediting of Narong had the hallmarks more of farce than of intrigue.

Arthit did not personally believe Narong was involved with illicit drugs, but his party's leader had apparently been condemned by association. There was good reason to believe that a brother of a Samakkitham member of parliament was indeed involved in narcotics, and this individual had visited Narong's house. The encounter had been detected by the DEA, which had an active presence in Thailand, and that was enough to put Narong on the American blacklist. No matter how vehemently Narong denied the accusation, his prospects for the premiership were sunk.

Who could replace him? Crucially, because Narong's nomination had not been put forward for royal assent, the National Peacekeeping Council still retained control of the nomination process. There was talk of Montri Pongpanich, the former communications minister and leader of Kukrit's Social Action Party. But Montri was one of nine cabinet ministers who had been singled out just the previous year after the NPKC's coup as 'unusually rich', and was intensely disliked by the military. Indeed, there were rumours that Montri was taken to a safe house by the military, where he was told not to even think of taking a run at the premiership. Some of the generals were meanwhile asking themselves why they needed to consider civilian alternatives at all. Samakkitham was now up and running as a parliamentary vehicle for military political ambitions. With Narong out of the picture, pressure was building within the junta, which never disguised its political ambitions well, to go for the premiership. During the drafting of the constitution in 1991, which was completed under military tutelage, some had feared an attempt to have the army chief serve concurrently as prime minister.

Before the storm

Following the general election in March 1992, but before the new prime minister was confirmed by royal proclamation, Anand's outgoing cabinet continued to function in a caretaker mode. The NPKC retained the power to nominate the next prime minister despite all the wrangling in the run-up to the December 1991 constitution. And, controversially, the position of prime minister still did not have to be filled by an elected politician. Whenever reporters asked questions about Suchinda's own political ambitions, he always parried them, declaring adamantly that he would not become prime minister. According to Arthit, Suchinda had promised, 'I maintain that I will not enter politics, not run for office, and will absolutely not be prime minister. There will be no politics.'

Suchinda's brother in law, General Issarapong Noonpakdee, and the air force chief, Air Chief Marshal Kaset Rojananil, had coveted political power quite openly, but evidently never enough to try and oust Anand. The US embassy always viewed Kaset as the junta's political ringleader. Sunthorn, meanwhile, always believed unity within the junta was paramount, and Issarapong always deferred to Suchinda.

Anand had therefore been confident in the second half of his government that no member of the NPKC would move against him. 'They knew Suchinda would not tolerate it,' he says. 'I could always explain my position to Suchinda. Once he understood, he would do the right thing. I was not concerned whether I stayed or not – that was always my basic position.'

When the NPKC met to discuss what should be done, with Narong discredited and gone, the decision was taken to nominate Suchinda to fill the vacuum. He was under pressure to prevent a fracture opening up. There was speculation in some quarters of tension within the junta relating to Kaset's political ambitions and willingness to step up if Suchinda refused – but Kaset would still have needed to be nominated.[6] Some have suggested that Suchinda was invited by the political parties to take the job for lack of a better choice. This did not happen. Indeed, their lack of the slightest loyalty towards Suchinda would become apparent soon enough.

Sunthorn was still the NPKC's chairman, and had technically been head of government throughout Anand's first term as prime minister. Sunthorn's relationship with Anand had been courteous on the surface but thorny beneath. Privately, Sunthorn was unhappy with the idea of Suchinda becoming premier. His preference was for his Class 1 contemporary, General Chavalit Yongchaiyudh, the former army chief who had fallen out of Chatichai's fractious cabinet. Chavalit had dusted himself off and returned to the political fray. He was now an elected member of parliament at the head of the New Aspiration Party, the second largest opposition party in terms of seats (but largest in terms of votes), with links to 'democratic' members of the military. Although he had machinated against Chatichai, Chavalit had at least sought power through the ballot box and not by military *fiat*.

Despite his personal reservations about Suchinda stepping up to the premiership, Sunthorn knew he could not expect any support for Chavalit from the other members of the junta. Unwilling to cause a split on the issue, he agreed to sign off on Suchinda's nomination. In the end, Sunthorn abided by his personal motto: 'Never kill your brothers or sell your friends.'[7] Like French musketeers, the NPKC generals would finish their days 'one for all and all for one'. However, Sunthorn returned from the junta's fateful meeting in a dark mood, smoking furiously in the back of his car. 'The country will go up in flames in ten days,' he told his aide.

'I must go against my words that I would never accept the premiership,' Suchinda explained. 'This is because as soldiers we have been drilled to make sacrifices – even our lives – for the nation. Therefore, when the need arises, we must work for the nation.'

Suchinda could argue that Prem Tinsulanond had been generally accepted as prime minister without being elected. Chatichai had been elected but was tarnished. Anand had been widely praised without being elected. 'I think Suchinda felt this was not out of the ordinary and could be done,' says Abhisit. 'From his point of view, Suchinda was going back on his word for good reasons.'

Suchinda's premiership

The royal proclamation appointing Suchinda as Thailand's 19th prime minister since 1932 was signed by King Bhumibol on 7 April 1992 at 5:25pm. The signature took place at an audience granted to Sunthorn and Issarapong from the NPKC, and to Arthit as president of the National Legislative Assembly. The presence of one civilian politician and two generals represented a strange confluence of democratic and undemocratic processes. In a Thai context, this somehow did not seem quite as contradictory as it might to an outsider. The archive of the king's principal private secretary records the audience without mentioning the name of the new prime minister. There is no official photographic record of the occasion.

Twenty years later, Arthit described the audience to a class of political science students. He remembered King Bhumibol ordering all the photographers and TV crews to leave, and then asking questions. As a constitutional monarch, the king could ask for clarification, or perhaps slow matters down, but he could not halt a process that was in accordance with the constitution: he reigned but he did not rule. Many regarded Suchinda's appointment as both unwise and fundamentally wrong, but it did not breach the letter of the constitution. However, the king wanted to know if Suchinda was proposing to be prime minister and remain a serving general. 'Has he resigned as army commander in chief?' the king asked pointedly, according to Arthit.

King Bhumibol was told that under the constitution a prime minister who was not a member of parliament could be approved by a parliamentary majority. Arthit also explained that a clause in the new constitution would disband the NPKC once the new government was formed. Suchinda could therefore have the junta or the premiership, but not both. King Bhumibol knew all this, but saw fit to remind everybody. His final suggestion was that Suchinda make a TV broadcast to explain all these matters to the public – with General Issarapong and Arthit providing clarifications. Arthit remembered the king then telling those present that the public wanted the prime minister to be an elected member of parliament. 'If a party's leader cannot be prime minister, doesn't that party have a deputy leader?' the king asked.

Suchinda had indeed been replaced as army chief on 7 April, the day of the audience, by Issarapong. The next day, he took an emotional leave of his brother officers. 'He farewelled a gathering of 500 military officers and, with tears streaming down his face, said he had to swallow his pride and go back on his word "for the sake of the country",' according to one account.[8]

When Suchinda revealed his 50-portfolio cabinet on 17 April, it was the largest in Thai history – before or since.[9] It included many of the politicians the NPKC's coup the previous year was supposed to have removed from public office. His five deputy prime ministers were Meechai Ruchupan, Montri Pongpanich, Narong Wongwan, Samak Sundaravej, and Somboon Rahong. Anand's comment when he saw the ministerial line-up was 'Aiyah!'

Usually, new cabinets are presented to the king for swearing in with minimum delay, but on this occasion Suchinda requested that the audience take place after a visit from UN Secretary General Boutros Boutros-Ghali, who was passing through Bangkok on his way to Cambodia. Suchinda felt Anand had a much better understanding of the UN and its workings, and requested he remain in place as caretaker prime minister to handle the visit. The last duty Anand performed in this capacity was therefore to accompany the world's top diplomat to an audience with King Bhumibol at 4:45pm on 21 April.

Boutros-Ghali was taking a close interest in the United Nations Transitional Authority in Cambodia, whose creation the Anand government had done its bit to facilitate. The secretary general would come to regard the breakthrough in Cambodia as one of the few successes in his difficult single-term tenure at the UN. On this occasion, he could only visit Thailand on one particular day. That afternoon, while Sunthorn, Suchinda, and the new cabinet were arriving elsewhere in the palace, Anand went through the normal introduction formalities in the second-floor drawing room King Bhumibol preferred for more intimate audiences. As they all sat down, the king commented to his Egyptian guest, 'When Khun Anand formally introduced you to me, he did not follow the convention of identifying himself as the prime minister – he is leaving this afternoon.'

The audience with Boutros-Ghali lasted less than an hour, and the secretary general left with Anand – no doubt still largely unaware of the political drama unfolding in the palace. The next order of business scheduled by the principal private secretary, *ML* Thawisan Ladawan, was at 5:45pm when Sunthorn arrived to notify King Bhumibol of the dissolution of the NPKC. Exactly 20 minutes later, Suchinda and his cabinet were received for the swearing-in ceremony.

Sunthorn had kept his personal misgivings about Suchinda's appointment to himself, and had no reason to confide in Arthit at any stage. He was stepping down as supreme commander to be replaced by Kaset. With the NPKC disbanded, Sunthorn flew off to Paris where his mistress owned a Thai restaurant. His long military career was over, and he would observe whatever transpired from a distance.

Suchinda's decision to take the premiership was a disaster from the outset, a misjudgement of epic proportions. For whatever reason, he had broken his word and become involved in a naked power grab. Some suggest that he wanted to save the country from bad politicians, but that had been one of the justifications for his coup the year before. That excuse was by now thin and tired. Military self-interest seemed a much more likely motive to most.

'Suchinda promised in public that he would not become prime minister,' recalls Karuna Buakamsri, a student at Chulalongkorn University at the time and vice secretary general of the Student Federation of Thailand. 'The day he was nominated, we picked up on the lie.'

The outrage was remarkable, even when people generally expect their politicians to lie about everything – as they do in most countries. In the hothouse of Bangkok gossip, rumours began to swirl to the effect that Suchinda had been asked to take the position by the king or the queen. However, the grilling to which King Bhumibol had subjected Arthit, Sunthorn, and Issarapong during their audience suggests a different story, and a degree of exasperation with what was transpiring.

Anand gave the rumours no credence, but remained curious. Some months later, he encountered Suchinda at a social event and asked him outright what had happened. Suchinda answered: 'How could I ever allow somebody like Montri Pongpanich to become prime minister?' He did not try to excuse himself by claiming he had been asked to take the position, and made no mention of the king or queen. 'Having heard that, I let it rest,' says Anand. Looking back, Anand recalls being less dismayed by Suchinda's appointment than by his policy statement to parliament when he talked about self-sacrifice. 'That was unfortunate,' says Anand. 'He claimed he had to do it for the nation.'

Anand's first period as prime minister had technically come to an end with the general election on 22 March, and he handed over to Suchinda in April. After leaving, Anand dropped completely from sight. He was hoping to take a holiday abroad with Sodsee before rejoining Saha Union. He was also due to take over as chairman of the Thailand Development Research Institute, replacing Snoh Unakul.

A clinical severance after his unexpected 14-month period in politics might have been Anand's intention, but public perceptions had changed. The Thailand Anand handed back was not the one he had started with. His persona had not been erased from the public mind.

Trouble on the streets

Parliament was besieged by protesters in the weeks after Suchinda began his premiership. Some went on hunger strike, including Chalard Worachat, an activist and former parliamentarian. Another hunger striker, Palang Tham leader Chamlong Srimuang was back on the streets and a warpath. The ascetic Chamlong had been secretary to Prime Minister Prem Tinsulanond, and later a popular and effective governor of Bangkok; he had a large and loyal political following. The historic rivalry between Suchinda's Class 5 and Chamlong's Class 7 was boiling up once more. This was a battle between two generals.

The rallies around parliament and mass rallies at Sanam Luang were nevertheless peaceful and good-natured. A stage was erected at Sanam Luang. There were speeches and entertainment, and people and families flocked in their tens of thousands to participate, particularly at weekends. At one point, the army sent in a spotter plane to drop pamphlets urging the crowds outside parliament to disperse, but these all landed in Dusit Zoo next door. The zoo was in lock-down, not to keep the animals in but to keep humans out.

Phaisith Phipatanakul, who had been appointed secretary general of parliament under Chatichai (and would spend eight years in the position), remembers crowds climbing into the parliamentary compound and damaging the fence after Suchinda delivered his policy speech on 6 May. The debate that was under way was exceptionally lively, with opposition leaders all dressed in black and in raucous full voice. 'As for sacrifices for the nation, can the prime minister please not make his actions contradict his words too often,' Chavalit Yongchaiyudh needled. 'Please resign as prime minister today,' Prachuab Chaiyasan demanded. Chuan Leekpai bemoaned a lack of substance, particularly with regard to farmers and land reform. Others griped that it was sham democracy – a continuation of the junta in civilian attire.

At 5:45pm, Ukrit Mongkolnavin, the president of the senate, caught everybody by surprise by closing the debate while it was still in full flight. The crowd outside had swelled dramatically from some 10,000 earlier, and was by then too large to count. Suchinda, his ministers, senators, and government members of parliament conferred, and all left hurriedly by the Rajavithi Road exit, which was still clear of the mob. Leaving 800 prepared dinners uneaten, the opposition went triumphantly out the front door to greet their supporters. 'People were shouting, "Where is Suchinda?"' Phaisith recalls.

It was all downhill from there for Suchinda. He lacked any kind of secure base among the coalition parties, and his unmanageably large cabinet was soon in disarray. Ministers openly sniped at the beleaguered new premier when not bickering over their pickings.

There was no end in sight to the demonstrations. The foreign media came and went from the protests, and grew weary. When the military leaned down on the local press and attempted censorship, the *Bangkok Post* took a leaf out of founding editor Alexander MacDonald's book by printing blank pages rather than running stories that had been self-censored. This proved embarrassing when the *Bangkok Post*'s rival, *The Nation*, carried on defiantly printing uncensored articles. Battery acid was poured on the car of *The Nation*'s editor, Suthichai Yoon, after he returned home from speaking at the FCCT one night. 'The military got angry because I went on the radio,' Suthichai recalls.

Others were also threatened behind the scenes. Following intimidation, technicians at Nippon Production Services, a local company set up with Japanese backing to supply satellite services and crews based at TV Channel 9, refused to provide satellite uplinks for some foreign television crews. This prompted a formal complaint from the FCCT's professional committee.[10]

The FCCT letter was conveyed directly to cabinet by the foreign ministry's director general of information, Sakthip Krairiksh. Suchinda personally directed that the foreign news transmissions should not be hindered. It was an instruction that seemed more in keeping with the pragmatic individual who had interacted with Anand the previous year, but it would soon help make Suchinda known around the world.

Arsa Sarasin, Anand's former foreign minister, knew better than most how important a stabilising factor Suchinda had been for the Anand government. His recollections of Suchinda at that earlier time was of a thoughtful and constructive man; however, when Arsa encountered Suchinda on 20 May, he seemed changed and distracted. Indeed, others had noticed that Suchinda appeared muddled and groggy during this period. With the city in uproar, Arsa asked Suchinda if he meant to carry on. 'He was taken aback,' says Arsa. 'It seemed to me he was not aware of what was going on outside.'

In Thai street politics it has often been the case that the build-up to a crisis takes weeks, even months, before a point is reached when events suddenly move forward fast and dangerously. In 1992, the violent eruption came on Sunday 17 May, some six weeks into Suchinda's premiership. The Royal hotel, overlooking Sanam Luang, served as the centre of operations for Chamlong and his supporters. Not far off stood a raised stage with a powerful sound system. 'If you controlled the stage, you controlled the crowd,' recalls Karuna Buakamsri, a student activist. She was one of the people responsible for scheduling events, but not involved with security issues. The controlling committee included Chamlong, Prateep Unsongtham Hata, and Parinya Thewanarumitkul, a student leader and future vice rector of Thammasat.

The involvement of others was more opaque. Squadron Leader Prasong Soonsiri, who was in contact with Chamlong, had quit as secretary general of Chavalit's New Aspiration Party just before the March general election, and later joined Chamlong's Palang Tham Party. Prasong was seen at the hotel that afternoon. Chavalit was thought to be stirring developments in the background, but nobody was quite sure how. Chamlong himself had not been at the Royal hotel on that Sunday afternoon, but Karuna remembers that there was some talk among the organisers that the crowd should be moved if the protest's momentum was not to be lost. The concern was that the demonstrations were reaching a peak with no obvious conclusion – the whole process might falter and fizzle out.

It was after 7pm, and darkness had fallen. Ad Carabao, one of Thailand's most popular musicians, had finished his performance. Jatuporn Prompan, a politician who was to acquire a much higher profile in the years to come, was talking to Karuna on stage. She remembers Prasarn Marukpitak, who was not supposed to be there, suddenly appearing on stage and taking over.

'He took the microphone and shouted, "We are moving now".' There was great confusion. Karuna and Jatuporn tried to intervene, but it was too late. The instructions had come from the stage, after all, and seemed to onlookers therefore in some way 'official'. The huge crowd began to move off along both sides of Ratchadamnoen Avenue towards Democracy Monument, a development that must have been sanctioned by Chamlong – but without reference to most of the other organisers. 'Even up until now, I cannot forgive Chamlong for that,' says

Karuna. She had no choice but to tag along with the huge crowd. 'We stopped at Democracy Monument and used the Sorn Daeng restaurant as a centre,' she recalls.

Democracy Monument was the first landmark along a route that ultimately led to the Chitralada Villa of Dusit Palace, the main residence of King Bhumibol. The huge crowd was made up of people of all ages and from all walks of life. These were not the radicalised, leftist protesters of the 1970s: they included older, educated, middle-class people with good jobs and prospects. They came from safe, comfortable homes. Some were equipped with early mobile phones, including cumbersome grey Motorolas with long, rubberised antennas. This was no disorganised mob running amok.

Beyond Democracy Monument was Paan Faa bridge, 'Heaven's Gate', a choke-point on the route into Dusit, the administrative heart of the city. Terrified and ill-equipped police more used to battling traffic had pulled coiled razor-wire across the road. Fire engines with water cannons were parked behind. There was a clash and people were hosed, but the police somehow held the line. Concrete pots were smashed and rocks thrown, but the mood in the main body of the crowd behind was not violent. Most simply sat down on the ground on the approach to the bridge, beneath the Mahakan fort, and waited. The Golden Mount temple twinkled high above them in the tropical darkness.

In Thanon Paribatra, a narrower street nearby, a deadlier running battle had already erupted as provocateurs confronted the police on a smaller bridge over the canal. More organised but shadowy elements with radios and signs of military training were occasionally spotted in the background. The shop-houses along the approach to the bridge were secured by steel shutters, turning it into a deadly alley. There was no way of escaping through the shops; retreat was the only option. Guns were fired and Molotov cocktails lobbed. The police charged, brutally pummelling with truncheons anybody who got in their way, foreign journalists included. US journalist Nate Thayer – who six years later would interview Pol Pot along the Cambodia–Thailand border – was left dazed and bruised, and without his expensive mobile phone. As the night went on, the situation on the fringes of the main demonstration turned uglier. Karuna and Jatuporn ended up on the frontline, in a truck with a public-address system mounted on the back. During a lull, Karuna fell asleep, only to wake up because someone was shooting at the loudspeaker. Eventually, she ran off.

As ordinary demonstrators along the main route fell away and went home, a smaller hard core remained. Paan Faa was overrun, and a nearby police station torched. Police vehicles also started going up in flames. Some believed the police – keen to discredit protesters and secure replacement equipment – were involved in the arson. At about 11pm, the news filtered through that martial law had been declared. The military would now be keeping the peace.

By Monday morning, troops had secured Paan Faa. They spent the day attempting to disperse thousands of demonstrators along Ratchadamnoen Avenue. There, Chamlong was arrested in the late afternoon as he was about to be interviewed by a US journalist, Paul Handley. The moment was captured on the front page of *Thai Rath*, the country's largest-circulation newspaper. On the other side of Sanam Luang, marines held Pinklao bridge, trying to prevent people crossing the Chao Phraya from the Thonburi side to join the demonstrations. On the Bangkok side, thunderous barrages of gunfire, mostly blanks, filled the air at regular intervals through the day, but to no effect. The crowds did not disperse. Some live rounds were fired, one of which claimed the life of the translator for the supreme patriarch, a New Zealander. Ten days later, a noodle vendor who had developed a splitting headache was found to have a spent round lodged on her brain. It had come to earth and penetrated her skull, miraculously doing no further damage.

Anand stayed in Bangkok, watching Suchinda's government fall apart without knowing where the crisis was heading. Nobody knew. The kind of chaos he had feared after the coup the previous year had become a reality. 'The second time was a terrible surprise,' he recalls. 'From Sunday onwards [17 May], my telephone kept ringing.' He heard accounts from all sides, including from doctors and nurses who were dealing with the wounded. 'The message was quite clear: the army was being high-handed.' Some callers urged Anand to contact the king, but he was concerned not to overestimate his influence: 'I was no longer the prime minister, and it was not easy for me to walk up to the palace and ask for an audience.'

The bloodiest night was that of Monday 18 May. A huge crowd had spread along Ratchadamnoen from Sanam Luang to Democracy Monument, where troops were holding their ground. Buses and lorries had been hijacked and were being driven at the army lines. When barrages of military gunfire went up into the air, the demonstrators dropped close to the ground and waited. After the firing stopped, they popped up with huge cheers and drummed empty water bottles defiantly on the tarmac. However, some bullets were finding their marks. Snipers also wounded at least three foreigners, including a Frenchman whose location had been revealed by the flash of his camera.

Wounded demonstrators were brought into the lobby of the Royal hotel and treated by medics, then if possible evacuated to hospital. At least five were already dead, or died in the hotel, and another five were not expected to reach hospital alive. As the night wore on, smoke drifted in and set off the hotel's fire alarms. The situation deteriorated on the streets and the crowd thinned. Many took refuge in the hotel rather than risk crossing open spaces. A couple of dozen foreign journalists realised they had no way out, and hunkered down for the night. When serious firing erupted outside, the hotel rooms were darkened, and people dropped down and hugged the concrete floors.

Around midnight, firebugs went methodically to work on nearby government buildings. The tax department, lottery building, and public relations department were all torched and by morning were gutted hulks. In the small hours, there was intermittent heavy-calibre machine-gun fire.

Around 6am, just before dawn, whistles blew and the Royal hotel was stormed by seasoned infantrymen. They used rifle butts and boots to quell any lingering resistance, although no shots were fired inside the building. Everybody was arrested and herded out of the hotel, men stripped to the waist and hands tied with their own shirts. Journalists were rounded up, although not arrested. Outside, hundreds of protesters, so defiant the night before, were squatting under guard with their hands tied behind them. Ratchadamnoen was lined with burned buildings and smouldering cars. So many vehicle windows had been smashed that the surface of the street crunched underfoot. A packed layer of hard, sharp glass looked like snow spattered here and there with bloodstains.

The unrest was contained more successfully during the course of Tuesday, but come nightfall there was a resurgence that spread across the city into the suburbs, including Hua Mark and Ramkhamhaeng. There was shooting along Sathorn Road in central Bangkok, where bodies were left floating in the canal. There were even shots outside the Dusit Thani hotel. Events were moving beyond straight political violence. Scores were being settled; and as often happens under cover of civil unrest, unwanted squatters were being burned out of their homes. The city was descending in an ever-deeper spiral of anarchy and chaos. There were rumours of death squads and assassination lists.

On Wednesday morning, tyres were burned outside the Royal hotel, sending black plumes into the sky. There were false reports that the hotel had been set ablaze. Increasingly, the continuing silence from the palace became a focus of speculation. Foreign news organisations were calling correspondents in Bangkok and asking if King Bhumibol would say anything. Was he being held incommunicado? Was he aware of how serious the situation had become? There was no answer – only a sense that if the crisis were to run any deeper, any royal intervention might be too late. Both Crown Prince Maha Vajiralongkorn and his second sister, Princess Maha Chakri Sirindhorn, were outside the country, but made public appeals for reconciliation and an end to the violence.

After hearing accounts from all quarters, Anand was horrified by the bloodshed. 'It was just a mess,' he says. The violence was deepening, and on the Wednesday afternoon he heard of troop deployments in the Ramkhamhaeng area of the city, a northeastern suburb with a massive open university that had become increasingly restive. At 6pm, Anand finally put in a call to the office of Thawisan, King Bhumibol's principal private secretary. He was not requesting an audience; he simply wanted to ascertain if the palace was aware of how serious the situation had become.

'The king is well aware of developments,' he was told. 'Just watch the television later tonight.'

Crisis defused

Unbeknownst to Anand, King Bhumibol would soon be sitting on a sofa in the Chitralada Villa of Dusit Palace, delivering a stern rebuke to two retired generals – Chamlong Srimuang, leader of the opposition on the streets, and Suchinda Kraprayoon, the prime minister. Their long-standing political feud threatened to destroy the country, he admonished. Also present were two former premiers: Sanya Dhammasakdi, president of the Privy Council, and his deputy, Prem Tinsulanond.

The scene was filmed by a palace crew with the rickety equipment they had at hand. King Bhumibol's words were barely audible on the tape, but the image of rebuke was stunning: enough was enough – the country was more important than power grabs and personal political vendettas. The confrontation 'would only lead to the utter destruction of Thailand,' the king said. A line had finally been drawn in the sand, and the situation defused – at least for the time being.

The dramatic images from the palace were not released for transmission until about 9pm; when they went out, they immediately riveted world attention. The scenes days earlier from the Royal hotel, in particular, were appalling. In three nights of violence, over 50 people had been killed, hundreds had been injured, and the whereabouts of thousands were unknown. More than 40 journalists had been hurt, some seriously – it was a near-miracle none were dead.

This was the second time in King Bhumibol's reign that he had stepped in after serious civilian bloodshed caused by the military. The previous occasion was in October 1973, when the king appointed the president of the Privy Council, Sanya, to be prime minister. In a rare interview in 1979, the king gave a personal perspective of his statecraft at such times:

> We keep in the middle, neutral, and in peaceful co-existence with everybody. That is the way of doing it. We are in the middle. We could be crushed by both sides, but we are impartial. One day it would be very handy to have somebody impartial, because you have in a country only groups or political parties which still have their own interest at heart, what about those who don't have the power, who don't … who are just ordinary people who cannot make their view known?[11]

That night, King Bhumibol reminded Chamlong and Suchinda of his birthday speech when he had said the constitution could always be amended. 'I think if possible we should consider the alternative suggested in my address of the 4th December to solve the original problem with a view to solving the present problem,' he said. Suchinda, the king noted, had already agreed to constitutional revisions, and some interpreted this as an implicit scolding of Chamlong for bringing people on to the streets. At this juncture, however, the king's manifest purpose was to bring peace and not to assign blame. Whatever his personal thoughts, which have never been revealed, he was sitting on the sofa not as a judge but as a peacemaker. The issue he was confronting at that juncture was not which of the two sitting on the carpet was the most culpable, but who might still be the most volatile.

Another broadcast followed that evening, which, given the recent violence, was almost surreal. Chamlong and Suchinda appeared seated side-by-side at a desk, flanked by national flags. Suchinda announced that Chamlong and other protesters were to be released and amnestied, and parliament would consider constitutional amendments the following Monday. Chamlong then asked people not to 'support or cooperate with those who are causing chaos in the nation'. This was interpreted to mean both demonstrators and security forces.[12]

After King Bhumibol's intervention that night, and the broadcast by Suchinda and Chamlong, peace returned. On Thursday morning, everything was quiet. Troops fanned out across Sanam Luang, picking up spent shell casings before boarding trucks and returning to their barracks. The violence had abated completely.

However, the calm was more superficial than it appeared to an outside world suddenly rather impressed by royal interventions. Silver bullets are rare, and there remained a question nobody would ask publicly: if for any reason violence were to kick off again, would King Bhumibol be able to make a second successful intervention? 'If you use the word intervention, you put it in inverted commas,' says Anand. He dislikes the notion of the king guiding politics, and prefers the word 'facilitation' when discussing these exercises in statecraft.

Whatever the correct term might be, failure was a dangerous possibility. 'There were a lot of complaints about the king acting too slowly – as if he could have prevented any of this,' says Anand. 'From the point of view of the king, it was timing. If he came down too early, he ran the risk of not being successful, and that would be the end of the king's reserve power. The timing was very important.'

Parliamentary moves

As president of parliament and speaker of the house, Arthit had all along wanted to find a way to bring the issues stirring the demonstrations off the streets and into parliament for proper, orderly debate. Everybody had seen King Bhumibol's intervention on 23 May halt the violence, but the unasked question was for how long it could last. The king had defused the crisis and created a crucial breathing space. However, the underlying political problems remained. These centred on installing a representative prime minister and other constitutional issues that were the responsibility of parliament. In a more mature democratic framework, these would have been issues for an elected chamber to resolve through debate.

Parliamentary efforts had nevertheless been attempted. On 9 May, over a month into Suchinda's premiership amid considerable political wrangling, Arthit had tabled two constitutional amendments that passed their first reading and were widely accepted, including by Chamlong: these laid down that future prime ministers be chosen from elected members of the house, and that the speaker of the house should also be president of parliament – and not appointed from the unelected, military-appointed senate, with only 116 civilians among its 270 members.

Such amendments required three readings, and the third was not due to take place until 10 June. On that day, parliament would pass the amendments and forward them to the king for the royal assent, a constitutional formality. On the night of the day when the king signed, whichever day it might be, the new laws would be posted in the *Royal Gazette* – the mechanism by which all new legislation is promulgated. Even then, the amendments would not actually have come into effect for another three months.

Although he could not confide in anyone, these dates would preoccupy Arthit for the most turbulent weeks of his life. As it turned out, General Suchinda did not resign until the Sunday, five days after his televised dressing down by the king with Chamlong. 'In a four-and-a-half-minute resignation speech that ended his 48-day tenure as Prime Minister, General Suchinda said that he was "deeply sorry about the unrest and violence between government officers and the people, which led to many lost lives and physical damage",' *The New York Times* reported. 'His face drawn with fatigue but otherwise without emotion, General Suchinda said he had submitted his resignation to King Bhumibol Adjulyadej as a demonstration of his "political responsibility" for last week's violence.'[13]

Suchinda's departure was not unconditional. Hours before, King Bhumibol had signed an amnesty decree that on paper provided the military and everyone involved in the violence with an avenue of escape from retribution. After the broadcast, Suchinda and his aides vanished from sight. There had been rumours that he might flee to Sweden or Taiwan, and that another coup was in the works. Chamlong meanwhile disappeared to a remote forest retreat in Kanchanaburi where he usually mentored followers and kept buffaloes and other cattle saved from the slaughterhouse. The fiery leader of the street protests now refused to speak about politics as he sat in a bamboo armchair, meditating beside a cool stream.

Opposition politicians dressed in black threatened to revoke the amnesty, although that never actually happened. 'In the future the military will try to come back, so be careful,' predicted Chalard, the political activist on hunger strike outside parliament, when he heard of Suchinda's resignation. Observers noted Chalard to be 'in a surprisingly strong voice'.[14]

Parliament's attention turned to constitutional amendments and finding a successor to Suchinda. The assumption was that the successor would emerge from the ruling coalition parties, and be Air Chief Marshal Somboon Rahong, a deputy prime minister. In a good example of the complexity of Thai political deals, Somboon was put up for the premiership as head of the third largest party, Chart Thai, the old vehicle of former Prime Minister Chatichai Choonhavan, who had been deposed in the coup staged by Somboon's boss, Air Chief Marshal Kaset Rojananil. Somboon had been one of Suchinda's five deputy prime ministers. While Chatichai remained influential behind the scenes, Chart Thai's key dealmaker was the diminutive Banharn Silpa-archa, nicknamed '1.5' by the Thai press (a reference to his height in metres), and 'Walking ATM' for other reasons. Banharn had been Suchinda's minister of transport and communications, Nukul Prachuabmoh's successor.

Arthit was deeply aware of how unwise it would be to challenge the amnesty or rely on a second royal intervention if things went wrong again. Deep down, after two spectacular failures in Narong and Suchinda, he believed there was a good chance of another serious political derailment if the parties persisted in trying to draw a prime minister from the same range of candidates.

A fresh election would have been infinitely preferable, but impossible in practice. The issue facing Arthit was that disbanding parliament – and providing a cooling-off period to give the electorate time to reconsider – was not an option. The powers of Suchinda's interim replacement, Acting Prime Minister Meechai Ruchupan, another of his five deputy prime ministers, were limited. Only an incumbent full prime minister could call an election and dissolve parliament. In effect, with Suchinda gone, parliament was an aircraft without a pilot that could not be landed safely. It would eventually crash.

Arthit viewed Somboon's proposed assumption of the premiership with dismay. While the appointment would not have been illegal – and was in some ways less controversial than Suchinda's appointment – Somboon was still a retired military figure, and from the air force wing of Class 5. Even though it appeared that Chamlong could be counted on at this point to respect the king's wishes and remain in the background, nobody could rule out further violence if another prime minister were to be nominated from the same clique.

'Deep down I knew it was a conflict between military people – innocent people had joined with Chamlong,' says Arthit. 'The information from all sides was that there would be bloodshed. The protests would boil up again and the military would do more killing.' With the NPKC disbanded, the 'burden and responsibility' of nominating a new prime minister for the king's assent now lay with Arthit alone as speaker of the house and president of parliament. He was in a very lonely place.

'I didn't know what to do,' Arthit confesses. Convinced that appointing Somboon prime minister would lead to more mayhem, he spent the next week working back channels to see if there was a safer alternative. Arthit's first approach was to Sanya, the president of the Privy Council, who had been at the audience when King Bhumibol carpeted Suchinda and Chamlong. Arthit asked Sanya to request on his behalf an audience with the king for some 'discreet guidance'. He knew royal audiences were always private and could go unrecorded.

Sanya said he was unsure of the protocol, but took Arthit's request to the king's personal private secretary, Thawisan. Within an hour, the answer came in the negative. There would be no audience with the king, and no guidance 'from above' as to what should be done next. The ball was back in Arthit's court.

With the palace gates shut, Arthit recalls feeling more isolated than ever. His next call was on Prem Tinsulanond, the former prime minister and heir apparent to Sanya as president of the Privy Council. Like Sunthorn, Prem thought Chavalit Yongchaiyudh was the best available candidate.

Chavalit had been key to Prem's peaceful – and very effective – counter-communist programme in the early 1980s, before becoming army chief. His other merits included the fact that he had retired early as army chief prior to entering politics, and his public condemnation of military coups in general. Chavalit was an elected member of parliament, and headed the New Aspiration Party, which had won the most votes in the March election. On paper, he was as democratic a soldier as anyone could wish for.

However, Arthit could immediately see that proposing Chavalit as prime minister raised problems. He was from Class 1 and unpopular with Class 5, which had never even considered him for the job given to Anand in 1991. As army chief, Chavalit had tied up a lot of budget and upset Class 5 with his handling of promotions. More relevant to the immediate moment, there was the simple fact that although Chavalit's party had won the most votes, it had ended up with fewer seats than Samakkitham, the military's proxy. Any alternative coalition would have had to include the second largest opposition party, the Democrats, led by Chuan Leekpai.

Arthit therefore knew there was no point approaching Chavalit without first seeking Chuan's perspective. When Arthit asked Chuan if he thought a minority government could be formed, Chuan was brutal in his response: 'It would not survive even one day.' That knocked out the Chavalit option. An approach to the third opposition party, Chamlong's Palang Tham, was pointless – the king had just asked Chamlong and Suchinda to step back from politics in the national interest.

So now, Arthit knew he had a major crisis on his hands. He played for time and told everybody to be patient until the third reading of the constitutional amendments that would ensure that future prime ministers had to be elected, and that the speaker of the house automatically became president of parliament – and also had to be elected.

According to Arthit, there were efforts at this time to bribe him with political inducements. He was told that if he went along with the nomination of Somboon, he would be allowed to resign his parliamentary positions and become interior minister, one of the most powerful portfolios. Arthit said nothing in response. He was promptly smeared. It was alleged that he had asked for 200 million baht to ensure Somboon's name reached the king.

Arthit was not swayed. He had much more to worry about than offers of money and position, neither of which would take him anywhere worthwhile or for very long. He was certain that any Somboon-led cabinet had a minimal life-expectancy. The fear that gripped him most was being complicit in another round of bloodshed. The only way forward that he could see was another general election that would produce both an elected prime minister and an elected president of parliament from the lower house. Other things might start to fall into place after that.

But how was this going to happen? It was a Catch-22 situation. Arthit needed a prime minister who didn't want to be prime minister.

Threading the needle

The perfect candidate would be someone with real experience in the job who could be relied upon to return power to the people by taking the country swiftly to another election.

There was only one person with these qualifications. Early in June, Arthit made his first telephone call to Anand. As it happened, Anand had taught Arthit

English at Chulalongkorn in 1956, but they barely knew each other. Anand was stunned by Arthit's request, and responded firmly: 'I don't want the position any more – please appoint someone else.'

'I am not asking you to take the position,' Arthit protested. 'I am requesting that you come back to dissolve parliament.'

Arthit had not been granted an audience with King Bhumibol; Prem's recommendation of Chavalit was unworkable; and now Anand had rebuffed him. And yet his life was about to become even more interesting.

Arthit remained a member of Samakkitham. Its beleaguered leader, Narong, thought it would be a good idea for his battered parliamentarians to retreat to the provinces, to enable them to regroup and reflect. Narong told Arthit that the rest would do him good. Considering what Narong had just been through courtesy of the US DEA, the choice of venue for the party retreat was provocative: Narong's Delta Golden Triangle Resort, a luxury hotel overlooking the Mekong at the Golden Triangle where Thailand, Burma, and Laos meet. This has long been an area infamous for its association with the opium trade and narcotics.

Although he does not actually use the word 'kidnapped', Arthit found himself being held virtually incommunicado in a luxurious suite there during this edgy period. His fellow Samakkitham parliamentarians passed the time gambling. They were evidently mistrustful and keen to know of his whereabouts at all times. 'All the MPs were playing cards in front of my room so I could not contact anyone,' he says. The group also included some key coalition dealmakers, Sompong Amornvivat and Pairoj Piempongsant, who always stayed close to Arthit. The party finally flew back to Bangkok via Chiang Mai, where there was an overnight delay. It was all very stressful for Arthit, but there was a major upside to his absence from the capital: he was spared having to explain himself to the press.

Before he left the Delta Golden Triangle Resort, Arthit did manage to place a phone call. It was to Anand. This time Anand was less abrupt although just as non-committal. 'I said nothing,' says Anand. According to Arthit, '[Anand] said to find somebody else, but I said there wasn't anybody else to form a government. It went on and on.'

By now, history was repeating itself. Once again, somebody was whispering in Anand's ear the unbelievable possibility of becoming prime minister – a position he had genuinely never sought. The first time it had been his nephew, MR Charnvudhi Varavarn, calling to test his mood just before Suchinda made his actual invitation. This time it was Arthit.

Anand did not know what was about to transpire, but he did sense that Arthit was desperate. Although he confided in nobody, Anand now had to ponder the unthinkable: the possibility of being appointed prime minister again. What Arthit did not know was that with all the rumours swirling and strange approaches to him, Anand had requested an audience with King Bhumibol to obtain some clarification. As with Arthit's request, this was refused. Although Anand saw the king at some ceremonies during this period, there were no audiences or conversations between the two from the end of his first premiership to the start of his second one.

Arthit returned to Bangkok, and on the morning of 10 June, the constitutional amendments passed their third readings smoothly. If things continued to run to plan, the amendments would be sent to King Bhumibol for the royal assent, become law from about midnight the same day after being posted in the *Royal Gazette*, and take effect in early September – absence of coups permitting.

The provenance of the prime minister designate was technically not an especially pressing issue this time, since Somboon had been elected to parliament. Everybody continued to assume that his name would be taken to the king in the afternoon. Although Banharn was very much in evidence as secretary general of Chart Thai, Chatichai Choonhavan, its most senior member, had also given the nod from the wings in support of Somboon's nomination.

Somboon was thus the man of the hour. As the critical moment approached, he donned his official white tunic, and waited at his home in front of a picture of King Bhumibol, according to the usual protocol. The proclamation appointing him was expected to arrive from the palace in the early evening, and the local and foreign press and television crews were present in force. They were given refreshments and the chance to peruse Somboon's unfamiliar *curriculum vitae*.

That afternoon, Anand had gone home at 4pm and found a solitary reporter outside his gate. He wondered if some rumour might have leaked out, but did not stop to ask. When he got inside, he found Sodsee sitting in front of the television weeping. 'I asked her what she was crying about and she said she felt sorry for the king that there was another crisis.' Anand said nothing. He had earlier called his daughters from his Saha Union office and asked them to come to the house and wait for him. Daranee was already there when he got home, and they all carried on watching the television coverage of preparations for the ceremony at Somboon's home.

When Daranee arrived, she too saw the reporter at the gate, who showed no inclination to leave. 'The reporter said he had come to the house to cover the news that Khun Anand would be the new prime minister,' she recalls. 'We said, no, it's Khun Somboon who is going to be prime minister. It's on television now.' The reporter remained.

The day before, a businessman and lobbyist, Pairoj Piempongsant, who had never let Arthit out of his sight during the Golden Triangle retreat up north, watched the proclamation being typed up – it had Somboon Rahong's name on it. 'He came to the parliament nearly every day to see how we would propose the new prime minister,' recalls Phaisith Phipatanakul, the secretary general of parliament. Pairoj hoped to be Somboon's secretary general. On the afternoon of 10 June, he followed the unescorted official car transporting Arthit and Phaisith to the palace gates, then peeled off and went home. As the car entered the palace, all was in order: Arthit was sticking to the coalition's agreement – or so it seemed. The two men arrived at the palace at about 2pm, well ahead of the audience. King Bhumibol usually gave audiences late in the afternoon.

Phaisith was responsible for actually carrying the document inside a folder – Somboon's name was typed below a magnificent red-and-gold official Garuda. However, once safely inside the Chitralada Villa of Dusit Palace, Arthit revealed the change of plan to Phaisith. 'I told him I would not nominate Somboon because if I did the country would be in chaos.'

Although Phaisith had no say in the decision, and made no attempt to dissuade Arthit, he advised him to think carefully on the matter. He remembers Arthit explaining his thinking very quickly. 'At first, I thought Mr Anand would not accept,' Phaisith says. He has no recollection of Arthit arriving with another proclamation sheet, however, and believes one could easily have been found within the palace.

'I said I would be responsible and asked for a typist,' says Arthit. He had another piece of paper with the embossed Garuda. He says that he had accessed the parliamentary stationery, but another name had not been typed in. As a precaution, he would only have that done after reaching the safety of the palace.

Arthit had one last thing to do before the typist arrived to prepare the new document, and before going in for his audience with King Bhumibol. He went to the telephone under the stairs and called Anand. 'I am about to have the audience,' he told his old English tutor. 'Teacher had better get ready.' As Arthit later wrote in his memoir, 'After this sentence, what could Anand say?'

Anand says he has no recollection of this conversation. According to Arthit, however, Anand asked if the press would know about his appointment. Arthit says he told Anand the the press would know soon enough. The solitary Thai reporter had appeared that afternoon outside Anand's gate, but what prompted his presence is unknown. Whatever Anand knew or suspected at this stage, he had confided in nobody. Perhaps the reporter was just there to get Anand's comments on Somboon's appointment – but that was not what the reporter told Daranee earlier.

Phaisith distinctly remembers Arthit going off and placing a call, and that it was very brief. When Arthit reappeared, he told Phaisith that Anand had accepted, but Phaisith has no idea of what was actually said between the two. Arthit then disappeared for at least 30 minutes with Thawisan, King Bhumibol's principal private secretary, to prepare the document. 'I think Mom Thawisan already knew,' says Phaisith. 'It took quite a long while. I don't know if they went off and had an audience with the king.'

There remain numerous questions to ponder. What would have transpired if Arthit had taken Somboon's nomination forward? Did King Bhumibol know which name was on the proclamation before the doors to the audience chamber opened? How could he not have? When and how did Anand know his name would be put forward? He will not say, but his movements that afternoon suggest it predated the final call Arthit says he made from the palace.

The palace has of course never issued its version of these opaque events. However, the wording on the short proclamation clearly indicates the king was directly involved in the choice of Anand, and was not simply giving his assent as a constitutional formality: 'After General Suchinda Kraprayoon left the position of prime minister, the president of the house of representatives informed the king that it had been done according to democratic processes. The king thought that Anand Panyarachun should be prime minister.' No other parties are alluded to in that decision. This can be compared with the first time Anand was appointed to the position, when the proclamation's wording showed him to be the junta's choice: 'The National Peacekeeping Council (NPKC) informed the king that Anand Panyarachun should be appointed prime minister.'[15]

And many still wonder: who was Arthit most afraid of? The switch to Anand was made inside the palace and obviously did not conform to any normal protocol. The upheaval caused by finding a typist to fill in the blank proclamation could not have gone unremarked. Did news of the change leak? Because the constitutional amendment stipulating that prime ministers must be elected had not yet received the royal assent and therefore not appeared in the *Royal Gazette*, the new law was not being violated – although its intent was certainly being bruised. But bruises fade, and there was parliamentary consensus that a full prime minister was needed. It just wasn't going to be Somboon.

'It was in accordance with the constitution,' says Anand. 'The procedure was correct. As to how my name happened to be the one, it is irrelevant.'

After weeks of uncertainty, the audience finally granted to Arthit was almost cursory. Inside the audience chamber, Arthit knelt on both knees before a small table, for the king to sign the proclamation appointing Anand prime minister a second time. According to Phaisith's recollection, this was around 3:30pm in the afternoon, but it might have been later. The king's preference was usually for around 5pm. 'The country has already suffered a lot,' Arthit told the king. 'I have no alternative, except to propose a prime minister in order to dissolve parliament.'

King Bhumibol signed the document without comment, and Phaisith immediately picked it up and left the audience chamber. Phaisith retained the unsigned proclamation for Somboon, which he still has in his possession. The king told Arthit to remain, and they talked.

Arthit remembers explaining that he had to take this course or there would have been more bloodshed. He recalls the king saying that he was 'very brave, like a statesman'. He was suddenly overcome with relief. 'I kneeled down and *kraab*ed him.'[16] After the three strained calls to Anand, and the exchanges in the palace with Thawisan and Phaisith, Arthit could at last confide in others. There had indeed been good reason to be fearful of many people. 'It was the most difficult period in my life. It is unthinkable that someone should be responsible for that very difficult situation alone. I could not leak it to anyone – not even my secretary. It was not done for whether the people liked it or not. I just had to do it.' Arthit still thinks it was the best decision he ever made. 'I kicked the ball into touch and said, "Let's do it all again."'

Phaisith meanwhile took the proclamation back to parliament where a seal was applied, and it was photocopied. That took about 20 minutes. He telephoned Anand from parliament to inform him that he was on his way over. 'Anand didn't say anything – he knew,' Phaisith recalls. The journey across town with his assistants to Anand's home took another 30 minutes, and he remembers Anand receiving him in person. By Anand's recollection, dusk was approaching. Phaisith did not notice the reporter at the gate, and there was no other press. A small table had been set up in front of a portrait of King Bhumibol. Phaisith laid out the document before it so that Anand could formally receive it.

Although a court photographer recorded King Bhumibol signing the second proclamation appointing Anand prime minister, royal audiences are rarely televised unless they are for a new cabinet, or for the presentation of other newly appointed senior officials such as judges. Nevertheless, word of what had just happened in the palace soon found its way to Somboon's house. The telephone call was taken in full view of the cameras by an astonished Banharn with Somboon standing nearby. The expression on Banharn's face was one of shock.

With remarkable dignity, a bemused Somboon commented that Anand was a good man before withdrawing upstairs to try and figure out what on earth had just transpired. It had not helped that the assembled press had broken into applause at the news of his replacement. The media then roared off across town to Anand's home. The new prime minister met them on his doorstep dressed in a grey suit as usual.

'My wife, not knowing what had happened, felt sorry for Somboon,' Anand recalls. A few months later, he met Somboon, and told him of Sodsee's reaction. 'Please tell your wife not to worry,' Somboon replied. 'I was very relieved not to get the job.'

Palpable relief

To this day, Arsa Sarasin believes Suchinda should have gone the Chavalit route and entered politics openly within a properly elected party. 'I think he would have become a very good prime minister – if he had waited a while, stayed outside, and kept his promise not to be involved in politics, then Somboon would have taken over and not have been successful.'

'I think he has several good qualities,' Anand later said of Suchinda. 'I happen to believe that he did not want to inherit the mantle of power.'[17] Others saw things differently. It was not about what Suchinda had inherited, but what he had assumed – for whatever reason. The military, with their commissions on arms purchases, property holdings, interests in construction and the stock market, and concessions on fishing, logging and mining, had major interests to protect.

It was largely a matter of ownership, and the military's sense of entitlement was increasingly at odds with a larger, wealthier, and more politically aware middle class. Professor Michael Leifer of the London School of Economics and Political Science commented that political conflict in Thailand could not 'be resolved until the military come to realise that a country that depends on educated and professional people is one that cannot be ruled by military dictatorships'.[18]

'The May events happened partly because of Anand – in a good way,' comments Ammar Siamwalla, one of Thailand's most distinguished economists, as he reflects on the jagged military-civilian divide at that time. 'The military came and made a big song and dance about Chatichai being corrupt. The one thing they did wrong from their point of view was to appoint Anand. I think Anand showed the Thai people – at least the middle classes among the demonstrators in May – that a clean government was possible. When all the shuffling was done, the military wanted to go back to the old style. It was exactly the same type of government that Chatichai left except that it was headed by Suchinda. That's why the May events happened. People were mad. They had been through the coup and all that, and nothing changed – zero.'

It is difficult to overstate the sense of foreboding that had remained prior to Anand's second appointment, even with Suchinda gone. There had been killing; the country was rudderless; there was no break in the clouds. The State Department in Washington had told its diplomats in Bangkok to do the rounds of the political parties and encourage dialogue and democratic solutions. Although there was concern at the embassy that this might appear as undue interference, they had their orders and duly met with Chuan, Banharn, Chatichai, Chavalit, and others. Preachers of democracy always have it far easier than aspiring practitioners.

'It was very depressing,' recalls Skip Boyce, the political counsellor at the US embassy who made the political rounds. 'Nobody knew what was going to happen.' On that pivotal night, when everyone had expected Somboon to be appointed, it was Boyce's job to file the cable to Washington as soon as the proclamation came through. Boyce remembers tuning into a local television station that opened its nightly news bulletin with a furiously spinning globe. It always made him dizzy. The channel flashed up images of Anand involved in some kind of ceremony. Boyce's initial reaction was irritation: a careless technician must have used an old tape by mistake, he thought. Then there was a shot of Somboon disappearing upstairs at his home, and the realisation of what had actually just transpired dawned on the political counsellor. 'How embarrassing was that?' Boyce remembers thinking.

For Arsa, this was the second time he had watched Anand become prime minister on television with no advance warning. Others were equally surprised: 'I was waiting for him in Italy,' recalls Prida Tiasuwan, a friend.

There was similar astonishment in the Thammasat University auditorium where students had gathered to watch Somboon's appointment. Thammasat commanded huge political symbolism, and was close to Sanam Luang where so much political drama had occurred over the decades. There had been Seni Pramoj's motorcade upon his return home after the Second World War, the triumphant leader of the Free Thai resistance in the US; the terrible lynching of students in October 1976; and, most recently, May's popular revolt.

The mood at Thammasat was exceptionally sombre that night. 'We had been through a lot, and it was quite painful because of the killing,' recalls Karuna. 'I watched Somboon Rahong dressed in white at his house and thought, "I almost got killed, and we end up with this guy?"' Her thoughts drifted back to the protests and the battering the students and others had taken. 'When they started shooting, we lay down. When they stopped, we stood up and sang the King's Anthem. Apart from my dad, the only person I was thinking about was the king.'

The remarkable turnaround triggered by the ceremony at the palace that afternoon then began to unfold beneath the unrelenting gaze of the cameras. The students watched Banharn take the call, and the news that Anand had been appointed break. They saw the press cast objectivity to the winds and break into spontaneous applause.

The extraordinary scenes were being transmitted live without buffers, unlike King Bhumibol's encounter with Suchinda and Chamlong a few weeks earlier. Initially, only one channel was carrying the alternative footage from Anand's house that explained the true story unfolding that night. The students suddenly saw Anand in a grey suit after receiving the proclamation delivered by Phaisith, and then kneeling down with only Sodsee.

'It was so ironic – Somboon was elected,' says Karuna. 'In the auditorium, there were thousands of people cheering. Some belonged to a group called We Love Democracy. I was crying, thinking we are safe – the country is safe in this guy's hands. We were all laughing and crying. A fortnight before, we had been surrounded by the army with guns.'

Questions over the legitimacy of an unelected prime minister being drafted in were largely lost in the warmth of the reception for Anand's return. King Bhumibol's earlier intervention had stayed the violence and bought time, but it was not until Anand's appointment 19 days later that the nation experienced a genuine sense of deliverance – a reassurance that peace had really returned, that political lunacy had been contained, and that there was a chance things might finally be set right.

Looking back, Anand feels he had less choice in accepting the role of prime minister this second time than at the beginning of his first administration, when Suchinda asked him to take the job. Arthit's hurried third phone call from under the stairs at the Chitralada Villa represented, in effect, a *fait accompli*. As Arthit himself observed, could Anand realistically have said no at that stage? Another version of events is that Anand had already agreed through an unidentified channel, and it suited the palace to leave Arthit in the spotlight.

Anand remains to this day very judicious with his words about his second appointment to the premiership. 'I might jokingly say I was drafted into it, but I never said I was forced into it. Every opportunity I had, I said I had "accepted" the prime ministership. If you say you "did it for the nation", it sounds as if the people owe you something. That wouldn't go down well.'

CHAPTER 15

ANAND'S SECOND TERM (1992)

Déjà vu

Anand vividly remembers the audience with King Bhumibol after being appointed prime minister for the second time. As usual, he entered the audience chamber with the king standing some distance away, bowed, and prostrated himself. 'And then I stood up, and he said to me, "Shane! Come back!"' The king's Hollywood allusion was a moment of humour and relief after the very dark weeks Thailand had experienced since their previous meeting.

Shane was a classic Western; the main character was a very righteous man, sheriff of a town which had some very serious problems, and he effectively pacified the place. Everybody of Anand's generation had seen the film in their youth. 'He got rid of all the gangsters and whatever,' says Anand, 'and then he hung up his pistols and retired into the country. And then the violence erupted again … and he was called back to come and pacify the city.'

One film critic interpreted the call to Shane in the film's closing scene as an appeal to 'the audience's longing for a pure man, a once-and-future hero who may reappear when we need him most'.[1] Anand was back, not wounded and bleeding like Shane, but he was a white knight. Once more, the surprise appointment came at a personal cost. 'We were in shock for Anand II,' his younger daughter Daranee recalls. 'I remember my friends calling up – they were celebrating. The country was in a very jubilant mood. My friends asked why the three of us looked so sad on television. My sister and I could handle it, but there was so much concern about my mother. We had all told Mom that it was over after Anand I. I felt awful, like we had gone back on our word to her. We said we would support whatever decision he thought was right. I think talking to our mum about it was one of the most difficult things we had to do because she had gone through a very difficult period the first time. She was still in shock.' Indeed, Sodsee went to stay with Daranee for a while.

Reporters immediately camped around the house in the mid-Sukhumvit residential area. To Anand's bemusement, Sumet Jumsai, an Anglophile architect and painter who lived just up the road, had decked out the lampposts with the national flag even though there was no official occasion at the time. Anand turned up on his doorstep to remind him that there were limits to exuberance. 'You can't do this,' he admonished Sumet lightly. 'This is the national flag – there are laws.'

For Anand, it was not to be a simple question of picking up where he had left off two months earlier, and he had no plans to regroup his old team. Apart from being composed of unusually competent, unelected technocrats, his two cabinets were quite different from one another. During the much longer first premiership, the head of government was technically not the prime minister but General Sunthorn Kongsompong, chairman of the National Peacekeeping Council (NPKC). With the junta gone, on his second watch Anand was actually fully head of government. Although Sunthorn had remained passive, and the junta had allowed Anand a free hand and executive authority, the NPKC had always retained the power to remove him and appoint an alternative. In the Anand II government, Anand had full executive authority – the power to appoint and to dismiss. He could even intervene in military affairs if he deemed it necessary. But would any civilian risk such an adventure in Thailand? The last person to trespass into this territory, Prime Minister Chatichai Choonhavan, had been removed in the 1991 coup.

Although he was unelected on both occasions, the difference in Anand's situations was not merely semantic. After being asked to take the position first by Suchinda, he was appointed under a short-interim military constitution. The second time, he was appointed after being nominated by an elected president of parliament, Arthit Ourairat, under the rules of the new, full constitution – albeit a controversial one drafted by a military-appointed national legislative assembly, and one adopted without referendum.

The circumstances of Anand's second appointment have always been the subject of much debate, but its legality is not in doubt. The fact that Anand was not an elected member of parliament was not proscribed by law at the time. It was also but a short step back to the five governments of Prem Tinsulanond in the 1980s. Prem had always been nominated by the elected parties, and approved according to the parliamentary rules of the day. Chatichai had been elected, but after getting rid of him the NPKC had fiddled with the rules to enable an unelected prime minister to slip into office – which is how Suchinda briefly and disastrously became prime minister after being nominated by the junta. The junta had been disbanded in April following Suchinda's nomination as prime minister, and just before he presented his cabinet to the king. The power to nominate future prime ministers then reverted to the president of parliament – Arthit Ourairat by this time – who was himself an elected member of parliament.

While the constitution had already been revised by an elected parliament to block the president's nominating an unelected prime minister, the new article had not yet received the royal assent and come into force.

King Bhumibol signed three other constitutional amendments on 20 June, ten days after Anand was appointed prime minister, but he did not sign the amendment requiring the prime minister be an elected member of parliament until September, a few days ahead of the next general election.

Anand's second appointment therefore slipped through a closing window. It did more than raise eyebrows. Arthit was regarded by many elected politicians as a traitor for his facilitating role. After all the lonely anguish he had experienced, Arthit was unfazed. He told reporters that Anand's government should last the four months necessary for the constitutional amendments to be implemented, but not more than seven. In the event, it lasted just 104 days – less than four months.

Anand honoured the understanding and ensured that he left as soon as possible. The plan was always to be gone in the shortest time. His stated order of business was to restore peace and tranquillity, alleviate rural hardships caused by drought and weak commodity prices, restore consumer confidence, restart infrastructure projects, recover international confidence, promote freedom of the media and debate, and to celebrate Queen Sirikit's 60th birthday in August. Above all, it was to encourage public participation in free and fair elections that would generate a new parliament and a viable government without delay. The Anand paradox was once again apparent: an unelected prime minister coaxing the emergence of democratic norms.

Reduced cabinet

Anand's first cabinet was formed in just four days. The second was sworn in at an audience with King Bhumibol on the afternoon of 15 June, five days after his surprise appointment, and had 11 members fewer than his first cabinet at full strength. Seven of the missing members were from the military.

'His Majesty told Mr Anand and his team that their administration is rather special because it has come at a time when the country needs people who are ready to make sacrifices to restore peace and stability,' the *Bangkok Post* reported.[2]

With the addition of some deputy portfolios in mid-1991, Anand's first cabinet had 36 members of whom eight were from the military. His second cabinet had 25 members – half as many as Suchinda's – with General Pow Sarasin serving as both deputy prime minister and minister of the interior. Anand drafted in a retired general, Banchob Bunnag, as the new minister of defence, and he was the sole military officer in the cabinet. 'I knew he would follow my directions,' Anand says.

Anand kept 11 ministers from his previous cabinet with the same portfolios. Among these, Mechai Viravaidya and Saisuree Chutikul were again ministers in the Office of the Prime Minister. Anand did not restore Mechai's responsibility for the tourism sector, however, which was left to its own devices. Mechai had had tense relations with the travel sector, both public and private. Among many disputes, Mechai disapproved of TAT's business interests. There was a golf course and a resort in Khao Yai with 'terrible bungalows' which he had bulldozed. His anti-HIV/AIDS campaign was a constant source of tension in tourism circles, but it had now acquired its own momentum. Anand knew that there would simply not be enough time for his new government to get embroiled afresh in many deeply entrenched issues.

Arsa Sarasin returned as foreign minister; Nukul Prachuabmoh as minister of transport and communications; Amaret Sila-on as commerce minister. Kaw Swasdi Panich took on education again; Pairoj Ningsanonda health; Phaichitr Uathavikul science, technology and environment; and Sipphanondha Ketudat industry.

Kosit Penpiemras was promoted to minister of agriculture as Anat Arbhabhirama had already committed himself to the preliminary stages of a major infrastructure project, the future BTS SkyTrain in Bangkok. In Kosit's view, Anand's most influential advisers during the previous government had been Pow, Arsa, Snoh, Suthee Singsaneh, Nukul Prachuabmoh, and Vidhya

Raiyananonda, his self-effacing deputy secretary general. Snoh could not return for health and personal reasons. Vidhya became his secretary general, replacing Staporn Kavitanon, who had returned to his position as secretary general at the Board of Investment. Anand thought Staporn was better placed there to drum up foreign investment damaged by the May events. With the NPKC dissolved and the military in disgrace, he also no longer had the same need for Staporn's diplomatic talents in finessing issues with the generals.

Anand particularly wanted Suthee Singsaneh back as finance minister. 'In a way, I had absorbed a lot of his patience and discretion,' Anand recalls. But it was not to be. Suthee was always noted for his good relations and tact with the military. During the first Anand government, Suthee had been one of the ministers appearing most frequently in parliament to explain new legislation. After the dissolution of that government, Suthee had been co-opted to serve as Suchinda's finance minister. He was wounded by a comment one day in the corridors of parliament from Chuan Leekpai, the Democrat Party leader. 'Here comes the man who can paddle in a boat with a monk and a robber,' Chuan chided him.

'It hurt Suthee very much,' Anand recalled. 'That's why he avoided me. He knew he would have been persuaded to come back.' After the terrible fireworks surrounding Suchinda, the affable Suthee simply could not face another thankless stint at the finance ministry. When Anand tracked him down at a golf course to ask him to reconsider, Suthee had been tipped off and made a hasty departure in a golf buggy just as Anand entered the clubhouse. He thereby dodged Anand's second draft, and was replaced by Panas Simasathien, a 30-year finance ministry veteran. 'I am confident he will be able to continue with the policy laid down by me and Mr Suthee,' Anand told reporters. Virabongsa Ramangkura, Suthee's former deputy, had also served in the Suchinda cabinet and was left out on Anand's second watch. 'He was a very good economist, but he became too close to Class 5,' Anand recalls.

Another missing face was Meechai Ruchupan, the third deputy prime minister in the first Anand government. Meechai became one of Suchinda's five deputy prime ministers, and served as caretaker prime minister for the weeks when Arthit was struggling to find a successor. Those issues aside, there was actually little need for Meechai in the second government. The Council of State[3] was available to provide the government with any technical advice on legislation it might need. Meechai had previously been occupied drafting the constitution and a mountain of new legislation. The new constitution was already in place, amendments had been approved by parliament, and were already awaiting the king's assent. Most importantly, Anand's new government had no legislative agenda – that was not its purpose.

Wissanu Krea-ngam was back, this time as cabinet secretary general and working more closely with Anand. 'Anand came with one intention and that was to dissolve the parliament ahead of elections,' Wissanu recalls. On his first day back at Government House, Anand summoned him and asked if there was any way he could dissolve the elected assembly immediately. Wissanu said it was out of the question. He had to first convene parliament and announce his policies, Wissanu explained. 'What policies? My only policy is to dissolve parliament,' Anand retorted. Indeed, at the audience for the new cabinet, Anand had already informed King Bhumibol his draft speech to parliament would be the shortest policy statement ever written.[4]

Anand immediately met with all the party leaders. 'I came to ask one question,' he told them. 'When do you want me to dissolve parliament?' The leaders were aghast. Things might not have gone to plan, and there had been carnage in the streets, but they had hoped that perhaps something could still be salvaged from their heavy outlays on the general election. 'We can work together,' they pleaded. Anand would have none of it, and not one of them had been offered a place in what he always regarded as an interim cabinet – once more entirely unelected.

A group of 20 'Young Turks' from the Samakkitham, Social Action, Chart Thai, and New Aspiration parties tried to derail Anand's determination to dissolve parliament. They believed some kind of government of national reconciliation might be possible. Chuan Leekpai meanwhile fended off attempts to push him forward as an alternative prime minister, pointing out that it was 'a little bit too late'. New Aspiration spokesman Chaturon Chaisang disavowed the blocking moves, saying they ran counter to the public mood, and endorsed Anand's plans for dissolution.[5] In August, PollWatch Secretary General Gothom Arya supported 115 academics led by Professor Chai-Anan Samudavanija, one of Thailand's foremost political scientists, who wanted to form a so-called 'mirror assembly' with 1,500 representatives appointed by the king to offer counsel. It had a vaguely French precedent. One of the issues they pressed was postponing King Bhumibol's assent to the constitutional amendment requiring the prime minister to be elected. 'This was primarily aimed at preventing the status of non-elected Prime Minister Anand

Panyarachun from being put into question,' the *Bangkok Post* reported.[6]

The mirror assembly was condemned by both the Law Society of Thailand and the police Special Branch on the grounds that it would only sow confusion.[7] Anand avoided being drawn into this particular controversy, but did express support for input more generally. 'It's the duty of all Thai people to protect democracy, to make it a viable instrument of national politics,' he told reporters. 'People must have a participatory role in all decision-making. Don't expect the government to come up with all the initiatives.'

A blistering speech

Even though he planned to leave office at the first opportunity, Anand could not avoid reading a policy speech of some kind at the re-opening of parliament. Wissanu was assigned to draft it, with Kasem Suwanakul, Mechai, and Pow mentoring him. That day, Monday 22 June, Anand went to parliament in the morning, read the unusually brief speech, and immediately returned to Government House for a cabinet meeting while parliament debated the statement. He reappeared in the chamber for a joint sitting of the upper and lower houses at 7pm, and listened to criticisms of his government. Chart Thai co-founder Praman Adireksan dismissed it as an '*ad hoc*' administration. Ignoring the objections of some members of parliament, Arthit as the president of parliament invited Anand to respond. He did so with a powerful, unscripted address.

'This situation is a tragedy for everyone – the people, the army, the police,' he declared. 'We have maintained our independence for 800 years. We have created prosperity. It may not be perfect, but this is a society in which we are proud to be Thai under His Majesty the King and the institution of the monarchy. Are we going to act rashly or in the short-term to destroy ourselves? If the answer to all this was easy, I wouldn't be here in the first place.'

'He made a really good speech,' recalls Supakorn Vejjajiva, one of Anand's young aides. 'They were quite shocked and there was a lot of heckling. One of the most vocal people giving him a hard time was a Democrat member of parliament, Surin Pitsuwan, who was tough without being uncivil. Other people were shouting, saying he was not an elected member of parliament.' Anand was unmoved. 'I enjoyed it,' he recalls.

Anand went on the attack over money politics. 'Some of my actions may go against the feelings of many members of parliament, and I sympathise, but my private sympathy does not override my respect for principles,' he said. 'I have appointed an able interior minister, Pow Sarasin, to make a cleaner election than last time. I cannot deny that the last election was the one that used up the most money. I would like to ask who is spending this money? Where did it come from? Why are they spending it? Every country has laws against corruption, murder, or theft. The effectiveness of those laws does not depend only on their being sacrosanct, but also on the people involved. I don't know which members of parliament have been elected by spending money. I don't know how those members of parliament got their money, or from where it came, who gave it and why, but we must listen to the people.'

'People were shocked by events,' he added. 'When I took this position, there were phone calls until 2am and thousands of letters from people of all ages. Reading those letters brings home how desperate the situation had become.'

Anand recalls of that night in parliament: 'I was very critical of them. It was off the cuff. At the end, they started applauding me and then stopped. They suddenly realised what they were doing – I was telling them off.' 'It was a blistering speech,' recalls Ammar Siamwalla of the Thailand Development Research Institute (TDRI). Like many, Ammar noticed that Anand can seem defensive about the circumstances of his second premiership. 'It is one thing that he is very un-transparent about,' says Ammar. 'How was it that he got to be prime minister?'

On a later occasion, Anand similarly took an association of Thai journalists to task over their professional shortcomings. His words were always widely followed and their unusual candour seemed to resonate wherever they were heard. A friend once told Anand that his 84-year-old mother would race out of the bathroom every time he came on the air. Queen Sirikit told him her driver had listened to the second speech, and mentioned it to her.

Thailand's development czar and founder of the TDRI, Snoh Unakul, was in poor health and afflicted by profound grief after the death of his son. Snoh concluded he could not continue as TDRI chairman. 'I could not see anyone who could be more appropriate to replace me than Khun Anand,' he recalls. 'While still bedridden, I begged him to accept the chairmanship.' But it was at exactly the time Anand was meant to be replacing Snoh at TDRI that he emerged out of all the chaos to become prime minister again.

Ammar remembers one TDRI meeting when Anand was actually in the process of forming his new cabinet. The new prime minister leaned across and asked him to suggest an expert on agriculture. Ammar's recommendation was Ampon Senarong, a future privy councillor. Anand chose Kosit, his deputy agriculture minister from the previous cabinet, and made Ampon deputy. The TDRI board met quarterly, usually for less than half a day, and it was Anand's intention to no longer be prime minister when the next meeting came around. 'You don't need to be an academic to be chairman,' says Ammar. 'The board is our link to the outside world, but we did not plan to have a sitting prime minister as our chairman.'

Anand was once again stepping into a position for which he had no specific qualifications. He had certainly never done any formal research work. Anand's involvement put the TDRI, which was again extremely well represented in the cabinet, in an interesting situation. In theory, Anand found himself both prime minister and chairman of its most important advisory body. In practice, it meant little because this was an interim government with no policy agenda to formulate.

This was a contrast to the Prem years, when TDRI had effectively been a part of government. 'We were almost a ministry,' Ammar recalls. 'At every cabinet meeting, we had an inner group of technocrats sitting around.' Both TDRI's presidents in the 1980s, Anat Arbhabhirama and Phaichitr Uathavikul, were particularly close to the government, and went on to hold portfolios in the first Anand administration.

'My policy has always been that we should distance ourselves as an institution from the government – not that I had anything against Prem,' says Ammar. 'I was very happy because I got on well with Anand. He is an academic's dream of a prime minister – very transparent and very clear-headed about what he wants to do. He is always clear in his point of view, so we don't have to psyche him out. I like that style.'[8]

Energy, environment, privatisation

Anand had quickly put the political parties in check. While he had no policy plans, his second government did provide an opportunity to see how the bureaucracy was handling legislation promulgated under his previous government. For full implementation, ministerial regulations needed to be in place. 'We found that some of the ministerial rules did not comply with the intent of the acts of parliament, and we were able to amend those regulations,' he recalls. The environmental law was one such example. Another was foreign ownership of condominiums. This had been a 30 per cent cap on foreign ownership of individual property developments, and this was increased to 49 per cent. 'You have to watch bureaucrats in Thailand at every step,' says Anand. 'Implementation can at times undermine good laws.'

Phaichitr Uathavikul, Anand's returning minister of science, technology and environment, seized the opportunity to add to the emission controls he initiated on his previous watch. In July, lead levels were set to be reduced further in 1993 from 0.15 gram per litre, and tighter limits were applied to benzene, aromatics, and sulphur content. The aim was to bring Thailand up to European standards within five years. 'Surprisingly, resistance was very strong from oil refineries, car manufacturers, academics,' recalls Piyasvasti Amranand, chairman of PTT, Thailand's national energy conglomerate. 'The civil service itself put forward counter arguments like Thai people are different from [foreigners], and that lead would not have an impact on their health, or that Bangkok was not yet polluted.'

Much of the policy on liberalising power generation originated under Chatichai and predated the Anand governments, but it had run into strong opposition from elements in EGAT's management and more importantly EGAT's labour union. It was a primary target in the NPKC's knockdown of state unions after the 1991 coup.

One law on which follow-up was needed was the Electricity Generating Authority of Thailand (EGAT) Act, which had been amended in March just ahead of the general election. That opened the way to small and independent power-producers feeding the national grid, breaking EGAT's 30-year-old monopoly. Small power-producers were looking to a future with energy produced from cogeneration processes and renewable resources. The expanding agricultural processing and livestock industries were producing enormous amounts of waste and byproducts that were potentially polluting and costly to dispose of. Paddy husk, wood chips, sugar cane pulp (bagasse), and waste from animal rearing, tapioca processing plants, and palm oil refineries could all be put to use generating energy. After regulations to purchase power from small power producers came into effect in May 1992, an increasing amount of previously untapped energy could be distributed on the national grid through EGAT, which retained its distribution monopoly.

Between 1986 and 1991, Thailand's electricity demand was increasing at around 14 per cent per annum – requiring an additional 800 megawatts of generating capacity each year. The long-term impact of the introduction of small power providers cannot be understated. By 2016, these were supplying 20 per cent of the

King Bhumibol Adulyadej pours lustral water on Anand during an audience in late 1977 ahead of his last diplomatic posting to Bonn, capital of the Federal Republic of Germany.
(PANYARACHUN FAMILY COLLECTION)

The board of Saha Union after Anand became chairman in early 1991. Sitting (from left) are Amorn Chantarasomboon, Amnuay Viravan, Anand, Damri Darakanonda, and Sumet Darakanonda. (SAHA UNION ARCHIVE)

TOP: *Prime Minister Anand Panyarachun attending a parade with army chief General Suchinda Kraprayoon in 1991. Standing behind Anand is Police General Pow Sarasin, one of three deputy prime ministers.* (PANYARACHUN FAMILY COLLECTION)

MIDDLE: *Prime Minister Anand at a reception in 1991 with former Prime Minister Prem Tinsulanond, the then deputy president of the Privy Council.*

ABOVE: *Anand with Air Chief Marshal Kaset Rojananil.*
(BOTH PHOTOS BY WARISARA WUTHIKUL - BUREAU BANGKOK)

TOP: *From left, US Secretary of State James Baker and Singapore's Senior Minister Lee Kuan Yew dining in Singapore in early 1992. Anand is sitting second from right.*

ABOVE: *Guests in Bangkok for the 1991 World Bank/IMF annual meetings included World Bank President Lewis T. Preston (sitting second from left) and Michel Camdessus, the longest-serving managing director of the IMF (sitting second from right).*

(BOTH PHOTOS FROM THE PANYARACHUN FAMILY COLLECTION)

TOP LEFT: *Prime Minister Chavalit Yongchaiyudh stepped out of uniform to form the New Aspiration Party as his political vehicle.* (MANIT SRIWANICHPOOM – BUREAU BANGKOK)

TOP RIGHT: *Prime Minister Chatichai Choonhavan juggled difficult coalitions as Thailand experienced double-digit economic growth.* (MANIT SRIWANICHPOOM – BUREAU BANGKOK)

ABOVE LEFT: *Future Prime Minister Abhisit Vejjajiva as a neophyte politician for the Democrat Party in the early 1990s.* (WARISARA WUTTHICHAI – BUREAU BANGKOK)

ABOVE RIGHT: *Prime Minister Banharn Silpa-archa allowed a constitutional adjustment that paved the way for the progressive 'People's Constitution' in 1997.* (BUREAU BANGKOK)

TOP: *The only occasion King Bhumibol Adulyadej sat for a photograph with a cabinet during his long reign; this photograph was taken at the Chitralada Villa of Dusit Palace in April 1992 towards the end of the first Anand government.*

ABOVE: *Anand and Sodsee were invited to tea with Princess Srinagarindra, the princess mother, at the end of Anand's first term in office.*

(ALL PHOTOS FROM THE PANYARACHUN FAMILY COLLECTION)

LEFT: *Queen Sirikit and Sodsee in 1992.*

MIDDLE: *Crown Prince Maha Vajiralongkorn and Princess Maha Chakri Sirindhorn arrive at a reception at Government House to mark the birthday of King Bhumibol Adulyadej on 5 December 1991. Princess Chulabhorn and Princess Bajrakitiyabha Mahidol are standing right and second from right.*

BELOW: *Princess Maha Chakri Sirindhorn and her niece, Princess Bajrakitiyabha Mahidol, with Anand and Sodsee.*

(ALL PHOTOS FROM THE PANYARACHUN FAMILY COLLECTION)

TOP: *Arthit Ourairat at a press conference given by Samakkitham, the military's proxy party, after the election in March 1992.*

ABOVE: *Samakkitham's leader Narong Wongwan speaking after his nomination for prime minister failed.*

(*BOTH PHOTOS BY DOMINIC FAULDER*)

TOP: *Government reception when army chief General Suchinda Kraprayoon became prime minister in April 1992.*

MIDDLE: *Chamlong Srimuang rallying opposition to Suchinda's government at Sanam Luang*

(*BOTH PHOTOS BY WARISARA WUTHIKUL – BUREAU BANGKOK*)

BELOW: *Troops rounded up hundreds of demonstrators outside the Royal hotel after a night of rioting and arson in May 1992.* (*DOMINIC FAULDER*)

TOP LEFT: *In June 1992, Anand met the press on the doorstep of his home after unexpectedly being appointed premier for a second brief term.* (WARISARA WUTHIKUL - BUREAU BANGKOK)

TOP RIGHT: *Anand's first finance minister, Suthee Singsaneh, was instrumental in the introduction of value added tax and other key financial reforms during the first Anand government.*

ABOVE LEFT: *'Development czar' Snoh Unakul returned to prominence in the first Anand government.* (BOTH PHOTOS BY MANIT SRIWANICHPOOM - BUREAU BANGKOK)

ABOVE RIGHT: *Population planning advocate Mechai Viravaidya strove to ensure that addressing HIV/AIDS became a top government priority.* (DOMINIC FAULDER)

TOP: *The second Anand government organised an election that returned a coalition led by the Democrat Party with Chuan Leekpai as prime minister.*

ABOVE LEFT: *Minister of Industry Sipphanondha Ketudat streamlined Thai manufacturing, particularly in automotives and electronics.*

ABOVE RIGHT: *Saisuree Chutikul, the minister in the prime minister's office who broke glass ceilings and championed the rights of women and children.*

(ALL PHOTOS BY DOMINIC FAULDER)

TOP LEFT: *With former US President George H.W. Bush in the late 1990s.*

TOP RIGHT: *With UN Secretary General Kofi Annan in 2004.*

MIDDLE LEFT: *Touring Ayutthaya with Henry Kissinger in 1998.*

MIDDLE RIGHT: *MR Sodsee and Anand with George H.W. Bush at an evening hosted by Thaksin Shinawatra (right) at his home.*

ABOVE: *Kofi Annan with the members and secretariat of his UN high-level panel on threats to global security in 2004. Former Australian Foreign Minister Gareth Evans is standing behind Anand to the left.* (ALL PHOTOS FROM THE PANYARACHUN FAMILY COLLECTION)

Moment of reconciliation – Thanat Khoman, the former foreign minister, points out Anand at a function to welcome Prince Alfred of Liechtenstein and his wife Princess Raffaella in 2003 on their first visit to Thailand. Thanat had been Anand's mentor at the foreign ministry, and the pair spontaneously reconciled on this occasion after a split that lasted a few years. It was an auspicious start to the 'Bridges – Dialogues Towards a Culture of Peace' programme organised by Uwe Morawetz (above, left). (BOTH PHOTOS FROM THE PANYARACHUN FAMILY COLLECTION)

TOP LEFT: *Anand making his way on foot through the crowds around the Grand Palace at the start of the one-year mourning period for King Bhumibol Adulyadej, October 2016.* (JONATHAN HEAD)

TOP RIGHT: *With social critic Sulak Sivaraksa in late 2017.* (AMARTYA SEN LECTURE SERIES)

ABOVE: *A recent Old Alleynian dinner in Bangkok with (from left) Mike Smith, Mike Holloway, Anand, Dulwich College founder Edward Alleyn (in cutout), Arsa Sarasin, Sally Holloway, Dibhyaraks Sukhum, Jonathan Head, Anusorn Thavisin, MR Chanvudhi Varavarn, and Chai Chalitaporn.* (MIKE SMITH)

LEFT: *Anand's fundraising activities for UNICEF over the past two decades have brought in over US$160 million for the benefit of children around the world.* (UNICEF)

BELOW: *Anand as chair of Siam Commercial Bank addresses the board. Sitting opposite him (second from left) is his predecessor in the position, Chirayu Isarangkun Na Ayuthaya.* (SIAM COMMERCIAL BANK)

TOP LEFT: *Anand at his Saha Union office in Bangkok.* (DOMINIC FAULDER)

TOP RIGHT: *Anand shares a quiet moment with his great grandson, Wyn Srifuengfung.*

ABOVE: *Close family occasion: sitting from left, Nanda Krairiksh, Anand, MR Sodsee, and Daranee. Standing from left, Kraithip Krairiksh, Thawin Srifuengfung, Tipanan Srifuengfung, Sirinda Charoen-Rajapark, Tanawin Charoen-Rajapark, and Chatchawin Charoen-Rajapark.*

(BOTH PHOTOS FROM THE PANYARACHUN FAMILY COLLECTION)

power to the national grid. 'The small power supplier programme is probably the single most important policy measure to promote renewable energy in Thailand,' says Piyasvasti. 'There have been some changes over the past 25 years, but the current form of regulations still reflect those issued by the Anand government.'

Nearly three years later, when Anand was once more chairman of Saha Union, the group formed Union Power Development as an independent power-provider to operate a $1.2-billion coal-burning 1,400-megawatt power plant at Hin Krut, in Prachuap Khiri Khan. It was the largest of seven projects approved initially to supply EGAT with an aggregate 5,200 megawatts. Union Power was later renamed Ratchaburi Power, with Saha Union retaining a minority shareholding. The project moved to Ratchaburi, where it could run on offshore natural gas piped overland from Myanmar. Plans to liberalise the energy sector clearly predated Saha Union's decision to become an independent power producer; it was a conglomerate always looking to invest in profitable new lines of business, and the fact that Anand was prime minister when related laws were adjusted was never a barrier to entry. Even so, it was one of the few areas in either of his two administrations for which he later took flak.

An important innovation in October 1991 that remains largely unchanged to this day was the fuel adjustment clause, a mechanism to adjust electricity prices in line with changes in the cost of generating fuels. This passed the real cost of energy to users, encouraging responsible usage. The Energy Conservation Promotion Act was passed in February 1992 towards the end of Anand's first government. This was all complemented by a demand-side management programme undertaken by EGAT – again a greener alternative to simply building more power stations. One of the most obvious and lasting manifestations was the prominent labelling of refrigerators and other household appliances to indicate energy efficiency.

Privatisation of all suitable state enterprises was strongly advocated by Anand's first finance minister, Suthee, to raise capital, introduce technology, and modernise management. As a first step in the power sector, EGAT set up the Electricity Generating Public Company (EGCO). This occurred during the troubled month of May between the two Anand governments, and created a vehicle whereby a power station in Rayong could be divested. Later EGCO bought another plant from EGAT at Khanom, in the southern province of Nakhon Si Thammarat. EGCO was floated on the stock exchange with EGAT initially retaining over 48 per cent, but this stake was subsequently diluted to below 20 per cent.

Nukul Prachuabmoh, the returned minister of transport and communications, was as bullish as ever. The Telecom Asia problem had been largely resolved earlier in the year, during the first cabinet. With the military now in disarray, there was an opportunity to clean house at Thai Airways International, the national flag-carrier, where the air force had been causing ructions.

The national airline had been experiencing serious internal upheavals since the late 1980s. Chatrachai Bunya-Ananta, who had joined the company in 1972 and been key to making the flag-carrier a top regional player by the 1980s, became executive vice president in 1986.[9] The airline won awards for exemplary service, and competed effectively at this time with Singapore Airlines and Hong Kong's Cathay Pacific.[10]

In the 1980s, Myanmar was stirring slightly and Indochina showing signs of opening up, but Thailand, uniquely placed to exploit hub-and-spoke network opportunities, was squandering a chance to become the centre of regional aviation in Southeast Asia. At that time Thai Airways could have forged strong, lasting relations with fledgling regional airlines had it not been so bound up with its own challenges, particularly involving the military. The airline's structure was complicated and faction-ridden, and air force meddling and corruption exacerbated the problems. The air force had always been deeply engaged in maintenance and other operational aspects, and viewed board positions as a birthright. By the 1980s, succession issues had again come to the fore. It had not always been thus. Chatrachai remembered many early air chief marshals as being gentlemanly, even rather stand-offish chairmen, but their successors in the late 1980s had become assertive and avaricious.

The airline had accumulated far too many different aircraft and engine types, and there was concern that it might be beyond reform. Before Anand and Nukul appeared on the scene, there certainly seemed no prospect of Chatrachai assuming the airline's presidency, a role that manifestly should already have been his on merit. 'I have only one year to retirement, so give me peace,' Chatrachai pleaded with Anand.

Anand and Nukul were determined to curb the air force's influence and prevent further damage. Chatrachai remembered being surprised by their resolution and willingness to tangle with the military. The prime minister called him directly one night and ordered him to chase down a recalcitrant senior air force officer who was being elusive.

'No airline in the world is monopolised by the chief of the air force,' says Nukul.

'If he is good enough, he can be head on merit but not by right.' Nukul duly fired the air force chairman of Thai Airways International, and changed the rules mandating that his successors be senior air force officers. Such firm steps against military interests were virtually unprecedented during a civilian government.[11]

After Anand and Nukul shook up the national flag-carrier's hierarchy, Chatrachai became its first non-air force president prior to his mandatory retirement at the age of 60 later in 1992. By then, the airline was among seven Asia-Pacific carriers in the top ten most profitable airlines in the world. For Chatrachai, it was a bittersweet vindication marked by a tragedy when an airbus crashed in Kathmandu.[12]

'What a year it was,' he later recalled. 'Anand would not take no for an answer.'

Back to the barracks

The greatest weight bearing down on the second Anand government was not in fact forcing an election, but deciding what to do with the military responsible for the May bloodshed. Academics were vocal and the press would not back off; the latter had witnessed too much at first hand. When Anand, at a keynote address to the Foreign Correspondents' Club of Thailand (FCCT), commented unguardedly that he had lived for many years in New York, and thousands of people were reported missing at any given time, it played badly. A sharp US reporter from the Associated Press pressed him for a clear answer to give to the families of missing people. Anand immediately corrected himself, and later apologised for the comment. 'Perhaps I was a little lighthearted, and I apologise if my statement was misconveyed,' he told a foreign reporter. He nevertheless remained sceptical about some of the higher casualty claims. 'I find it hard to believe that hundreds of bodies were taken away without any photographic evidence,' he told the reporter.[13]

At least 52 people had died, and hundreds were maimed for life. A list compiled by Mahidol University had thousands missing initially, but this became somewhat discredited when missing people started showing up alive without being removed promptly from the tally. Nevertheless, it was not in Anand's interests to signpost his true intentions towards the military. How far could he go without triggering a backlash – or even another coup? 'I must tread rather carefully,' he said in the interview. 'I hope you understand that issues of this kind need to be resolved more or less in a quiet manner.'[14]

'He had to do something,' recalls Vidhya Raiyananonda, Anand's trusted secretary general. 'It was very hard for a civilian to make that decision.' Unlike in 1973, when a civilian upheaval had effectively overthrown a military government, this time those responsible for the mayhem had not gone into exile. In fact, they had remained at the top of the military chain of command. Various committees had been established to investigate the May events, including one headed by Sophon Rattanakorn, a former supreme court president, which was set up under Meechai Ruchupan's caretaker government. Sophon's committee was asked, among other things, to suggest ways that a repeat of May's events could be prevented. At Anand's behest, the defence ministry conducted its own investigation under the chairmanship of General Pichit Kullavanijaya, who was not considered close to any particular military faction.[15]

'My only motive at that time was to defuse the situation by identifying the individuals who had to take political responsibility,' says Anand. 'My priority was to find out the truth of events, not to try and bring them to court. I had a limited aim. The military's report would come to a conclusion as to who was politically responsible for the events, and I was looking for a way to remove those people from command positions.'

Prosecution of those responsible was a different issue. The duration of Anand's government was to be short and the agenda very limited. If his government became embroiled in prosecutions, Anand would have had to extend his term. 'If I were to have launched a criminal investigation, it would have been out of my hands and up to the court, and have carried over to the next government,' he says. While the democratic mandate to see justice done lay with an elected government, such an entity might not even contemplate disciplinary action such as transfers. Anand felt strongly that these measures needed to be accomplished on his fleeting watch.

When he became prime minister, various activists wanted to present him publicly with flowers and petition him to take action against the military. Anand asked them to visit him privately at his Saha Union office. 'What I planned was to take steps to identify those who were politically responsible for the incident,' he says. 'I have only about three or four months so don't expect me to begin a process of criminal investigation,' he remembers telling the activists. He also asked them to refrain from creating any trouble while he was working on the problem. 'They willingly agreed,' he recalls.

The first step against the military came on 29 June with the abolition of the Internal Peacekeeping Law, which had facilitated the use of military force against unarmed demonstrators as if a communist uprising were under way. Kaset lost control of the Capital Peacekeeping Command, which had directed the suppression operations in May.

Anand let July pass before he made any further move. On Monday 27 July, Pichit delivered the military's internal report on the handling of the May unrest. It confirmed that troops had been high-handed, and had used lethal force against unarmed people without justification. Supakorn Vejjajiva, the son of Vitthya, the permanent secretary at the foreign ministry, had volunteered to be an assistant to Anand during his second term. Late one Friday afternoon, he was instructed to set up a typewriter in Anand's office. Nobody at Government House knew what this slightly irregular instruction was all about.

Anand came in after lunch the next day. There were two other people in his office: Vidhya and Defence Minister Banchob. No secretary or typist was involved. The three were about to prepare a military transfer order without anyone else knowing. Anand knew that precise timing was critical to his plan succeeding.

'I knew I had to do it that Saturday, the first day of August,' says Anand. 'This was the only matter in the Anand I or II governments I never broached with anybody – definitely not in cabinet or with the Ministry of Defence, which was supposed to be handling the matter. Nobody knew about it – not even the deputy prime ministers. It was all in my head from the very first day. I had my own game plan and timetable. I chose that particular date because I could have an audience with the king and ask for his signature. It was just before the beginning of celebrations for the queen's 60th birthday. Sunday would be quiet. In my mind, once the celebration process began on Monday, nobody would dare to do a counter-coup. I asked the minister of defence, General Banchob Bunnag, to come to my office together with the registry of the military. Vidhya was the typist. Nobody was around except the janitors, so it was just Banchob and Vidhya at three o'clock. We finished about four, and the audience was about five, so we left at 4:30. When we got to the palace, King Bhumibol asked me many questions, and whether it should be delayed because celebrations of the queen's birthday were about to start. I said it had to be done that day. I knew the military would not dare disrupt the celebration period of the queen. The audience lasted about 45 minutes, and the king looked at all the ramifications – he was very methodical.

His final question was: "Do you think it will work and that there will be no more disturbances?" I said yes, and informed him about my promise to the activists, and said they could be trusted. The king then signed the document. I gambled on all that, and was confident it would all work – but it had to be that Saturday.'

Anand called the activists at 7pm to alert them to what was transpiring. Later that night, a statement was issued from the prime minister's office saying that a total of 16 senior military figures had been transferred or replaced. Air Chief Marshal Kaset Rojananil, who had already been stripped of the Capital Security Command, was removed as military supreme commander and head of the air force. General Issarapong Noonpakdee was transferred from army chief to the position of deputy permanent secretary at the Ministry of Defence. His cousin, Lieutenant General Chainarong Noonpakdee, the commander of the army's first region covering Bangkok and surrounding areas, was also moved.

Issarapong was replaced by General Wimol Wongwanich, who was also a member of Class 5. Wimol had served in the first Anand cabinet as deputy minister of defence, and was widely regarded as a professional, apolitical soldier. Anand selected him over another candidate because he had more time to retirement – two years. Kaset was replaced as supreme commander by Air Chief Marshal Voranart Apicharee, and as air force chief by Air Chief Marshal Gun Pimantip.

'I think the military knew they were going to get canned, but not in such a way,' says Supakorn. 'They were surprised.' But would they also retaliate? Such an order from a civilian government was unprecedented. If they chose to stage a coup against Anand, it would have been unpopular without doubt, but probably successful. It would also have been very damaging to the national interest and image.

Importantly, a coup would also have violated King Bhumibol's assent, both to Anand as prime minister and to the document placed before him that Saturday evening. Anand had picked his moment carefully. It would also have interrupted Queen Sirikit's milestone birthday on 12 August, the Wednesday of the following week. Unusually elaborate celebrations were scheduled. The main event was a colourful outdoor gathering at Sanam Luang beneath a massive, glamorous full-length portrait of the queen. It was all in striking contrast to the violent unrest seen in previous weeks in the same part of the city. After May's mayhem, Anand knew that any further disruption at this time would be unacceptable to virtually everybody. For his purposes, this fortnight was the best of all possible periods during his fleeting premiership to push the military high command into limbo.

There were some mutterings to the effect that Anand had overreacted, but the tanks were not rolled out from the cavalry bays in Dusit, the administrative heart of the capital. Anand, however, did not escape entirely unscathed. There was an indignant telephone call from a senior lady in the court who feared he had destroyed the armed forces. When he attended a dinner given by the foreign ministry on the Monday night to honour the queen, it was a different story. He sat beside Queen Sirikit for two hours, and she said nothing of his unprecedented disciplining of the military. The conversation was friendly and non-political. Indeed, the chief of police called the next day to say the queen had requested Anand be given extra security when he travelled. Heavily armed security personnel were sent as escorts to ride alongside his car. Anand felt such precautions were unwarranted, and sent the bodyguards away after a few days. His security detail would, however, be stepped up again in the week before September's general election.

There were more relaxed moments amid the tension. Supakorn remembers that the mood would usually lighten at Government House after 6pm, when good food would be brought in and bottles of fine whisky opened. Anand's own 60th birthday fell on 9 August, a Sunday. He had been led to believe that there would be a small family gathering in the old Tiara Lounge at the top of the Dusit Thani. In the lift, Anand encountered Amnuay Viravan and his wife, who said no more than they were on their way up for dinner – which was perfectly true. Anand entered to find the room filled for a surprise party. 'You guys are all fired,' he told his grinning staff. Later in the evening, the party was joined by the king's oldest daughter, Tunkramom Ying Ubol Ratana, who sang. 'That was a surprise. I don't know who told her,' says Anand.

On 10 September, a further military shakeup was announced ahead of the annual military promotions that always take effect in October, but this was entirely an internal affair. 'I had nothing to do with that,' Anand recalls. On that occasion, 557 officers were involved. Chainarong's chief of staff in the first army region, Major General Sompong Muangklam, was the only officer to be demoted. Three other major generals – Panom Chinavichairaiya, Suvinai Boriboonangkoon, and Thitipong Chunnuwat – were 'promoted' to more senior, but less powerful, positions.

The earlier transfer of military officers by a civilian government was without precedent in Thailand. Normally the king would give his assent to promotions and transfers on the recommendation of the military council. Wimol, the new army chief, and other senior officers, including General Surayud Chulanont, who had commanded special forces in the capital in May, pledged to professionalise the armed forces and keep the military out of politics. Ironically, when that pledge was shattered after the next coup in 2006, it would be Surayud who stepped out from the Privy Council to be appointed prime minister.

'I didn't expect that everything was going to change overnight, but I did think that things would be better,' says Anand. 'I was fairly sure there would be no more *coups d'état*. I was quite confident I had put the military back into their barracks. That went on for over ten years, which was quite an achievement. There was a time when generals would always make political comments. After I left, there were three or four elections that were free and fair – although you could never rid the election process of money politics.'

In the May aftermath, there were some attempts made to get at the truth and address the issues of impunity. 'Although we have not been successful as yet, there is a memorial,' says Gothom Arya. 'I think Anand made a strong contribution to show that these events were very important to our society's struggle towards democratisation.'

There were annual demonstrations outside Suchinda's house for at least a decade. Among the junta, Suchinda was the only member to express some remorse for Black May, after which he essentially removed himself from public life. He became chairman of Telecom Holding, the holding company for Telecom Asia (which became True Corporation in 2004); played golf with Kaset and Issarapong; and was from time to time a low-key but knowledgeable presence at fine wine tastings.

In 2000, Suchinda broke his silence and called publicly for the release of all reports relating to the May 1992 events. 'I would like full disclosure of every report on the crackdown, especially the army's own inquiry,' he told the *Bangkok Post* in June of that year. His call was supported by the then army chief, Surayud Chulanont, and Issarapong. The defence ministry report ran to 714 pages. However, when it was released after much public pressure, more than 60 per cent had been redacted.[16] Suchinda evidently felt a better explanation would have been in his interests.

Looking back, Anand's concern is not that he could be accused of letting the military off the hook in 1992. That was a failing of the elected governments that followed. 'I should have done more to curb corruption within the military,' he reflects. Even so, there is a common perception that Anand's two cabinets were the least corrupt and in many respects the most effective Thailand has seen: that he was the best prime minister Thailand never elected.

'I am almost 100 per cent certain that while I was prime minister among cabinet members on the civilian side there was no corruption,' he says. 'Bad policies take two to three years to show up. The effects of corruption show up straight away.'

Image repair

Following the dramatic scenes in May, Thailand's image was tainted more by the military's violence against civilians than by any perception of corruption. King Bhumibol's admonishment of Chamlong and Suchinda on the palace carpet followed scenes of terrible unrest and bloodshed. Thailand was on the verge of an economic boom, and investors and foreign visitors needed to be reassured. There was an urgent need to send out positive images and messages, and to restore confidence. But pictures of everything looking normal have never made for particularly interesting television.

Anand instructed the Tourism Authority of Thailand (TAT) to call tenders for a public relations campaign. 'I think this was probably the first time a Thai prime minister said, "Let's do this professionally with a communications programme,"' says Hasan Basar, who at the time co-managed Presko, Thailand's first dedicated public-relations company. It had been established in the 1960s by Esko Pajasalmi, a Thai-speaking Finnish missionary who was still chairman, and by this time was co-managed by Esko's son, Norman.

Presko was to execute The World, Our Guest (TWOG) campaign. It was the brainchild of Bert Van Walbeek, who was chairing a TAT marketing working group and the 1992 Recovery Committee. Van Walbeek's strategy was quite simple: open Thailand up to the world, and say, 'Come and be our guests.' The programme was hastily formulated in late June and early July to tie in with the celebrations of Queen Sirikit's 60th birthday in August. The support of the entire hospitality industry was enlisted, and some 700 hotels came on board. It was to be more than a simple marketing campaign with discounts and giveaway nights or special packages.

'It was not a tourism programme to increase arrivals,' says Basar, 'but a public relations programme to change perceptions. Showing people partying on the streets would implant the idea that everything was okay again. We had to go back on the very same channels that delivered the bad news with as powerful a message as possible – with something else that stuck in people's minds. The old experience had to be pushed back into history. That is how you eliminate this negative stuff – not by diving in and trying to scrub it.'

The campaign had to be prepared and executed immediately after the bidding was completed in early July even though the contract was not signed until the middle of the month. TAT was simply unused to moving at such a pace, and showed little interest in the corrective public-relations programme. Funding was therefore an immediate problem, and with time so short Presko raised the matter directly with Government House. The younger Pajasalmi and Basar were summoned two days later for a meeting with Anand, a senior tourism official, and the official's two assistants.

With an unlit cigar in hand, Anand read the riot act to the TAT official. 'It was probably one of the harshest attacks I have ever seen delivered by one adult to another in civilised company,' Basar recalls. 'Anand was completely unambiguous about what he was doing, and why he was being so tough. He wanted to know what was going on, and why nothing was happening.'

'What sort of a man are you?' Anand excoriated the official. 'Our country is in national crisis, and you don't sign a contract when the money has already been transferred to you?'

The two PR men watched in disbelief as the dressing down continued for what seemed like an eternity. 'It got so bad, the official placed his hands under his legs and looked up at the ceiling,' Basar recalls. 'He must have regretted bringing his two subordinates along.'

Anand then asked Basar about the programme, wagging his cigar. 'I had not spoken 30 seconds when Khun Anand said, "That's an excellent programme. Approved!"' Basar recalls. 'It was not a long meeting, but Anand got the ball moving. It was probably one of 50 hugely important things he was trying to manage at the time. He made his decision very clear, with no ambiguity about whether this was going to happen. He also said, "In two weeks, I want a report." Everything got done on time, and we were paid. In terms of management style, he listened, he responded. He had a sense of responsibility for delivering – ownership of the project. He was not just the prime minister who nodded, and that's it. He was also responsible for the outcome.'

Basar recalls the The World, Our Guest campaign as a Herculean task. 'Once Anand felt the project was in relatively competent hands, and had heard a story that made sense about the theory and what we wanted to do, he just let it run. He knew people were making up their minds about Thailand, and that the country had to have a hand in that process.'

The World, Our Guest was subsequently recognised at the annual World Travel Mart in London for its ambition and effectiveness. Indeed, it was compared favourably to a campaign by British Airways to get people flying again after the First Gulf War.

Run-in with the law

After King Mongkut (r.1851–1868) signed the Bowring Treaty with Great Britain in 1855, extraterritorial courts were developed in Siam that lasted well into the 20th century. Thirteen more 'unequal treaties' with European nations, and another with Japan, were signed subsequently. Although disadvantageous in important respects to Siam, these courts and treaties were important to the conduct of trade. Siam's ancient laws were replaced by modern codes drafted between King Chulalongkorn's reign (r.1868–1910) and the 1930s. These were influenced by the codified systems of countries such as France, Germany, and Japan rather than the Anglo-American common-law system. The extraterritorial courts were abolished by new treaties concluded in the 1930s.

Because Siam never fell directly under any colonial yoke, the judiciary evolved idiosyncratically. Judges are appointed by the independent Judicial Commission to serve in the various courts. These comprise the courts of first instance, the courts of appeal, and the Supreme Court in Bangkok, which is the court of last resort and holds sway over all courts in the nation's 77 provinces. Latterly, a constitutional court (1997) and an administrative court (2000) have been added, and there also exist a central bankruptcy court (1999), a central tax court, a central intellectual property and international trade court, juvenile and family courts, and labour courts. There are also military courts, which become much more influential during periods of military rule. Under the contempt of court legislation – part of Thailand's suite of ferocious defamation laws – it is illegal to belittle or ridicule the courts. Rulings can only be critiqued in measured terms, although there is more latitude when it comes to the Constitutional Court. 'You can criticise but not reprimand or scold the courts – you can't abuse them,' says Phongthep Thepkanjana, a former judge and deputy prime minister. Anand still finds it shocking that the judiciary cannot always be critiqued constructively, and is disturbed by the lack of awareness of the need for change. 'It's a very archaic system,' he says.

There was also some muddling. In times past, a few senior judges were educated in France and Germany. More were trained in Britain under a quite different system, incorporating common law and trial by jury. 'I don't know if that was one of the weaknesses in the Thai court system,' says Anand.

Anand's connection to Thailand's legal establishment was somewhat tenuous. Although he had studied law at Cambridge, he was well aware of his limited understanding of Thailand's legal system, which he views as something of a 'hodgepodge'. 'The Thai system is topsy-turvy – it is neither here nor there,' he says. Sodsee's grandfather, a judge who had studied law at Cambridge, was influential in developing the Thai justice system. One of Anand's sisters had married a judge, but he was conscious of how few people he knew in the judiciary. He recalls judges in the mid-20th century being part of a close-knit community sealed off from the outside world. There has been limited reform of the judiciary in the past 60 or 70 years. Even so, Anand was unprepared for the high price he would pay for this lack of familiarity.

For his first cabinet, Anand had picked Prapasna Auychai for minister of justice. Prapasna was three years his senior, and they had known each other moderately well in England, where Prapasna had studied law and been called to the bar. As a judge, Prapasna had a reputation for honesty and integrity, and had served as vice president of the Supreme Court before his retirement. However, the Supreme Court chose its own judges, and Prapasna was no longer a part of it.

Anand was broadly aware that the public impression of the justice system was poor, and of the rumours of corruption, but he was completely unprepared for the intense rivalries between different factions within the judiciary. The competition to get judges elected from different sides was fierce.

'I picked Prapasna not realising the disputes and factions the Ministry of Justice was suffering,' Anand recalls. Indeed, the ministry was barely functioning because of the factional undercurrents. Prapasna on one side wanted to weaken the grip of another faction, which brought him into conflict with Praman Chansue, the permanent secretary and future president and chief justice of the Supreme Court.

Prapasna vetoed Praman's selection for Supreme Court president, preferring Sawad Chotipanich. The normal process required the minister of justice to nominate judges, and for the Judicial Commission to then elect, which was meant to ensure underlying consensus. There followed a wrangle over the composition of the Judicial Commission after some of its members reached retirement. Against this highly politicised backdrop, the promotion of a group of judges got held up by the change of government after the March 1992 election.

Appointments in all quarters of the public sector were constantly being forwarded from Government House for King Bhumibol's signature, and lists of judges went through about every six months. New appointments were generally handled by other members of the cabinet. 'I allowed my ministers a high degree of freedom,' Anand recalls. 'I didn't micro-manage, particularly in matters that were beyond my knowledge and expertise. The foreign ministry was my cup of tea.'

A list of new judges arrived in the last week of the first Anand government, when it was already in caretaker mode. With everything in the prime minister's office in limbo, the names were never put before Anand. The list was still sitting in an in-tray when Suchinda's government came into office with Sawat Khumprakob serving briefly as minister of justice. Despite the upheavals in May, the list was sent to the palace, and would normally have been routinely reviewed by members of the Privy Council. In this instance, however, it was not sent to the Privy Council because two judges on the list were the sons of privy councillors.

When Anand came back into office unexpectedly, the list was still in the hands of *ML* Thawisan Ladawan, the king's principal private secretary, and had not been signed. Procedurally, appointments forwarded from the cabinet must receive the royal assent within the same term of office. If there is a change of cabinet, or an election, all documents need to be returned to the new government for its consideration. In this instance, the list of judges was returned to the prime minister's office for forwarding to the justice ministry. It was sent initially to Kasem Suwanakul, one of Anand's new deputy prime ministers with responsibility for the justice ministry.

'It did not come to me,' Anand recalls. 'I had nothing to do with it – I am not sure I was even aware of it because all the papers that had been returned did not come to my office, or to my personal attention, but to the deputy prime ministers in charge of various portfolios. It was a bureaucratic procedure, so when I was taken to court I knew I was not in the wrong.'

Kasem had sufficient authority to simply resubmit the list to the palace, but instead returned it to the justice ministry. He was new to the job, and this was a prudent move. The situation at the justice ministry had changed yet again, however. When he constituted his new cabinet, Anand decided not to reappoint Prapasna. 'I thought he was part of the problem, too,' he recalls. With all the infighting, he suspected 'a lot of inbreeding' in the ministry and the judiciary, with officials and judges living in worlds apart from the rest of society. Anand therefore decided to appoint an outsider. He settled on Wichian Wattanakun, who had been deputy foreign minister in his first cabinet, and ambassador to Tokyo for seven years from 1980. 'The idea was to bring in a new person,' says Anand. Although he was a career diplomat, Wichian was a Thammasat University law graduate and had studied further in France.

When Wichian reviewed the list, he got drawn into the feud between the factions. 'So long as these could be managed by the cabinet minister, I never interfered – it was up to them,' says Anand. 'If it became unmanageable at the ministerial level, then I would join in. When I started to get involved personally on this occasion, I became a target of criticism.'

A key problem seemed to be the 12-person Judicial Commission (eight elected, four *ex officio*), which appointed judges. Anand came to the conclusion that the committee should be dissolved and a new one constituted with some outside blood to make it more relevant, and better protected against dubious individuals. 'Ill feelings were very prevalent at that time,' Anand recalls. 'We thought if we could reform the commission, we could make everything more transparent.'

Anand's plan was to introduce four outsiders. 'Our reform efforts were opposed not only by the judiciary but also the deans of all the law schools. I was very much criticised by them – they felt I was overstretching the issue,' he recalls. Among the legal minds who remonstrated with him at the time were Phongthep Thepkanjana, a former judge; Borwornsak Uwanno, the dean of a law school; and three other academics. 'It was a cliquish thing,' says Anand. At one point, he invited five judges to meet with him, but it resolved nothing.

Wissanu recalls being invited to Anand's home for lunch or dinner on a few occasions, usually to discuss the Supreme Court issue. Anand asked him to get some discreet advice from Sanya Dhammasakdi, the president of the Privy Council, on how to proceed with the matter. Sanya asked Wissanu who had sent him. Wissanu did not say it was Anand, but who else would Sanya have presumed? 'I was his student before,' Wissanu recalls. 'Sanya was very neutral. He gave advice as a judge who knew the traditions and habits of the courts very well.'

Wissanu took the view that Anand could simply wait for the list of judges to be resubmitted, and that there was no reason for him to be involved pre-emptively in adjusting the selection mechanism. Anand considered the matter urgent, and time was against him. Controversially, he wanted to pass an emergency decree with royal assent and produce a fast-track solution. 'I don't know who suggested it or told him how to do it, but it was not me,' says Wissanu, who firmly opposed the idea. 'I should warn you that this is not safe because there is not an emergency,' Wissanu told Anand. 'There is no war or riots.' With his legal background, Wissanu firmly believed in the separation of powers, and did not think the government – particularly an unelected one – should become embroiled with the judiciary. Wissanu also wanted to be recused from the whole issue for personal reasons. His brother-in-law was the secretary of Praman Chansue, and Anand always teased him about being a spy.

More seriously, Anand told Wissanu to go off and think his arguments through. Wissanu returned the next day, and laid out his arguments. 'I don't want to convince you,' Anand told him. 'I want to find the loopholes I may be confronted with in the future. You are the presumed enemy, and I am looking for the weaknesses in my story.' After a while, however, Wissanu found himself wondering who he was to question the prime minister. 'Excellency, it is my duty to caution you,' he said. 'I have done this already, and that is enough.'

Feeling emboldened, Anand was not dissuaded. It was discussed at a cabinet meeting with all non-cabinet members told to leave the room. Only Wissanu remained behind as a 'resource person'. Wissanu was closely questioned by some of the ministers, who concurred with his arguments. They were with Wissanu, and their recommendation was to send the list to the king for signing and not get involved with emergency decrees to dissolve and reconstitute the Judicial Council.

'Are you happy now?' Anand asked Wissanu. 'I am not happy,' Wissanu replied. 'It is my duty to protect the government, and this is not safe.'

'I felt that we were fighting against time,' says Anand, reflecting on his bid to push through an emergency decree to reform the Judicial Commission. 'It was festering over a year.' In the end, the elected parliament rejected the decree. Wissanu had advised Anand that there was no emergency to justify issuing a decree, but how the vote was produced is unclear. 'There was a lot of lobbying from both sides of judges, but we don't know why parliament voted it down,' says Phongthep.

'The debate highlighted the need for reform. The situation is much better now,' says Anand. 'A lot of my critics have changed their minds, and I have no enemies in judicial circles.' With hindsight, Anand believes a significant part of the argument was to do with the characters involved. 'The problem with Thai society is everything is always personalised,' he says. 'As time goes by, you lose sight of the substance and issues.' He believes people in Thailand have a particular proclivity for assuming personal interests must always be in play – as in the case of Saha Union's decision to become an independent power producer after he had left office. This makes them susceptible to conspiracy theories. 'They cannot believe somebody else has a different mentality – they fail to see that others can do things without friendship or cronyism. It's a mindset among some Thais.'

In the end, Anand's problem with senior members of the judiciary was not policy-related but administrative. After he left office, one judge in Praman's camp filed a criminal case against him on the grounds that he had been mistreated and his career damaged. On paper, it was a personal complaint, not one lodged by a body of judges. 'That's how I got into trouble,' says Anand. 'That justice sued me for not having presented the list to the king for signature.'

The complaint could just as easily have been lodged against his deputy prime minister, Kasem Suwanakul, who had full signing authority. The case was eventually dismissed in the court of first instance, but only after four years during which Anand had to appear from time to time because he was facing a criminal charge. For a civil charge, he would not have had to attend every hearing.

Sanya tried to mediate at one point later on by inviting Anand and Praman to lunch. 'You have to make an apology to me,' Praman told Anand, who refused point-blank. He felt he had nothing to apologise for. Thawisan, the king's principal private secretary, and Wissanu, Anand's own secretary general, were both called as witnesses for the prosecution, but with no benefit to the plaintiff. In their view, Anand had not been obstructive. 'I testified according to the truth,' Wissanu recalls. 'They dismissed the case citing my testimony. Khun Anand did nothing wrong.'

'They both cleared me because I was not involved in the process,' says Anand. 'It was cumbersome and rather inconvenient for me.' Phongthep believes the prominence of the people involved certainly made the case interesting, but that there was no long-term negative damage to the judiciary.[17]

For Wissanu, the experience of being summoned to testify in court against his former boss was disturbing. 'Anand used the term "presumed enemy" with many people,' he recalls. It was simply a part of the way Anand interacted and jousted with government officials and others as he formulated ideas and strategies.

Wissanu remembers Anand's friendliness to staff, and how on his final day in office the departing prime minister toured Government House and the surrounding buildings to say farewell to everyone. Wissanu was startled when Anand entered his office that day without warning. 'Is this the room in which you conspire against me?' Anand joked. 'I took it very seriously, but he laughed and sat down,' Wissanu recalls. Many years later, Wissanu sent Anand a New Year card thanking him for everything he had learned from him over the years. Anand sent a note back: 'That is because you are a good student, not because I am a good teacher.'

The people speak

The general election of 13 September 1992 succeeded where the election in March had so spectacularly failed: it facilitated an orderly and peaceful transfer of power, and created a government sufficiently stable to last until 1995. The fact that this outcome had been finessed by unelected individuals including Anand did not make it any less democratic. The controversial and often maligned NPKC constitution of 1992 managed to produce two more elected governments, in 1995 and 1996. Both were flawed, but with the aid of coalitions and reshuffles the latter saw out the 20th century.

The military-backed Samakkitham Party had dissolved itself in the wake of Black May. The September election tilted the balance away from so-called 'devil' parties in favour of supposed 'angel' parties, but not by the margins liberal observers predicted. The reality of Thailand's political landscape remained hard to read. With the exception of the disgraced military, most of the old familiar faces were back in play, including Chamlong who was strongly tipped in some polls to become prime minister. Others predicted Chatichai Choonhavan would be premier, aboard his new vehicle, Chart Pattana, the National Development Party, which would remain among the top four strongest-polling parties for more than a decade. After the May events, and the public humiliation of Somboon Rahong, Chatichai had dumped 'satanic' Chart Thai. Chart Pattana managed to beat it into fourth place on votes but not seats – winning 60 compared to Chart Thai's

77. Perhaps Chatichai, who died in 1998, could have spared himself the trouble.

'The distinction between "angels" and "devils" meant little outside Bangkok and some of the major provincial towns,' notes one academic. 'The middle-class character of the anti-Suchinda movement has often since been overstated, but Black May had been for the most part an urban affair.'[18]

Even with the Anand-inspired PollWatch on its second outing, and an army of 60,000 poll monitors recruited and dispatched – some soon to be put in fear for their lives – money politics was still in play. A few days ahead of the poll, the Bank of Thailand reported ominously that in the first nine days of September 1992 nearly six billion baht was withdrawn from banks – up 15 per cent compared to the same period the previous year when there was no election. The inference was that some 780 million baht (over US$30 million) was withdrawn for election-related reasons.[19] That was likely only a fraction of the total election slush money, and hardly an earth-shattering amount. A dozen or so parties were competing for 360 seats, after all, and each candidate was allowed to spend a million baht campaigning. The parties were also still relatively impoverished by the March election, particularly Chavalit's New Aspiration, which slumped from nearly ten million votes and 72 seats to just under 6.6 million votes and 51 seats. It was an exasperating state of affairs for Chavalit, who in his speeches made much of having retired early from the military to pursue a legitimate political career and become prime minister.

PollWatch continued to press for the public display of electoral rolls to try and tackle the problem of 'ghost' voters. It investigated a familiar raft of election law violations that ranged from outright bribery and purchase of identity cards, to lavish banquets, and paid-for visits to casinos and massage parlours. The new democracy watchdog's primary aim was to get voters to the polling stations. The Public Relations Department also ran a campaign to bring out voters, and for the first time parties were allotted fixed mass-media slots for campaign broadcasts.

Also for the first time, military bases were opened up – not that 'angel' parties were always well received. Following the transfers of senior military figures in August, much had been made about the military removing itself from politics, becoming more professional, and focusing on defence of the nation. The new supreme commander, Air Chief Marshal Voranart Apicharee, made a point of ordering all military personnel to vote freely, proving that with even with the best will in the world old habits die hard. It was a bit late for the generals to start experimenting with public relations, and they would maintain a downward trajectory for the rest of the 1990s.[20]

After the heady days of May, the election revealed once more the shortcomings of Thailand's political class. Its performance was often underwhelming according to author David Murray's detailed account *Angels and Devils*:

> The election campaign in general was lacklustre. Few parties put forward coherent party platforms; the 'devilish' parties and their leaders (apart from Chatichai) kept their heads down and went about doing what they did best – buying votes; the pro-democracy parties were diverted by squabbles amongst themselves; few issues of great moment were raised; and there was little coherent structure to the electioneering. The public's response was a general sense of apathy, and it was feared that even fewer would vote in September than had done in March.[21]

That concern was overly pessimistic. Turnout was up to 61.6 per cent from March's 59.2 per cent, with spoiled and invalid ballots down marginally to under 2.6 per cent, although that was still poor compared to the latter half of the 1980s. With 79 seats – 13 more than had been predicted in polls – Chuan Leekpai, as head of the Democrat Party, was able to form a comfortable 208-seat coalition comprising the New Aspiration, Chart Pattana, Palang Tham, and Social Action parties.

Chuan would often be criticised later for indecisiveness and a lack of vision, but he came to the premiership as an experienced politician. A lawyer of humble origin in the South, he had no family, military, or bureaucratic connections underpinning his rise to power. This lent credibility to his victory and to the election process. Thailand was without doubt back on a democratic track. Anand's short second government had served its purpose.

CHAPTER 16

FROM COURT TO CONSTITUTION
(1993–1997)

Days of trial

Anand's problems with senior members of the judiciary returned to haunt him long after he left office. In 1993, a former Supreme Court judge, Prawit Khamparat, filed a criminal complaint of nonfeasance against Anand, Wichian Wattanakun (former minister of justice), Prasert Boonsri (former permanent secretary at the justice ministry), and Sawad Chotipanich (former president of the Supreme Court). The accusation was that they had delayed his promotion as a regional appeals court chief justice sitting in Bangkok approved by the Judicial Commission on 11 May 1992. His complaint alleged a failure to secure the necessary royal assent before September 1992, by which date he had reached the mandatory retirement age.

While Anand had tangled with Praman Chansue, the future president of the Supreme Court who had been appointed right after Anand left office for the second time, this case was not overtly linked to their earlier differences. Prawit's contention was that his new appointment should have been confirmed in June after Anand returned to office. Prison terms of up to ten years were in the balance with five years usually handed down, though nobody expected matters to go that far. Much of the bad blood stemmed from Anand's failed attempt to change the composition of the Judicial Commission, which had ended up being blocked in parliament. Given the limited time available to him, some questioned why Anand had even attempted this. 'If I had a chance to do it all over again, I would do it differently,' he conceded in a television interview at the time.

Anand had recently given a talk in the Philippines about political development.

Weng Tojirakarn and San Hatteerat of the Federation of Democracy wanted him to broadcast some programmes about Thailand's problems with Jermsak Pinthong as host. The broadcasts contributed to a significant display of support for Anand. The month before he was due in court, Anand's neighbour Sumet Jumsai, the Anglophile architect who had draped their street with flags when he was appointed prime minister the second time, decided to rally informally behind Anand. He was joined by MR Sukhumbhand Paribatra.

Sumet approached top diplomats such as MR Kasemsomosorn Kasemsri and Vitthya Vejjajiva, and also Suthep Bulakul from the old English student network. This networking developed more or less spontaneously into the 'Friends of Anand' movement. Thousands of people wanted to join, and made enquiries about membership fees. With his office and fax machines overwhelmed, Sumet reassured everyone that he only needed names and addresses, not money – and then fretted over what to do with all the unsolicited donations that had poured in.

Sumet believed it was important to support Anand, who he believed had done so much for Thailand's international standing, if lessons were to be learned. 'Look at his fate,' he said. 'It was almost as if every time the country was in crisis, Anand's life would be affected.'

Sympathetic foreigners also came on board, including a group of ambassadors. Sukhumbhand, Suthep, Noranit Setthabut, and Mechai Viravaidya structured working groups from the private sector; they also arranged for Thammasat University to get involved, and created awareness by lobbying the media. For some who stepped up, there was a lingering sense of guilt. It was linked to October 1976 and the Thammasat University events, when Anand had been attacked for his work at the foreign ministry, and most had not lifted a finger to help him. 'We also learned from the case of Puey Ungphakorn, who was a good man,' said Sumet. 'We did not want to stay quiet because it is a shame people don't get support when they are in crisis after doing so much for the country.'

Some started wearing 'We love Anand Panyarachun' badges.[1] When Anand arrived at court in April with his daughters at his side, over 1,000 people were waiting, including relatives of victims of the May 1992 violence. The next hearing was scheduled for late May.

The legal process was to drag on for three years. Some politicians also were antagonistic towards Anand. Chuan Leekpai's coalition government had usurped the so-called devil parties from Suchinda's disastrous, short-lived government.

Now in opposition, the Social Action Party's Montri Pongpanich and others tried to pick holes in the legacies of the Anand administrations. Wattana Asavahame and Nipon Wisityutasart of Chart Thai questioned the sale of Thai Oil, the state refinery, for eight billion baht. Wattana offered to buy it back for 15 billion.

Busarakham Nilavajara, Anand's personal assistant at Saha Union, found herself having to cope with the unexpected wave of support, with hundreds of people contacting the office directly. 'They were ordinary people from all walks of life,' she recalls. She would vet the people who could actually come and meet Anand. Many of the hundreds of letters he received were answered individually. She remembers people coming up from the provinces by train to attend the court hearing. One of Anand's most loyal supporters in 1976, Pridi Boonyobhas, had by this time been posted abroad again. 'Whenever I was in Bangkok, I went to court,' he recalls. He knew Anand's personality well, and how difficult his old boss found it to keep still. In court, however, Anand was impassive, almost serene. 'He was very calm – I was surprised,' Pridi recalls. 'I think he thought there was no reason to show any feelings. If he had, they would have taken advantage.'

One reason for Anand's silence was a measure of boredom. Although he had studied law at Cambridge, he often found it hard to concentrate on the protracted and arcane court proceedings that ultimately led to his acquittal. While it dissipated over the course of the trial, the Friends of Anand movement had lifted his spirits. 'Most of them I did not know personally, but they felt I was being victimised unfairly,' he recalls. 'It helped my family, and I was happy because it meant there were still people with principles in Thailand.'

People's constitution

Anand and his first cabinet had had no collective involvement in drafting the military's 1992 constitution, which had formed an important part of the backdrop to the violence of May 1992. At one point during the drafting, former Prime Minister Chatichai Choonhavan requested an audience with King Bhumibol and offered to oversee work on an alternative constitution using Borwornsak Uwanno as the main drafter.

Borwornsak was far from enamoured with this idea, and not tempted by the offer of Chatichai's apartment in London as a place to do the work. Borwornsak had been one of the former prime minister's closest advisers, and was the man carrying his briefcase at the time of the plane hijacking during the coup that toppled his government. He had no involvement with either of Anand's governments, and could see trouble brewing as a consequence of the military-drafted constitution. After the constitution's promulgation in early 1992, he secured himself a four-month fellowship in Paris, and was there when violence erupted in May.

Later, during the first Chuan government, Borwornsak joined the house committee for revising the constitution, which had been set up after one of political activist Chalard Worachat's hunger strikes. Marut Bunnag was then president of parliament, and Prawase Wasi chaired the Commission on Democratic Reform.

'In this country, we don't like the word "reform",' notes Borwornsak. The prime minister at the time was certainly not much associated with reform or progressive tendencies. Banharn Silpa-archa had replaced Chatichai as leader of the Chart Thai Party. He had made his fortune in construction during the Vietnam War and was always staunchly pro-US. A consummate pork-barrel, upcountry politician, he was first appointed to the national legislative assembly in 1974, and from 1976 was properly elected to parliament 11 times.[2]

During his election campaign in 1995, Banharn promised to carry on Prawase's reform work. One of the most important developments during Banharn's elected, but troubled, 1995–6 government was the passage of a constitutional amendment that opened the way to establishing a constitutional drafting assembly, a body intended to somehow discern the will of the people and produce an enduring constitution. Although the drafting process did go ahead at this time, the signs were not propitious and Banharn himself seldom enjoyed good press – as this report at the time of his death shows:

> Banharn, or members of his government, were accused – sometimes unfairly – of accepting bribes for arms contracts and bank licences, looting a bank of more than US$3 billion, appointing incompetent cronies to the cabinet and state enterprises, firing corruption fighters, politicising the central bank, engaging in land scams and illegal logging, muzzling the press and blocking political reform.[3]

Banharn certainly provided plenty of colour: he locked himself out of his hotel room in his underwear during a visit to the United Nations in New York; he referred to Queen Elizabeth as Elizabeth Taylor; he reintroduced the ten baht note to stimulate the grassroots economy; and he made Cambodia's two prime ministers hold hands publicly during a political spat that eventually ended in bloodshed. Economic mismanagement on his watch was, rightly or wrongly, considered a factor in the collapse of the baht in 1997 under his successor Chavalit Yongchaiyudh, and the Asian financial crisis that ensued. He left office in 1997 when his coalition fractured. The Democrat Party had earlier tabled a no-confidence motion calling into question his father's nationality, but that was defeated.

On account of his ethnicity and his devotion to his constituents in Suphanburi, Banharn's many nicknames included Deng Xiaoharn and the Dragon of Suphan. Located in a rich rice-growing area northwest of Bangkok, Suphanburi was duly dubbed Banharnburi. The classic Thai political patron-client relationship Banharn developed in his home constituency gave him a robust operating platform, but it amounted almost to a cult of personality. The first names of Banharn and his wife, Khunying Jamsai, were stamped on everything from bus shelters to litter bins. Anand only came to know Banharn personally much later when the two would be seated together at royal ceremonies as former prime ministers. Like Anand, Banharn always attended such events.

'One has to give credit to Banharn, the prime minister at the time,' says Anand. 'Being a traditionalist, one would have assumed that he would resist any attempts to change the constitution or widen its context. I don't know whether it was for his own personal reasons, or whether he was persuaded by the force of arguments by the more liberal wing of the establishment, but he was instrumental in amending one provision to create a constituent assembly to draft a new constitution.'

That process spanned 1995 and 1996, with various academics and non-governmental organisations contributing ideas. Anand was approached to play a part quite early on. He expressed some interest, but not to the extent of wanting to be directly involved. Apart from anything, his expertise was limited. 'I had never read any past constitutions of Thailand,' he admits. His first practical exposure had been as prime minister when he tested the limits of his power and executive authority, and learned about the interaction between the government and legislature.

There had been constant talk of amending the constitution throughout the 1990s since Chatichai's government, and of the need to strike a new, more liberal balance of power between the three pillars of state under the monarchy: the government, legislature, and judiciary. Conservatives feared it would raise undeliverable expectations. 'Some thinkers began to expound concepts pertaining to more rights for the individual, greater access to information, justice, resources, environmental protection,' Anand recalls. 'Many of these ideas did not exist 30 or 40 years ago.' There was at this time a shift in the establishment's mindset, a recognition that something more in tune with the modern world was required. A way had to be found to balance effective prime ministerial power with more participation at lower levels, breaking 'the cycle of Thai politics'. Study groups and commissions had been at work, and academics and the media had been stirring awareness and interest. There was a broader willingness to engage in discussion on constitutional reform to improve civic participation and guarantee ordinary citizens their rights.

Representatives for the Constitution Drafting Assembly were put forward from all 72 provinces at the time. A former judge, Phongthep Thepkanjana was an unusual inclusion, but he was elected with one of the highest votes. Another 17 – mostly academics, political scientists, lawyers, economists – were selected by parliament for their expertise in different areas. Anand was included in the latter group because of his recent political experience. The total assembly numbered 99, and included no military or active civil servants, except academics.

The assembly's first order of business was to elect a president, but there was to be no campaigning. It was purely a reputational affair. Anand was one of three nominees. He came second to Uthai Pimchaichon, a veteran politician and a former president of parliament with excellent grass-roots connections. 'I suppose some people thought I was disappointed,' Anand recalls of his brush with the ballot box. 'Far from it. I was rather happy because I knew in advance what the job entailed.'

The following day, Anand was approached by two legal experts who were delighted that he had not been elected as the assembly's president. They wanted him instead to chair the actual drafting committee, which had only 25 members. Anand was elected committee chairman, with Borwornsak Uwanno as his secretary and Phongthep as deputy secretary.

Borwornsak had been drafted in as an expert in public law. He was happy to act in a supporting role on the drafting committee, and voted for Anand's chairmanship himself. 'Anand was not a constitutionalist, but he was a person with vision and experience,' Borwornsak recalls. He compares Anand in some respects to Chatichai, particularly in the way both men knew instinctively how to react to situations. 'They both treat people with respect. I learned how to be patient, and to listen to people with stupid ideas without insulting them.'

Anand's chairmanship of the drafting committee was one of the few occasions when he was elected rather than appointed to a powerful position. He approached the task in a completely different manner from running his cabinet, when he had taken personal responsibility for every decision. Drafting a new, representative constitution was a quite different undertaking. It was to be a departure from its 15 predecessors, all of which were handed down in one way or another.

Anand wanted to be in charge of the proceedings as a facilitator, ensuring that they ran smoothly and on time. He wanted to stir a wider sense of involvement, and refrained almost entirely from expressing his own opinions during drafting sessions. There were only two particularly contentious issues relating to religion and education in which he took part in a vote. 'That required a lot of patience,' he recalls. Considerable restraint was required when speakers went on for one or two hours. When the process became interminable, Anand sometimes threatened to keep everyone up all night.

He chose not to wear a suit and tie, another departure from the grey apparel of his premierships. Many members of the committee insisted on attending in suits, however, adding a certain formality to the proceedings. Among the 25, a conservative faction and a progressive faction emerged. There were also some personality conflicts in play. 'Whatever you do must be trusted by the two opposing sides, and I remained sincerely friendly to all,' Anand recalls.

'He worked well with people whose selection he had not been involved with,' recalls Phongthep. 'He was good at getting the members of the committee to think and reach a resolution.' Anand used the media, making the proceedings open to the press to ensure everything was on the record. These were heavily reported on each day and kept very much in the public eye to encourage more productive debate. 'It meant the members of this drafting committee could not talk nonsense or flip-flop,' Anand says. 'I coined the word transparency in Thai – *prongsai*. The media behaved very well – they were a great help.'

The draft constitution had to be approved by both houses of parliament. If that failed, under the terms of the existing constitution, it could be put to national referendum. 'My firm belief,' Anand says, 'is that if you persuade the public to be with you, you can overcome any parliamentary opposition.'

Government bodies were allowed to send representatives to listen, but unlike the media they could not just walk in on the hearings. They also could not contribute verbally. Their participation was limited to the submission of memoranda and position papers. Had this been a parliamentary subcommittee at work, it could not have completed its task within the 240 days allotted. 'There are so many procedural rules that could stall or subvert the drafting process,' Anand says of normal procedures. He always sought consensus. 'By consensus, I mean there should be no opposition – you could abstain,' he says.

The two issues that caused Anand the most difficulty were related to religion and education. Both arose out of hearings conducted in virtually every province by Uthai, who was credited with doing a good job. One issue was the inclusion of Buddhism as the national religion, a notion which King Bhumibol, as a defender of all faiths, had always opposed in the background. Making Buddhism a state religion would have affected interfaith relations, risking sectarian conflict. However, Uthai had been quite receptive to this idea; he saw it as a way of enlisting the support of the influential *sangha*, the Buddhist clergy.

'There was not much substantive discussion of this,' Anand recalls. 'Quietly, I was working against it. Most felt obliged to raise the issue because of what they had heard from the public hearings.' Uthai had been lobbied during the hearings by both monks and lay people. He was looking for votes at some point in the future and believed 200,000 Buddhist monks would be able to swing a referendum one day. In the end, the only drafting committee meeting held *in camera*, without media present, was about religion. 'There were no outbursts,' Anand recalls. 'It was reasoned, logical debate with no accusations or name calling, and the proposal was defeated.'

An issue on which Anand failed to prevail, however, was the fundamentally undemocratic requirement that all members of parliament should have university degrees. This was not some elitist proposal to keep the uneducated masses in check. Far from it. During his public consultations in the provinces, Uthai had found very strong public support for the idea – 75–80 per cent among those canvassed. 'The irony was that we who had BAs, MAs, and PhDs fundamentally opposed the requirement,' Anand recalls. 'How many farmers have degrees? How can you exclude all these people?' With nearly half the population coming from farming families, the degree requirement effectively denied them direct representation.

Anand could not fathom why provincial people should feel so strongly about something he believed was so contrary to their interests. Uthai's interpretation was that poor farmers expected their problems to be handled by provincial officials and governors, and members of parliament. They therefore wanted to be represented in parliament by people who could stand up to centralised power. Such people were pictured in uniforms with medals and sashes, and all had degrees. Rural folk, Uthai said, believed they needed people with comparable qualifications to represent them. This might have made some pragmatic sense, but in practice it meant that a huge swathe of the population was marginalising itself; it also demonstrated how limited the popular understanding of participatory democracy was. 'That was one of the few matters on which I requested a vote, and we lost in both the committee and the assembly,' Anand recalls. One of the unforeseen downsides of the new requirement was to be shameless cheating by politicians who, come election time, would need a degree from some institution or another to carry on.

Another thorny issue was disallowing members of parliament from serving concurrently as ministers, as in France. Political parties saw this rule as running counter to their interests. Anand also put this to the vote, calling out names in public to hold everyone accountable. The provision was voted through. 'If it had been a secret ballot, we would have lost,' he says. 'When you expose them to TV, people change their behaviour.'

One of the aims of the new constitution was to do away with the small parties and individuals who fed on money politics, shifting their loyalties whenever opportunities arose to recoup their investment. Smaller players also did not benefit from the party list system that was being introduced to provide an element of proportional representation. This was one way of ensuring the election of senior members of big parties, and spared them the hard graft of campaigning. Anand had personal reservations about the ban on independent members of parliament, which he felt undermined democratic credentials. Another contentious issue was decentralisation, including the roles of provinces and local *amphurs*. In terms of democratic furniture, the senate was henceforth to be elected; there would be a constitutional court; and election and human rights commissions were established; the office of auditor general, part of the civil service, was brought into parliamentary purview. These were all major innovations.

Thailand's first Election Commission had not only a political mandate but also significant resources. It aimed to improve the electoral process by making the public more aware of its significance, creating political consciousness, and helping people to understand how they could vote tactically – how they could make their vote count. It was about promoting 'the spirit of a democratic party', according to PollWatch's Gothom Arya, one of the first election commissioners. On its first outing in the 2001 general election, the commission would investigate over half the senate for transgressions.

The adoption process was not seamless. One day, many of the 72 provincial representatives revolted against the drafting committee. They were unhappy with the way the draft had been completed, and wanted everyone replaced except Anand and Borwornsak. Anand had overslept and arrived after the usual 9am start, and Borwornsak informed him that the rest of the committee had been voted off. 'I cannot accept this kind of conspiracy,' Anand declared loudly to reporters, threatening to resign. Borwornsak said he would do the same, and bring the whole house down. Anand reckoned that those who craved power would beg to be readmitted. A compromise was reached, but it involved doubling the number of deputies.

'That was the kind of lesson you cannot learn in class,' Borwornsak recalls.

The People's Constitution, as it was dubbed, was promulgated on 1 October 1997 with the country gripped in the worst financial crisis in its history. There was a widespread sense that Thailand needed to mend its careless ways. Chavalit Yongchaiyudh's government was in its last gasp, and the economy lay all around in ruins.

'When it came out, the constitution was generally endorsed, including by foreign governments,' Anand observes. 'It raised the democracy index by several notches.' Its many articles and provisions went into effect at that time, but its impact on party politics would not be tested for more than three years – not until the general election of early 2001. That was won decisively by Thaksin Shinawatra and his Thai Rak Thai Party, opening the way to a whole new era of modern big-party politics.

CHAPTER 17

THE ASIAN FINANCIAL CRISIS & THAI-US RELATIONS (1997)

An end to aid

By the mid-1990s, Thailand was considered 'newly industrialised' – a significant second-division economy ranked in the top 40 globally. Economic liberals such as Anand had worked hard to build credibility and economic stability, dispelling the image of a nation lurching helplessly from coup to coup. Indeed, Thailand was booming as never before, and many Thai businessmen seemed to believe the economy would never see a downturn. But the fundamentals underpinning it often remained rickety, and the country was on a giddy, dangerous course.

One implication of Thailand's rapid economic expansion was that direct foreign aid was much harder to justify. Thailand could now afford to pay its own way, as it had done in the early 1990s in the war on HIV/AIDS. However, there was still a need for foreign expertise in key areas, particularly the environment, public health, and education. In 1990, Tom Reese, the head of USAID in Thailand, saw scope for 'more market-based US services and technology, as well as the need for solutions to problems created by such accelerated development'. The US-Thailand Development Programme (US-TDP) was introduced to wean Thailand off traditional aid programmes.

In 1995, with the US congress itching to cut spending, the USAID mission to Thailand was closed. The following year, US-TDP was wound up early. It was a USAID-funded, US$8-million development collaboration between Kenan Institute of Private Enterprise (KIPE – part of the Kenan-Flagler Business School at the University of North Carolina at Chapel Hill), Chulalongkorn University, and the

Brooker Group, a Bangkok consulting company. The purpose of US-TDP was to enlist the US and Thai private sectors to 'develop an institutional arrangement that would provide ways to continue this sort of assistance after the closure of the USAID bilateral mission in Thailand'.[1]

The US-TDP and its residual funding were taken over by the Kenan Institute Asia, which was established in early 1996 as a Thai non-profit foundation for development cooperation. The Thai government granted the foundation funds that had been reserved to match USAID funding and, with the strong backing of the Kenan family, KIPE made a roughly equal donation of its own. Rather than being withdrawn completely, American assistance to Thailand was thus being essentially privatised via the creation of a non-governmental organisation.

Kenan's first executive director was Paul Wedel, an American fluent in Thai and a former Bangkok bureau chief of United Press International. He recalls that Anand, when first approached as a potential trustee, was supportive of the Kenan goals of enlisting private involvement in national development. He particularly favoured the idea of a development partnership that would not be a client-patron relationship, but one of mutual benefit and mutual cost. Anand was happy to lend his name to the project as a trustee, and to attend one meeting a year.

As the project picked up pace, Anand's interest in it increased. It appealed to his growing interest in non-governmental approaches to development issues. 'When we decided to set up an executive committee to meet at least quarterly, we asked Anand who among the trustees would be best to serve as the chairman,' Wedel recalls. 'He thought for a moment and then said that it would be best if he took that position. From that time on, he chaired every committee meeting, and I cannot recall that he missed more than one in a decade as chairman.'

Also sitting on the first board of trustees were US Ambassador William Itoh, with whom Anand got along particularly well; and Pichet Soontornpipit, director general of Thailand's Department of Technical and Economic Cooperation. Both were included *ex-officio* as non-voting trustees in recognition of the two governments' contributions to the institute. Another key figure on the Thai side was Asavin Chintakananda, an economist and business academic. Kenan carried on with US-TDP-type projects, such as affordable HIV diagnostic kits, waste-water treatment, and alternative energy. There were also capacity-building training projects in public health, the environment, urban management, and information technology.

Anand proved to be an extremely active chairman. 'When an issue arose during the discussion where he felt he could help, he took immediate action,' says Wedel. 'When we reported on difficulties getting mid-level Bangkok Metropolitan Administration officials to cooperate on a project to improve waste-water management for Bangkok, Khun Anand immediately picked up his cell phone and got the governor of Bangkok on the line. He told the governor that the project was good for the environment and good for Bangkok, so he should have a word with his officials to make sure the project moved ahead. It did.'

Anand was a hard taskmaster when it came to the other trustees. He expected them to pull their weight, and if he found out a particular trustee had not been helpful, he immediately called to let the individual concerned know he should resign. If he wanted a particular person to join the board, he would make a personal invitation, which he did not expect to be rejected. He did not stand by diplomatic niceties when he thought something was amiss. Down the road, he was very critical of the US in the aftermath of 9-11. 'I recall a number of board meetings in which he was particularly harsh about the US misadventures in Iraq,' says Wedel. 'I suspect that some of those ambassadors privately agreed with him, but they certainly did not take him on in debating the issue.'

The termination of USAID and the creation of Kenan Institute Asia was a remarkable piece of timing. US policymakers may have imagined they were taking a step back. However, precisely the opposite was to transpire, when Thailand's increasingly troubled economy finally tanked in 1997.

The US had always had an important impact on Thailand's economy. The Great Depression in the late 1920s and 1930s had caused a crash in the commodity market, hurting Siam's exports and contributing to the revolutionary restiveness of the period. World War II, with Thailand cut off from the West and sanctioned as an ally of the Axis powers, made matters worse. The Americans, however, proved more forgiving than their European allies when peace returned, and largely shielded Thailand from demands for war reparations. In the years that followed, as the Cold War deepened, Thailand's strategic importance grew. US aid poured into the country in the late 1950s, much to the satisfaction of the then prime ministers, Field Marshals Plaek Phibunsongkhram and Sarit Thanarat. Thailand saw steady annual growth of 7 per cent from the 1950s to the 1970s. Despite a dip in the early 1980s, when three devaluations of the baht had to be applied, growth averaged 7.6 per cent from 1977 to 1996 overall, hitting double digits during Chatichai's government in the late 1980s. By then, Japan had long since overtaken the US as Thailand's most important business partner. The golden age of the technocrats was passing, and Anand's two governments in the early 1990s were in some respects their last triumph.

Road to disaster

East Asian investment, from Japan and Taiwan in particular, had transformed the Thai economy. In 1985, Japan's overvalued yen created a business imperative to shift factories to Thailand, where the Eastern Seaboard was being promoted as an industrialised corridor. Manufacturing fuelled spectacular, export-led growth.

At the same time, half the working population remained locked into low-value agricultural production, contributing only about 15 per cent to Thailand's gross domestic product.

By the early 1990s, the East Asian industrial push was abating. Thailand was being encouraged by the World Bank and others to liberalise its financial market. Opening up Indochina had been a central policy plank of Chatichai's administration, and Thailand had ambitions to become a regional financial hub, competing with Hong Kong and Singapore. It wanted to liberalise its capital market, maintain a pegged exchange rate, and run its own monetary policy simultaneously – an unrealistic ambition, many economists argued, but one that successive Thai governments hung on to until the 1997 crash.

Anand freely admits his debt to Amnuay Viravan for tutoring him at Saha Union on corporate finance. He had always been modest about his understanding of public finance and macroeconomics. As prime minister, he had felt he needed to learn more about these intricate topics. Ekamol Kiriwat, a deputy governor of the Bank of Thailand, remembers Anand as prime minister visiting the central bank at least one day a month for briefings. He was particularly interested in tax reform, and finding ways to promote foreign direct investment.

Ekamol was instrumental in establishing the Securities and Exchange Commission (SEC) in 1991 at the direction of Suthee Singsaneh, who as finance minister became its first chairman. With Ekamol as secretary general, the SEC set out to tackle rampant stock manipulation. In 1992, it made enemies when it took on some share-ramping rings with powerful political connections.[2] Money borrowed on one declared pretext often went elsewhere, such as into the stock market with its improbably high yields. Many regarded the stock market as the best casino available in a country where gaming is illegal but widespread. Some of the big players, puffing Havanas, would weekend in Hong Kong, planning which stocks to ramp the following week as they lorded it in the lobby of The Peninsula hotel. Chan Bulakul notes the Thai delight in gambling and getting rich without working. 'In Thai, it is to "play" the stock market, not invest in it,' he says.

The government wanted to get beyond this, to give the stock market credibility, and to improve Bangkok's standing as a finance hub. 'Our immediate aim is not to compete with regional financial centres,' said Anand in a written interview as prime minister. 'The main idea is to begin setting up facilities so that some of the intermediation of international capital can be done in Bangkok, with participation from both foreign and Thai financial institutions. Geographical proximity and the existing close political and economic ties with ASEAN and Indochinese countries should give Bangkok an advantage to assume this specialised role. In the longer term, we would hope to see Bangkok developing into a "full service" regional financial centre, specialising in the intermediation of medium- and long-term capital.'[3]

One of the subjects Ekamol remembers discussing most with Anand as prime minister was flotation of the baht in relation to making the economy more competitive and responsive. The Thai currency had long been pegged at around 25 to the US dollar. The dollar was relatively weak at the time, so the baht was not in a bad place. Nobody bothered with hedging. 'It was not an issue then,' Anand recalls. Ekamol favoured flotation, but the governor of the Bank of Thailand, Vijit Supinit,[4] felt Thailand was not yet strong enough to float free. This issue was not resolved until the spectacular collapse of the baht in the 1997 financial crisis, when in July there was no choice left but to release it into free fall.

In May 1990 under Chatichai, Thailand had formally accepted Article VIII of the articles of agreement of the International Monetary Fund, which enabled commercial banks to approve foreign exchange transactions without prior approval by the Bank of Thailand. The Anand government further liberalised capital transactions in April 1991. These developments made it easier for Thais to borrow from abroad at far more competitive rates. Dollar debt was secure enough so long as the fixed exchange-rate regime remained in place. There was little obvious risk, and the private sector borrowed heavily over the next six years for business development, property purchases, and speculation. There was ample official support all along for making it easier to borrow more cheaply from overseas. Suthee, Anand's finance minister in 1991, believed local interest rates had to come down from as high as 16 per cent. 'We cannot keep them this high. We can borrow at a cheaper level – it is also good for the private sector,' he argued.

Who could possibly argue with lower interest rates? With easy and cheap dollar loans, foreign money rushed in. Anand remembers concern over what Alan Greenspan, the gnomic chairman of the US Federal Reserve for nearly 20 years from 1986, would have termed 'irrational exuberance'. Money was being borrowed and used for non-core businesses. Hotels and golf courses were popping up everywhere. Efforts were made to curb credit expansion, and the current account deficit was trimmed back from around 5 to 6 per cent of gross domestic product – a 'danger level' – to about 4 per cent by the second quarter of 1992, 'a more manageable level', according to Anand at the time.

Vijit Supinit, the business-minded governor of the Bank of Thailand, presided over the introduction of the Bangkok International Banking Facilities in 1993, which facilitated the inflow of Western capital through local and foreign commercial banks and branches – more than US$30 billion over the next three years. With reduced demand for industrial investment, the funds filtered through banks and finance companies into more speculative areas, creating oversupply and bubbles. 'Money was lent without due diligence to family members and political and business cronies,' *Asia Times* noted in a 1999 editorial when failed finance company assets were being auctioned. 'Asset values backing up loans were deliberately and fraudulently overstated. A significant portion of loans was backed up by nothing at all. Simply deducting for the risk factors implied by such practices would have brought asset values down by 20–30 per cent from book value.'[5]

The Bank of Thailand had historically been regarded as detached, neutral, beyond reproach – a vital, always sober steward of Thailand's post-war economic miracle. Its reputation at this time hit an all-time low. There had been private feuds between officials at the Bank of Thailand and those at the SEC trying to regulate the stock market, disastrous personality conflicts within the Bank of Thailand, and spats with the Ministry of Finance. Because he could see numerous problems but felt his opinions were being disregarded in cabinet and outside, Finance Minister Amnuay Viravan, who was also deputy prime minister, finally resigned in June 1997. He was replaced by Thanong Bidaya, who lasted until October when the government of Prime Minister Chavalit Yongchaiyudh resigned.

Chavalit's New Aspiration Party had been feuding with a major coalition partner, Chatichai's Chart Pattana.

Amnuay and Chavalit, born a week apart in 1932, had become good friends. Chavalit at one point wanted him to lead New Aspiration, but Amnuay declined. He did not want to be a party leader by invitation. 'I have to earn it,' he told Chavalit, who came to him twice with the request. On both occasions he declined but agreed to help in cabinet. Although Amnuay lasted a year, he clashed with other cabinet members and felt maligned. Finally, he told Chavalit he had had enough and wanted to stand down in May when he reached 65. Prime Minister Goh Chok Tong of Singapore was visiting at about this time, and played golf with Amnuay at the exclusive Rajpruek Club in the northern Bangkok suburbs. They were on good terms, and he remembers Goh asking him to stay on to avert a financial crisis. Amnuay said his decision was irreversible. He speculates that if he had stayed, the crisis might have been of a 'lesser degree'. Amnuay was particularly alarmed by private debt levels. 'One day we are going to have trouble,' he remembers warning everyone.

In July 1996 Governor Vijit resigned from the Bank of Thailand in a blaze of bad publicity over a number of issues, including his handling of some scandal-plagued banks, the Bangkok Bank of Commerce in particular. The bank had numerous links to politicians and was later closed. Vijit's replacement, Rerngchai Marakanond, had never expected to be in the job and was simply not up to the task.

'I regret making one bad decision,' says Amnuay reflecting on the appointment of Rerngchai, who was favoured by Prime Minister Banharn Silpa-archa. Amnuay would have preferred MR Chatumongkol Sonakul, the permanent secretary of finance, for the position. But Chatumongkol had strong ideas about who should succeed him at the finance ministry. 'I usually don't accept conditions,' says Amnuay. 'The decision is my own.'

Rerngchai's appointment turned out to be a major mistake. 'He couldn't handle the problem and did things that made it worse,' says Amnuay. How things might have been different had Chatumongkol been appointed in 1996 is a matter of pure speculation. In 1998, he was finally appointed governor, and was credited with restoring the central bank's credibility, only to be dismissed in 2001 by Prime Minister Thaksin Shinawatra a few months after he entered office.

The general consensus of economists is that the commitment to maintaining an exchange rate pegged against a small basket of currencies, 80 per cent of which was the US dollar, was disastrous. All these circumstances would prove to be a toxic cocktail, increasingly so as foreign confidence in the management of the economy and the Bank of Thailand slipped as the roaring 1990s progressed. No economic boom could be limitless, and a serious current-account deficit had settled in.

The month Rerngchai came into office, the baht came under attack again from speculators, this time in the Singapore and Hong Kong markets. In subsequent desperate efforts to defend it, Thailand's foreign exchange reserves were depleted at an eye-watering rate from nearly US$40 billion at the end of 1996 to just over US$1.1 billion by late May 1997. Ekamol believes Rerngchai was the wrong person to handle the growing exchange rate crisis. He failed to inform his minister that foreign exchange reserves were being so rapidly depleted.

According to one academic account, '[during] the second week of May 1997, in an all-out attack, international hedge funds, including [George] Soros's Quantum Fund and traders at US financial institutions such as J.P. Morgan and Goldman Sachs, took short positions in spot, forward and option markets, betting as much as US$10 billion on Thailand devaluing. In return, on three different days, May 8, 13, and 14, the BOT used or committed US$6.1 billion, US$9.7 billion and US$10 billion respectively defending the baht's dollar peg – considered key to maintaining the confidence of foreign investors.'[6]

The Bank of Thailand's return barrage failed, and some of its officials were literally reduced to tears on 14 May, the blackest day in the institution's history. By then, the economy and the banking system, drowning in a rising tide of non-performing loans, were effectively insolvent. In due course, an International Monetary Fund bailout of over US$17.2 billion would be required. Economic mayhem followed in South Korea and Indonesia, where the bailouts were even larger. This was to be the largest contributing factor to the downfall in 1998 of President Suharto, Indonesia's elderly dictator. Malaysia and the Philippines were also sucked in as the contagion spread.

When the baht was finally cut loose, on 2 July 1997, it plunged so far that hard currencies spiked at around twice their normal parities. Some people buying condominiums with offshore loans suddenly found their entire monthly salary, denominated in baht, was insufficient to cover their next mortgage payment. The Bank of Thailand was also considered to have gravely mishandled support to floundering finance companies through the Financial Institution Development Fund. Rerngchai, its hapless governor, was later prosecuted for 'serious negligence' in the financial disaster. In 2005, he was fined US$4.6 billion in a civil court. That verdict would not be overturned until 2016, when the Supreme Court acquitted Rerngchai on the grounds that he alone could not be held accountable.

The baht plummeted from its regular haunt at about 25 on the US dollar to a low around 56, settling back to near 48 before gradually recovering (the rate at the time of writing is about 33 on the dollar). The IMF prescription for recovery was strong and bitter medicine. As a precondition for any assistance, 56 insolvent finance companies were shuttered initially, followed by more the next year. The government was forced into austerity mode with heavy spending cuts; the economy shrank by 15 per cent in 18 months with two million people forced out of work, and industrial output decreased 30 per cent. Among the employment casualties were some 6,000 local journalists whose publications had prospered during the boom years on the back of property advertising.

US response

As a result of financial liberalisation, Thailand's capital inflows rose from some US$7 billion annually around 1990 to about US$20 billion annually in 1995 and 1996. Some question the role of the first Anand government in all this, but economic mismanagement under the three elected governments that followed must also be considered. The connection to Anand's administration was not binary: liberalisation in 1991 did not create the circumstances for the crash of 1997. Had the baht been floated sooner after the Anand governments, compelling more responsible borrowing practices, the 1997 iceberg might have been avoided. In the event, even the conservative Crown Property Bureau, which administers the finances and investments of the monarchy, did not see it coming. Two of the Bureau's main financial pillars, Siam Commercial Bank and Siam Cement Group, were both badly hit.

The economic fallout was all too apparent, but there were other, less visible consequences. Barely beneath the surface, there was considerable damage to official relations between Thailand and the US. The US reaction to the Thai economy's meltdown was widely regarded as cold and unfriendly, almost as if Americans felt the Thais had got their comeuppance.

'Ours is a friendship which goes back 165 years, back to 1833 when Siam became the first Asian country to establish diplomatic ties with America,' Prime

Minister Chuan Leekpai reminded everyone on a cap-in-hand visit to New York in early 1998. However, many felt Washington's support for Thailand, its military ally since the 1950s, was strikingly impersonal, channelled coldly through the IMF and other international financial institutions.

US Treasury Secretary Robert Rubin, himself a 25-year veteran of Goldman Sachs, was fulsome in his public praise for the financial recovery team Thailand had assembled, but privately many US officials felt Thailand was itself largely to blame for bringing the financial roof down on its own head. These included Timothy Geithner, who had finished his high school years in Bangkok.[7] In the late 1980s, Geithner worked for Kissinger Associates in Washington. He served as undersecretary of state of the treasury for international affairs from 1998 to 2001, among other things advising the Bank of Thailand on belated US government assistance.

Rubin promised that up to another US$5 billion would be available in reserve funds should Thailand need them. 'Thailand's really on a very good track,' Rubin told the press when Chuan and finance minister Tarrin Nimmanahaeminda came to Washington in March 1998. In the event, Tarrin only drew down US$14.2 billion from the US$17 billion-plus the IMF initially made available, and went all out to clear the borrowing ahead of schedule.

'It takes two to tango,' says Asda Jayanama, who was posted to the United Nations in New York at the time. 'They didn't talk about the bankers who were so keen to lend to Thailand. We should have bargained and argued more – the system would then correct itself.'

Many Thais were profoundly shocked when Thailand, a country that had escaped colonisation, suddenly found itself in hock to overbearing Western financial institutions; there was a sense that Thailand had opened up its economy too soon, almost innocently, and been gobbled up by a sophisticated modern capitalist attack machine. George Soros, the head of the Quantum Fund, was singled out for particular demonisation, and mention of his name will for ever evoke strong reactions in nationalistic circles around the region, regardless of his philanthropic credentials.

Although a study of the currency crisis sparked by Mexico's late 1994 devaluation of the peso might have provided some clues, Thailand had crashed and burned in a crisis nobody had adequately foreseen. It was, as a result, forced to take extremely tough corrective measures – humiliating punishment for economic mismanagement, foolhardiness, and naïveté. No one doubted that Chavalit's replacement as prime minister, Chuan, had sincerity and integrity, but he was weak on economics. He also struggled to answer a question about Thailand's legal system at a special gathering of the Asia Society in New York.

At a joint press conference with Tarrin, Secretary of State Madeleine Albright commended the Thais for 'staying the course' and facing up to their responsibilities. 'We have great confidence in Thailand,' she said. 'That nation has acted firmly in seeking to restore confidence in the Thai economy and laying the groundwork for renewed growth. Moreover, its government is democratic, its press open, and its authorities accountable to the people.'

'The Thai people fully realise that hardship and sacrifice are necessary in this period of economic adjustment and reform,' Tarrin responded, striking just enough of the penitent tone Washington wanted to hear. He did not, however, point out that Thailand had got itself into this spectacular mess with democratically elected governments, a free press, and authorities accountable to the people all in place. The international media were meanwhile in the doghouse for failing to see the crash coming – perhaps more so than the domestic media which at least brought down Vijit and nagged at the many problems besetting the economy.

Chuan was even more conciliatory and confessional in his address to the Council on Foreign Relations and the Asia Society in New York. 'From day one of my present government, I have insisted that responsibility is the key,' he said. 'I have insisted that we must be brave enough, courageous enough, to face up to our responsibilities. We must know what we did wrong, and we must seek to put things right. Nor can we put things right if we do not help ourselves first and only expect others to help us.'

'We became a part of the globalised world and felt proud ... while much of our law and governance and many of our instruments for macro-economic, financial and business management are waiting to be modified, modernised, and upgraded to international standards and practices.'

Tarrin, the Harvard- and Stanford-educated finance minister from 1997 to 2001, had also been finance minister in Chuan's previous government from 1992 to 1995. When he returned to office, he appointed Nukul Prachuabmoh, an unimpeachable former Bank of Thailand governor, to investigate what went wrong. In 1991 and 1992, Nukul had been minister of transport and communications in both Anand's cabinets, and was his toughest, most uncompromising minister. Senior officials and financiers on the Nukul Commission spent three months analysing what had caused the economic meltdown, and their conclusions were unflattering to the institutions concerned. Much of the blame was put on the Bank of Thailand's mismanagement of the baht; it had been warned in March by the IMF of what might lie ahead. Rerngchai's successor, Governor Chaiyawat Wibulswasdi, resigned in May 1998 to avoid dismissal, as did some of his colleagues. The Nukul Commmission's criticisms were broad and withering:

> Having decided to liberalise the capital market, the BOT should have adopted a more flexible exchange policy, but it preferred to maintain a narrow trading band for the baht instead. It began to reconsider this policy in April 1996, only a few months before economic conditions began to worsen considerably. With such worsening ... the BOT became reluctant to change the exchange rate regime, fearing that such an action would send the wrong signal to the market.

The commission also criticised the BOT's methods:

> Worse, by using swap transactions to defend the baht, the BOT was able to circumvent both the market constraints as well as the legal constraints imposed by the Currency Act. The BOT poured an enormous amount of its reserves to defend the currency. By July 2, 1997, foreign reserves had declined to only US$2.8 billion.

Anand decided to contact Henry Kissinger, the US former secretary of state and national security adviser. 'Kissinger was very upset with the Clinton administration for not helping Thailand more,' Asda recalls. With funding support from Kenan, Anand flew to the US and was active setting up meetings for Thai officials in Washington and New York. He got Kissinger to speak up for an aid package for Thailand. With the help of Kissinger and Maurice 'Hank' Greenberg, who was the head of American International Group (AIG) and chairman of the board of the Asia Society, meetings were arranged for Chuan and other ministers with US business people and politicians. An assistance package was eventually approved. 'It was slow and small, but symbolically useful to both sides,' says Wedel.

Anand was the prime mover in setting up a Kenan programme, American Corporations for Thailand (ACT), which focused on retraining Thais who had lost their jobs in the crisis. Its two biggest funders, AIG and Unocal, were brought in personally by Anand through his direct connections. Others followed, no doubt eager to have their pictures taken handing over large cheques to Anand – American Express, Chase Manhattan Bank, Dow Chemical, GE, Motorola, Raytheon. Anand described ACT as an endorsement of Kenan's 'central premise that the most effective long-term development depends on an enlightened and well-balanced free enterprise system'. Kissinger visited Thailand and agreed to co-chair the committee with Anand. He was satisfied with results in the first year. 'It's extremely satisfying to see a programme do what it sets out to do,' he commented.[8] The former US secretary of state also gave a lunchtime address supportive of positive bilateral relations to the American Chamber of Commerce.

'ACT was important, not only for the assistance to the economy and the unemployed, but also in showing the US government that the US private sector was coming to the aid of Thailand while it held back,' says Wedel.

When it came to decide on a structure to oversee the US programme, USAID considered re-establishing its office in Thailand to administer the national component of its regional programme, Accelerating Economic Recovery in Asia (AERA). Both Anand and Ambassador Itoh opposed this idea as cumbersome and costly. Instead, Kenan was appointed to administer the program with a binational oversight committee that included representatives of both governments. The only contentious point was who should chair the committee. Neither government wanted to be in a minority, even though it was unlikely any issues would come down to a vote. The problem was solved when Anand agreed to chair the committee. Both sides were satisfied he had the clout to make things work. The programme ran from 1998 to 2005, executed over 50 projects involving some 27,000 Thais, and handled more than US$30 million, of which US$23 million was from USAID. That was a significant improvement on the US$10 million initially budgeted. In a case of better late than never, one project saw 2,000 bank managers from all 17 local commercial banks trained in risk management, credit analysis, and internal control.[9]

'I believe this was a very rare – perhaps unique – arrangement in which a significant USAID program without any USAID personnel on the ground was overseen by a body in which US officials were in a minority,' says Wedel. The oversight committee functioned well until USAID finally returned to Bangkok in 2003, when it established its Asia-Pacific regional office as an adjunct to what remains one of the world's largest US embassies.

The 1997 fallout

As the severity of the crash became apparent, there were calls for those responsible to be prosecuted. Nukul Commission member Amaret Sila-on, a 65-year-old former commerce minister and the new chairman of the stock exchange, counselled patience. 'If they committed criminal acts, we have ten years to go after them,' he said. 'We don't have ten years to restructure the financial system. We have to get on with that job first.'[10] Ironically, Amaret was himself handed a suspended two-year prison sentence for supposedly negligent oversight of the Financial Sector Restructuring Authority (FRA), which was established to handle the assets of the shuttered finance companies. A civil court ruled that 'under his guidance, the FRA did not press for the payment of 2.3 billion baht from Lehman Brothers, for bad loans formerly belonging to 56 financially-ailing finance companies'.[11]

All along, Amaret had had to struggle with highly inflated asset valuations on the Thai side. 'I think the main thing really, which a lot of people miss, is that all these things we have been doing for the last year is not to raise money,' he told a reporter. 'Everything we have been doing is all designed to create or recreate the confidence of investors in the financial system of Thailand. Now if we have done that and we get 40 per cent instead of 50 per cent recovery [of the assets' cost], but we gain 100 per cent of the confidence back, then I say that is worth it.'[12]

Amaret was damned if he did sell and damned if he did not. *The Economist* faulted the FRA for not selling off enough:

> The whole point of the auction was to find out what the highest bidders would offer for the assets: not very much, it would seem. But if the FRA had sold more of the assets now, it would have done Thailand's economy a huge favour. By establishing rough market prices for a swathe of the banking sector's loan portfolios, it could have helped bankers to start making better guesses about the extent of their dud loans; and it could have given potential investors more confidence that a bottom has been found. Instead, those who are keen to sort through the rubbish for gems will have to wait a bit longer.[13]

During the 1990s, King Bhumibol had been warning about greed and irresponsible national growth strategies. His opinions gained greater resonance with the 1997 crash. In early 1998, a project based on his development work and talks over the years was launched to promulgate his ideas for a so-called Sufficiency Economy imbued with Buddhist notions of moderation. Topically, the central planks in the king's theory included prudence and the capacity to guard against outside shocks. Promotion of Sufficiency Economy thinking has been reenergised under the military government of General Prayut Chan-o-cha, who seized power with a coup in 2014. Nevertheless, its calls for moderation have always had limited appeal to an increasingly urbanised generation striving for growth and modernity.

The economic interests of the crown were directly impacted by the 1997 crash. Its immense wealth in land holdings and equity, valued in 2018 at in excess of US$50 billion, is managed by the Crown Property Bureau (CPB). After 1997, it was compelled to create a reserve fund to deal with future financial contingencies. The CPB was until 2018 a major shareholder in Siam Commercial Bank (SCB) and Siam Cement Group (SCG), both of which were severely damaged. Like other banks, SCB had lent heavily to the real estate sector, and a third of that portfolio turned non-performing. A bailout of 6 billion baht was needed. SCG was meanwhile carrying US$6.6 billion in debt, mostly foreign and unhedged as was common practice at the time, and became at one point technically insolvent. The CPB's investments in other listed companies were also damaged. The crash led to a complete review and overhaul of the CPB's operations, resulting in a more commercial approach to property leases and rents, and the structuring of a separate equity division which, because of the crash, unexpectedly came to include the Kempinski luxury hotel chain.[14]

Even before the final collapse, many loans by banks and other financial institutions were troubled or non-performing, particularly in the property sector. In 1998, there was 'negative uptake' in office leases, with over 265,000 square metres of space vacated largely as a result of finance-company closures. In 1996, the peak year, uptake had been around 550,000 square metres – a figure that has never been approached since. Some 300 major office, hotel, and apartment developments in Bangkok failed, leaving the city strewn with 'ghost' buildings that quickly deteriorated in the harsh sub-tropical conditions. Many remained untouched for a decade or more. Years on, a few are still visible, mostly in the outer reaches of the city.[15]

Chuan and the Democrats were criticised for being too soft, and kowtowing to Washington. Anand's efforts, also, were not always appreciated. At an annual dinner party for retiring diplomats at the foreign ministry, he was involved in a distressing row at the top table with his mentor, Thanat Khoman, the former foreign minister. Thanat had been chairman of Finance One. Thailand's flagship finance company, it had needed to be bailed out by the Bank of Thailand in March 1997 during a merger with Thai Danu Bank. Although Thanat's wife, Thanphuying Molee, was wealthy, Thanat had always made his own way financially. He was therefore gratified late in life to have become rather well off, on paper at least, through his shares in the finance company. Thanat was on the board at the behest of Pin Chakkapak, a friend of his son, who revered the old foreign minister.

'The major shareholders of Fin-One, who include Dr Thanat Khoman, the Srivikorns, Chumpol Pornprapha and others on the board, had been acting mostly as a rubber stamp,' reported Thanong Khanthong in *The Nation*. 'More often than not they went into board meetings without knowing the agenda because they were not given it in advance. In the firm's glory days, no shareholder dared question Pin because he seemed so successful at snapping up companies and adding capital gains to Fin-One's books. As long as the Fin-One stock kept rising, everybody was happy.'[17]

Pin was indeed widely regarded as a financial wizard before everything fell apart in early 1997.[18] 'Fin-One has management with a good track record,' Goldman Sachs reported in early 1996. 'We would describe Mr Pin's operating system as sharp, creative, nimble and opportunistic. We also sense that Mr Pin makes it a point to hire capable, professional managers for day-to-day operations, and to reward and retain good people via share participation and performance-based compensation.'[19]

Anand was not involved in the financial sector, but he did have plenty of connections to US business interests. During the annual dinner for current and former civil servants at the foreign ministry – the biggest social event in its calendar – Thanat seemed confused as he lambasted both the US and Anand. The old foreign minister had been blindsided by the closure of the finance companies, and started dishing out blame out to the Americans, the Democrats, Anand, whoever. At the heart of the misunderstanding was Thanat's misapprehension that the finance houses had been closed on Tarrin's watch as finance minister, when in fact this happened when Thanong Bidaya was in the post. Thanat viewed

Anand as somehow guilty by his closeness to Tarrin.

'He started attacking me at the table, and I just listened – it was so unlike him,' Anand recalls. 'After I had borne so much pain without reacting, I started talking back to him and we got into a real row. I stood up and *waied* him, and I said, "Well, if that's the way you feel about me, I am leaving." And I left the table, much to the consternation of everybody.'

Nobody in the room could be oblivious to the argument. 'It was a very embarrassing evening, very tense,' recalls Tej Bunnag. 'It had been brewing up for some time, but I don't think Anand thought it would turn bad at that function. It wasn't an event where something like that should have happened. They were literally shouting at each other. We didn't know what they were shouting about – they were both very upset. They are two very strong personalities who always stick to their principles.'

The problem did not blow over, however. Thanat continued to attack Anand publicly. He was a guest on Dusit Siriwan's television talk show where he alleged that Anand was being paid millions each month. 'Thanat appeared three or four times, and started blasting me publicly,' Anand recalls. 'He knew that I was sitting on the advisory board of General Electric. He was totally confused. What hurt me most, he gave a print media interview attacking me very harshly, and casting aspersions on my character. I never once responded, and kept quiet in the hope that it would be a passing aberration. He was not himself.'

Up until their falling out, Anand used to visit Thanat every three or four months. After there had been no contact for three years, Thanat's daughters came and asked Anand to relent. 'Somehow he added two and two and it became five,' Anand recalls. 'It was not fair. I showed his daughters the article, and said, "I have pride. You know I love your father. He is my mentor and nurtured my career, but enough is enough".'

Thanat's bellicosity finally subsided in 2003. The occasion was a reception at the Dusit Thani for Prince Alfred of Liechtenstein, the chairman of the advisory board of the Vienna-based International Peace Foundation. The prince was visiting Thailand for the first time with his wife, Princess Raffaella, to promote the foundation's forthcoming event series, 'Bridges – Dialogues Towards a Culture of Peace'. In the years that followed, the programme would bring a succession of Nobel laureates for keynote addresses in Thailand intended to foster global peace and understanding, and to support education in Thailand and in the ASEAN region. Anand served as the Thai honorary chairman for the series. 'He became the chief mentor of the "Bridges" programme in Thailand, and my personal Thai father figure,' says Uwe Morawetz, the foundation's German chairman and founder.

At the function, Anand was surprised to overhear himself being praised by Thanat to the guests. Somewhat bemused, he kept close to his old mentor for the next ten minutes without engaging him. It was Thanat who eventually broke the ice and spoke to him. 'I decided then and there to let it all pass, and after that I remember seeing him every three or four months,' says Anand. The personal détente between Thanat and Anand was an auspicious start for the International Peace Foundation in Thailand, even though Morawetz was unaware of it at the time. However, he does remember both men returning in each other's company for the 'Bridges' launch press conference later in the year.

When Thanat turned 100, many of his protégés came to pay their respects at Bangkok's Ramathibodi Hospital, where he had been kept on life support for some time. He lay serenely in a coma, a 'sleeping beauty', as Thais call such patients, and eventually died in March 2016, a few months short of his 102nd birthday. As the last of ASEAN's five founding fathers, his passing was truly the end of an era.

CHAPTER 18

BACK TO THE PRIVATE SECTOR & THE RISE OF THAKSIN (1998–2003)

Saha Union

During his brief second government, Anand had marked his 60th birthday. Buddhists regard it as an important time to reflect on what they have done, and where they have been, and to prepare for a long and hopefully satisfying old age. When soon after he left Government House for the second time, reporters asked Anand about his achievements, he was characteristically dismissive. He did not dwell on jobs undone, and expressed no desire to cling to power.

'I didn't have any lingering feelings,' he recalls. 'People with ambitions become addicted to power. I don't belong to that group – I am different, emotionally detached. Whenever I take up a job, when it is done it is done.'

After stepping down the first time, Anand had briefly returned to work at Saha Union as chairman. This stint lasted only six weeks, until early June 1992, when he became prime minister for the second time. Following his more permanent return in October, he remained with the company until August 2002.

Damri Darakananda, his employer and friend, was struck by how little the time as prime minister had changed him. Anand had not parlayed his premiership into another job, as many would have done, and did not seem to expect people at the office to treat him any differently from before. 'He got a lot of offers but he still came back here with the same salary,' says Damri. 'It was as if he had returned home,' says Jongrak, Damri's wife.

As before, Saha Union allowed Anand great flexibility. His work there was always at the policy level, and did not touch upon executive functions or administration.

He was able to organise his own time efficiently, exercise with tennis and squash, and travel more extensively than he had in the previous two decades.

In the early 1990s, the conglomerate was keen to move into China as the country opened up. Because Anand had played a key role in restoring diplomatic relations between China and Thailand, he was well known to the Chinese, and could get access to the most senior officials. On one visit he led, the Saha Union delegation met with Zhu Rongji, the former mayor of Shanghai who was at the time vice premier – in 1998 he would become premier, a position he occupied for five years.

'We had no idea at the time what kind of business we would be investing in,' Damri recalls. 'Zhu Rongji advised us that China lacked public infrastructure, such as roads and electricity. He said the power business had a lot of future potential. He recommended that we should not invest in construction because the business was volatile.'

China needed power stations, and there was little regulation of the sector. Non-state producers were therefore able largely to set their own prices and terms. A subsidiary, Saha Union Investment (China), was established in Shanghai in 1995, and went on to have joint ventures in ten co-generation power plants. 'We had never had this kind of business in Thailand,' says Damri. Retired senior officials from the Electricity Generating Authority of Thailand were recruited as consultants.

Meanwhile, Saha Union's business in Thailand was waning. It still produced hard disks for computers, and was moving into private power production, but contract manufacturing for Nike had gone and the textiles industry was being eroded by competition from lower-wage countries. 'We are not a garment or a power company today,' says Damri. 'We are more like an investor – a holding company. The world changes and Saha Union's business is changing with it. The Thai garment industry was not in a position to compete globally. We looked for other businesses to take its place. Our policy is not to be specific about products. We enter industries which provide opportunities to replace what we have lost. We have to constantly look for new businesses. Every business has a cycle. There will be birth, growth, decline, and death. If a business does not look for new products, that is dangerous.'

While Anand's re-entry into private-sector employment after his premiership appeared smooth, beneath the surface he was more introspective. Reflecting on his life at 60 and what he would do with the next 20 years or so, he sensed something was missing. He had spent over a third of his life overseas. 'Up to that age, I knew very little about Thailand. I had never been to the Northeast. Occasionally, Chiang Mai or Phuket, but I never knew how the other half of the people lived – I never knew about poverty.' As prime minister, he had visited some of the poorer provinces, seen flood damage, entered slums, tackled issues that were unfamiliar to him as a diplomat or senior figure in the corporate world. 'It was all new to me – a turning point. All these issues were brought to my desk, and I began to know the people involved. I was lucky in the sense that I was interested in people, but I wanted to find out what made people think this way or that. This is where Sulak Sivaraksa is not quite right when he says that before I became prime minister I had no interest in poverty. It's not that I had no interest – it's that I had no personal experience of it.'

As prime minister, Anand found that he enjoyed meeting people and that their issues interested him. It was also dawning on him that engagement with civil society might be more productive than the politics commonly practised in Thailand. 'I was discovering what Thailand was all about. I began to read more – economist Puey Ungphakorn, social critic Sulak Sivaraksa, author and political scientist Seksan Prasertkun, historian Nidhi Eoseewong, and political scientist Chai-Anan Samudavanija. I became more interested in social problems and social justice – and the debate as to whether economic development brings greater social justice.' Over the following decade, Anand would involve himself in numerous activities with a public-service component, both at home and abroad.

In Thailand in 1993, he became chairman of the Thailand Environment Institute and also of the Business Council for Sustainable Development, and vice chairman of the Suan Luang Rama IX Foundation. He was founding chairman in 1998 of the university council of Asian University, which had links to the UK's Imperial College in London, and taught in English. Anand also joined the advisory board of the National Social Policy Committee. From 1998, after his leading role in drafting a new constitution for Thailand, he chaired the National Commission for the Formulation of Policy and Action Plan on Human Rights for two years through to its completion.

International public service

In 1994, Anand became a member of the informal advisory group to the United Nations High Commissioner for Refugees, and remained there until 2000. The following year, he became a member of the advisory board to the Council on Foreign Relations in New York. He was invited to join the the InterAction Council in 1996 for five years – this had been established in 1983 to mobilise senior statesmen from around the world to offer recommendations and possible solutions to global political, economic, and social issues. In 1999, he was included in the World Bank's advisory group on anti-corruption in East Asia and the Pacific, and the following year became an international adviser to the International Committee of the Red Cross.

Anand lent his name to various private foundations, including two commemorating major international figures: U Thant, the Burmese secretary general of the United Nations for most of Anand's time there; and Carlos Romulo, the veteran Philippine foreign secretary in the 1970s and early 1980s, who had been president of the fourth session of the United Nations General Assembly (1949–1950), the first Asian to serve in that role, and a candidate for secretary general in 1953. 'There was no need to have meetings,' Anand recalls of helping memorialise these figures. U Thant and Romulo were both people to whom he felt an attachment and debt of gratitude. 'They were kind to me – they saw me grow up from the ranks,' he says.

Anand was invited to join the Club de Madrid, an organisation formed in 2001 by the Spanish government for 'serious deliberations on international topics, including conflict resolution'. Its motto is 'Democracy that Delivers'. The Club de Madrid has nearly 100 former heads of states and government from all over the world as full members. Anand admired the Club de Madrid's regional roundtables, and still contributes inputs from afar on issues of interest to him when he cannot attend in person. 'They had very good people,' he says. In 2008, he joined the Global Leadership Foundation for three years. This was founded in 2004 by F.W. de Klerk, the former president of South Africa, and has similar objectives to the Club de Madrid, but is much more low-key. Anand rarely attended meetings, but was aware of the foundation's particular interest in Myanmar. 'I was not optimistic,' he recalls.

During Anand's first government, Thailand played a useful facilitating role ahead of the United Nations Transitional Authority in Cambodia (UNTAC) in 1992. This had raised Anand's international profile. UNTAC had been considered a success for UN Secretary General Boutros Boutros-Ghali, even though some later faulted the UN for being in too much of a hurry to leave Cambodia. The incumbent prime minister, Hun Sen of the Cambodian People's Party, had come second to

Prince Norodom Ranariddh's royalist FUNCINPEC party in the May 1993 general election organised under UNTAC. Ranariddh's father, Prince Norodom Sihanouk, had parlayed an unusual co-prime minister arrangement with Hun Sen nominally taking second place. In practice, Hun Sen retained most of the levers of power with control over the military, bureaucracy, judiciary, and police.

Boutros-Ghali's term as secretary general was marked by the Rwandan genocide in 1994 that left over a million dead, and wars in the former Yugoslavia and Somalia. When he needed to be re-elected for a second term, a US presidential election was under way. There existed added tension over the US's unpaid dues to the UN. Madeleine Albright was secretary of state, and her chemistry with Boutros-Ghali was not good. His imperious style also played badly with smaller countries, who tended to feel ignored. In the end, the US went it alone and vetoed Boutros-Ghali – making him the first of six secretary generals not to be re-elected.

As it became clear that Boutros-Ghali would not be serving a second term, from 1997 to 2001, the question arose as to who should replace him. Most agreed that that it was Asia's turn to fill the post after Africa, but Africa had had only one term instead of the customary two. This boosted the prospects of Kofi Annan, an urbane and experienced Ghanaian UN insider. Before there was agreement to allow Africa a second term with another secretary general, there was talk about who from Asia might be suitable. Anand's name was floated informally by a senior figure in the United Nations Development Programme who had been in Thailand in the early 1990s.

The idea did not go far. Some doubted his suitability for the position, not least because he would have to campaign for the job and get himself elected. Anand would normally be appointed to a position and get on with it. Did he have the temperament for the endless politicking, sensitive diplomacy, and need to compromise necessary to be secretary general?

'He is more than capable of being one,' says Manaspas Xuto, 'but he knew it was the kind of thing that he would have to compete for. What if he lost?' Anand was a tested and effective diplomat with considerable direct UN experience from his years in New York in the 1960s and 1970s. There was also for that reason some interest in Tommy Koh in Singapore, who had a similar UN background. In that crucial respect, Anand was much more qualified than compatriots Surin Pitsuwan and Surakiart Sathirathai, whose names later hovered around the position as possible successors to Kofi Annan, both of whom were politicians. A stronger possibility in 1996 was veteran Indonesian foreign minister Ali Alatas, but he was facing serious health issues at the time after undergoing heart surgery.

Anand was aware that his name had come up as a possibility. 'I was asked by the Thai government about it, but I said no,' he recalls. 'I didn't have to think – it never entered my head. The main thing was I was not prepared to leave Thailand. I did not want to be parted from my daughters and grandchildren, and my wife would not have enjoyed the life either.'

'If it had become a reality, it would have been a great honour for Thailand,' reflects Saroj Chavanviraj, Anand's colleague at the UN during their New York years. A few years later, Yevgeny Primakov, a former Russian prime minister, foreign minister, and intelligence chief returned to the subject after the two had served on a United Nations' panel convened by Annan. 'Anand, if you ever did decide to run, we will vote for you,' he promised.

Advisory roles

It was fashionable in the late 20th century for multinational corporations to set up distinguished advisory boards, most of them based in the US or Europe. During his time in New York and Washington in the 1960s and 1970s, Anand had attended numerous functions as a diplomat, but had also come into contact with bankers and businessmen, which provided a basis for further development of relationships with these people. However, the first time he met Jack Welch, who in 1981 became chairman and chief executive of General Electric (GE), was when Henry Kissinger brought him to call on Anand at New York's Plaza hotel in 1991. They talked about Thailand and the general situation in Southeast Asia. 'I liked him,' says Anand.

Welch, a hard-driving, Irish-American chemical engineer, spent his entire career with GE. He believed that to succeed, companies needed to be first or second in their sector. He slashed GE headcounts and sold off unprofitable businesses, pushing up profits, turnover, and capitalisation. He was widely admired as being streetwise, and became a guru for US manufacturing generally. Welch approached Anand immediately after his first premiership, when he was briefly back at Saha Union. The US conglomerate at that time did some business with Thailand but had no significant corporate presence in the kingdom. Anand was surprised by the lack of interaction, and invited Welch to Bangkok. There was an audience with King Bhumibol, and Welch donated a scanner. 'I think he was impressed with Thailand in general,' Anand recalls.

In October 1992, the month Anand left office for the second time, he joined GE's international advisory board. He would soon befriend James McNerney, who was GE's Asia-Pacific president from 1993 to 1995, based in Hong Kong. On his Hong Kong watch, Welch asked McNerney to form a regional advisory group. Both regarded Anand as key to that body, and from 1994 to 1998 Anand chaired GE's Asia-Pacific Advisory Board. After that, until 2006, he remained GE's regional adviser.

Anand recalls very businesslike GE meetings every six months in New York or somewhere in Europe with distinguished speakers. The company meetings lasted four or five hours, and focused on the big scene, rather than operations or business. 'It was a very good format,' he says.

Anand's macro connection to GE was always well removed from any operations. He was never involved in bidding for business, for example when GE was competing to sell jet engines. He did, however, ask GE to persuade a Japanese partner to set up a plastics manufacturing base in Thailand rather than Malaysia around 2000. At the time, GE and another US company, Goldman Sachs, had been experiencing critical publicity over asset acquisitions. GE was a passive member in a group that had acquired bad assets rather cheaply. 'Many Thais felt they had exploited the situation by not paying higher prices,' Anand recalls. 'I actually called up Jack Welch. It was more than lobbying – more of a direct request. I told him: "You have a bad name in Thailand – this is a time to recover it".'[1]

Networking with some of the top people in their fields through advisory boards was extremely stimulating. 'You can contribute and you can learn,' says Anand. 'They were all experts in their fields, and I learned a lot from my association with them.' From 1992 to 2000, Anand also served on the Asia-Pacific board of IBM, and from 1995 to 2005 he was a member of Unocal's Asia-Pacific advisory board. His most enduring relationship, however, was on the international advisory board of Hank Greenberg's American International Group (AIG), from 1993 to 2011. He was invited to join by the board's chairman, Henry Kissinger. It was eventually disbanded following a corporate scandal in the US over the reinsurance business. The advisory board had from 15 to 20 members – much larger than GE with just ten.

In 2001, Anand became a member of the international advisory board of Toyota Motor Corporation. 'The difference with the American model is that the Japanese are very formal,' he says. In Japan, nobody ever spoke off the cuff. Everything was extremely measured, and the food always sublime. One meeting took place at a hot springs resort with bright sunshine blazing down outside. Everybody was dressed in business suits. Anand wondered aloud if such formal attire was really necessary. The matter was discussed, and Japanese members reappeared later still dressed in dark suits but without ties.

Anand's involvement with all these foreign corporates was not for financial gain, but for the insights he garnered and the exceptional networking opportunities the advisory boards provided.

'I never asked for speaking fees, but if I was invited anywhere first class travel and accommodation had to be provided,' says Anand. He declined two invitations to speak at the annual World Economic Forum at Davos because he would have had to bear the travel expenses personally. 'I never enjoy going to big events anyway,' he says. 'Many people go just to be seen.'

In Thailand, Anand stepped away from some of his business activities. He had served on the advisory council of the International Finance Corporation since 1991 and concluded his term in 1995. He resigned as chairman of Suthep Bulakul's Star Block Group in 1996. Anand had taken the position in 1982, and been instrumental in getting Malaysia's Sime Darby to take a shareholding. 'That's when we became close,' Suthep recalls. 'Once you have him as chairman, people work together. At our peak, we were building one house per day all over Thailand.' Suthep brought in housing technology from Norway and Japan, but struggled with the scale of the company. 'It needs a lot of very strong financial control,' he says. 'My failure was to trust people too much.'

'When the company's financial outlook was deteriorating, Suthep advised me to resign from the board,' Anand recalls. Although he resigned from the Star Block chairmanship, Anand retained the chairmanship of Eastern Star, a property developer in Rayong province in which Star Block had a major interest. Pairoj Piempongsant, the entrepreneur and political dealmaker who tracked Arthit Ourairat during the political crisis in mid 1992, had by then sold out his interest.

Thaksin and The Carlyle Group

Anand's most controversial international, private-sector association came after the 1997 crash. It was with The Carlyle Group, which is NASDAQ-listed and one of the world's largest private-equity companies. Anand served as a member of its Asian Advisory Board from 1998 to 2003. Another member of that board was Thaksin Shinawatra, the telecoms billionaire behind Shin Corporation, which owned AIS, Thailand's biggest mobile carrier.

The Carlyle Group was named after the New York hotel where its founders used to meet. In 1989, the group had taken on Frank Carlucci, President Ronald Reagan's defence secretary and deputy director of the CIA, who was highly connected in Washington and globally. George H.W. Bush had come on board after leaving office in 1994, and James Baker III, Bush's secretary of state, served as the group's senior counsellor. 'With door-openers of this calibre, along with shrewd investment skills, Carlyle has gone from an unknown in the world of private equity to one of its biggest players,' Leslie Wayne commented in *The New York Times*.

It acquired and maintained a reputation for powerful connections. In Europe, it had Karol Otto Pöhl, president of the Bundesbank in the 1980s; and John Major, the former British prime minister, would chair Carlyle Europe from 2001 to 2004.

In 1986, Thaksin Shinawatra, a former police colonel, had founded a modest computer rental company, Advance Info System (AIS). He later launched pager, mobile phone, cable, and satellite businesses that were eventually consolidated into ShinCorp. During the 1990s, as his wealth grew, Thaksin moved into politics, taking over the leadership of Chamlong Srimuang's Palang Tham Party. Chamlong's ascetic political instincts had failed him in Chuan's coalition government, and he believed that Thaksin, as an astute and dynamic businessman, would have a more practical understanding of the development needs of a modernising Thailand. Thaksin served briefly as Chuan's foreign minister in 1994, resigned from Palang Tham in 1996 as it fell apart, and in 1998 founded his own party, Thai Rak Thai. In the late 1990s, after the new constitution had been promulgated and Palang Tham was history, Thaksin starting seeing Anand on a regular basis, drawing from him political insights. Anand remembers lunches together every two or three months with Thaksin and his wife, Khunying Potjaman.

The relationship was strong enough for Thaksin at one stage to ask Anand to be the leader of Thai Rak Thai with himself as the party's secretary general. Anand declined, as always. Chamlong had asked him to take over as leader of Palang Tham before he approached Thaksin, and was similarly turned down. 'I was surprised when Chamlong handed over his party to Thaksin,' says Anand. 'The Democrats approached me too,' he recalls.

Former President Bush came to Bangkok on a speaking engagement in April 1998 at Thaksin's invitation, and specifically requested that Anand be included in the arrangements. Anand was invited to a private dinner with Bush at Thaksin's home, the first time he had visited. It was a pleasant evening, with the conversation mostly about Thailand. After the elaborate meal, Anand and Thaksin moved to a small sitting room with David Rubenstein, a former aide to President Jimmy Carter and the co-founder and co-chief executive of The Carlyle Group.[2] Anand had not met Rubenstein before, but both he and Thaksin agreed to join The Carlyle Group's new Asia-Pacific advisory board.

'I didn't know anything about The Carlyle Group until they approached me,' he recalls. His decision to join had been made at Bush's personal request. The former US president had always made friends easily, and never stood on ceremony or pulled rank. He had met Anand when the two were diplomats at the United Nations in New York, when they dealt with each other on China, Taiwan, and Indochina. 'Somehow we became good friends even though Thailand was a small entity in the UN context,' Anand recalls. 'We got along.' Bush had welcomed Anand warmly to Washington as prime minister, despite the circumstances of his appointment. 'Apart from not staying at Blair House, I was given a full range of engagements befitting a visiting prime minister,' Anand says. 'Bush is a special guy.'

The first meeting of the Carlyle Asia-Pacific advisory board was held a few months later in South Korea, and also included Fidel Ramos, a former president of the Philippines. Anand and Thaksin arrived separately. 'I think I spoke more than Thaksin,' Anand recalls. 'Everybody knew Thaksin was aiming for a political career.'

Anand got on well with Thaksin, but was uncertain how well he knew the exceptionally wealthy politician. Bush once asked Anand's opinion of Thaksin. 'I said I liked him as a person, and found him interesting, but I always had some doubts about his genuineness,' Anand recalls.

In the late 1990s, Carlyle was regarded with some trepidation by many in Thailand; they saw it as a giant vulture fund intent on scooping up undervalued assets in the aftermath of the financial crash. 'The Carlyle Group is a godsend for conspiracy theorists who are convinced that the world is run by, and on behalf of, a shadowy network of wealthy men,' *The Economist* later observed.[3]

'I'm just trying to be a matchmaker for those who want to invest in Thailand,' Thaksin told *The Nation* in April 1998. 'What our country needs most is capital.'

'As a member of the advisory board, I am not supposed to get involved in operations,' Anand later told the same reporter. 'I just give out advice when we meet to discuss about the economic or business opportunities in the region.'[4]

The board continued to meet annually. Its second outing, in 1999, was at the Mandarin Oriental in Bangkok with Bush present. The Carlyle Group was reported to be interested in steel and energy in Thailand. In May 1999, it was part of a five-company consortium that also included General Electric Capital Services bidding for Siam City Bank. Nothing came of that because the bank's asset values were on the slide. Indeed, despite having hundreds of millions of dollars available to invest in the region, The Carlyle Group never invested in Thailand, apart from an investment in a Charoen Pokphand offshore subsidiary in Hong Kong.

Thaksin stepped away from The Carlyle Group in 2001, when he became prime minister. Anand remained on the advisory board until 2003, but never felt he could generate much interest in rescuing distressed companies.

Although Anand was descended from the educated elite administrators of Siam in the 19th and early 20th century, he strived to be in tune with different social strata, and had strong ideas about where the country should be going. As prime minister, Thaksin cast himself as a humble, self-made man of the people, although he came from a rich and influential family in Chiang Mai. He came to be viewed by the old Thai establishment as a classic Sino-Thai businessman, and an existential threat. His personal wealth based on a mobile telephone concession represented full percentage points of Thailand's gross domestic product.

Thaksin excelled at addressing and motivating target groups, particularly at political rallies. Many of his campaign techniques were borrowed from abroad with scant acknowledgement. However, in a Thai context, they came across as fresh, dynamic, modern. Critics would later chide him for pandering to anything that seemed 'new' and spuriously progressive.

Thaksin's election in 2001 was widely viewed as an exciting opportunity to bring about a more prosperous, modern Thailand. It was a watershed in Thai politics with the country broadly united. From Prem Tinsulanond, president of the Privy Council, down, there was a desire to see Thaksin ride out his problematic asset declaration with the Constitutional Court – which he achieved by the vote of one judge – and to have the chance to succeed as prime minister. 'There was nothing wrong with Thaksin in the first place,' recalls Bill Heinecke, chairman of Minor Group, one of Thailand's highest-profile multinationals. 'He presents very well.'

Thaksin Shinawatra triumphed as no elected Thai politician had ever done before. With the benefit of the new electoral and party rules drafted for the 1997 constitution, the telecom billionaire swept into office on the back of an almost 70 per cent turnout with 248 seats in the elected 500-seat lower house. His party, Thai Rak Thai (TRT), went on to absorb the New Aspiration Party of former Prime Minister Chavalit Yongchaiyudh, which had won 36 seats, to form a comfortable parliamentary majority with Chavalit as a deputy prime minister.

Thaksin improved on this in 2005, when TRT won 375 seats in its own right and was beholden to no other party. The second result was all the more credible for an even higher 72 per cent turnout. No Thai government had ever gone full term or won re-election so convincingly. Thaksin had reinvented Thai representative politics, and the old ruling elites became deeply disquieted. They felt he had hijacked the liberal, progressive intentions of the People's Constitution that had emerged from a national consultative process, bent it to his advantage, and co-opted the new institutions that had been meant to provide checks and balances.

The Election Commission (EC), one of the newly minted independent institutions, started out well in 2001. In line with the 1997 constitution, this was the first time all senators were elected. The election commissioners delayed confirmation of more than half the newly elected senators while complaints against them were investigated. Although virtually all were allowed to pass, it was a warning that Thailand's traditional corrupt election habits would no longer be tolerated. 'It did not stop the practices, but it was an awakening,' recalls Gothom Arya, one of the first commissioners. The negative side of this was that the entrenched powers, who had always viewed the senate as a means of keeping the disorderly lower house in check, were concerned that the EC would become too zealous and powerful and sideline them. 'There was adjustment on both sides,' Gothom recalls.

An elected senate was a big switch from the days when the prime minister more or less controlled who was nominated. Even so, Anand's drafting commission had struggled in 1997 over how to make the senate genuinely representative. Thought had been given to a partitioning system whereby different sectors were given senate allocations – the judiciary, academia, labour, non-governmental organisations, and so forth. A major problem was finding representatives for farmers, the largest section of the population. The agricultural sector remained marginalised and disorganised – not least because this had always suited preceding governments; efforts to organise the sector had been regarded as 'socialistic' and threatening. Thaksin's strong political footing in the North and Northeast gave previously marginalised rural voters a new and real sense of representation.

Thaksin promoted greater national awareness. He laudably wanted to cut export dependency and develop domestic markets. He promoted distinctly Thai products in his celebrated One Tambon One Product scheme to promote local specialities. It was a popular idea that still resonates, but the economy remains heavily dependent on exports and tourism. A cosmetic attempt to promote Thai attire in the cabinet, in the way Prem had successfully done with smart *prarachatan* tunics, failed. Thaksin arrived with silk tailors from Chiang Mai, and other cabinet members came up with cotton specialists. The Thai outfits had unforeseen security implications. Ministers were left with insufficient pockets, and staff found papers and telephone numbers lying around the cabinet room. 'Sometimes, they left state secrets on the table,' then Cabinet Secretary General Wissanu Krea-ngam recalls.

'Thaksin raised the election process by a notch or two,' says Anand, noting his good use of study groups and research, clear policy formulation, and effective campaigning. 'It was the first election to concentrate on issues rather than personalities.' By the time of Thaksin's re-election in 2005, however, Thai politics had again become highly personalised. Thaksin's critics included the Yellow Shirts originally mobilised by Sondhi Limthongkul over a business dispute with Thaksin that went on to become conflated with loyalty to the monarchy. The Thai media also became politically polarised. Thaksin's opponents accused him of parliamentary dictatorship and tyranny. They beseeched the ailing King Bhumibol to invoke Article 7 of the constitution to dissolve parliament, but without success.

'I never had much sympathy with involving Article 7, and I think I did say that publicly at the time,' Anand says. 'I was sure the king would never make use of it. Thaksin went too far with some of his oratory, but I never believed he was anti-monarchy, or wanted to dismantle the system. I do not believe he is a republican.'

Anand was increasingly among Thaksin's critics, but in public comments stuck to specific points of contention. He had unwittingly played a vital role in Thaksin's electoral success because of his work drafting the liberal constitution of 1997. 'We wanted a strong executive – we knew that coalition governments did not work,' Anand recalls. The reforms had been intentionally drafted to favour large parties and produce decisive governments free of coalition compromises. Thaksin's brilliance was in seizing the opportunity, and ushering in an entirely new style of party politics with slick campaigning and popular manifestos. The plodding Democrats had been left at the starting gate.

Although Anand and Thaksin came into office through different doors, they stood apart from all other Thai prime ministers for their experience in the business world – Anand the captain of industry, Thaksin the entrepreneurial, self-made telecoms magnate. Thaksin's police background gave him an understanding of the bureaucracy and the Thai ways of doing things, but he had little of Anand's technocratic or diplomatic experience – he had been foreign minister for less than four months. Both men were widely perceived as being goal-driven, effective national chief executives – a profile Thaksin always made much more explicit when presenting himself.

The two had different working styles. Thaksin surrounded himself with a dozen telephones that enabled him to reach out as a commanding central presence. Anand had been unhurried and delegated as much as possible; he projected a certain effortlessness after arriving for work at 9am each day. 'On his desk, you could not see anything,' recalls Wissanu Krea-ngam, the cabinet secretary general. Anand might have had something out to read, but never stacks of files.

'Sometimes when I went to see Anand, he was reading a newspaper and smoking a cigar,' says Wissanu. He once found Anand perusing *Si Phaendin*, the acclaimed 1950s novel by a former prime minister, *MR* Kukrit Pramoj. 'I know the story but have never read it before,' Anand explained.

Both prime ministers shared an intolerance of long-windedness. Anand would give speakers, particularly civil servants, 'three minutes no more' to make their point. Thaksin also did not want to be lectured. 'His reaction would always be disagreement – he did not want anybody to teach him,' Wissanu recalls.

Although Anand read documents closely when necessary, he could also delegate and trust the opinions of people with more direct experience. Thaksin kept a tighter watch; he had a strong grasp of detail and regulations, particularly with regard to infrastructure. He could recite building codes, for example, and followed projects that interested him closely.

Anand immersed himself in no more detail than necessary, and openly recognised his ignorance in some areas. He recalls a conversation with Thaksin after the prime minister had upbraided some judges. Anand thought this unwise, and tried to broach the rule of law as a topic. Thaksin immediately cut him off. He said he had a doctorate from Sam Houston University in Texas in criminology, and his dissertation was on the rule of law. Anand was astonished by the remark.

Thaksin did not indulge in intellectual jousting with his advisers, and would never appoint 'presumed enemies' – sounding boards to find the weaknesses in his ideas and arguments. He charted his path through other means, and extracted information in his own way. 'If Thaksin invites you to come to see him and talk, then he is open,' says Wissanu. 'But it is upon his invitation.' During cabinet meetings, Thaksin would invite dissenting opinions to speak up, but he always warned ministers already in agreement to say nothing and not waste time.

It was all a marked contrast with Chuan's government, when everybody got their say as politicians wrestling interminably with complex, non-binary issues. If Thaksin's no-nonsense approach was suited to a corporate setting, it was sometimes vulnerable to failure in the political world with its awkward realities and certainty that all of the people could never be pleased all of the time.

Wissanu believes that the public always assumed Anand had good intentions and no inside agenda, and that this worked in his favour. 'People trust Anand's objectives but they don't trust yours,' he once warned Thaksin. 'You must choose the right way to go, not just where to go – how to go too.' When Wissanu pointed out to Thaksin that innocent people had likely been killed during his controversial war on drugs, he warned that it would rebound on the prime minister, not negligent officials. Thaksin's response was dismissive: 'That is significant but it is not my duty,' he said. 'I am the prime minister – I cannot handle the details.'

Many might regard the forthrightness of both Anand and Thaksin as not particularly Thai. They were so different from the placid outward demeanours of Prem and Chuan, or the cheerful vagueness of Chatichai. Many Thais were impressed when Thaksin stood up to foreigners and pushed back forcefully. Their pride in Anand was for speaking eloquently on their behalf – for presenting Thailand well. Thaksin's original party name, 'Thais Love Thais', fell short of outright jingoism but certainly alluded to some sort of collective resistance to outside predations and interference. 'The UN is not my father,' he famously told the press when Asma Jahangir, the UN special rapporteur on extrajudicial executions, expressed 'deep concern' about the conduct of his war on drugs, and the piled corpses it produced. 'Do not ask too much,' Thaksin warned. 'There is no problem.'[5]

CHAPTER 19

ON PUBLIC SERVICE
(2004–2011)

UN panel – threats, challenges, change

Nobody could have predicted Anand's brief return to international diplomacy in 2004 when UN Secretary General Kofi Annan beckoned him. The circumstances surrounding his appointment were also unforeseen. The purpose of the first Gulf War in February 1991 had been to liberate Kuwait from the Iraqi occupying forces of President Saddam Hussein. President George H.W. Bush had been careful to enlist UN and other international support for the US-led response. Once the liberation had been accomplished in early 1991, Bush did not press his overwhelming military advantage and take the war on to Baghdad, the Iraqi capital. It seemed to some in 2003 that Bush's son, President George W. Bush, was intent on making up for his father's omission with the second Gulf War.

In March 2003, the US and forces from Australia, Poland, and the UK invaded Iraq to effect regime change by military means. Following just three weeks of major combat operations, the Ba'athist government was unseated and Saddam went into hiding.

The invasion was deeply controversial. It raised issues about pre-emptive strikes, and the grounds on which war can be justified. On 11 September 2001, in an attack masterminded by Osama bin Laden, the Sunni Islamist terrorist organisation Al-Qaeda had brought down the Twin Towers of the World Trade Center in New York using hijacked passenger jets, killing almost 3,000 people. Although Saddam's secular regime was bellicose in the face of UN sanctions and unpalatable to many, Iraq was not involved in the '9-11' attack. Bin Laden came from a prominent Saudi Arabian family. Fifteen of the 19 Middle Eastern terrorists who hijacked four civilian aircraft were also from Saudi Arabia, an oil-rich country with strong business and strategic links to the West.

So why was Iraq invaded? In February 2003, US Secretary of State Colin Powell made a compelling presentation to the United Nations Security Council based on a variety of intelligence reports. He stated unequivocally that Iraq possessed weapons of mass destruction. This was not implausible since Saddam had developed chemical weapons in the 1980s during the war with Iran, and had deployed them in 1988 against the Kurdish minority in the north, and in 1991 against a rebellion in the south. Hans Blix, a former Swedish diplomat who headed the UN Monitoring, Verification and Inspection Commission for three years until June 2003, later told journalists in Bangkok that had his teams been allowed another 90 days, they would probably have been able to confirm that Iraq no longer possessed weapons of mass destruction. But that was too late.

For UN Secretary General Kofi Annan, the highly questionable second Gulf War and invasion of Iraq not only lacked UN endorsement, but turned the world of multilateral diplomacy upside down. Annan was being questioned from all sides on the role of the UN, and by May he had decided that a panel of some kind was needed to clarify matters. This gained further impetus in August at the annual Security Council retreat when Thant Myint-U, head of the UN's policy planning unit, drew up a list of the challenges and broad issues facing the organisation following US-led military action in Afghanistan and Iraq in the wake of 9-11.

Annan and his deputies immediately endorsed the idea of a panel, but it would take another three weeks to decide whom it should include. The objective would be to identify all threats to world peace, not just terrorism. It was not conceived as a direct response to Bush and his neocon administration in Washington; its brief would be to consider global peace and security in the widest frame, and to recommend policies and institutional changes to address them; it was not to obsess with the 'war on terror' or the 'axis of evil'. It should help formulate overall policies, not tinker with institutions, or look for ways to make the UN larger. Thant felt that if the panel could find four or five ways to make the UN more effective, it would have justified its existence.

The panel was to be made up of respected elder government and international figures. The usual UN concerns about continental and gender balance immediately came into play. Gro Harlem Brundtland, a former Norwegian prime minister who went on to serve as director general of the World Health Organization, was initially considered as a potential co-chairperson. She had chaired the World Commission on Environment and Development in the 1980s, which concerned sustainable development and came to be known as the Brundtland Commission. Brundtland, however, had experienced recent health problems, and made it clear that she was willing to participate but not lead. While Annan had considered Brundtland partnering somebody from the South, she favoured assigning the chair to one individual without fretting over the North-South balance.

'I suggested Anand Panyarachun and explained who he was to people who did not know him,' Thant recalls. Thant is a grandson of U Thant, the Burmese UN secretary general from 1965 to 1973, and his father Tyn Myint-U was a senior official at ESCAP, the UN's regional office in Bangkok. Although Anand had attended Thant's parents' wedding in 1960, Thant himself only knew Anand by repute as a political leader and statesman. 'I could not think of any other retired Asian head-of-government-level person who was as respected and had no downsides,' says Thant.

Anand also had the added lustre of direct, if historic, UN experience, having served as Thailand's permanent representative to the UN from 1967 effectively until 1975. Before Annan was chosen, some had even suggested Anand in 1996 as a possible UN secretary general, but this had no bearing on developments in 2003. Annan did not know Anand at all when he placed an exploratory call to Bangkok to test his interest in serving as the panel's co-chair with Brundtland. The second time Annan telephoned, it was to say that Brundtland did not want the position and to ask if Anand would take the lead on his own.

'That's the kind of challenge I like, so I readily accepted,' Anand recalls replying after hearing the secretary general's proposal that he chair the panel. By the start of the annual UN General Assembly in September, the panel had been fleshed out. Its 16 members included only four women. Critics faulted it initially for its high average age and lack of recent, if any, UN experience. But the report was due within a year, and younger people in government and public service would simply have been unable to allocate the time needed.[1] Also, by excluding diplomats assigned to the UN in New York, there was a better chance the panel would perform 'out of the box', and not get bogged down in endless debate over the outdated but deeply entrenched composition of the Security Council. It was undoubtedly an important issue, but only one of many.

Annan and his staff had taken great care picking out names from the detailed rosters kept on every country. In terms of career experience, the selection included three former prime ministers, including Anand; one vice prime minister; six former foreign ministers; a former justice minister; a spymaster; a national security adviser; two generals (one a peacekeeper); a development banker; four senior diplomats; and seven heads of major international organisations.

The five permanent members of the Security Council – China, France, Russia, the UK, and the US – all had one member on the panel. The geographic spread among the remaining 11 members was broadly acceptable for its North-South mix: two Africans, two Latin Americans, one Arab, four Asians, one European, and one Australian. The panel was supported by an 11-member secretariat with Stephen Stedman of Stanford University as research director, and Bruce Jones of New York University as his deputy. The secretariat, which included Thant, was crucial to drafting the final document.

Panellist David Hannay, a former British permanent representative to the UN, was critical of the panel's title. 'The UN Secretary-General's High-Level Panel on Threats, Challenges and Change, was a masterpiece of the sort of bureaucratic jargon for which the UN, like other international organisations, was so infamous,' he wrote. 'It epitomised one of the UN's greatest weaknesses: an inability to communicate with ordinary people in a language which they could understand.' Hannay consoled himself that the title was at least a non-starter as an acronym.[2]

Tommy Koh, Anand's Singaporean colleague at the UN in their younger days, was not at all surprised by the secretary general's choice for the chair: 'I think the UN community regarded Anand as a statesman of the world, and in Asia as one of the top few,' he says. 'He is seen as someone of integrity and principle who does not covet power.'

Anand was new to most of his fellow panel members, knowing only Salim Ahmed Salim of Tanzania, Gareth Evans of Australia, and Brent Scowcroft from previous encounters, but he knew none of them well. Evans was extremely well versed on most of the topics under discussion, but had a reputation for abrasiveness. 'He is very able and forthright, but has a hot temper and can be a bit overbearing,' Anand recalls. Both men had been involved in the 1991–2 UN-backed international intervention in Cambodia. There was a more tenuous personal connection. Anand had been friendly in New York with an Australian diplomat, Michael Cook, who went on to become head of Australian intelligence (director general of the Office of National Assessments) for most of the 1980s. He was the author of the Cook Report into Soviet infiltration of the Australian Security Intelligence Organisation during the Cold War. Evans viewed Cook as a 'Tory', and blocked his rise to secretary, the top bureaucratic position, at the Department of Foreign Affairs and Trade in 1993 following four years as ambassador in Washington.

Evans knew about Soviet moles in Australian intelligence well enough. As foreign minister under Prime Minister Paul Keating, he had written to Yevgeny Primakov, the head of the Foreign Intelligence Service of the Russian Federation from 1991 to 1996 (which replaced the Soviet Union's KGB), to inform him that six Russian diplomats were being secretly expelled as spies. 'Primakov replied to Evans – absurdly – that these six Russian agents were "rogue elements" and were not acting on behalf of the government in Moscow,' *The Australian* later reported.[3] Evans described the incident as part of 'the extraordinary, tumultuous rush of events surrounding the end of the Cold War' but could not recall ever having read Michael Cook's report.[4] Ten years on, Cook was retired and Primakov was sitting across the table from Evans as a fellow panellist, with Cook's old buddy Anand presiding.

Thant had the idea of holding the plenary sessions in different places. He had been tempted to suggest opening the proceedings in Las Vegas – rolling the dice so to speak. That was glitzy but impractical. The distinction fell to Princeton at a 'gloomy company training establishment'. When the panel members arrived there from all over world, Thant was reminded of an HBO series, or a scene from a John le Carré spy novel. A blizzard was blowing as Anand wandered around in the cold, puffing a cigar and greeting people in avuncular fashion.

Primakov and Qian Qichen, a former vice prime minister and foreign minister from China (who had also played an important role in the Cambodian peace process), both had minders close by, reminding everybody that they were not quite the independent participants attending in their own right that they were meant to be. Primakov and Qian would remain among the quietest members of the panel until the late stages, when the wording of drafts needed to be finalised, red lines drawn, and deals done.

Brent Scowcroft, a retired air force general and urbane Cold War warrior who had been national security adviser to President Gerald Ford and President Bush Senior, was personally sceptical of the younger Bush's unilateralist approach to

Iraq and his small 'coalition of the willing'. Even so, Scowcroft remained tapped into Washington thinking, and close to Henry Kissinger. Anand had met him first during his time as ambassador in Washington. Thant remembers Scowcroft as being detached from the drafting minutiae but a kind of 'safety check' keeping things real – 'always extremely polite, very engaging, and thoughtful'.

Kofi Annan launched the panel early in December 2003. It met six times for three days roughly every six weeks between 5 December 2003 and 5 November 2004. The first and last two meetings, held at Princeton, Tarrytown, and New York City respectively, were not too far from the UN headquarters. One, at Mont Pèlerin in Switzerland, and another, at Baden in Austria, were near UN offices in Geneva and Vienna respectively. The third meeting at the end of April was held in Addis Ababa, Ethiopia. Anand and the other panellists were struck by the politeness of the Ethiopians, but dismayed that there was insufficient time and security to get out and see anything of the country. 'We never had a day off,' Anand recalls. 'I wanted to walk down to the market but I was not allowed to go out – it was too dangerous.'

The penultimate meeting was held at Tarrytown on the Rockefeller Estate in the Pocantico Conference Center, which is used for annual gatherings of the presidents of major foundations and officials from the UN Security Council. The final meeting, in November, was held in a Lower Manhattan hotel in the most sombre of settings overlooking Ground Zero, the dark pits where the Twin Towers of the World Trade Center had once stood. It rained heavily for the three days the panel made its final deliberations, locked away together for meetings and meals.[5]

Attendance at the plenary sessions was remarkably good, with most panellists not missing more than a day here or there. Anand shepherded the process along, always mindful of his tight schedule. Amre Moussa, the Egyptian secretary general of the League of Arab States, was very concerned about the Security Council issue, but had a scheduling conflict for the final meeting in Lower Manhattan. He pleaded with Anand for another meeting, but was refused because of the immovable deadline. 'Otherwise the process would never have ended,' Anand recalls.

Equally important to the plenary sessions were some 40 complementary thematic regional consultations held all over the world – New York, Cairo, Shanghai, Rio de Janeiro, Singapore, Warsaw, Kyoto, Mexico City – organised by governments, think tanks, universities, and foundations at short notice to chime in with the deliberations of the UN panel. It was a global effort to engage leading thinkers on the key security issues of the day. The panel also engaged directly with key players, such as Mohamed ElBaradei, director general of the International Atomic Energy Agency.

An initial idea, that Kofi Annan be sent an interim report half-way through, was abandoned as onerous and impractical in the time available. Instead, Annan met with the panel for the last three sessions, so all parties were able to calibrate their thinking. The report's 2004 delivery date was pushed back from September to November–December. This provided more time and disentangled it from the General Assembly and the final stages of the US presidential election, which saw Bush return for a second term. The delay ensured more measured deliberation of the final outcome document – overseen by a different panel – in time for the 2005 General Assembly that marked the 60th anniversary of the UN.

In the early meetings, a palpable mutual antipathy could be discerned between some of the Western and non-Western members, between North and South. Thant watched Anand smooth out some of the initial tensions and conflicting world views, remaining genial and relatively passive. 'I spent the first fortnight getting to know them – and them getting to know me,' Anand recalls of his initial 'trust-building measures' in December. He introduced himself to some as 'Whisky Anand' to reduce confusion with Kofi Annan. Establishing personal relationships, he believed, would help with thorny issues later: 'It means they are more likely to deal with things they may not want to hear. I made friends with everybody, drinking and socialising. It was a good group, but it was not easy to chair a meeting of such prominent people.' He recalls having to shut down some early arguments between Evans and Nafis Sadik from Pakistan, the former executive director of the UN Population Fund.

'Nobody disliked him,' Thant says, recalling how Anand kept the process going and calmed any heated debate without pushing any substantive opinions of his own. 'Where that was useful – critically – was at the very end, when deals had to be cut, and people had to accept certain compromises,' says Thant. 'Then he would be the guy that everyone didn't have a problem with. In the end, he became very useful.'

'[Anand] had no strong view on the policy issues before the panel and was a champion of consensus at almost any price, which certainly irritated some of the stronger-minded members of the panel, but also helped to move business along and to ensure that the final report was indeed agreed by all,' Hannay recalled.[6]

Gareth Evans recalls Anand as 'a courtly and decent chair' who was liked and respected by the panel members. 'But I have to say he did not in any way drive the process, and was more anxious to avoid disharmony through lowest-common-denominator recommendations than to produce really substantive, cutting-edge results.'[7]

Anand largely concealed from Hannay and his fellow panel members his strong and long-held personal disapproval for the US invasion of Iraq – a topic on which he did not hesitate to hold forth to US ambassadors in Bangkok during Kenan Institute business. For a while, he had even stopped reading *The Economist* and other Western media that supported forceful regime change. During the plenary meetings, Anand allowed members the freedom to go back and forth on issues that needed to be debated. 'That gives them a feeling that the chair is being fair to them,' says Anand. 'It is very important that the chair has integrity, common sense, and trustworthiness – it must be held in high esteem, and seen to be impartial, but flexible in some ways.'

Evans and Hannay were the most proactive members in terms of actual drafting, and interacted closely with the secretariat. Both pressed more expansive concepts of multilateralism, intervention, and protection. The panel identified ten main threats to global peace and stability: poverty; infectious disease; environmental degradation; interstate war; civil war; genocide; atrocities such as trafficking people for sexual slavery or body parts; weapons of mass destruction; terrorism; and transnational crime. There were strong debates on the definition of terrorism – including state terrorism – and factors that might give rise to it, such as poverty and occupation.

There was also the issue of when war and pre-emptive strikes can be justified – topical given the events unfolding in Iraq. There was not much debate on peacekeeping; its value was mostly self-evident. The most important issue to be excluded was climate change. This was not because it was not recognised as a threat to humanity and stability. Stedman argued that climate change was still an emerging area of concern, and that more study was needed to take the topic forward. Infectious diseases, on the other hand, clearly threatened global peace and stability, and as an issue lent itself easily to building consensus, shared responses, and multilateral institutions. Severe Acute Respiratory Syndrome, commonly known as SARS, was a particular concern at the time, and the World Health Organization had won plaudits for rolling out an effective response to the global hazard.

Predictably, the main issue on which the panel failed to achieve consensus was reform of the Security Council – by far the most important topic to most permanent representatives at the UN. Anand conceded this in his submission to the secretary general: 'Members of the panel disagree about the models put forth for Security Council expansion and the method for determining the criteria for Security Council membership.'

Annan was more optimistic that there could be reform. 'Among the most significant recommendations is the expansion of the Security Council from 15 to 24 members, either by adding six new permanent members, without veto, or by creating a new category of four-year, renewable seats which could be regionally distributed,' he wrote in an article at the time. 'I believe either formula would strengthen the council's legitimacy in the eyes of the world, by bringing its membership closer to the realities of the 21st century – as opposed to those of 1945, when the UN Charter was drafted.'

Although there was much lobbying for reform in 2004 and 2005, the Security Council remains unreformed to this day. Obsolete references to 'enemy states' – Germany, Italy, and Japan, the vanquished Axis nations of World War II – in three articles of the UN Charter have not been removed. The Russian Federation continues to oppose their deletion on the grounds of historical context. The countries themselves – today prosperous, democratic, non-belligerent nations – meanwhile still want places on the Security Council, as do Brazil, Egypt, India, and South Africa, among others. Anand recalls many countries being mentioned, but no discussion of their individual merits.

With hindsight, Anand believes some of his panel's thunder may have been stolen by another report that Annan commissioned. At almost the same time, Jeffrey Sachs, director of the Earth Institute of Columbia University, was leading the UN Millennium Project and preparing an action plan based on the work of dedicated task forces over four years. The objective was to set Millennium Development Goals for 2015 in eight areas.[8] Sachs's report, 'Investing in Development: A Practical Plan to Achieve the Millennium Development Goals', was completed in January 2005 soon after Anand's report, and its key recommendations were adopted at a special session in September that year.

The two reports were complementary in some ways, but they inevitably competed for attention. Sachs had also generated considerable interest in December with his bestselling book, *The End of Poverty: Economic Possibilities for*

Our Time. His ideas provided some consolation to those who were dismayed by Bush's re-election in the US, and who feared that obsessiveness about the Middle East situation and the eradication of Al-Qaeda, might overshadow the greater global battle against poverty. Indeed, even if the Millennium Development Goals have not been achieved, significant progress has been made since and lives saved.

In terms of peace and stability, however, the world is not a safer place. In his final submission, Anand called for a redoubling of efforts to resolve 'longstanding disputes that continue to fester and to feed the new threats we now face. Foremost among these are the issues of Palestine, Kashmir and the Korean Peninsula.' To the unresolved conflicts with international dimensions Anand cited at that time, one can today add regions in Central and West Africa, Afghanistan, Iraq, Libya, Syria, Yemen, Ukraine, as well as the southern reaches of the Philippines. According to the Sydney-based Institute for Economics and Peace (IEP), the Global Peace Index has declined every year since 2008, with a slight improvement in 2016 and 2017. The IEP estimated that 'global peacefulness' had declined by over 2.1 per cent since 2008, and assessed the economic impact of violence on the global economy as US$14.3 trillion in 2016, or 12.6 per cent of gross world product.[9]

It is difficult to measure the success of international commissions – nobody can say what might have been without them – but there are plenty of sceptics. 'I have been on many commissions, and I have come to the conclusion in my old age that I will not serve on any more,' says Tommy Koh, Anand's Singaporean colleague at the UN. 'You work very hard on good recommendations and they get no traction. I have seen it again and again. There is a disconnect between these eminent guys looking at a problem – diagnosing it – and the people on the ground who are actually grappling with it. I guess they don't have any ownership of the policy. There is no conduit between these panels and commissions and the people on the ground.'

Others were more positive. Annan praised Anand's panel for 'reaching a consensus on a definition of terrorism'.[10] 'It's still a very good report for laying out the problems and issues,' says Thant, noting how it underlined the importance of strong and effective states in addressing all problems. The report also stimulated some UN institutional reforms that have endured – the creation of a peace-building commission, and reforms in the human rights commission, and in the secretary general's office. The panel also facilitated important debates, particularly through the 40 related meetings around the world that were usually attended by one or two of the panellists. 'This provided the main mechanism for governments to get together and discuss the post-9-11, post-Iraq invasion world,' says Thant. 'It meant that you had something that was at least state-of-the-art thinking on the whole range of most important issues of that decade.'

Evans recalls that composition of the Security Council was 'the biggest issue we were wrestling with, and where expectations of a breakthrough were highest, but politics as usual prevailed. The panel's biggest success in his view was endorsing the Responsibility to Protect (R2P) – a 'crucial precondition' for its adoption at the UN World Summit in September 2005, attended by over 170 world leaders. Evans thinks some of the Human Rights Council changes were good, although the jury is 'still out on whether these have been of much use'.

As Anand wound up his panel's deliberations on time, there was speculation about who should eventually succeed Kofi Annan as secretary general. It would be Asia's turn. Primakov shook hands as they all bade farewell, and said, 'Anand, if your government should nominate you, you'd get the Russian vote.' Anand laughed at the jocular endorsement from the old spymaster. 'I didn't take it seriously, but it was an indirect expression of his appreciation for the work I did as chair,' he says.

National Reconciliation Commission

Right on the heels of chairing the UN panel in 2004, Anand agreed to head a commission in southern Thailand, where the security situation had deteriorated alarmingly. The three Muslim-majority southern provinces, Narathiwat, Pattani, and Yala, had been annexed by Siam from a Malay sultanate in 1902, and saw renewed restiveness after World War II. In the late 1960s, the Pattani United Liberation Organisation (PULO) was founded. It needled the authorities with localised terrorist activity, but occasionally went further afield. In early 1981, for instance, a southbound train was stopped further north in the Isthmus of Kra, Thailand's narrowest point, near Nakhon Si Thammarat. The locomotive was uncoupled and blown up, but there was no loss of life. Sporadic terrorism of this kind was an irritant but had no significant impact on life in the rest of the country.

During the 1980s, when Prem Tinsulanond was prime minister, there were a number of successful national pacification initiatives. The Communist Party of Thailand was finally disbanded, and the situation in the deep south also calmed.

That continued through the 1990s with relatively peaceful coexistence and relaxed military control. Tensions began brewing again in late 2001, however, and worsened during Thaksin's 'war on drugs' in 2003. They ratcheted up in earnest in January 2004 with an attack on an army base in Narathiwat that left four dead.

On 28 April 2004, Islamic insurgents launched pre-dawn attacks on 11 government locations spread through Pattani, Songkhla, and Yala provinces. These were expected by security forces, which struck back. According to the government, 107 insurgents were killed along with five security personnel. The historic Krue Se mosque was seized by the attackers, and a nine-hour siege followed. Deputy Prime Minister Chavalit Yongchaiyudh gave orders that a negotiated solution be found, but this was ignored on the ground by General Pallop Pinmanee. The mosque was finally stormed, and all 32 people inside killed. Many of the dead were wearing shoes, suggesting they had taken refuge and were hoping to make an escape. The nature of the head wounds indicated extra-judicial executions.

Although Interior Minister Bhokin Balakula defended the heavy response, a subsequent official enquiry noted that 'the tactic of laying siege to the mosque, surrounding it with security forces, in tandem with the use of negotiations with the assailants, could have ultimately led to their surrender'.[11] Pallop was recalled from the South. He offered his resignation, but it was refused. He remained on active duty as deputy commander of the International Security Operations Command (ISOC). 'The Krue Se incident could be taken as a lesson in training our officials to look for more peaceful methods,' Thaksin commented after the report appeared.[12] The other ten incidents that day, which included the killing of an entire soccer team, were not publicly investigated.

The lessons in measured responses by security officials that Thaksin spoke of were not learned. On 25 October at Tak Bai in Narathiwat, close to the border with Malaysia, there was an even more serious incident after mostly farmers and fishermen gathered to protest the detention of village elders for alleged militancy. The heavy official response involved water cannons and live fire. Seven protesters were shot dead, and scores of young and old men arrested. Some were forced to crawl, then tied up and made to lie in trucks piled four layers high in some instances. At least 78 detainees were found suffocated or crushed to death by the time they reached prison six hours later.[13] Some officials suggested fatuously that the victims died because they were weak due to Ramadan fasting. Krue Se and Tak Bai together claimed almost 200 lives.

'While central to the story of the insurgency, both these episodes proved deeply unrepresentative of what followed,' noted the academic Duncan McCargo in a detailed study of the unrest in southern Thailand. 'Most subsequent deaths have been in ones and twos, and only very rarely has any single incident claimed more than ten lives. Put crudely, not enough people are being killed at once for the violence to claim serious international attention.'[14]

A remarkably hermetic lid has indeed been kept on the unrest in the South. It has had negligible impact on Thailand's thriving tourism industry not far north, in the island resorts of Phuket and Ko Samui. Yet since January 2004, the violence in the South has claimed over 7,000 lives – that is more than twice as many people as the 'troubles' in Northern Ireland from the 1960s to 1998, and more than seven times the number killed by Basque separatists in Spain between 1959 and 2011.[15]

A central theme in McCargo's analysis was that Bangkok had lost its legitimacy in governing the South. Regional indifference to central government had reverted to open hostility. The resurgence of violence and hostility towards the symbols of central government coincided with the election of Thaksin in 2001, although it is not clear that there was a causal relationship. However, the whole of the southern part of the country has long been the main bastion of the Democrat Party, which at that time served as a very weak opposition. Thaksin's election did not therefore bode well for the interests of Muslims, and some of his comments confirmed that he preferred to reward those who supported him.

There was a long history of second-rate functionaries being assigned to the bothersome South, which had been neglected and remained economically backward. Thaksin, as a former police colonel, instinctively pushed back against military influence. The national police force historically was the poor cousin; the fourth branch of the armed forces behind the army, navy, and air force – although this at least earned it a seat in any junta. In 2002, Thaksin abolished the Southern Border Provinces Administrative Centre (SBPAC) that had been established in 1981 on Prem's watch. Prem was himself a native of Songkhla, and he went on to use amnesties and other low-key cajolery to defuse tension. The SBPAC provided liaison with local government and security forces, and was credited with some success in building local trust. Thaksin's notorious war on drugs in 2003 may also have backfired by damaging intelligence gathering in the area, as informers there were among the nearly 2,000 people killed off across the country. The SBPAC was reinstated in 2006 after the coup that removed Thaksin, but never recovered its old stature and usefulness.

Thaksin may have been distracted at times. For example, in 2004, he was involved in a bid for a share of Liverpool Football Club in the UK. It was unsuccessful, but captured tremendous national interest. However, some are doubtful about laying too much blame for the deteriorating situation in the South on the prime minister personally. The upturn in irrational violence and other problems were already simmering when he came into office, and perhaps he failed to see the gathering storm. School burnings and beheadings of Buddhists were already going on as insurgents regrouped and retrained for their own internal reasons, not because of any links to a wider Islamic cause. Thaksin may also have misstepped after taking advice from advocates of normalising security arrangements at the wrong moment. People who believed the South should be treated like anywhere else in Thailand saw disbanding the SBPAC as a logical step.

Anand was returning to Thailand from the giddy international heights of a UN panel exploring paths to world peace. He was deeply critical of the government's handling of the South, which was under a state of emergency. People living there felt increasingly alienated. His relations with Prime Minister Thaksin by this time were cool and indirect. Meanwhile, Thaksin was at the height of his confidence, the master of his game, and unused to being challenged.

In March 2005, the month after Thaksin was returned to power with an unprecedented parliamentary majority, Anand accepted his invitation to become chairman of the National Reconciliation Commission, which was unexpectedly created to seek ways forward in the South. Its appearance followed well-publicised speeches of deep concern by Queen Sirikit and King Bhumibol in November. The queen was alarmed by the mounting violence after a two-month stay at the provincial palace in Narathiwat. In late February, Privy Council President Prem called on Thaksin publicly to respond to the 500 violent deaths in the South over the preceding year. 'Prem urged Prime Minister Thaksin Shinawatra to accept advice from the king and queen, adopting a peaceful and cautious approach to the problems of the South, rather than hastily sending in force without a proper understanding of the situation,' McCargo wrote.[16] With a nod to post-apartheid South Africa and inquiry commissions elsewhere, it was a first for Thailand and had a character of its own – not least its size. Where it differed, however, from commissions formed at different times in places like Cambodia, Rwanda, and

South Africa, was that it did not come after the events being investigated had reached some kind of conclusion; reconciliation usually takes place after violence has ceased. In Thailand's South, the bloodshed was worsening as the commission went to work, which made it a much bolder and riskier undertaking.

Whatever spurred Thaksin to appoint him, Anand did not consider he was accepting a poisoned chalice. He still does not believe it was an attempt to draw him in and stifle his criticism. 'I think Thaksin did it for his own reasons,' Anand says. 'It bolstered his position – at least reflected his "concern" for the South. But his heart was never in it. He was thinking of his short-term political advantage and political image.'

'I think Thaksin thought Anand was the most suitable person, and that he would be accepted by most people,' says Phongthep Thepkanjana, a co-founder of Thaksin's TRT party, and a deputy prime minister in Thaksin's cabinet at that time. Proposing anybody too close to the government would have made the work of the commission harder. Anand was a royalist, certainly, but not a member of the Privy Council, and certainly not in the lap of the Democrat Party. Indeed, he has often been sharply critical of the party for its lack of political vision and its indecisiveness.

Anand freely admits that he 'never knew anything about the three southernmost provinces' – but then nor was he an expert on the UN or world peace when Kofi Annan invited him to chair his panel in 2003. The challenge only grew more daunting as the security situation in the South worsened. His reconciliation commission had 50 commissioners, 17 drawn from local Muslim civil society, 12 from the broader civil society community in Thailand, 12 from the civil service and security forces, and seven politicians. Characteristically, Anand made independence a condition of acceptance, both for himself and in his selection of commissioners. The Muslim majority in the South was represented, and there was consensus among the commissioners that the country's largest religious minority had been badly treated. 'We listened to them very seriously – these people knew what was actually happening in the South,' recalls Phongthep.

'I took particular care in showing balance in the commission,' Anand recalls. He ensured there were Muslims not only from the South but also other parts of the country, and also women. 'I always include historians,' he adds. 'I have always felt that one of the reasons we have not had effective governments is that many of our leaders did not have a sense of history – they worked in a vacuum.'

He also appointed tried and trusted civil society figures such as Gothom Arya, and progressive politicians from Thaksin's fold, like Phongthep and Chaturon Chaisang, a former minister of justice. Phongthep prided himself on his impartiality. 'I don't mind talking to people of whatever political colour,' he says. Phongthep believes he and Chaturon were there not to represent Thaksin or the government in any way, but because Anand had worked with them previously on the 1997 constitution and wanted their involvement. Anand's vice chairman, Dr Prawase Wasi, was another progressive royalist he had worked with in the 1990s. Surin Pitsuwan, a Democrat member of parliament from the South, was also included.

One of Anand's most important inclusions was Chaiwat Satha-Anand, a Bangkok Muslim of Indian heritage and an academic from Thammasat University. Chaiwat always liked to sit with Chaturon, but also prided himself on his independence and objectivity. 'I am not connected with anything,' he says. Anand took many recommendations from Chaiwat for commissioners from the South; they included a number of academics who had graduated from Middle Eastern universities such as Medina. It was among many southern grievances that such centres of learning were not recognised in Thailand as they were in other Asian countries or in the West. The Thai security establishment viewed such institutions sceptically, and their degrees usually counted for little in academic and official circles.

Chaiwat believes commissioners were attracted to join as a result of Anand's stature and credibility. Chaiwat regards Anand as a very unusual figure in Thai society, a member of the so-called *ammart* but one who had been exceptionally ostracised and ill-treated after the Thammasat University massacre in October 1976. In Chaiwat's view, that experience was vital to shaping Anand's worldview, imbuing him with a quality often absent in Southeast Asian politics: empathy. 'Anand listens but with strange ears,' says Chaiwat. 'His unique experience provides him with the possibility to have contact with different groups. He is a bridge. He knows how bad Thai society can become. That puts him in a strange position because he is in the elite. It is a very interesting tension. He has lived through that – mastered it. That fascinates me.'

Chaiwat worried that Anand was making the reconciliation commission too large and unwieldy. He himself was given the title of technical director, which in practice meant he was the commission's chief draughtsman, the person who had to translate deliberations into words. The report he created had three parts: diagnosis, prognosis, therapy. The first draft took Chaiwat six months, and it went through nine edits. By and large, the commissioners accepted the report's structure, but struggled with the final therapy. So many of the problems they found were rooted in the past. 'Thai history is very biased and nationalistic,' says Chaiwat. 'There is no way you can solve this problem using standard Thai history to accommodate the historical consciousness of people who are now in conflict.'

Although Chaiwat was noted for being a fine writer, there were words that he simply could not employ. His chairman knew they would never fly in official circles. 'Khun Anand said we could not use the word "autonomy" so I took it out,' he recalls. 'It's a taboo that irks the military and the establishment.' Chaiwat found himself forced to resort to euphemisms like 'thick decentralisation' or 'higher degree of self-reliance'. Malays who were Thai citizens had to be called 'Thai Muslims with Malay lineage'. It was similar to the Thai official practice of referring critically, when necessary, to 'a country with a border to the west of Thailand'. There is only Myanmar, as Burma is now called, to the west, but its name sometimes cannot be uttered.

'We have no word in Thai for autonomy,' says Anand. 'The Thai word is *issarapap*, which is the same word as independence. Another factor is that Thais are not familiar with federal structures. We talk about the United States of America or the Federal Republic of Germany, but most Thais don't know what that implies.'

'Anand was like an anchor,' Chaiwat recalls. 'He was authoritarian when he chaired the commission, but he also listened. He kept us grounded in the Thai social reality that informed us how much we could push forward. It was good in that we became much more realistic. But sometimes he allowed me to be extremely adventurous. No one would have believed in an official document a proposal for an unarmed army.'

Autonomy was anathema to the Thai governing elites who were sensitive about preserving the unitary state developed by King Chulalongkorn in the 19th century. A search was initiated to find examples of an autonomous region within a unitary state with a monarchy, constitution, parliament, and democratic system of government. That turned up Okinawa in Japan and England in the United Kingdom. But any linkages were tenuous, and the whole notion unacceptable to Thailand's conservative, controlling, defence-minded establishment.

'We still have to educate the security community about the reality of Thai society,' says Chaiwat. 'They have a very outdated notion of what a unitary state is. It does not mean that when you have a unitary military state all kinds of autonomous regions are out of the question, or that anybody who talks about that is talking about federalism.'

One of the problems facing the commission was establishing the causes of unrest, which appeared to be largely internal, disconnected from developments in the wider world, Muslim or otherwise. There was no connection, for example, to the 9-11 attack on the World Trade Center in New York and the Pentagon in Washington. There were certainly central issues of religion and culture, and there was also incontrovertible evidence of ill-treatment by the central authorities beyond Krue Se and Tak Bai, which the commissioners all found deeply disturbing. But there were also criminal elements in the mix – smuggling, narcotics, trafficking, prostitution. Anand had been willing to admit that he had previously understood little about the South, but he felt others were unaware of their own ignorance about how convoluted the problems there were, and remain today. 'We are still in a period of denial,' he says. 'If you believe this is just a separatist movement, you are barking up the wrong tree.'

'Anand realised there was much more to the South than any of us would have thought,' says Chaiwat. 'Even now, we do not know why the situation escalated,' reflects Phongthep. 'It would be a wild guess if I said anything.' Some have suggested that Thaksin, the former policeman, was settling scores with the military and trying to undermine royalist networks in the far South. If so, why have Anand chair the commission?

Even with his egalitarian instincts, Anand was always the most important person in the room, the biggest *poo yai*, and everybody deferred to that. Sometimes he used his status to be counter-cultural, and to challenge preconceptions. He could get away with it. 'Look around this room,' he said at one meeting. 'Can anyone here really say that they are Thai?' Chaiwat found that sort of frankness remarkable in a Thai context. 'I really enjoyed that,' he says. 'Anand is Mon-Chinese, but Thai-Thai – what is it?'

Chaiwat was entranced by Anand's way of handling large groups of people, often playing the role of a *na hong* – head of the class. One of Chaiwat's assistants was thrilled whenever Anand scolded people, particularly Chaiwat himself. During one boisterous meeting at the foreign ministry, there was so much squabbling and ballyhoo that Anand called a halt and sent people out of the room – including generals and ministers. 'Don't come back until you've settled down,' he instructed them. 'Chaiwat, you go too.'

Relations between Anand and Thaksin hit another bump when the pair appeared on a TV talk show to discuss the crisis in the South. 'Anand, a two-time prime minister with long-standing international recognition, appeared a more mature figure,' noted Sopon Onkgara. 'Thaksin was there out of the necessity to regain credibility and public faith, following repeated failures in containing the expanding crisis.'[17] Anand spoke of a 'dirty war' and licences to kill, constantly besting the floundering prime minister who was no longer used to serious debate. 'This was no surprise,' Sopon observed. 'Until that night, Thaksin had been used to solo talks, particularly his one-sided Saturday radio chats.'

Sopon's prognosis was grim and prophetic: 'For the people in the South, what comes next is predictable. As long as Thaksin does not change his attitude or strategy, the crisis will persist, if not worsen, with yet more dead bodies piling up.' There were indeed plenty of corpses and atrocities. People also went missing. One of the most publicised cases was Somchai Neelapaijit, a Muslim lawyer kidnapped from his car off busy Ramkhamhaeng Road in Bangkok in March 2004. Somchai had been investigating the alleged torture of Muslim detainees suspected of raiding a military barracks in January 2004, when the troubles resumed in earnest. Five police officers were charged with robbery and assault, four of whom were later acquitted on appeal. Somchai's murder could not be proven because his remains were never found, and the Department of Special Investigation produced nothing more. In 2013, the case files were wrongly reported to have been lost.[18]

Thaksin was facing numerous headwinds at this time as the Yellow Shirt movement coalesced against him, gaining increasing momentum as a royalist movement. A controversy erupted around his multi-billion dollar sale of Shin Corporation (ShinCorp) to Temasek Holdings, a Singapore state-owned investment vehicle. He called a snap election in April 2006, more as a referendum on his mandate than out of any parliamentary necessity given his 375 majority in the 500-seat lower house. The election was boycotted by the opposition Democrats and other parties, and Thaksin 'resigned' despite winning 61 per cent of the vote and 460 seats. King Bhumibol, in a rare public comment on politics, called the election undemocratic. It was annulled by the Constitutional Court, and a new date was set for October. Thaksin returned to his job in time to oversee the lavish five-day celebration in June of the 60th anniversary of King Bhumibol's reign. Royal Plaza and the surrounding area were filled to capacity by people dressed in yellow. Heads and representatives of 25 royal families around the world attended, and an uneasy political truce descended.

Despite his criticism of Thaksin's policies, Anand had held back his commission's report until after the election to keep it apart from all the other political controversies raging at the time. It was handed to Borwornsak Uwanno, one of three cabinet secretary generals, on 5 June 2006 just ahead of the 60th anniversary celebrations. For unrelated reasons, Borwornsak resigned the following day, and would spend some time in the monkhood, but the report had been delivered. Its recommendations included allowing a bigger role for Sharia law (which had in fact been used to guide family and inheritance matters previously), and making the local Malay dialect an official language in the provinces where it was widely spoken. It also suggested that an unarmed peacekeeping force be deployed, and that SBPAC, the administrative liaison centre shuttered in 2002, be reopened. Prem, the military, and the education ministry were among those very critical of the report, particularly of the language recommendation. They believed there could only be one official language in Thailand. 'The authorities didn't like it,' Chaiwat recalls. 'They recognise religious differences, but not ethnicities.' The UNHCR was supportive and expressed hope that some of the recommendations could be implemented. The justice ministry did later pick up on some suggestions when Kittipong Kittayarak was permanent secretary. 'A lot of recommendations have been taken up by different agencies,' says Chaiwat.

The report was criticised by some for not tackling the autonomy issue openly, and for failing to quell the insurgency – which was always beyond its scope. Chaiwat believes that many had unrealistic expectations, and failed to grasp that the commission was created to make recommendations, not to tackle problems directly itself. Anand was criticised for being high-handed with the press, although that was not out of character. He had frequently dressed reporters down for their shortcomings in the past, sometimes very sharply, and always batted off speculative questions.

'Anand often overlooks some dimensions of the problem,' says Abhisit Vejjajiva, Thailand's prime minister from 2008 to 2011. 'He is not a details man. That is good because he sees the big picture and does not get bogged down, but sometimes there are details that need attention. I think the one he overlooks in the South is how hard it is to protect Buddhist communities. I think he underestimates the agenda of some of the extremists who want to drive Buddhist communities out.'

'Some of the criticism was quite unfair,' says Chaiwat. The commission was not a police inquiry, and its purpose was never to plough through layers of insurgency. It was meant to suggest ways of creating a better environment, but ended up on a dusty shelf.

'Some recommendations have been implemented in small doses,' says Abhisit, but he admits expectations were low when the Democrats were such feeble opposition to Thaksin. 'We never believed Anand and Thaksin had the same ideas,' he says. 'At no point did we feel that his ideas would get accepted let alone implemented. I think eventually Chaturon made some efforts, but he was then removed from responsibility. For us, it was almost a non-starter. For Thaksin, it was a way of defusing an issue he was having difficulty with.'

The academic McCargo argued that an opportunity had been squandered and nothing achieved. Subsequent governments have effectively carried on seeking military solutions to social, economic, political, and religious grievances. When Prime Minister Prayut Chan-o-cha conducted a rare regional cabinet meeting in the South in late November 2017, violence was at least at its lowest ebb since 2004, but nothing much else had been resolved. 'No government so far has confronted all these issues honestly, particularly the need for limited but real autonomy for the region,' the *Bangkok Post* noted in an editorial. 'It would take real and determined leadership at the top to make that possible.'[19]

Gothom believes there should be another independent commission, and he would like Anand to be involved. 'So far, I have not been able to move forward this idea,' he says. Anand for his part does not believe that the almost complete lack of follow-through should be blamed on his commission. 'My job was to do a report with recommendations,' he says. 'I enjoyed being involved in that process. If you ask me what has been achieved, it is that you leave that report behind for somebody who is interested to pick it up and do something. As far as I am concerned, I have done my part.'

Another coup

On 19 September 2006, General Sonthi Boonyaratglin, Thailand's first Muslim army commander in chief, staged a coup while Thaksin was attending the UN General Assembly in New York. Sonthi was close to a former army chief and supreme commander, Surayud Chulanont, who had entered King Bhumibol's Privy Council in November 2003, just six weeks after retiring from the military.

Surayud in turn was close to Prem, the president of the Privy Council, who himself had retired as army chief in 1980 to become prime minister, but retained a major say in military promotions. Because Prem and Surayud had backed Sonthi's rise to the top of the army, the coup that removed Thaksin was widely perceived to have had their backing. To the dismay of some senior courtiers, the coup-makers were granted an audience with King Bhumibol and Queen Sirikit the same evening. Audiences after coups are quite normal; it was the unusual promptness that sparked comment.

There were signs of poor planning. It took much longer to announce who should replace Thaksin as prime minister than it had in 1991 to replace Chatichai. The candidates included Surayud himself, whose popularity with the military was assured, but who would have to step out of the Privy Council. Other possibilities were MR Chatumongkol Sonakul, a former governor of the Bank of Thailand whom Thaksin had dismissed in May 2001 for not being a 'team player'. There was also MR Pridiyathorn Devakula, who had replaced Chatumongkol as central bank governor and survived through to the coup. Pridiyathorn knew about the coup two weeks ahead. In the event, he accepted the deputy premiership and finance portfolio, but soon resigned over cabinet flip-flops. 'I thought General Surayud, from his background and record, should perform well as a prime minister only to learn a few months after joining the government that I was wrong,' he says.

In hindsight, Pridiyathorn is ambivalent about whether Sonthi's coup was a mistake, but concedes that it would have been better to remove Thaksin by legal means. 'Picking Surayud was a mistake,' he says. 'If it was fair, Anand would have been proposed. No one can be better than Anand, but if the military is involved he will not be picked. If it was done by the people, he would be the first choice.'

Some did naively expect Anand to be a candidate for the premiership in 2006 given his effectiveness in 1991 and 1992. At 74, he was older than the other candidates, but still fit enough for the job. In the crisis of 1992, King Bhumibol had appointed Anand prime minister, not Prem, who at that time was deputy president of the Privy Council, and still vigorous in his early 70s. Anand has always distanced himself from Prem, and disdained military involvement in governance. In 1992, Anand sidelined the military culpable in the May violence without involving Prem. Anand's recommendations on the South in the months before the coup had also played badly in the Privy Council.

Anand was not in the least surprised by the coup against Thaksin. He believed

Thaksin had overstepped himself. 'He took full advantage of a strong political constitution, but later on he corrupted it,' says Anand. 'If he had continued on the same early path, he would have been a great statesman.' Anand particularly faulted Thaksin for his winner-takes-all approach. TRT had easily attained a clear majority in its first election, but Thaksin carried on mopping up smaller parties that he did not need in order to govern. 'He had to have everything,' says Anand. 'That was his downfall.'

Others believe the ineptness of the Democrat Party, which had grown listless on its sense of entitlement as the default ruling party, was also a major part of the problem. 'The reason TRT gained so many seats was not because of the constitution but because of the platform the party introduced,' says Phongthep. 'If it was about the constitution, the Democrats should have done better – they had been in politics for much longer than TRT.' When Thaksin won re-election in 2005 by a landslide, the Democrats led by Banyat Bantadtan were left with only 96 seats and just 16 per cent of the popular vote compared to nearly 27 per cent in the 2001 election. Banyat immediately resigned as party leader and was replaced by Abhisit.

A major drawback to appointing Surayud was that it implied palace involvement in the seizure of power. When Sanya Dhammasakdi stepped down from the Privy Council in 1973 to become prime minister, he was a former academic, not a former general; nobody imputed to him a personal agenda or involvement in a conspiracy. After Surayud finished his term as prime minister, he was reinstated in the Privy Council in January 2008.

On the surface, Surayud seemed to take a leaf out of Anand's book, putting together a technocrat cabinet that included a number of respected figures. His choice for foreign minister, Nitya Pibulsonggram, was at pains to tell correspondents it was only an 'interim' government that would be gone in a year. Kosit Panpiemras was given one of the finance portfolios. He observed some efforts to emulate the philosophy of the Anand cabinets, but Surayud's management style was entirely different. 'Surayud's cabinet engaged much more in debate – "for and against" kind of thing,' Kosit recalled. 'Surayud listened, and if he was convinced it was for the good of the country, he made very quick decisions.'

However, when Surayud was not convinced, he would postpone. Pridiyathorn regarded this as indecisiveness when it came to vital financial reforms, and resigned in February 2007 after a Thaksin stalwart, Somkid Jatusripitak, had been brought into the cabinet. But Surayud was decisive in some respects. 'Anything with a hint of corruption, he was at the forefront against it,' says Pridiyathorn.

Apart from his superior understanding of the civil service and familiarity with the top technocrats of his day, Anand had as prime minister enjoyed other advantages over Surayud. There was an appointed parliament again in 2006, but this time it often had ideas of its own. The Anand government had been efficient, pushing a steady train of legislation through the NLA; but on Surayud's watch a backlog built up to a frenzied final fortnight when legislation was hurriedly pushed through, including the deeply controversial Computer Crimes Act. There were also a number of agendas in play without Surayud's direct involvement. One of the most important was the prosecution of Thaksin for his alleged crimes – the justification for staging the coup in the first place. This was handled by a separate committee that essentially failed, with only one case against Thaksin going forward. Surayud himself had to be careful not to show any bias while the investigations were ongoing. 'I don't think it's fair to blame him,' said Kosit. 'If this particular group of people had finished their work, then the government could have done something.'

Surayud warned his cabinet how difficult their job would be. He showed no sign of being a power-seeker personally, and came across as friendly and humble. He resisted suggestions that his government use populist spending tactics; he was not going to try and convince people he was more generous than Thaksin. 'We were not politicians,' said Kosit. There was no need for crowd-pleasing tactics to win re-election. 'I think Surayud was good in the sense that he tried his best not to do any damage. He reminded us that he could do only so much. The parliament was beyond him. There were a bunch of different ideologies and the government had no means to organise them.'

Anand had always been able to talk through with Suchinda any problems that arose, which gave him a much firmer grasp on executive power. After the coup in 1991, Chatichai had essentially rolled over and gone away. Thaksin on the other hand was still fighting back. 'Surayud had to face a well-organised and well-financed opposition,' notes Abhisit. 'I felt pity for him. In fairness to Surayud, the luxury that Anand had was that Chatichai was never a problem.'

A major casualty of the 2006 coup was the 1997 so-called People's Constitution that Anand had been instrumental in drafting. The constitutional crisis of 2006 developed after Thaksin called a snap election and the opposition refused to participate. The overwhelming TRT majority was already a major problem in a country where the notion of the 'loyal opposition' playing a constructive role was anyway undeveloped. With TRT holding more than three-fifths of the seats, the opposition was unable even to table motions.

'We did not expect the opposition not to be able to censure the government – they did not have the numbers,' says Phongthep, who had helped draft the 1997 constitution. By 2005, he was serving as the TRT's whip in parliament and seeing little of Thaksin. From a legal standpoint, he believes Thaksin could have been sanctioned in a court of law for any wrongdoing, and that throwing out Thailand's most carefully crafted and successful constitution since 1932 was unwarranted. 'That constitution could have been amended in a positive way,' he maintains. 'Even Thaksin was considering it. The constitution was not perfect, but there was nothing very wrong with it.'

In the time preceding the coup, Phongthep was dismayed when some members of the judiciary became embroiled in the constitutional row. 'They not only took sides but took some action,' he recalls. 'That was bad for the judiciary and bad for the country. We need neutral judges in any court so that they can decide cases impartially.' The situation did not improve in the years that followed. Three elected prime ministers in the Thaksin camp have been dismissed by court rulings that critics dubbed 'judicial coups', and politicians and parties were suspended.

For the new constitution, Anand was consulted indirectly at the working level by a few individuals, but took negligible interest in any changes. 'I did not want to be involved,' he recalls. The revised constitution was approved in 2007, for the first time by a national referendum. 'If I am not directly involved, I am not in the habit of making suggestions,' he says. He did, however, approve of lifting the undemocratic ban on non-graduates entering parliament. As the redrafting went forward, he noticed the absence of a figurehead capable of generating public trust in the process. He thought back to the public consultation process undertaken by Uthai Pimchaichon, the president of the Constitution Drafting Assembly, and the countless speeches he himself had made in 1997 to explain the salient points of the constitution. But who could have done all that for Surayud's administration? 'That's why every now and again my name was dragged into the public domain,' says Anand.

Borwornsak Uwanno believes the 1997 constitution failed because of the prevailing political culture and the subsequent poor appointments to the NCC,

Election Commission, and other independent bodies created at that time – there were also the Office of the Auditor General, and the National Human Rights Commission. 'Thai political culture is cronyism,' he says. 'It is not to obey and respect the law and constitution. Thais are good at finding loopholes – how do you change the culture? It is a question that cannot be answered.' He believes that if change cannot come through parliament, the powerful will always resort to extra-constitutional movements in the belief that they know better. But the risk is that what then emerges is framed to benefit those with the upper hand. 'The constitution should be a law for everyone, not victors trying to dominate the losers,' Borwornsak argues.

National Reform Commission

Although it was unofficially translated into English and Yawi, the Kelantan-Pattani dialect of Malay, the recommendations of the National Reconciliation Commission were largely lost in the rush of events in 2006. Anand nevertheless persevered along a reformist path. In 2010, he embarked on another commission in partnership with Dr Prawase Wasi, the political activist who until 2005 had also been a personal physician to King Bhumibol. Prawase had resigned that position to dive into political reform. 'I didn't want to belong to the palace,' he says. Prawase continued to work at Siriraj Hospital in the Chalermprakiat Building, however, a few floors below the ailing king. He had a magnificent view, virtually identical to that enjoyed by the king out over the Chao Phraya river, Thammasat University, and the Grand Palace. Despite their daily proximity, Prawase only encountered the king one more time in the years that followed, and that was as part of a committee of 20 doctors gathered to make a diagnosis. When the king opened his eyes and beheld his familiar old physician among the assembled white coats, he asked: 'Is this a professional visit or a social visit?' Prawase recalls he was the only doctor in that group not to be paid: 'It was an honour not to receive money.'

Anand also had fewer meetings with the king, although these audiences always lasted some time. There was a private audience in 2004 after his 72nd birthday, and the last was at Klai Kangwan Palace in Hua Hin in 2007. He also attended some ceremonies presided over by the king, notably the Diamond Jubilee celebrations in 2006 at the Ananta Samakhom Throne Hall overlooking Bangkok's Royal Plaza, and the funeral ceremonies for Princess Galyani, the king's sister, in 2008. There was also King Bhumibol's final speech, given at Hua Hin on 5 May 2014 on coronation day – when the king paused at one point for 17 seconds to recover his train of thought. For Anand, the weekly audiences in the early 1990s were happy but distant memories. Access to the king in his final years was governed by a small number of palace gatekeepers, and audiences grew increasingly infrequent. Because the king was a car enthusiast, Australian F1 racing driver Mark Webber (with his Red Bull car) was granted one in late 2010, as was President Barack Obama in late 2012. As the king's health declined, and the circle around him grew tighter, old royalists like Anand and Prawase carried on in their own way. Both men were disillusioned with constitutions and politics, and looking for other avenues to progress. 'We have had 18 constitutions, and they won't work because we don't have active citizenship,' says Prawase. 'I have lost interest – I have devoted a lot of time and labour to them and it hasn't worked.' The fabric of society, he believes, is stressed. 'If we believe Buddhism is good, and Thais are Buddhist, why are there so many crimes?' he asks. 'Monks want to be promoted to a high rank, *somdech*.'

Like most, Prawase traces centralisation in Siam/Thailand back to King Chulalongkorn (r.1868–1910). In his view, it has become onerous and outlived its usefulness, and this has led to six major problems: local organisations are undeveloped and weak while central government is overloaded; regional cultures are in conflict with and not respected by central government – the South is the best example but not unique; the bureaucratic system is weak because it relies on power rather than wisdom, leading to chronic poverty and insoluble environmental problems that may eventually produce a failed state; the quality of politics is poor with over-investment in power – with such high stakes, the winner takes all and even violence becomes acceptable; concentration of power fuels corruption; *coups d'état* are easy, and only require a few hundred soldiers to capture the capital, the seat of power.

Prawase sometimes looks abroad for inspiration. For example, Switzerland has become much less corrupt because of its system of cantons, and power is impossible to seize in India with its 29 states and two administrative regions. 'No matter how poor India is, nobody can stage a coup there,' he says.

Anand and Prawase go back to the mid-1990s together when Prawase's reform work was an important precursor to the 1997 constitution. In 2010, when the National Reform Commission idea came up, Prime Minister Abhisit Vejjajiva was on the rebound from the 2010 violent political meltdown. Thaksin's Red Shirts had been violently cleared from the capital's streets, leaving 91 dead. 'He was in crisis and tried to find something to hang on to,' says Prawase.

During this new push for reform, Prawase's initial idea was to suggest not one but three commissions. One was to be headed by Anand; it would oversee the process and serve as the think tank. The second would be a reform assembly run by Prawase; it was meant to identify people and ways to implement big ideas. And the third commission would be run by the National Economic and Social Development Board, and play a role in implementing recommendations. Anand rejected the idea of the third commission because he wanted no direct involvement in implementation. The commission was established by cabinet resolution on 29 June 2010 with a budget of 13 million baht. Its purpose was 'to research and consolidate approaches to national reform, and to draft an action plan for implementation by the government, civil service, and private sectors to resolve issues concerning injustice and inequality'.

In July, Anand announced the names of his 20 commissioners, including himself as chairman. He brought on board some quite radical personalities. One was Nidhi Eoseewong, the writer and historian whom Anand had previously invited to join the board of trustees of the Thailand Development Research Institute. 'After about six months, he asked to resign – I think he thought it was a losing battle to convince the TDRI economists,' says Anand of that particular failed experiment. Another was Seksan Prasertkun, a student leader from the 1970s who had risen to become dean of political science at Thammasat University. 'Seksan was out in the wilderness,' Anand recalls. 'He honestly did not want to be part of any group.' Both joined the reform commission on condition that Anand would chair it and choose his own people. Even with those preconditions, Pasuk Pongpaichit, a lauded political science professor at Chulalongkorn, declined to get involved. Like many, Nidhi and Seksan had no confidence in the Democrats, and did not want to be associated officially or publicly in any way with the government.

Prawase's National Reform Assembly was a 2,000-strong gathering of community leaders and civil society representatives divided into eight discussion groups, which delivered a 'declaration of the people'. Anand convened his discussions separately. These covered 14 key topics in five broad areas: the economy; resource allocation; human rights; opportunities; and bargaining power. There were no particular structure or agenda to this, and a consensus approach was adopted without voting. Anand chose the venues, which included Baan Phitsanulok, technically the official residence of the prime minister, but rarely used as such. Following a quick lunch, discussions would run from 1:30pm for five or six hours. Anand remembers vigorous, civil debating with nobody storming out. 'It was hard work, but not stressful – a great opportunity,' he recalls. 'We had to go beyond the Red and Yellow divide and get down to basics.' The commission met twice a week for eight months.

'My original thesis was that the basic problem was poverty and unequal opportunities,' Anand recalls. He believed schooling and environmental conditions were also factors, adding to inequality from the time of birth. 'It goes up the ladder, and as a result those who have less access to opportunities and employment feel there is no equal treatment in this society,' he says. This would be reinforced in their dealings with the bureaucracy and judicial system. Both Nidhi and Seksan disputed this view. They argued that a sense of inequality sets in when people feel themselves blocked from communication with the more powerful. The root problem, they argued, was communication, including between the government and the people; there was a strong sense of unequal bargaining power. Anand recalls how when drafting the 1997 constitution, rural people had felt inferior, and were keen to be represented by more qualified people who could negotiate on their behalf.

Such vertical blockages meant addressing the national power structure, which in turn meant addressing the question of decentralisation – reversing the administrative legacy of the 19th century. There had also been heightened nationalism in the early 20th century under King Vajiravudh (r. 1910–1925) as an antidote to foreign predations; and promotion of the notion of a Thai diaspora under Field Marshal Plaek Phibunsongkhram (Phibun) in the mid-20th century. It was Phibun who had changed the country's old name, Siam, which did not connote the predominance of any particular ethnic group or race. All these influences promoted a sense of specifically Thai nationhood within a strong unitary state that the commissioners felt needed to be softened in the 21st century. 'I don't see any dangers in having regionalism in Thailand – it should promote economic well-being,' says Anand. 'You can't deal with this problem in the South unless you have a new mindset.' He believes the North and Northeast should be treated in the same way as the southernmost provinces. 'You don't do things just for the people in the South but for every region,' he argues. 'It boils down to empowering people.'

Although it has not happened yet, tackling problems in the South effectively could lead to resentment elsewhere, which is why any solutions found there should be applied nationwide. The issue is why should politicians and bureaucrats in Bangkok continue to determine the use of resources in the South, North, or Northeast? 'The roots of many problems pertain to the history, traditions, and culture of the country, which have developed over so many centuries,' says Anand. 'We need to think more about the future than the present. It is no longer viable for us to do patchwork. We need to think out of the box and be more daring in our objectives.'

'At the moment, those who advocate decentralisation still want power to be vested in central government,' Anand continues. 'It must be vested in the people of the region. I prefer the term devolution to decentralisation.' Effective decentralisation, he believes, enables people to handle more of their own affairs, including the local economy, policing, and development. The unitary state remains, with central government looking after national issues, such as defence, the macro economy, and foreign relations. Far from being a threat to the unitary state, Anand views decentralisation as a means of enhancing it. 'Nidhi, Seksan, and I felt quite strongly about that, and we convinced a lot of the members who were very rightist in the beginning to switch their position,' he says.

Without a new mindset and shift of paradigm, new answers cannot be expected. 'It cannot be a top-down resolution,' Anand says. 'Change has to be nurtured in a series of consultations, a process involving several sectors of society. It is not instant medicine.' To this day, only Bangkok, as a special administrative area, elects its own governor (in normal circumstances); the governors of Thailand's other 76 provinces are all appointed by the Ministry of the Interior. Electing governors would, however, only be one step in the right direction. 'It is not the device that alone would reflect our view on the devolution of power,' he says. 'Even the governor of Bangkok does not have very much power.'

As speculation about an election heightened in 2011, Anand decided to wrap up the reform commission early. All the commissioners resigned as soon as the poll's date emerged. 'Once an election date is announced, it is a government in transition in a way,' says Anand. He reasoned that ultimately his commission was accountable not to a government or parliament, but to the people. He believed the next government should have a free hand to decide on whether or not to act on the report. 'They could do whatever they liked,' he says. He informed Abhisit that he would be standing down. 'I think he knew that if there was a change of government he would not enjoy whatever relationship came after,' says Abhisit.

'It's a very good report,' says Anand. Unlike the reconciliation report on the South, the 300-page document was circulated to members of parliament, senators, the media, and libraries, but it has not been translated. 'There was no organised system of distribution or propagating the report,' says Anand. 'It was for political parties and academic institutions to add value and take ownership.'

The government of Yingluck Shinawatra, which took office in early August 2011, was widely regarded as being strongly influenced from abroad by her older brother, Thaksin. It had essentially three options relating to the reform commission. It could have invited Anand to resume the review process; implement the reforms already proposed according to its own modalities; or do nothing. It chose the last. By resigning early, Anand, of course, deprived the new government of the chance to sack him. 'In Thai society, they would not have fired me,' he says. 'They would have let it lapse.'

Wissanu claims to know little of the relationship between Prawase and Anand; he formed the impression that Thaksin might lend an ear to Prawase's ideas but never to Anand's suggestions. It was perhaps to be expected that the report, entitled *Thailand's Reform Road Map: Proposals for Political Parties and Eligible Voters*, would be buried in the oncoming rush of another overwhelming Shinawatra election victory. Anand, however, does not disguise his disappointment that the Democrats made such little use of it at the time. After all, they commissioned it, and initially showed interest. 'To me that's stupid,' says Anand. 'They could have picked up on all these points and made it into their own platform.'

'The NRC's work will eventually be influential in structural change,' says Abhisit. 'Anand resigned out of respect for the electoral process – the very least he thought would happen is that the government would appoint a new committee. It didn't happen. I think this is something close to his heart, which he didn't really have a go at when he was prime minister. He wants to do good work on this, but the best he can do is offer it to political parties. I think he now feels he has done his job – he has put it down on the table.'

Phongthep credits both of Anand's commissions with having some impact. 'The reports have been read and some of the recommendation have been implemented,' he says. 'But many of the things he proposed are ideas without the detail needed for implementation – for example, educational reform.'

In 2013, veteran journalist and commentator Suthichai Yoon noted gloomily that the reform commission had been created 'amid great hopes that the political leaders were serious' about taking the country forward. 'The report, one of the most comprehensive proposals for national reform, has since been gathering dust on a shelf at Government House.'[20]

Anand, ever the good bureaucrat, still believes both his commission reports can be picked up by future governments, academics, and the media. 'I am happy that they are there,' he says. But as to meaningful national reform any time soon, he is not optimistic: 'It is something that has been weighing on my mind for quite some time, but I do not expect to live to see any changes.'

CHAPTER 20

REPRESENTING THAILAND

Facing the world

When Foreign Minister Thanat Khoman sent Anand to join the Thai permanent mission at the United Nations in New York in 1965, he hoped to raise Thailand's profile, and lift its public relations game. He wanted to improve understanding of the then little-known country, and cast it in a favourable light. Anand quickly showed a talent for the task, gaining experience by scheduling his own speaking engagements at educational institutions, and later engaging with journalists, think tanks, and international organisations. As a young but seasoned ambassador, he began appearing on the most-watched US talk shows of the day, explaining everything from Field Marshal Thanom Kittikachorn's baffling coup against his own government in 1971, when Thanat was ejected from the cabinet, to the reasons for Prime Minister Kukrit Pramoj's outrage at the US government for blithely violating Thai sovereignty at the time of SS *Mayaguez* incident in Cambodia.

As Thailand's prime minister in 1991 and 1992, Anand presented Thailand to the world in an open and frank way that blunted critics hostile to a government installed by the military. Thailand's subsequent unelected prime ministers – Surayud Chulanont and Prayut Chan-o-cha, both non-technocrat former army chiefs – were viewed much more critically by the foreign media, diplomats, governments, international civil society, and free-society watchdogs. Surayud endured the disdain, and left office as quickly as he could reasonably manage. Prayut has stayed on much longer, and has failed to establish any kind of constructive rapport with the international media, which he often criticises. Relations with Western diplomats have also often been strained during both governments.

As a respected elder statesman, Anand has continued to engage with the local and foreign media. Very seldom has he declined to comment; if he has, it has usually been on the grounds that the time is not right. Because he was more accessible and willing to talk, the foreign media were sometimes attacked for speaking to only Anand. In practice, journalists can only quote those willing to speak on the record. It is a bonus if their subjects interview well.

Anand's notable absence from the Privy Council afforded him the independence to speak on all matters as he saw fit, including the monarchy under King Bhumibol, whom, nobody ever doubted, he held in the highest regard. Indeed, some regard Anand as 'Bhumibolist' first, and a royalist second. He was in some ways the 'outsider on the inside' who always reserved a measure of detachment and objectivity.

Broadly speaking, successive elected Thai governments have been willing to allow Anand free reign to speak his mind. He has occasionally overcome his writer's block and penned commentaries for high-profile publications such as *The International Herald Tribune*. When Anand appeared on the BBC's *HardTalk* programme in mid-2011 with the combative Stephen Sackur, he seemed a little subdued. There had been a technical glitch with the sound recording, and the interview had to be started again. 'If they had been able to broadcast the first recording, it would have been better – I was quite fresh,' Anand recalls. 'The questions were not identical.'

Anand's profile has been raised by the shortage of other Thais capable of speaking effectively on the international stage. Supachai Panitchpakdi obviously spoke not about Thailand but about international trade when he ran the World Trade Organization from 2002 to 2005, and then the UN Conference on Trade and Development from 2005 to 2013. Exceptions have included Surin Pitsuwan, a gifted orator who served as Thailand's foreign minister and later became secretary general of the Association of Southeast Asian Nations.

Sulak Sivaraksa, an 'engaged Buddhist' and the country's best known social critic, has always spoken well and provocatively, relishing debate and controversy. He has been deeply critical of what he considers Thailand's mindless pursuit of Western development agendas, globalisation, and materialism at the expense of the poor. Sulak has always presented himself as a monarchist prepared to criticise the institution openly for its benefit – a habit that has seen him entangled with the kingdom's law of *lèse-majesté* on at least four occasions – in 1984, 1991, 2008, and 2016. 'Monarchy must be constitutional,' he told Sackur on another episode of *HardTalk* aired around the same time as Anand's interview. 'It should not be something sacred, something beyond criticism.'

Anand is sometimes critical of Sulak's intentional abrasiveness and attention seeking. Sulak often dresses as a 19th-century Siamese gentleman, and refers to Thailand as Siam – but he does not portray Siam as some lost Utopia. For him, it has always been a country with qualities and faults. Both he and Anand blend patriotism into their critiques of national shortcomings. These are acts of love, not sedition.

Thais, Anand argues, would not need to be such good crisis managers if they were better at avoiding crises in the first place, and had better self-understanding. 'It's not the issues, but the way we manage them that worries me,' he says. 'We are generally not organisers or planners. There is a lack of long-term planning. We just roll with the punches – we are an adhocracy.'

Anand's innate rationalism makes him highly critical of the susceptibility to self-fascination that he sees in many of his compatriots. 'There is no such thing as Thainess,' he asserts. 'I don't like the term – it's a myth. We are not conscious of our own diversity. Most Thais do not know their own history. Eight-hundred years ago, we were very much like the princely states in Italy or Germany. There was no kingdom of Siam. Then we became preoccupied with this false concept of Thainess – of Thailand as a unitary state. This obsession to me is a threat to the kingdom.'

If he regards criticism of Thailand as unfair, Anand reacts forcefully. He once verbally eviscerated an expert on pollution who was visiting from the UK for talking about poor air quality in Bangkok without mentioning the problems London faced in the 1950s, when toxic fogs, or 'pea soupers', killed thousands. Nothing so bad has happened in Bangkok, and it took London three rounds of clean air legislation spread over four decades to eradicate its problems. 'We had to touch the shoulder of the person in front to go anyhere,' Anand recalls of his schooldays in southeast London. 'It was pitch dark with soot. When I first went to England, I could not understand why people wore detachable collars, but of course they got dirty so quickly. Nowadays, nobody wears them.'

Anand was far more restrained in 2009, when a lot of Thai feathers were ruffled after the 1967 farewell cable of a former British ambassador, Sir Anthony

Rumbold, surfaced in a new book reviewed by the BBC. It was a kind of proto-Wikileaks, with Rumbold writing in what he presumed at the time was complete confidence to George Brown, the secretary of state for foreign affairs in London from 1966 to 1968. Rumbold made some deeply offensive observations, that only look worse with the passage of time. 'The general level of intelligence of the Thais is rather low, a good deal lower than ours and much lower than that of the Chinese,' he wrote. 'They have no literature, no painting and only a very odd kind of music; their sculpture, ceramics and dancing are borrowed from others, and their architecture is monotonous and interior decoration hideous.' The offensive diplomat described Bangkok as 'fast becoming one of the ugliest towns in the world, indistinguishable from the meaner parts of Tokyo or Los Angeles'. The Thai elites fared no better: 'Nobody can deny that gambling and golf are the chief pleasures of the rich and that licentiousness is the chief pleasure of all of them.'[1]

Bobbing haplessly upon a sea of outrage and hurt, Quinton Quayle, Rumbold's distant successor as British ambassador from 2007 to 2010, felt compelled to issue a statement. 'My own views differ from my predecessor of 42 years ago,' wrote Quayle, a Thai speaker. 'Ever since I was first posted to Thailand 30 years ago, I have been impressed by the richness of Thai culture, be it art, sculpture, dance, music or literature.' Quayle eulogised the natural beauty of the landscape and the charm and warmth of the Thai people. 'The country for me certainly lives up to its brand name "Amazing Thailand,"' he said.[2]

What many missed in the brouhaha was that Rumbold's cable went some way beyond a condescending skewering of his hosts. It contained a perceptive analysis of the US presence in Thailand, and of Thai politics in general. It also praised Thais for their excellent manners, fastidiousness, grace, and elegance. 'If we are elephants and oxen they are gazelles and butterflies,' he observed. 'The Thais are past-masters at taking it out on foreign interests which have incurred their displeasure and conversely they respond quickly to quite small gestures.' Rumbold also singled out individuals like Pote Sarasin and Puey Ungphakorn for high praise.

There was a certain British eccentricity in Rumbold's valedictory message, a throwback to lost empire. As was apparent, such cables could all too easily leak, and the practice of sending them was ended by the British foreign office in 2006.

When Anand went over Rumbold's assault on Thai sensibilities nearly half a century later, puffing lightly on a cigar, he chuckled over what the haughty diplomat got wrong – and what he got right. 'I disagree with half the things I read, but that's all right,' says Anand. 'I enjoy reading the reasoning more than the conclusions – it enriches me one way or another.' Holocaust deniers undoubtedly take matters to an unacceptable extreme for most, but Anand is still surprised that their works are not allowed to be published in Germany. Contrariness can also be engaging. Anand was impressed by an obituary of Eric Hobsbawm. When he died in 2012, Hobsbawm was considered one of the leading Marxist historians of the 20th century, principally for his 'Age of ...' trilogy covering Europe's history, the French Revolution and World War I. Anand was impressed by the fact that Hobsbawm achieved greatness despite almost nobody agreeing with him. That alone was a reason to read him.

When something catches his attention, Anand runs a thin black line under the point of interest, possibly just a single word. Clippings are circulated to others he thinks might be interested. Anand also sends online material, sometimes quite provocative, by email to various groups – foreign journalists and writers, Dulwich College alumni, his Cambridge group, as well as his Thai circles. He does not necessarily participate in any exchanges these generate.

Anand does not read newspapers as much as he once did, preferring biographies and books on social history, particularly those about Thailand. He prefers British newspapers, principally the *Financial Times*, to US ones. 'I used to read *The Economist* religiously before the war in Iraq,' he says. He enjoys the *New York Review of Books* and the *Times Literary Supplement*, and picks up *The Atlantic*, *The Spectator*, *New Statesman*, and *The New Yorker*. He misses *Punch* and the *Far Eastern Economic Review* in their heydays. 'In the 1960s, the only regional publication was the *Far Eastern Economic Review*,' Anand recalls. 'Now I read the sports news.'

Most Thai newspapers are still full of accidents, murders, rapes, and gossip, but Anand thinks the columnists are improving. He regards the local English-language newspapers as 'passable', but never hesitates to pick up the phone to admonish the editors if he spots errors or poor reporting. He does not read gossip columns, and enjoys Thai-PBS on television for its documentaries. He does not regularly watch Channels 3, 5, 7, 9, or 11. 'Sometimes they have good programmes,' he says. The big screens in his offices at Saha Union and Siam Commercial Bank are often tuned to sports channels. He often gets up in the middle of the night to watch his beloved FC Barcelona play in the Champions League.

Academic accolades

Anand has garnered over 26 honorary degrees and academic honours since 1990, when Chulalongkorn University awarded him a doctorate in business administration, *honoris causa*. Arguably the most useful of these was an honorary diploma in 1991 from the National Defence College, which Anand did not get around to attending when he was permanent secretary at the foreign ministry in 1976. For most senior civil servants, attendance at the college is a rite of passage designed to cement ties with the military and security forces. Of the 26 degrees and honours, 16 are from Thai universities and institutions – an exhaustive list from Prince of Songkla University in the South to Chiang Mai University (political science) and Khon Kaen University (business administration) in the Northeast. There are a couple of degrees from Canada, three from Japan, one from the University of Hong Kong, and one from the US.

The most recent honour is the most personal, and the most quietly prized. In June 2017, Anand was elected an honorary fellow of his Cambridge *alma mater*, Trinity College. Sir Gregory Winter, the master of the college, wrote to say the proposed citation described Anand as 'distinguished for his key contributions, *inter alia*, to an effective HIV/AIDS policy in Thailand and to the ASEAN Free Trade Agreement, as Thai diplomat, businessman (and briefly prime minister)'. Signing off as 'Greg', Winter reminded Anand that Trinity honorary fellows are a 'select band', attaching the short list of just 36 with 21 professors among them. Winter did not mention that it is decidedly a select band of brothers, with Professor Dame Marilyn Strathern elected in 1999 as the sole woman.

When Anand was an undergraduate at Trinity, he preferred to dine at nearby Chinese and Indian restaurants on account of the austere and uninviting English fare on offer. Times have changed, and the catering has improved in his old haunt. As an honorary fellow, he can have lunch or dinner at the college up to 90 times in any quarter, and also bring guests. The select band of honorary fellows includes Prince Charles. The Prince of Wales read anthropology, archaeology, and history at Trinity in the late 1960s, and was elected in 1988. Justin Welby, the Archbishop of Canterbury, was elected in 2015. Predating them all, Prince Philip, the Duke of Edinburgh, was elected in 1977, although he attended the Royal Naval College, Dartmouth, prior to his naval career in World War II.

When his grandson, Tanawin Charoen-Rajapark, got into Churchill College,

Cambridge, Anand threw a party at which he made an emotional address and pulled out an old jumper from his own student days. 'It was a very memorable speech,' his daughter Daranee recalls. Anand's links to Cambridge remain very active. He has chaired the Cambridge Thai Foundation (CTF) since 1990. It offers scholarships to undergraduate and graduate Thai students attending the university in all subjects, and has Queen Sirikit as its patron. The CTF partners the Cambridge Trust in the UK, which provides basic scholarships for the CTF to top up. CTF has sent well over 100 students to the UK over the past two decades, mostly for postgraduate studies. Over half the students are from the provinces, and Anand takes pride in their loyalty to home. So far, they have all returned to Thailand. 'It's a mindset that's rather unique,' he says.

One of the prime movers behind the CTF was Sumet Jumsai, the well-known architect who helped create the Friends of Anand group when Anand was taken to court after his second premiership in 1992. Sumet was inspired by the Cambridge Malaysia Trust, which was sending about 30 students each year to the university. Even Singapore, with a fraction of Thailand's population, was sending about that number. Some 200 such alumni organisations around the world helped raise funds in 2009 when Cambridge mounted a drive to raise £1 billion to mark the 800th anniversary of its founding, and help secure the future of one of the world's five oldest universities.

Anand has always served the CTF well, drumming up donations from corporate sponsors and affluent individuals. Bill Heinecke, a man who built a career on dropping out and never going to university, and who is very selective about philanthropic donations, remembers giving a million baht to CTF. 'I didn't even know it was a fund-raising dinner,' he recalls. 'I have ties to Anand so I am happy to support any charity he is a part of – he was a very positive influence in my life.'

Anand attends the annual Oxford and Cambridge dinners, from which spouses and non-alumni are generally banned. There is plenty of political debate at the tables, however. 'I know he doesn't like it, but I do keep pointing out that the ones who actually go through elections usually come from Oxford – *MR* Seni Pramoj, *MR* Kukrit Pramoj, *MR* Sukhumbhand Paribatra, Korn Chotikavanij,' says Abhisit Vejjajiva, himself a graduate of St John's College, Oxford. 'We don't recall a Cambridge-educated member of parliament elected from a constituency.' Anand has been known to have lively exchanges at these Oxbridge dinners with

Abhisit and Korn, the former Democrat minister of finance who also attended St John's College, jabbing hard at the failings of Thailand's political system.

The Dulwich experiment

As an honorary international adviser to the college governors, Anand maintains active links with his beloved Dulwich College. He is sent the academic league tables that appear in the British newspapers – the controversial metrics used to assess the performance of schools and universities. He has occasionally testy exchanges with the Master, as the headmaster is known, if the college appears to be slipping.

As prime minister in the early 1990s, Anand was instrumental in lowering Thailand's barriers to entry for foreign schools. Originally these were erected largely to prevent Chinese schools from gaining a foothold and subverting Thai culture. All children were to be educated as Thais and in Thai, and have a Thai given name and family name. These requirements, solidified during the reign of King Vajiravudh (r.1910–1925), are among the reasons Thailand has the most assimilated ethnic Chinese population in Southeast Asia. Sino-Thais have been taught from birth to think of themselves as Thai, and this principle has been extended to other children of mixed or foreign ancestry.

In around 1994, with Thailand booming as never before, and the 1997 financial crash still well over the horizon, Dulwich College was already on the way to establishing its first franchise overseas. It hoped to turn a 400-year-old school with a proven brand into a successful multinational educational enterprise. The project was strongly backed by Anthony Verity, Dulwich's master at that time.

Thai boys had been going to Dulwich for over 70 years, and Old Alleynians, as they are known, have for decades been getting together regularly for dinners in Bangkok presided over by Anand. Thai culture dictates respect for teachers and elders, and educational alumni groups play an important role in society. The Old Alleynians in Bangkok are truly an old boy's network, and can usually muster more than 20 for a dinner, discussing their old school, cricket, rugby, and academic leagues, all the while consuming large amounts of alcohol. Some of the non-Thai Old Alleynians are permanent residents or on postings to Bangkok. They have included Paul Sizeland, the UK's deputy ambassador in Bangkok in the 1990s when Anand received his knighthood from Queen Elizabeth. There is also Jonathan Head, the BBC's often misquoted Southeast Asia correspondent, who has proved controversial in royalist circles. Head's reports have often tested Anand's patience, but that did not prevent Anand doing what he could to help the British correspondent when he was the victim of trumped-up *lèse-majesté* charges. However, when the *lèse-majesté* cases reached four, an exasperated Anand asked Head outright if he was making a habit of attracting them. Their exchanges added sparks to the dinners.

After one false start in Thailand in the early 1990s, Dulwich identified a local business partner in Arthit Ourairat, the former president of parliament who had played such a pivotal role in Anand's appointment as prime minister for a second time in 1992. Arthit had since gone into the education business, and was president of Rangsit University in Pathum Thani in the northern reaches of Greater Bangkok. It was established in 1990 on what had previously been Rangsit College.

In December 1994, Verity attended a dinner in Bangkok hosted by Arsa Sarasin, the former foreign minister who had attended Dulwich with Anand. Arthit was there to seal the deal in the presence of Christian Adams, the British ambassador. The school was to be built in the island province of Phuket. Apart from the new school's board, a consultative committee was set up, chaired by Anand. He had led a convoy of jubilant Old Alleynians on a visit to the project in the early days, and expectations were very high. The main buildings had a red-brick finish, in a style best described as faux Gothic with Thai tweaks that, despite the hot, lush setting, was intended to hark back to Charles Barry Junior's 19th-century design for the school in southeast London. Dulwich International College (DIC) opened in 1996 with 150 children, and this rose to 800 in under five years despite the national economic headwinds. A measure of the prestige of the project, Princess Maha Chakri Sirindhorn presided at the official opening and a plaque was erected to mark the occasion.

Although the school did well enough academically and in terms of enrolment, relations between Arthit and Dulwich College Enterprises (DCEL) in London became strained over the years, particularly in regard to senior teaching appointments and finances. 'As time went on, ever-increasing differences in opinion and expectations became more evident and tensions mounted,' DIC said in a statement in 2005 attributed to Arthit. 'At each stage, while efforts were made by each party to resolve these differences, it became clear that the number of unresolved issues would remain outstanding. Consequently, from the viewpoint of DIC Phuket, there was little alternative [but] to terminate the franchise agreement.'[3]

The franchise was officially terminated in June 2005 with 850 students enrolled. It was announced that the school would be renamed, and it is today known as the British International School, Phuket, or BISP. 'Despite many hours of discussion between DCEL and Arthit, it was impossible to find a way forward to continue the franchise: the DIC board were determined to manage the school in a way that would marginalise the [headmaster's] role and compromise the essential Dulwich ethos,' Dulwich College recorded in its official history. An olive branch of sorts was extended: 'There is something of "unfinished business" about it, however, and who knows what the future may bring?'[4]

Dulwich has not returned to Thailand, but it has expanded immensely in Asia with a 'family' of eight international schools, a pair of international high schools and a sister school, encompassing Beijing, Suzhou, Shanghai, and Zhuhai in China; Yangon in Myanmar; Singapore; and Seoul in South Korea. The difficult path Dulwich pioneered in Thailand provided lessons for the other major British school franchises that have followed – Bromsgrove International School Thailand, Harrow International School, Shrewsbury International School, and most recently in 2017 Brighton College Bangkok, Rugby School Thailand, and Wellington College International Bangkok.

The nub of Dulwich's problem, Anand believes, was whether the head of the school should be the manager in all matters, academic and business. For Arthit, while he was commited to educational ideals, it was also a business concern in which he was heavily invested and returns were slow. He wanted the headmaster to function not as the chief executive but the chief education officer. From his perspective, Anand's consultative board – essentially an independent board of governors – simply added complexity to an already difficult relationship.

Arthit found the representative sent from London to negotiate with him to be high-handed and unreasonable, even though he believed the terms given to Dulwich were always advantageous. However, the final, overarching reason for the split, according to Arthit, was his unwillingness to invest in a proposed second Dulwich campus that was to be built on a 66-rai plot on Ko Samui, an island in the Gulf of Thailand. It would simply have overextended him.

In the bigger picture, Anand's government had been instrumental in promoting international schools in Thailand. Anand believes these institutions are generally doing well, and that the country's educational paradigm has been permanently altered for the better. With some 170 international schools, affluent parents have more choice for their children, and no longer have to send them away for long periods for a foreign education.

Honours

Anand has seven Thai honours, starting with the Royal Cypher Medal (Third Class) that King Bhumibol awarded him in 1967 following the royal visits to Canada and the US, the last time the king travelled outside Thailand. Significantly, Anand was made a Knight Grand Cross (First Class) of the Most Exalted Order of the White Elephant in 1977, just after he was exonerated from false charges of being a communist sympathiser in the aftermath of the massacre of students at Thammasat University in October 1976. Anand was raised a final notch to Special Class in the Order of the White Elephant in 1992, after his service as prime minister. He holds similarly high ranks in the Most Noble Order of the Crown of Thailand, the Most Illustrious Order of Chula Chom Klao, and the Most Admirable Order of Direkgunabhorn. As a non-royal, there are few higher Thai honours he could conceivably aspire to.

Internationally, Anand has been honoured by Italy, South Korea, Indonesia, Belgium, Japan, the UK, and Sweden. He was awarded Japan's Grand Cordon of the Rising Sun in 1991, and became a Commander Grand Cross of Sweden's Royal Order of the Polar Star in 2007. In 1996, he was appointed an Honorary Knight Commander of the Civil Division of the Most Excellent Order of the British Empire (KBE). Over the years, the same honorary knighthood has been bestowed on other foreigners, including Placido Domingo, Dean Rusk, Franco Zefirelli, Bill Gates, Akio Morita, J. Edgar Hoover, Bob Geldof, Brent Scowcroft, and Bob Hope. They could all add KBE after their names if they wished, but not use 'Sir' as an honorific because their countries did not have a British head of state. Although Anand can never be addressed as 'Sir Anand', he has done better than most British ambassadors, who used routinely to be given knighthoods. They are now more commonly appointed Companions of the Order of St Michael and St George (CMG). Of the 12 British ambassadors to Thailand since 1978, only two were given knighthoods, Sir Ramsey Melhuish (KBE CMG) and Sir James Hodge (KCVO CMG).

Literary tastes

Anand laments that biographies do not have much of a tradition in Thai literature, and those that do appear tend to lack critical and analytical content. Historically, biographies were most likely to appear in funeral books, commemorative tomes which constitute an important strand in the country's publishing history. Prominent figures in other Southeast Asian countries – for example Lee Kuan Yew and S.R. Nathan in Singapore, and Dr Mahathir Mohamad in Malaysia – have been careful to leave detailed accounts of their life stories. Others have been the subjects of critical biographies, usually written by foreigners – King Bhumibol and Thaksin Shinawatra in Thailand; Aung San Suu Kyi in Myanmar; Hun Sen and Pol Pot in Cambodia; Ho Chi Minh and Vo Nguyen Giap in Vietnam.

'I am not a natural writer,' Anand admits. He relishes direct interaction with audiences when he speaks, and excuses himself for not producing a memoir with a joke about what would have to be left out; but he reads widely in both Thai and English. 'Our literature is quite rich, but what is lacking is social content.' He does find such material in Khamsing Srinawk, for example, an acclaimed short story writer and former journalist who fled into the forests after the Thammasat massacre. Khamsing is considered an heir to Jit Phumisak, the young leftist writer killed by the authorities in 1966. Anand meets Khamsing from time to time, and says he would make him compulsory reading in all schools if he were minister of education. Khamsing writes from the perspective of ordinary rural folk, describing how people in the Northeast view modernisation, and how Bangkokians misunderstand northeasterners.

'There is a big gap – no mutual understanding,' says Anand. 'In my younger days, Isaan [northeastern] people would be portrayed as lazy, poor, uneducated fools, which is far from the truth. Wherever you go in Thailand, the people who really work are from Isaan.' He also reads Seksan Prasertkun, the student leader from the 1970s turned political scientist, author, and orator; historian Nidhi Eoseewong, the historian and political thinker; social critic Sulak Sivaraksa; and older writers such as Sakchai Bamrungphong, a retired diplomat who was once ambassador to Burma and wrote under the pen name Seni Saowaphong. He also enjoys the poetry of Naowarat Pongpaiboon, who is among 30 or 40 people he regularly socialises with.

Anand likes writers who challenge preconceptions, and has always been deeply critical of official histories. 'I firmly believe that most Thais do not know what Thailand is all about,' he says. 'When authorities believe there is an official history, that is a most misguided viewpoint – they don't understand the word "history".' Among political columnists, he has read everyone from Pansak Vinyaratn, latterly chief policy adviser to Thaksin Shinawatra, to Chai-Anan Samudavanija, a former professor of political science and president of the Royal Institute.

Anand's reading of foreign political thinkers has been less rigorous. 'I knew about Rousseau, but I never read John Locke or John Stuart Mill, or philosophical books – no Plato or Marx,' he says. 'I never read Keynes – I heard about his theory but never anything deeper than that. I read Chaucer and Shakespeare, but never understood them. I loved Thomas Hardy. I think the most classical books I ever read were *Jude the Obscure* and *Tess of the D'Urbervilles*.' There was no Tolstoy or Proust, but he enjoyed John Buchan, the Brontës, Jane Austen, W. Somerset Maugham, as well as C.S. Forester, Raymond Chandler, and P.G. Wodehouse – the latter three all Old Alleynians. He does not consider himself well read. Among his more eclectic recent choices: *Jews in Thailand* by Ruth Gerson and Stephen Mallinger.

Print media

In 1994, Anand became chairman of Post Publishing, which owns the *Bangkok Post* newspaper. Saha Union had a small shareholding in the company, and there was a sentimental connection to Anand's own father, Sern, one of the eight original shareholders who, in 1946, backed Alexander MacDonald, the newspaper's American founding editor. It was Sern who in August 1946 switched on the old Japanese press that printed the first edition. Anand was reminded also of his father's own *Siam Chronicle*, an earlier English-language newspaper. There was a link to Anand's early diplomatic career as well: in the 1960s, James Linen, the president of Time Inc., had invested personally in Darrel Berrigan's *Bangkok World*. The *World* was taken over by the *Post* in 1971, and shuttered in the 1980s, but one of Linen's daughters remained a minor shareholder in Post Publishing.

Anand was asked to chair Post Publishing by Robert Kuok, a wealthy Malaysian businessman resident in Hong Kong. In 1993, Kuok had bought a controlling interest in the South China Morning Post Group, which was a major shareholder in Post Publishing. Chairing the *Bangkok Post* on a barely remunerated basis proved to be one of Anand's less happy involvements. 'People were very pleased, certainly among the liberal editorial group,' recalls David Pratt, the 'Outlook' section editor at the time of Anand's appointment. 'I think things were expected, but nothing really materialised. As chairman, he was quite remote.' The newspaper was run with some distance between the editorial sections in the back building and the management at the front. There was some historic bad chemistry between Anand and one of the key board members, although this did not surface at meetings. 'It was not a fruitful relationship,' Anand recalls. He came to regard the newspaper as somewhat 'spineless'.

'There were times Anand felt the paper did not do its job, and he let his views be known forcefully,' recalls Pichai Chuensuksawadi, the *Post*'s newly appointed editor at that time. The board met every two months, and Pichai recalls that Anand brought to the position a 'lot of charisma' and a certain egalitarianism. He enlisted Anand's support sometimes on staffing issues. In 1996, the management wanted to award all members of staff a month's bonus to mark the 50th anniversary of the newspaper's founding. The board's inner executive committee turned down the proposal an hour ahead of a board meeting. Anand knew about the proposal and supported it. When he asked each board member individually to vote on the motion the same day, the staff got their bonus.

Anand supported a project to develop an independent Thai-language sister newspaper, *Siam Post*, under Paisal Sricharatchanya, a feisty former bureau chief for the *Far Eastern Economic Review* and the previous editor of the *Bangkok Post*. In the end, it failed for financial reasons. The management formula was faulty, and the confrontational editorial tone attracted litigation.

'There was not enough sense of public service,' Anand reflects on his involvement with the *Post*. '*The Nation* was more adventurous.' In 1997, as he became increasingly involved in drafting the new national constitution, Anand felt it was time to move on and resigned.

Anand personally never attempted to impose any particular editorial line on the *Bangkok Post*, but he was the moving force behind *Thailand's Guiding Light*, a 180-page coffee-table book produced in 1996 by Post Publishing to mark the 50th anniversary of King Bhumibol's accession to the throne. Pichai took charge of the editing. He recognised the uncomfortable editorial constraints bearing down on such a project, and asked only for voluntary involvement from staff. The biggest problem turned out to be obtaining photographs from the massive but inaccessible palace archive.

When the proofs were ready, Anand perused them, making some adjustments that were mostly minor – except for one. He judged the balance of photographs between Crown Prince Maha Vajiralongkorn and Princess Maha Chakri Sirindhorn to be skewed too much towards the princess. This may well have been essentially a reflection of comparative photo opportunities: the princess was the most visible member of the royal family after King Bhumibol, whom she often accompanied upcountry, and she simply appeared more often than any other member of the royal family in public. Anand instructed that more pictures of the crown prince be added, and that the last photograph in the book be of the heir to the throne. The book should imply no ambiguity about the path of succession.

An audience with King Bhumibol was granted after publication. It was an extremely formal affair. Anand had ensured that those sitting in the front row were the writers and editors – in front of the sponsors that Anand himself had rounded up. It was Pichai who presented the book to the king, and Anand who presented the customary cheque for the royal charities.

At the same time as he was involved with *Thailand's Guiding Light*, Anand became chairman of the editorial advisory board for a project produced by an outside publisher, Archipelago Press, an imprint of Editions Didier Millet (the publisher of this book). A larger, more lavish 280-page coffee-table book, *Thailand: King Bhumibol Adulyadej: The Golden Jubilee, 1946–1996* featured polished essays from some notable contributors, including ML Thawisan Ladawan, the king's personal private secretary; Likhit Dhiravegin, a top political scientist of the day; and Ammar Siamwalla, Thailand's most erudite economist. With a rare byline, Anand himself contributed a detailed essay on Thai diplomacy.

The publisher, Didier Millet, struck up a good working relationship with Khwankeo Vajarodaya, the grand chamberlain in the Bureau of the Royal Household, who had been in the king's service for around half a century since the years in Switzerland. Kwankeo personally had probably the best collection of photographs of King Bhumibol's state visits and travels abroad in the late 1950s and 1960s, many of which he had taken himself, and these featured prominently in the book.

Anand's genuine interest in publishing projects did not go unnoticed. In October 1997, he was asked to attend the Frankfurt Book Fair to introduce *Mahajanaka*. The illustrated book was a retelling for a Thai readership of an ancient allegorical tale about an incarnation of the Lord Buddha that King

Bhumibol had written over a 20-year period. A few years later, he was asked to review a manuscript that had been in preparation for a decade with considerable assistance from the Crown Property Bureau, the Bureau of the Royal Household, and the Office of His Majesty's Principal Private Secretary. *The Revolutionary King* was written by William Stevenson, author of *A Man Called Intrepid: The Secret War*, published by Macmillan in 1976. This earlier book was the colourful story of Sir William Stephenson, a Canadian Allied 'spymaster' during World War II with the codename Intrepid. After the war ended, Intrepid was believed to have been supportive of Thailand, particularly in its dealing with onerous British demands for reparations. Unlike Lord Louis Mountbatten, the supreme Allied commander in Southeast Asia from 1943 to 1946, Stephenson the spymaster was, by Stevenson the author's account, sympathetic to young King Bhumibol after his accession when rumours were swirling over his brother's unexplained death by gunshot.[5] King Bhumibol once described *Intrepid* as an 'exciting secret war book', and produced a personal translation titled *Nai In Phu Pid Tong Laang Phra*, which can be rendered in English as 'Mr In, Who Puts Gold on the Back of the Buddha Image'. The idiom refers to the practice of earning merit by putting gold leaf on Buddha images: those who apply gold to the back of an image do good without seeking attention or credit.

There had long been serious doubts about the accuracy of Stevenson's work, including *Intrepid*. In 1990, he and his wife, Monika Jensen-Stevenson, co-authored *Kiss the Boys Goodbye: How the United States Betrayed Its Own POWs in Vietnam*. The book alleged a conspiracy by the US to conceal the 'fact' that prisoners of war were knowingly left behind in Indochina when the wars there ended. Critics were concerned by the way in which the book interwove fact and rumour. Malcolm McConnell, with the benefit of access to previously unavailable North Vietnamese material, later wrote in *Inside Hanoi's Secret Archives* that the Stevensons had produced a 'flawed' book.

Although the king's translation was not published until 1993, King Bhumibol and Stevenson exchanged letters about *Intrepid* in the late 1970s. At the king's invitation, they first met in 1987 at Thaksin Ratchaniwet Palace in Narathiwat, a Muslim-majority province in southern Thailand. 'He was waiting for me on a journey that I now sometimes think must have started for us a great time ago,' Stevenson opened his prologue portentously.

In 1989, the author and his wife moved to Thailand, where he resided at Sra

Pathum Palace, the Princess Mother's home in Bangkok. The couple's daughter, Alexandra, was enrolled in the Chitralada School, and Stevenson became for the next six years or so essentially a biographer in residence. He had exceptional access to the king and Queen Sirikit, and to others who almost never gave interviews, including the Princess Mother, but he did not record his interviews. He met Anand once. According to Stevenson's own account, Anand commented, perhaps with a measure of concern, 'The king must trust you.'

Stevenson had a remarkable opportunity and produced an extraordinary book – one filled on almost every page with glaring factual errors. He conjured up unique theories utterly detached from history. He had no grasp of the basic geography of Southeast Asia. Sensitive royal lineages were muddled so badly that King Taksin was listed in the index as 'the First Rama'. In fact, Taksin moved the capital from Ayutthaya to Thonburi, across the Chao Phraya from Bangkok, and his reign predated the Chakri dynasty's founding in 1782.[6]

Stevenson's description of Anand gives a fair indication of the book's accuracy:

> Khun Anand Panyarachun was a diplomat and a scholar. He had been charged with subversion and jailed, with nothing but rumour and gossip for evidence. After months of investigation that produced nothing untoward, he had escaped to West Germany where, in his outrage, he declared, 'I am no longer a Thai!' Now he returned and agreed to serve a year as premier. At his formal royal audience, the Ninth Rama said, 'Ah – Zorro rides again!'

Though he has always read widely, nobody would ever describe Anand as a scholar. He was never jailed, and the attack on him was mounted by Thailand's security establishment, not Bangkok's infamous rumour mill. He was assigned to Bonn as Thailand's ambassador following a routine audience with King Bhumibol, and being Thai throughout that period also qualified him to serve as ASEAN's top negotiator with the European Economic Community. Having resigned from the diplomatic service, he had been living happily as a businessman in Thailand for more than a dozen years before he became prime minister. Stevenson's Hollywood allusion not only muddled Anand's two premierships: it also got the film wrong – and the true sense of the king's joking allusion to *Shane*.

According to Stevenson, Prime Minister Chatichai Choonhavan was not removed in the 1991 coup, but 'resigned' after mishandling a terrible storm in southern Thailand. Stevenson claimed the economic crash of 1997 reduced Bangkok's population by half from ten million, and left the 'neo-Nazi' Grand Hyatt Erawan hotel 'derelict'.[7]

Anand read the manuscript through and realised that a great deal was seriously amiss. 'It could never be revised,' he says. 'There were innumerable inaccuracies, and I recommended that it be spiked.' There was no binding contract in place, however, and the book was published uncorrected in London by Constable in 1999, and reprinted, still largely uncorrected, in 2001. Its appearance coincided with the release of *Anna and the King* starring Jodie Foster and Chow Yun-fat, a reworking of 1953's *The King and I*, starring Yul Brynner and Deborah Kerr. The subtitle of *The Revolutionary King* was 'The True-Life Sequel to "The King and I"'. This laid bare an effort to connect the book, presumably for marketing purposes, to the two films – both of which are officially banned in Thailand.

'I'd never heard of Stevenson or this project, but happened to be in London and walked into Foyles on the day it was launched,' historian Chris Baker recalls. 'I remember later that evening rolling around on the floor in laughter.' The book has never been banned in Thailand explicitly, but it is not stocked openly by bookshops. Newspaper editors were instructed at the time not to mention it.

'The king had made it clear from the beginning that he did not want the book published inside Thailand,' Stevenson told *The International Herald Tribune*. 'But I never fully understood what his concern was until there was this reported backlash of it being banned.' Among many issues, the Thai authorities were upset by Stevenson's reference to the king throughout the book by a family nickname. 'If he has a good enough perspective about Thailand and the royal household, he should know how to address the king,' said Don Pramudwinai, the foreign ministry's spokesman.[8]

In his 2012 memoir, *Past to Present*, Stevenson gives an account of his time in Thailand that confirms how well treated he was in royal circles, but does not address criticisms of *The Revolutionary King*. Indeed, he comes up with further inventions. The king's father, Prince Mahidol Adulyadej na Songkla, Stevenson wrote, while 'at university in Heidelberg, was shaken by the discovery of Auschwitz and other death camps'. In fact, Prince Mahidol received medical treatment in Heidelberg in 1926, which is how Prince Ananda Mahidol came to be born there. Auschwitz was not opened until 1940.[9]

According to Chirayu Isarangkun Na Ayuthaya, the former director general of the Crown Property Bureau, King Bhumibol never spoke about the book, so his reaction is unknown. If he felt disappointed, even betrayed, nobody can say. There would, however, be no more interviews or help from him with biographical projects of any kind. King Bhumibol's door closed permanently.

In mid-2006, the government attempted to foil the publication of *The King Never Smiles,* a critical biography of King Bhumibol by Paul Handley, an American former correspondent in Thailand for the Hong Kong-based *Far Eastern Economic Review.* Borwornsak Uwanno, a secretary general to the cabinet, was assigned to the task and consulted Anand. 'Not having the full facts of what they were trying to do, I told Borwornsak that it was Mission Impossible, and that world-class universities could not be swayed,' Anand recalls. 'You merely dignify the publication and draw attention to it.' The book was indeed published by Yale University Press soon after the celebrations in July marking the 60th anniversary of the king's accession in 1946. Its distribution has always been banned in Thailand.

Not long after, Arsa Sarasin, King Bhumibol's principal private secretary, approached the Foreign Correspondents' Club of Thailand (FCCT) to find out if there was any chance of reprinting *The King of Thailand in World Focus*, a book first published in 1988. The palace had wanted to present a copy to Emperor Akihito of Japan, and found it no longer had any spare. *World Focus* was simply a compilation of foreign print media coverage of King Bhumibol's life since his birth in Cambridge, Massachusetts, in 1927. It also included a fine genealogy of the Chakri dynasty by Owen Wrigley, a club member. There were very few copies left from the 5,000 originally printed; the book had been a moderate success in Thailand, a relatively small English-speaking market.

A small group from the FCCT met with Arsa and Tej Bunnag, who had briefly served as foreign minister in 2005 under Thaksin, and it was agreed that a second edition would be produced if sponsors could be found to underwrite the substantial cost of the project since the FCCT could not afford the significant financial exposure.[10] The project's original editor in chief, Denis Gray, who had been the Associated Press bureau chief in Bangkok since 1975 after the fall of Phnom Penh, reassumed his old position. Australian photographer John Everingham returned as photo editor. Owen Wrigley, Yvan Van Outrive, and Rosemary Whitcraft, the elderly American expatriate who in 1987 located the king's original birth certificate, also rejoined. The author, who had not been involved with the first edition, became editor.

A much larger 260-page coffee table book emerged from the second project due to the wide variety of articles that had been written about King Bhumibol in the intervening years, and also the inclusion of a number of old articles that had previously been overlooked. Although he had no formal role on the project, Anand joined some lunches and was given updates on it. He had no involvement in the book's production or content, and neither did the palace nor the sponsors, but Thanphuying Putrie Viravaidya, the king's deputy principal private secretary, was consulted to ensure the Chakri genealogy was up to date with correct spellings of names and titles.

Anand agreed to be guest of honour and give an address at the book's official launch in August 2007 at The Mandarin Oriental. 'You will never see a monarch like this in any other country,' he said. '[Thais] still retain pomp and circumstance, they still retain rituals and rites, they still retain traditions and so forth, but they retain mystique too.'

It was a lively evening, with Amy Kazmin of the *Financial Times*, the FCCT's president at the time, reminding everyone that reporting the monarchy was subject to some 'unique constraints, not least the law of *lèse-majesté*'. In her welcome, she said, 'Thailand is extremely protective of the reputation of its monarchy, and all foreign journalists face a difficult juggling act in trying to report about the institution.'

Anand had been one of the first prominent people in Thailand to broach the subject of *lèse-majesté* for broader discussion, and had privately been disappointed by the lack of response. The foreign press were keen to probe the topic, however, and the first question that night was about *lèse-majesté*. 'My own personal view is that I do not like the law,' Anand responded, reminding them of his foreign education. 'And yet you have to understand that the king is held in a certain position which is inviolable by the will of his people … You may have to wait for 20 more years, 50 more years, I do not know, but the Thai people, rightly or wrongly, will not tolerate any "criticism" against our king.' Anand also said he felt sure King Bhumibol did not mind if the law existed or not.

Anand's address covered the place of the monarchy in Thai life, and the closeness of King Bhumibol to his people, particularly outside Bangkok. 'The reverence that the Thai people hold for His Majesty in my view is the only reason for the existence of such a law,' he argued. The king, he said, 'never made use or took advantage of this legal recourse to silence critics'.

But others have certainly used the law of *lèse-majesté* to silence critics, and in the intervening years Anand has adopted a more critical view. 'I can accept the existence of the law in light of the special relationship our people have with the king,' Anand said during an interview in April 2016, some months before the passing of King Bhumibol. His view was that the king would be 'a hostage to criticism if he were not protected'. That said, he believed the law was being applied too broadly and should cover only the king, the queen, the crown prince, and the regent. 'My thinking on this matter has evolved because of the growing number of abuses not only by the authorities, but also by individuals in their private capacities,' says Anand. 'These have become more serious as time has gone by.'

Anand now feels that amendments should be made to the law. 'Firstly, *lèse-majesté* should be decriminalised and replaced with a system of fines commensurate with the infringements,' he says. 'Secondly, a mechanism should be created, under the chairmanship of either the minister of interior or the minister of justice, to undertake a full and fair review of the merits of a case before deciding whether to proceed with legal action or to dismiss.'

He believes such changes would relieve police and prosecutors of responsibility. State officials, he argues, regard themselves as messengers in *lèse-majesté* cases, and pass them on up lest they themselves be accused of obstruction. 'The attorney general has the same feeling when it reaches him, and in my view this is unfair,' says Anand. 'The attorney general is still a civil servant.' Most importantly, Anand believes the authorities should not involve the palace in any way.

There is still a belief in some quarters that senior members of the royal family must be fully protected from defamation and criticism. In practice, particularly since the government of Prayut Chan-o-cha took power in May 2014, the law of *lèse-majesté* has been used to prosecute an increasingly broad range of people and their alleged slights against the institution.

A notable example was charging the social critic Sulak Sivaraksa in October 2016 two years after he questioned an official narrative of a battle in 1593 involving King Naresuan. Sulak had faced *lèse-majesté* charges on numerous occasions in his 84 years, but this instance involving a long-dead king was by far the most tendentious. Chris Baker, Japan's Fukuoka Grand Prize winner in 2017 and co-author of a history of Ayutthaya, noted that there are at least ten different accounts in English, French, and Thai of the celebrated elephant battle to repel invading Burmese forces. 'Academic freedom and free speech in Thailand will suffer devastating blows if the trial against Mr Sulak proceeds,' warned Brad Adams, the Asia director of Human Rights Watch. Unusually, the case was dropped by the military court after Sulak sent a petition to the king. Sulak believes that this was 'due to the grace of the king'. He has since been fulsome in his praise for King Maha Vajiralongkorn Bodindradebayavarangkun, who acceded to the throne in 2016.

World Focus was entirely an FCCT project editorially, and the club retained the copyright unconditionally. It was, however, produced and printed by Editions Didier Millet (EDM), the publishing company that had published on its own initiative in 1996 *Thailand: King Bhumibol Adulyadej: The Golden Jubilee, 1946–1996* (and is also the publisher of this book). The Singapore-based company had produced numerous books on Thailand over the years. Publisher Didier Millet liked to enlist distinguished editorial boards to help navigate the local scene, and to peg his projects to national milestones.

King Bhumibol marked his Diamond Jubilee in 2006, his 80th birthday in 2007, and his 84th birthday in 2011. The latter marked the completion of the seventh 12-year cycle in his lifetime. In late 2010, Nicholas Grossman, EDM's managing editor in Bangkok (and one of the editors of this book), was scouting around for publishing projects. Sensing there could be demand for a biography of King Bhumibol that could exist in both the local and international market, he sent an outline to Chirayu at the Crown Property Bureau (CPB), a longtime supporter of EDM projects. Chirayu recommended approaching Anand, who had the 'intellectual energy' for such an undertaking. After some deliberation and suggesting some revisions to the outline, Anand agreed to select his own editorial advisory board for *King Bhumibol Adulyadej – A Life's Work*.

Anand's board was very much royalist establishment. It included Thanphuying Putrie Viravaidya, the king's deputy principal private secretary and a leading authority on the monarchy, and Sumet Tantivejkul, secretary general to the Chaipattana Foundation, which runs the numerous projects set up by King Bhumibol over the years.[12]

Anand hosted a dinner to introduce his advisory board to the publishing and editorial teams at the Fireplace Grill – the restaurant where in 1991 it was suggested to General Suchinda Kraprayoon that he consider approaching Anand to become prime minister. Anand said he believed chapters on both the Privy

Council and Crown Property Bureau should be included because both were so poorly understood. This meant finding more specialist writers. Academics Chris Baker, Porphant Ouyyanont, and David Streckfuss were approached. Baker and Porphant had collaborated on ground-breaking research into the Crown Property Bureau, and Streckfuss, an American political scientist based at Khon Kaen University, is arguably the world's leading authority on *lèse-majesté*. At the first editorial meeting, the editors (including the author of this book) took the additions further by recommending that chapters on the law of *lèse-majesté* and the law of succession also be included.

The editors recruited journalists, both retired and working, to file different sections of the book, which eventually ran to over 380 pages.[13] No chapter in the book was credited to any of its authors since the process involved so many inputs from different individuals. There was therefore concern that bylines would lead to writers being quoted for something they had not in fact written.

The drafting of *King Bhumibol Adulyadej* was completed on a very tight eight-month schedule in 2011. Grossman recalled: 'We wanted to bridge a tricky divide with this project and bring Thais and foreigners together to produce something more credible on King Bhumibol than existed at the time in the local market. Anand was perfect for this role. He can see both sides of issues and knew how far we might be able to go. The results may not have pleased everyone, but without Anand's leadership we likely would not have been able to release a book on these topics in Thailand at all.' Grossman was impressed by Anand's hands-on working style: 'For someone of his stature he was remarkably involved. He can be very sharp, but he's also affable and clearly loves rolling up his sleeves and getting to work. It's refreshing to collaborate with someone like that. He also promotes efficiency in meetings and he's decisive. From a publishing standpoint, that's ideal.'

The editors met the editorial advisory board every month or so, when drafts in progress were critiqued. The editorial board responded to what it was asked to read, and initiated very little about what should be included. There was no brief from the palace, and no offers of inside interviews – certainly no repeat of the opportunities afforded to Stevenson a few decades earlier. There was some access to the Crown Property Bureau, Privy Council, and Ministry of Justice, however, and Pisoot Vijarnsorn and Pramote Maiklad, who had both worked on royal projects over many years, were meticulous in responding to queries.

Putrie was key to the chapter on ceremonies and regalia; nobody else could match her grasp of such arcane material. 'That was the only chapter where I had no contribution to make,' recalls Anand. Perhaps its more mystical elements jarred with his rationalism. It was also the only part of the book for which a strong case was made for leaving some material out: the description of the ancient – and in parts gruesome – royal cremation ceremony based on a 1931 account by Horace Geoffrey (H.G.) Quaritch Wales in his book *Siamese State Ceremonies*. The editorial board saw no justification for including a section on royal funerary rites while King Bhumibol was still alive. The board also knew by then that the king's cremation would involve a coffin rather than the traditional royal funerary urn encased in sandalwood, so many of the details from the 1931 description of King Vajiravudh's cremation would not apply. The ceremonies for both the Princess Mother, the king's mother, in 1996 and Princess Galyani, his only sister, in 2008, had involved coffins instead of urns.

The editorial board was adamant that nothing should be projected on to the king. There were to be no references to his thinking or reasons for doing things, because this was deemed to be speculation about unknown processes. Mystique was anyway an important element in King Bhumibol's persona; he seldom set out to be open and revealing. Reporters covering the king's public addresses often huddled together to try and work out what had actually been said. An effort by the editors to establish if the king had any 'friends' in the normal sense failed.

Anand clearly cared about the project and worked very hard on it, running marathon meetings and placing phone calls to the editors up until the deadline. When *King Bhumibol Adulyadej – A Life's Work* was launched toward the end of 2011, it was an immediate hit in the local market, thanks in part to Anand's personal lobbying on behalf of the title.

CHAPTER 21

TWILIGHT YEARS

Elusive retirement

At the time of writing, Anand, approaching 86, is still chairman of Siam Commercial Bank (SCB), Thailand's third-largest bank by assets with over 1,260 branches. His present term ends in April 2019. He long ago wrote a letter of resignation to be delivered in the event of his incapacitation. The chairman of the executive committee is Vichit Suraphongchai. Anand goes to his office at the massive SCB headquarters in Ratchayothin, northern Bangkok, once a week on Wednesdays, and once a month for board meetings. These are meant to last four hours, but sometimes run longer. Before becoming chairman, he used to sit on the corporate and social responsibility committee. 'I listen a lot,' he says of his monthly lunches with the SCB team. 'I think one of the troubles with Thailand is that most people only talk. They don't listen.'

Anand first joined the board of SCB in 1981. He stepped away in 1991 when he became prime minister, and returned in late 1992. When he reached the age of 69 in 2001, he proposed that retirement for board members should be mandatory at 70, but this was turned down. He made the same suggestion for 72 and 75, but these waymarkers were also rejected. When Anand reached 76, Chirayu Isarangkun Na Ayuthaya, the director general of the Crown Property Bureau (CPB) who became chairman of both SCB and Siam Cement Group (SCG) following the 1997 financial crash, finally dashed Anand's exit hopes by asking him to take over the bank's chair. 'I knew that being chairman of two big companies listed on the Stock Exchange of Thailand wasn't illegal, but it wasn't good practice and is not recommended,' says Chirayu.

Chirayu felt the bank's chair should be independent, and not the representative of a major shareholder. The CPB had diluted its shareholding in SCB when Chirayu became chairman, and retained just over 20 per cent of the stock; it was its largest individual shareholder until the shares were transferred to King Maha Vajiralongkorn Bodindradebayavarangkun in mid-2018. When he handed over to Anand, Chirayu's intention was to focus on SCG, where he believed his background in Thai industry would be better applied.

'Prior to the 1997 crisis, Anand was a good member of the board but he did not play such a strong role,' says Chirayu. 'He was a non-executive member – he contributed but it was not significant. After the crisis, he played a very major role.'

In the wake of the 1997 crash, the bank's governance, both macro and micro, was found wanting, much like the country's. SCB was probably no worse off in terms of non-performing loans than other banks that ended up with shares trading for mere satang. 'There had been too much optimism and not enough diligence,' Chirayu reflects. After CPB reduced its shareholding, some 64 billion baht was needed for recapitalisation. SCB was only able to raise half that amount. The government offered to match this, buying shares that could be sold back later at market price.

Tarrin Nimmanahaeminda, the former president and chief executive of SCB, was finance minister at the time, so critics found it easy to impute some sort of cosy relationship even though the lifeboat scheme was open to all banks. 'Only a few took advantage of it because not many banks wanted such a government influence – one that completely altered the structure of the shareholding,' Chirayu recalls. Thai Military Bank was another that took up the offer. Others, such as Kasikornbank, opted to raise capital in ways that cost significantly more.

Recapitalising the beached banks was an obvious priority, but there had to be institutional reform too. In SCB's case, this meant effective implementation of a change programme drawn up by the management consultants McKinsey and Company. The plan always made good sense to Anand, and it was during this period that he and Chirayu first really got the chance to work together. A cornerstone of the implementation was that nobody should be fired. As chairman then, Chirayu credits Anand with working to ensure old staff were properly treated and meaningful reforms were put in place to avoid a repeat disaster. 'I think Anand played a role in getting the right degree of change going,' he says.

As chairman, Anand has always insisted that the SCB board should be composed of an odd number of directors. 'He stood firm on his principle that the chairman must never vote,' says Chirayu, recalling some lively debate when the issue first arose. 'With reason, you listen to everyone, state your opinions, and you don't need to vote after that,' he says.

The rule has yet to be applied universally to other SCB boards and committees, and Anand admits it is a more aspirational than enforceable policy. 'In my time as chairman, I cannot recall any specific vote,' he says. 'We all tried to reach consensus.' Chirayu remembers Anand sometimes taking cautionary positions, but not digging in if the flow of discussion went against him. If something later went wrong, as he had warned, Anand would not say, 'I told you so.'

Anand has always particularly liked attending the twice-yearly SCB retreats for top-level management, when medium-term plans are discussed. The meetings run from a Thursday to Sunday, and are usually held within driving distance of Bangkok in places such as Khao Yai or Hua Hin. 'He comes early and leaves late,' says Chirayu. 'He likes dialogues as long as there is good reasoning – it does not matter how long it takes.'

At the time of writing, SCB has 15 main board directors, of whom three are women. The gender balance does not compare with Saha Union's 60 per cent female board, but is considerably better than the Privy Council, which remains all-male; seven of its 13 members are retired generals. On Anand's watch, privy councillors have been phased out of the SCB main board and the company's subsidiaries. Vacancies have been filled through a nomination committee to respect principles of good governance and rules laid down by the Stock Exchange of Thailand. 'Anand would probably feel that privy councillors are not truly independent,' says Chirayu.

Helping hand

Despite being ostracised in 1976 for alleged communist sympathies, Anand has never had any overtly leftist tendencies. He has, however, always had a liberal streak and genuinely empathises with people who are disadvantaged in some way. 'Although in some senses, he is very conservative, Anand was always a bit of a protector for NGOs being harried by the more conservative sides of the state,' says Kraisak Choonhavan, a former senator and social activist.

As a student activist protesting about pharmaceutical procurements in a capitalist world, Karuna Buakamsri was astonished when Anand once invited her group outside on the pavement into Government House for a chat. They expected him, as somebody privileged and foreign-educated, to be stiff and autocratic; but they found him very accessible – even when to his exasperation he failed to change their thinking. 'When you are a prime minister, you don't normally have contact with ordinary people,' says Karuna.

Anand's enduring openness to the NGO community is shared by people like Gothom Arya and Prawase Wasi, who believe there is a need for a third space beyond the government and its parliamentary opposition. 'Many things are happening at the local level and have been quite successful,' says Anand. 'It is part of the overall campaign to empower people at the grassroots, but unfortunately, no party has picked up on this, including Pheu Thai.'

It was Saisuree Chutikul, the only woman in Anand's two cabinets, who was instrumental in having Anand personally sign Thailand up to the United Nations Convention on the Rights of the Child. In 1996, Anand became directly involved with the United Nations Children's Fund (UNICEF) as a national goodwill ambassador. The relationship has lasted over 20 years, garnering him special awards in 2003 and 2016. UNICEF estimates that Anand has raised over five billion baht (US$160 million) for impoverished children in Thailand and elsewhere, including for the ebola crisis in Africa, the war in Syria, and the 2015 earthquake in Nepal. The money comes from over 25,000 donors, both individual and corporate, who contribute small and large amounts, sometimes monthly. In Thailand, he has campaigned for the iodisation of salt (which is crucial for physical and cognitive development), online birth registration, and child-support schemes.

'Poverty denies children their rights,' said Anand. 'It blights their lives with ill-health, malnutrition, and impaired physical and mental development. Poverty is transmitted from one generation to the next. To break this cycle, we need to invest in children's wellbeing and education.'

Even in his mid-80s, Anand continued with one or two field trips and four or five engagements for UNICEF each year. He raised nearly US$12 million in 2012, a nearly 12 per cent increase year on year. Sometimes he travels with Saisuree, who is now almost blind. 'He has to lead me by the hand,' she says. 'Some of the villagers thought I was his wife. If he is committed, he works on it and asks the kids good questions.'

Even with the best will in the world, things occasionally went awry on the UNICEF trips. In the aftermath of the 2004 tsunami, there was concern about employment prospects for youngsters in the South, and developing their skills for life. Anand visited Ban Bakan, a Muslim community that was promoting batik print-making, a hot-wax process. The hoped-for informal interaction between Anand and the youngsters was overtaken by hordes of local officials, non-governmental workers, and business sponsors. One of the boys demonstrating the batik process lost his focus and accidentally tipped very hot wax on Anand's hand, causing him a great deal of pain and irritation.

Anand still takes on the occasional new charity, and gets involved in new areas. In early 2015, he became honorary chairman of Operation Smile Thailand, a charitable organisation complementing the public health system. Since 2001, it has performed 9,000 surgical operations on children with cleft lips and cleft palates in Thailand and neighbouring countries. The facial deformity affects one in 700 children at birth. Anand set out to raise 50 million baht each year to bridge the charity's funding shortfalls. 'I can see that these patients have no confidence in themselves, and some children do not even have access to education for fear of going to school and being ridiculed,' Anand said. 'My main goal is to fully help patients by integrating financial sustainability into the core of the foundation.'

Anand hosts a fundraising party for Special Olympics Thailand each December at his country home in Rayong. In some of his speeches, he pushes the concept of 'strategic donations' for similar charities, particularly in education. He has never thrown birthday parties for himself. Cash gifts he received at the 84th birthday party organised for him by various friends all went to charity – UNICEF, UNAIDS, Operation Smile, and various schools – along with a substantial personal donation. He also planned to contribute to the restoration of the old family temple in Ratchaburi built by his grandfather and father. 'Normally, I don't give money to temples,' he says.

Reform agenda

Anand has phased out most of his non-charitable involvements because of advancing age. Over the years, he has been involved with a remarkable variety of non-governmental organisations, including the Business Council for Sustainable Development and Transparency International, which he chaired in Thailand.

He sat on Transparency International's advisory council, contributing from afar without attending meetings.

Anand chaired the influential Asian Institute of Technology (AIT), a postgraduate greenhouse for engineering and sustainable development, after being approached by four ambassadors on the board of trustees. Gothom Arya was the registrar at the time. Anand handed the chairmanship on to his old foreign ministry colleague, Tej Bunnag, and worked through the transition meticulously.

Anand was the longest-serving chairman of the Thailand Development Research Institute (TDRI), the country's most influential think tank. He took over from Snoh Unakul in 1992. Ammar Siamwalla remembers Anand striking a deal with him then. 'He came in and he said to me, "If you are the president, I'll be the chairman." In other words, it was a condition. After he judges somebody, he lets go.'

Ammar was never comfortable in the role of president, however, and in 1995 asked Anand for permission to step down so that he could once more concentrate on being an academic. 'You have to make unpleasant decisions, which I am too scared to do – dressing downs and so forth,' says Ammar. 'It is not my interest. I am as lazy as Khun Anand claims he is, but that is not true – that is his one big piece of false modesty.'

Being TDRI chairman came easily to Anand. 'He works in a very un-Thai way,' says Ammar. 'He sees all the reports and reads a lot – I don't know where he finds the time between his dinners and parties and so on.' Ammar credits Anand with getting non-governmental organisations more involved with TDRI, and more women on board, but not for having much personal impact on the research side. 'We became more like a consulting house – a kind of homegrown McKinsey. My value added was to distance ourselves from the government.' In the Thaksin years, the government took that a step further, and consciously froze out TDRI from government consultations. On one occasion, Thaksin took strong issue publicly with some of Ammar's criticisms of what had been dubbed 'Thaksinomics'.

Anand continued as chairman through the Thaksin years. In mid-2008, he passed the chair to Kosit Panpiemras, at much the same time as he handed over the Kenan Institute to Nitya Pibulsonggram. Snoh praised Anand at the TDRI retirement party for his efforts to involve civil society members, and for inviting community leaders and villagers to attend year-end conferences. 'This policy has helped to soften the image of TDRI as an elitist institution, making it more down to earth, and also more relevant to a wider spectrum of Thai society,' Snoh observed.

The Thai condition

Guests at Anand's 84th birthday celebration at the Siam Society, soon after the constitutional referendum in 2016, included Sulak Sivaraksa, Snoh Unakul, Ammar Siamwalla, Nukul Prachuabmoh, Mechai Viravaidya, and Jermsak Pinthong. There was a poem from Naowarat Pongpaiboon, who sometimes accompanied Anand on trips upcountry, and a painting from Preecha Thaothong, both national artists. Thirayuth Boonmi, the leftist student firebrand from the 1970s, was also there. In his speech, Anand said he was sorry more of his Red Shirt friends had not been invited by the organiser. He said many of the issues raised by the reds were understandable and needed to be discussed. Some were surprised that he would even mention the topic at such a non-red event, even if Anand himself was not completely yellow. 'I don't hide the fact that I am a royalist, but that's a separate matter,' he says.

'He is light yellow – pale yellow,' says Prida Tiasuwan, a businessman friend who had a leading role in organising the yellow movement's People's Alliance for Democracy in early 2006. Anand donated 50,000 baht 'as a gesture', he says, but never addressed any rallies. 'They never asked me to speak,' he recalls. 'They knew I would not accept – I never engage in political activities.' He did, however, attend the funeral on 14 October of a Yellow Shirt protester killed during heavy-handed attempts by the authorities to retake Government House. 'I attended after numerous requests from my activist friends,' he recalls without regret.

Thailand at that time had never been more polarised politically. 'I still believe that whatever dividing lines we have, these things can be contained. I cannot see Thais killing Thais,' he says. Since the coup led by the then army chief, General Prayut Chan-o-cha, in 2014, the country has been in a state of political suspension. The military has imposed peace, a new constitution, and is bringing on its own 20-year vision for the future. The present calm may be deceptive. It is often said that nothing much happens in Thailand until there is a crisis – until it absolutely has to happen. Anand believes Thais are overly protective and reactionary 'out of fear for the future', and are so preoccupied with everyday problems that nobody is much interested in addressing core issues. There is never any time for the big picture, he argues, yet the civil service, judiciary, military, and police all need to be reformed.

'Thai society is basically very conservative,' he says. 'The initial, instinctive resistance to change is very strong and combative, but once you overcome that obstacle the Thais are good at adapting to new situations – they are very pragmatic people.'

Steadfastness, conviction, and persuasiveness are therefore very important for any leader wishing to effect meaningful change. 'The words weak and strong have different meanings to me than to most other Thai people,' he says. 'A strong prime minister does not use power or influence arbitrarily. A strong prime minister takes into account all aspects of an argument, the pros and cons, and is sincere in that effort. But then, he has to make a decision. That is what governments are for. At the end of the day, you cannot afford to have a weak prime minister.'

'Change could take decades,' he believes. 'The weak point is that everything tends to be personal in this country. There are unrecoverable differences of opinion. Thais start off with issues, but as time goes by these are submerged and things become very personalised. If a traditional Thai has an argument with a friend to the disadvantage of their friendship, and tells his wife, the wife would take quite a strong decision vis-à-vis that friend. As a people, we are not in tune with democratic values. The essence of democracy is that the majority has to protect the interests of the minority. It is a game of accommodation, of compromise – accommodating the interests of all the people. We have not learned this and that is why democracy has not worked here. We have never been interested in building up democratic institutions. Italian politicians are much like ours. They kept on electing Berlusconi.'

A possible upside of the apparent inability of Thais to make constitutional democracy work is that they seem usefully immune to other outside ideologies and imported ideas. Christian missionaries succeeded as school teachers but never converted the general population from Buddhism; immigrants have been largely absorbed and naturalised; and Communist insurgents failed in the Cold War.

'Thais are open to foreign ideas and concepts, but tend to focus on form more than substance,' says Anand. 'They never really absorb the content. A clear-cut example is democracy. The process of writing a new constitution, forming political parties, administering an election process, forming a government – that's their idea of democracy.'

Indeed, few countries have had more constitutions than Thailand. The Dominican Republic has had over 30, but it began in 1844, almost a century ahead of Siam. Even Italy, with its revolving-door coalition governments, has had only one constitution since 1948.[1]

Thailand's great distinction is the unmatched frequency with which it shreds its charters. The people who draft each new constitution have familiar faces and infinite experience, but have yet to produce anything lasting. The constitutions are replaced – often twice – whenever there is a successful coup. There have been 13 coups since 1932 and nine failures. The military's interim constitutions are at least relatively short. The latest in 2014 had only 48 articles, the 44th of which is a notorious catch-all inclusion that permits virtually any measure the prime minister considers appropriate.

Thailand's 'permanent' constitutions, on the other hand are remarkably long. These are not distillations of the fundamental principles and beliefs that bind and unify the people of a sovereign state, but full-blown national operating manuals intended to thwart nefarious elements at every turn. Among 200 national constitutions around the world, Thailand's have long ranked in the top 10 for length. The 1997 charter drafted under Anand's chairmanship, and incorporating a groundbreaking public consultation process, included 336 articles in 12 chapters, the last of which usefully prescribed how to amend the preceding 11 without a coup. The revised constitution of 2007 had two more chapters but only 309 articles. The latest adopted by national referendum in 2016 had only 279.[2] It was promulgated in 2017, and is difficult to amend.

'The constitution should be a law for everyone, not victors trying to dominate the losers,' argues Borwornsak Uwanno, whose draft in 2015 was rejected by the military. With all Thailand's wasted charters, Borwornsak ponders the problem of stimulating collective political responsibility. Perhaps the answer lies in Anand's approach of generating reports and paper trails.

'As with everything in Thailand, when an idea is adopted with good intentions, it doesn't always work out in practice,' says Anand. Thailand is inherently stable in other ways, however. Respect for elders and teachers remain. Crucially, it will always be able to feed itself, and to export food to other countries. In Anand's view, it should concentrate on public health and education – improving the quality of life and raising the level of national happiness. 'We complain a lot, just like the French, but very few Thais would decide to emigrate for ever,' he says. 'After 20 or 25 years, they would come back. You hardly see any Thai professional settling down abroad for good.' He notes how his own wife Sodsee, who spent so many years abroad, never contemplated leaving Bangkok permanently. 'It has a lot to do with family cohesion,' he says – where the children and grandchildren are.

Anand's daughters were brought up and educated in the US, but never considered staying there. He depends on them to look after their mother. 'My wife's health has been bad for the past 30 years,' he says. At his birthday party, Anand mentioned Sodsee being asked by her family about the happiest time of her life. 'Right now,' she said.

That same powerful sense of home can be found elsewhere in the region. Most refugees who have ended up in Thailand have wanted to go home in safer times rather than find resettlement. With the working population changing, many Karens, Kachins, and Shans have come from Myanmar in search of employment. They have a strong work ethic, but often leave without warning when it suits them. 'Their hearts and minds are still back there in Myanmar,' Anand says. The sense of family, of belonging prevails.

Anand refuses, however, to generalise from the particular, and does not suggest that what goes in Thailand applies elsewhere in Asia. 'I don't know Asians well enough to say that,' he says. 'Privately we Thais are very liberal, yet public displays of affection are frowned upon. It is a society full of contradictions. Individually, Thais bathe twice a day and keep their houses clean, but they don't care as much about cleanliness in public places.'

Anand sees the region as being divided into hard and soft cultures. China, Japan, Singapore, South Korea, and Vietnam are hard. Cambodia, Laos, and Thailand are soft. 'I don't know about Myanmar,' he says. 'I don't know whether we can ever aspire to being South Korea, Taiwan, Singapore, or China. We may always remain middle-ranking, second division. I don't see anything basically wrong with that, but of course I would like to see us move up from the second division to the first. We should aspire to do better.'

Being himself

Anand recalls that his father, Sern, spent six months in Sweden on non-academic pursuits such as carpentry. 'He picked up quite a few dishes from Europe that he could cook,' Anand recalls. This practical streak is not something Anand has inherited. He has always enjoyed a reputation among his friends for being somewhat challenged in technical matters. Half-seriously, Anand threatened to resign the chairmanship of SCB when iPads were issued to the entire board. He still uses *The Economist* pocket book for his diary, and has never got along with computers, DVD players, and gadgets. He opens his iPad for incoming messages, but dictates his responses to Busarakham at Saha Union or another assistant. He has, however, become much more adept at using an iPhone since the arrival of his great grandson, Wyn, and plays recordings to guests showing the boy's development.

Constantly protective, Nanda and Daranee track their father in sometimes quite wifely ways. 'Both my daughters thought I was drinking too much.' Anand admits. 'I sometimes went a bit tipsy at parties and they didn't like it.' When they invited him out for dinner one night, he was surprised that it was just the three of them. 'They asked me to stop drinking and I blew my top. I said, "Don't be silly!"' Even so, they sometimes deliver him to parties and ask the hosts to keep an eye on him.

'I tell the story to everybody,' says Anand. 'To me, social drinking is part of a conversational environment, and I rarely drink at home. The problem is that I go out two or three nights a week with friends. My daughters were worried about the impact on my health. They force me to have a medical every year, and I am as healthy as ever – a stress-free person. I think my daughters' concern for my drinking "habit" stems from their concern for my public appearance.' He exercises three times a week, walking at the Polo Club or visiting a fitness club, mostly for stretching.

Anand's daughters don't smoke or drink, and neither do his grandchildren. He views himself as a man of normal habits, not as an abbot; to him, alcohol and tobacco are 'Siamese twins'. He supports non-smoking areas, but not in public parks. Although road safety remains a national disaster, he points out that Thailand, by being sensible, has done well on its public health campaigns in terms of smoking and family planning – so much so that it now faces the problems of an aging society with one of the most pronounced elderly demographics in Asia. 'In five years' time, we won't have to build any more schools,' he says.

In hindsight, Anand feels vindicated in most of his personal choices. He believes his two governments, which contained no politicians, were 'democratic in essence', much as they were disliked by much of the political establishment.

'When the second government came along, I capitalised on my successes. By that time, I had people on my side,' Anand says. 'I made some decisions that luckily turned out be successful ones. But leadership *per se* has never been on my radar screen. Even though I accepted the premiership, I was never seen as an opportunist. I enjoyed every minute of my prime ministership – the work. I was glad I was given the chance to do something for Thailand. But to be there for another 10 or 15 years as a professional politician, that I would not have been able to survive. I do not like manipulation and intrigue, and for long-term politics you just cannot get away from that game.'

'How can you combine capability with politicking?' asks Snoh Unakul, an archetypal Thai technocrat with a deeply ingrained distrust of party politics. He was not alone in lauding Anand's approach. When Anand stepped down the second time, Lee Kuan Yew wrote him a personal letter.

Abhisit speaks of Anand-era policies that shape Thailand's regulatory environment to this day: 'He was not just there to give some reassurance to the international and business community. He seized the opportunity to get some reforms going, particularly on the economic side.' According to Abhisit, 'Anand keeps his integrity by not participating, and I respect him for that. It is not a reflection of him but of the country that this is a huge challenge. How can we get a political environment where people like Anand, and the ideas and agenda that he has, actually gain support?'

White knight

'Everywhere I go, to this day, people will say that they wish my father had continued as prime minister,' says Daranee. 'I just smile.'

The question never arises within the family, however. Sodsee's abiding fear is that her husband will be drawn into public life and persecuted as he was in 1976. His daughters are also wary of the pitfalls of public life, and the daggers behind the smiles.

'Personally, I could stand the heat,' says Anand. 'I have the temperament for it, but I would not do it at the expense of my wife and my daughters. What I refrain from engaging in is party politics and in political life. I remain engaged in a lot of things without being directly involved in traditional politics. I promote education and environmental protection – issues politicians need to be involved with.'

He does see political consciousness in the general population rising as deference to the old elites erodes in 'a gradual process'. He does not expect respect for the old, ill-defined *ammart* class ever to recover. Provincial politicians have evolved, and they have been able to send their children to good universities; the political dynasties continue but the choices are gradually improving. 'Technocrats are still used, but their roles have been subsumed by politicians, and they no longer go unchallenged,' says Anand. 'In the past, they ran the country.'

King Bhumibol often commented that 'good people' did not seem to want to go into politics, and that idea still resonates in parts of the conservative establishment, particularly the military. The king's sceptical view of politicians was expressed as early as 1973, and certainly endured into the 1990s. But his support for the progressive 1997 constitution suggests he did envisage a rules-based way forward for the Thai polity, however often it ran into problems. He called on judges during the constitutional crisis preceding the 2006 coup that removed Thaksin to enforce the law, but that had some questionable consequences. Following the coup, 105 Thai Rak Thai former members of parliament were suspended from political life for five years and a number of parties were dissolved in 2008. The suspensions excluded some of the brightest and most promising politicians of the day from an active public role. The cabinets of both Samak and Somchai were filled with second division ministers, many of whom were virtually unknown. The dicey notion of 'good' and 'bad' politicians – never mind if they had been duly elected – regained currency after the 2014 coup. 'Bad' politicians were those at odds with the military government and its establishment backers.

In March 2018, Seksan Prasertkun delivered a scathing attack on this moribund line of thinking in a talk at Thammasat University. 'It can be inferred that the front line of the "good people" in this context are bureaucrats, major business groups, and upper middle class people while "bad people" are politicians and their voters,' the *Bangkok Post* reported Seksan saying. Conservative elements, which have held the upper hand in the wake of the 2014 coup, feel threatened by civic movements, particularly those advocating decentralisation. Those who do not conform to this reactionary mindset are criticised for lacking Thainess. 'The creators of such discourses are usually those who are close to the centre of power, in this case the elites such as civil servants,' Assistant Professor Wanwichit Boonprong of Rangsit University commented. 'These elites feel threatened if other groups who hold different opinions attempt to disrupt their share of power.'[3]

Seksan was part of Anand's 2011 National Reform Commission, and his comments in 2018 are an echo of its largely ignored recommendations, particularly regarding civil society, decentralisation, and freedom of thought. Anand's own thinking predates the reform commission. In June 2008, he delivered in Belgium the third in the Amartya Sen Lecture Series, which honour his fellow Trinity alumnus, the Indian-born economist and 1998 Nobel laureate. Sen has set a liberal agenda on numerous socio-economic issues, including the cost of austerity and the centrality of human freedom to development.

Anand spoke in Brussels on sustainable democracy, describing the 'seven pillars' needed to support it: elections; political tolerance; the rule of law; freedom of expression; accountability and transparency; decentralisation; and civil society. The lecture went beyond Thailand, with its wobbly governments, coups, and transient constitutions. A central Anand tenet is that every society needs time to find its own way in the world, politically, economically, and socially. Trees grow in different shapes, he argues, but they all cast cooling shade.

As he approached his 84th birthday in 2016, Anand's seven pillars all remained undermined or stunted, not just in Thailand but to varying degrees in each of the other nine member countries of the Association of Southeast Asian Nations (ASEAN). Contemplating the future, he gave keynote addresses to the Bank of Thailand and the Foreign Correspondents' Club of Thailand: Democratic Governance: Striving for Thailand's New Normal.[4] His talks in 2015 and 2016 drew on the seven universal pillars he described in 2008 to identify four elements specifically missing in Thailand if it is to achieve a 'new normal' and functioning democracy: sustainable and widespread economic development; open and inclusive society; the rule of law; responsive government and decentralisation.

Underpinning these four elements are the need for collective responsibility and a break with the top-down governing mentality of the past. Anand finds that collective awareness still missing. He always pours scorn on the tendency to look for 'white knights' when crises strike, and its implicit abdication of political responsibility. 'I was never really in politics,' he once told *Asiaweek* about the possibility one day of a third stint. 'It would be a sad commentary on our political life.' Speaking to a journalist when he received his Magsaysay award, he observed: 'They will have succeeded when no one thinks that the country needs me.'[5] He was not being coy. Anand always had to consider the circumstances of his second even more unexpected second premiership. The possibility of a third appointment due to some unforeseeable juxtaposition of events was always there, however small. 'I couldn't prevent some people thinking about it, but personally I ruled it out completely,' he says.

But the critical moments when a third Anand government might have been contemplated have always passed. He was not made prime minister when the economy melted down in 1997, or when a coup removed Thaksin from power in 2006. He was at that time a spry 74, in excellent physical and mental health. Maybe he could have righted the capsized ship of state, maybe not. Whatever, he was not asked.

In an encounter with US Ambassador Skip Boyce, Anand said he had no foreknowledge of the move against Thaksin, whom he had publicly criticised the month before, but also that he had not been surprised by the turn of events that brought the prime minister down. Boyce said Anand had been 'generally sympathetic' to the junta, and 'understanding of its motives'.

'Interesting and not surprising was Anand's disparaging reference to Thaksin's manipulation of the "uninformed" electorate,' Boyce reported in a cable to Washington. 'This elitist point of view – shared by many wealthy and educated Thais, especially in Bangkok – gets to the heart of Thaksin's claim about revolutionising Thai politics, precisely by taking on these entrenched elites.'[6]

'I don't think it's an elitist point of view at all,' says Anand. 'It is a view shared by many other people. And right now in 2018, you could say we are disappointed with the Americans themselves for what an uninformed US electorate has done.'

Ambassador Boyce's successor, Eric John, sent a cable to Washington in early September 2008 relating a conversation with Privy Councillor Siddhi Savetsila. That same evening during a dinner with King Bhumibol, Siddhi told John he was planning to recommend Anand as a replacement to Prime Minister Samak Sundaravej to 'rehabilitate democracy'.[7]

Given Siddhi's critical view of Anand in 1976, there was some historical irony in any notion of him putting Anand forward in 2008, but the events that soon followed tell a rather different story. Since Anand was not an elected member of parliament, nothing short of a coup would have been needed to install him in the premiership. Samak was instead removed from office by order of the Constitutional Court a few days later on 9 September, and replaced by his deputy, Somchai Wongsawat. The impeachment ruling was based on Samak's alleged conflict of interest in receiving a monthly retainer for his popular cookery and talk show, '*Tasting, Grumbling*', which he had hosted for eight years. There was no mention in any quarter at this time of Anand replacing Samak; it was a constitutional impossibility.

In a later cable revealed by Wikileaks, John reported on conversations with Siddhi, Prem, and Anand about the royal succession. With no direct quotes included, it is not clear exactly what any of the three actually said, but the gross breach of confidence Wikileaks represented was a disaster for the US. 'Exposing information and opinions clearly understood by both parties as more complete, sensitive, strategic, and candid than that intended for the public domain, the site uniquely damaged US-Thai relations,' noted Benjamin Zawacki in an analysis of Thailand's changing relations with the US and China. 'Wikileaks would leave the generational shift in bilateral relations with a bitter aftertaste – and the Chinese with a diplomatic windfall.'[8]

By the time of the next coup in 2014, Anand was 82, but still in good shape. Again, he was not considered. The premiership at such an age would have been an extremely unfair burden on anybody, but it was never on the cards. The agenda of the government of General Prayut Chan-o-cha was stewarding the impending royal succession and reasserting the military's role in political life. Anand's limited contact with Prayut's government has been verbal; he has always declined invitations to submit policy suggestions in writing, and he contributed nothing to redrafting the constitution.

A perennial question is what might have been if Anand's time at Government House had somehow been extended, but in June 1992 there was no question of this happening. Anand forestalled any possibility by immediately announcing the dissolution of parliament and setting the country on course for another general election – the second that year and one of the more important in Thai history.

People like Ekamol Kiriwat have never regarded the circumscribed Anand interludes as any sort of model for democracy, but argue that Thailand would have been much better off after a five-year technocrat government run by him. Mechai Viravaidya views him as simply Thailand's best prime minister. Wissanu Krea-ngam, the secretary general to six prime ministers, agrees. 'If he had stayed longer, he would have been in trouble, but I still believe he was the best prime minister we have ever had,' says Wissanu. 'Everything he does seems to have intention and some purpose.'

Saisuree Chutikul on the other hand laments lost opportunities. She believes much more could have been achieved, particularly with education, and continues to call for a total overhaul of the education ministry. She sees money being squandered, not least on pointless high-level study tours overseas. 'If you look at their budget, it is all big shots going abroad,' she says. 'It goes on and on – none of this goes to the children.' She believes the flood of international schools also needed more attention at the outset under Anand to ensure quality control.

Some in the foreign business community remain nostalgic for the distant Anand cloud breaks. 'This country would still be stuck in the Middle Ages if it had not been for him,' says David Lyman, the lawyer and former AmCham president. 'He just kept getting better and better as prime minister,' said James Rooney, another former AmCham president and old acquaintance. 'He filled the role of prime minister probably as well as it can be done. Normally jobs like that tend to beat you down, but that was Thailand's Camelot – all the ministers were working in the same direction. Anand was not subject to the tremendous political infighting normal to a Thai government. He could tackle legal reforms benefiting the entire business sector. He knew what to expect and how the government worked – it was uncharacteristically honest.'

'I think he could have done much more,' says Bhichai Rattakul, Anand's former boss as foreign minister. 'It wouldn't have been possible for Anand to stay on,' counters Nukul Prachuabmoh, Anand's toughest minister. 'People like me are not good for politics – we are not politicians,' he says. 'Another government came and just spoiled everything.'

'In a way, Anand is a very egotistical man, but at a broader level he could just walk away,' says Suthichai Yoon. 'He realised he had a problem with legitimacy, but his contribution to politics was preventing the coup from deteriorating into a real mess. If Anand had not come in, it would have been a disaster. He raised awareness of transparency, of ethics, and he did not get too attached to power – he gave it back.'

'Clearly he would have done more good things if he had stayed, but whether that would have served Thailand well in the longer run is another matter,' says Abhisit. 'Had it not been Anand, you could have had the same amount of legislation coming out in the opposite direction. You continue to wonder how well he would have done on the less familiar issues that were left untouched.'

Networks

Anand remains devoted to the memory of King Bhumibol, whom he served and defended without being drawn into the Privy Council or the palace. 'The king was there when he was needed to defuse a crisis, but he always knew it was not his constitutional role to resolve political issues,' Anand says, reiterating the position he has always maintained. 'He was very clear about his mandate, his political role. His influence derived from his moral authority and commitment to justice.'

Anand never disputes the central role the monarchy has played in Thai life since the 1960s, but he is very dismissive of the 'network monarchy' theory. 'Thailand's political order is characterised by network-based politics,' Duncan McCargo, professor of Southeast Asian politics at the University of Leeds, posited in 2005.[9] 'From 1973 to 2001, Thailand's leading political network was that of the reigning monarch, King Bhumibol. Since 2001, the primacy of palace-based networks has been challenged by the remarkable rise of the billionaire telecommunications magnate-turned-prime-minister, Thaksin Shinawatra.'

McCargo argued: 'From 1980 onwards, the manager of Thailand's network monarchy was in place: Prem Tinsulanond, handpicked by the king as army commander and later prime minister. His installation as prime minister might have appeared democratic but was actually a "royal coup" ... Prem's power was never absolute, though it was always considerable.'[10]

'Royalists such as Anand and Prawase worked hard to reinvent network monarchy as a more liberal construct, not paralysed by anachronistic military and bureaucratic preferences for stability and order,' McCargo argued. 'Anand and Prawase were liberals by comparison with many of the king's closest confidant[s], yet objectively speaking, they were also deeply conservative.'[11]

Prem, 'the ideal royal proxy, the architect of network monarchy', as McCargo pictures the president of the Privy Council, gets little credit for his personal consensus building and pacification efforts as prime minister in the 1980s, or the incremental democratisation and economic leap forward he stewarded at that time.

King Bhumibol also gets faint praise for his intervention in 1992: 'While the May 1992 protests were clearly not scripted by the palace, the belated and fuzzy royal intervention that ended the bloodshed and led to Suchinda's resignation was subsequently mythologised into a triumph for the monarchy.'[12]

While the spectacle of King Bhumibol scolding two feuding generals on the palace carpet in 1992 certainly garnered enormous publicity, there is no mention in this analysis of how and why Anand was returned very briefly to Government House afterwards – a much more important development at the time that has never been mythologised or indeed clearly explained. Indeed, Anand's second premiership, his transfer of senior military officers, and his subsequent appointment as chairman of the National Reconciliation Commission in 2005 do not support the notion of Prem's supposed omniscience. Meanwhile, the poor relations between General Suchinda Kraprayoon's Class 5 and Prem suggest that it is unlikely that 'the palace was involved in the ousting of Chatichai' in 1991, as McCargo suggests in a footnote.[13]

Nobody would dispute that Thailand has a myriad of complex networks, some very dark and many quite innocuous. But the network monarchy theory has about it an overarching inference of nefariousness; nobody ever gets much credit for trying to do the right thing or for being pragmatic; reformers are liberals of convenience; it's all a deep state plot. King Bhumibol telling *The New York Times* perfectly openly that the monarchy 'must be in the middle, and working in every field' is described as 'a neat summary of network monarchical governance, as it operated in Thailand after 1973'.[14]

Anand sees in all this a convoluted, somewhat obsessive conspiracy theory woven together largely by academics, mostly foreign, quoting each other endlessly. 'We have so many conspiracy theories, and so many so-called insiders,' he says of the way doubtful stories about the monarchy circulate and go unchallenged – more so with the advent of social media.'Those on the fringe try to portray themselves as being close. It's all about self-promotion,' he says.

The reality for Anand is something far less tidy: not some well-oiled, interlocking, cynical control mechanism but the messy swirl of Thai political life, and the scrum of many interacting stakeholders scrambling over each other. 'Our development path has been one of muddling along, an "adhocracy" you might say,' he said in 2016 in his 'new normal' address. 'Little has been done in the way of strategic long-term planning or effective implementation.'[15]

'Which country does not have networking?' he asks. 'It is a fact of life. There is an Anand network – a very large one. Do I direct it or organise it? No. So why is it there? I suppose because I have so many friends, and they happen to like me. That's all. It's a natural phenomenon. Anyone who has *baramee* inherently has a network, but it is not a planned thing.'

Indeed, Anand continues to be visited by people of all backgrounds and political hues. 'I like to talk to those who disagree with me,' he says. 'If you talk with those who agree with you, what is there to discuss?' He maintains his own 'instantaneous' social network broken up into separate groups that do not interact: old diplomats, other civil servants, school friends, Cambridge friends, businessmen, activists, artists, singing friends, drinking friends. 'These groups have no personal agendas,' he says.

Does he feel the need to explain himself? 'Many people ask why I have not written an autobiography,' he muses. 'It has been in the back of my mind all along, but I am not a writer.' He laments that so many Thais – including MR Kukrit Pramoj with his formidable literary skills and great wit – did not leave autobiographies. 'I think in a way it's Thai modesty – they don't want to write about themselves,' he says. 'It's in our culture subconsciously that we can never write autobiographies. Thais get confused between a critique and criticism. If anything is cast in a negative light, they take offence.'

He faults Thai academics for inertia. 'They have yet to take an interest in Prince Wan Waithayakon or Thanat Khoman,' he says. 'They did a lot about Pridi Banomyong, but that is an exception, and a lot for Puey Ungphakorn. I am not in the same class. Pridi and Puey's names remain unforgettable. Prince Wan and Thanat 50 years from now will be forgotten.'

Some of Anand's closest friends once suggested establishing a foundation as a legacy, but Anand immediately vetoed the idea of funds being solicited in his name. 'He is very concerned about his influence and his reputation,' says Chan Bulakul. 'He won't accept anything that is just about using his name.'

'My name might last another 20 or 30 years after I die, but who is going to run the organisation?' Anand asks. 'There will come a time when people will start asking who is running it, and who is spending the money, and on what activities. I have no interest in building such a legacy. My daughters were not too happy when I said history will forget me. I meant it.'

Anand is never maudlin, though. He has always looked over the horizon; obstacles are there to be overcome. The Chinese, he reminds us, have two words for crisis – one is for danger and the other is for opportunity. 'I always concentrated on the opportunity aspect,' he says. He is fond of paraphrasing Winston Churchill: the pessimist sees difficulty in every opportunity; the optimist sees the opportunity in every difficulty. 'It is a common trait among leaders in some countries never to miss an opportunity to miss an opportunity,' he laughs.

When talking about the art of the possible, he likes to quote Reinhold Niebuhr, the 20th-century American theologian:

> God grant me the serenity to accept the things I cannot change,
> Courage to change the things I can,
> And the wisdom to know the difference.[16]

Anand's many aphorisms come mostly from a world that has already vastly changed in his long lifetime. The Thai economy has been transformed in a globalised world; Cambodia, Laos, Myanmar, and Vietnam are part of ASEAN, as he predicted they would be in 1975; Chinese and Russians, the kingdom's former Cold War foes, are today welcomed to Thailand in their millions as tourists; and US, European, and Japanese influence have all waned in the face of a rising China.

Truth, he believes, helps both friends and enemies to negotiate; fear encourages evasiveness, and is counterproductive; and proof of sincerity comes with time. 'If you can get your counterpart to be equally objective, there is no reason for animosity or enmity. If you speak the truth, and are honest with your friends and enemies, you will never waiver. Whatever you say today, you can repeat the same sentence two years from now because you speak from your heart. The moment you are dishonest and don't speak the truth, you begin to fail – you have got to remember what you said. If you speak the truth, you can be very consistent naturally. The moment you have ego, a superiority complex, you get into trouble – you lose your objectivity.'

'Anand is a very healthy man largely because he is very happy,' says Ammar Siamwalla. 'He is a man, I would say, at peace and at home with himself. He knows who he is. He knows how powerful he is. Insecurity is never a word I would use for Anand – he is the most secure person I have ever met.'

Chaiwat Satha-Anand recalls how domineering Anand could be when chairing the National Reconciliation Commission, but also how open to new ideas he remained. 'He is there to challenge people on things they have not thought about before,' says Chaiwat. 'It is quite conscious – no doubt about it. His role is to push Thai society to experiment with new ideas.' The two examples Chaiwat picks out are Article 65 of the 1997 constitution,[17] which gave citizens the right to oppose military coups and the unlawful usurpation of power in non-violent ways, and the proposal for an unarmed army in the South by the National Reconciliation Commission in 2006.

'He is a realist, but adventurous,' says Chaiwat, 'a royalist and also a liberal – you can be both.'

ENDNOTES

CHAPTER 1

1. More so in the 1930s than today, Buddhist monks were asked to name babies. Sometimes the names from the temple were taxing and polysyllabic, lacking even vowels. The process could take months, so an easy nickname was needed in the interim and it could last a lifetime.

2. Siam's *'ammart'* predate the 1932 revolution, and included bureaucrats or mandarins upon whom non-royal titles were conferred. The term *phrai*, which has a more derogatory connotation, was given fresh currency in the political strife of the early 21st century to describe a purported underclass. Broadly, these 19th- and early-20th-century terms were revived to label mutually antagonistic political groups: the Yellow-Shirt *ammart* establishment pitted against the rebelling Red-Shirt *phrai*.

3. One of Anand's great aunts married into Malaya's Perak royal family, introducing Thai blood there. Another distinguished Malay with Thai ancestry was Tunku Abdul Rahman, the first prime minister of the Federation of Malaya after independence from Britain in 1957. His mother, Che Manjalera, was born Nueng Nandanakorn in Siam. As a ten-year-old, the Tunku began two years at Bangkok's Debsirin School, learning Siamese and acquiring a great love of Thai food. He later studied law at Cambridge University, where he mingled mostly with Malay and Thai students.

4. Nicholas Grossman and Dominic Faulder (eds), *King Bhumibol Adulyadej – A Life's Work*. Singapore: Editions Didier Millet, 2011, p. 37.

5. In the UK, Prince Vajiravudh attended the Royal Military Academy Sandhurst, and Christ Church, Oxford, where he studied law and history but did not graduate. He served briefly in the Durham Light Infantry. In 1917, King Vajiravudh sided against Germany in World War I, and sent Siamese forces to Europe to support the British and their allies.

6. The royal ranks of the northern royal family were not reduced with passing generations like the Thai royal family.

7. Permanent secretaries, the top civil servants in ministries, were then known as undersecretaries.

8. Prince Dhani Nivat (1885–1974), a member of the Sonakul family, was a grandson of King Mongkut, and educated in England at Rugby School and Merton College, Oxford. After World War II, he succeeded Prince Rangsit in 1949 as president of the first Privy Council to serve King Bhumibol Adulyadej. A leading authority on Thai culture and history, he was also a prominent Rotarian.

9. Chao Phya Thammasak Montri (Sanan Thephasadin Na Ayutthaya), the new education minister in 1932, had also served as education minister from 1915 to 1926.

10. Sern Panyarachun was one of seven local investors in the *Bangkok Post* when Alexander MacDonald, the former station chief of the Office of Strategic Services (OSS) in Bangkok, launched it in August 1946. The others were Prasit Lulitanond, Thawee Tavedikul, Major Vilas Osathanon, Ajint Unhanatana, Damrong Duritarek, and Chavala Sukumalnantana.

11. The Press Association of Thailand still exists in Bangkok's Dusit area (http://th.kompass.com/c/the-press-association-of-thailand/th0053682/).

12. Genevieve Caulfield, an American teacher, established Thailand's first school for the blind and visually impaired in 1938 on Silom Road. During the Japanese occupation in the early 1940s, Caulfield was not interned as most other Westerners were. Confined to her home, she was allowed to keep the school open. Caulfield was awarded a Ramon Magsaysay Award for International Understanding in 1961.

13. See Kenneth Barrett, *22 Walks in Bangkok – Exploring the City's Historic Back Lanes and Byways*. Singapore: Tuttle Publishing, 2013, p. 248.

14. Anand's closest brother, Chatchawan, shortened his name to Chat in later life.

15. Dee later became nanny to Anand's second daughter, Daranee, and then to his granddaughter Sirinda. She was with the family during all of Anand's postings overseas in the 1960s and 1970s, and was always regarded as a member of the family. She lived with Daranee until her death at the age of 91 in 2017.

16. Anand's niece Charatsri is the daughter of Pritha, his second sister and third sibling. Pritha was 15 years older than Anand. Her husband, Krasae, served as a judge in Nakhon Sri Thammarat in the South. Charatsri spent six years there before coming to Bangkok at 12 for education at Mater Dei and Chulalongkorn University. Naturally, she moved in with her grandparents and to all intents became the 13th child in the family.

17. When talking of gender balance, Thais sometimes describe wives as the 'hind legs of the elephant' to imply indispensability. The idiom has recently acquired greater political correctness. Richard Lair, an American expert on elephants resident in Thailand since 1980, has contributed to three recent 'definitive' papers concerning elephantine locomotion. 'We showed, rather unexpectedly, that the elephant is one of the rare mammals that is pretty much four-wheel drive, with the front and back legs equally sharing all duties,' he reports. 'With most mammals the back legs are mostly for propulsion and the front ones for braking.'

18. Porphant Ouyyanont, 'Bangkok's Population and the Ministry of the Capital in Early 20th Century Thai History'. Kyoto University: Centre for Southeast Asian Studies, Vol. 35, No. 2, September 1997, p. 244.

19. Porphant Ouyyanont, 'Transformation of Bangkok and Concomitant Changes in Urban-Rural Interaction in Thailand in the 19th and 20th Centuries' in 'The Chao Phraya Delta: Historical Development, Dynamics and Challenges of Thailand's Rice Bowl', *Proceedings of the International Conference*. Bangkok: Kasetsart University, December 2000.

20. Bangkok's trams were originally horse-drawn and date from the 1880s. Bangkok's second mass-transit system, the Bangkok SkyTrain (BTS), opened in 1999, a century after the electric trams were powered up, with a little over 50 kilometres of track on two lines. Bangkok's last tram ran in 1968.

21. A statue of King Vajiravudh – the sixth king in the Chakri dynasty, which took power in 1782, the year it founded Bangkok – has stood on the park's southwest corner since 1942. Its Italian sculptor, Corrodo Feroci, is better known by his Thai name, Silpa Bhirasri. In a city of villas and shophouses, Bhirasri was responsible during this period for numerous statues,

portentous monuments, and Western flourishes around the city. These included the Democracy Monument in 1939 along the sweep of Rajadamnoen Avenue, and the Victory Monument a few years later.

22. Wong Bunnag.

23. The Hotel Ratchathani was shut down in 1968. The original building today houses offices of the State Railway of Thailand.

24. The first Sarasin villa in Hua Hin was bought by Pote in the late 1920s at about the time King Prajadhipok built Klai Kangwol Palace as a seaside retreat. The Sarasins, who have been dubbed the Kennedys of Thailand, retain units in a Hua Hin condominium where they often gather for holidays and long weekends.

25. Long before Anand's birth, when the railway had not been extended all the way, the family had to disembark and travel the last part of the journey by cart. The station at Hua Hin was completed in 1920.

26. Founded in 1926 for boys, Amnuay Silpa School is today co-ed with a Thai-UK curriculum. It has produced six prime ministers: Kriangsak Chomanand (1977–1980); Chatichai Choonhavan (1988–1991); Anand Panyarachun (1991–2); Suchinda Kraprayoon (1992); Chavalit Yongchaiyudh (1996–7); and Somchai Wongsawat (2008).

27. The Thai education system has *prathom* grades 1–6 corresponding to grades 1–6 in the US system, and *mathayom* grades 1–6 corresponding to grades 7–12.

28. Ajarn Kamchai taught later at the Chitralada School, which was set up in 1958 and attended by the four children of King Bhumibol and Queen Sirikit.

29. Though a nominal Axis ally, and an enemy target for the British, Thailand took no active part in hostilities during the war. Field Marshal Plaek Phibunsongkhram (Phibun) did, however, push territorial claims in Burma's Shan states and Cambodia's Battambang province.

30. The Panyarachun Chidlom compound was in the vicinity of the Alma Link Building and Central Department Store today. Another plot on Sukhumvit Soi 18 had been bought earlier for Rak, the eldest son.

31. For some years, Rak Panyarachun and Thanat Khoman, Thailand's noted foreign minister, were the most senior Thai law graduates from France.

32. During an interview with the author in 1984, *MR* Seni Pramoj suggested that his reluctance to deliver Thailand's declaration of war on the US was more than matched by Cordell Hunt's disinclination to accept it, so Seni returned the document to a drawer in his office. Hunt, the longest-serving US secretary of state, left in 1944 after 11 years in the post.

33. Ceylon, which reverted to its old name, Sri Lanka, in 1972, gained independence from the British in 1948. During the war, the Southeast Asia Allied Command under Lord Louis Mountbatten was headquartered at Kandy.

CHAPTER 2

1. By the war's end, the Thais were radioing to the Allies target and timing information relating to Japanese troop dispositions. See Direk Jayanama, *Thailand and World War II*. Chiang Mai: Silkworm Books, 2008, p. 151.

2. Idem, p. 205.

3. Prior to *MR* Seni Pramoj's return, Tawee Boonyaket served briefly as interim prime minister.

4. The king's death, described as an accident initially, has never been clearly explained. Suicide or a self-inflicted accident has been ruled out, leaving assassination or accidental discharge of the firearm by another person as the only remaining possibilities. More blood was spilled in 1955 when two pages and a secretary were executed for complicity in regicide, but their killings did not bring any closure to the mystery. Whatever the circumstances, there was no dispute as to King Ananda's successor: Prince Bhumibol acceded to the throne on the evening of the day of his brother's death.

5. Field Marshal Plaek Phibunsongkhram (Phibun) first changed Siam's name to Thailand in 1939. The latter sounded more modern, but also had an irredentist undertone with regard to the lands beyond its borders inhabited by Thai (Tai) people.

6. Gakushuin was established in 1847 by Emperor Kinko to educate children of the aristocracy.

7. Jakarta was called Batavia until the Dutch East Indies became Indonesia in 1949.

8. Chavalit Yodmani, a distinguished retired police general, headed Thailand's Office of Narcotics Control Board in the 1980s and 1990s.

9. The term Old Alleynian derives from Edward Alleyn, a celebrated Elizabethan-era actor who founded the 'College of God's Gift' in Dulwich in 1619.

10. Usnisa Sukhvsasti, 'Outlook', *Bangkok Post*, 11 March 2003.

11. Jan Pigott, *Dulwich College, A History 1616–2006*. London: Dulwich College Enterprises, 2008, p. 280.

12. Two more athletic houses have been added since Anand's time. The eight houses are Sir Francis Drake (seafarer); Sir Richard Grenville (seafarer); Lord Charles Howard (seafarer); Ben Jonson (playwright); Christopher Marlowe (playwright); Sir Walter Raleigh (seafarer); Sir Philip Sidney (poet, courtier and soldier); Edmund Spenser (poet). William Shakespeare has always been considered too much of a colossus for inclusion.

13. Rationing was not fully lifted in the UK until July 1954.

14. Usnisa Sukhvsasti, ibid.

15. Roland Dallas authored *King Hussein: Life on the Edge* (1999).

16. Arsa Sarasin left Singapore to embark on the 17-day sea passage to Southampton as a charge of the returning British ambassador, Richard Whittington, who was close to his parents. Always slightly accident prone, he was seasick for a week but well enough to spend the rest of the passage chatting up all the girls on board. He started as a junior boarder in Orchard House in 1949, and stayed until 1953.

17. Sern's granddaughter, Vivan [Kukai], a daughter of Chat, was also a teacher. She set up the well-known Kukai Kindergarten in Bangkok.

18. Bob Nunes's father, the great cricketer Robert Karl Nunes CBE, was captain and wicketkeeper in 1928 of the first West Indies test team to tour England, and later president of the West Indies Cricket Board. Nunes senior was also an Old Alleynian (1910–1912) and boarder at Blew House.

19. In April 1949, the Junior Training Corps (army), the Air Training Corps and the Sea Cadet Corps were brought together as the Combined Cadet Corps. School cadets were more prominent after Word War II, but later abolished at many schools, including Eton, St Paul's, and Westminster. In March 1952, 20 Dulwich cadets marched in the funeral procession of King George VI.

20. Boys sometimes put on gloves and sparred informally at Bangkok Christian College, but not Anand or Suthep Bulakul,

who were discouraged from such sports by their mothers. The main institutional Western boxing, observing Queensberry Rules, among schoolboys pitted Presbyterian Bangkok Christian College against Catholic Assumption College. The two Christian-run schools also clashed regularly on the football pitch, but the boys were almost all Buddhist.

21. Lord Valentine Charles Thynne (1937–1979) was the youngest of five children of Viscount Weymouth, the 6th Marquess of Bath. Thynne married three times, and took his own life.

22. *The Alleynian*, 1951, p. 234.

23. Chatrachai Bunya-Ananta's sporting prowess in tennis, squash, and badminton earned him a Sportsman of the Year accolade at Cardiff University. 'We thought that in Wales only the rugby players would get recognition, but they were very fair,' he recalled.

24. C.H. Gilkes was the third son of the Reverend Arthur Herman Gilkes, who was the master at Dulwich from 1885 to 1915. One of his brothers, Antony Newcombe Gilkes, was High Master of St Paul's, another leading London public school, from 1953 to 1962.

25. Midway through Anand's stay in 1950, with the onset of the Korean War and Soviet atomic tests, the question of evacuation contingency plans for the school arose again.

26. 'After Fleming – New Policy at Dulwich' by C.H. Gilkes, *The Times Educational Supplement*, 17 June 1949.

27. Jan Piggott, *Dulwich College, A History 1616–2006*. London: Dulwich College Enterprises, 2008, pp. 272–277.

28. Idem, p. 214.

29. Walter Reynolds Booth, Gilkes's predecessor, had attended a grammar school and had similar egalitarian inclinations.

30. This Dulwich College tradition continues in the Boardroom, which is identical in size to the Masters' Library and on the other side of the Great Hall. It is conducted by the deputy master pastoral.

31. A few months later, the school was dealt a second tragic blow when the charismatic head of music, Stanley Wilson, succumbed to heart failure while still in his early 50s. William Darby, whose family Anand first lodged with at Dulwich, also died young at 52 in 1968 having been fortunate to survive hazardous service during the war. Anand had felt guilty about losing touch with Darby, but did later make contact with his wife, Molly.

32. Nicholas Drummond was captain of rugby and a few years ahead of Anand at Dulwich College. He attended Trinity College Cambridge at the same time (1952–5) after a two-year break for National Service, and is also unsure whether Gilkes helped directly with his university entry. The Oxford and Cambridge entrance process was more opaque in those years, and colleges often had close ties with particular schools.

33. Field Marshal Sir John Chapple retired in 1992 as chief of general staff, Britain's highest-ranking soldier.

34. Edward Stourton, *Trinity: A Portrait*. London: Third Millennium, 2011, p. 256.

35. To form Trinity College in 1546, King Henry VIII consolidated two earlier institutions: Michael House, which was founded in 1324 in the reign of King Edward II by Hervey of Stanton, and King's Hall, which was established in 1337 by King Edward III. In ancient Siamese terms, the origins of Trinity date from the mid-Sukhothai era (c.1249–1378), and its consolidation from the mid-Ayutthaya era (c.1351–1767). The foundation of Cambridge in the very early 13th century as a breakaway from Oxford University predates the Sukhothai kingdom.

36. Lord John Vaizey, *Scenes from Institutional Life and Other Writings – My Cambridge*. London: Weidenfeld and Nicolson, 1977, pp. 91–108.

37. Times have changed greatly. These days, a Thai restaurant, Bangkok City, sits on Green Street along Anand's old path to Trinity Street, and the route is often choked with Chinese tourists meandering through the ancient bicycle routes.

38. The Magpie and Stump debating society dated from the mid-19th century, and in 1907 elected Kaiser Wilhelm II a permanent member of its committee. As Kaiser Bill, he is remembered not for debate but for World War I.

39. The Cambridge University Footlights Dramatic Club, founded in 1883, is a major force in British theatre, and has played a leading role in the development of post-war comedy and satire.

40. *The Adventures of Mr Verdant Green*, a novel by Cuthbert M. Bede (Edward Bradley, 1827–1899), depicted life as a freshman at Oxford in the mid-19th century.

41. The three other members of the Cambridge Five to be identified were Donald Maclean and Guy Burgess – who like Philby became diplomats – and Anthony Blunt. Maclean attended Trinity Hall and Burgess Trinity College, where he belonged to the Cambridge Apostles, a secretive and elitist discussion group with only 12 members. Blunt was the oldest known member of the group and a fellow of Trinity College. A distinguished art historian, he was knighted in the 1950s and counselled King George VI and Queen Elizabeth II as keeper of the royal art collection. When Blunt was finally exposed as the 'fourth man' in 1979, he was stripped of his honours. There have been a number of candidates for the fifth member including Sir Anthony Rumbold, who was posted as ambassador to Thailand (1965–7). Rumbold attended Oxford, but Maclean was best man at his wedding. Some believe the group was actually larger.

42. Umesh Pandey, 'Lifelong Learner', *Bangkok Post*, 11 January 2016.

43. In his Nobel acceptance speech, Amartya Sen observed: 'The major debates in political economy at Cambridge were rather firmly geared to the pros and cons of Keynesian economics and the diverse contributions of Keynes's followers at Cambridge (Richard Kahn, Nicholas Kaldor, Joan Robinson, among them), on the one hand, and of "neo-classical" economists sceptical of Keynes, on the other (including, in different ways, Dennis Robertson, Harry Johnson, Peter Bauer, Michael Farrell, among others).'

44. Bachelor degrees at Cambridge are awarded after the completion of a nine-term, three-year 'Tripos' divided into a part one and a part two, sometimes with different subjects. Part one usually lasts only a year, but for some courses it can be two.

45. Elizabeth S. Johnson and Harry Gordon Johnson, *The Shadow of Keynes, Understanding Keynes, Cambridge and Keynesian Economics*. Chicago: University of Chicago Press; Oxford: Basil Blackwell, 1978.

46. Lord John Vaizey, ibid.

47. Anand was in good company. MR Kukrit Pramoj, a future prime minister of Thailand, took a third at Queen's College, University of Oxford, in philosophy, politics, and economics (PPE); and Aung San Suu Kyi, the future Nobel peace laureate and state counsellor of Myanmar, took a third in the same degree at St Hugh's, also Oxford.

48. 'Sir Elihu 'Eli' Lauterpacht, international lawyer – obituary', *The Daily Telegraph*, London, 13 February 2017. This recorded that in early 2014 Lauterpacht appeared as counsel before the

International Court of Justice in his last case over 60 years since his first appearance there. He successfully represented Timor-Leste in challenging the seizure by Australia of papers relating to a maritime dispute between the two countries.

49. Edward Stourton, ibid.

50. J.M.F. Wright, *Alma Mater or Seven Years at the University of Cambridge*. London and Cambridge, 1827, pp. 166–167. A mathematician and fellow of the college, Wright reported that Lord Byron's bear occupied a small hexagonal room in a corner turret of the courtyard, Merton Hall Corner. The turret room, which is now thought to be K-8, was close above Byron's substantial chambers. Many legends have sprung up around the tale, including the alleged loophole that initially allowed Bruin entry to the college. Byron had a passion for dogs, particularly the Newfoundland breed. He noticed that while dogs were expressly banned from the college, there was no mention of bears. Prior to Bruin's inevitable eviction, Byron paraded him around the college grounds and along the streets of Cambridge. He once disguised Bruin beneath a peaked cap for a train journey, leaving fellow passengers traumatised. Other accounts place Byron in staircase I-1 in Nevile's Court and Bruin in Ram Yard on Bridge Street. Some speculate that Bruin ended up in Ram Yard after his eviction.

51. Edward Stourton, ibid.

52. Nukul Prachuabmoh was a recent graduate of Melbourne University working for the finance ministry. He passed through London in late 1954 on his way to postgraduate studies at George Washington University in the US, and a trainee position with the International Monetary Fund.

53. Elizabeth S. Johnson and Harry Gordon Johnson, ibid.

54. Anand wrote the forewords to his cousin Teddy Spha Palasthira's books: *Addresses – Siamese Memoirs in Wartime England and Post-War Europe and Siam* and *The Last Siamese – Journeys in War and Peace*. Bangkok: Post Publishing Public Company Limited, 2010 and 2013.

CHAPTER 3

1. As a US military veteran of World War II, Kusa Panyarachun had educational entitlements under the GI Bill of Rights and attended Wharton School of Business at the University of Pennsylvania.

2. Cesar R. Bacani Jr, *The Ramon Magsaysay Awards, Vol XIII*. Manila: Ramon Magsaysay Award Foundation, 2005.

3. Some of these recollections of life in late-1950s Thailand are sourced from *Yesteryear – Bangkok in 1956: What Life Was Like When AMCHAM Thailand Was Born* by David Lyman (Bangkok: Tilleke and Gibbins, April 2006); and from Mark Whitcraft, AMCHAM's oldest member at the time of his death in 2015, who arrived in Thailand as a Goodyear regional salesman in May 1958.

4. These included Anand's cousin Arsa Sarasin and nephew ML Birabhongse Kasemsri, Chawan Chawanid, MR Kasemsomosorn Kasemsri, Kosol Sindhvananda, Nitya Pibulsonggram, Manaspas Xuto, Pracha Guna-Kasem, Thepkamol Devakul, Sakol Vanabriksha, Sompong Sucharitkul, Sudhee Prasasvinitchai, Tej Bunnag, and Vitthya Vejjajiva. Vitthya, for example, is about five years Anand's junior; he attended Cambridge University on a foreign ministry scholarship, and later Harvard University. He was one of ten such scholars sent to the UK and the US during this period. Vitthya never worked directly under Anand,

but remembers him as 'young, brilliant – someone for my generation to look up to'.

5. https://m.youtube.com/watch?v=JVpLCsA-NCo

6. The United Nations' Economic Commission for Asia and the Far East (ECAFE) was set up in 1947, and became ESCAP (Economic and Social Commission for Asia and the Pacific) in 1974. One of five United Nations regional commissions, ESCAP has 58 Asia-Pacific members plus France, the Netherlands, the UK, and the US.

7. SEATO came out of the Southeast Asia Collective Defense Treaty, or Manila Pact, signed in the Philippines in September 1954. It was a product of the Truman Doctrine creating anti-communist alliances, including the North Atlantic Treaty Organization (NATO). Within Southeast Asia, only Thailand and the Philippines joined. SEATO's other members were Australia, France, New Zealand, Pakistan, the UK, and the US, with Cambodia, Laos, and the Republic of [South] Vietnam taking observer status in the early years. Its principal purpose was countering the perceived communist threat from the People's Republic of China. SEATO was dissolved in 1977.

8. Speech given by Snoh Unakul at the dinner honouring Anand Panyarachun's retirement from the chairmanship of the Thailand Development Research Institute, 9 July 2008.

9. Sir Anthony Rumbold, 'Goodbye to Thailand', a confidential cable to George Brown, the secretary of state for foreign affairs in London, at the time of Rumbold's departure from Bangkok, 18 July 1967, p. 8.

10. Apart from his role in the creation of SEATO, Prince Wan Waithayakon's career milestones included helping negotiate the end of the unequal treaties imposed on Siam by European powers in the 19th century; representing Thailand at the Greater East Asia Conference in Tokyo in 1943; stewarding Thailand's admission to the United Nations in 1946; representing Thailand at the Bandung Conference in 1955; and serving as president of the United Nations General Assembly in 1956 – for which he was accorded a standing ovation when he drew proceedings to a close.

11. Renamed the Walter Reed Army Medical Center in 2011.

12. The Thai delegation's elaborate extraction from Thailand by an Allied flying boat was codenamed Operation Violet, but did not result in a meeting with Lord Louis Mountbatten, the supreme Allied commander in Southeast Asia, at his headquarters in Kandy, Ceylon. Mountbatten saw himself as a military figure with no political mandate to deal with Thailand, which was technically a hostile state. Instead, the delegation met with Maberly Dening, Mountbatten's political adviser, and Major General Mackenzie, the head of Force 136 which was working in concert with the Free Thai Movement. See Direk Jayanama, *Thailand and World War II*. Chiang Mai: Silkworm Books, 2008, pp. 127–9.

13. Luang Wichit Wathakarn had been a leading proponent of a greater Thai national identity and after the war was initially detained as a war criminal along with Field Marshal Plaek Phibunsongkhram (Phibun) at the behest of the British. The US had, however, never been officially at war with Thailand, and was far more conciliatory. The charges against both men were subsequently dropped.

14. Thanphuying Vichitra, Field Marshal Sarit Thanarat's wife, told Amnuay Viravan that on the morning of his death, Sarit asked to see Amnuay for reasons nobody ever discovered. 'I know he really cared about me but he was so sick that I never got to

see him,' says Amnuay.

15. Amnuay Viravan has no knowledge of what became of the weekly briefings he sent directly to Field Marshal Sarit Thanarat after his death at 55 in late 1963. Sarit was the only Thai prime minister to die in office.

16. The National Economic and Social Development Board was set up in 1950 as the National Economic Board (NEB); it was renamed National Economic Development Board (NEDB) in 1959; and re-formed as the NESDB in 1972 as part of the Office of the Prime Minister.

17. Associate Professor Thitinan Pongsudhirak is director of Chulalongkorn University's Institute of Security and International Studies (ISIS).

18. King Bhumibol Adulyadej placed a crown upon King Ananda Mahidol's head after his brother had been embalmed.

19. Prince Wan Waithayakon was reinstated as foreign minister all through 1958 until 20 October. Although he came back from the US at that time, Thanat did not formally replace Prince Wan until 10 February 1959, and remained foreign minister until late 1971.

20. John F. Kennedy, 'Public Papers of the Presidents of the United States: John F. Kennedy', 1962, p. 192.

21. MR Kukrit Pramoj penned for many years one of Thailand's best-read columns in *Siam Rath*, the newspaper he founded. Speaking as Thailand's real prime minister, Kukrit made light of his latest change of career: 'As you may know, I have been most of my life a newspaper man, and am proud of it. I had to turn in my press credentials recently when the present job was offered to me. They told me this was a better-paying job, so I took it. Now that I have held the job for a while, I would like to share a couple of secrets with you: I do miss my old calling. And, it is certainly less cumbersome to wield a pen than to wield competing political parties. Anyway, I am consoled by the thought that when I return to the newspaper (if they will take me back), I certainly will have a lot to write about.' Speech to the Foreign Correspondents' Association of Southeast Asia, Raffles Hotel, Singapore, 25 July 1975.

22. The postings of a number of Kenneth Young's predecessors as US ambassador in Siam/Thailand also came to unfortunate ends. Hamilton King died at his post after nine years in 1912. Wilys R. Peck was interned for five months after the Japanese occupation in 1941. John E. Peurifoy and a son were killed in a collision with a lorry near Hua Hin in 1955 after less than three months in the kingdom.

23. Siamese diplomats lobbying against the unequal treaties in the 1930s were helped by Francis Bowes Sayre, a Harvard-trained lawyer and son in law of US President Woodrow Wilson, who served as a foreign affairs adviser to Siam in the 1920s during the reign of King Vajiravudh.

24. The agreement was signed in July 1962 between Laos and 14 other states including the US, China, the Democratic Republic of (North) Vietnam, the USSR, and Thailand. The Ho Chi Minh Trail, along which *matériel* was supplied from North Vietnam to the Vietcong fighting in South Vietnam, was but one of many violations on all sides.

25. 'Malcolm MacDonald, British Envoy and Son of Ex-Prime Minister', The Associated Press, 12 January 1981.

26. Geritol is an iron and vitamin dietary supplement first sold in 1950.

27. Although SEATO was dissolved in 1977 in the aftermath of the Vietnam War, Thailand remained a treaty ally of the US because of the Cold War security pacts signed in the 1950s and 1960s. In 2003, following the 9-11 terrorist attacks on American soil in late 2001, the US officially designated Thailand a Major Non-NATO Ally (MNNA).

28. Arne Kislenko, 'The Vietnam War, Thailand, and the United States', in Richard J. Jensen, Jon Thares Davidann, Yoneyuki Sugita (eds), *Trans-Pacific Relations: America, Europe, and Asia in the Twentieth Century*. Westport, Connecticut: Greenwood Publishing, 2003, p. 224.

29. The other six full SEATO members were Australia, France, New Zealand, Pakistan, the UK, and the US.

30. Sompong Sucharitkul participated in the International Commission of Jurists (ICJ) congress in New Delhi, India, in 1959 that produced the Declaration of Delhi on the rule of law.

31. Report on a talk given by Charnvit Kasetsiri, the former rector of Thammasat University, at the Foreign Correspondents' Club of Thailand. Subhatra Bhumiprabhas, *The Nation*, 7 October 2009.

32. Phya Arthakarinibhonda was formerly Sitthi Chunnanda.

33. Robert Woodrow, 'Princes, Poets & Premiers', *Asiaweek*, 23 April 1982.

34. Charnvit Kasetsiri, Pou Sothirak, and Pavin Chachavalpongpun, *Preah Vihear – A Guide to the Thai-Cambodian Conflict and Its Solutions*. Bangkok: White Lotus Press, 2013, p. 8.

CHAPTER 4

1. Editorial, 'A Vital Post for Anand', *Bangkok Post*, 27 July 1972.

2. Private letter from Rak Panyarachun to old family friends, 29 March 1974.

3. ML Birabhongse Kasemsri served with Anand as his deputy at the UN, and as ambassador in Washington and Tokyo, and permanent secretary. After his retirement, he was appointed principal private secretary to King Bhumibol Adulyadej. He died of a heart attack in 2000 following what had been considered successful treatment for cancer at the Mayo Clinic in the US.

4. Linen installed John Millington at the *Bangkok World*. He later worked at the US Council for Foreign Relations. Millington had five children with his wife Didi, *née* Deirdre Sharon Kelley (1932–2010). She became wrapped up in Thailand's liberal and leftist circles, and close to Pansak Vinyaratn, a future adviser to several prime ministers, notably Chatichai Choonhavan and Thaksin and Yingluck Shinawatra. A pacifist and outspoken critic of US foreign policy at the time, she wrote for the *Bangkok World* and *Chaturat*, a left-wing monthly that she co-owned and which Pansak briefly revived in 1981. The Millingtons later divorced. See also *Chicago Tribune*, 25 April 2010 and *The New York Times*, 18 April 2010.

5. According to Ashley South's *Mon Nationalism and Civil War in Burma*, U Thant, then secretary general of the UN, spoke at a 1970 UN conference on minorities, declaring that 'the last Mon is dead'. U Thant (whose mother was half-Mon) apparently meant that the Mon and Burmese cultures and ethnic identities had been fully integrated. Anand then cited his own Mon heritage and insisted that the Mon ethnic identity was still very much alive, winning praise from Mon nationalists.

6. Louis Halasz, 'Thailand: United We Stand', *Far Eastern Economic Review*, Hong Kong, Vol. 58, No. 4, 22/28 October 1967.

7. Ibid.

8. Sir Anthony Rumbold, 'Goodbye to Thailand', a confidential cable to George Brown, the secretary of state for foreign affairs in London, at the time of Rumbold's departure from Bangkok,

18 July 1967.

9. The Domino Theory dated from a comment made by President Dwight D. Eisenhower in 1954.

10. Cesar R. Bacani Jr, 'Biographical Profile of Anand Panyarachun', in *The Ramon Magsaysay Awards, Vol XIII*. Manila: Ramon Magsaysay Award Foundation, 2005.

11. S.R. Nathan with Timothy Auger. *An Unexpected Journey: Path to the Presidency*. Singapore: Editions Didier Millet, 2013, p. 353.

12. Negotiations for the Bangkok Declaration at Bang Saen were gruelling at times. An added complication was the appearance of two diplomats from Sri Lanka. Somewhat illogically in terms of its geography, Sri Lanka had been mooted as a sixth founding member. As the deadline approached, Colombo drew back and the candidacy fizzled out.

13. S.R. Nathan writes in his autobiography of the academic tome *Southeast Asia in United States Foreign Policy* by Russell H. Fifield: 'I went to the National Library, got hold of the book and found the reference. It seemed that the name ASEAN had been suggested by the US during the early 1960s for a regional co-operation organisation. It was an embarrassing coincidence. If nothing else, the conversation showed how thoroughly the Russians went through US publications.'

14. A canal across the Isthmus of Kra was first conceived in the 16th century for defensive purposes. Later, it would have had an impact similar to the Panama and Suez canals, and dramatically altered commercial shipping between the Indian Ocean to the west and the South China Sea and the North Pacific to the east. The Kra Canal would have relieved congestion in the Strait of Malacca, but also reduced the strategic value of Singapore as a port and centre for regional commerce. Apart from the expense, Thai security concerns over the years about introducing a body of water in its troubled South was another reason the project has never got off the ground.

15. S.R. Nathan with Timothy Auger, idem, pp. 427–8.

16. Professor Tommy Koh was not yet 30 when he was posted to the UN for the first time in 1968 for three years. He returned for a second stint in 1974.

17. EQ = emotional intelligence quotient.

18. The Six-Day War, 5–10 June 1967, was launched preemptively by Israel against the United Arab Republic (Egypt), Jordan, and Syria. In quick order, Israel secured the Gaza Strip, the Sinai Peninsula, the West Bank, East Jerusalem, and the Golan Heights from the Arab neighbours, expanding its territory threefold.

19. United Nations Information System on the Question of Palestine (UNISPAL): Resolution 242 (1967) of 22 November 1967. https://unispal.un.org/DPA/DPR/unispal.nsf/udc.htm.

20. WAIF was established in 1955 by the Hollywood actress Jane Russell.

21. Poonperm Krairiksh's son Kraithip would later marry Nanda, Anand's older daughter.

22. King Bhumibol has been awarded countless honorary degrees over the years, and personally presented more degrees to students than anyone on earth. Ironically, his own graduation from the University of Lausanne was prevented by a near-fatal car accident in 1949 that cost him an eye, and necessitated long convalescence and specialist treatment.

23. *Chronicle of Thailand – Headline News Since 1946*. Singapore: Editions Didier Millet, 2009, p. 168.

24. National Broadcasting Company (NBC), 11 September 1969.

25. China was a charter member of the UN after World War II, but its seat was occupied by the Republic of China (Taiwan) following the Communist Revolution of 1949. The entry of the People's Republic of China in 1971 was therefore also the re-entry of mainland China into the body.

26. In 1936, Huang Hua interpreted interviews with Mao Zedong and other communist leaders for Edgar Snow, the US journalist who in 1937 published *Red Star Over China*, about the Communist Party of China after the Long March retreat in the mid-1930s. Huang was China's permanent representative at the UN from 1971 to 1976, when he returned to Beijing and became foreign minister. He retired in 1982.

27. In a controversial legal ruling, Prime Minister Samak Sundaravej was dismissed as prime minister in September 2008 almost as soon as Saroj Chavanviraj received the royal assent as foreign minister.

28. Asda is a member of the distinguished Jayanama family of diplomats. During World War II, his father became the youngest director general of the Propaganda Department of Field Marshal Plaek Phibunsongkhram (Phibun), and was on good terms with the press, including Sern Panyarachun, Anand's father. He organised a fact-finding trip to Japanese-occupied Manchuria in China, which Sern joined. Direk, his uncle, was ambassador to Tokyo and briefly foreign minister during the war, and was also one of the 'Promoters' in the 1932 revolution.

29. Foreshadowing the Non-Aligned Movement of the 1960s, the Bandung Conference took place in April 1955 in Bandung, Indonesia, and was attended by 29 African and Asian nations. Espousing a non-racist, post-colonial world, the conference issued a declaration containing ten principles that should govern international relations:

    1. *Respect for fundamental human rights and for the purpose and principles of the Charter of the United Nations.*
    2. *Respect for the sovereignty and territorial integrity of all countries.*
    3. *Recognition of the equality of all races and the equality of all nations.*
    4. *Non-intervention in the internal affairs of other countries.*
    5. *Respect for the right of each nation to defend itself singly or collectively, in conformity with the Charter of the United Nations.*
    6. *(a) Abstention from the use of arrangements of collective defence to serve any particular interests of the big powers. (b) Abstention by any countries from exerting pressures on other countries.*
    7. *Refraining from acts or threats of aggression or the use of force against the territorial integrity or political independence of any countries.*
    8. *Settlement of all international disputes by peaceful means, such as negotiation, conciliation, arbitration or judicial settlement as well as other peaceful means of the parties' own choice, in conformity with the Charter of the United Nations.*
    9. *Promotion for mutual interest and cooperation.*
    10. *Respect for justice and international obligations.*

30. Interview with Fareed Zakaria in the television programme *GPS*, CNN, 4 January 2013.

31. CNN, *Cold War*. Turner Original Productions, 1998.

32. Resolution 2758, 25 October 1971.

33. The original permanent five members with veto powers in 1946 were China, France, Soviet Union, the UK, and the US.

34. The official name of Burma was changed controversially to Myanmar in 1989 by a junta, the State Law and Order

Restoration Council (SLORC).

35. Louis Halasz, ibid.

36. Manaspas Xuto demonstrated a degree of daring by getting himself posted in 1965 to Burma, which had fallen to General Ne Win's Revolutionary Council in a coup in 1962. 'I considered it a challenge to find out what was going on,' recalls Manaspas. 'Thanat Khoman did not like to hear Field Marshal Praphas complaining in cabinet that we did not know what was going on in Burma.' Manaspas served three years in Rangoon as second secretary, developing links with the Directorate of Defence Services Intelligence, Burma's military intelligence. He found the cost of living remarkably low and the social scene good.

37. The second ground-up popular political triumph was the forced resignation of General Suchinda Kraprayoon as prime minister in May 1992.

38. 'King asks students to maintain unity, warns of infiltrators', *Bangkok Post*, 24 October 1973, p. 3.

39. Communist Party of Thailand statement of 16 October 1973 transmitted on 21 October by Voice of the People of Thailand clandestine radio.

40. Funding for the *Social Science Review* originally came from the Asia Foundation. The foundation was funded by the US Central Intelligence Agency (CIA) from its incarnation in 1954 until 1967, when the covert relationship was revealed in the US media.

41. 'The *Social Science Review* was supported by grants from the Asia Foundation. Its unusual political views were made somewhat palatable by its connection with Prince Wan Waithayakon, president of the Social Science Association of Thailand that sponsored the journal. The first magazine of its type to be read widely by intellectuals and students, it became very popular because of the high quality of its critical analyses of society and government. Much of the revitalised spirit of intellectual curiosity and skepticism during the 1963–8 period may be attributed to the energetic work and contributions of Sulak and his journal ... By 1968, the journal had virtually become the intellectual voice of the nation, thereby exercising great influence upon an entire younger generation then in the various universities.' David Morell, Chai-Anan Samudavanija, *Political Conflict in Thailand*. Cambridge, Massachusetts: Oelgesclager, Gunn & Hain, 1981, p. 140.

CHAPTER 5

1. US Embassy assessment, mid-October 1976.

2. MR Seni Pramoj (1905–1997) and his younger brother Kukrit (1911–1995) were grandsons of Prince Pramoj, the 61st child of King Buddha Loet La Nabhalai, Rama II (b.1768; r.1809–1824). Prince Pramoj handled foreign affairs during the reign of his younger first cousin, King Mongkut, Rama IV (b.1788; r.1851–1868).

3. Robert Woodrow, 'Princes, Poets & Premiers', *Asiaweek*, 23 April 1982. Kukrit founded the Progressive Party in 1945, which merged into the Democrat Party in 1946. He founded the Social Action Party in 1974.

4. Prince Norodom Sihanouk acceded to the Cambodian throne in 1941, but abdicated in favour of his father in 1955 in order to pursue a more overtly political career. He was overthrown in a coup in 1970 staged by General Lon Nol, and headed an alliance against the new US-backed government in which the principal military muscle was the Khmer Rouge. He was imprisoned from 1975 to late 1978 by the Khmer Rouge, and

five of his acknowledged children and 14 grandchildren were murdered by the genocidal regime of Pol Pot. Because of their time incarcerated together in the palace in Phnom Penh, Prince Norodom Sihamoni became the son closest to his father, and succeeded him as king when King Sihanouk abdicated for a second time in 2004. Sihanouk had re-ascended the throne in 1993.

5. After the fall, Saigon was renamed Ho Chi Minh City and Independence Palace became Reunification Palace. Lonely Planet Guides give it a 'Top Choice' rating as a visitor attraction: 'The 2nd floor contributes a shagadelic card-playing room, complete with a cheesy round leather banquette, a barrel-shaped bar, hubcap light fixtures and groovy three-legged chairs set around a flared-legged card table. There's also a cinema and a rooftop nightclub, complete with helipad: James Bond/Austin Powers – eat your heart out.'

6. For an exhaustive and highly readable 384-page account of the *Mayaguez* incident from US and Cambodian sources with extensive investigations on the ground, see Ralph Wetterhahn, *The Last Battle – The Mayaguez Incident and the End of the Vietnam War*. New York: Carroll & Graf, 2001.

7. Kenton Clymer, *The United States and Cambodia, 1969–2000: A Troubled Relationship*. New York: Routledge, 2004, p. 102. The suggestion that the *Mayaguez* 'clipped a corner' en route to Sattahip and was five miles inside Cambodian waters was never accepted by the US.

8. Walter Isaacson, *Kissinger – A Biography*. New York: Simon & Schuster, 1992 and 2005, p. 649.

9. Gerald Ford was a Republican congressman appointed by Richard Nixon to replace Vice President Spiro Agnew, who resigned in October 1973. In August 1974, following the Watergate scandal, Nixon became the first and only US president to resign from office, and Ford became president. Ford contested the 1976 election but lost to Jimmy Carter.

10. The BLU-82 resembles a concrete mixer on a pogo stick, which serves as a detonator. It was delivered on a parachute from an ML-130 transport aircraft rather than a conventional bomber. Nicknamed the Daisy Cutter, its preferred application is clearing forests for airstrips by exploding just above ground. The US air war in Indochina was by far the largest bombing campaign in history, and the last bomb to be dropped was the largest in the USAF's sub-nuclear armoury.

11. Charles Stuart Kennedy, Interview with Edward C. Masters. 'Frontline Diplomacy: The Foreign Affairs Oral History Collection of the Association for Diplomatic Studies and Training', Library of Congress, 14 March 1989.

12. Ibid.

13. Ibid.

14. Ministry of Foreign Affairs transcript of an interview with Michael Morrow, a correspondent with Hong Kong's *Far Eastern Economic Review*, 23 March 1976.

15. Chatichai Choonhavan, the foreign minister who later became prime minister, was once asked to name his favourite US ambassador. He joked that it was Ed Masters – who was never ambassador but spent five years in Thailand as deputy chief of mission.

16. 'Thailand policy on China is wary – cautious moves are made for increased relations', *The New York Times*, 1 April 1973.

17. '180. Memorandum of Conversation, Washington, October 2, 1972, 3pm,' in *Foreign relations of the United States, 1969–1976, Volume XX, Southeast Asia: Thailand, 1969–1972*, p. 384.

18. Sirin Phathanothai with James Peck, *The Dragon's Pearl*. New York: Simon & Schuster, 1994.

19. Some of the best photographs of this historic visit were taken by Phichai Wasanasong. They were stored at his home in Muang Ake, northern Bangkok, and lost in the great flood of 2011, much to Tej Bunnag's distress.

20. Thailand struck oil deals with China well before the 1959 Revolutionary Party Announcement No. 53 was ditched. An aide memoir at the time suggested likely exports from Thailand as kenaf, natural rubber, tobacco leaf, timber, sugar, maize and rice; and from China as raw silk, crude oil and petroleum products, chemicals, medicines, fertiliser, iron and steel, and hand tools.

21. Extracts from Tej Bunnag's notes were included in *Phan Pheua Phandin* by Vitthya Vejjajiva, a biography of Phan Wannamethee, the head of the Red Cross in Thailand and president of the World Fellowship of Buddhists. It was published in 2014 by Post Publishing and won a national literary award.

22. Purificacion C.V. Quisumbing, 'ASEAN and China: Some Policy and Security Concerns', *Foreign Relations Journal*, Vol. 1, No. 1, January 1986, p. 134.

23. Idem, pp. 131–2.

24. Ibid.

25. 'Anand carries extra for China communiqué', *The Voice of the Nation*, 17 June 1975.

26. Purificacion C.V. Quisumbing, idem, p. 134.

27. 'Thai envoy en route to Peking', *South China Morning Post*, 17 June 1975.

28. Philip Short, *Pol Pot – The History of a Nightmare*. London: John Murray, 2004, p. 299.

29. Jung Chang and Jon Halliday, *Mao – The Unknown Story*. London: Jonathan Cape, 2005, p. 650.

30. Obituary of Clare Hollingworth – 'Doyenne of foreign correspondents who as a novice *Daily Telegraph* stringer reported the outbreak of the Second World War', *The Daily Telegraph*, London, 11 January 2017.

31. Chulacheeb Chinwanno, *Thirty-five Years of Thai-Chinese Relations*.

32. From an interview with Vilas Manivat, 17 February 1980, reproduced in Steve Van Beek (ed.), *Kukrit Pramoj: His Wit and Wisdom, Writings, Speeches and Interviews*. Bangkok: Editions Duang Kamol, 1983.

33. Tang Wengsheng, or Nancy Tang, was born in New York in 1943 where her father Tang Mingzhao later became China's first deputy secretary general of the United Nations. The family came home to the 'New China' in the 1950s. Tang rose high in the foreign ministry and Communist Party of China. In an interview given to Wu Jia, she gave some indication of her proficiency in foreign affairs in the 1970s: 'At that time we were just interpreters, and there were many things we didn't know much about. But they encouraged us to study, not to just settle for being a basic interpreter. They encouraged us to learn more about the people we translated for, the issues they were discussing, and the background and culture of the foreign guests. I think it was through being at these discussions – and they also made us feel we were a part of it. I think it was great these leaders treated us young people in that way. That was actually how we grew up, how we later came to understand life and our responsibilities, how we should work through life – we learned to do as they had done.' *Life in China*, 12 March 2006.

34. Chulacheeb Chinwanno, ibid.

35. Ibid.

36. US Department of State Memorandum of Conversation, Washington, 26 November 1975.

37. Thailand's long-standing concern about Chinese hegemony in Asia is reflected in Clause 5 of the Thai-Chinese joint communiqué signed on 1 July 1975 in Beijing, which states: 'The two governments are also opposed to any attempt by any country or group of countries to establish hegemony or create spheres of influence in any part of the world.'

38. Although Deng Xiaoping's lively expectorations were well known in diplomatic circles, they startled British prime minister Margaret Thatcher over a decade later when she met with the Chinese premier in a rather one-sided dialogue on the future of Hong Kong: Deng bluntly informed her it would revert to China without any conditions, and sounded the spittoon like a gong.

39. Purificacion C.V. Quisumbing, idem, p. 132.

40. Apart from Cambodia and Thailand, China was at this time building relations with the Philippines, Indonesia, and Malaysia, and had made first contact with the Singaporeans in 1974 at the UN in New York through their permanent representative, Tommy Koh. Among the countries of ASEAN, Thailand with its Cold War US connections and military bases presented some of the thorniest issues for China.

41. Premier Zhou Enlai died on 8 January 1976 and Chairman Mao on 9 September the same year.

42. Voice of Free Asia was originally set up beside the foreign ministry at Saranrom Palace in what had been the first Western-style garden in Bangkok. The garden was created in the 19th century by Henry Alabaster, an American adviser to King Chulalongkorn and the grandfather of Air Chief Marshal Siddhi Savetsila (Savetsila can be translated as 'white stone' or 'alabaster'). The site is today occupied by the Privy Council Chambers, and Voice of Free Asia (which was renamed Radio Saranrom in 1998) has been revitalised with Manaspas Xuto as a consultant. Manaspas recalls with evident pride that when President Sheikh Mujib of Bangladesh was killed in a coup in 1975, the Thai ambassador in Dacca first heard the news from Voice of Free Asia.

CHAPTER 6

1. Speech by Prime Minister *MR* Kukrit Pramoj at the Foreign Correspondents' Association of Southeast Asia, Raffles Hotel, Singapore, 25 July 1975.

2. Aderholt gave three very free and frank background briefings not intended for publication to a female reporter, in a six-day period from 19 May 1976, at around the time of U-Tapao's closure.

3. The lunch, at 1pm on 26 November 1975 at the State Department, was also attended by Koson Sinthawanon, director general, Ministry of Foreign Affairs; Siddhi Savetsila, secretary general of the National Security Council; General Saiyud Kerdphol, deputy director, Internal Security Operations Command; Sudhee Prasasvinitchai. On the State Department side was Philip C. Habib, assistant secretary for East Asian and Pacific Affairs; Brent Scowcroft, National Security Council; Winston Lord, director of policy planning; and George B. Roberts.

4. Kissinger became national security adviser to President Nixon in January 1969, and secretary of state in September 1973. He is the only person to have held the two positions concurrently.

5. Chatichai Choonhavan's successor as foreign minister, Bhichai Rattakul, remembers being infuriated when the new minister of defence, Admiral Sangad Chaloryu, produced a shopping list for the US of planes, ammunition, and surveillance equipment. 'It was like a baby asking for toys,' Bhichai recalls. 'We were talking about the national interest, the survival of the country, and he was talking about antennae, dammit.'

6. The European Economic Community, or Common Market, was formed in 1957 by the Treaty of Rome, and morphed into the Economic Community in 1993 (Treaty of Maastricht) and finally the European Union in 2009 (Treaty of Lisbon). The latter name changes imply growing political union within Europe which has not been mirrored in Southeast Asia.

7. The Rajakhru Clan (or Group) takes its name from an area near the Victory Monument in Bangkok where the family of Chatichai Choonhavan lived. It originated with Chatichai's father, Field Marshal Phin Choonhavan, as a vehicle for political and business interests, and coalesced in 1974 into the right-of-centre Chart Thai (Thai Nation) Party with General Pramarn Adireksarn, a hardline rightist, as chairman. The party headed coalition governments in 1988 and 1995 when Chatichai Choonhavan and Banharn Silpa-archa respectively served as elected prime ministers. The party was among a number dissolved in 2008 by the Constitutional Court, and mutated into the Chartthaipattana (Thai Nation Development) Party.

8. Surin Masdit's daughter, Khunying Supatra, became a well-known Democrat member of parliament and minister.

9. Puey Ungphakorn (1916–1999), a Ramon Magsaysay Award winner in 1965, was honoured by UNESCO on the centenary of his birth as one of the world's most important people, 'a prominent educator and civil servant of impeccable ethics' who played a key role in laying the foundations of the modern Thai economy. *Bangkok Post*, 20 November 2015.

10. Rick Newman and Don Shepperd, *Bury Us Upside Down – The Misty Pilots and the Secret Battle for the Ho Chi Minh Trail*. New York: Presidio Press, 2007, p. 181.

11. Thailand today remains a non-NATO ally of the US, which has over a hundred military personnel stationed in Thailand. U-Tapao continues to be used by the USAF for logistics. The huge runway was one of the few worldwide designated as a suitable alternate landing site for emergency use in the NASA Space Shuttle programme, which concluded in 2012.

12. Department of Information, Ministry of Foreign Affairs, transcript of interview of Prime Minister Seni Pramoj by Masahiro Nagata, NHK Bangkok bureau chief, Government House, 21 May 1976.

13. Article I (3) of 'Agreement Respecting the establishment, conduct and support of radio communications research and development activities in Thailand' – a 'secret' agreement between Ambassador Graham Martin of the US and Deputy Defence Minister Dawee Chullasapya of Thailand, signed in Bangkok on 19 January 1965.

14. A similar but older Cold War AN/FLR-9 listening station with a Wullenweber antenna array went into service in 1965 at the Misawa Air Base in northern Japan to monitor transmissions in the Soviet Union and People's Republic of China. It too was nicknamed the Elephant Cage, and had 40-metre aerials placed in a circle some 440 metres in diameter. The old technology at Misawa was dismantled in late 2014, seven years after the decommissioning of Japan's only other listening facility at Yomitan, Okinawa prefecture (*Nikkei Asian Review*, 15 October

2014). During the Cold War, eight AN/FLR-9 signals intelligence stations formed a global network known as the Iron Horse which could monitor virtually the entire planet in radiuses of almost 7,500 kilometres. Apart from Ramasun in northeastern Thailand and Misawa in northern Japan, stations were built at Augsburg, Germany; Chicksands, UK; Clark Air Force Base, the Philippines; Elmendorf Air Force Base, Alaska; Karamursel, Turkey; and San Vito dei Normanni Air Station, Italy.

15. Charles Stuart Kennedy, Interview with Edward C. Masters, 'Frontline Diplomacy: The Foreign Affairs Oral History Collection of the Association for Diplomatic Studies and Training', Library of Congress, 14 March 1989.

16. 'Seni, Whitehouse touch on ammo and Ramasoon', *The Voice of the Nation*, 5 June 1976.

17. 'US planes to use Takhli to refuel', *Bangkok Post*, 6 June 1976.

18. Christian Oesterheld, 'Cambodian-Thai Relations during the Khmer Rouge Regime: Evidence from the East German Diplomatic Archives', *Silpakorn University Journal of Social Sciences, Humanities, and Arts*, Bangkok, 2014, Vol. 14, No. 2, pp. 1331–154.

19. Bhichai Rattakul was elected president of Rotary International in 2002 and chairman of the Rotary Foundation in 2007, the highest positions attainable in the international philanthropic organisation. Bhichai remembers playing golf on a Rotary visit to South Vietnam in the late 1960s with Truong Dinh Dzu. 'As long as you have a government as corrupt as this, you will lose the war,' Bhichai warned Truong, with shelling audible in the background. Truong had failed to win election in 1967 as president of US-backed South Vietnam against General Nguyen Van Thieu, and was subsequently imprisoned for five months on trumped-up charges of currency manipulation.

20. Prominent Thai Rotarians included the former foreign minister Prince Wan Waithayakon; diplomat and literary figure Prince Prem Purachatra; Prince Dhani Nivat, the president of the Privy Council; and Sern Panyarachun, Anand's father.

21. 'Yellow Rain' was an airborne toxin allegedly used by the communist government in Laos against Hmong minorities in the late 1970s. Its use was never proven and has been strongly disputed.

22. 'Asia Yearbook 1977', *Far Eastern Economic Review*, p. 318.

23. Warren A. Trest, *Air Command One – Heinie Aderholt and America's Secret Wars*. Washington and London: Smithsonian Institution Press, 2000, p. 252.

24. Aderholt gave three free and frank background briefings not intended for publication to a female reporter, 19–25 May 1976, at around the time of U-Tapao's closure.

25. *The Nation* started out in 1971 as *The Voice of the Nation*.

26. James J. Gormley's recollections from his career as a US diplomat were recorded in an interview with Charles Stuart Kennedy for the Association for Diplomatic Studies and Training Foreign Affairs Oral History Project, 20 October 1992.

27. Ministry of Foreign Affairs transcript of interview with unidentified reporters, 18 March 1976.

28. Ambassador Daniel A. O'Donohue's recollections from his career as a US diplomat were recorded in an interview with Charles Stuart Kennedy for the Association for Diplomatic Studies and Training Foreign Affairs Oral History Project, 28 May 1996.

CHAPTER 7

1. Robert Woodrow, 'Princes, Poets & Premiers', *Asiaweek*, 23

April 1982.

2. David Morell and Chai-Anan Samudavanija, *Political Reform in Thailand: Reform, Reaction and Revolution*. Cambridge, Massachusetts: Oelgesclager, Gunn & Hain, 1982, p. 271.

3. In 1988, His Holiness the Supreme Patriarch Somdet Phra Yanasangvara was appointed the 19th supreme patriarch of the Chakri dynasty, founded in 1782; he died on 24 October 2013, aged 100. A 30-day period of national mourning was announced.

4. Nicholas Grossman and Dominic Faulder (eds), *King Bhumibol Adulyadej – A Life's Work*. Singapore: Editions Didier Millet, 2011, p. 103.

5. 'A Letter from Dr Puey Ungphakorn, The Violence and the October 6, 1976, Coup', The Union of Democratic Thais (USA), 1976, para 7.

6. Lewis M. Simons, 'Civilian rule in Thailand overthrown – Admiral takes power after leftists crushed', *The Washington Post*, 7 October 1976.

7. 'Trends in Thailand – Seminar with Dr Puey Ungphakorn', moderator Dr Sevina Carlson. Center for Strategic and International Studies, Georgetown University, Washington DC, 15 February 1977.

8. As deputy interior minister in 1976, Samak Sundaravej led a rightist faction in the Democrat Party and was prominent in the anti-leftist campaign. In a television interview with Selina Downes for Al Jazeera English after he became prime minister in early 2008, Samak claimed that only one person had died among the more than 3,000 students caught up in the 6 October bloodletting. He dismissed high casualty claims as 'dirty history', and said Downes had not been in Bangkok at the time and was too young to know the truth. Samak was widely criticised in the Thai press for this revisionism in the face of ample evidence. The violence at Thammasat was well covered in the Western media. Indeed, photographer Neal Ulevich, on assignment for the Associated Press, won a third-place World Press Award followed by the 1977 Pulitzer Prize for Spot News with his graphic pictures from that day. Unbeknownst to Samak, the cameraman filming his interview with Downes in 2008, Derek Williams, had filmed the violence of 6 October 1976 for CBS News. A veteran of numerous battles in Cambodia and Vietnam, Williams still looks back on that day as the most horrific of his life. Noted for his professionalism, the New Zealander carried on filming Samak's effort to rewrite history. It ended with a shameless admonition from Samak to Downes to do her homework better in future. 'I found it very hard to shut up,' said Williams of the encounter. 'I cannot think of another event that is so burned in my memory, and I have seen some bad stuff.'

9. *The Japan Times*, 7 October 1976.

10. *Time*, 18 October 1976.

11. Joel Henri, 'Thais welcome "timely" coup', Agence France-Presse, 7 October 1976.

12. Alan Dawson, 'Loss of democracy has attractions for Thai people', United Press International, October 1976.

13. Sulak Sivaraksa, *Siamese Resurgence*. Bangkok: Asian Cultural Forum on Development, 1985, pp. 454–463.

14. Lewis M. Simons, ibid.

15. Commentary in *Quan Doi Nhan Dan* newspaper quoted by Vietnam News Agency, Hanoi, 8 October 1976.

16. 'Counter-coup fears: Thai general is sacked', *New Straits Times*, 12 October 1976.

17. Gray's Inn is one of London's four Inns of Court, the professional associations of barristers and judges.

18. Private letter from Anand to his daughters, Nanda and Daranee, on foreign ministry stationery, 15 October 1976.

19. Norman Peagam, 'Challenges for the New Order', *Far Eastern Economic Review*, 5 November 1976.

20. US Embassy assessment filed after 13 October 1976.

21. David Morell and Chai-Anan Samudavanija, idem, p. 271.

22. 'A Letter from Dr Puey Ungphakorn, The Violence and the October 6, 1976, Coup', The Union of Democratic Thais (USA), 1976, para. 15.

23. Ibid.

24. *Bangkok Post*, 25 October 1976.

25. David A. Andelman, 'Key Thailand negotiator with US over bases is ousted from cabinet', *The New York Times*, 25 October 1975.

26. The finance ministry's Bureau of the Budget was also purged. Its director, Boontham Thonghaimuk, and his deputy, Metha Phumchoosri, were both sacked for connections to Air Siam, a private airline competing with the national flag-carrier Thai International Airways. The latter had strong links to the Royal Thai Air Force.

27. The civil service panel included the permanent secretaries from the prime minister's office and the Ministry of Justice.

28. Private email correspondence with Tuptim Malakul, 19 June 2013, concerning a profile of Anand Panyarachun she was writing for the Royal Bangkok Sports Club (RBSC) magazine.

29. 'Victims of Détente', *Asiaweek*, 12 November 1976.

30. US Embassy cable, 'Conversation with former foreign minister Thanat Khoman regarding military takeover', Bangkok, 14 October 1976.

31. *Moscow News*, 42 (2718), 16 October 1976.

32. The only national capitals at higher altitude than Ethiopia's Addis Ababa are Bogotá in Colombia, La Paz in Bolivia, Quito in Ecuador, and Thimphu in Bhutan. Chawan Chawanid moved on from Addis Ababa to Lagos in Nigeria, and was brought back to Thailand as deputy permanent secretary in 1980 when ACM Siddhi Savetsila became foreign minister in the first Prem Tinsulanond government.

33. Private letter from Anand to his daughters, Nanda and Daranee, on foreign ministry stationery, 29 October 1976.

34. *The Nation Review*, 14 November 1976.

35. Ibid.

36. Private letter from Anand to his daughters, Nanda and Daranee, 15 October 1976.

37. *Bangkok Post*, 30 October 1977.

38. Private letter from Anand to his daughters, 4 November 1976.

39. Private letter from Anand to his daughters, 18 November 1976.

40. *Khun Ya* is an affectionate but quite formal term of address for a paternal grandmother; *Khun Yai* is used for a maternal grandmother.

41. Private letter from Anand to his daughters, 25 November 1976.

42. Ibid.

43. Private letter from Anand to his daughters, 2 December 1976.

44. Private letter from Anand to his daughters, 15 December 1976.

45. Ibid.

46. Private correspondence from Professor Frank C. Darling, head of DePauw University, Greencastle, Indiana, 4 January 1977.

47. Private correspondence from T.T.B. Koh, Permanent Representative of the Republic of Singapore to the UN, 10 January 1977.

48. Private letter from Tan Boon Seng, Minister for Foreign Affairs, Singapore, 13 January 1977.

49. *Bangkok Post*, 13 January 1977.

50. Message relayed in a private letter from Manuel T. Tan, ambassador of the Philippines, Bangkok, 17 January 1977.

51. Private letter from Reuven Dafni, ambassador of Israel, Bangkok, 14 January 1977.

52. Private letter from Charles S. Whitehouse, US ambassador, Bangkok, 13 January 1977.

53. Private letter from Anand to his daughters, 13 January 1977.

54. *The Nation Review*, 26 January 1977.

55. The titles of permanent secretary and undersecretary of state are interchangeable and describe the most senior civil service position in a ministry. 'Permanent secretary' is preferred in modern usage because in the Thai system cabinet ministers are not referred to as secretaries. Thailand has a foreign minister not a secretary of state, as in the US.

56. Thailand's Civil Service Commission uses the Position Classification system with grades 1–10. The PC10 rank of an ambassador is usually rendered simply as C10.

57. *Bangkok Post*, 3 June 1977.

58. Puey Ungphakorn spent his remaining 23 years in the UK; he returned to Thailand for a private visit in 1997.

59. In paragraphs 33-35 of 'A Letter from Dr Puey Ungphakorn, The Violence and the October 6, 1976, Coup' (published by The Union of Democratic Thais (USA) in 1976), Puey gives a harrowing account of his near lynching after being detained in the departure lounge of Don Muang International Airport while waiting to board a flight to Kuala Lumpur. The military's Armoured Brigade Radio had been alerted, and was calling on Village Scouts to arrest him. Puey was manhandled by a police lieutenant colonel while talking on the telephone. 'With a very rude manner, he slapped the earphone, which dropped from my hand,' Puey wrote. 'He scolded me and said he wanted to seize me and take me to the police chief.' Puey said nothing, but air force military police and customs officers did not want him taken into any landside public areas where 'herds of Village Scouts' were milling around. He was confined in a customs office, and searched by police officers from the Crime Suppression Division, who confiscated a notebook and Father Brown novel by G.K. Chesterton. 'At about 8pm, the police informed me that "words from above" had ordered my release,' Puey wrote. Before he boarded a late flight to Europe, a police officer who had searched him returned the notebook. 'I thanked him and told him that he had committed a grave sin, for I was innocent,' Puey wrote. 'That police officer retorted that three arrested students mentioned me as a stage manager of the hanging play intended to destroy the King, on Monday October 4. He also added that the students who accused me had their stomachs burnt with fire by the Red Gaur members. They then "confessed" and incriminated me.'

60. Puey had also spent several years in exile during the dictatorship of Field Marshal Thanom Kittikachorn.

CHAPTER 8

1. Amnuay Viravan had taken on military business interests before. He once forced military strongman Field Marshal Thanom Kittikachorn to move his deputy, Field Marshal Praphas Charusathien, from the chairmanship of a failing slaughterhouse owned by the Bangkok Metropolitan Administration. After three letters on the problem, Amnuay had finally rebuked Thanom for failing to safeguard the public interest. Within a year of Amnuay taking over, the slaughterhouse was profitable, breeders placated, and the price of pork reduced for consumers. Amnuay was, however, unable to prevent board members voting themselves a Mercedes Benz each as a bonus – but declined one for himself. Similarly, when he was director general of the customs department, Amnuay opted out of the lucrative reward scheme, which goes with the position. Instead, he had the money put into an account and transferred to the department's provident fund when he left. 'I was the only who did not accept the reward,' he says.

2. The US-ASEAN Center for Technology Exchange was recast as the US-ASEAN Council for Business and Technology in 1989 when it merged with the US Chamber of Commerce's ten-year-old ASEAN-US Business Council.

3. NIFCO owns *The Japan Times*. Toshiaki Ogasawara became the newspaper's chairman in 2001, and is also its chief executive officer and publisher. He has numerous links to the US, including as a trustee for the University of Southern California, and Thunderbird, the American Graduate School of International Management. He is a director of the Los Angeles Philharmonic Society and a governor of Cedars-Sinai Medical Center in Los Angeles. Source: Bloomberg.

4. Pavida Pananond is an associate professor at Thammasat Business School, Thammasat University.

5. Pavida Pananond, 'Thai Coup: Gains mask looming pains', *Nikkei Asian Review*, 15–21 September 2014, p. 56.

6. Unocal was merged into Chevron Corporation in 2005.

7. The Nong Ngu Hao ('Cobra Swamp') airport project east of Bangkok had been first mooted in the early 1960s when Field Marshal Sarit Thanarat was prime minister. Prime Minister Thaksin Shinawatra finally brought the project to fruition in late 2006 when it opened as Suvarnabhumi Airport amid allegations of massive graft. Thaksin was removed from power in a coup the same month.

8. William Warren, *Chronicles of American Business in Thailand*. Bangkok: The American Chamber of Commerce in Thailand, 2006, p. 76.

9. When he arrived in Thailand as a teenager in the 1960s, Heinecke remembers being interested mostly 'in motorcycles, go karts, and girls'. He married at 18, never went to university and never learned to speak Thai – he commands perhaps a hundred words of this tonal language. The ultimate outsider inside, Heinecke treasures his Thai friends and supporters. 'There are too many to mention,' he says, cautioning: 'You would hate to have any Thai actually against you.' Heinecke went so far as to relinquish his US citizenship in 1991 and become a naturalised Thai citizen – making it unlikely that he will ever be AmCham president again.

10. John McBeth, 'Steel beneath the saintliness', *Far Eastern Economic Review*, Hong Kong, 21 March 1980.

11. Major General Chamlong Srimuang graduated from Chulachomklao Military Academy in Class 7 but refused to join other Young Turks in the first of two failed coup attempts against Prem on 1 April 1981 – the so-called April Fool's Day Coup. A devout Buddhist and member of the Santi Asoke Buddhist fundamentalist group, Chamlong stepped away from Prem following a controversy over abortion legislation. He became a popular Bangkok governor for six years, founded the Palang Tham Party in the 1990s which launched Thaksin

Shinawatra's political career, led demonstrations that brought down the short-lived government of General Suchinda Kraprayoon, and carried on into old age as a tenacious pro-establishment political agitator.

12. Originally a German song, 'Oh, mein Papa' was a number one hit in the US in 1954 for singer Eddie Fisher, and topped the UK charts for trumpeter Eddie Calvert. It was covered by numerous other singers.

13. *Baramee* is a Thai concept that is often wrongly translated as charisma. *Baramee* is accumulated through meritorious efforts and always positive. It is a perception of an individual held by others. Likhit Dhiravegin, Felllow of the Royal Institute, wrote: '*Baramee* is a significant attribute for one's standing in Thai society in general and for holders of positions in organisations in particular. This is most especially true for those who are the power wielders in politics. One may hear every now and then, in effect, that that person is not suitable for the ministerial post [because] he does not have enough *baramee* … '

14. Giles G. Ungpakorn, 'Thailand: Democratic Audit 2014', *Ugly Truth Thailand* blog, 11 April 2014.

CHAPTER 9

1. Grissarin Chungsiriwat and Nicholas Grossman (eds), *Thailand at Random*. Bangkok: Editions Didier Millet, 2012.
2. Ibid.
3. Paul Handley, 'Politics and business, 1987–96', in Kevin Hewison (ed.), *Political Change in Thailand: Democracy and Participation*. New York and London: Routledge, 1997.
4. Like many Thais, Manoonkrit Roopkachorn changed his name in later life. In his Class 7 years, he was known as Manoon.
5. 'Immediately after the coup, [the NPKC] ordered mutual fund managers, banks and brokers to support the market. The NPKC's Kaset [Rojananil], the air force commander, made repeated statements encouraging confidence in the SET. Not many other coup leaders have shown such sensitivity to a stock market.' Paul Handley, 'Politics and business, 1987–96', in Kevin Hewison (ed.), *Political Change in Thailand: Democracy and Participation*. New York and London: Routledge, 1997, p. 107.

CHAPTER 10

1. The Heritage Club was a businessmen's networking club created in a modern office block near the Rajaprasong intersection in central Bangkok in 1986. It offered Chinese, Japanese, and Western dining. The Heritage was followed by the Pacific City Club and the Bangkok Club, both of which were more health-conscious and offered spa and workout facilities. In a more competitive 21st-century environment, the Heritage Club went out of business, and the Pacific Club closed its doors temporarily in 2011. In their heyday in the early 1990s, these clubs had prestigious chairmen, including former Prime Minister General Prem Tinsulanond, former Supreme Commander General Saiyud Kerdphol, and former Foreign Minister Arsa Sarasin. (*The Nation*, 25 September 1997).
2. MR Pridiyathorn Devakula and Charoenjit Na Songkhla were added as deputy ministers of commerce and interior respectively in July 1991.
3. *Pi* is a term of respect and affection meaning older brother or sister. *Nong* is used for younger people.
4. Speech given by Snoh Unakul honouring Anand's retirement

after 17 years as chairman of the TDRI, 9 July 2008.
5. Interview with Ambassador Daniel A. O'Donohue by Charles Stuart Kennedy on 28 May 1996, The Association for Diplomatic Studies and Training Foreign Affairs Oral History Project, Library of Congress.
6. See Tyrell Haberkorn, 'Article 17, a Totalitarian Movement, and a Military Dictatorship', Hot Spots, Cultural Anthropology website, 23 September 2014 (https://culanth.org/fieldsights/566-article-17-a-totalitarian-movement-and-a-military-dictatorship). 'Article 17 was put in place during the dictatorship of Field Marshal Sarit Thanarat (1958–1963), used extensively during the regime of Field Marshal Thanom Kittikachorn (1963–1973), and finally repealed following a transition to a more democratic government under Prime Minister Sanya [Dhammasakdi] after the student and peoples' movement of October 14, 1973. Under Sarit, Article 17 was used 11 times to authorise executions. Under Thanom, it was used 65 times to authorise executions and 113 times to authorise detentions (Premchai 2517 [1974], 21). A similar order providing executive power has been present in several constitutions under military dictatorships, including Article 21 of the 1976 charter and Article 27 of the 1977 and 1991 charters. The three most recent of Thailand's 18 constitutions since the end of the absolute monarchy – 1997, 2006, and 2007 – have not contained such a measure.
7. Respect for the status and feelings of others, particularly elders, is governed by the Thai concept of *krieng jai*. Actions and words that might cause discomfort or offence are generally avoided.
8. Staporn Kavitanon died in early 2012. He was secretary general of the Board of Investment (BOI) from 1991 to 2001, when he retired three months early and established a consulting company, the eponymous Khun Staporn Kavitanon (KSK), to continue in the same line of business. His stint at the BOI earned him the accolade of 'Thailand's Leading Salesman'. One of his last roles was as an economic adviser to Prime Minister Abhisit Vejjajiva, who was in office from 2008 to 2011.
9. Chawadee Nualkhjair, 'Staporn Kavitanon: Still aiming high', *Asia Times Online*, 8 June 2002.
10. The author had been elected for a second year as FCCT president a few weeks before the NPKC coup in 1991.

CHAPTER 11

1. United Front for an Independent, Neutral, Peaceful and Cooperative Cambodia (FUNCINPEC).
2. William Shawcross, 'Thailand Still Wary of Accepting Swarms of Desperate Refugees', *The Washington Post*, 19 March 1980.
3. In late 1986, Squadron Leader Prasong Soonsiri, secretary general to Prime Minister Prem Tinsulanond, declared, 'There will be no new UNHCR camps for Khmer.' This particular occasion was the relocation of 26,000 refugees and the closure of Khao-I-Dang, which at its height housed 140,000 Cambodians. In 'Thai refugee camp, door of hope, will be closed', *The New York Times*, 20 December 1986, Barbara Crossette reported Prasong Soonsiri telling reporters that 665,354 Cambodians, Laotians and Vietnamese had fled to Thailand since the fall of Indochina to communist forces in 1975.
4. It was attended by the four Cambodian factions, all six ASEAN countries, Vietnam, the five permanent members of the UN Security Council, a representative of UN Secretary General

Javier Pérez de Cuéllar, plus Australia, Canada, India and Laos. Zimbabwe attended to represent the Non-Aligned Movement.

5. Gareth Evans, 'Cambodia: The Peace Process – And After', Presentation as chancellor of The Australian National University to Cambodia Roundtable, Monash University, 2 November 2012.

6. MacAlister Brown and Joseph Jermiah Zasloff, *Cambodia Confounds the Peacemakers, 1979–1998*. Ithaca: Cornell University Press, 1998, p. 58.

7. Gareth Evans, ibid. Gareth Evans later said, 'This process was considerably assisted by an extraordinary feat of diplomatically effective endurance by Michael Costello, then the Department of Foreign Affairs and Trade's Deputy Secretary. I had tasked him early in December 1989 to pay a quick visit to Hanoi – in between talks scheduled on other matters in Hawaii and Tokyo – to take preliminary soundings. This initial detour turned into a series of thirty major meetings with key players in thirteen countries over a period of just twenty-one days.'

8. Aix-Marseille University.

9. Reuters, 12 June 1990.

10. 'Chinese president arrives in Bangkok', United Press International, 10 June 1991.

11. Gareth Evans, ibid.

12. Don Oberdorfer, 'Pol Pot reportedly had role in talks', *The Washington Post*, 7 August 1991. Reported by *The Washington Post* special correspondent Mary Kay Magistad.

13. Dominic Faulder, 'Old Cambodian Puzzle', Intelligence, *Asiaweek*, 13 March 1999.

14. Gareth Evans, '*Incorrigible Optimist: A Political Memoir*', Melbourne University Press, 2017, p. 178.

15. Idem, p. 179.

16. Louis de Guiringaud was France's permanent representative at the United Nations from 1972 to 1976, and as such a permanent member of the Security Council. He returned to Paris as foreign minister (1976–1978) under President Raymond Barre. He committed suicide in April 1982 after a nervous breakdown.

17. *Bangkok Post*, 17 January 1991.

18. Emperor Akihito of Japan was among 13 reigning monarchs to attend King Bhumibol Adulyadej's Diamond Jubilee celebrations in Bangkok in June 2006 marking the 60th anniversary of his accession. Representatives of another 12 monarchs also attended.

19. Conversation with the author prior to Anand Panyarachun addressing visiting correspondents during the Annual Meetings of the World Bank and International Monetary Fund in Bangkok, 15–17 October 1991.

20. Other ASEAN collective initiatives failed to gain traction. Just before the first Anand government, the six members signed a US$320-million ASEAN joint venture agreement for potash mining in northeastern Thailand, that was expected to produce a million tons of potash annually. Thailand had a 70 per cent stake, and Indonesia and Malaysia shared most of the rest. Brunei, the Philippines, and Singapore had 1 per cent each. Production was planned for 1996, but the scheme ran into serious headwinds, particularly from the environmental lobby. 'Up to now, it has not been implemented,' says Anand.

21. Dominic Faulder, 'Punching above his weight in ASEAN and beyond', *Nikkei Asian Review*, 23 March 2015.

22. Anand never forgot Lee's courtesy during his visit to Singapore, and personally gives importance to such details – etiquette matters to him. While Anand is never bothered by a breach of protocol by people uninformed in such matters, he can be unforgiving and prickly with people he feels should know better. Many years later, a new British ambassador to Thailand made the mistake of inviting Anand for lunch without first paying him a courtesy call. The invitation went unanswered for some time.

23. Lee Kuan Yew, '*From Third World to First – Singapore and the Asian Economic Boom*', New York: Harper Business, 2000, p. 341.

24. The East Asia Economic Caucus (EAEC) was proposed by Malaysian Prime Minister Dr Mahathir Mohamad in 1990 to offset the influence of Western economies in Asia-Pacific Economic Cooperation (APEC). In 1997, EAEC mutated into ASEAN Plus Three for cooperation between the ASEAN bloc, China, Japan, and South Korea.

25. The original schedule for the AFTA common effective preferential tariff scheme was 15 years dating from 1 January 1993, but this was brought forward five years in 1995, and by another year to 2002 in the aftermath of the 1997 Asian financial crisis. The 15 product categories originally marked for accelerated tariff reduction were vegetable oil, cement, ceramic and glass products, chemicals, copper cathodes, electronics, fertiliser, leather products, pharmaceuticals, plastics, pulp, rubber products, textiles, and wooden and rattan furniture. When ASEAN expanded to include Vietnam (1995), Laos (1997), Myanmar (1997) and Cambodia (1999), the new members were allowed longer grace periods for CEPT compliance. Singapore was the first country in the grouping to achieve it.

CHAPTER 12

1. Founded in 1990, Telecom Asia was consolidated as True Corporation in 2004.

2. Duncan McCargo, *The Thaksinization of Thailand*. Copenhagen: NIAS Press, 2005, p. 28.

3. Brian C. Folk and K.S. Som, *Ethnic Business: Chinese Capitalism in Southeast Asia*. Routledge, 7 March 2013, p. 198.

4. Arterial highways constructed during Nukul Prachuabmoh's stint at the highways department included Bangpa-in–Nakhon Sawan (central plains), Lampang–Chiang Mai (north), Saraburi–Petchaboon (northeast), Bangkok–Sriracha (southeast), and Nakhon Pathom–Pattani (south) – the last named 'a route infested by Chinese bandits'.

5. http://prachatai.com/english/node/6541

6. Nicholas Grossman and Dominic Faulder (eds), *King Bhumibol Adulyadej – A Life's Work*. Singapore: Editions Didier Millet, 2011, p. 295.

7. Phil Robertson was with the Solidarity Center of the American Federation of Labor and Congress of Industrial Organizations (AFL-CIO), a programme manager of the UN Inter-Agency Project on Human Trafficking (UNIAP); in 2009 he became deputy director, Asia Division, of US-based Human Rights Watch.

8. Andrew Brown, 'Locating Working-Class Power', in Kevin Hewison (ed.), *Political Change in Thailand: Democracy and Participation*. London: Routledge, 1997, p. 236.

9. Nicholas Grossman (ed.), *Thailand's Sustainable Business Guide – How to future-proof your business in the name of a better world*. Bangkok: Editions Didier Millet, 2017, pp. 238–41.

10. T. Brown and Werasit Sittitrai, 'Estimates of Recent HIV Infection Levels in Thailand'. Research Report No. 9, Program on AIDS, Thai Red Cross Society, Bangkok, 1993.

11. Scott Bamber, Kevin Hewison, and Peter Underwood, 'Dangerous Liaisons: A History of Sexually Transmitted Diseases

in Thailand', in *Sex, Disease and Society: A Comparative History of Sexually Transmitted Diseases and HIV/AIDS in Asia and the Pacific*. Westport and London: Greenwood Press, Contributions in Medical Studies No. 43, 1997, pp. 37–65.

12. Steve Kraus was the World Health Organisation's technical adviser for HIV/AIDS based in Bangkok at the Ministry of Public Health from 1989 to 1994, and assigned to help the national response to the health crisis.

13. During the failed coup of 9 September 1985 attempted by members of Class 7 against the government of Prime Minister Prem Tinsulanond, two foreign journalists, NBC cameraman Neil Davis and his soundman Bill Latch, were killed by wild firing from rebel tanks. The tanks were attempting to knock out a military radio station loyal to the government that refused to stop broadcasting. Two soldiers and a civilian were also killed that morning, and 62 wounded – 27 seriously. The number of people who may have perished inside the radio station has never been revealed. One Thai reporter who entered the shattered station believed there were eight bodies beneath curtains that had been pulled down from the windows and thrown over them.

14. There were six conventional TV stations in the early 1990s (Channels 3,4 [9 today], 5,7, and 11) and 488 radio stations at the time of the Anand governments. There has been a digital and social media revolution since, and numerous international channels have become available on cable subscription or through the internet. However, in 2016 Thailand's mass media remained restricted. Community radio stations provided alternatives in the provinces, but were mostly silenced after the coup in May 2014. AM and FM radio stations with talk components are generally government-compliant. Among conventional analogue television channels, the military still own Channels 5 and 7. Channel 5 has the most explicit army influence. It is relatively light on entertainment content, but has more than Channel 9. Channel 7 is also owned by the army, but programming is created by BBTV, which is owned by the Ratanarak family. It has the highest viewership, ahead of Channel 3. The government indirectly controls Channels 3 and 9 through the Mass Communication Organization of Thailand (MCOT). Channel 3 is run by BEC Tero and controlled by the Maleenont family. NBT, the old Channel 11, is owned and run by the Public Relations Department. TV Pool meanwhile exists to provide a shared feed to the four analogue channels, and has been used by the National Council for Peace and Order for a 15-minute daily feed after the national anthem at 6pm. New digital channels in recent years include ones belonging to influential newspapers, including *Thai Rath* and *The Nation*, but have generally done badly financially because of the internet and changed viewing habits. More than half Thailand's viewership is still analogue, however.

15. HIV prevalence in Thailand in 2013 was about 1.1 per cent of the population, or about 440,000 people, according to AVERT. It was about 1.3 per cent in 2009. Nearly 600,000 Thais are known to have died from AIDS since 1984, but the figure is probably higher since it is the immediate cause of death that is often recorded, not the underlying HIV.

16. 'Thailand's Response to to HIV/AIDS: Progress and Challenges', United Nations Development Programme, Thematic MDG Report, Bangkok, 2004, p. 16.

17. 'Thailand's Response to to HIV/AIDS: Progress and Challenges', idem, p. 14.

18. Wiwat Rojanapithayakorn, Peter Cox, Robert Bennoun, Chawalit Natpratan, and Usa Duongsaa, 'Governance and HIV. Decentralization: An Aspect of Governance Critical to an Effective Response. A Case Study from Northern Thailand'. New Delhi: United Nations Development Programme, 1997.

19. Idem, p. 14.

20. http://www.unicef.org/media/media_14534.html

CHAPTER 13

1. Snoh Unakul was governor of the Bank of Thailand from 24 May 1975 to 31 October 1979. He took up the position under finance minister Sommai Hoontrakul, who had originally wanted Amnuay Viravan. Amnuay recommended Snoh instead.

2. In order not to burden his family, Snoh Unakul, who is still alive, wrote his own funeral book by hand in 2009 using his left arm. Thai funeral books commemorate the deceased, and can be very sophisticated. They usually contain biographical material and photographs, but can also be used as vehicles for other texts of merit, which gives them an important place in the history of Thai publishing. One of the finest funeral book libraries is at Wat Bowornniwet in Bangkok.

3. In another misadventure, one of Anand's ministers had a fall late in the year and suffered a blow to the head that impaired his performance for some months.

4. Snoh Unakul was honoured by Japan in 2009 with the Grand Cordon of the Order of the Rising Sun.

5. This figure is slightly more than 10 per cent of the nearly 33 million tourists who arrived in Thailand in 2016.

6. Interview with the author, 9 July 1991.

7. Interview with *Siam Rath*, September 1991.

8. Steven Erlanger, 'A Fast Fire, and a Thai Slum's Slow Poisoning', *The New York Times*, 21 March 1991.

9. Law Changes Project Steering Committee: David Lyman of Tilleke & Gibbins; Albert T. Chandler of Chandler & Thong-ek Law Offices; Leonard Chinitz of International Legal Counsellors Thailand; John W. Hancock of Baker & McKenzie; Simon Makinson of Denton Hall Burgin & Warrens; Harold K. Vickery of Vickery, Prapone, Pramuan & Worachai.

10. Chambers of commerce participating in the Law Changes Project: American, Australian, British, Canadian, German, French, Indian, Japanese, and Swedish.

CHAPTER 14

1. 'A Night To Remember – Launching *The King of Thailand in World Focus*', Foreign Correspondents' Club of Thailand, The Oriental, 23 August 2007.

2. 'The year of Anand: an empty political legacy', *The Nation*, 15 March 1992.

3. Federico Ferrara, *The Political Development of Modern Thailand*. Cambridge: Cambridge University Press, 2015, p. 208.

4. 'Election Observation Mission: Kingdom of Thailand', International Foundation for Electoral Systems (IFES) report, 31 January 1997.

5. Samak Sundaravej, who served as prime minister from January to September 2008, was also removed by court order for receiving payment for a popular TV cooking show he hosted. In what many described as a second judicial coup, his successor Somchai Wongsawat, who lasted only until December, was also ruled out of office by a court order. Both politicians belonged to the People's Power Party of Thaksin Shinawatra. Somchai's

wife, Yaowapha, is another of Thaksin's sisters.

6. David Murray, *Angels and Devils, Thai Politics from February 1991 to September 1992 – A Struggle for Democracy?* Bangkok: Orchid Press, 2000, p. 123.

7. 'Spotlight', *Bangkok Post*, 21 November 2015, p. 11.

8. David Murray, ibid.

9. Thai cabinets were contained to within 30 members until Field Marshal Plaek Phibunsongkhram's last in 1957. The number rose to 44 with Kriangsak Chomanand's second cabinet in 1979; Chatichai Choonhavan's first in 1988 had 45. This was not simply down to added ministries. Indeed, both of Thaksin Shinawatra's in the 21st century were modest at around 35. Suchinda's abnormally large cabinet contained five deputy prime ministers, eight ministers attached to the prime minister's office, and large numbers of deputy ministers, particularly in the ministries of agriculture, commerce, education, interior, and transport and communications.

10. The FCCT letter to Prime Minister Suchinda Kraprayoon was written by the author, who as past president of the club continued to chair its professional committee.

11. David Lomax interview, 'Soul of a Nation', BBC, London, 1979. Transcribed in *The King of Thailand in World Focus* (3rd ed.). Bangkok: Foreign Correspondents' Club of Thailand, 2008, pp. 162–4.

12. William Branigin, 'Thai King Tells Rivals to Settle Crisis', *The Washington Post*, 21 May 1992.

13. Philip Shenon, 'Thailand Premier Quits Over Unrest', *The New York Times*, 25 May 1992.

14. Ibid.

15. On some previous occasions when King Bhumibol appointed unelected prime ministers, the wording was also varied and nuanced: 15 October 1973: 'King Rama IX previously ordered Field Marshal Thanom Kittikachorn to be prime minister of Thailand on 18 December 1972. As Field Marshal Thanom left the post on October 14, 1973, the king considered Sanya Dharmasakti could be trusted to be appointed the next prime minister.' 28 May 1974: 'As Sanya Dhammasakdi left the post on May 22, 1973, the president of the National Legislative Assembly informed the king that he had received votes from the assembly's members. The assembly still trusts Sanya Dhammasakdi, and would like him to continue as prime minister … Therefore, the king thought that Sanya deserved to continue in the position.' 10 October 1976: 'The head of the National Administrative Reform Council informed the king that at this time Thailand should have a civilian government to administer the country. He said that Tanin Kraivixien deserved the position of prime minister and to set up a cabinet. The king thought that the country should have a civilian government and that Tanin Kraivixien should be prime minister.'

16. A *kraab* involves full prostration before the king.

17. Cesar R. Bacani Jr, 'Biographical Profile of Anand Panyarachun', in *The Ramon Magsaysay Awards, Vol XIII*. Manila: Ramon Magsaysay Award Foundation, 2005, p. 17.

18. Michael Richardson, 'Lingering Issue: Military Influence', *The New York Times*, 22 May 1992.

CHAPTER 15

1. The 1953 classic Hollywood Western *Shane*, set in Wyoming, starred Alan Ladd as Shane with Jack Palance as the sadistic gunslinger Jack Wilson. In the famous closing scene, a wounded but resolute Shane rides off into the darkness with young Joey Starrett, played by Brandon DeWilde, calling after his hero: 'Shane! … Shane! Come back!' Film critic Elizabeth Abele writes: 'His longing cry for Shane at the movie's conclusion becomes the audience's longing for a pure man, a once-and-future hero who may reappear when we need him most.' 'A Night To Remember', in *The King of Thailand In World Focus* (3rd ed.). Bangkok: Foreign Correspondents' Club of Thailand, 2008, p. 275.

2. 'Freedoms to be stressed in policy speech', *Bangkok Post*, 16 June 1992.

3. Thailand's Council of State was originally created in 1874 by King Chulalongkorn, and provides legal counsel to the government. It vets draft legislation for technical details more than substance. Prime ministers appoint the council's secretary general, who while technically a civil servant is also therefore a political appointee. Meechai Ruchupan held this position quite early in his career, and has provided legal counsel to prime ministers since 1973; he has been involved to varying degrees in drafting all of Thailand's new constitutions since 1974, apart from the one in 1997. Meechai has always been a strong defender of the law of lèse-majesté.

4. 'Freedoms to be stressed in policy speech', *Bangkok Post*, 16 June 1992.

5. 'House dissolution move', *Bangkok Post*, 19 June 1992.

6. 'Kasem adds weight to setting up of assembly', *Bangkok Post*, 20 June 1992.

7. 'Assembly hailed – and condemned', *Bangkok Post*, 19 June 1992.

8. Ammar Siamwalla was also grateful to the Anand government for establishing the Thai Research Fund. Although TDRI did not get much benefit initially, in the 21st century it would receive funding for bigger projects with broader concepts that were less agency-based.

9. Flying Douglas DC-6s, Convairs and later Caravelles, Thai International was set up in 1960 as a joint venture with Scandinavian Airlines System (SAS). Chatrachai Bunya-Ananta came across from the UK's BOAC two years later. Thai International absorbed domestic carrier Thai Airways in the 1980s, after a number of crashes in the South. 'The Scandinavians were the best partners because they themselves were partners from three countries,' said Chatrachai in one of his final interviews in 2014. In 1977, the Scandinavians were asked to 'let Thai be Thai' and relinquish the last of their equity at par. 'I offered to take over SAS at that time, but they laughed,' said Chatrachai. Marketing and technical co-operation between the two airlines continued, however, and Chatrachai maintained a particularly close working relationship with Niels Lumholdt, one of the 'Vikings' who stayed on and made Thailand his home. See Chatrachai Bunya-Ananta obituary, *The Nation*, 20 April 2015.

10. Chatrachai Bunya-Ananta was the most visible personality in an exceptionally strong team that included Danish aviation guru Niels Lumholdt; Thamnoon Wanglee in charge of finance; Captain Yothin Pamon-Montri, flight operations; Captain Udom Krisnampok, ground operations; Captain Chusak Bhachaiyud, vice president for technical services; and Chitdee Rangavara, public relations. As the management face of Thai International, Chatrachai instituted the Marketing Activity Plan (MAP) as an annual event in 1972, drawing in the airline's representatives from all over its widening route net. The gatherings promoted different parts of Thailand and were

thrown open to the press. On Chatrachai's watch, the airline engaged and financed numerous national tourism promotions in partnership with the Tourism Authority of Thailand and other industry bodies.

11. The civilianisation of Thai Airways International's uppermost reaches lasted for over 20 years, until Air Chief Marshal Prajin Juntong was appointed its chairman on 10 March 2014 during the caretaker government of Prime Minister Yingluck Shinawatra, who was removed from office on 7 May after the Constitutional Court ruled her guilty of abuse of power. Prajin became a minister in the military government that seized power on 20 May.

12. In July 1992, a Thai Airways Airbus 310 crashed while trying to land at Kathmandu's Tribhuvan International Airport. The aircraft had experienced a transient technical problem and communication between an inexperienced air traffic controller and the flight deck was poor. It was the airline's worst international accident, killing 99 passengers and 14 crew. Two months earlier, a Pakistan International Airways flight had crashed nearby with 167 dead.

13. Philip Shenon, 'Bangkok Journal; A Tall Order: To March the Soldier Out of Politics', *The New York Times*, 10 July 1992.

14. Ibid.

15. Among other investigations, the Foreign Correspondents' Club of Thailand's professional committee looked into the damage sustained by local and foreign media.

16. Newsmakers, 'You Wonder What He Knows', *Asiaweek*, Hong Kong, Vol. 29, No. 25, 30 June 2000.

17. Praman Chansue remained influential until his retirement as president of the Supreme Court in 2003. He died in early 2007, and was given a royally sponsored cremation at Wat Thepsirin on 3 June.

18. Federico Ferrara, *The Political Development of Modern Thailand*. Cambridge: Cambridge University Press, 2015, p. 213.

19. 'B5.9b withdrawn from banks in week', *Bangkok Post*, 12 September 1992.

20. 'The military's political decline continued through the mid-1990s. When half the Senate came up for renewal in 1995, many military men were replaced by civilians. Generals disappeared from most boardrooms. The military's share of the government budget declined from 22 per cent in 1985 to 13 per cent in 1996, and 6 per cent in 2006. Unofficial income sources were cut because arms-buying, construction, and other military projects came under close public scrutiny … Some 700 generals (almost half the total) had no substantive job. Many played a lot of golf, and some exercised their leadership skills by heading national sports associations.' Chris Baker and Pasuk Phongpaichit, *A History of Thailand* (2nd ed.), Cambridge: Cambridge University Press, 2009, p. 249.

21. David Murray, *Angels and Devils: Thai Politics from February 1991 to September 1992 – A Struggle for Democracy?* Bangkok: Orchid Press, 2000, pp. 236–7.

CHAPTER 16

1. Pranee Srithongnoy, 'Former Thai prime minister charged with official misconduct', United Press International, 21 April 1993.

2. Banharn Silpa-archa's final election in 2007 under the Chart Thai Pattana banner was by the widest margin of any politician. His Chart Thai Pattana Party was banned after the 2006 coup.

3. Grant Peck, 'Banharn Silpa-archa, former Thai prime minister, dead at 83', Associated Press, 23 April 2016.

CHAPTER 17

1. http://www.kenan-asia.org/en

2. Ekamol Kiriwat later received high praise: 'In a town where corruption is taken for granted, the 25-year Bank of Thailand veteran had a spotless reputation, and his bold defiance of political interference helped establish the SEC's fairness and independence,' US banking magazine *Institutional Investor* noted (February 1996, p. 15).

3. Written answer to questions from *Institutional Investor*, 10 July 1991.

4. Vijit Supinit was governor of the Bank of Thailand from 13 July 1996 to 28 July 1997. His successor, Rerngchai Marakanond, served from 13 July 1996 to 28 July 1997.

5. 'Thailand: Was It a Firesale?' *Asia Times*, 19 November 1999.

6. Shahendra Sharma, *The Asian Financial Crisis: New International Financial Architecture: Crisis, Reform and Recovery*. Manchester University Press, 2003, p. 91.

7. Timothy Geithner completed high school in the 1970s at the International School Bangkok (ISB). His father, Peter, was assigned to Thailand at the time within the United States Agency for International Development (USAID).

8. http://www.kenan-asia.org/en

9. Ibid.

10. *Bloomberg*, 29 June 1998.

11. *The Nation*, 17 September 2012.

12. Julian Gearing, 'Swapping assets for confidence – Thailand prepares a blockbuster auction', *Asiaweek*, 18 December 1998.

13. 'Thailand's asset sale', *The Economist*, 17 December 1998.

14. In the fallout from 1997, the CPB acquired the Kempinski luxury hotel chain, which by mid-2017 ran 73 properties in 31 countries. Kempinski was originally bought (52 per cent) in 1994 by Dusit Sindhorn, which had CPB as a shareholder and was bought by the Dusit Thani Group in equal partnership with SCB in 1996 ahead of the financial crash. In 1998, Dusit sold out to SCB entirely, which at the time was about 25 per cent owned by the CPB. CPB then appears to have acquired it from SCB, and held the equity until February 2017 when the majority stake was sold to the minority shareholder, the Bahraini royal family, for an undisclosed sum rumoured to be about US$1 billion. The deal received little publicity but was reported at the time in Germany's *Die Welt*. The CPB previously owned 83 per cent, and it is not known exactly how much it retains.

15. The most infamous of these, the so-called Ghost Tower overlooking the Chao Phraya river, is covered with black mould and graffiti. The reasons for the project's failure are more complicated than just the 1997 crash, however. It was a development by architect Professor Rangsan Torsuwan, an assistant professor at Chulalongkorn University, who had designed the very similar State Tower at the bottom of Silom Road, which is featured in the film *The Hangover Part II*. Before that, Rangsan also designed the Grand Hyatt Erawan. Both are fine examples of the Bangkok school of wedding cake architecture. Rangsan's failed 1990 condominium project, the 600-unit Sathorn Unique, ran into funding problems and finally foundered in the 1997 crisis. It remains unfinished to this day, unlike 95 per cent of leftover projects from the time.

16. Former Prime Minister Yingluck Shinawatra was in 2017 sent a multi-billion-baht court-ordered bill for her alleged failure to prevent a corrupt rice subsidy scheme.

17. Thanong Khanthong, 'Bear Chews Up Takeover King', *The Nation*, 1 March 1997.

18. Pin Chakkapak returned quietly to Bangkok in August 2012 after defeating extradition proceedings in London in 2001 and reaching the 15-year statute of limitations on his cases. '"Takeover king" Pin Ends Exile, back in Bangkok', *The Nation*, 20 August 2012.

19. Julian Gearing, 'From One to Zero – The Story of Pin Chakkapak and FinOne', *Asiaweek*, 23 June 2000.

CHAPTER 18

1. General Electric's business in contemporary Thailand is very significant, with a presence in the aviation, energy, healthcare, petrochemical, power, and water supply sectors. The US conglomerate also took a strategic shareholding in Bank of Ayudhya (Krungsri), Thailand's fifth-largest bank by assets, which in 2013 became a subsidiary of Japan's Bank of Tokyo-Mitsubishi UFJ (BTMU), the core banking unit of Mitsubishi UFJ Financial Group.

2. David Rubenstein was already a noted and well-connected philanthropist by the late 1990s. In 2010, he joined Bill Gates and Warren Buffett among 40 billionaires who pledged to give half their wealth to charity.

3. 'The Carlyle Group – C for Capitalism', *The Economist*, 26 June 2003.

4. Thanong Khanthong, 'Anand outlines ties to group of giants', *The Nation*, 7 March 2001.

5. 'Not Enough Graves: The War on Drugs, HIV/AIDS, and Violations of Human Rights', *Human Rights Watch*, New York, Vol. 16, No. 8 (C), June 2004, p. 11.

CHAPTER 19

1. Members of UN Secretary General's High-Level Panel on Threats, Challenges and Change: Anand Panyarachun (chairman), former prime minister, Thailand; Robert Badinter, former justice minister, France; João Clemente Baena Soares, former secretary general of the Organization of American States, Brazil; Gro Harlem Brundtland, former prime minister, Norway; Mary Chinery-Hesse, former deputy director general of the International Labour Organization, Ghana; Gareth Evans, president of the International Crisis Group and former foreign minister, Australia; David Hannay, former permanent representative to the United Nations, United Kingdom; Enrique Iglesias, president of the Inter-American Development Bank, Uruguay; Amre Moussa, secretary general of the League of Arab States, Egypt; Satish Nambiar, former Lt General and UNPROFOR force commander, India; Sadako Ogata, former UN high commissioner for refugees, Japan; Yevgeny Primakov, former prime minister of the Russian Federation, Russia; Qian Qichen, former vice prime minister and foreign minister, China; Nafis Sadik, former executive director of the UN Population Fund, Pakistan; Salim Ahmed Salim, former secretary general of the Organization of African Unity, United Republic of Tanzania; Brent Scowcroft, former national security adviser, United States.

2. David Hannay, *New World Disorder, The UN After the Cold War: An Insider's View*. London: I.B. Tauris, 2008, p. 215.

3. Cameron Stewart, 'The KGB spy who came in from the heat', *The Australian*, 8 November 2014.

4. Michael Cook's daughter, Genevieve, was Barack Obama's girlfriend in New York from 1984 to 1985. See David Maraniss,

'Becoming Obama', *Vanity Fair*, 2 May 2012.

5. The six three-day plenary sessions were held at Princeton, New Jersey, US, 5–7 December 2003; Mont Pèlerin, Lake Geneva, Switzerland, 13–15 February 2004; Addis Ababa, Ethiopia, 30 April–2 May 2004; Baden, Austria, 16–18 July 2004; Tarrytown, New York, US, 24–26 September 2004; Ground Zero, Lower Manhattan, New York, US, 3–5 November 2004.

6. David Hannay, idem, p. 212.

7. Email correspondence with the author, November 2017.

8. Eight UN Millennium Development Goals: 1. Eradicate extreme poverty and hunger. 2. Achieve universal primary education. 3. Promote gender equality and empower women. 4. Reduce child mortality. 5. Improve maternal health. 6. Combat HIV/AIDS, malaria, and other diseases. 7. Ensure environmental sustainability. 8. Develop a global partnership for development.

9. Global Peace Index 2017, IEP Report 48, Institute for Economics and Peace, Sydney, June 2017.

10. Kofi Annan, 'A way forward on global security', *International Herald Tribune*, 3 December 2004.

11. Human Rights Watch, 'Thailand: Investigate Krue Se Mosque Raid – No Justice Two Years After Deadly Clashes in the South', New York, 28 April 2006.

12. Ibid.

13. Ibid.

14. Duncan McCargo, 'Mapping National Anxieties – Thailand's Southern Conflict'. Nordic Institute of Asian Studies (NIAS), Copenhagen, 2012, pp. 3–4.

15. Dominic Faulder, 'From ballots to bombings, it's been a long week for Thailand', *Nikkei Asian Review*, 18 August 2016.

16. Duncan McCargo, 'Network monarchy and legitimacy crises in Thailand', *The Pacific Review*, Vol. 18, No. 4, December 2005, p. 499.

17. Sopon Ongara, 'Thaksin the Loser in Televised Head-to-head', *The Nation*, 31 July 2005.

18. BenarNews, 'Thailand: Wife of Missing Lawyer Calls for New Investigation', 12 March 2015.

19. 'Opinion', *Bangkok Post*, 28 November 2017.

20. Suthichai Yoon, 'Reform: Separating political rhetoric from substance', *The Nation*, Bangkok, 23 December 2013.

CHAPTER 20

1. Sir Anthony Rumbold, 'Goodbye to Thailand', a confidential cable to George Brown, the secretary of state for foreign affairs in London, at the time of Rumbold's departure from Bangkok, 18 July 1967, after a two-year posting. Rumbold was best man at the wedding of Donald Maclean, a member of the Cambridge Five spy ring. The group included diplomats Guy Burgess and Kim Philby. Maclean attended Trinity Hall and Burgess Trinity College, where he belonged to the Cambridge Apostles, a secretive and elitist discussion group with only twelve members. Anthony Blunt was the oldest known member of the group, and a fellow of Trinity College. A distinguished art historian, he was knighted in the 1950s and counselled King George VI and Queen Elizabeth I as keeper of the royal art collection. When Blunt was finally exposed as the fourth man in 1979, he was stripped of his honours. There have been a number of candidates for the fifth man including Rumbold, but an MI5 investigation produced nothing actionable against him. Rumbold attended Magdelen

College, Oxford, not Cambridge. Some believe the spy ring was actually larger.

2. 'British envoy puts record straight on Thai image', *The Nation*, Bangkok, 20 October 2009; 'British envoy defends Thailand from predecessor's "sex and culture" attack', *The Daily Telegraph*, London, 21 October 2009.

3. 'Dulwich divorce is final', *Phuket Gazette*, 13 May 2005.

4. Jan Piggott, *Dulwich College: A History 1616–2008*. London: Dulwich College Enterprises, 2008, p. 329.

5. William Stevenson, *The Revolutionary King – The True-Life Sequel to The King and I*. London: Constable, 1999, p. 4.

6. King Taksin was certainly not a Rama, but neither were the first five Chakri kings in their day. The practice of titling the Siamese kings as Ramas was devised in the early 20th century by King Vajiravudh – the sixth Chakri king who thenceforth also became known as Rama VI. One reason for the simplified system was to help non-Thais, who often have great difficulty with names and titles – as Stevenson amply demonstrated.

7. Dominic Faulder, 'Cashing In – A New Book on the Royals Is Unessential Reading', *Asiaweek*, 3 December 1999.

8. Thomas Crampton, 'Bangkok May Ban King's Biography', *International Herald Tribune*, Paris, 27 August 1999.

9. William Stevenson, *Past to Present – A Reporter's Story of War, Spies, People, and Politics*. Guilford, Connecticut: Lyons Press, 2012, p. 217.

10. The eight sponsors for the second edition of *The King of Thailand in World Focus* were Sarcar Geneve, Thai Beverage, Kasikornbank, Exxon Mobil, Siam Commercial Bank, Siam Cement Group, Pfizer, and Toyota.

11. 'Military court struggles with Sulak lèse-majesté case', *Bangkok Post*, 8 December 2017.

12. *King Bhumibol Adulyadej – A Life's Work* editorial advisory board: Chaired by Anand Panyarachun, it included Thanphuying Putrie Viravaidya, the king's deputy principal private secretary; Sumet Tantivejkul, secretary general to the Chaipattana Foundation; Pramote Maiklad, a former director general of the Royal Irrigation Department; Pisoot Vijarnsorn, a specialist in land development; Dhiravat na Pombejra, a retired historian from Chulalongkorn University; Duangtip Surintatip, president of the Thai Association of Conference Interpreters; Sondhi Tejanant, a former governor of Songkhla province in the south with an interest in contemporary political history; Wissanu Krea-ngam, Anand's former cabinet secretary and a former deputy prime minister; Theerakun Niyom, permanent secretary at the foreign ministry. Theerakun was represented at all editorial meetings by Thani Thongphadki, the ministry's director general of information. Parames Krairiksh of the Crown Property Bureau also attended.

13. *King Bhumibol Adulyadej – A Life's Work* editorial contributors: Nicholas Grossman, editor in chief; Dominic Faulder, senior editor; Julian Gearing, former bureau chief in Bangkok for *Asiaweek*; Paul Wedel, bureau chief for United Press International before becoming director of the Kenan Institute; Robert Horn, a contributor to *Time* magazine; Richard Ehrlich, correspondent for *The Washington Times*; Robert Woodrow, retired deputy editor of *Asiaweek*; and Joe Cummings, original author of the *Lonely Planet* guide to Thailand. Simon Wallace, a dentist and Thai consul in Australia, also contributed material from a book project on King Bhumibol and his music that had fizzled out. Deputy editor Grissarin Chungsiriwat handled research, picture editing, and fact checking.

CHAPTER 21

1. Dominic Faulder, 'Thailand's constitution illusion', *Nikkei Asian Review*, 5 May 2016.

2. Ecuador and India are still ahead of Thailand with around 400 articles each. The U.S. has the shortest, with just seven originally. Drafted in 1787, it is also the oldest.

3. Patpon Sabpaitoon and Aekarach Sattaburuth, 'Seksan blasts divisive politics', *Bangkok Post*, 10 March 2018.

4. Keynote addresses to the Bank of Thailand Annual Seminar, 17 September 2015, and the Foreign Correspondents' Club of Thailand, 23 March 2016.

5. The Ramon Magsaysay Award Foundation, Manila, 2005.

6. Wikileaks 06BANGKOK5832, 'Former Premier Anand: Coup forestalled violence', US Embassy Bangkok, 21 September 2006.

7. Wikileaks 08BANGKOK2619, 'Thailand: Senior Statesmen Seeking The King's Approval To Push Aside Pm Samak', US Embassy Bangkok, 3 September 2008.

8. Benjamin Zawacki, *Thailand: Shifting ground between the US and a rising China*. London: Zed Books, 2017, pp. 202–3.

9. Duncan McCargo, 'Network monarchy and legitimacy crises in Thailand', *The Pacific Review*, Vol. 18, No. 4, December 2005, p. 500.

10. Idem, p. 506.

11. Idem, p. 508.

12. Idem, p. 507.

13. Idem, p. 517.

14. Idem, p. 502.

15. Anand Panyarachun, 'Democratic governance: striving for Thailand's new normal', Keynote address to the Foreign Correspondents' Club of Thailand, 23 March 2016.

16. This is the popular short form of a quote with many versions. A longer one reads: 'God, give me grace to accept with serenity the things that cannot be changed; courage to change the things which should be changed; and the wisdom to distinguish the one from the other.'

17. Section 65 of Thailand's 1997 constitution: 'A person shall have the right to resist peacefully any act committed for the acquisition of the power to rule the country by a means which is not in accordance with the modes provided in this Constitution.' This was retained as Section 69 in the 2007 constitution, but was dropped from its replacement in 2017.

THE PANYARACHUN FAMILY TREE

Originally spelled Panyarjun, Anand's family name was bestowed on 7 July 1911 by King Vajiravudh (r.1910-1925). *Panya* is a reference to wisdom; Arjun was a heroic king from the *Mahabharata*, a Sanskrit epic that recounts the history of the ancient Bharata dynasty. Running to nearly two million words, the *Mahabharata* is much longer than another great Hindu epic, the *Ramayana*, which is known in its Thai version as the *Ramakien*. The name Panyarjun is arguably better suited than most to a leader, diplomat, or mediator. Arjun's banner depicted a monkey, and he believed fighting among kinsfolk to be morally wrong. The family seal depicts a chariot bearing Arjun and Krishna, an incarnation of Vishnu, the Hindu god. The name Panyarjun was changed to its phonetically more correct modern version by Rak Panyarachun in 1956 when he was Thailand's deputy foreign minister.

Phya Prichanusat
(Sern Panyarachun) (1890-1974)

Khunying Prichanusat
(Pruek Jotikasthira) (1889-1987)

Rak Panyarachun (1914-2007)

Jeerawat Panyarachun
(née Pibulsonggram) (1921-2017)

Suthira Kasemsri Na Ayudhaya
(née Panyarachun) (1915-2009)

MR Rambibandh Kasemsri (1904-1969)

Pritha Vajrabhaya
(née Panyarachun) (1916-2006)

Krasae Vajrabhaya (1906-1947)

Koonti Bijayendrayodhin
(née Panyarachun) (1917-2012)

Krierk-Ith Bijayendrayodhin (1910-1994)

Supanee Bencharit (divorced) (1926-)

Kusa Panyarachun (1918-)

Naruvorn Panyarachun (née Taweesin)
(1941-)

Mom Chitra Varavarn Na Ayudhaya
(née Panyarachun) (1919-2008)

MC Vodhayakara Varavarn (1900-1981)

Dusadee Osathanondh
(née Panyarachun) (1920-)

Jajaval Osathanondh (1909-1999)

Prasat Panyarachun
(1923-2018)

Suksi Panyarachun (née Santawa) (1929-)

Kanthana Isarasena Na Ayudhya
(née Panyarachun) (1924-)

Ayus Isarasena Na Ayudhya (1919-1997)

Supapan Jumbala Na Ayudhya
(née Panyarachun) (1927-)

MR Bajarisan Jumbala (1928-2016)

Chat Panyarachun (1928-)

Mullika Panyarachun
(née Snidvongs Na Ayudhya) (1933-1963)

Anand Panyarachun (1932-)

MR Sodsee Panyarachun
(née Chakrabandh) (1936-)

ML Suratee Israsena
Bajr Isarasena Na Ayudhya (1933-2012)

ML Birabhongse Kasemsri (1935-2000)
MR Rampiapha Kasemsri

Charatsri Vajrabhaya

Viravudhi Vajrabhaya (1940-2017) (divorced)
Srichanok Wattanasiri

Sutdya Vajrabhaya (1944-2017)

Nantha Prempridi (1935-2012)
Thomrong Prempridi

Aporn Poompanna (divorced)
Sahas Bukhamana

Samrith Bijayendrayodhin (1937-1938)

Pachree Bijayendrayodhin
Pinai Sukhawarn (1935-2015)

Pannee Karunpak
Suporn Karunpak

Itthi Bijayendrayodhin
Thavida Bijayendrayodhin

Krid Panyarachun (divorced)
Supawan Lamsam

Krai Panyarachun
Rassamee Panyarachun

Vie Panyarachun
Candy Panyarachun

MR Chanvudhi Varavarn
Kasama Varavarn Na Ayudhaya

Rapin Osathanondh
Suellen O' Neill

Tipsuda Suwanraks (1944-1971)
Chinda Suwanraks

Warittha Chang (1952-2016)
Henry Chang

Kritkasem Panyarachun
Jaruporn Panyarachun

Chutima Isarasena Na Ayudhya (divorced)
Thirawit Leetavorn

Thippa Praneeprachachon (divorced)
ML Supat Jumbala
Samapasse Jumbala Na Ayudhya

ML Patreesa Ma
Eric Ma

Vivan Sarakitprija
Wirapich Sarakitprija

Pimpa Bencharit
Adit Bencharit

Janejit Panyarachun

Nanda Krairiksh
Kraithip Krairiksh

Daranee Charoen-Rajapark
Chatchawin Charoen-Rajapark

Saravudh Israsena Na Ayudhya
Vasinee Israsena Na Ayudhya

Achara Sangruji
Norachet Sangruji

Vanasobhin Kasemsri Na Ayudhya
Joel Martin Farnworth

Thivakorn Kasemsri Na Ayudhya
Elizabeth Kasemsri Na Ayudhya

Birathon Kasemsri Na Ayudhya
Kazuko Kasemsri Na Ayudhya

Praire Vajrabhaya
Prao Vajrabhaya

Saangjit Prempridi

Pithan Prempridi
Chonticha Khumwang

Thinawat Bukhamana
Jariya Bukhamana

Pornsiri Bukhamana

Norasi Bukhamana
Suphatra Bukhamana

Orapin Sukhawarn (1971-1977)

Korapin Karunpak

Karn Karunpak
Nasaraporn Karunpak

Anak Bijayendrayodhin
Mitsara Bijayendrayodhin

Supaprat Panyarachun
Tanika Panyarachun

Sakthip Panyarachun

Akra Panyarachun

ML Varudh Varavarn
Nisakorn Varavarn Na Ayudhya

Ryratana Rangsitpol
Nattapol Rangsitpol

Christopher Natawon Chang

Jonathan Kasadit Chang

Anthony Chayan Chang

Thanakrit Panyarachun

Kritikorn Panyarachun

Kris Leetavorn
Pannisa Leetavorn

Tanya Jumbala Na Ayudhya

Gavin Ma

Warren Ma

Vipa Sarakitprija
Jeremy Ross

Voramon Sarakitprija
Thanaphol Sutthibut

Pim Bencharit

Tipanan Srifuengfung
Thawin Srifuengfung

Sirinda Charoen-Rajapark
Tanawin Charoen-Rajapark

Patcharaporn Israsena Na Ayudhya

Isr Israsena Na Ayudhya

Naruj Sangruji

Bhrus Sangruji

Pana Farnworth

Sobha Farnworth

Sulissa Kasemsri Na Ayudhya

Vudhavadhi Kasemsri Na Ayudhya

Dhirapa Kasemsri Na Ayudhya

Ponrapi Kasemsri Na Ayudhya

Phaka Bukhamana

Noraphat Bukhamana

Phuri Karunpak

Anissara Bijayendrayodhin

Napakorn Varavarn Na Ayudhaya

Krydda Varavarn Na Ayudhaya

Veerin Varavarn Na Ayudhaya

Parin Leetavorn

Aaron Jade Ross

Thanat Sutthibut

Thanakrit Sutthibut

Wyn Srifuengfung

TEXT OF RUSK-THANAT COMMUNIQUÉ

U.S. Department of State Press Release 145; dated 6 March 1962

The Foreign Minister of Thailand, Thanat Khoman, and the Secretary of State, Dean Rusk, met on several occasions during the past few days for discussions on the current situation in Southeast Asia, the Southeast Asia Collective Defense Treaty and the Security of Thailand.

The Secretary of State reaffirmed that the United States regards the preservation of the independence and integrity of Thailand as vital to the national interest of the United States and to world peace. He expressed the firm intention of the United States to aid Thailand, its ally and historic friend, in resisting Communist aggression and subversion.

The Foreign Minister and Secretary of State reviewed the close association of Thailand and the United States in the Southeast Asia Collective Defense Treaty and agreed that such association is an effective deterrent to direct Communist aggression against Thailand. They agreed that the Treaty provides the basis for the signatories collectively to assist Thailand in case of Communist armed attack against that country. The Secretary of State assured the Foreign Minister that in the event of such aggression, the United States intends to give full effect to its obligations under the Treaty to act to meet the common danger in accordance with its constitutional processes. The Secretary of State reaffirmed that this obligation of the United States does not depend upon the prior agreement of all other parties to the Treaty, since this Treaty obligation is individual as well as collective.

In reviewing measures to meet indirect aggression, the Secretary of State stated that the United States regards its commitments to Thailand under the Southeast Asia Collective Defense Treaty and under its bilateral economic and military assistance agreements with Thailand as providing an important basis for United States actions to help Thailand meet indirect aggression. In this connection the Secretary reviewed with the Foreign Minister the actions being taken by the United States to assist the Republic of Vietnam to meet the threat of indirect aggression.

The Foreign Minister assured the Secretary of State of the determination of the Government of Thailand to meet the threat of indirect aggression by pursuing vigorously measures for the economic and social welfare and the safety of its people.

The situation in Laos was reviewed in detail and full agreement was reached on the necessity for the stability of Southeast Asia, of achieving a free, independent and truly neutral Laos.

The Foreign Minister and the Secretary of State reviewed the mutual efforts of their governments to increase the capabilities and readiness of the Thai armed forces to defend the Kingdom. They noted also that the United States is making a significant contribution to this effort and that the United States intends to accelerate future deliveries to the greatest extent possible. The Secretary and the Foreign Minister also took note of the work of the Joint Thai-United States Committee which has been established in Bangkok to assure effective cooperation in social, economic, and military measures to increase Thailand's national capabilities. They agreed that this Joint Committee and its subcommittees should continue to work toward the most effective utilisation of Thailand's resources and those provided by the United States to promote Thailand's development and security.

The Foreign Minister and the Secretary were in full agreement that continued economic and social progress is essential to the stability of Thailand. They reviewed Thailand's impressive economic and social progress and the Thai Government's plans to accelerate development, particularly Thailand's continuing determination fully to utilise its own resources in moving toward its development goals.

The Foreign Minister and the Secretary of State also discussed the desirability of an early conclusion of a treaty of friendship, commerce and navigation between the two countries which would bring into accord with current conditions the existing treaty of 1937.

Source: Department of State Bulletin, 'The Realities of Foreign Policy', remarks by Secretary Rusk, Vol. XLVI, No. ll87 (6 March 1962), pp.498–9.

RAMASUN AGREEMENT

SECRET . . . SECRET . . . SECRET . . . SECRET . . .

Agreement Respecting the Establishment, Conduct and Support of Radio Communications Research and Development Activities in Thailand.

The Government of the United States of America and the Government of Thailand: Desiring to take those actions which will further their capability to provide an adequate defense against Communist insurgency and aggression in Thailand:

Have agreed as follows:

ARTICLE I

1. Each Government, pursuant to the Agreement respecting military assistance signed at Bangkok on 24th June 1964, will make available to the other, such equipment, training, and authorization as is mutually deemed necessary for the success of the respective Radio Communications Research and Development missions.

2. The Government of the United States of America undertakes to provide equipment requested in the Armed Forces Security Center letter of 7 August 1964. Such equipment will be delivered by the Armed Forces Security Center in two shipments, the initial by 1 December 1965 and the final by 1 June 1966. In addition the Government of the United States of America undertakes to provide normal material support to four Signal Research Companies as may be from time to time mutually agreed by the two Governments. If desired, training and advisory assistance will be provided by a team not to exceed two officers and ten enlisted men. Such training and advice to include search, intercept, direction finding, translation, recording and reporting of enemy plain text voice communications.

3. The Government of Thailand undertakes to authorize the conduct by the Government of the United States of America of a Radio Communications Research and Development effort in Thailand with a personnel ceiling not to exceed one thousand except as may be specifically authorized by the Government of Thailand. In addition, the Government of Thailand agrees to make available for unrestricted use by the Government of the United States land near Udorn, not to exceed five hundred acres, as may be required for this purpose. It is understood that title to this land will remain with the Thai Government and it will remain available to unrestricted United States Government use as long as the United States requires it. The Government of the United States shall provide funds for the acquisition of privately owned land by the Thai Government as required by the United States.

ARTICLE II

1. Additional arrangements necessitated by this agreement will be in consonance with the agreements signed on October 17, 1950 and June 24, 1964. Commitments of these agreements remain in force and apply to this agreement.

2. The provisions of this agreement are effective upon signature.

IN WITNESS WHEREOF, the respective representatives, duly authorized for this purpose, have signed the present agreement.

DONE in duplicate at Bangkok on this 19th day of January of the 2508 year of the Buddhist Era.

For the Government of the United States of America	For the Government of Thailand
/s/ *Graham Martin*	/s/ *Dawee Chullasapya*
Ambassador of the United States of America	Deputy Minister of Defense

---

SECRET . . . SECRET . . . SECRET . . . SECRET . . .

Agreement Respecting Radio Communications Research and Development Activities by the United States in Thailand.

Pursuant to the terms of the Agreement respecting military assistance between the Government of the United States of America and the Government of Thailand signed at Bangkok on October 17, 1950.

The Government of the United States of America and the Government of Thailand have agreed as follows:

ARTICLE I

A. The Royal Thai Government authorizes and provides for the conduct of radio communications research and development activities by the United States Government in Thailand in the following manner:

(1) Unrestricted use by the United States Government for radio communications research and development of 286 rai of land to be procured by the Royal Thai Government adjacent to the southern boundary of the Royal Thai Armed Forces Security Center at Bang Khen and of other land presently being used by the United States Government for this purpose, excluding 11th regiment, RTA, land until the United States Government has no further requirement for the land or facilities thereon.

(2) Limitation, insofar as is practical, of technical interference with the radio environment.

B. The Government of the United States of America, in consideration of the military assistance provided by the Royal Thai Government in para A, agrees to provide a one time payment to the Royal Thai Government not to exceed ten million one hundred and forty seven thousand one hundred and fifty five Baht; this sum to be utilized by the Royal Thai Government to cover all expenses in connection with the procurement of the land, including payment to private landowners for sale of their land to the Royal Thai Government. It is further understood that no other payment will be effected for use of this land. The Government of the United States further agrees that:

(1) Title to all land described herein to be with the Ministry of Defense of the Royal Thai Government.

(2) All buildings constructed on and/or improvement to real estate will be turned over, free of charge, to the Royal Thai Government when the United States Government's requirement for use of land and structures no longer exists.

ARTICLE II

A. Additional arrangements necessitated by this agreement will be in consonance with the Agreement respecting military assistance signed on October 17, 1950, and are subject to the mutual agreement of the United States and the Royal Thai Governments.

B. The provisions of the agreement are effective upon signature.

IN WITNESS WHEREOF, the respective representatives, duly authorized for this purpose, have signed the present agreement.

DONE in duplicate at Bangkok, Thailand, on this 24th day of June of the 2507 year of the Buddhist Era, corresponding to the 24th day of June 1964 of the Christian Era.

For the Government of the United States of America	For the Government of Thailand
/s/ *Graham Martin*	/s/ *Dawee Chullasapya*
Ambassador of the United States of America	Deputy Minister of Defense

ASSEMBLY XLVII
2 MARCH 1991 – 22 MARCH 1992

Anand Panyarachun was appointed prime minister, by royal decree of King Rama IX, on 2 March 1991, and he, in turn, on 6 March 1991, appointed the cabinet, whose names are shown below.

Cabinet

Snoh Unakul	Deputy Prime Minister
Police General Pow Sarasin	Deputy Prime Minister
Meechai Ruchupan	Deputy Prime Minister
MR Kasemsomosorn Kasemsri	Minister to the Office of the Prime Minister
Phaichitr Uathavikul	Minister to the Office of the Prime Minister
Mechai Viravaidya	Minister to the Office of the Prime Minister
Saisuree Chutikul	Minister to the Office of the Prime Minister
Admiral Prapat Krisnachan	Minister of Defence
General Wimol Wongwanich	Deputy Minister of Defence
Air Chief Marshal Pisit Saligupta	Deputy Minister of Defence
Suthee Singsaneh	Minister of Finance
Virabongsa Ramangkura	Deputy Minister of Finance
Arsa Sarasin	Minister of Foreign Affairs
Wichian Wattanakun	Deputy Minister of Foreign Affairs
Anat Arbhabhirama	Minister of Agriculture and Co-operatives
Ajva Taulananda	Deputy Minister of Agriculture and Co-operatives
Kosit Panpiemras	Deputy Minister of Agriculture and Co-operatives
Nukul Prachuabmoh	Minister of Transport
ML Joengjan Kambhu	Deputy Minister of Transport
General Viroj Saengsanit	Deputy Minister of Transport
Air Chief Marshal Suthep Teparak	Deputy Minister of Transport
Amaret Sila-on	Minister of Commerce
General Issarapong Noonpakdee	Minister of Interior
Air Chief Marshal Anan Kalinta	Deputy Minister of Interior
Admiral Vichet Karunyavanij	Deputy Minister of Interior
Prapasna Auychai	Minister of Justice
Sanga Sabhasri	Minister of Science, Technology and Energy
Kaw Swasdi Panich	Minister of Education
Somchai Wudhipreecha	Deputy Minister of Education
Pairoj Ningsanonda	Minister of Public Health
Attasit Vejjajiva	Deputy Minister of Health
Sipphanondha Ketudat	Minister of Industry
Vira Susangkarakan	Deputy Minister of Industry
Kasem Suwanakul	Minister of University Affairs

On July 10, 1991, MR *Pridiyathorn Devakula was appointed Deputy Minister of Commerce.*
On July 29, 1991, Jaroenjit Na Songkhla was appointed Deputy Minister of Interior.

Remark: This cabinet left office when the general election was held on 22 March 1992.

ASSEMBLY XLVIII
7 APRIL 1992 – 9 JUNE 1992

General Suchinda Kraprayoon was appointed prime minister by royal decree of King Rama IX, on 7 April 1992, and he, in turn, on 17 April 1992 appointed the cabinet, whose names are shown below.

Cabinet

Meechai Ruchupan	Deputy Prime Minister
Narong Wongwan	Deputy Prime Minister
Air Chief Marshal Somboon Rahong	Deputy Prime Minister
Montri Pongpanich	Deputy Prime Minister
Samak Sundaravej	Deputy Prime Minister
Mai Sirinawakul	Minister to the Office of the Prime Minister
Chatchawal Chomphudaeng	Minister to the Office of the Prime Minister
Korn Dabbaransi	Minister to the Office of the Prime Minister
Suchon Charmpoonod	Minister to the Office of the Prime Minister
Vatana Asavahame	Minister to the Office of the Prime Minister
Piyanat Watcharaporn	Minister to the Office of the Prime Minister
Chaiyapak Siriwat	Minister to the Office of the Prime Minister
Thinaphan Nakata	Minister to the Office of the Prime Minister
General Suchinda Kraprayoon	Minister of Defence
General Chatchom Kanlong	Deputy Minister of Defence
Suthee Singsaneh	Minister of Finance
Chawalit Austhanukror	Deputy Minister of Finance
Pongpol Adireksarn	Minister of Foreign Affairs
Sombat Srisurin	Deputy Minister of Foreign Affairs
Pinit Chandrasurin	Minister of Agriculture and Co-operatives
Sunti Chaiviratana	Deputy Minister of Agriculture and Co-operatives
Yuth Angiranan	Deputy Minister of Agriculture and Co-operatives
Warothai Pinyasasana	Deputy Minister of Agriculture and Co-operatives
Banharn Silpa-archa	Minister of Transport
Sanoh Thienthong	Deputy Minister of Transport
Suwat Liptapanlop	Deputy Minister of Transport
Kamchai Ruangkanjanasetra	Deputy Minister of Transport
Anuwat Wattanapongsiri	Minister of Commerce
MR Pridiyathorn Devakula	Deputy Minister of Commerce
Samphan Lertnuwat	Deputy Minister of Commerce
Puanglek Boonchiang	Deputy Minister of Commerce
Air Chief Marshal Anan Kalinta	Minister of Interior
Police Lieutenant General Wiroj Pao-in	Deputy Minister of Interior
Weera Pitrachart	Deputy Minister of Interior
Suchart Tancharoen	Deputy Minister of Interior
Prapat Pothasuthon	Deputy Minister of Interior
Sawat Khumprakob	Minister of Justice
Prayuth Siripanich	Minister of Science, Technology and Environment
Kittisak Hathasongkror	Deputy Minister of Science, Technology and Environment
Air Chief Marshal Somboon Rahong	Minister of Education
Shucheep Hansaward	Deputy Minister of Education

Pairoj Kruerattana	Deputy Minister of Education
Ngern Boonsupha	Deputy Minister of Education
Boonphan Kaewattana	Minister of Public Health
Somsak Thepsuthin	Deputy Minister of Public Health
Jaroon Ngarmpichet	Deputy Minister of Public Health
Sompong Amornvivat	Minister of Industry
Ruengwit Linga	Deputy Minister of Industry
Udomsak Thangthong	Deputy Minister of Industry
Thavich Klinprathum	Minister of University Affairs

On 26 May 1992, Police Lieutenant General Wiroj Pao-in, Deputy Minister of Interior, resigned from the position.

Remark: This cabinet left office when the Bloody May unrest broke out.

ASSEMBLY XLIX
10 JUNE 1992 – 22 SEPTEMBER 1992

Anand Panyarachun was appointed prime minister, by royal decree of King Rama IX on 10 June 1992, and he, in turn, on 18 June 1992, appointed the cabinet, whose names are shown below.

Cabinet

Police General Pow Sarasin	Deputy Prime Minister
Kasem Suwanakul	Deputy Prime Minister
MR Kasemsomosorn Kasemsri	Deputy Prime Minister
Mechai Viravaidya	Minister to the Office of the Prime Minister
Saisuree Chutikul	Minister to the Office of the Prime Minister
General Banchob Bunnag	Minister of Defence
Panas Simasathien	Minister of Finance
Arsa Sarasin	Minister of Foreign Affairs
Kosit Panpiemras	Minister of Agriculture and Co-operatives
Amphol Senanarong	Deputy Minister of Agriculture and Co-operatives
Nukul Prachuabmoh	Minister of Transport
ML Joengjan Kambhu	Deputy Minister of Transport
Amaret Sila-on	Minister of Commerce
MR Pridiyathorn Devakula	Deputy Minister of Commerce
Police General Pow Sarasin	Minister of Interior
Jaroenjit Na Songkhla	Deputy Minister of Interior
Anek Sitthipasasana	Deputy Minister of Interior
Wichian Wattanakun	Minister of Justice
Phaichitr Uathavikul	Minister of Science, Technology and Environment
Kop Kristayakirana	Deputy Minister of Science, Technology and Environment
Kaw Swasdi Panich	Minister of Education
Somchai Wudhipreecha	Deputy Minister of Education
Pairoj Ningsanonda	Minister of Public Health
Sipphanondha Ketudat	Minister of Industry
Vira Susangkarakan	Deputy Minister of Industry
Kasem Suwanakul	Minister of University Affairs

Remark: This cabinet left office when the general election was held on 13 September 1992.

DEMOCRATIC GOVERNANCE: STRIVING FOR THAILAND'S NEW NORMAL

Full text of the keynote addresses given by Anand Panyarachun in the Thai language to the Bank of Thailand Annual Seminar, 17 September 2015, and then subsequently in English to the Foreign Correspondents' Club of Thailand, 23 March 2016.

We are at an interesting time of political transition, and many of you may be trying to envisage what Thailand's new normal will be when we finally emerge. My predictions are probably as good as yours. With the benefit of hindsight, however, we can see that globalisation, consumerism, extravagance, dishonesty, and immoderation have led to management failures in both government and business.

It is therefore time to have a better understanding of our past behaviour and how it contributed to the present situation. We should be mindful of the Sufficiency Economy thinking formulated by His Majesty King Bhumibol Adulyadej in terms of its key principles of moderation, rationality, and immunity. A better grasp of these concepts can help us confront problems or crises and find solutions.

I would like to suggest what I believe to be the four essential elements of the new normal in the development of Thailand – the elements that will contribute to true and enduring change.

Element one

The first element in Thailand's new normal rests on sustainable and widespread economic development. I emphasise *sustainable* and *widespread*. In the past, we focussed on the overall rate of economic growth but neglected the quality of that growth as well as the equitable distribution of income and opportunities. The Asian financial crisis of 1997, and the more recent global financial crisis, both illustrate the dangers of unbridled economic growth. We have also been reminded that growth fuelled by populist measures which disregard fiscal discipline are unsustainable and leave problems in their wake. In Thailand, the first car-purchasing and rice-pledging schemes were both examples of short-term stimulus measures. Policies of this kind are pushed by governments the world over to secure quick popular support with inadequate regard for their negative economic repercussions.

Sustainable economic development must focus on strengthening the foundations of the economy. This entails raising underlying economic competitiveness, be it through improving public sector efficiency, state enterprise reforms, developing skilled and flexible labour, or upgrading education and research. Raising competitiveness requires appropriate incentives through effective market mechanisms.

The state's role should largely be as an enabler, establishing an environment that is conducive for market competition to enhance economic efficiency. Things the state *should do* include providing regulations to limit monopolies and establishing frameworks for consumer protection. Things the state *should not do* include competing directly with the private sector or issuing laws and regulations that undermine efficient market mechanisms.

These principles were in fact enshrined in Thailand's 1997 constitution and reflected in the Trade Competition Act of 1999, but enforcement of the laws was never sufficiently exacting. As a result, competition in many sectors, particularly in basic services such as transportation, communications, and energy, remains inadequate. Improving the efficiency of state-owned enterprises is an important element in this regard, and I shall return to it later.

For development to be sustainable, the fruits of economic growth must be spread widely and fairly to foster social cohesion and continued economic and political legitimacy. Many of the economic and social problems we currently face, including the simmering political tensions and sporadic clashes we have suffered in the past decade, can be traced back to the injustice and inequality inherent in our society. Studies also suggest that economic disparity in itself retards economic growth, which is why the topic is of such interest in so many countries. Even the United States, the world's leading economic power, is home to some of the greatest economic inequality in the developed world. Unless seriously addressed, inequality and injustice in all their forms will eventually hold back a country's development and breed political upheaval, even violence.

Element two

The second element in Thailand's new normal is promoting an open and inclusive society. Apart from the equitable distribution of income discussed earlier, we must ensure equal rights, liberties, and opportunities for all segments of society. Every group, every religion, every region, every rung of society must enjoy these to be able to participate collectively in directing national development. This will instil a critical sense of ownership in the nation's destiny that encourages each and every member of society to keep the state under constant scrutiny.

Liberty and equal rights are not simply about the right to vote. The demands and views of everyone must be heard and respected – not just those of the victors in elections. Majoritarian rule does not give a mandate to the winning party to do as it pleases in a winner-takes-all fashion. As the American libertarian James Bovard once observed, 'Democracy must be something more than two wolves and a sheep voting on what to have for dinner.' If democracy is to survive in the long term and create happiness, there has to be tolerance and an acceptance of diversity in society. Minority groups must receive equal benefit from the electoral process.

An open and inclusive society goes hand in hand with freedom of expression and respect for diversity of views and beliefs. In much of Asia, including Thailand, where harmony is a core value and conflict avoidance a first response, our challenge is to embrace criticism, the weighing of pros and cons and disagreements, and accept them all as part of the maturation of the democratic process. In a democracy things are not always strictly black and white, right or wrong. Often there is no absolute right or wrong, just different perspectives and judgments. In striving towards a genuinely open and inclusive society, we must learn to move forward together on the basis of diversity without causing division or conflict.

In an open and participatory society, the media have a very important role to play in reporting opinion neutrally, creating balance and preventing distortion. Modern technology has opened the way to the rapid dissemination of information, and opened up unprecedented space for public discourse. The internet has revolutionised participation in debate and the political process, and fostered many online communities. There are a multitude of voices. Some may be contradictory, some more informed than others, and some personal opinion, gossip, or speculation.

It is a vast marketplace of ideas and, as in all markets, not everything is of equal value. So long as our institutions enable people to understand how to assess ideas in this marketplace – selecting the rigorous and reasonable, rejecting the shoddy and reckless – democracy is not simply sustained but thrives.

As Thailand approaches elections in the near future, it will be imperative for the winners to consider themselves representatives of the entire country, and not just of the people who voted them in. They have a duty to address the concerns of all interest groups and promote consensus in society. Striking that balance is an art. I hope all political parties have learned important lessons from our painful past, and will do their utmost to pursue this vital principle of governance.

Element three

The third element of the new normal in Thailand is the rule of law. This goes beyond simply the application of the law. It requires adherence to both the spirit of the law as well as its underlying moral principles. Rule of law entails not only the clear enunciation of principled rules and regulations, but that they be applied across the board to all citizens without exception. Every individual and organisation, private and public, and even the government itself, must be subject to the law. The legislative and enforcement processes must be transparent and just. The judicial system must be neutral, independent, efficient, and have full integrity. Most importantly, the law must not be used as a means for attaining political goals. State actions must not be arbitrary and based on whims. Dissidents must not be prosecuted or deprived of their legal rights. The human rights of every citizen must be strictly upheld bar none.

Lawful governance does not imply using the law to govern people or enforce the state's will. We must have rule *of* law rather than rule *by* law. This is a crucial albeit subtle distinction. Here in Thailand, a semblance of calm and stability belies tensions beneath the surface. Society cannot flourish in the long run if order and stability are rooted in measures that inhibit public discourse. When order and stability are imposed rather than allowed to emerge naturally in accordance with the rules and norms of society, there can be no transparency.

The World Justice Project has attempted to make global comparisons of the rule of law. The figures for 2015 see the four top places occupied by the Nordic countries: Denmark, Norway, Sweden, and Finland. With a score of 0.52 out of one, Thailand ranks 56th among 102 countries and 11th out of 15 in the region. Thailand trails the Philippines, Greece, and Ghana, and this should remind us that we still have far to travel on our journey to attaining the rule of law.

When the rule of law is weak, corruption flourishes. Democracy becomes dysfunctional if politicians, civil servants, the private sector, the judiciary, the police, and the military use their power to enrich themselves and advance their own interests at the expense of civil society.

We read about the impunity of the rich and powerful in our newspapers every day. An independent and neutral judiciary is fundamental to the rule of law. If judges use one law for the powerful and another for the powerless, the entire political and judicial system is degraded, and the people's trust in the government to see justice dispensed is eroded.

The rule of law demands public responsibility and the transparency of state institutions and their personnel. Accountability and transparency have the same objective: to protect citizens from misguided policies or decisions that unfairly favour a minority at the expense of the majority. A government that is not held accountable, not answerable to anyone, and its actions not subject to public scrutiny, is more likely to abuse its power and disregard the public interest. Preventing such outcomes requires that the decision-making process be transparent and subject to scrutiny. There must be full and timely disclosure of information about policy and public projects. Such checks and balances are at the core of the state's responsibility to society.

Element four

Governance through the rule of law together with public accountability and transparency form the basis of responsible government. This is related to the fourth and final element of the new normal that I would like to talk about: the need to recalibrate the balance of power between the state and the people.

Responsive government lies at the core of true democracy, and can occur only when there is comprehensive decentralisation and local political empowerment.

The closer the government is to the people governed, the more responsive the government is going to be. A centralised system of governance cannot keep pace with the increasing complexity of today's society. Decentralisation enables the participation of more diverse interest groups and represents one way to curb the concentration of power and influence exercised by political forces.

By decentralisation, I do not mean the distribution of power to local government bodies that report to the central authority. I mean dispersion of power directly into the hands of people or their representatives. In the past, we have established local institutions but always retained centralised control over them. Going forward, we must reform these local bodies so that they become answerable to the needs and demands of the local populace rather than to the central government.

The heart of democracy beats only with the participation of all citizens in exercising their rights on issues that affect them directly. In each locality, province, and region, the demands and solutions to various challenges may be similar or dissimilar. The formulation of policies and plans of action should give precedence to the input of local communities. The state's role is to provide support with knowledge, data, funding, and other forms of assistance as needed.

Obviously, on issues such as national security, international relations, or macroeconomic management, the responsibility and authority must rest with the central government. But on matters that affect them directly, people must have a say. Take the education system as an example. Why should the ministry of education stipulate the curriculum for every village, district, and province? The role of the ministry should evolve from one of setting and imposing requirements to one of providing support and assistance to teachers in terms of information and training.

In the areas of natural resource management, transportation or public safety, the decentralisation of power to the local level will not only help to increase flexibility in meeting the needs of ordinary people, it will also lower the burden on central government. As things stand, every time a problem or conflict arises, the aggrieved descend upon Government House or various ministries in Bangkok. Why can't we let local institutions handle these matters directly when it has been amply demonstrated that the central government is incapable of resolving problems in an effective and timely manner?

Importantly, once the political process is decentralised, citizens become more aware, interested, and willing to participate in shaping collective outcomes. This entrenches democracy in society, and nurtures its longevity.

The success of decentralisation hinges on a balanced and diverse flow of information, and this brings me to the critical role of civil society. An active civil society generates a wealth of information for constructive debate on matters of public interest. Civil society also provides a mechanism whereby the collective views of citizens can shape and influence government policy. By bringing arguments and information into the public domain, policies can be examined and challenged, and 'activist citizenship' is fostered by people informing themselves better on matters that affect them. A genuinely democratic government will feel obliged to present counterarguments or to modify its position. Such interactions are healthy for democracy, and improve the decision-making process.

A vibrant civil society relies on the wisdom of the populace and its ability to make rational and informed decisions. Democracy becomes a force for meaningful progress when voters not only understand the issues at hand, but are also conscious of their context, the various alternatives available, as well as their responsibilities as democratic citizens. We must therefore urgently reform our education system from one that simply produces graduates to one that nurtures the ability of people to think critically and make constructive changes in society.

There has been much discussion on this topic over the years but little tangible progress. We must take a step back and carefully reassess our fundamental approach. As things stand, a child starting out in first grade this year will retire in about 2069. No one here, or anywhere else for that matter, can predict with confidence what the world will be like five years from now, let alone in that distant future. Yet we are tasked with educating our children for that world – to ensure they are equipped to solve the problems of their time.

In my view, the best way to do this is to shift the emphasis of education away from memorising facts and rote learning to focus instead on nurturing creativity and adaptability. This all starts with getting teachers to teach less, encouraging students to read more diversely, and ensuring teachers engage in dialogues with students. The main focus should not be on getting the right answer but on instilling confidence to think problems through, to voice opinions and to articulate reasoned arguments.

In an age where a staggering amount of information is available at the touch of a button or the swipe of a smartphone, learning will be more important than knowing. If our children are to be able to solve the complex problems of the future – and climate change is but one – they will need a high degree of creativity. This is something I feel has been sadly neglected so far.

The enemy of creativity is the fear of being wrong or making mistakes. I believe every child is born with an immense amount of creativity and the capacity to innovate. But an education system that stigmatises mistakes, focuses on correct answers, and penalises wrong ones, serves to retard creativity. By the time children grow into adults, they have been deprived of their creative impulse by the fear of being wrong.

Innovation does not come from a fear of being wrong. On the contrary, the courage to risk making mistakes, the relentless process of trial and error, and the ability to bounce back from repeated failures are the seeds of innovation and advancement. Let us not forget that the iPhone many of you carry around was regarded with some scepticism when it was first released in 2007. Its success is a testament to the willingness of Steve Jobs to be wrong rather than his fear of not being right.

Human development does not follow a linear trajectory, and success does not come from a set formula. The learning process is unique for each child – it is not one size fits all. The education system in Finland stands out as a success, but it does not rely on a centralised curriculum or standardised tests. Instead, curriculums are set by schools on their own and experimental teaching approaches are encouraged. Education is individualised, and tests are used to identify and build on each student's comparative strengths rather than to rank them. The emphasis on education for practical, everyday life is conveyed by the fact that over a third of Finnish students attend vocational school.

An education system that promotes good learning skills in children will contribute to a citizenry capable of grasping issues of concern and placing them in the right context. This contributes to well-informed, rational decisions, and helps ensure that the responsibilities of society under democratic rule are met.

A new normal for Thailand

What I have laid out so far is a vision for a new normal for Thailand built upon the foundation of democratic governance. It broadly represents a framework for governance that Thailand has lacked up to now.

We have a tendency to focus on democracy in form rather than in substance.

We follow procedures and go through the motions of elections. Yet we have paid little attention to developing the institutions that are critical to sustaining democracy. The challenges that we are presently facing have their roots in the fact that we have never had a true democratic transition – a genuine change in our political system.

Change has always been superficial, old wine in a new bottle – or you could even say old wine in an old bottle but with a new cork. Critically, we have not dug deeply enough to uncover the true underlying cause of current divisions in Thai society.

Much of this is unrelated to the actual policies of governments, present or past, nor is it about a fight between pro-government and anti-government forces. Rather it is about poverty, social injustice, unequal rights and opportunities, and about the way power is divided between the state and the people – or even among groups of people.

Thais have traditionally been good at creating problems. Some say that they are also good at solving them, but is this not really a bit of a myth? Our development path has been one of muddling along, an 'adhocracy' you might say. Little has been done in the way of strategic long-term planning or effective implementation.

While substantial progress has been achieved in terms of economic development, we have not taken sufficient note of its negative political and social impact. At this juncture, it has become patently clear that many of our institutions are inadequate when faced with the challenges of globalisation. Against a backdrop of rapid global change, our economic, political, and social institutions have simply not kept up.

Democratic governance can serve as a basis for a more balanced path to development. By paying heed to the diverse views and opinions of a wide variety of interest groups, the government can pursue a more rounded and sustainable development model.

We Thais often yearn for a knight in shining armour to ride to the rescue when there are problems. But the time for that kind of 'I-know-best' style of management has passed. For all the information and broad powers that the state possesses, it does not know best on all issues, particularly when it comes to increasingly complex modern economic systems.

Why is good governance the key to good economic management? Let me take the example of state-owned enterprises where performances in recent years have been worrying, where competitiveness has declined markedly – and so have operating profits. Those that enjoy monopoly rights remain profitable, while those that face competition mostly operate at a loss. The root of the problems lies squarely in governance. Regulatory frameworks are complicated, with large overlaps and a lack of overriding authority. Management of state enterprises is vulnerable to political interference and corruption, as well as competing social and business objectives. Importantly, there is no clear separation among the relevant government agencies in terms of their responsibilities as policymakers, regulators, and owners. The uneven playing field state enterprises and private companies play upon has meanwhile dulled the impetus to improve efficiency.

Such problems need to be tackled urgently. State enterprises account for a large part of the economy and exert significant influence on overall economic efficiency. Their role as providers of basic infrastructure in many forms – electricity, water, telecommunications, transportation, airports, ports – make them integral to private sector operations. Inefficient state enterprises not only undermine their own profitability but also impede the performance of all related private activity. Expensive and low-quality basic infrastructure translates directly into reduced competitiveness in private companies. The current reform agenda, including the proposed establishment of the National State Enterprise Corporation, warrants attention as it promises significant improvements in resource allocation. This is conditional, of course, on the integrity and competence of the management of such an institution.

More broadly, government efficiency has become one of the most important determinants of a country's competitiveness. And government efficiency typically is associated with the strength of democracy. Efficient government, however, does not necessarily mean small government. The key lies in the degree of competence with which government affairs are managed, and responsiveness to the needs of the people. A development model that emphasises the role of the state in promoting the freedoms and opportunities of individuals represents the essence of true democracy. Such a model is described in *Development as Freedom* by Professor Amartya Sen, a Nobel laureate for economic sciences.

The road to reform

To make headway towards the new normal that I have described, we must embark on comprehensive structural reforms today. Reforms inevitably create winners and losers. The winners are often diffused and dispersed. Conversely, the losers can be easily identified; they are powerful and well organised. Ensuring that the prospective losers do not impede changes that benefit the public good requires a mechanism to ensure balanced distribution of the gains from reforms among various segments of society. This entails inclusive economic and political institutions, as well as a healthy dose of opportunism. Successful reforms often result from leveraging on opportunities that arise, such as at times of crisis. I have always held the view that we did not make the most of the 1997 financial crisis.

Thus at this point we should not waste time debating where we are, or if we got here in the right or wrong way. These are important and legitimate questions that deserve study and reflection, but they should not prevent us moving forward or seeking solutions to the problems at hand.

A reform strategy must always be assessed within the context of the bigger picture. In the past, the main thrust has been through constitutional reform, which is not ideal and may even be counterproductive. We have been rather profligate with our constitutions. We are on our 19th – or is it 20th? – in the space of 83 years, which happens to coincide exactly with my age.

As one of the people involved in drafting Thailand's 1997 constitution, which for the first time involved broad-based public participation, I had hoped it would make Thai democracy more open, transparent and accountable, and that electoral reforms would limit money politics and corruption. That said, I always recognised that a constitution is not a silver bullet for all that ails society. For a constitution to make a real difference, society must first embrace the underlying values it espouses. As subsequently became apparent, the constitution alone cannot bring about meaningful change absent reforms to other key democratic pillars, particularly political institutions and the mindsets of people.

Structural reform is a continuous process rather than a one-shot exercise. It might begin with drafting a new constitution, but the process must evolve. We must not fall into the trap of using shortcuts or quick wins to achieve our goals. We must not imagine that certain initiatives today will bring about lasting change and forever resolve prevailing problems. There are no once-and-for-all solutions. With constant change, everything eventually needs to adapt and evolve. Developed countries do not stand still. They are continuously changing and adapting. A society with no reform is static and prone to stagnation. And in the process of reform, it is pointless to ask whether success can be guaranteed of each proposal tabled. Nothing can be guaranteed except that all the effort expended is based on goodwill and the best of intentions. We must then stand ready to adapt and adjust down the road as necessary.

There is no unique blueprint for reforms to bring about true democracy. It is quite unlike building a house where there are step-by-step instructions based on clear plans that can be amended as desired or applied to build hundreds of identical houses. Much like a tree that depends on a host of supporting factors to flourish – good soil, water, air – true democracy emerges organically with no predetermined outcome or shape. Its development is path-dependent, and the most that can be done to cultivate it is to provide a supportive environment for it to grow. No two trees are identical, but each one can do just as well providing shade from the sun.

The seeds of democracy must be sown from within each society for the shoots to be accepted and nurtured. As Mahatma Gandhi once observed, 'The spirit of democracy cannot be imposed from without. It has to come from within.' People must want democracy for it to take hold. Each society must find its own way out of conflict and prioritise its needs in accordance with its unique experience. The elements of democratic governance that I have outlined can serve as overarching supports to encourage democracy to evolve in the right direction.

As a nation, we have come far – and there is no turning back to the way things were. Change is unavoidable and permanent. Each and every one of us has a stake in the future of our country. We must contribute to ensuring that the change is constructive. All the forces of goodwill and empathy that bind our society must come out into the open. We must forge a collective vision that is progressive and contributes to change that is constructive.

Democratic governance ultimately is a state of mind rather than some tangible rule or procedure. Over and above the implementation of critical reforms, moving forward towards a prosperous new normal requires that we fundamentally change our way of thinking, attitudes, and mindsets to embrace openness, a diversity of views, as well as values that support societal change. Democratic governance opens up channels through which the diversity in our society can come together to foster political, economic, and social development. It thus represents the most direct route to true sustainability.

BIOGRAPHICAL DATA

Present Positions

Business

2007	:	Chairman of the Board of Directors of Siam Commercial Bank Public Co., Ltd.
1984	:	Director of Siam Commercial Bank Public Co., Ltd.
1989	:	Chairman of Eastern Star Real Estate Public Co., Ltd.
May 2006	:	Consultant of Chevron Asia South Ltd.

Non-business

1988	:	Member of the Advisory Council of SASIN Graduate Institute of Business Administration of Chulalongkorn University
1990	:	Chairman of the Cambridge Thai Foundation
January 1996	:	Distinguished International ISIS Fellow (Malaysia)
	:	UNICEF Ambassador for Thailand
August 1996	:	Chairman of International Advisory Board of the Carlos P. Romulo Foundation
January 1998	:	Board of Trustees of Thailand Management Association
July 1999	:	Honorary International Advisor to the Governors of Dulwich College, London
January 2000	:	Member of the Advisory Council of Transparency International (TI)
November 2003	:	Trustee of U Thant Institute
	:	Fellow of Dulwich College
2005	:	Member of the Club de Madrid
2007	:	Member of Asian Wise Person's Group
January 2012	:	Honorary Patron of Global Leadership Foundation
January 2015	:	Honorary Chairman of Operation Smile Thailand
May 2015	:	Honorary Mentor to the Caux Round Table
12 May 2016	:	Chairman of the Advisory Board of Vidyasirimedhi Institute of Science and Technology (VISTEC)
1 March 2017	:	Honorary Advisor of "AIDS Almost Zero" Project under Thai National AIDS Foundation
29 May 2017	:	Honorary Chairman of Green Globe Institute
June 2017	:	Honorary Fellow of Trinity College, Cambridge

Place and Date of Birth: Bangkok, Thailand
9 August 1932

Education

1943–1945	:	Amnuay Silpa School
1945–1948	:	Bangkok Christian College
1948–1952	:	Dulwich College, London
1952–1955	:	Trinity College, University of Cambridge B.A. (Honours)

Marital Status : Married to *MR* Sodsee (née Chakrabandh)
       Two daughters (Nanda, Daranee)

Awards   : Man of the Year 1997; Management Training Center, Thailand
       : 1997 Ramon Magsaysay Awardee for Government Service
       : 2003 UNICEF Recognition Award for Outstanding Service to Children
       : Outstanding Democrat award, 2003, by People's Constitution Association
       : International Integrity Medal, The Kuala Lumpur Society for Transparency and
         Integrity in February 2004
       : Honorary Fellow of Trinity, Cambridge in June 2017

Thai Honorary Degrees

1.	1990	: Doctor of Business Administration, Honoris Causa, Chulalongkorn University
2.	1991	: Honorary Diploma, The National Defence College
3.	1992	: Honorary Doctoral Degree in Business Administration, The National Institute of Development Administration (NIDA)
4.		: Honorary Doctorate Degree of Industrial Technology, King Mongkut's Institute of Technology North Bangkok
5.		: Honorary Doctoral Degree in Communication Arts, Bangkok University
6.	1993	: Honorary Doctorate Degree in Economics, Thammasat University
7.		: Honorary Doctorate Degree in Political Science, Prince of Songkla University
8.		: Honorary Doctor of Science (Environment Technology), King Mongkut's Institute of Technology Thonburi
9.	1994	: Honorary Doctoral Degree in Political Science, Chiangmai University
10.		: Honorary Doctoral Degree in Development Economics, The National Institute of Development Administration (NIDA)
11.		: The Degree of Doctor of Philosophy (Social Sciences), Honoris Causa, Mahidol University
12.		: Honorary Doctor of Political Science, Sukhothai Thammathirat Open University
13.		: Honorary Degree of Doctor of Philosophy in Political Science, Burapha University
14.	1995	: Honorary Doctor in Political Science, Srinakharinwirot University
15.	1996	: Honorary Doctor of Business Administration, Khon Kaen University
16.	1997	: Honorary Doctorate in Laws, Ramkhamhaeng University
17.	2006	: Doctor of Philosophy Degree in Political Science Honoris Causa (International Relations), Thammasat University
18.	2007	: Doctor of Philosophy (Honoris Causa), Asian Institute of Technology
19.	2009	: Honorary Doctoral Degree in Philosophy (Communications), Maejo University

International Honorary Degrees

1.	1993	: Honorary Doctor of Laws Degree, University of Victoria, Canada
2.	1994	: Honorary Doctor of Laws Degree, Queen's University, Canada
3.	1996	: Honorary Degree of Doctor of Social Sciences, University of Hong Kong, Hong Kong
4.	2000	: Degree of Doctor, Honoris Causa, Soka University, Japan
5.	2005	: Honorary Degree of Doctor of Laws, The University of North Carolina at Chapel Hill, U.S.A.
6.	2008	: Honorary Doctor of Government, National Graduate Institute for Policy Studies, Japan

Government Service

1955	: Joined the Ministry of Foreign Affairs
1959–1964	: Secretary to the Minister of Foreign Affairs
1964–1966	: First Secretary and then Counsellor, Permanent Mission of Thailand to the United Nations
1967–1972	: Ambassador, Acting Permanent Representative of Thailand to the United Nations and concurrently Ambassador to Canada
1972–1975	: Ambassador to the United States of America and concurrently Permanent Representative of Thailand to the United Nations
1976–1977	: Permanent Secretary for Foreign Affairs
1977	: Ambassador-at-large
1977–1979	: Ambassador to the Federal Republic of Germany
2 March 1991–21 April 1992	: Prime Minister of Thailand
10 June–1 October 1992	: Prime Minister of Thailand

Private Sector & Civil Society

1979–1990	: Vice Chairman of Saha-Union Public Co., Ltd.
1979–1992	: Member of the Council of the National Institute of Development Administration (NIDA)
1980–1986	: Member of the International Council of the Asia Society Inc.
1980–1987	: Vice President of the Association of Thai Industries
1981–2002	: Vice Chairman of Union Textile Industries Public Co., Ltd.
1981–1984	: Member of the Board of Governors of the American Chamber of Commerce in Thailand
1981–March 1991	: President of the Association of Thai International Trading Companies
1982–1983	: Chairman of ASEAN Task Force on ASEAN Cooperation
1982–1984	: President of the ASEAN-CCI (ASEAN Chambers of Commerce and Industry)
1982–1996	: Chairman of Star Block Group Public Co., Ltd.
1982–November 1998	: Director of Sime Darby Berhad, Malaysia
1984–1989	: Vice President of ASEAN-CCI
1984–1991	: Member of Council of Trustees of Thailand Development Research Institute Foundation
1985–March 1991	: Director of US-ASEAN Center for Technology Exchange
1986–1990	: Chairman of the ASEAN Section of the ASEAN-U.S. Business Council
	: Director of the John E. Peurifoy Foundation
1986–March 1991	: Director of the Science and Technology Development Board
1987–1989	: Member of University Bureau Committee
1987–1990	: Member of the Export Development Committee
1987–March 1991	: Advisor to the Standing Committee on Foreign Affairs of the House of Representatives
1988–1989	: Member of the Ad Hoc Committee on the OMNIBUS Trade and Competitiveness Act of 1988 of the House of Representatives
1988–1990	: Vice Chairman of the Federation of Thai Industries (FTI)
1989–1997	: President of the Old England Students Association
1989–April 1994	: Director of Union Thread Industries Co., Ltd.
1989–October 1997	: Director of Union Plastic Public Co., Ltd.
1989–December 1999	: Director of Union-Footwear Public Co., Ltd.
1990–March 1991	: Chairman of the Federation of Thai Industries
1990–1994	: Member of Chulalongkorn University Council

1990–2006	:	Member of the Board of Trustees of the Asian Institute of Technology (AIT)
1 January–13 March 1991	:	Chairman of Saha-Union Co., Ltd.
10 January–2 March 1991	:	Chairman of the Advisory Committee on Administrative System
1991–1995	:	Member of Business Advisory Council of International Finance Corporation (IFC)
23 April–10 June 1992	:	Chairman of Saha-Union Co., Ltd.
April 1992–October 2012	:	Chairman of Chiang Mai Night Bazaar Co., Ltd.
June 1992–February 2008	:	Chairman of the Council of Trustees and the Board of Directors of Thailand Development Research Institute (TDRI)
October 1992–1998	:	Member of International Advisory Board of General Electric Company (GE)
15 October 1992–31 August 2002	:	Chairman of Saha-Union Public Co., Ltd.
December 1992–December 2000	:	Member of IBM Asia Pacific Board
1993–1994	:	Chairman of Business Council for Sustainable Development (Geneva)
1993–April 1998	:	Director of Samitivej Public Co., Ltd.
April 1993–December 2007	:	Chairman of the Council of Trustees of Thailand Environment Institute (TEI)
April 1993–2011	:	Member of International Advisory Board of American International Group, Inc. (AIG)
October 1993–December 2007	:	Chairman of Thailand Business Council for Sustainable Development (TBCSD)
1994–1997	:	Chairman of The Post Publishing Public Co., Ltd.
July 1994–1998	:	Chairman of General Electric's Asia Pacific Advisory Board
September 1994–2000	:	Informal Advisory Group, United Nations High Commissioner for Refugees (UNHCR)
1995–1997	:	Juror for the Conrad N. Hilton Humanitarian Prize
August 1995–1999	:	Member of International Advisory Board of Council on Foreign Relations (New York)
August 1995–2005	:	Member of the Asia-Pacific Advisory Board of Unocal Asia-Pacific Ventures, Ltd.
August 1995–January 2008	:	Chairman of the Board of Imperial Technology Management Services Public Co., Ltd.
September 1995–August 2009	:	Vice Chairman of Suan Luang Rama 9 Foundation
October 1995–2011	:	Chairman of the Board of Trustees, Mekong Region Law Center
November 1995–February 2006	:	Chairman of Kenan Institute Asia
May 1996–May 2001	:	Member of Inter-Action Council
January–May 1997	:	Chairman of the Drafting Committee of the Constitution Drafting Assembly
May–July 1997	:	Chairman of the Scrutiny Committee of the Constitution Drafting Assembly
December 1997–January 2008	:	Chairman of University Council of Asian University
June 1998–2001	:	Member of Advisory Board, National Social Policy Committee
July 1998–2000	:	Chairman of the National Commission for the Formulation of Policy and Action Plan on Human Rights
August 1998–2003	:	Member of Asian Advisory Board of the Carlyle Group
January 1999–2006	:	Regional Advisor of General Electric Company (GE)
March 1999–2007	:	Advisory Group on Anti-Corruption Issues for the East Asia and Pacific Region, World Bank
July 1999–2005	:	Chairman of the Board of Advisors of Dulwich International College, Phuket
January 2000–December 2003	:	Member of the Group of International Advisers of International Committee of the Red Cross
September 2000–October 2006	:	Chairman of the Board of Trustees of the Asian Institute of Technology (AIT)

October 2000–March 2002	:	Chairman of the Public Consultation Committee on the Future of Chulalongkorn University
August 2001–August 2005	:	Chairman of the National Economic and Social Advisory Council
September 2001–2002	:	Chairman of the Committee to Follow Up on the Missing and to Assist the Injured Parties Caused by the May 1992 Events
November 2001–2008	:	Member of the International Advisory Board of Toyota Motor Corporation
October 2003–2005	:	Chairman of the Steering Committee, Asia Pacific Leadership Forum on HIV/AIDS and Development (APLF)
November 2003–December 2004	:	Chairman of High-Level Panel on Threats, Challenges and Change of the United Nations
March 2005–June 2006	:	Chairman of the National Reconciliation Commission (NRC)
February 2008–2011	:	Member of Global Leadership Foundation
30 October 2009–29 May 2017	:	Chairman of Green Globe Institute
5 July 2010–May 2011	:	Chairman of Reform Commission

Thai Decorations

1967	:	The Royal Cypher Medal (Third Class)
1968	:	Knight Commander (Second Class, lower grade) of the Most Illustrious Order of Chula Chom Klao
1977	:	Knight Grand Cross (First Class) of the Most Exalted Order of the White Elephant
1988	:	Knight Grand Cordon (Special Class) of the Most Noble Order of the Crown of Thailand
1991	:	Knight Grand Commander (Second Class, higher grade) of the Most Illustrious Order of Chula Chom Klao
1992	:	Knight Grand Cordon (Special Class) of the Most Exalted Order of the White Elephant
2003	:	Knight Grand Cross (First Class) of the Most Admirable Order of the Direkgunabhorn

Foreign Decorations

1961	:	Ordine al Merito della Repubblica Italiana (Third Class), Italy
1970	:	Order of Diplomatic Service Merit, (First Class), Republic of Korea
1971	:	Ringtang Jasa (First Class), Indonesia
1990	:	Grand Officier de L'ordre de la Couronne (Second Class), Belgium
1991	:	Grand Cordon of the Order of the Rising Sun, Japan
1996	:	Honorary Knight Commander of the Civil Division of the Most Excellent Order of the British Empire (KBE), United Kingdom
2007	:	The Commander Grand Cross of the Royal Order of the Polar Star, Sweden

DRAMATIS PERSONAE

Abhisit Vejjajiva, prime minister of Thailand 2008-11, remained as Democrat Party leader after election defeat by the Shinawatra family's Pheu Thai Party.

Amaret Sila-on, commerce minister in the Anand governments who later chaired the Stock Exchange of Thailand and the Financial Sector Restructuring Authority after the 1997 financial collapse. He played an important role in the formation of the ASEAN Free Trade Area.

Amnuay Viravan, economist and permanent secretary at the finance ministry who later entered the private sector and politics. Started career in the early 1960s as an economic advisor to the prime minister, Field Marshal Sarit Thanarat. His private sector peaks included chairing Saha Union and Bangkok Bank. He served as deputy prime minister and finance minister at different times.

Anat Arbhabhirama, the first president of the Thailand Development Research Institute in the late 1980s, minister of agriculture in the 1991 Anand Panyarachun government, and later executive director of the BTS SkyTrain.

Arsa Sarasin, a career diplomat who served as ambassador to Belgium and the US, was permanent secretary of the foreign ministry in the 1980s, and Anand's foreign minister in 1991 and 1992; he became principal private secretary to King Bhumibol Adulyadej in 2000.

Arthit Ourairat, a former politician and member of the Samakkitham Party. Elected to parliament in 1988, he was president of parliament and speaker of the house in 1992. His ministerial experience includes foreign affairs, public health, and science and technology. Latterly, he has been the president of Rangsit University for over 20 years.

Asda Jayanama, a career diplomat who served as Thailand's permanent representative to the United Nations in New York in the 1990s. He was actively involved in UN and regional affairs.

Banharn Silpa-archa, prime minister of Thailand 1995-6, joined the Chart Thai Party in 1974, and was elected to parliament 11 times. His premiership produced a constitutional amendment that facilitated the drafting of the 1997 constitution.

ML Birabhongse Kasemsri, the son of Anand's oldest sister, Suthira. A career diplomat trained at Oxford University and Fletcher School of Law and Diplomacy, he served as Thailand's permanent representative to the UN and subsequently ambassador to the US. He also served as King Bhumibol's principal private secretary.

Bhichai Rattakul, one of the world's leading Rotarians, the former Democrat Party leader, was foreign minister in 1976; he also served as deputy prime minister, speaker of the house of representatives, and president of parliament.

Borwornsak Uwanno, a professor of law at Chulalongkorn University and former senator who belonged to the Baan Phitsanulok advisory group of Prime Minister Chatichai Choonhavan. He later served on the 1997 constitution drafting committee, as secretary general of the King Prajadhipok Institute, and as a cabinet secretary general to Prime Minister Thaksin Shinawatra.

Major General Chamlong Srimuang, a member of the Class Seven 'Young Turks' military faction, served as secretary to Prime Minister Prem Tinsulanond, and later in the 1980s as a popular governor of Bangkok. He founded the Palang Tham Party in 1988, and led street protests against the Suchinda Kraprayoon government in May 1992. He handed leadership of Palang Tham to Thaksin Shinawatra in the mid-1990s, but the two later became estranged.

Charatsri Vajrabhaya, the daughter of Anand's second eldest sister, Pritha, and only two years his junior. She followed in her grandfather Sern's footsteps as an educator, and worked at the Ministry of Education and UNESCO in Bangkok.

Chat Panyarachun, the 11th child of Sern and Pruek Panyarachun, is four years older than Anand and the closest in age of his siblings. He joined the travel industry after returning from studies in the US.

Chatichai Choonhavan, a soldier, diplomat, and politician, was foreign minister during *MR* Kukrit Pramoj's government (1975-6) and served as Thailand's prime minister 1988-91. He was ousted in a coup in 1991 by the National Peacekeeping Council chaired by General Sunthorn Kongsompong.

General Chavalit Yongchaiyudh, a former army chief, served as Thailand's prime minister 1996-7 as head of the New Aspiration Party, which he founded in the late 1980s.

Chuan Leekpai, a lawyer and politician from the South who led the Democrat Party for many years. He served as prime minister twice, in 1992-5 and 1997-2001.

Damri Darakananda, founder, former president, and former chairman of Saha Union, and a pioneer in the textile industry.

Ekamol Kiriwat, a deputy governor of the Bank of Thailand who was instrumental in establishing the Securities and Exchange Commission (SEC) in 1991, and was its first secretary general.

Gothom Arya, an electrical engineer by training turned civil society activist, he was the first secretary general of PollWatch, a government-funded electoral monitoring organisation, a member of Thailand's first election commission, and also director of the Institute of Human Rights and Peace Studies.

General Issarapong Noonpakdee, the army chief of staff who became interior minister in the first Anand government in 1991. A hardliner, he was also the brother in law of General Suchinda Kraprayoon, the army chief.

Air Chief Marshal Kaset Rojananil, the air force chief who carried out the coup against Prime Minister Chatichai Choonhavan in February 1991, and was viewed by some observers as the main ideologue in the National Peacekeeping Council.

Kusa Panyarachun, Anand's second oldest brother, enlisted in the US army during World War II, established and headed the World Travel Service, and later became a major force in Thailand's travel industry.

Kraisak Choonhavan, the son of Prime Minister Chatichai Choonhavan was a member of his Baan Phitsanulok advisory team, and later a senator with particular interests in foreign relations and human rights.

General Kriangsak Chomanand, the army chief who became Thailand's prime minister in 1977 following the second coup staged by Admiral Sangad Chaloryu, which ousted Prime Minister Tanin Kraivixien.

MR **Kukrit Pramoj,** Thailand's prime minister 1975-6, younger brother of Prime Minister *MR* Seni Pramoj, leader of the Social Action Party, writer, columnist, actor, and cultural icon. Kukrit is particularly remembered for establishing diplomatic relations with China after a historic meeting with Mao Zedong in 1975.

Manaspas Xuto, a career diplomat trained at the Fletcher School of Law and Diplomacy, served as Thailand's permanent representative to the United Nations, and was instrumental in developing Voice of Free Asia (today Saranrom Radio) at the foreign ministry.

Mechai Viravaidya, a minister in the Anand governments best known internationally for his pioneering work in family planning, rural development, and poverty reduction, and his campaign to improve HIV/AIDS awareness and education in the 1990s.

Meechai Ruchupan, a legal expert and former secretary general of the Judicial Council, was a deputy prime minister in 1991 and 1992, and briefly served as acting prime minister following political violence in 1992. He has been involved in drafting new Thai constitutions since 1973, except in 1997.

Nukul Prachuabmoh, an economist and former governor of the Bank of Thailand who headed the Nukul Commission to investigate the causes of the 1997 Asian financial crisis. He previously held positions in the Ministry of Finance, and was minister for transport and communications in both Anand governments.

Field Marshal Plaek Phibunsongkhram (Phibun) played a pivotal role in the revolutionary coup of 1932, and was prime minister twice (1938-44 and 1948-57). After allying with Japan in 1941, he later pursued a modernising nationalist agenda. He was responsible for changing the name of Siam to Thailand in 1939.

Pote Sarasin was very briefly prime minister from September 1957 to January 1958, and foreign minister from 1949 to 1951. He was the first secretary general of the Southeast Asia Treaty Organization (SEATO), which was formed in 1954.

Field Marshal Praphas Charusathien was deputy prime minister to Field Marshal Thanom Kittikachorn, and also interior minister and army commander in chief. He was removed from power along with Thanom in 1973, and sent into exile.

Squadron Leader Prasong Soonsiri, a former secretary general of the National Security Council, served as foreign minister, 1992-4.

Dr Prawase Wasi, a haematologist at Siriraj Hospital, activist on public health issues and national reform, and royal physician. He laid important groundwork for the 1997 constitution, and was deeply involved in the National Reform Commission of 2010 in the aftermath of political unrest.

General Prayut Chan-o-cha, the current prime minister of Thailand and head of the National Council for Peace and Order, entered office after a coup in May 2014 that ousted the caretaker Yingluck Shinawatra government.

General Prem Tinsulanond, Thailand's prime minister 1980-88, came into office after the tumultuous 1970s. Oversaw a crucial transformational period, tackling economic setbacks in the mid-1980s, and stewarding incremental democratisation. He is the current president of the Privy Council and has been a member since 1988.

Pridi Banomyong, the prime minister of Thailand from March to August 1946, was a key figure in the revolutionary coup that ended absolute monarchy in 1932. Forced into permanent exile in 1946 by political and royalist enemies, he died in Paris in 1984.

Pruek Panyarachun, the mother of Anand, was titled Khunying Prichanusat and was from the Jotikasthira Hokkien Chinese clan.

Puey Ungphakorn, the economist, technocrat, and Free Thai veteran who was governor of the Bank of Thailand from 1959 to 1971. He was also the dean of the faculty of economics at Thammasat University, and eventually became its rector.

Rak Panyarachun, Anand's oldest brother was 18 years his senior. He graduated from the University of Lille, France, in 1940 and served as deputy foreign minister in the 1950s.

Admiral Sangad Chaloryu staged the 1976 coup that overthrew *MR* Seni Pramoj's government as head of the National Administrative Reform Council. A year later, in October 1977, he ousted Prime Minister Tanin Kraivixien, Seni's replacement.

Saisuree Chutikul, the only woman in Anand's cabinets, is renowned for promoting and protecting the rights of women and children and for combatting human trafficking.

Samak Sundaravej, firebrand Democrat Party politician in the 1970s who served briefly as Thailand's prime minister in 2008.

Sanya Dhammasakdi was appointed prime minister by King Bhumibol in 1973 following the removal of Field Marshal Thanom Kittikachorn. He was president of the Privy Council at the time, and a former rector of Thammasat University.

Field Marshal Sarit Thanarat, prime minister of Thailand 1959-63, ousted Field Marshal Plaek Phibunsongkhram in 1957. The monarchy saw a major revival on his watch. Sarit was the only Thai prime minister to die in office.

MR Seni Pramoj, a lawyer, diplomat, Democrat Party politician, became prime minister of Thailand for three short terms in 1945, 1975, and 1976. During World War II, while serving as Thai ambassador in Washington, he formed the US branch of the Free Thai resistance.

Sern Panyarachun, Anand's father, served as permanent secretary of the Ministry of Education. He also served as headmaster of Vajiravudh College and the first president of the Press Association of Thailand, after moving into the private sector in the early 1930s.

Air Chief Marshal Siddhi Savetsila was secretary general of the National Security Council in the late 1970s and foreign minister from 1980 to 1990, mostly under Prime Minister Prem Tinsulanond.

Snoh Unakul, an economist dubbed Thailand's 'development czar', headed the National Economic and Social Development Board, which formulates Thailand's five-year plans. He was governor of the Bank of Thailand (1975-9), founded the influential Thailand Development Research Institute in 1984, and was deputy prime minister in the first Anand government.

MR Sodsrisuriya Chakrabhandhu (Sodsee), Anand's wife, was studying in London when they met. Upon returning to Thailand, she worked at the United Nations regional office and later resigned to accompany Anand when he was posted abroad. The couple married on 4 May 1956, and have two daughters, Nanda and Daranee.

Sompong Sucharitkul, a distinguished international lawyer, academic, and linguist, succeeded Anand as secretary to Foreign Minister Thanat Khoman. He was involved in forming ASEAN in 1967, and later served as ambassador to The Hague and Japan.

Staporn Kavitanon started his civil service career in the planning commission and subsequently served as the secretary general of the Board of Investment of Thailand, 1991-2001.

General Suchinda Krapayoon served as army chief, leader of the National Peace Keeping Council, and became Thailand's Prime Minister for 48 days in 1992. Protests led by General Chamlong Srimuang ended with the violence of Black May and Suchinda's resignation following an intervention by King Bhumibol.

Sulak Sivaraksa, a prominent social critic and intellectual, is the founder of the International Network of Engaged Buddhists.

General Sunthorn Kongsompong, the supreme commander of the Royal Thai Armed Forces who led the military coup that deposed Chatichai Choonhavan in 1991, served as the chairman of the junta, the National Peacekeeping Council, and was *de facto* head of government until May 1992.

Supapan Jumbala Na Ayudhya (née Panyarachun) is Anand's closest sister in age, and arrived for studies in London in 1950 while Anand was attending Dulwich College.

General Surayud Chulanont, a former army chief and supreme commander, stepped out of the Privy Council to become prime minister after a coup in 2006 ousted Thaksin Shinawatra.

Suthee Singsaneh, a leading technocrat who served as finance minister under Prem Tinsulanond, Anand, and Suchinda Krapayoon.

Suthichai Yoon, a veteran journalist and commentator who co-founded *The Nation* newspaper.

ML Thawisan Ladawan was the principal private secretary to King Bhumibol (1969-95), a privy counciller, and was husband of Queen Sirikit's sister, Thanpuying *MR* Busba Kitiyakara.

Tanin Kraivixien, a former supreme court judge and former privy councillor, served as Thailand's prime minister following a violent coup in October 1976. His government was overthrown a year later.

Tej Bunnag, a distinguished diplomat and historian trained at Cambridge and Oxford universities, served as Thai ambassador to China, and was foreign minister in 2008.

Thaksin Shinawatra, a telecoms billionaire who founded the progressive Thai Rak Thai Party in the late 1990s. He won election as prime minister in 2001, and an unprecented re-election in 2005, but was ousted in a coup in 2006. He went into exile in 2008 to escape prosecution.

Thanat Khoman served as ambassador in Washington prior to being appointed foreign minister (1959-71) by Field Marshal Sarit Thanarat. He was one of five founding fathers of the Association of Southeast Asian Nations, and also served as deputy prime minister from 1980-1982.

Field Marshal Thanom Kittikachorn, the prime minister of Thailand in 1958 returned for a nine-year term in 1963, and was removed after a popular student-led uprising in 1973.

Prince Wan Waithayakon, one of Thailand's most distinguished diplomats, was appointed ambassador in Washington at the age of only 29. He was later foreign minister, and permanent representative to the UN, where he served as president of the General Assembly in 1956.

Wissanu Krea-ngam, a professor of law and member of the Council of State of Thailand who has served as cabinet secretary general to seven prime ministers, and as a deputy prime minister under Prayut Chan-o-cha.

Yingluck Shinawatra became the first woman prime minister of Thailand in 2011. She is the youngest sister of Thaksin Shinawatra, and was removed from office by court order in 2014 a few weeks before her caretaker government was ousted by a coup. She went into exile in the UK after facing criminal prosecution.

INDEX